T0202918

Lecture Notes in Artificial Intelligence 13548

Subseries of Lecture Notes in Computer Science

Series Editors

Randy Goebel
University of Alberta, Edmonton, Canada

Wolfgang Wahlster
DFKI, Berlin, Germany

Zhi-Hua Zhou
Nanjing University, Nanjing, China

Founding Editor

Jörg Siekmann
DFKI and Saarland University, Saarbrücken, Germany

More information about this subseries at https://link.springer.com/bookseries/1244

Alexander Hunt · Vasiliki Vouloutsi ·
Kenneth Moses · Roger Quinn · Anna Mura ·
Tony Prescott · Paul F. M. J. Verschure (Eds.)

Biomimetic and Biohybrid Systems

11th International Conference, Living Machines 2022
Virtual Event, July 19–22, 2022
Proceedings

Springer

Editors
Alexander Hunt 🄳
Portland State University
Portland, OR, USA

Vasiliki Vouloutsi 🄳
Technology Innovation Institute
Masdar City, United Arab Emirates

Kenneth Moses 🄳
Case Western Reserve University
Cleveland, OH, USA

Roger Quinn 🄳
Case Western Reserve University
Cleveland, OH, USA

Anna Mura 🄳
Institute for Bioengineering of Cataloni
Barcelona, Spain

Tony Prescott 🄳
University of Sheffield
Sheffield, UK

Paul F. M. J. Verschure 🄳
Radboud University
Nijmegen, The Netherlands

ISSN 0302-9743   ISSN 1611-3349 (electronic)
Lecture Notes in Artificial Intelligence
ISBN 978-3-031-20469-2   ISBN 978-3-031-20470-8 (eBook)
https://doi.org/10.1007/978-3-031-20470-8

LNCS Sublibrary: SL7 – Artificial Intelligence

© The Editor(s) (if applicable) and The Author(s), under exclusive license
to Springer Nature Switzerland AG 2022, corrected publication 2022
This work is subject to copyright. All rights are reserved by the Publisher, whether the whole or part of the material is concerned, specifically the rights of translation, reprinting, reuse of illustrations, recitation, broadcasting, reproduction on microfilms or in any other physical way, and transmission or information storage and retrieval, electronic adaptation, computer software, or by similar or dissimilar methodology now known or hereafter developed.
The use of general descriptive names, registered names, trademarks, service marks, etc. in this publication does not imply, even in the absence of a specific statement, that such names are exempt from the relevant protective laws and regulations and therefore free for general use.
The publisher, the authors, and the editors are safe to assume that the advice and information in this book are believed to be true and accurate at the date of publication. Neither the publisher nor the authors or the editors give a warranty, expressed or implied, with respect to the material contained herein or for any errors or omissions that may have been made. The publisher remains neutral with regard to jurisdictional claims in published maps and institutional affiliations.

This Springer imprint is published by the registered company Springer Nature Switzerland AG
The registered company address is: Gewerbestrasse 11, 6330 Cham, Switzerland

Preface

These proceedings contain the papers presented at the 11th International Conference on Biomimetic and Biohybrid Systems (Living Machines 2022), held online during July 19–22, 2022. The international conferences in the Living Machines series are targeted at the intersection of research on novel life-like technologies inspired by the scientific investigation of biological systems, biomimetics, and research that seeks to interface biological and artificial systems to create biohybrid systems. The conference aims to highlight the most exciting international research in both of these fields united by the theme of "Living Machines."

The development of biomimetic and biohybrid systems is multidisciplinary at its core. It requires knowledge of both biology and engineering to develop working systems, the results of which can be mutually beneficial. Billions of years have shaped biological systems to solve problems through evolutionary pressures. These pressures have enabled biological systems to thrive in harsh environments, maneuver with efficiency and grace, and adapt to their ever changing surroundings. Careful scientific studies of these systems are able to reveal many of the qualities that are important for these behaviors. Hundreds of years of human experience has shown that we can then adapt these qualities in our engineered systems in order to improve the behavior and outcomes.

However, despite our efforts and careful studies, there is still much about biological systems that we do not know. Engineering attempts at mimicking these systems can help test competing theories of what components are important, and how those components interact with other parts of the system. Additionally, with the right tools and knowledge, we can even interface directly with biological systems, creating biohybrid systems. These systems are formed by combining at least one biological component - an existing living system - and at least one artificial, newly engineered component. These systems either enhance the ability of the biological system to carry out specific tasks, or use the biological capabilities to develop systems that are not feasible with traditional engineered systems.

Effective creation of biomimetic and biohybrid systems requires clear and constant communication between the two fields, and experts that constantly work at the boundaries. Language, techniques, limitations, and new advancements must be shared on a regular basis. The Living Machines conference series was first organized by the Convergent Science Network (CSN) of biomimetic and biohybrid systems to provide a mechanism for ensuring this communication. It provides a focal point for the gathering of world-leading researchers and the presentation and discussion of cutting-edge research at the boundary of biology and engineering. This year's edition of Living Machines continued that proud tradition, featuring biologists and engineers who have spent their careers developing biomimetic and biohybrid systems. Additionally, the conference provided an opportunity to introduce and support many young researchers in the growing field.

The main conference was hosted by Case Western Reserve University in Cleveland, USA, and took the form of three days of single-track oral presentations during July 20–22, 2022. The Program Committee received 48 papers, of which 30 full papers and eight short papers were accepted and are printed in this volume. During the conference, they were divided up between 18 regular talks and 20 short talk spotlights. Each paper received two to three reviews from the Program Committee and other external reviewers in a single-blind process. The conference also included three plenary lectures from leading international researchers in biomimetic and biohybrid systems: Hillel Chiel (Case Western Reserve University, USA) spoke on "From Living Organism to Living Machines"; Mirko Kovac (Imperial College London, UK, and Empa Material Science Institute, Switzerland) spoke on "Bio-inspired Drones for Sustainability"; and Victoria Webster-Wood (Carnegie Mellon University, USA) spoke on "Beyond Bioinspired: Living and organic materials for living machines". Session themes included biomimetic robots, neural models of control, neural models of behavior, modeling approaches, and navigation. Additionally, there were discussions on "What makes something living?", "What are potential jobs and career paths?", and "Equity, Accessibility, and Inclusion".

The conference was complemented by a one day workshop on July 19 led by Roger Quinn and Hillel Chiel on "How do animal neuromechanical systems perform communication, coordination, and control?". Cross-disciplinary talks featured biologists and engineers investigating the neural and biomechanical mechanisms that lead to robust and adaptive control across the animal kingdom.

We wish to thank the many people that were involved in making Living Machines 2022 possible. Additional guidance and support were provided by the Living Machines International Advisory Board. We would also like to thank the authors and speakers who contributed their work, and the members of the international Program Committee for their detailed and considerate reviews. We are grateful to the three keynote speakers who shared with us their vision of the future of Living Machines.

August 2022

Alexander Hunt
Vasiliki Vouloutsi
Kenneth Moses
Roger Quinn

Organization

Program Chairs

Hunt, Alexander	Portland State University, USA
Quinn, Roger	Case Western Reserve University, USA
Mura, Anna	Institute for Bioengineering of Catalonia, Spain
Vouloutsi, Vasiliki	Technology Innovation Institute, UAE
Moses, Kenneth	Case Western Reserve University, USA
Prescott, Tony	University of Sheffield, UK
Verschure, Paul F. M. J.	Radboud University, The Netherlands

Local Organization

Chiel, Hillel	Case Western Reserve University, USA
Moses, Kenneth	Case Western Reserve University, USA
Quinn, Roger	Case Western Reserve University, USA

International Steering Committee

Asada, Minoru	Osaka University, Japan
Ayers, Joseph	Northeastern University, USA
Chiel, Hillel	Case Western Reserve University, USA
Cutkosky, Mark	Stanford University, USA
Desmulliez, Marc	Heriot-Watt University, UK
Halloy, Jose	Universitzé Paris Cité, France
Hosoda, Koh	Osaka University, Japan
Hunt, Alexander	Portland State University, USA
Krapp, Holger G.	Imperial College London, UK
Laschi, Cecilia	National University of Singapore, Singapore
Lepora, Nathan	University of Bristol, UK
Martinez-Hernandez, Uriel	University of Bath, UK
Mazzolai, Barbara	Istituto Italiano die Tecnologia, Italy
Meder, Fabian	Italian Institute of Technology, Italy
Mura, Anna	Institute for Bioengineering of Catalonia, Spain
Prescott, Tony	University of Sheffield, UK
Quinn, Roger	Case Western Reserve University, USA
Shimizu, Masahiro	Osaka University, Japan
Speck, Thomas	Albert-Ludwigs-Universität Freiburg, Germany

Szczecinski, Nicholas	West Virginia University, USA
Tauber, Falk	Albert-Ludwigs-Universität Freiburg, Germany
Verschure, Paul F. M. J.	Radboud University, The Netherlands
Vouloutsi, Vasiliki	Technology Innovation Institute, UAE
Webster-Wood, Victoria	Carnegie Mellon University, USA

Reviewers

Abhimanyu	Carnegie Mellon University, USA
Andrada, Emanuel	Friedrich Schiller University Jena, Germany
Ayers, Joseph	Northeastern University, USA
Bal, Cafer	Firat University, Turkey
Bennington, Michael	Carnegie Mellon University, USA
Bhat, Anoop	Carnegie Mellon University, USA
Cai, Yilin	Carnegie Mellon University, USA
Cal, Raul	Portland State University, USA
Cuayáhuitl, Heriberto	University of Lincoln, UK
Cutkosky, Mark	Stanford University, USA
Cutsuridis, Vassilis	University of Lincoln, UK
Dai, Kevin	Carnegie Mellon University, USA
Danner, Simon	Drexel University, USA
Dickerson, Bradley	Princeton University, USA
Dupeyroux, Julien	Delft University of Technology, The Netherlands
Etesami, Faryar	Portland State University, USA
Fischer, Martin	Friedrich Schiller University Jena, Germany
Freire, Ismael	University of Pompeu Fabra, Spain
Gao, Ya	Carnegie Mellon University, USA
Gebehart, Corinna	Champalimaud Foundation, Portugal
Girard, Benoît	Sorbonne University and CNRS, France
Goldsmith, Clarissa	West Virginia University, USA
Guie, Chloe	West Virginia University, USA
Guix, Maria	Institute for Bioengineering of Catalonia, Spain
Hauser, Helmut	University of Bristol and Bristol Robotics Laboratory, UK
Hosoda, Koh	Osaka University, Japan
Hunt, Alexander	Portland State University, USA
Ijspeert, Auke	Swiss Federal Institute of Technology in Lausanne (EPFL), Switzerland
Jimenez Rodriguez, Alejandro	University of Sheffield, UK
Kandhari, Akhil	Case Western Reserve University, USA
Kimura, Hiroshi	Kyoto Institute of Technology, Japan
Kodono, Kodai	Kyoto Institute of Technology, Japan
Li, Lu	Carnegie Mellon University, USA

Liao, Ashlee S.	Carnegie Mellon University, USA
Lipor, John	Portland State University, USA
Manoonpong, Poramate	University of Southern Denmark, Denmark; Vidyasirimedhi Institute of Science and Technology (VISTEC), Thailand, and Nanjing University of Aeronautics and Astronautics, China
Martinez-Hernandez, Uriel	University of Bath, UK
Meder, Fabian	Italian Institute of Technology, Italy
Mitchener, Ludovico	PhycoWorks, UK
Moses, Kenneth	Case Western Reserve University, USA
Mura, Anna	Institute for Bioengineering of Catalonia, Spain
Nagel, Katherine	New York University Langone Health, USA
Najem, Joseph	Pennsylvania State University, USA
Pearson, Martin	University of the West England and Bristol Robotics Laboratory, UK
Peterka, Robert	Portland VA Medical Center and Oregon Health and Science University, USA
Philamore, Hemma	University of the West England and Bristol Robotics Laboratory, UK
Philippides, Andy	University of Sussex, UK
Pickard, Shanel	University of Illinois Urbana-Champaign, USA
Prescott, Tony	University of Sheffield, UK
Quinn, Roger	Case Western Reserve University, USA
Raman, Ritu	Massachusetts Institute of Technology, USA
Recktenwald, Gerald	Portland State University, USA
Saal, Hannes	University of Sheffield, UK
Santos-Pata, Diogo	Institute for Bioengineering of Catalonia, Spain
Schaffer, Saul	Carnegie Mellon University, USA
Sinibaldi, Edoardo	Italian Institute of Technology, Italy
Sukhnandan, Ravesh	Carngie Mellon University, USA
Sun, Xuelong	University of Lincoln, UK
Sun, Wenhuan	Carnegie Mellon University, USA
Sutton, Greg	University of Lincoln, UK
Swallow, Ben	University of Glasgow, UK
Szczecinski, Nicholas	West Virginia University, USA
Tauber, Falk	Albert-Ludwigs-Universität Freiburg, Germany
Taylor, Brian	University of North Carolina at Chapel Hill, USA
Tresch, Matthew	Northwestern University, USA
Umedachi, Takuya	University of Tokyo, Japan
Varona, Pablo	Autonomous University of Madrid, Spain
Vouloutsi, Vasiliki	Technology Innovation Institute, UAE
Ward-Cherrier, Benjamin	University of Bristol, UK

Webster-Wood, Victoria   Carnegie Mellon University, USA
Wilson, Stuart   University of Sheffield, UK
Young, Fletcher   Case Western Reserve University, USA
Yuan, Wenzhen   Carnegie Mellon University, USA
Zareh, Hormoz   Portland State University, USA
Zhang, Ketao   Queen Mary University of London, UK
Zucca, Riccardo   University of Pompeu Fabra, Spain
Zyhowski, William   West Virginia University, USA

Contents

Unit Cell Based Artificial Venus Flytrap

Falk J. Tauber[1,2](✉) ⓘ, Laura Riechert[1] ⓘ, Joscha Teichmann[1] ⓘ,
Nivedya Poovathody[1,2] ⓘ, Uwe Jonas[2,3], Stefan Schiller[2,3] ⓘ,
and Thomas Speck[1,2,4] ⓘ

[1] Plant Biomechanics Group (PBG) Freiburg, Botanic Garden of the University of Freiburg,
Freiburg im Breisgau, Germany
falk.tauber@biologie.uni-freiburg.de
[2] Cluster of Excellence livMatS @ FIT–Freiburg Center for Interactive Materials and
Bioinspired Technologies, University of Freiburg, Freiburg im Breisgau, Germany
[3] Hilde Mangold Haus - Centre for Integrative Biological Signalling Studies (CIBSS),
University of Freiburg, Freiburg im Breisgau, Germany
[4] Freiburg Center for Interactive Materials and Bioinspired Technologies (FIT), University of
Freiburg, Freiburg im Breisgau, Germany

Abstract. Nature's "inventions" have inspired designers, researchers and engineers for centuries. Over the past 25 years, progressive improvements in analytical and manufacturing technologies allowed us to understand more and more biological principles and to apply them to engineered systems. In recent years, this has led to the advancement and use of metamaterials in bioinspired systems. These material systems, mostly based on unit cells, allow engineering systems to be equipped with ever-new nature-like capabilities. In this study, we use novel bending elements to create doubly curved surfaces that can snap from concave to convex like the lobes of a Venus flytrap. By connecting two of these surfaces using a central actuator unit cell, an artificial Venus flytrap based on unit cells can be created for the first time. In this study, the closing behavior and the force required for the movement are characterized. Based on these results, a suitable environmentally activated actuator will be selected to generate an autonomous and adaptive artificial Venus flytrap system that can be used as a gripper for autonomous systems in the future.

Keywords: Artificial venus flytrap · Unit cell · Metamaterial · Snapping mechanics · Biomimetics

1 Introduction

Metamaterials fascinate researchers since late 20th century, by definition these materials inherit properties beyond natural occurring materials from there designed structural geometry [1, 2]. Often based on a confluence of several self-repeating unit cells, in which the exact geometry of the underlying unit cell determines the properties of the

© The Author(s), under exclusive license to Springer Nature Switzerland AG 2022
A. Hunt et al. (Eds.): Living Machines 2022, LNAI 13548, pp. 1–12, 2022.
https://doi.org/10.1007/978-3-031-20470-8_1

overall metamaterial. Through the combination of different unit cell geometries, the material can achieve different states and properties.

The most prominent feature of metamaterials is the possibility to create materials with negative Poisson ratios, which are called auxetic (meta-)materials. Poisson's ratio is defined as the negative transverse strain divided by the axial strain in the direction of stretching force [3]. Meaning, a material either expands in all directions or contracts in all directions if a one-dimensional force is applied [2]. Materials with negative Poisson's ratio do not expand under pressure but thicken under the compression point as material is pulled inward, as well as they do not thin under tension but extend laterally due to their internal auxetic structuring [4]. However, mechanical metamaterials have since evolved to include structures that exhibit pattern or shape change when force is applied, or that can propagate waves or motion in desired directions [1, 2]. For example, Raney et al. (2016) [5] presented metamaterials that are based upon unstable elements, using these bistable elements to develop mechanical, lossless signal propagation that can also be used to implement logic circuits.

The origins of the mechanical metamaterial used in this study lay in work of Ou et al. (2018) who created "KinetiX" structures [6]. Rotating polygon type auxetic structures which are simplified to a four-bar linkage of rigid plates and elastic or rotary hinges (Fig. 1 A), enabling planar and spatial shape changes by varying the plate and hinge positions and angles, such as uniform scaling, shearing, bending and rotating (Fig. 1 B). Ou et al. (2018) theoretically described an out-of-plane rotation unit, in which all rigid plates were tilted in a 45° angle, which was not used in their final bending unit, which only had one set of angled plates.

The use of these metamaterial systems enabled us to create unprecedented structures like doubly curved surfaces changing from concave to convex by applying force to only one unit cell. These doubly curved surfaces can be used as lobes for a metamaterial-based artificial Venus flytrap (AVF).

Venus flytraps (*Dionaea muscipula*) are carnivorous plants with active snapping traps. These traps are modified leaves consisting two of bilaterally symmetric, doubly curved trapezoidal lobes connected by a midrib and typically close within 100–500 ms (Fig. 2 A) [7–10]. Trap closure of *Dionaea muscipula* is a combination of a first turgor change-based slower motion, and a second passive, fast motion based on the release of stored elastic energy in an abrupt geometric change of its trap lobes snap-buckling from a concave to a convex state (looking at the outer lobe side) [7–10].

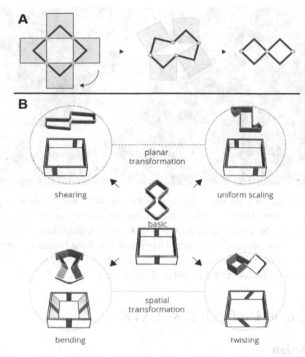

Fig. 1. KinetiX metamaterial structures. A) KinetiX principle is based on rotating polygons auxetic geometry, four squares rotate at the junctions (blue circles). Fixed corners at 90° to each other (red lines) replace grey squares, reducing the structure to bars and hinges that exhibit planar transformation if moved. B) Changing certain parameters (joint position, joint- and wall-angle) of the basic KinetiX shape (center) creates four different structures with novel properties for planar and spatial transformation. (Figures in A and B are reprinted from publication [6], Computers & Graphics, Volume 75, October 2018, Pages 72–81, with permission from Elsevier Ltd.)

In this study, we designed a unit cell based on the theoretical examples presented by Ou et al. (2018) with two sets of angled rigid plates to allow not only a bending but also a curving motion. Negating the need to use a bending and shearing unit in combination, as Ou et al. (2018) did, to create a curvature. This study´s goal is to create a metamaterial based skeleton for an AVF [11, 12] with lobes that mimic the bilaterally symmetric and doubly curved trapezoidal geometry of *Dionaea muscipula* snap-traps and their snap-buckling behavior (Fig. 2 B). To achieve this goal we create for the first time a doubly curved concave surface from KinetiX like unit cells connected by a central actuation unit cell mimicking the midrib in the biological model. In this study, the motion of the system as well as the force necessary to move and close the system via the central unit are characterized, to afterwards allow for choosing a suitable autonomous actuator for the system. This unit cell based AVF (UC AVF) shall function as a basis for the development of a metamaterial based autonomous actuating AVF.

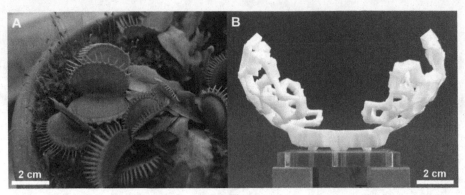

Fig. 2. The biological model plant Venus flytrap (*Dionaea muscipula*) (A) shows one of the fastest and most complex trap motion behaviors in the plant kingdom. After a sequential stimulation of the trigger hairs within 20 s, the trap closes within 100–500 ms in a snap buckling motion, changing their lobe curvatures from concave to convex. Using unit cell based meta-materials an artificial Venus flytrap (B) has been built able to change lobe curvature from concave to convex like the biological model and thus performing a snap-buckling motion.

2 Construction of Unit Cell Based AVF

2.1 Unit Cell Design

Our unit cell design is based on the theoretical hingeout-plane rotation model described in Ou et al. (2018). Yet the design varies from the KinetiX bending unit in one crucial aspect as it uses two sets of angled rigid plates to allow not only for a bending but also for a curving motion of the designed surface. Negating the need for a combination of a bending and shearing unit to achieve curvature.

Fig. 3. Two inward and outward inclined walls, perpendicular to each other, form a double bending element (A). Combing nine bending elements in a 3x3x3 array (B) creates a concave or convex bending surface, if actuated horizontally or perpendicular. Two bending surfaces are connected by a central actuation unit, which as a whole forms an artificial Venus flytrap based on unit cells (C).

The following wall configurations and design steps were used to create the novel double bending element in this study that enables to obtain a double curved surface. For this purpose, an inward inclined at 67.5° rigid wall was constructed and perpendicular oriented to an outward inclined wall with the same angle, resulting in the bending element (Fig. 3 A). Because of the inclination, the wall length is different at the top and bottom. The long section is 12.07 mm and the short section is 7.93 mm long. The actual height of the model kept at 10 mm, so the distance at the inclined wall is fixed at the angle of 67.5° to 10.82 mm.

For the first functional test prints, joints made of flexible materials were used, which were initially simple rectangles and then redesigned into a triangular and hourglass design. The demonstrators were printed with PolyJet multi-material 3D printers (Object260 Connex3, Stratasys). TangoBlackPlus™ was used as a material for the flexible joints and Rigur™ (RGD450) for the rigid walls and pin joints (Table 1).

Table 1. Properties of the printing materials[*]

Material	Tensile strength [MPa]	Elongation at break [%]	Shore hardness [Scale]	Modulus of elasticity [MPa]
Tango BlackPlus™	1.3–1.8	110–130	A 35–40	–
Rigur™	40–45	20–35	D 80–84	1700–2100

[*] Material datasheet values (https://3dprinting.co.uk/wp-content/uploads/2016/11/Polyjet-Materials-Data-Sheet.pdf accessed 14 June 2022 3:30 pm)

Pin joints were used for the final actuator as these show an improved motion transmission compared to the flexible joints. A preceding comparative parameter study of the curvature behavior of the bending units, using different joint materials and geometries (data not shown), showed that the flexible joints made of TangoBlackPlus™ exhibit a poor durability. The flexible joints did not sufficiently transmit the motion and force from compression of the central actuation unit to the surrounding unit cells. Additionally, a stiffness gradient was introduced into the system by varying the material composition of the flexible joints. However, this only slightly improved the force transmission but not the relaxation over time. For the bending elements with flexible joints a decrease in curvature over time was observed, which was not the case in bending units with rigid material pin joints. However, the tolerances within the pin joints must be maintained rigorously, otherwise the joints will fuse during printing. A tolerance of 0.25 mm for straight joints and 0.20 mm for angled joints was considered feasible. The height of the lobe surfaces was reduced to 5 mm and the height of the central actuation unit and the two adjacent bending elements was set at 10 mm to ensure better force transmission. For scaling the system (up or down) the percentage ratios of wall height from the lobe units to the central unit of 50%, the width of the lobe unit to the width of the central units of 78% and the pin joint tolerance to the outer joint diameter of 12% should be kept. It should be noted here that the hinge tolerance was limited by the printer resolution.

2.2 Motion and Actuation Force Characterization

In order to characterize the developed UC AVF, three identical replicates of the demonstrators (further mentioned as demonstrator 1, 2 and 3) with pin joints have been designed and fabricated. The snapping motion of UC AVF lobes was analyzed via video recordings in a horizontal orientation during manual actuation. The necessary actuation force to close the UC AVF was measured using a universal testing machine (Inspekt table 5 kN, Hegewald & Peschke). The UC AVF were attached vertically in a concave open state to a specifically designed 3D printed sample mount. The central actuator of each demonstrator was compressed 30 times via a 3D-printed pressure pin that allowed localized force application to the hinge. Video recordings of the force measurements were used for analyzing the motion response of the UC AVF to the localized force application. Blender was used to track the circumference of the lobes, and Python to synchronize the data with the video, which allowed a determination of the point during the motion where the lowest force is required.

3   Results

All of the produced UC AVF demonstrators showed the expected motion behavior and achieved inversion of lobe curvature from concave to convex after compression of the central actuation unit. With reduced lobes surface height of 5 mm and the higher central unit the UC AVF achieves an open concave curvature $\kappa = -0.124$ cm^{-1} (median $\sigma = 0.002$ cm^{-1}, n = 8), a closed convex curvature of $\kappa = 0.134$ cm^{-1} directly after actuation and $\kappa = 0.133$ cm^{-1} after 30 s (median in each case, $\sigma = 0.027$ cm^{-1}, n = 8). As described above using pin joints no relaxation over time was observed. Actuated manually the lobes closed within 300 to 600 ms and the lobe tips achieved average speeds of 1.19 m/s (right lobe) to 1.69 m/s (left lobe) after passage of the 0° curvature point (Fig. 4 A–D). Only marginal differences between the three demonstrators were observed during manual actuation in closing behavior or speeds.

In contrast, in measuring the necessary force for lobe closure in a universal testing machine with a constant movement speed of the compression anvil, differences between the three demonstrators were found in the force necessary for closure. The force required to close the lobes initially increases to 1.5–2 N (depending on the demonstrator) and then drops to a local minimum of 0.25–1 N after the lobes pass the 0° point of curvature (Fig. 5 A). As the lobes continue to close, the force increases again until the steric hindrance of the geometry prevents further closure without damaging the demonstrator at 60% compression and 2–4 N (Fig. 5 A, E). For demonstrator 1 with a peak force average

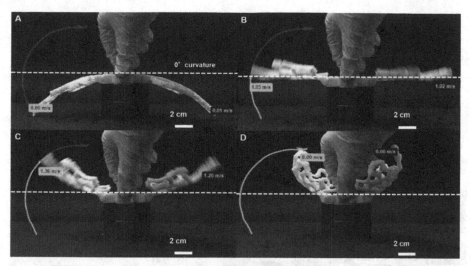

Fig. 4. Closing motion of the UC AVF: Exemplary manual actuation of UC AVF. Central actuation is followed by a closure motion (A-D) with an inversion of the lobe curvature from a concave (A) to convex (D), due to the kinematic coupling of the central unit to the lobes. The lobes accelerate and achieve tip speeds of up to 1.36 m/s (C).

of 1.5 N during curvature inversion and an overall average force of 0.79 ± 0.42 N, the necessary force to close the lobes is the lowest observed (Fig. 5 A). For demonstrator 2 the highest values were observed, with a peak force average of 2 N during curvature inversion and an overall average force of 1.72 ± 0.76 N (Fig. 5 A). Significant differences were observed between the three demonstrators force values at 0° curvature (4.13 ± 0.08 mm or ~ 16% of compression), here demonstrator 1 (median 0.75 N) shows significantly lower values than demonstrator 2 (median 1.11 N) and demonstrator 3 (median 1.08 N) (Fig. 5 B). No significant difference in force values for the latter two were observed.

The circumferential analysis, from the videos of the measurements described above, tracking the change in the circumference of demonstrator over time in response to the applied force, allows to link the circumferential change to the applied force (orange line in Fig. 5 C–E). Indicating that the lowest force for the closing motion is required after the transition point of 0° curvature at 20% compression. This is exemplary shown for a measurement of demonstrator 3 in Fig. 5 C at 20% perimeter response when the force value drops below 0.4 N. Since the demonstrator is viewed from above, the transition point here corresponds to the largest measured circumference.

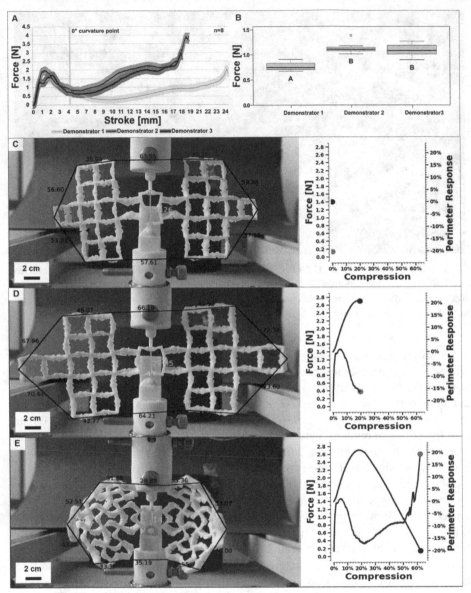

Fig. 5. Characterization of the closure force of the three demonstrators. A): The force necessary to close the lobes varies between the three demonstrators, with highest values observed in demonstrator 2. The load curve follows the same trajectories in a three demonstrators, with an initial rise of force. After passing the 0° curvature point a force drop can be observed followed by a constant rise of force as the lobes close further until maximum closure. B): Significant difference between the demonstrators were observed in the amount of force necessary to achieve 0° curvature. The capital letters represent significance levels. Different letters indicate a significant difference in force with p-values below 0.01. C-E): Exemplary force measurement of demonstrator 3 with tracked perimeter response to the applied force. The circumference analysis indicates that the least amount of force is necessary at a central actuation unit compression of 20% after passing of the 0° curvature point (C).

4 Discussion

4.1 Snapping Motion of UC AVF

In the UC AVF we successfully transferred the snap buckling behavior of *Dionaea mus-cipula* trap into a unit cell based technical demonstrator. Curvature inversion of the trap lobes was achieved via specifically designed double bending unit cells. The designed models are based on a derivate of the KinetiX bending structures which were only the-oretically described by Ou et al. (2018), but not further explained or the combination to a surface shown. Within this study several parameters were investigated which were not addressed in Ou et al. (2018), i.e. the variations in flexible joint geometry, a hardness gra-dient due to material mixtures within a model, and different structure heights. The double bending unit cells, presented in this study, allowed for the creation of two double-curved surfaces connected via central actuation unit, representing the midrib of the biological model. A structure height reduction of the lobes, allowed to obtain a stronger actuation in bending cells, and a structure height increase in the central actuation unit, resulted in a significantly higher and more robust lobe curvature. One parameter that has not been changed within in this study, was the wall angle of the bending elements, for which an increase would probably result in a higher curvature. Here, further investigations are needed to establish a relation between angle to height and wall lengths and the resulting greater curvature.

By manually actuating the UC AVF the snapping behavior could be investigated and lobe curvature and motion speeds could be analyzed. The observed lobe speeds marginally varied in between the demonstrators. In the case of manual actuation, it is simple to reverse the snapping motion. Since it is only necessary to compress the cen-tral part in the opposite direction in order to reverse the movement and the snapping, thus reopening UC AVF through the kinematic coupling of the central unit to the lobes. However, the manual actuation only enabled a qualitative analysis and comparison of the UC AVF snapping behavior to the biological model. The manual actuation is highly test person dependent and biased in applied force and speed. As a quantitative analysis, force displacement measurements were performed to analyze the behavior and the force necessary for the closure motion. The force displacement curves show that an internal force maximum–due to inner joint resistance and friction–must first be overcome to initially set the trap halves in motion and reach the 0° curvature horizontal orientation. After passing the 0° curvature point, a local force minimum occurs when the closing movement commences, followed by an increase of the force during further closing and reaching the maximum when the steric hindrance by the geometry occurs (Fig. 4 A–D, Fig. 5 A, C–D). The joint tolerances in the UC AVF allow for a bit of movement and play resulting in slightly tilted joints. At the 0° curvature point, the joints adjacent to the central actuator unit change their angle from slightly outward tilted over a perpendicular orien-tation to an inward tilt. During this change in orientation, the joint resistance changes and the force necessary to move drops. If the joint tolerance could be reduced further the play would vanish. For an ideal system friction-less joints with high force transition would be ideal, but such systems cannot be generated via 3D printed and without the use of lubricant. Within the measurements significant differences between the demon-strators were observed (Fig. 5 A, B). We attribute the observed differences between the demonstrators to small variations of the joints and possible variations in clamping in the test machine. To keep differences small, the demonstrators were manufactured with the same material- and print-settings, and cleaned with the same procedures. However, the smallest variations may have occurred during cleaning, as the joints are small and delicate (0.25 mm gap), it may not have been possible to completely remove all support material from all joints. The scalability of the system and of the pin joints markedly depends on the used printing method. The resolution of the printer limited the gap size to 0.25 mm, otherwise it would not have been possible to remove the support from the pin joints. If a high-resolution printing system such as a multiphoton lithography printer would be used, the pin joints and the entire system could significantly be reduced in size. However, with this method the printing time for a full-size model would be several days instead of several hours. If the ratios are maintained, the only factor limiting the upscaling of the model with the current printer system is the build volume of the printer.

If the closure motion is stopped before the steric hindrance of the geometry occurs, the necessary actuation force to fully close the UC AVF can be kept at the first maximum of curvature inversion. Thus, this first peak can be seen as a minimum force requirement for a possible actuator, so that it "only" has to overcome the internal friction forces of the joints at the beginning of the movement, which amount to 2 N and 1.6 mm of stroke on average.

An electric linear motor could easily drive the system, but as the system is intended to be used in autonomous applications as grippers or support structures for solar energy harvesters, an autonomous actuator system is needed. For this, possible actuation schemes could be shape memory alloy springs attached to the inner walls or pneumatic cushions compressing the outer walls of the central actuation unit, as these systems would be able to generate the necessary force [11, 12]. A reduction of joint friction with lubricants could enable the use of shape memory polymers developing up 3.6 N restoring force and stresses up to 0.65 MPa [13–16]. The central actuation unit has to be redesigned for an integrated actuation system. For the generation of an autonomous system the actuation system could be driven via an environmental temperature change in case of shape memory alloys/polymers and an on board pressure generation in case of the pneumatic cushions.

Using compliant mechanisms, the central actuation unit could be redesigned to a snap outward and trigger the closure of the UC AVF [17–20]. The central actuation unit could be replaced by a bistable beam actuator, in which the left and right joint of the central actuation unit (viewed from above see Fig. 3 C) would be replaced by bistable beams. The upper and lower joint would be replaced by struts fixed to a frame. This would allow the bistable snap to actuate the entire system, resulting in a reduction of actuation force and enabling the use of less powerful thermo-responsive actuators.

5 Conclusion

Complex meta-material structures can be used to build artificial bioinspired systems performing complex motion sequences. In this study, we developed and characterized a unit cell based artificial Venus flytrap (UC AVF). The basic unit cell used in this study was inspired by the KinetiX structures. We redesigned the unit cell to enable the formation of a double curved surface by using two sets of tilted walls with rigid pin joints. This novel bending unit cell was used to create an artificial Venus flytrap consisting of two concave lobes connected via central unit, like the trap of the biological model *Dionaea muscipula*. By compressing the central actuation unit the lobes snap from a concave to convex configuration. The motion of the central actuation unit's compression is transmitted via kinematic coupling of the adjacent unit cells to the lobe unit cells. Here we characterized not only the motion but also the force necessary to close the lobes. Revealing, that a higher force is initially required to overcome the internal resistance of the joints to initiate the motion. Thereafter the required force drops to a minimum when the lobes pass the 0° curvature point.

Identifying the force requirements enables us in the next step to select a suitable actuator for an autonomous actuation. This novel UC AVF will enable us to build unit cell based autonomous grippers and support structures for soft machines performing complex motion sequences in the future.

Acknowledgement. Funded by the Deutsche Forschungsgemeinschaft (DFG, German Research Foundation) under Germany's Excellence Strategy–EXC-2193/1–390951807.

References

1. Bertoldi, K., Vitelli, V., Christensen, J., van Hecke, M.: Flexible mechanical metamaterials. Nat. Rev. Mater. **2**, 17066 (2017). https://doi.org/10.1038/natrevmats.2017.66
2. Saxena, K.K., Das, R., Calius, E.P.: Three decades of auxetics research – materials with negative poisson's ratio: a review. Adv. Eng. Mater. **18**, 1847–1870 (2016). https://doi.org/10.1002/adem.201600053
3. Lakes, R.: Foam structures with a negative poisson's ratio. Science **235**, 1038–1040 (1987). https://doi.org/10.1126/science.235.4792.1038
4. Evans, K.E., Alderson, A.: Auxetic materials: functional materials and structures from lateral thinking! Adv. Mater. **12**, 617–628 (2000). https://doi.org/10.1002/(SICI)1521-4095(200005)12:9%3c617:AID-ADMA617%3e3.0.CO;2-3
5. Raney, J.R., Nadkarni, N., Daraio, C., Kochmann, D.M., Lewis, J.A., Bertoldi, K.: Stable propagation of mechanical signals in soft media using stored elastic energy. Proc. Natl. Acad. Sci. **113**(35), 9722–9727 (2016). https://doi.org/10.1073/pnas.1604838113
6. Ou, J., Ma, Z., Peters, J., Vlavianos, N., Ishiii, H.: KinetiX–designing auxetic-inspired deformable material structures. Comput. Graph. **75**, 72–81 (2018). https://doi.org/10.1016/j.cag.2018.06.003
7. Westermeier, A.S., et al.: How the carnivorous waterwheel plant (Aldrovanda vesiculosa) snaps. Proc. Biol. Sci. **285**, 1–10 (2018). https://doi.org/10.1098/rspb.2018.0012
8. Poppinga, S., Bauer, U., Speck, T., Volkov, A.G.: Motile traps. In: Ellison, A., Adamec, L. (eds.) Carnivorous Plants: Physiology, Ecology, and Evolution, pp. 180–193. Oxford University Press (2018)
9. Poppinga, S., Kampowski, T., Metzger, A., Speck, O., Speck, T.: Comparative kinematical analyses of Venus flytrap (Dionaea muscipula) snap traps. Beilstein J. Nanotechnol **7**, 664–674 (2016). https://doi.org/10.3762/bjnano.7.59
10. Poppinga, S., Joyeux, M.: Different mechanics of snap-trapping in the two closely related carnivorous plants Dionaea muscipula and Aldrovanda vesiculosa. Phys. Rev. E **84**, 041928–041935 (2011). https://doi.org/10.1103/PhysRevE.84.041928

11. Esser, F.J., Auth, P., Speck, T.: Artificial Venus flytraps: a research review and outlook on their importance for novel bioinspired materials systems. Front Robot AI **7**, 75 (2020). https://doi.org/10.3389/frobt.2020.00075
12. Esser, F., et al.: Adaptive biomimetic actuator systems reacting to various stimuli by and combining two biological snap-trap mechanics. In: Martinez-Hernandez, U., et al. (eds.) Living Machines 2019. LNCS (LNAI), vol. 11556, pp. 114–121. Springer, Cham (2019). https://doi.org/10.1007/978-3-030-24741-6_10
13. Lendlein, A., Balk, M., Tarazona, N.A., Gould, O.E.C.: Bioperspectives for shape-memory polymers as shape programmable, active materials. Biomacromolecules **20**, 3627–3640 (2019). https://doi.org/10.1021/acs.biomac.9b01074
14. Monzón, M.D., et al.: 4D printing: processability and measurement of recovery force in shape memory polymers. The Int. J. Adv. Manuf. Technol. **89**(5–8), 1827–1836 (2016). https://doi.org/10.1007/s00170-016-9233-9
15. Song, J.J., Chang, H.H., Naguib, H.E.: Biocompatible shape memory polymer actuators with high force capabilities. Eur. Polymer J. **67**, 186–198 (2015). https://doi.org/10.1016/j.eurpolymj.2015.03.067
16. Lendlein, A., Kelch, S.: Shape-memory polymers. Angew. Chem. Int. Ed. **41**, 2034 (2002). https://doi.org/10.1002/1521-3773(20020617)41:12%3c2034:AID-ANIE2034%3e3.0.CO;2-M
17. Jeong, H.Y., et al.: 3D printing of twisting and rotational bistable structures with tuning elements. Sci Rep **9**, 324 (2019). https://doi.org/10.1038/s41598-018-36936-6
18. Howell, L.L., Magleby, S.P., Olsen, B.M. (eds.): Handbook of Compliant Mechanisms. Wiley, Chichester, West Sussex, United Kingdom, Hoboken, New Jersey (2013)
19. Greenberg, H.C., Gong, M.L., Magleby, S.P., Howell, L.L.: Identifying links between origami and compliant mechanisms. Mech. Sci. **2**, 217–225 (2011). https://doi.org/10.5194/ms-2-217-2011
20. Lobontiu, N.: Compliant Mechanisms. CRC Press (2002)

Ten Years of Living Machines Conferences: Transformers-Based Automated Topic Grouping

Théophile Carniel[1,2(✉)], Leo Cazenille[1], Jean-Michel Dalle[2,3,4], and José Halloy[1]

[1] Université Paris Cité, CNRS, LIED UMR 8236, 75006 Paris, France
[2] Agoranov, Paris, France
tc@agoranov.com
[3] Sorbonne Université, Paris, France
[4] École Polytechnique, Palaiseau, France

Abstract. The overwhelming growth in the number of scientific publications has its drawbacks: it is difficult to cope with it. Researchers need to constantly process the information contained in a very large and increasing number of articles to be up-to-date with their research community. This is especially difficult when interdisciplinary research requires knowledge of the state of the art in different fields. High interdisciplinarity is at the heart of the Living Machines conferences, which bring together scientists from different fields of biology, neuroscience, physics, robotics, artificial intelligence and other engineering fields. Here, using algorithmic AI methods, we analyze the publications of the ten "Living Machines" conferences to automatically discover clusters of research topics. We show that neural networks for natural language processing can find a set of thematic clusters that correspond to different research topics within this community.

Keywords: Text mining · Bibliography · Natural language processing · Emerging topics · BERT · Transformers · Clustering

1 Introduction

The first edition of the Living Machines conference took place 10 years ago. This new conference was created on the premise that "the development of future real-world technologies will depend strongly on our understanding and harnessing of the principles underlying living systems and the flow of communication signals between living and artificial systems," which translates into the emergence of a bio-inspired and bio-based [17] interdisciplinary scientific field that draws expertise from robotics, computer science, biology and the natural sciences in order to design and build machines capable of interacting with their environments on a near-human level. The interdisciplinary nature and rapid development of this nascent field, however, makes it difficult for any given individual to have a global knowledge of the state-of-the-art in the field of Living Machines.

© The Author(s), under exclusive license to Springer Nature Switzerland AG 2022
A. Hunt et al. (Eds.): Living Machines 2022, LNAI 13548, pp. 13–26, 2022.
https://doi.org/10.1007/978-3-031-20470-8_2

Even for a relatively young and small conference such as Living Machines, getting up-to-date with the current production is an arduous task. Indeed, reading and understanding of about 500 articles that have so far been published in the conference proceedings [8, 15, 16, 20, 22, 28, 36, 37, 40] represents a sizable investment in terms of human resources with no guarantees as to the pertinence of their contents. The magnitude of the problem scales with the complexity of a given domain of interest. Recent developments in the field of text mining [7, 38] can however offer substantial solutions to this problem by processing, analyzing and summarizing scientific corpora in an automated and efficient manner, thus providing tools to easily characterize a new corpus. One can imagine that text analysis algorithms can be useful in many ways, such as categorizing articles, writing summaries of groups of articles, identifying areas that emerge in research. These results can then contribute to the state of the art of a field. It can also allow experts in the field to identify research efforts that are not sufficiently developed.

Objectives
Our goal is to discover a list of overarching research topics presented in publications from Living Machines conferences between 2012 and 2020. We analyze the complete set of published articles to perform their automatic grouping by research topic. To perform this automatic analysis, we develop a methodology based on natural language processing by transformers. Once the main themes are automatically identified, we evaluate their proximity. Then, we analyze the proportions of each theme and their temporal evolution. Finally, we define the co-author network between the authors participating in the conferences.

2   Methods

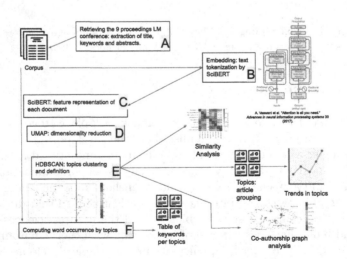

Fig. 1. Workflow of the proposed methodology to automate the clustering of all Living Machines articles by theme. The Transformer BERT model is described by a picture from [35].

We propose a methodology based on [12] that will automatically read the corpus of Living Machine articles, create a vectoral representation ("embedding") of each article and use that representation to automatically cluster similar articles together based on the topic of the article. Additional analysis is performed on the basis of these topics. The general workflow is described in Fig. 1.

The proceedings of the 2012–2020 Living Machines conferences are read and analyzed using the PyMuPDF[1] package to separate the articles and extract the authors, abstract, title, body and references of each article (Fig. 1**A**). Here we only use the title, abstract and keywords when provided and not the whole article text.

After eliminating 33 articles that do not have abstracts, 461 articles remain in our sample down from the original 494 articles available in the proceedings. The title, abstract and keywords of each article are entered into the algorithm, which transforms this data into a latent description of the topics studied in the article (articles corresponding to similar topics are closer in the latent space). The embedding of each article is done using a recent and effective deep learning technique for natural language processing, called *Transformers* [35] (Fig. 1**B**). Transformers have in recent years become the main method to work with natural language thanks to their particular self-attention mechanism. This mechanism has the benefit (among others) of giving the model a better "understanding" of language achieved through an improved learning of the general context of words and of the interdependence of terms in the context of a sentence. Here we use a pre-trained version of the Bidirectional Encoder Representations from Transformers (BERT) model [6] called SciBERT [1] specifically trained on scientific literature (Fig. 1**C**).

In applying this model, each token (sequence of characters, or morphemes) is embedded in a 768-dimensional embedding space. As this space is not latent, we reduce the dimension of this space to a projected latent space of dimension 5 using the UMAP algorithm [24] (Fig. 1**D**). This dimensionality reduction step condenses the information and increases the performance of the HDBSCAN community detection algorithm [23]. This dimensionality reduction also provides the added benefits of significantly reducing memory requirements and subsequent computation time, which turn out to be particularly important when working with much larger amounts of data such as complete corpora of scientific articles. Dimension 5 is chosen empirically as it is a low-dimensional representation that provides both a good interpretability (in term of human comprehension) of the results and a low number of unlabeled articles. We note that the results presented are qualitatively valid for higher dimensional UMAP projections.

Using this latent space projection, the HDBSCAN [23] algorithm is applied to our projected vectorial representations to perform unsupervised clustering in latent space, automatically grouping items based on their main themes (Fig. 1**E**). Unlike most clustering algorithm, HDBSCAN has the ability to consider points of the dataset as *noise*; these points are considered unlabeled.

---

[1] https://github.com/pymupdf/PyMuPDF.

We then find the vocabulary specific to each cluster using a model called class-based TF-IDF (c-TF-IDF) as defined in Eq. 1, which consists in applying the standard TF-IDF method [29] treating each cluster as a single document (Fig. 1F). As TF-IDF reflects how important an ngram is to a document in a corpus, c-TF-IDF is well-suited to our use case as it reflects how important an ngram is to a cluster in a collection of clusters. Using both this cluster-specific vocabulary and looking at the individual articles in the various clusters, we label each of the resulting groupings by their research theme. It is calculated with the following equation:

$$x_{w,c} = \frac{w_c}{A_c} \times \log \frac{m}{\sum_{j=0}^{n} t_j} \tag{1}$$

where $x_{w,c}$ represents the importance of ngram w within class c, w_c the number of occurences of ngram w in class c, A_c the total number of ngrams in class c, m the number of documents in the sample, n the number of different classes and t_j the frequency of ngram t across all classes.

Preprocessing and analysis scripts are all written in Python 3.8, with the BERT models provided by the Hugging Face framework [41] and implemented with PyTorch [27].

3   Results

Applying the proposed methodology, we run the topic clustering algorithm which results in eight thematic clusters and roughly 7% of articles being unlabeled. As seen in Fig. 2, most of the unlabeled articles lay in the space between clusters 4, 5 and 6. The clusters also seem to be relatively well-separated, meaning that we retrieve fairly well-defined topics despite the small size of the corpus. As the breadth of research topics is in reality a continuum, we therefore still expect some fuzziness in terms of topic for the articles close to the border between two clusters since we work in a latent space where similar articles lay close to each other.

In order to interpret the topics for each of the clusters, we generate a specific vocabulary based on the corpora of each cluster and present the top 10 most significant words for each grouping in Table 1. The vocabulary is coherent for the individual clusters, and looking at the general concepts in each cluster we can draw three major overarching themes with Locomotion-based clusters 0, 1, 2, and 3 on the left, Sensing-based clusters 4 and 5 in the middle and Behavior-based cluster 6 and 7 on the right. This is in line with the position of individual clusters in latent space shown in Fig. 2 where similar clusters lie closer.

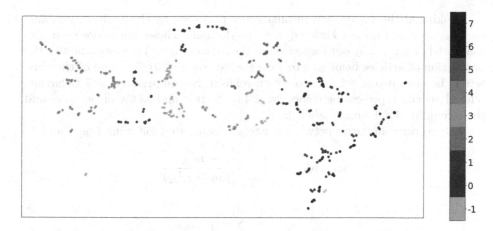

Fig. 2. Two-dimensional projection computed using UMAP of the latent representation of articles computed using the SciBERT model. The colors represent the topic labels as assigned by the HDBSCAN clustering applied to a 5-dimensional projection of the SciBERT latent representations. The gray dots represent unlabeled articles. All dimensionality reductions are performed with UMAP. We set HDBSCAN parameters $m_{clSize} = 25$, $\epsilon = 0.6$, $min\_samples = 1$ and UMAP parameter $n = 3$.

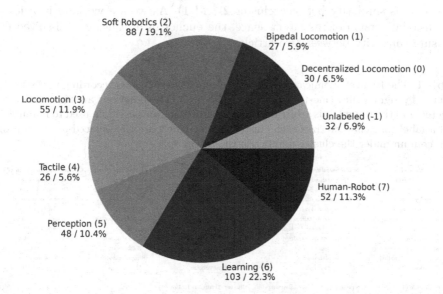

Fig. 3. Number and proportion of articles in each cluster. Cluster labels are given by the authors by looking at the top words in Table 1 for each cluster and then manually checking some articles in each cluster.

Looking at the vocabulary automatically produced by the analysis, we name each group based on our knowledge of the domain. These names are then corroborated or refined by our inspection of the article titles. Then, we quantify the proportion of articles belonging to each theme (see Fig. 3). The size of the clusters is heterogeneous, with Locomotion-related, Sensing-related and Behavior-related articles representing respectively 43.4%, 16% and 33.6% of the total and the remaining 7% being unlabeled.

The average similarity between clusters is computed following Eqs. 2 and 3:

$$s(p_k, p_l) = 1 - \frac{||p_k - p_l||_2}{\max\limits_{k,l}(||p_k - p_l||_2)} \tag{2}$$

$$S(c_i, c_j) = \frac{\sum\limits_{k=0}^{n_i} \sum\limits_{l=0}^{n_j} s(p_k, p_l)}{n_i n_j} \tag{3}$$

where $S(c_i, c_i)$ denotes the final similarity between clusters i and j, n_i the number of articles in cluster i, p_k the latent space projection of the $k - th$ article in cluster i with $k \in [0, n_i]$ and $s(p_k, p_l)$ the euclidean similarity between articles p_k and p_l. Since we perform minmax scaling on each row of the matrix, this similarity measure is asymmetrical (i.e. similarity between cluster 1 and 2 is not the same as similarity between cluster 2 and 1). As we are working in a low-dimensional version of the latent space, the euclidean distance is well-suited to measure similarity between two articles.

Table 1. The 10 most significant ngrams for each of the 9 clusters according to the Eq. 1 ordered by significance (most significant at the top). These ngrams are automatically selected and their number is arbitrarily chosen. These ngrams are then used to manually find a label that characterizes each cluster. These labels are then placed at the top of each column under the cluster number in the latent space (see Fig. 2).

Cluster -1Unlabeled (-1)	Cluster 0Decentralized Locomotion (0)	Cluster 1Bipedal Locomotion (1)	Cluster 2Soft Robotics (2)	**Cluster 3Locomotion (3)**
Manduca sexta	Decentralized control	Biarticular muscles	Soft robotics	Human balance
Visual navigation	Control scheme	Bipedal robot	Peristaltic pumping	Quadruped robot
Sexta hawkmoth	Interlimb coordination	Moment arm	Direct laser	Neural network
Hippocampal replay	Tegotaebased control	Octopus arm	Work present	Cat model
Manduca sexta hawkmoth	Autonomous decentralized control	Behavioral diversity	Mechanical properties	Balance control
Flapping wing	Decentralized control scheme	Kinetics model	Tactile sensor	Central pattern
Object identification	Autonomous decentralized	Continuum manipulator	Artificial muscle	Central pattern generator
Soft robotic fish	Snakelike robot	Biarticular actuators	Soft robotic	Pattern generator
Thermoregulatory huddling	Bipedal walking	Tail fin	Ring actuators	Neural control
Reverse replays	Optic flow	Legged robots	Muscle cells	Human balance control

Cluster 4Tactile (4)	Cluster 5Perception (5)	Cluster 6Learning (6)	**Cluster 7Human-Robot (7)**
Tactile sensors	Flyrobot interface	Neural networks	Humanrobot interaction
Tactile sensing	Machine interface	Reinforcement learning	Humanoid robot
Efficient coding	Brain machine	Motor control	Distributed adaptive control
Stick insect	Brain machine interface	Autobiographical memory	Social robots
Biomimetic tactile	Spike rate	Deep learning	Distributed adaptive
Insect antennae	Odor source	Computational model	Vocal fold
Static stability	Eye movements	Social interaction	Cognitive architecture
Virtual reality	Turning radius	Neural network	Facial expressions
Cell types	Virtual chameleon	Social interactions	Adaptive control
Climbing stick	Mobile treadmill	Collective behaviour	Sensorimotor contingencies

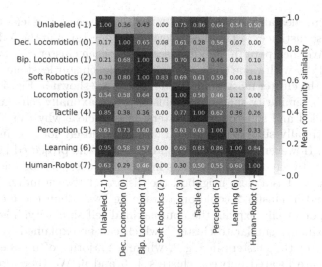

Fig. 4. Pairwise row-normalized cluster similarity matrix. The pairwise euclidean similarity between all clusters was computed according to Eq. 3; min-max scaling was then applied to each row of the matrix, making this similarity measure asymmetrical. The row for a given cluster thus gives information about the ranked similarity of the other clusters. The column for a given cluster gives global information about this cluster ranks for each of the other clusters.

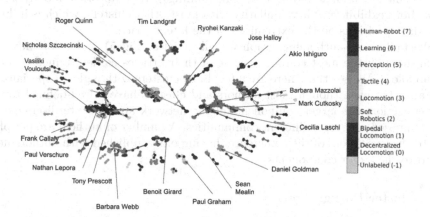

Fig. 5. Coauthorship network with nodes colored following the cluster allocation for individual authors. An author is allocated to the cluster where he has the most publications. To reduce the network, only a few selected author nodes are annotated. We remove components that have less than 3 nodes in the graph to reduce visual clutter, label the top 8 most active authors in the whole conference and, for each individual component with 10 nodes or more, we label the most active author.

We compute the pairwise euclidean similarity between all articles (Eq. 2) and aggregate these distances at the cluster level following Eq. 3 in the 5-dimensional latent space. We then perform min-max scaling for each cluster $\hat{c}$ in order to have $S(\hat{c}, c_j) \in [0, 1]$ $\forall j$ with value 0 corresponding to the cluster least similar to cluster $\hat{c}$ and 1 to the cluster most similar. The results are shown in Fig. 4 as an adjacency matrix in similarity-space. Most clusters are maximally self-similar except for the unlabeled and soft robotics clusters. It is unclear why the soft robotics cluster is maximally similar to cluster 1, which is closely located in the latent space (Fig. 2). However, as cluster 2 is spread out in the projected latent space, the distances between individual articles inside the cluster can be relatively high and, since cluster 1 is a close neighbor, the distance between individual articles in cluster 1 and in cluster 2 could on average be lower than those of cluster 2, which could potentially explain the non-maximal self-similarity. The unlabeled cluster is maximally similar to cluster 5 which can be explained by looking at the projection of the clusters in Fig. 2, where a majority of unlabeled articles (gray points) are located between clusters 4, 5 and 6. We therefore postulate that the topics of unlabeled articles are related to learning through interaction with the environment, that fall between the themes of groups 4 and 5 on the one hand and group 6 on the other. The central position of the Sensing-based clusters in terms of similarity can be explained by the necessity of sensory feedback loops for machines to operate in their environment both on a physical level (locomotion, physically interacting with their surroundings) and on a cognitive level (behavior, understanding their surroundings). *Soft Robotics* and *Human-Robot* both exhibit very low similarity with most other clusters, which is in line with their positions on the extremities of the latent space.

We build a co-authorship graph for all articles (Fig. 5) and color individual authors by the most common theme of their articles as determined by our methodology. We see that there are a few large clusters with a global specialization and that even though most authors and clusters have a well-defined topic of predilection, the larger components of the network are still interdisciplinary and composed of several different communities. A number of authors are peripheral to the social core of the conference, having only published with authors not linked to the larger components.

3.1   Cluster Backgrounds

Cluster 0 is focused on Decentralized Locomotion, with articles such as [14] which describes a decentralized control scheme for snake robots based on the *Tegotae* concept, and [5] which presents the results from a simulation of the adaptive crawling of a worm-like robot.

Cluster 1 contains articles concerning Bipedal Locomotion, such as [26] which details an algorithm for optimal placement of actuators on a bipedal robot, and [3], a study on the modeling and simulation of a novel human-inspired bipedal robot.

Cluster 2 is comprised of articles on Soft Robotics, with topics such as the design of octopus-inspired artificial suction cups [9], the design and manufacturing process of a three-finger adaptable soft gripper [21] and a collagen-based scaffold for the fabrication of living machines [39].

The selected representative works from Cluster 3 deal with Locomotion-related subjects such as a Central Pattern Generator model of quadruped locomotion [32] and a canine-inspired quadruped robot as a platform for synthetic neural network control [31].

Cluster 4's articles tend to be centered around matters of tactile perception, with subjects such as a bio-inspired antennal control model for antennal behavior in climbing stick insects [13], new sensors for biomimetic force sensing [10] and dynamical models for the description of adaptive responses to insect cuticular strain [33].

Cluster 5 contains works on perception such as [34] which presents a complete eye-head stabilization model based on vestibular reflexes, or [18] which deals with the implementation of insect-based odor classification and localization models on autonomous wheeled robots.

Cluster 6 is focused on the processes of Learning, such as a hippocampal model for learning in a navigational task [2], a biophysical model of the striatum for arbitrary sequence learning and reproduction [19] or the individual and collective biomimetic fish behavior modeling using artificial neural networks [4].

Cluster 7's articles deal with Human-Robot interactions, such as [25] which touches upon the design of a biomimetic brain-based prototype companion robot, [30] which presents the developments and insights gained from a European project designing a robot in educational settings and [11], an article about the reproduction of the Milgram experiment on a robot in order to induce an empathic state in the human subjects in the experiment.

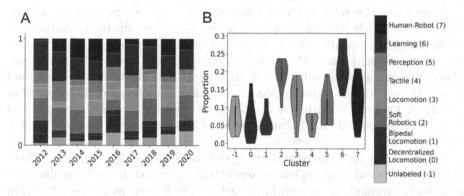

Fig. 6. Temporal evolution of the proportion of articles in each theme over the editions of the Living Machines conference (**A**) and the associated violin plots (**B**). No clear trend is discernible, which is probably due to the large fluctuations in a relatively small total number of articles. The *Soft Robotics (2)* and *Learning (6)* topics are regulars of the conference, being well-represented every edition. Topics *Bipedal Locomotion (1)* and *Tactile (4)* receive comparatively low interest throughout the whole period.

3.2   Temporal Evolution

We finally study the temporal evolution of the number of articles published in each theme for each edition of the Living Machines conference (see Fig. 6). There are no clear trends in the temporal evolution of the proportion of the different themes.This is most likely due to the fact that the study period is quite short (only 9 editions of the conference are available) and that the number of available articles is relatively small, 494 articles are available in the corpus. This relatively small corpus size automatically increases the relative importance of random fluctuations in the results. The importance of the fluctuations is illustrated in Fig. 6.B which shows the dispersion of the proportions of each theme for all edition of the conference.

4   Discussions and Conclusion

We presented a novel methodology to analyze all articles in a given corpus of interest and group them by research topic. This methodology was then applied on all editions of the Living Machines conference to identify eight thematic clusters. The algorithm classifies articles as part of one of these clusters according to their most prevalent research subject. We were able to empirically assign labels to each cluster by computing word occurrence in their respective articles: "Decentralized Locomotion", "Bipedal Locomotion", "Soft robotics", "Locomotion", "Tactile", "Perception", "Learning", and "Human-Robot". In turn, these clusters could be regrouped into three overarching topical categories: robotic locomotion, sensing and behavior. This is not surprising, as they are intuitively the most general research themes in robotic conferences.

Nonetheless this topic grouping could still be improved to some extent: the subject of an article will often not be clear-cut as the various topics determined by the algorithm are interrelated; the allocation of an article to a single topic is therefore necessarily simplistic. As a consequence, some articles also find themselves unlabeled as their subject matters fall squarely between two topics and the algorithm is unable to make a decision on their classification. As the number of unlabeled articles is fairly low compared to the total size of the corpus and as this classification difficulty can be seen as inherent to the problem, forcing allocation might not be necessary.

Note that our methodology currently only analyzes the abstract and title of each article, instead of taking into account their entire text. Indeed, the abstracts are already summarized versions of the articles, so it is easier for the algorithm to correctly identify the research subject from them compared to the whole text. Moreover, the latter may be written differently depending on the writing style of the authors, or on the type of article (review vs research article), which would render their analysis more complex to the algorithm.

It would be possible to improve further our methodology by finding several complementary groupings of the articles, identifying not only the main research theme as is done here, but also other relevant information, such as the type of article (e.g., review vs research article vs commentary), the type of method proposed or the kind of robots used. These groupings could be formulated according to a query specified by the user: the algorithm would then extract the related information in each article and group them accordingly.

Finally, we hope to use and extend our approach to larger corpora. For instance, it would be interesting how our current findings based on the Living Machines conferences relate to the broader literature in biomimetics, soft-robotics and interdisciplinary robotics.

References

1. Beltagy, I., Lo, K., Cohan, A.: Scibert: a pretrained language model for scientific text. arXiv preprint arXiv:1903.10676 (2019)
2. Boorman, L.W., Damianou, A.C., Martinez-Hernandez, U., Prescott, T.J.: Extending a hippocampal model for navigation around a maze generated from real-world data. In: Wilson, S.P., Verschure, P.F.M.J., Mura, A., Prescott, T.J. (eds.) LIVINGMACHINES 2015. LNCS (LNAI), vol. 9222, pp. 441–452. Springer, Cham (2015). https://doi.org/10.1007/978-3-319-22979-9_44
3. Bortoletto, R., Sartori, M., He, F., Pagello, E.: Simulating an elastic bipedal robot based on musculoskeletal modeling. In: Prescott, T.J., Lepora, N.F., Mura, A., Verschure, P.F.M.J. (eds.) Living Machines 2012. LNCS (LNAI), vol. 7375, pp. 26–37. Springer, Heidelberg (2012). https://doi.org/10.1007/978-3-642-31525-1_3
4. Cazenille, L., Bredeche, N., Halloy, J.: Evolutionary optimisation of neural network models for fish collective behaviours in mixed groups of robots and zebrafish. In: Vouloutsi, V., et al. (eds.) Living Machines 2018. LNCS (LNAI), vol. 10928, pp. 85–96. Springer, Cham (2018). https://doi.org/10.1007/978-3-319-95972-6_10
5. Daltorio, K.A., Horchler, A.D., Shaw, K.M., Chiel, H.J., Quinn, R.D.: Stable heteroclinic channels for slip control of a peristaltic crawling robot. In: Lepora, N.F., Mura, A., Krapp, H.G., Verschure, P.F.M.J., Prescott, T.J. (eds.) Living Machines 2013. LNCS (LNAI), vol. 8064, pp. 59–70. Springer, Heidelberg (2013). https://doi.org/10.1007/978-3-642-39802-5_6
6. Devlin, J., Chang, M.W., Lee, K., Toutanova, K.: Bert: Pre-training of deep bidirectional transformers for language understanding. arXiv preprint arXiv:1810.04805 (2018)
7. van Dinter, R., Tekinerdogan, B., Catal, C.: Automation of systematic literature reviews: a systematic literature review. Inf. Softw. Technol. **136**, 106589 (2021)
8. Duff, A., Lepora, N.F., Mura, A., Prescott, T.J., Verschure, P.F.: Biomimetic and biohybrid systems. In: Third International Conference, Living Machines 2014, Milan, Italy, July 30-August 1, 2014, Proceedings, vol. 8608. Springer,, Cham (2014).https://doi.org/10.1007/978-3-030-64313-3
9. Follador, M., et al.: Octopus-inspired innovative suction cups. In: Lepora, N.F., Mura, A., Krapp, H.G., Verschure, P.F.M.J., Prescott, T.J. (eds.) Living Machines 2013. LNCS (LNAI), vol. 8064, pp. 368–370. Springer, Heidelberg (2013). https://doi.org/10.1007/978-3-642-39802-5_37
10. Giannaccini, M.E., Whyle, S., Lepora, N.F.: Force sensing with a biomimetic fingertip. In: Lepora, N.F.F., Mura, A., Mangan, M., Verschure, P.F.M.J.F.M.J., Desmulliez, M., Prescott, T.J.J. (eds.) Living Machines 2016. LNCS (LNAI), vol. 9793, pp. 436–440. Springer, Cham (2016). https://doi.org/10.1007/978-3-319-42417-0_43

11. Gou, M.S., Vouloutsi, V., Grechuta, K., Lallée, S., Verschure, P.F.M.J.: Empathy in Humanoid robots. In: Duff, A., Lepora, N.F., Mura, A., Prescott, T.J., Verschure, P.F.M.J. (eds.) Living Machines 2014. LNCS (LNAI), vol. 8608, pp. 423–426. Springer, Cham (2014). https://doi.org/10.1007/978-3-319-09435-9_50
12. Grootendorst, M.: Bertopic: leveraging bert and C-TF-IDF to create easily interpretable topics. (2020). https://doi.org/10.5281/zenodo.4381785, https://doi.org/10.5281/zenodo.4381785
13. Hoinville, T., Harischandra, N., Krause, A.F., Dürr, V.: Insect-inspired tactile contour sampling using vibration-based robotic antennae. In: Duff, A., Lepora, N.F., Mura, A., Prescott, T.J., Verschure, P.F.M.J. (eds.) Living Machines 2014. LNCS (LNAI), vol. 8608, pp. 118–129. Springer, Cham (2014). https://doi.org/10.1007/978-3-319-09435-9_11
14. Kano, T., Matsui, N., Ishiguro, A.: 3D movement of snake robot driven by *Tegotae*-based control. In: Martinez-Hernandez, J.M., et al. (eds.) Living Machines 2019. LNCS (LNAI), vol. 11556, pp. 346–350. Springer, Cham (2019). https://doi.org/10.1007/978-3-030-24741-6_35
15. Lepora, N.F., Mura, A., Krapp, H.G., Verschure, P.F., Prescott, T.J.: Biomimetic and Biohybrid Systems: Second International Conference, Living Machines 2013, London, UK, July 29-August 2, 2013, Proceedings, vol. 8064. Springer, Cham (2013). https://doi.org/10.1007/978-3-319-63537-8
16. Lepora, N.F., Mura, A., Mangan, M., Verschure, P.F., Desmulliez, M., Prescott, T.J.: Biomimetic and biohybrid systems. In: 5th International Conference, Living Machines 2016, Edinburgh, UK, July 19–22, 2016. Proceedings, vol. 9793. Springer, Cham (2016). https://doi.org/10.1007/978-3-030-64313-3
17. Lepora, N.F., Verschure, P., Prescott, T.J.: The state of the art in biomimetics. Bioinsp. Biomimet. **8**(1), 013001 (2013)
18. López-Serrano, L.L., Vouloutsi, V., Escudero Chimeno, A., Mathews, Z., Verschure, P.F.M.J.: Insect-like odor classification and localization on an autonomous robot. In: Prescott, T.J., Lepora, N.F., Mura, A., Verschure, P.F.M.J. (eds.) Living Machines 2012. LNCS (LNAI), vol. 7375, pp. 371–372. Springer, Heidelberg (2012). https://doi.org/10.1007/978-3-642-31525-1_47
19. Maffei, G., Puigbò, J.-Y., Verschure, P.F.M.J.: Learning modular sequences in the striatum. In: Mangan, M., Cutkosky, M., Mura, A., Verschure, P.F.M.J., Prescott, T., Lepora, N. (eds.) Living Machines 2017. LNCS (LNAI), vol. 10384, pp. 574–578. Springer, Cham (2017). https://doi.org/10.1007/978-3-319-63537-8_52
20. Mangan, M., Cutkosky, M., Mura, A., Verschure, P.F., Prescott, T., Lepora, N.: Biomimetic and biohybrid systems. In: 6th International Conference, Living Machines 2017, Stanford, CA, USA, July 26–28, 2017, Proceedings, vol. 10384. Springer, Cham (2017). https://doi.org/10.1007/978-3-030-64313-3
21. Manti, M., Hassan, T., Passetti, G., d'Elia, N., Cianchetti, M., Laschi, C.: An under-actuated and adaptable soft robotic gripper. In: Wilson, S.P., Verschure, P.F.M.J., Mura, A., Prescott, T.J. (eds.) LIVINGMACHINES 2015. LNCS (LNAI), vol. 9222, pp. 64–74. Springer, Cham (2015). https://doi.org/10.1007/978-3-319-22979-9_6
22. Martinez-Hernandez, U., et al.: Biomimetic and biohybrid systems. In: 8th International Conference, Living Machines 2019, Nara, Japan, July 9–12, 2019, Proceedings, vol. 11556. Springer (2019). https://doi.org/10.1007/978-3-030-64313-3
23. McInnes, L., Healy, J., Astels, S.: hdbscan: hierarchical density based clustering. J. Open Sour. Softw. **2**(11), 205 (2017)
24. McInnes, L., Healy, J., Melville, J.: Umap: uniform manifold approximation and projection for dimension reduction. arXiv preprint arXiv:1802.03426 (2018)

25. Mitchinson, B., Prescott, T.J.: MIRO: a robot mammal with a biomimetic brain-based control system. In: Lepora, N.F.F., Mura, A., Mangan, M., Verschure, P.F.M.J.F.M.J., Desmulliez, M., Prescott, T.J.J. (eds.) Living Machines 2016. LNCS (LNAI), vol. 9793, pp. 179–191. Springer, Cham (2016). https://doi.org/10.1007/978-3-319-42417-0_17

26. Morrow, C., Bolen, B., Hunt, A.J.: Optimization of artificial muscle placements for a humanoid bipedal robot. In: Living Machines 2020. LNCS (LNAI), vol. 12413, pp. 257–269. Springer, Cham (2020). https://doi.org/10.1007/978-3-030-64313-3_25

27. Paszke, A., G et al.: Pytorch: an imperative style, high-performance deep learning library. In: 32th Proceedings of the International Conference on Advances in Neural information Processing Systems (2019)

28. Prescott, T.T., Lepora, N.F., Mura, A., Verschure, P.F.: Biomimetic and Biohybrid Systems: First International Conference, Living Machines 2012, Barcelona, Spain, July 9–12, 2012, Proceedings, vol. 7375. Springer (2012). https://doi.org/10.1007/978-3-319-63537-8

29. Ramos, J., et al.: Using TF-IDF to determine word relevance in document queries. In: Proceedings of the First Instructional Conference on Machine Learning, vol. 242, pp. 29–48. Citeseer (2003)

30. Reidsma, D., et al.: The EASEL project: towards educational human-robot symbiotic interaction. In: Lepora, N.F.F., Mura, A., Mangan, M., Verschure, P.F.M.J.F.M.J., Desmulliez, M., Prescott, T.J.J. (eds.) Living Machines 2016. LNCS (LNAI), vol. 9793, pp. 297–306. Springer, Cham (2016). https://doi.org/10.1007/978-3-319-42417-0_27

31. Scharzenberger, C., Mendoza, J., Hunt, A.: Design of a canine inspired quadruped robot as a platform for synthetic neural network control. In: Martinez-Hernandez, U., Vouloutsi, V., Mura, A., Mangan, M., Asada, M., Prescott, T.J., Verschure, P.F.M.J. (eds.) Living Machines 2019. LNCS (LNAI), vol. 11556, pp. 228–239. Springer, Cham (2019). https://doi.org/10.1007/978-3-030-24741-6_20

32. Suzuki, S., Owaki, D., Fukuhara, A., Ishiguro, A.: Quadruped gait transition from walk to pace to rotary gallop by exploiting head movement. In: Lepora, N.F.F., et al. (eds.) Living Machines 2016. LNCS (LNAI), vol. 9793, pp. 532–539. Springer, Cham (2016). https://doi.org/10.1007/978-3-319-42417-0_58

33. Szczecinski, N.S., Zill, S.N., Dallmann, C.J., Quinn, R.D.: Modeling the dynamic sensory discharges of insect campaniform sensilla. In: Living Machines 2020. LNCS (LNAI), vol. 12413, pp. 342–353. Springer, Cham (2020). https://doi.org/10.1007/978-3-030-64313-3_33

34. Vannucci, L., Falotico, E., Tolu, S., Dario, P., Lund, H.H., Laschi, C.: Eye-head stabilization mechanism for a humanoid robot tested on human inertial data. In: Lepora, N.F.F., Mura, A., Mangan, M., Verschure, P.F.M.J.F.M.J., Desmulliez, M., Prescott, T.J.J. (eds.) Living Machines 2016. LNCS (LNAI), vol. 9793, pp. 341–352. Springer, Cham (2016). https://doi.org/10.1007/978-3-319-42417-0_31

35. Vaswani, A., et al.: Attention is all you need. In:30th Proceedings of the international Conference on Advances in Neural Information Processing Systems (2017)

36. Vouloutsi, V., et al.: Biomimetic and Biohybrid Systems. In: 7th International Conference, Living Machines 2018, Paris, France, July 17–20, 2018, Proceedings, vol. 10928. Springer, Cham (2018). https://doi.org/10.1007/978-3-319-63537-8

37. Vouloutsi, V., Mura, A., Tauber, F., Speck, T., Prescott, T.J., Verschure, P.F.: Biomimetic and biohybrid systems. In: 9th International Conference, Living Machines 2020, Freiburg, Germany, July 28–30, 2020, Proceedings, vol. 12413. Springer, Cham (2020). https://doi.org/10.1007/978-3-030-64313-3

38. Wang, L.L., Lo, K.: Text mining approaches for dealing with the rapidly expanding literature on Covid-19. Brief. Bioinform. **22**(2), 781–799 (2021)
39. Webster, V.A., Hawley, E.L., Akkus, O., Chiel, H.J., Quinn, R.D.: Fabrication of electrocompacted aligned collagen morphs for cardiomyocyte powered living machines. In: Wilson, S.P., Verschure, P.F.M.J., Mura, A., Prescott, T.J. (eds.) LIVINGMACHINES 2015. LNCS (LNAI), vol. 9222, pp. 429–440. Springer, Cham (2015). https://doi.org/10.1007/978-3-319-22979-9_43
40. Wilson, S.P., Verschure, P.F., Mura, A., Prescott, T.J.: Biomimetic and biohybrid systems. In: 4th International Conference, Living Machines 2015, Barcelona, Spain, July 28–31, 2015, Proceedings, vol. 9222. Springer, Cham (2015).https://doi.org/10.1007/978-3-030-64313-3
41. Wolf, T., et al.: Transformers: State-of-the-art natural language processing. In: Proceedings of the 2020 Conference on Empirical Methods in Natural Language Processing: System Demonstrations, pp. 38–45 (2020)

Multi-material FDM 3D Printed Arm with Integrated Pneumatic Actuator

Stefan Conrad[1,2](✉) (ID), Thomas Speck[1,2,3] (ID), and Falk J. Tauber[1,2] (ID)

[1] Plant Biomechanics Group (PBG) Freiburg, Botanic Garden of the University of Freiburg, Freiburg im Breisgau, Germany
stefan.conrad@biologie.uni-freiburg.de

[2] Cluster of Excellence livMatS @ FIT – Freiburg Center for Interactive Materials and Bioinspired Technologies, University of Freiburg, Freiburg im Breisgau, Germany

[3] Freiburg Center for Interactive Materials and Bioinspired Technologies (FIT), University of Freiburg, Freiburg im Breisgau, Germany

Abstract. One approach to realize more life-like soft robots is the use of pneumatically contracting structures, acting as muscles. Fabricating such systems usually requires manual assembly or molding steps, which extend the time between designing and testing of a new concept. In order to streamline rapid prototyping this study used a multi-material FDM 3D printer for producing a simplified robotic arm with an integrated pneumatic muscle. The actuator working as a pneumatic bicep is printed from thermoplastic polyurethane with a shore hardness of A70, while the arm itself is made of rigid polylactic acid. During the printing process the muscle is, while being printed itself, embedded into the arm by a physical joint, through which the arm assembly can change its angle according to the actuation. In this work, we describe the challenges appearing in such a combined processing of two different materials and how they are addressed. Through its design the resulting soft robotic arm is printed without the need of any support material inside its hollow structures and is ready for testing right after the printing finished. By applying negative pressure to the actuator's inlet, the arm was able to lift up to 270 g load.

Keywords: Soft robotics · Multi-material 3D printer · Pneumatic actuator · Biomimetics

1 Introduction

In today's society, evermore robots are integrated for various tasks into our daily life for which the classic metal-based robots are unfit. Especially when it comes to direct human interaction, engineers have to deal with multiple safety and acceptance concerns [1]. This is one reason why the research on soft robots, that are based on polymers rather than metal, is of high interest [2, 3]. One approach to achieve this is to use muscles with "biomimetic function, but not biomimetic mechanism" [4] like presented in Yang *et al.* (2016) [5]. The presented actuator systems are based on periodic pneumatic chamber structures that contract under evacuation. One of the main challenges in the development

© The Author(s), under exclusive license to Springer Nature Switzerland AG 2022
A. Hunt et al. (Eds.): Living Machines 2022, LNAI 13548, pp. 27–31, 2022.
https://doi.org/10.1007/978-3-031-20470-8_3

of such pressure-based actuation systems is their rapid prototyping. Especially the rapid simultaneous processing of multiple materials with a minimum of manual interventions would accelerate production of and research on more advanced soft robots. FDM 3D printers have proven their potential for the fast fabrication of complex structures, but printing highly flexible filament and combining different materials is still complicated. Substances with varying melting temperature and viscosity require separate extruders, which are ideally spatially separated to avoid cross contamination. As a step in this direction, Conrad *et al.* (2020) presented a new tool changing 3D printer optimized for soft filaments [6]. The platform can switch between independent extruders, which are loaded with individual materials. It was already shown how the device can combine flexible TPU and rigid PLA to form airtight multi-material chambers. Conrad *et al.* (2021) then demonstrated the platform's potential to fabricate customizable pneumatic actuators (CPA) that can be manually configured to perform linear contraction or bending after printing [7]. In this study, we will go the next logical step and integrate such an actuator into a simultaneously printed hinge structure resulting in a functional, soft robotic arm with an artificial "bicep". The fabrication required additional settings and precautions compared to a single-material print, which are discussed in detail. This will be the first example for a basic demonstrator of a soft robotic arm or leg with fully integrated pneumatic muscles ready to use directly after FDM printing without additional assembly steps.

2   Materials and Methods

2.1   Multi-Material 3D Printing Procedure and Parameters

The soft robotic arm presented in this study was made of "Recreus FilaFlex TPU A70" and "Filamentworld PLA Plus". Due to its low Young's-modulus, the TPU A70 filament can clog the printer because of twisting and entanglement inside the extruder. Since the pneumatic actuator has to be airtight, all chosen print parameters and design features have the goal of guaranteeing a consistent extrusion and well fusing layers. The newly developed multi-material 3D printing platform presented in S. Conrad *et al.* (2020) has proven its ability to print pneumatic actuators from highly flexible polymers [6]. This platform is able to create thin expandable membranes of 0.5 mm thickness and ensures their airtightness using over extrusion [7]. In over extrusion the printer extrudes more material than needed for the volume it is building. Since a constant over extrusion on all areas of the object would lead to swelling surfaces, the device uses a "feature adapted extrusion factor" to ensure that non-critical regions are printed normally [7].

The printer is able to switch between different materials by placing one tool in a docking station and picking up another tool that is being held in standby conditions. Tool changes are the most sensitive activity while printing a multi-material object and the soft robotic arm shown in this study requires 180 of them since the actuator ends on a height of 18 mm and the printer has to switch tools once per 0.1 mm layer. As such, additional hardware has been introduced into the existing system to ensure a reliable changing procedure. Each docking position was upgraded with sensors that allow the device to supervise the tool change sequence and to repeat it in case of failure. In addition, each docking position was outfitted with a wiper station so the printer could clean the print heads before usage. In order to minimize oozing after a tool change, the object was placed as close as possible to the wiper station. To reestablish a consistent flow rate of TPU after nozzle cleaning, an additional cuboid of $20 \times 20 \times 15$ mm was placed close to the CPA to act as a purge tower. The tower was always printed before the actuator and each layer required enough material to assume the nozzle was free of air afterwards and ready for the functional object. As a third precaution, the order of infill and perimeters were reversed. The whole object was printed with three perimeters and an infill density of 90%. Furthermore, by choosing the "avoid crossing parameters" option in PrusaSlicer, the print head was forced to travel only along existing perimeters to avoid unwanted material in channels and chambers (Fig. 2 Conrad *et al.* (2021)) [7]. This inhibited cross contamination of TPU and PLA, since actuator and arm were spatially separated by design (Fig. 1 A).

2.2 Soft Robotic Arm Design

The soft robotic arm shown in Fig. 1 A is composed of a rigid PLA arm structure and an embedded CPA forming its soft robotic bicep. The rigid arm has a height of 20 mm and is made of two pieces representing upper arm and forearm, which are connected by a compliant hinge with a thickness of 0.5 mm. The bicep is anchored to the arm by two PLA rods going through two rings at the ends of the CPA forming two hinges. The actuator has a height and width of 15 mm and a length of 72 mm with a connector inlet at the bottom side for pneumatic positive or negative pressure actuation. Since TPU has poor bridging properties and does not work as support material itself, the design includes a PLA platform on which the actuator can start building.

2.3 Print Results and Lift Capability

After a print time of approximately 20 h and 180 tool changes, the multi-material 3D print was finished without any issues and no observable cross contaminations of TPU and PLA. Stringing was only observed between actuator, purge tower and wiper station, and the print itself showed a high surface quality. After cooling the object was removed from the build plate and the CPA could be directly configured for linear expansion by cutting all struts in correspondence with Conrad *et al.* (2021) [7]. When connected to a "vacuubrand PC 3004 VARIO" vacuum pump and loaded with up to 270 g, it showed the targeted behavior.

Under atmospheric conditions, the weight stretches the bicep and bends the compliant hinge of the arm to 130(2) ° (Fig. 1 C). If additionally pressurized with 1 bar, the bicep extends further and the forearm bends to 150(2) ° (Fig. 1 B). Applying negative pressure, the actuator contracts and lifts the load until the arm is in its 93(2) ° default state (Fig. 1 D).

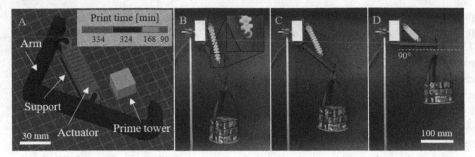

Fig. 1. Multi-material FDM 3D printed soft robotic arm (SRA). **A:** Sliced SRA made of PLA (red) and TPU (green) (PrusaSlicer 2.4.0). Print time color marked (Tool changes in blue). **B:** SRA overstretched state (+1.0 bar). **C:** SRA relaxed state (atmospheric pressure). **D:** SRA in actuated state (−0.996 bar).

3 Conclusion and Outlook

This study demonstrates using a simple arm-muscle combination how multi-material FDM 3D printing can be used for the rapid prototyping of complex fully integrated soft robots. The presented system was composed of a rigid arm made of PLA with a compliant hinge and a CPA actuator made of TPU A70 acting as a pneumatic muscle. Both components were fabricated in one simultaneous 3D print and unlike in most other 3D printing techniques, do not contain any kind of support material. The challenges appearing in such a process have been described as well as the strategies to solve them. Despite being about 1/3 the size of the "VAMP-actuated arm" presented in Yang *et al.* (2016) our arm can lift the same mass of 270 g against gravity [5]. Based on the described parameters and design specifics our FDM printer platform offers a high potential for rapid prototyping of novel fully integrated soft robotic motion systems, in which the pneumatic muscles are directly embedded into the robot skeleton.

Funding. Funded by the Deutsche Forschungsgemeinschaft (DFG, German Research Foundation) under Germany's Excellence Strategy – EXC-2193/1-390951807.

References

1. Abidi, H., Cianchetti, M.: On intrinsic safety of soft robots. Front Robot AI **4**, 6 (2017). https://doi.org/10.3389/frobt.2017.00005
2. Rus, D., Tolley, M.T.: Design, fabrication and control of soft robots. Nature **521**, 467–475 (2015). https://doi.org/10.1038/nature14543
3. Mazzolai, B., et al.: Roadmap on soft robotics: multifunctionality, adaptability and growth without borders. Multifunct. Mater. **5**, 032001 (2022). https://doi.org/10.1088/2399-7532/ac4c95
4. Whitesides, G.M.: Soft robotics. Angew. Chem. Int. Ed. **57**, 4258–4273 (2018). https://doi.org/10.1002/anie.201800907
5. Yang, D., et al.: Buckling pneumatic linear actuators inspired by muscle. Adv. Mater. Technol. **1**, 1600055 (2016). https://doi.org/10.1002/admt.201600055

6. Conrad, S., Speck, T., Tauber, F.: Multi-material 3D-printer for rapid prototyping of bio-inspired soft robotic elements. In: Vouloutsi, V., Mura, A., Tauber, F., Speck, T., Prescott, T.J., Verschure, P.F.M.J. (eds.) Biomimetic and Biohybrid Systems: 9th International Conference, Living Machines 2020, Freiburg, Germany, July 28–30, 2020, Proceedings, pp. 46–54. Springer International Publishing, Cham (2020). https://doi.org/10.1007/978-3-030-64313-3_6
7. Conrad, S., Speck, T., Tauber, F.J.: Tool changing 3D printer for rapid prototyping of advanced soft robotic elements. Bioinspir. Biomim. **16**, 55010 (2021). https://doi.org/10.1088/1748-3190/ac095a

SNS-Toolbox: A Tool for Efficient Simulation of Synthetic Nervous Systems

William R. P. Nourse[1]([✉]) [iD], Nicholas S. Szczecinski[2] [iD], and Roger D. Quinn[3] [iD]

[1] Department of Electrical, Computer, and Systems Engineering, Case Western Reserve University, Cleveland, OH 44106, USA
nourse@case.edu
[2] Department of Mechanical and Aerospace Engineering, West Virginia University, Morgantown, WV 26506, USA
[3] Department of Mechanical and Aerospace Engineering, Case Western Reserve University, Cleveland, OH 44106, USA

Abstract. We introduce SNS-Toolbox, a Python software package for the design and simulation of networks of conductance-based neurons and synapses, also called Synthetic Nervous Systems (SNS). SNS-Toolbox implements non-spiking and spiking neurons in multiple software backends, and is capable of simulating networks with thousands of neurons in real-time. We benchmark the toolbox simulation speed across multiple network sizes, characterize upper limits on network size in various scenarios, and showcase the design of a two-layer convolutional network inspired by circuits within the *Drosophila melanogaster* optic lobe. SNS-Toolbox, as well as the code to generate all of the figures in this work, is located at https://github.com/wnourse05/SNS-Toolbox.

Keywords: Conductance based modeling · Synthetic nervous systems · Simulation · Neurorobotics · Neural networks

1 Introduction

In recent years, more and more research has been done on implementing control systems for robots using networks of biologically-inspired neurons [6,11,14,20] with an end goal of creating robots with the adaptability and generalization of animals. One particular approach in this field is using Synthetic Nervous Systems (SNS) [21], which are networks of conductance-based neurons and synapses connected using analytic design rules. The predominant tool used for designing SNS controllers until now has been Animatlab [5], a visual tool that combines neural simulation, physics simulation, and plotting within one software platform. Robot controllers have been successfully developed using this software [11,14]. However, as the body of neuroscience knowledge increases and control networks

This work was funded by National Science Foundation (NSF) Award #1704436, as well as by NSF DBI 2015317 as part of the NSF/CIHR/DFG/FRQ/UKRI-MRC Next Generation Networks for Neuroscience Program.

© The Author(s), under exclusive license to Springer Nature Switzerland AG 2022
A. Hunt et al. (Eds.): Living Machines 2022, LNAI 13548, pp. 32–43, 2022.
https://doi.org/10.1007/978-3-031-20470-8_4

become larger, it is becoming more difficult to maintain and develop these large networks and simulate them in a sufficiently fast manner [19].

Simulators capable of designing conductance-based neurons have existed for years, such as NEURON [13], NEST [15], and Brian [15]. There are also simulators capable of designing large neural networks using principles of machine learning, albeit using reduced neural models, such as snnTorch [8], SpykeTorch [17], and BindsNET [15]. Although many simulators are available, it is difficult to interface any of these programs with hardware. Many of these were designed around collecting data over long simulation runs, so interfacing with hardware becomes an exercise in creative engineering [20]. There are solutions for robotic interfacing in simulation [9], but due to the overhead associated with these programs it is not practical to execute the network in real-time. High-performance robots have been developed which are controlled using spiking neurons [6], but these rely on specialized neuromorphic hardware and software specially designed for these platforms, which are not widely available [1]. As of now the best software for implementing conductance-based networks and applying them to real hardware is Nengo [15], but this software is primarily designed for networks using the Neural Engineering Framework [7] and contains enough overhead to slow down performance without the use of specialized hardware.

We present SNS-Toolbox, a Python software package for designing and simulating networks of conductance-based neurons and synapses. External inputs are processed and transformed into neural state outputs on a timestep-by-timestep basis. These outputs can then be used with any software or external hardware which is capable of communicating with Python code. By not interfacing with a dedicated physics simulator and optimizing for two specific neural models, we can simulate networks of thousands of neurons and synapses in real-time or faster using consumer-grade computer hardware.

2   Neural Models

When designing SNS-Toolbox, we chose to focus on designing and simulating two neural models that have often been used in previous SNS work: a non-spiking model and a spiking model.

2.1   Non-spiking Neurons and Synapses

Non-spiking neurons are simulated as leaky integrators, the same model as those used in continuous-time recurrent neural networks [2,21]. The membrane depolarization above rest, U, behaves according to the differential equation

$$C_{mem}\frac{dU}{dt} = -G_{mem} \cdot U + I_{syn} + I_{bias} + I_{app}, \tag{1}$$

where C_{mem} is the membrane capacitance, G_{mem} is the membrane leak conductance, I_{bias} is a constant offset current, and I_{app} is an external applied current. I_{syn} is the current induced by incoming conductance-based synapses to the neuron,

$$I_{syn} = \sum_{i=1}^{n} G_{syn}^i \cdot (E_{syn}^i - U). \tag{2}$$

E_{syn}^i is the reversal potential of the ith incoming synapse relative to the neuron's rest potential, and G_{syn}^i is the instantaneous synaptic conductance. This conductance is defined as a function of the pre-synaptic neuron depolarization,

$$G_{syn}^i = max\left(0, min\left(G_{max,non}^i \cdot \frac{U_{pre}}{R}, G_{max,non}^i\right)\right) \tag{3}$$

$G_{max,non}^i$ is the maximum possible conductance for the synapse, and R is the maximum desired membrane depolarization of any neuron throughout the network [21]. In general, $G_{max,non}^i$ controls the strength of a synapse while E_{syn} determines the behavior (excitatory, inhibitory, or modulatory) [21]. Substituting Eq. 2 into Eq. 1, the full non-spiking neural model can be written as

$$C_{mem}\frac{dU}{dt} = -G_{mem} \cdot U + \sum_{i=1}^{n} G_{syn}^i \cdot (E_{syn}^i - U) + I_{bias} + I_{app}. \tag{4}$$

2.2   Spiking Neurons and Synapses

For the spiking model, the membrane depolarization dynamics are similar to the non-spiking model (see Eq. 4), with an additional dynamical variable for a firing threshold θ [22],

$$\tau_\theta \frac{d\theta}{dt} = -\theta + \theta_0 + m \cdot U, \tag{5}$$

where τ_θ is the threshold time constant, θ_0 is the initial threshold voltage, and m is a proportionality constant describing how changes in U affect θ. We also define a spiking variable δ, which represents a spike and resets the membrane state,

$$\delta = \begin{cases} 1, & \text{if } U > \theta \\ 0, & \text{otherwise.} \end{cases} \tag{6}$$

$$\text{if } \delta = 1, 0 \leftarrow U. \tag{7}$$

Unlike the non-spiking model, the synaptic conductance for spiking synapses G_{syn} is a dynamical variable. It is reset to a maximum value $G_{max,spike}$ whenever its corresponding pre-synaptic neuron spikes, and otherwise decays to 0 with a time constant τ_{syn}.

$$\tau_{syn}\frac{dG_{syn}}{dt} = -G_{syn} \tag{8}$$

$$\text{if } \delta = 1, G_{max,spike} \leftarrow G_{syn} \tag{9}$$

In order to perform more dynamic computation with spiking neurons, a mechanism for synaptic propagation delay can also be incorporated. If the synapse from neuron i to neuron j has a delay of d timesteps, the delayed spike can be defined as

$$\delta^{j,i}_{delay}[t] = \delta^{j,i}[d - \Delta t] \tag{10}$$

3   Software Design and Workflow

SNS-Toolbox allows for the design and implementation of synthetic nervous systems, and operates in three phases: design, compilation, and simulation.

3.1   Design Phase

When designing a network, users add neurons and populations of neurons to an overall *Network* object, with defined synaptic connections between the neurons. These connections can take on any topology desired, including feedback loops, and can be either individual synapses or patterns of synapses (an example of patterned synapses is given in Sect. 4.3). For applying external stimulus to a network, one-dimensional vectors can be added as input sources. To observe neural states during simulation, output monitors can be added. These monitors can be voltage-based or spike-based, for which the output is the direct voltage or spiking state of the source neuron.

This *Network* object by itself is not capable of being simulated, it merely acts as a defined storage container which describes the network parameters and structure. In the compilation phase, the object is referenced as a building plan to construct a network which can be simulated. Any network can also be used as an element within another network. In this way, a large network can be designed using large collections of predefined subnetworks. A collection of subnetworks that perform simple arithmetic and dynamic functions is available within SNS-Toolbox. For a complete explanation of these networks please refer to [21].

3.2   Compilation

Once a network is designed, it needs to be converted from a dictionary of parameters into an executable network. Given a *Network* object, SNS-Toolbox is able to build a new object which simulates a given network in one of four software backends: NumPy [12], PyTorch [18], a PyTorch-based sparse matrix library (torch.sparse), and a NumPy-based iterative evaluator which evaluates each synapse individually.

In order to improve simulation performance, the multiplication constant for the membrane voltage, firing threshold, and synapse dynamics are pre-computed. Instead of handling the timestep Δt and a time constant τ at each step, a time factor T is used instead where $T = \frac{\Delta t}{\tau}$.

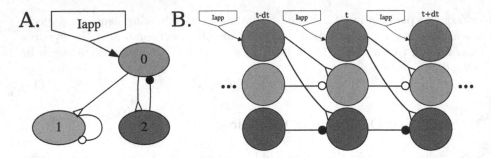

Fig. 1. Simulation method for a small example network using SNS-Toolbox. **A.** Overall network diagram generated within the toolbox. **B.** Diagram of the general computational flow when simulating the network.

3.3   Simulation

Commonly used high-performance frameworks focus on neural networks structured around massively connected individual layers [18], but SNS-Toolbox focuses on smaller networks connected with multiple levels of feedback loops [2, 14] found in animal nervous systems. Since these networks are more cyclic in nature, all networks simulated by SNS-Toolbox are unfolded through time, similar to the method pioneered by backpropagation through time [23]. For a visual representation of this unfolding, please see Fig. 1. At every timestep, each neuron can receive synaptic input from any neuron at the previous timestep, including an autapse from itself. These connections retain the same properties from step to step, and these properties are stored in NxN matrices for a network of N neurons.

At a given timestep t, a user applies an external input vector $\vec{In}[t]$. This vector could come from any source (e.g., static data, real-time sensors), but must be formatted in the dominant datatype of the software backend (either Numpy array or Torch tensor). Within the forward pass of simulation, first the memory states are updated as $\vec{U}_{last}[t] \leftarrow \vec{U}[t - \Delta t]$ and $\vec{\theta}_{last}[t] \leftarrow \vec{\theta}[t - \Delta t]$. Next the external input is applied to the correct neurons,

$$\vec{I}_{app}[t] \leftarrow \mathbf{C_{in}} \cdot \vec{In}[t], \tag{11}$$

where $\mathbf{C_{in}}$ is an LxN (L is the number of input elements, N is the number of neurons in the network) binary masking matrix which routes each input element to its correct target neuron.

Adapting Eqs. 3 and 8, the non-spiking synaptic conductance matrix $\mathbf{G_{non}}$ and spiking counterpart $\mathbf{G_{spike}}$ are computed as

$$\mathbf{G_{non}}[t] \leftarrow max\left(0, min\left(\mathbf{G_{max,non}} \cdot \frac{\vec{U}_{last}[t]}{R}, \mathbf{G_{max,non}}\right)\right), \tag{12}$$

$$\mathbf{G_{spike}}[t] \leftarrow \mathbf{G_{spike}}[t-1] \cdot (1 - \mathbf{T_{syn}}), \tag{13}$$

These conductances are summed to form the total synaptic conductance matrix $\mathbf{G}_{\mathbf{syn}}[t]$. The synaptic current vector follows Eq. 2, adapted to matrix form using row-wise sums

$$\vec{I}_{syn}[t] \leftarrow \sum_{j} \mathbf{G}_{\mathbf{syn}}^{i,j}[t] \cdot \mathbf{E}^{i,j} - \vec{U}_{last}[t] \odot \sum_{j} \mathbf{G}_{\mathbf{syn}}^{i,j}, \tag{14}$$

where $\odot$ denotes the element-wise Hadamard product. The new neural state $\vec{U}[t]$ and firing threshold $\vec{\theta}[t]$ are computed as

$$\vec{U}[t] \leftarrow \vec{U}_{last}[t] + \vec{T}_{mem} \odot \left(-\vec{G}_{mem} \odot \vec{U}_{last}[t] + \vec{I}_b + \vec{I}_{syn} + \vec{I}_{app} \right), \tag{15}$$

$$\vec{\theta}[t] \leftarrow \vec{\theta}_{last}[t] + \vec{T}_{\theta}[t] \odot \left(-\vec{\theta}_{last}[t] + \vec{\theta}_0 + \vec{m} \odot \vec{U}_{last}[t] \right). \tag{16}$$

Based on Eq. 16, the spiking states are also updated,

$$\vec{\delta}[t] \leftarrow sign\left(min\left(0, \vec{\theta} - \vec{U}\right)\right). \tag{17}$$

For ease of implementation, SNS-Toolbox internally represents spikes as impulses with a magnitude of –1.

Synaptic propagation delay is accomplished using a buffer matrix δ_{buffer} with N columns and D rows, where D is the longest delay time in timesteps within the network. At each timestep, the rows of δ_{buffer} are shifted down by 1, and the first row is replaced with the spike state vector of the current timestep $\vec{\delta}[t]$. A matrix of delayed spikes δ_{delay} is then generated by rearranging δ_{buffer} based on the amount of delay of each spiking synapse in the network. δ_{delay} is used to implement the spiking synapse reset dynamics in 9,

$$\mathbf{G}_{\mathbf{spike}}[t] \leftarrow max\left(\mathbf{G}_{\mathbf{spike}}[t], -\delta_{delay}[t] \odot \mathbf{G}_{\mathbf{max,spike}}\right). \tag{18}$$

Using the spike states, the neural membrane voltage of each neuron that spiked is reset to zero.

$$\vec{U}[t] \leftarrow \vec{U}[t] \odot \left(\vec{\delta}[t] + 1\right) \tag{19}$$

The vector output is then computed,

$$\overrightarrow{Out}[t] \leftarrow \mathbf{C}_{\mathbf{out,voltage}} \cdot \vec{U}[t] + \mathbf{C}_{\mathbf{out,spike}} \cdot \vec{\delta}[t]. \tag{20}$$

This output is a general vector, which can subsequently be formatted or distributed to external systems based on the intention of the user.

Variants. Each software backend implements the behavior of Eqs. 11–20, but also has two variants available for improved performance. When no synaptic propagation delay is needed for any spiking synapses, one backend variant can be used where δ_{buffer} and δ_{delay} are never computed. The spiking state vector $\vec{\delta}[t]$ is used instead of δ_{delay}. Similarly, when there are no spiking neurons in the network a variant can be used where no spiking parameters or variables are computed and Eqs. 13, 16–19 are not implemented. The performance difference of these variants is explored in Sect. 4.2.

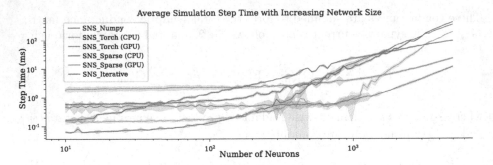

Fig. 2. Comparison of average wall-clock time to simulate a network for one simulation time-step. Solid lines represent the mean elapsed time per step over 100 steps, shaded areas show one standard deviation from the mean.

4 Results

4.1 Backend Simulation Performance

100 networks were run in a logarithmic spacing between 10 and 5000 spiking neurons, connected in the following structure: number of inputs = 8% of N, outputs = 12% of N, number of synapses = N. This structure is derived from a previous large-scale synthetic nervous system [14]. The mechanism for propagation delay was enabled. Each network was run for 100 steps, and the time to compute the forward pass was saved for each step. Results are shown in Fig. 2. SNS_Numpy was the fastest until 158 neurons, then the CPU version of SNS_Torch until 358 neurons. Both versions of SNS_Torch are tied until 978 neurons, after which point the GPU version is the fastest.

Real-Time Performance. If SNS-Toolbox were to be interfaced with a real-world robotic system, a 1:1 correlation between the simulated and real step time (or better) would be desired. For non-spiking neurons with a time constant τ_{mem} of 5 ms, the coarsest timestep producing accurate dynamics would also be 5 ms. Looking at Fig. 2, the largest network that could be theoretically simulated in real-time under these conditions would be 3,240 neurons, using the full GPU SNS_Torch backend. If the non-spiking variant were used, the maximum network size would be larger. For spiking networks, depending on the firing rate and synaptic dynamics the coarsest timestep will be smaller. Assuming a simulation timestep of 1 ms, the largest network which could be simulated would be 1,190 neurons. For step-times below 10 ms a relatively large variance can be observed, potentially due to interference from other processes in the operating system. Further benchmarking will be done on dedicated hardware systems with less overhead than a consumer desktop system.

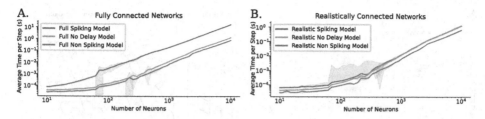

Fig. 3. Average wall-clock time to simulate a network for one simulation time-step, using three different variations of the SNS_Numpy backend. Network size was varied from 10 neurons to 10,000 neurons. Solid lines represent the mean elapsed time per step over 100 steps, shaded areas show one standard deviation from the mean. **A.** Networks are fully connected. **B.** The number of synaptic connections is equal to the number of neurons.

4.2   Backend Variant Performance

Isolating one backend family, we can examine the performance difference between different variants of the same backend. For this experiment, we chose to analyze SNS_Numpy. The number of neurons in a network was varied from 10 to 10,000, and the average timestep was measured for a backend implementing the full neural model, one without synaptic propagation delay, and one with no spiking whatsoever. The data is presented in Fig. 3. For fully connected networks, after 20 neurons the full model is consistently one order of magnitude slower than the other models. When the network connectivity is more constrained, the performance difference between the backends reduces. Non-spiking is always the fastest, but for realistically connected networks the speed difference between the full model with and without synaptic propagation delay becomes relatively small.

4.3   Example Network Design

Using SNS-Toolbox, we implemented a network that models an anatomical circuit and performs a useful function, but would be complicated and tedious to manually route all of the synaptic connections. In the *Drosophila melanogaster* nervous system, the optic lobe contains circuits for processing motion in the visual field [3]. The first two layers of this visual system are the retina and the lamina, which perform two distinct visual processing operations. Retinal neurons R1-R6 encode incoming photons as changing neural activity [4], and the lamina primarily consists of two pathways: the L2 neurons have an antagonistic center-surround receptive field, and L1 neurons have a traditional center-surround receptive field [10]. Based on this structure, modeling the retina and L1 cells results in a circuit that performs high-pass filtering of an input image.

Previous work has created a synthetic nervous system model of the *Drosophila* optic lobe motion circuitry [19] using the Animatlab software [5]. This model was constrained to one-dimensional images, in part due to the difficulty of implementing the model. In this previous approach neurons and synapses had to be placed

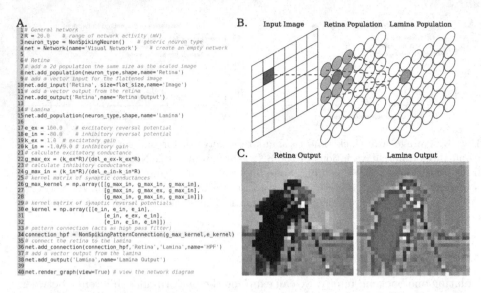

A.

```
1 # General network
2 R = 20.0      # range of network activity (mV)
3 neuron_type = NonSpikingNeuron()   # generic neuron type
4 net = Network(name='Visual Network')   # create an empty network
5
6 # Retina
7 # add a 2d population the same size as the scaled image
8 net.add_population(neuron_type,shape,name='Retina')
9 # add a vector input for the flattened image
10 net.add_input('Retina', size=flat_size,name='Image')
11 # add a vector output from the retina
12 net.add_output('Retina',name='Retina Output')
13
14 # Lamina
15 net.add_population(neuron_type,shape,name='Lamina')
16
17 e_ex = 160.0     # excitatory reversal potential
18 e_in = -80.0     # inhibitory reversal potential
19 k_ex = 1.0  # excitatory gain
20 k_in = -1.0/9.0 # inhibitory gain
21 # calculate excitatory conductance
22 g_max_ex = (k_ex*R)/(del_e_ex-k_ex*R)
23 # calculate inhibitory conductance
24 g_max_in = (k_in*R)/(del_e_in-k_in*R)
25 # kernel matrix of synaptic conductances
26 g_max_kernel = np.array([[g_max_in, g_max_in, g_max_in],
27                          [g_max_in, g_max_ex, g_max_in],
28                          [g_max_in, g_max_in, g_max_in]])
29 # kernel matrix of synaptic reversal potentials
30 e_kernel = np.array([[e_in, e_in, e_in],
31                      [e_in, e_ex, e_in],
32                      [e_in, e_in, e_in]])
33 # pattern connection (acts as high pass filter)
34 connection_hpf = NonSpikingPatternConnection(g_max_kernel,e_kernel)
35 # connect the retina to the lamina
36 net.add_connection(connection_hpf,'Retina','Lamina',name='HPF')
37 # add a vector output from the lamina
38 net.add_output('Lamina',name='Lamina Output')
39
40 net.render_graph(view=True) # view the network diagram
```

B. Input Image   Retina Population   Lamina Population

C. Retina Output   Lamina Output

Fig. 4. Using SNS-Toolbox to design a two-layer visual processing system. **A.** Python code to generate the desired network. Image preprocessing and output plotting are omitted. **B.** Network visual representation. An input image is converted to stimulus current for a population of neurons, representing the insect retina. From the retina, a 3×3 kernel of inhibitory (light blue) and excitatory (purple) synapses is applied to create a high-pass filtering effect in the next layer, representing the L1 insect lamina neurons. **C.** Output of retina and lamina neurons, respectively. Voltages are mapped to grayscale intensities. (Color figure online)

and routed by hand, which is time-intensive and tedious to produce a simplified model with 510 neurons and 1574 synapses for one-dimensional images [19]. To demonstrate the effectiveness of SNS-Toolbox, we created a model of the retina and L1 cells of the optic lobe capable of processing two-dimensional images, consisting of 2048 neurons and 8476 synapses and generated in only 18 lines of Python code (see Fig. 4A).

We assumed that input images are grayscale. Since a single *Drosophila* eye consists of around 800 ommatidia arranged in 32–34 columns [16], we also designed for input images which are 32×32 pixels. After creating two 32×32 populations of neurons and attaching an input source, the last step was to define the connection between the retina and the lamina. Our lamina model only consists of L1 neurons, so each neuron has center-on surround-off receptive field. Since each L1 cell receives input from the directly adjacent ommatidia, we can implement these receptive fields as a 3×3 connection kernel:

$$\mathbf{K} = \begin{bmatrix} k_{in} & k_{in} & k_{in} \\ k_{in} & k_{ex} & k_{in} \\ k_{in} & k_{in} & k_{in} \end{bmatrix},$$

where k_{in} and k_{ex} are the desired gains for inhibitory and excitatory synapses, respectively. For desired behavior, these gains were chosen as $k_{in} = -\frac{1}{9}$ and $k_{ex} = 1$. These synaptic gains are transformed into synaptic conductances and relative reversal potentials using the method described in [21].

The results of simulating the network are shown in Fig. 4. The output of the lamina layer correctly implements a rudimentary high-pass filter or edge-detector, as expected.

5   Discussion and Future Work

In this work, we introduced SNS-Toolbox, a software tool for designing and simulating recurrent networks of biologically-inspired spiking and non-spiking neurons with conductance-based synapses. For networks with a few hundred neurons, the CPU-based backends are the fastest simulation approach; for networks with more neurons, GPU-based backends are fastest.

There are existing software packages [13,15] for simulating conductance-based neurons and synapses, but are primarily designed for offline simulation. Methods to interface these simulators with robotic hardware are impractical [20]. Other software packages are efficient simulators, but not designed to efficiently simulate conductance-based neurons [15,18]. Others still simulate networks of neurons, but these packages are inherently tied to physics engines and overhead such that it is impossible to simulate large networks in real-time or faster [5,9]. Future work will provide quantitative speed comparisons between SNS-Toolbox and other simulation systems.

SNS-Toolbox implements two specific neural models commonly used in the SNS literature, and aims to simulate them as fast as possible on consumer computer hardware. Networks can contain both of these models, but cannot be expanded by the user to include new models since SNS-Toolbox is a specific accelerator for these models. Larger models could be approximated by treating these neurons as compartments within a larger model, an approach commonly employed with neuromorphic hardware [1], but this has not been explored at this time. These neural models are also lacking any voltage-gated ion-specific channels, which can be used to create pattern-generators [11]. Future work will implement an optional voltage-gated ion channel for these oscillatory networks.

Section 4.3 details the design and simulation of an example network which performs vision processing. While this network demonstrates some of the features of SNS-Toolbox, the example is not the best to showcase the strengths of the toolbox over other software. Future work will use SNS-Toolbox to implement motor systems, an area for which SNS-Toolbox is better suited.

In this work, we focus on using SNS-Toolbox to simulate networks of neurons in isolation. At its heart, SNS-Toolbox takes an input vector at each timestep and generates an output vector. These inputs and outputs can be arbitrary data (as they are in this work), but could include data streams from a robot, camera, or any continuous source. Future work will implement interfaces for interaction with physics simulators, as well as an interface for external robotic hardware. In its current state the whole codebase is developed in Python for ease of maintenance and development. In the future, the addition of a C++-based backend would allow for additional improvements in performance.

References

1. Lava software framework (2021)
2. Beer, R.D., Gallagher, J.C.: Evolving dynamical neural networks for adaptive behavior. Adapt. Behav. **1**, 91–122 (1992)
3. Borst, A.: Drosophila's view on insect vision. Curr. Biol. **19**, R36–R47 (2009)
4. Clark, D.A., Demb, J.B.: Parallel computations in insect and mammalian visual motion processing. Curr Biol. **24** (20), R1062–R1072 (2016)
5. Cofer, D., et al.: A 3D graphics environment for neuromechanical simulations. J. Neurosci. Methods **187**, 280–288 (2010)
6. Cohen, G.: Gooaall!!!: Why we built a neuromorphic robot to play foosball. IEEE Spect. **59**, 44–50 (3 2022)
7. Eliasmith, C., Anderson, C.H.: Neural Engineering: Computation, Representation, and Dynamics in Neurobiological Systems. MIT Press (2003)
8. Eshraghian, J.K., et al.: Training spiking neural networks using lessons from deep learning (2021)
9. Falotico, E., et al.: Connecting artificial brains to robots in a comprehensive simulation framework: the neurorobotics platform. Front. Neurorobot. **11**, 2 (2017)
10. Freifeld, L., Clark, D.A., Schnitzer, M.J., Horowitz, M.A., Clandinin, T.R.: Gabaergic lateral interactions tune the early stages of visual processing in drosophila. Neuron **78**, 1075–1089 (2013)
11. Goldsmith, C.A., Szczecinski, N.S., Quinn, R.D.: Neurodynamic modeling of the fruit fly Drosophila melanogaster. Bioinspir. Biomimet. **15**, 065003 (2020)
12. Harris, C.R., et al.: Array programming with numpy. Nature **585**(7825), 357–362 (2020)
13. Hines, M.L., Carnevale, N.T.: Neuron: a tool for neuroscientists. Neuroscientist **7**(2), 123–135 (2001). http://www.neu
14. Hunt, A., Szczecinski, N., Quinn, R.: Development and training of a neural controller for hind leg walking in a dog robot. Front. Neurorobot. **11** (2017)
15. Kulkarni, S.R., Parsa, M., Mitchell, J.P., Schuman, C.D.: Benchmarking the performance of neuromorphic and spiking neural network simulators. Neurocomputing **447**, 145–160 (2021)
16. Kumar, J.P.: Building an ommatidium one cell at a time. Dev. Dyn. **241**(1), 136-149 (2012)
17. Mozafari, M., Ganjtabesh, M., Nowzari-Dalini, A., Masquelier, T.: Spyketorch: efficient simulation of convolutional spiking neural networks with at most one spike per neuron. Front. Neurosci. **13** (2019)
18. Paszke, A., et al.: PyTorch: An Imperative style, high-performance deep learning library. In: NIPS'19: Proceedings of the 33rd International Conference on Neural Information Processing Systems. Curran Associates, Inc. (2019)
19. Sedlackova, A., Szczecinski, N.S., Quinn, R.D.: A synthetic nervous system model of the insect optomotor response. In: Living Machines 2020. LNCS (LNAI), vol. 12413, pp. 312–324. Springer, Cham (2020). https://doi.org/10.1007/978-3-030-64313-3_30

20. Strohmer, B., Manoonpong, P., Larsen, L.B.: Flexible spiking CPGs for online manipulation during hexapod walking. Front. Neurorobot. **14** (2020)
21. Szczecinski, N.S., Hunt, A.J., Quinn, R.D.: A functional subnetwork approach to designing synthetic nervous systems that control legged robot locomotion. Front. Neurorobot. **11** (2017)
22. Szczecinski, N.S., Quinn, R.D., Hunt, A.J.: Extending the functional subnetwork approach to a generalized linear integrate-and-fire neuron model. Front. Neurorobot. **14** (2020)
23. Werbos, P.J.: Bacpropagation through time: what it does and how to do it. In: Proceedings of the IEEE 78 (1990)

Scaling a Hippocampus Model with GPU Parallelisation and Test-Driven Refactoring

Jack Stevenson and Charles Fox[✉]

School of Computer Science, University of Lincoln, Lincoln, UK
{jastevenson,chfox}@lincoln.ac.uk

Abstract. The hippocampus is the brain area used for localisation, mapping and episodic memory. Humans and animals can outperform robotic systems in these tasks, so functional models of hippocampus may be useful to improve robotic navigation, such as for self-driving cars. Previous work developed a biologically plausible model of hippocampus based on Unitary Coherent Particle Filter (UCPF) and Temporal Restricted Boltzmann Machine, which was able to learn to navigate around small test environments. However it was implemented in serial software, which becomes very slow as the environments and numbers of neurons scale up. Modern GPUs can parallelize execution of neural networks. The present Neural Software Engineering study develops a GPU accelerated version of the UCPF hippocampus software, using the formal Software Engineering techniques of profiling, optimisation and test-driven refactoring. Results show that the model can greatly benefit from parallel execution, which may enable it to scale from toy environments and applications to real-world ones such as self-driving car navigation. The refactored parallel code is released to the community as open source software as part of this publication.

1 Introduction

The hippocampus [2] is an important area of the brain involved in spatial memory. It is known to represent self-location and views of high-level objects, and to compute with them for current, replayed, and predicted times, forming an ego-centric map, planner, and episodic memory. These are tasks also required by mobile robots such as self-driving cars as they localise, map, and plan around their environments [2]. Hippocampal models might thus be used to improve these robots' abilities beyond current Simultaneous Localisation and Mapping (SLAM) systems towards more human levels.

A recent model of the hippocampus is the Unitary Coherent Particle Filter (UCPF) [6,7]. This model maps the wake-sleep algorithm [9] in a Temporal Restricted Boltzmann machine [12] onto biologically plausible structures and processes of hippocampal areas. The model is notable for predicting the need for after-depolarisation potential (ADP) to be found and used in region CA3

© The Author(s), under exclusive license to Springer Nature Switzerland AG 2022
A. Hunt et al. (Eds.): Living Machines 2022, LNAI 13548, pp. 44–53, 2022.
https://doi.org/10.1007/978-3-031-20470-8_5

(sub-field 3 of the cornu ammonis), as occurs in the biology, to enable the wake-sleep phases via the theta rhythm. The model also makes use of a cholinergic Subiculum-Septum (Sub-Sep) pathway to detect and correct for lostness of localisation. The model architecture is reviewed in more detail below.

The UCPF model was then scaled up [11], on a serial CPU, to perform a robotic navigation task shown in Fig. 1b. Here a simulated agent random walks around 13 discrete locations, with four possible orientations at each, and each having a pre-computed bag of SURF (Speeded Up Robust Features) visual features taken from a real world mobile robot environment. Simulated odometry is also computed and used to create grid cell activations. Entorhinal Cortex (EC) thus contains visual and grid cell inputs. The UCPF model was able to successfully learn and navigate around this environment in the presence of realistic sensory noise and visual ambiguity, including recovering from loss of localisation using the Sub-Sep system.

However, at the software implementation level, this serial software becomes slow as the environments and numbers of neurons scale up. The plus maze task Fig. 1b was limited to 13 locations and 86 CA3 neurons for this reason. Modern GPU architectures [10] can massively parallelize execution of neural networks. This is usually done to accelerate backpropagation of multilayer perceptrons for non-biologically plausible machine learning [3]. But they similarly offer the possibility of speeding up more realistic biological networks such as the UCPF hippocampus.

We here use GPUs, together with the formal software engineering techniques of profiling, optimisation and test-driven refactoring [5], to parallelise the learning process of the UCPF hippocampus software. By parallelising, we enable the easy horizontal scaling of the model by reducing the workload on a given processing unit. The software engineering techniques used to ensure compatibility with the original model and to guide optimisation are intended as a case study for similar accelerations of other neurally plausible models. The newly engineered fast and scalable code is released to the community as open source software as part of this publication, as may be useful to applied robotics researchers in self-driving and similar fields.

2   Hippocampus Review

2.1   Neuroanatomy

The hippocampus is part of hippocampal formation system along with the EC and Dentate Gyrus (DG) [2]. EC may be divided into superficial layers (ECs) and deep layers (ECd) The hippocampus is comprised of four main sub-fields: CA1, CA2, CA3 and CA4. However, the classical view of the hippocampal circuit only considers the CA1 and CA3 sub-fields, along with the EC and DG. The circuit accepts sensory input from external sources via ECs. ECs input can include high level object perception from cortical areas, and an odometric percept encoded in EC grid cells. ECs output is then passed to the DG which sparsifies the EC representation. DG and ECs output are passed to the CA3, which has strong recurrent connections, which are disabled by the presence of Septal acetylcholine (ACh). CA3 then projects its output to CA1, which projects the apparent output of the system to ECd. ECs and CA1 also project to Subiculum (Sub), which projects to Septum (Sep) to activate ACh.

2.2 Unitary Coherent Particle Filter Model

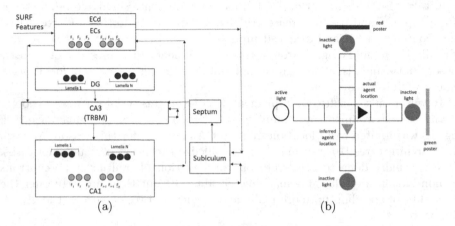

Fig. 1. (a) Illustration of the hippocampus model showing data flows and hippocampus regions. SURF features are used in this case as the visual inputs, from [11]. (b) The plus maze environment the model is learning, from [6].

UCPF models the areas ECs, DG, CA3, CA1, ECd, Sub and Sep as seen in Fig. 1a. Sensor input from any available modality is placed in ECs as input. This can include biologically realistic sensors such as high level object detectors and grid cells, and/or machine vision and robotics sensors such as visual SIFT or lidar features at egocentric locations. As in many hippocampal models [2], DG is assumed to sparsify this representation using PCA encoding. CA1 is assumed to be an output using the same sparsified encoding in the same basis as DG, and ECd a de-sparsified output encoding in the same basis as ECs.

DG and ECs project to the CA3, which functions in the model as the hidden layer in a modified Temporal Restricted Boltzmann Machine (TRBM) [9], whose hidden variable (neurons) have joint probability distribution:

$$P(x_t, x_{t-1}, z_t) = \frac{1}{Z} \exp \sum_t (-x_t' W_{x_t' x_t'} x_{t-1}' - x_t' W_{x_t' z_t'} z_t'), \tag{1}$$

where z represents a Boolean observation vector from DG and ECs, x represents the Boolean hidden state vector of CA3, the prime symbol (') denotes appending an extra dimension containing bias 1 to a vector, and $W_{x_t' x_t'}$ and $W_{x_t' z_t'}$ are the weight matrices connecting these vectors.

The hidden variables function similarly to those in a Hidden Markov model which is most commonly used to fuse sensory input over time with prior memories in order to de-noise the current input and accurately localise from noise inputs. They can also be used to replay memories and predict future plans when disconnected from sensor inputs.

The TRBM is thus a fundamentally serial processing method, with each successive sample of the CA3 state over time requiring the previous sample's result as input. This means that there are limited points of parallelisation in the learning process. However x is a vector state so within each sequential step, the computation can be parallized as the individual CA3 neurons.

UCPF uses a modification of the TRBM, computing a deterministic maximum *a posteriori* (MAP) estimate $\hat{x}_t$ rather than drawing probabilistic samples,

$$\hat{x}_t \leftarrow \arg\max P(x_t|\hat{x}_{t-1}, z_t) = \{\hat{x}_t(i) = (P(x_t(i)|\hat{x}_{t-1}, z_t) > \frac{1}{2})\}_i. \tag{2}$$

This makes CA3 track the MAP states of location and de-noised sensors, in the sparsified basis, which is decoded by CA1 and placed in ECd as output.

Sub/Sep detect loss of tracking by comparing the input and output sensor values (including localization estimates), and sending tonic ACh to CA3 when they differ above a threshold. Thus when tracking is lost, CA3 disables the use of prior information and uses only the current sensory input to relocalise. This can occur both when exploring novel environments and when tracking has been lost by the algorithm in known environments.

The first version of UCPF used hand-set weights throughout, in order to demonstrate the biological plausibility of localisation. The model was then extended [7] to replace these with learning of the weights, in a biologically plausible way. This mapped stages within 10 Hz theta oscillation [2], controlled by phasic ACh, to the inference and learning stages of the wake-sleep algorithm,

$$\Delta w_{ij} = \alpha(\langle x_i pop_j \rangle_{P(x|pop,b)} - \langle x_i pop_j \rangle_{P(pop,x|b)}), \tag{3}$$

where the input population *pop* includes all of the CA3 input populations: ECs, DG and CA3 recurrents, and b are prior biases (detailed in [6]). The UCPF model thus integrates inference and learning, which are performed in alternating states of the theta cycle. There are no distinct 'offline training' and 'on-line inference' runs of the model – the two steps always run together, as postulated in the real, awake hippocampus.[1] Software optimisation should thus target both learning and inferring together.

3   Experiment Design

We would like to locate each of the bottlenecks in the serial implementation and then optimise them with TensorFlow parallelizations. Our first experiment

---

[1] The 'wake-sleep' algorithm is a machine learning structure which is here unrelated to night time sleep behaviour of the hippocampus. Night time slow wave sleep is thought to be involved in consolidating memories from hippocampus to cortex so is outside the scope of the UCPF model.

thus consists of an iterated process of profiling and parallalization refactoring in response to each bottleneck found. It is of general interest to report the sequence of bottlenecks found as they may be common to other biologically realistic neural models and give some insight into what optimisations could be useful in this class of models. Many algorithms have some inherently serial component in addition to parallelizable components, so when the bottleneck becomes an inherently serial component we stop doing refactorings.

Second, we would then like to know and report what total speedup is created once all parallelizable optimisations have been made, and how it varies as a function of the size of the hippocampus simulated, i.e. the number of neurons in CA3. While currently available GPUs are limited in size, trends observed here may suggest how real-time simulation will be able to grow as GPUs become larger.

4   Methods

4.1   Task Configuration

For all experiments, we run the UCPF model in the same configuration. The plus maze environment of Fig. 1b was simulated, and a random walk paths for the agent within this environment simulated for 3000 steps per epoch over 10 epochs, as in [11]. Times were recorded using the Python *time* function on an i5-8700@3.20 GHz, 24 GB DDR4 RAM@2600 MHz and an 11 GB NVidia Geforce 1080TI. Open source code is available from http://github.com/A-Yakkus/hclearn.

4.2   TensorFlow

For each refactoring step, we rewrite the top bottleneck model using TensorFlow [1], a data flow library that performs low level math operations in parallel on GPU. This level is suitable for mimicking biological models in software, at the level of modelling particular biological characteristics of individual neurons. In TensorFlow is it possible to define a function to represent a neurons's mapping from its inputs to its output, then make many parallel copies of this function to make a population of neurons and deploy them on the GPU. This method is used here.

4.3   Formal Refactoring Process

At each refactoring step, we wish to speed up the top bottleneck whilst keeping the code's behaviour the same. A well known challenge of refactoring is ensuring that each modified version retains the same external behaviour as its predecessors. To ensure this, we apply Fowler's formal refactoring methodology [5]. This consists of three stages for each refactoring:

First we profile the code, this tells us which functions are using the most amount of time to run, in terms of the total time spent running the function and the cumulative time, which includes the run time of external functions. This provides the list of program bottlenecks to refactor, which we can rank based on the total time spent in the function.

Second, we write a suite of unit tests around the top bottleneck of the code. This is done by running the original units with various inputs, observing their outputs, and writing tests which assert these outputs follow from these inputs.

Third, we refactor the code in the bottleneck unit using TensorFlow, and rerun the refactored version through the unit tests. These identify any bugs in the new version which can be fixed. A refactoring is only considered complete when it passes the unit tests.

5   Results

We present two types of result from the above experiments. First, we report on what bottlenecks were found and how each was optimised away. These results may be of interest to authors of other neural models as they may suggest similar bottlenecks in them.

Second, we test the performance of the final optimised system as a function of CA3 size. This shows how the speedups scale with larger models, and suggests how they might continue to scale with larger future GPUs beyond what is currently available.

5.1   Bottleneck Locations

The profiling results for the original, unoptimised *serial* code, are shown in Fig. 2a. These show that there were three main bottlenecks, each taking similar total time: computation of the Boltzmann probabilities functions; the Kronecker outer product between vectors; and Bayesian fusion of probabilities.

Computation of Boltzmann probabilities is used to calculate the probability P_{on} of a single neuron being on given its input vector x and weight vector w, used in Eq. 1. The exp(0) term is the probability of the neuron being off, equal to $\exp(-(\mathbf{0}.\mathbf{w})) = 1$, and is here used to compute the normalizing factor Z in that equation,

$$P_{on} = \frac{\exp(-(\mathbf{x}.\mathbf{w}))}{\exp(-(\mathbf{x}.\mathbf{w})) + \exp(0)} \tag{4}$$

The Kronecker outer product $\mathbf{x} \otimes \mathbf{pop}$ is used in the computation of Eq. 3, for the expectations in the wake and sleep terms.

Bayesian fusion is used both in inference (Eq. 1) to fuse probabilities computed for sensory and recurrent connections, and also in learning (Eq. 3) to fuse probabilities arising from observations and biases,

$$f(p_{x1}, p_{x2}) = \frac{p_{x1}p_{x2}}{(p_{x1}p_{x2}) + (1 - p_{x1})(1 - p_{x2})} \tag{5}$$

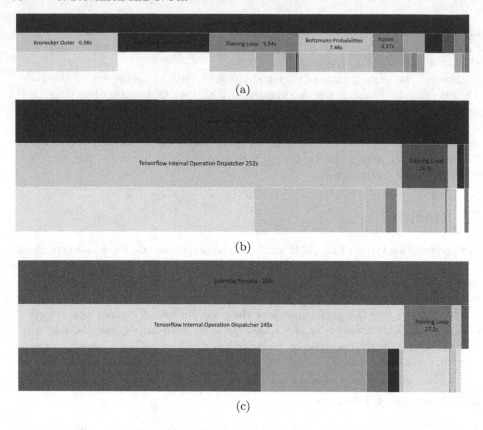

Fig. 2. Profile diagrams at each stage of the refactoring process. Each row is one level of the program call stack, with the top row being the lowest point. Each bar represents the percentage of time the named function took of the above row, with the times provided being the cumulative time of each function in the entries execution. (a) Initial profile of the learning process. (b) Profiling after the first round of optimisations as described by Eqs. 4 - 6 (c) Final profiling of the system. This shows that most of the time is spent in passing data between the CPU and GPU.

An additional bottleneck occurred in computing the sigmoid function for neuron activations,

$$f(x) = -\log(\frac{1}{x} - 1) \tag{6}$$

We refactored each of these functions using parallel TensorFlow. The Boltzmann probabilities and Bayesian fusion are easily parallelized: Eqs. 4 and 5 are functions performed by single, independent neurons. These were thus coded in TensorFlow then deployed on the GPU as many parallel copies for all the neurons in each relevant population. TensorFlow does not have a native implementation of the Kronecker outer product, so we created our own. The sigmoid functions were changed to be computed for all neurons simultaneously on the GPU rather than in series on CPU.[2] Profiling results after these optimisations can be seen in Fig. 2b.

Interestingly, after refactoring, the time to execute on the original model first *increased* by 9× on the original task. This effect comes from the Tensorflow operation dispatcher, which handles the compilation of the neural graph and transfers data between the system memory and GPU Memory. Thus at smaller scales, the refactoring process appears to be detrimental to system performance. However as we will discuss in Sect. 5.2, the move to Tensorflow shows benefits as we scale up.

Casting. At this point in the refactoring process, the new bottleneck can be seen to be in casting between the datatypes used in the CPU and GPU as data is transferred between them.

This is an issue which had arisen from the introduction of our own new TensorFlow refactorings rather than from the original code. The original system loaded weights in CPU as 64-bit floats while TensorFlow initialises variables as 32-bit floats. Bottleneck time was spend converting between them. This lead to an investigation in how to use a Boolean tensor as a tensor of integers of zeros and ones for math operations. TensorFlow provides two ways to handle this: type casting and the *where* function. Type casting creates a new tensor of the requested data type and populates it with the original values made to fit into the requested data type. On the other hand, the where function takes a condition, and returns one of two values based on if the condition is true or false. Table 1 shows that there is an approximate 33% time reduction when casting to a given data type to using the *where* function.

Table 1. Timing 100000 invocations of each function over different numbers of nodes. The times reported are cumulative of all 100000 invocations.

Number of Nodes	Time for tf.cast (s)	Time for tf.where (s)
10	62.073	43.839
100	62.091	43.934
1000	62.208	44.035
10000	61.614	44.288

Profiling results after removing unnecessary casting operations can be seen in Fig. 2c. The bottleneck is now in transferring data between inherently serial CPU and parallel GPU functions which is not easily further optimised, so we stop refactoring here.

---

[2] Sigmoid functions were found to be a bottleneck in pure machine learning DNNs, where they are now replaced by rectified linear units (ReLUs) for speed. However sigmoids are required in UCPF for biological plausibility, and our aim in refactoring is to preserve neural functionality rather than make such approximations.

5.2 Final System Performance

Figure 3a shows the total time to run the model as a function of CA3 size on CPU and GPU. Figure 3b shows the same GPU time curve zoomed in on the y-axis to better show its shape. As the size of CA3, measured in number of neurons, is increased, the GPU implementation's advantage over the original CPU implementation increases, reaching a 23× speedup at the maximum 20,000 neurons size CA3 tested. This maximum is the limit of neurons possible to physically instantiate in parallel on the available GPU hardware.

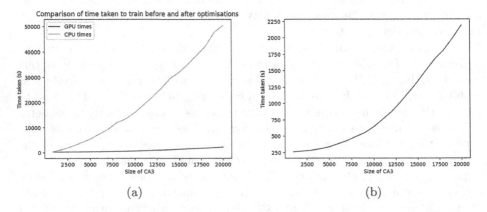

(a)   (b)

Fig. 3. Line graphs showing the time taken to train the model with extra nodes in steps of 1000 from 1000 to 20000. (a) Comparison between CPU and GPU models. (b) The same GPU times as in the comparison, shown alone with a zoomed y-axis.

6 Discussion

If larger GPU's were available, we would expect the trends in Fig. 3a and 3b to continue to larger CA3s. When comparing the two lines in Fig. 3a, the growth of the GPU line appears to linear, but on further inspection, the growth follows a more quadratic curve (Fig. 3b). This indicates that whilst using a GPU does provide significant benefits over the CPU, there are still further optimisations within the training process that can be made. This may be because the UCPF model assumes that all N CA3 cells are mutually connected by N^2 recurrent connections. While FPGA style parallelism might compute these N^2 signals in $\mathcal{O}(1)$ time using N^2 physical wires, GPUs do not immediately connect all their processing elements in this way, and require additional time to move information around hierarchies of elements. The model could be easily modified to be more like the biological hippocampus, which is thought to have many but not fully connected recurrent connections, which could reduce this complexity. (A similar idea has recently worked well to speed up machine learning DNNs as attention and transformers.)

The original implementation was designed to run with a CA3 size of 86 neurons, so scaling to 20,000 is a large improvement. For comparison, the real biological hippocampus in Wistar rats has around 320,000 neurons [4], and in humans around 2 million [8]. The current GPU used cannot fit these biological scales of neurons into memory, but is now only one power of ten away from the rat, and two powers of ten from the human.

The aim of this study is only to show speed gains and the ability to scale up the number of simulated neurons – not to test for the localisation accuracy of the larger CA3 systems enabled by the software. We used the same constrained plus maze task as the original implementation in all tests. This task was designed to be solvable by a small number (86) of CA3 neurons. It is likely that the larger CA3s enabled by the new implementation, perhaps in conjunction with larger GPUs or other neural hardware accelerators such as FGPAs and ASICs will allow future work to try mapping and localising in larger environments, such as those of self-driving cars.

References

1. Abadi, M.: Tensorflow: learning functions at scale. In: Proceedings of the 21st ACM SIGPLAN International Conference on Functional Programming, pp. 1–1 (2016)
2. Andersen, P., Morris, R., Amaral, D., Bliss, T., O'Keefe, J.: The Hippocampus Book. Oxford University Press, London (2006)
3. Bengio, Y., Goodfellow, I., Courville, A.: Deep Learning, vol. 1. MIT Press, Cambridge (2017)
4. Boss, B.D., Turlejski, K., Stanfield, B.B., Cowan, W.M.: On the numbers of neurons on fields ca1 and ca3 of the hippocampus of sprague-dawley and wistar rats. Brain Res. **406**(1–2), 280–287 (1987)
5. Fowler, M.: Refactoring: Improving the Design of Existing Code. Addison-Wesley Professional, Boston (2018)
6. Fox, C., Prescott, T.: Hippocampus as unitary coherent particle filter. In: The 2010 International Joint Conference on. Neural Networks (IJCNN), pp. 1–8 (2010)
7. Fox, C., Prescott, T.: Learning in a unitary coherent hippocampus. In: Artificial Neural Networks (ICANN) (2010)
8. Harding, A., Halliday, G., Kril, J.: Variation in hippocampal neuron number with age and brain volume. Cerebral Cortex (New York, NY: 1991) **8**(8), 710–718 (1998)
9. Hinton, G.E., Osindero, S., Teh, Y.W.: A fast learning algorithm for deep belief nets. Neural Comput. **18**(7), 1527–1554 (2006)
10. Owens, J.: GPU architecture overview. In: ACM SIGGRAPH 2007 Courses, pp. 2-es (2007)
11. Saul, A., Prescott, T., Fox, C.: Scaling up a boltzmann machine model of hippocampus with visual features for mobile robots. In: 2011 IEEE International Conference on Robotics and Biomimetics, pp. 835–840 (2011)
12. Sutskever, I., Hinton, G.E., Taylor, G.W.: The recurrent temporal restricted boltzmann machine. In: 21st Proceedings of the International Conference on Advances in Neural Information Processing Systems (2008)

Application-Oriented Comparison of Two 3D Printing Processes for the Manufacture of Pneumatic Bending Actuators for Bioinspired Macroscopic Soft Gripper Systems

Peter Kappel[1,2] ⓘ, Corinna Kramp[1,2] ⓘ, Thomas Speck[1,2,3] ⓘ,
and Falk J. Tauber[1,2(✉)] ⓘ

[1] Plant Biomechanics Group (PBG) Freiburg, Botanic Garden of the University of Freiburg, University of Freiburg, Freiburg im Breisgau, Germany
{peter.kappel,falk.tauber}@biologie.uni-freiburg.de
[2] Cluster of Excellence livMatS @ FIT – Freiburg Center for Interactive Materials and Bioinspired Technologies, University of Freiburg, Freiburg im Breisgau, Germany
[3] Freiburg Center for Interactive Materials and Bioinspired Technologies (FIT), University of Freiburg, Freiburg im Breisgau, Germany

Abstract. Soft robotic systems are ideally suited for adaptive bioinspired grippers due to their intrinsic properties. The advent of flexible 3D printing materials has made soft robotic actuator designs that were previously difficult or impossible to produce now implementable. In this study, we present an application-oriented comparison of the suitability for the printing of pneumatic actuators of two state-of-the-art 3D printing processes for flexible material, fused deposition modeling (FDM) and material jetting (PolyJet). While the FDM method affects the actuator designs, e.g., by the lack of practicable support material for flexible materials and its nozzle size, PolyJet uses support material but requires a design that allows the removal of it afterward. To compare how the two 3D printer technologies are suited for fabricating bending actuators, we have developed a pneumatic mono-material bending actuator that meets the design requirements to be printed with both printers. The design process itself and the characterization by bending angle and torque provided information about which design concepts could be better implemented with which method. The PolyJet process seems more suited for pneumatic actuators with large chambers and complex overhangs that show a sensitive response in the bending angle, but have low robustness. In contrast, the FDM method appears more suited for actuators with small chambers and complex geometries that feature high robustness and higher absolute tip force. These results form the basis for translating new inspirations from the elastic movements of living nature into our actuators by fully exploiting the advantages of each additive manufacturing process.

Keywords: Soft robotics · Soft machines · Additive manufacturing · Material jetting · PolyJet · FDM printing

© The Author(s), under exclusive license to Springer Nature Switzerland AG 2022
A. Hunt et al. (Eds.): Living Machines 2022, LNAI 13548, pp. 54–67, 2022.
https://doi.org/10.1007/978-3-031-20470-8_6

1 Introduction

Living nature offers an enormous variety of inspiration for energy-efficient, locally controlled elastic movements in the animal and plant kingdoms. Soft machines are particularly suitable for transferring these inspirations to technology because they offer flexible and often self-adapting properties. Movements of soft machines are initiated by actuators, which work principles could be based on materials, for example, dielectric elastomer actuators (DEA) [1], liquid crystal elastomers (LCE) [2], and shape memory alloys (SMAs) [3] or on the use of mechanical principles like granular particle jamming [4] or cable-drives [5]. A further principle is fluidic actuation (hydraulic or pneumatic), which has been widely used for bioinspired actuators and grippers [6–8]. Pneumatic actuators are relatively easily manufactured and can make use of the pneumatic infrastructure available in most laboratories. They are usually made from a flexible material like silicone or other elastomers and consist of one or more pneumatic chambers, often with strain-limiting elements, e.g., asymmetries in its cross-section, layers, or fibers [9–11]. When pressurized with air, the pressure chamber expands and induces movement, while design determines the type of movement performed. Artificial muscles, for example, produce a change in length (contraction) upon actuation [12, 13], while other actuator designs result in torsional, closing, or bending motions or combinations of all of the above [14–16]. A classic bending actuator, for example, bends through a one-sided restriction by an expansion-limiting layer on its underside as opposing air cushions push away from each other [17].

How soft robotic actuators are tested depends on their design and the type of motion they perform. Commonly, the experimental characterization is conducted by specific parameters that are needed to validate simulations. A fundamental parameter to describe the movement of a bending actuator is the displacement of the tip relative to the axis of the fixated actuator base from the side view. This two-dimensional displacement is often sufficiently specified in the form of an angle [18]. Otherwise, for a more in-depth analysis, a position evaluation of the tip is performed [19] or even of many points along the actuator [20] for complex bending deformations. For three-dimensional movements, e.g., helical movements caused by combined bending and torsion, the evaluation is done from several views [21]. The second main parameter of an actuator is the blocked force or torque it generates, typically measured at the tip by a force gauge or sensor [18, 19, 22].

Up until now, soft robotic pneumatic actuators have been mostly cast, e.g., from silicone [23, 24], which has some advantages, such as the possibility to embed easily strain limiting layers or sensors. Disadvantages are the need to mold hollow actuators from at least two parts with often complex molds and glue them together, which is a challenge to obtain airtight and mechanically robust pressure chambers.

With the advent of flexible materials for additive manufacturing, more and more soft robotic actuators are 3D printed [25–27]. The advantages of additive manufacturing are fewer work steps, faster production, printing airtight pressure chambers as one part, and the possibility of using multi-materials. These methods open up the possibility of fabricating directly ready-to-use actuators after printing. Material jetting is an established 3D printing technology that can print a wide range of flexible materials (PolyJet, Fig. 1B). The principle of material jetting is similar to inkjet printing, but instead of the dispersal of liquid ink dots, resulting in a two-dimensional picture, layer by layer, three-dimensional voxels of photopolymers are dispersed. The use of voxels enables multi-material prints, support material, and even material mixtures; so-called digital materials (DMs) are possible. PolyJet printers have already been used in various studies to print various types of actuators. For example, one study made complete multi-material actuators [28], and another was able to simultaneously print both a soft robotic gripper and with included strain sensors [29]. These examples show that complex geometries and overhangs are made possible through the use of support material. However, hollow parts must always be designed to be large enough so that the support material can be mechanically or chemically removed after printing. Even the technology allows theoretically very small and branched designs, it is practically not applicable if the support material could not be removed sufficiently. There are also printers that work on other principles, which are able to print flexible materials, such as fused deposition modeling (FDM, Fig. 1A) printers [20]. Some 3D printing systems are developed specifically for the fabrication of pneumatic actuators and allow multi-material printing and embedment of pneumatic cushions and membranes into 3D printed structures from hard material [30, 31].

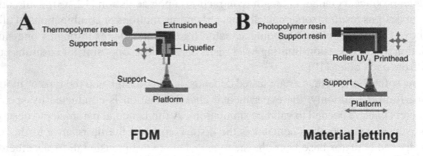

Fig. 1. Schematic description of the two compared 3D printing processes, fused deposition modelling (FDM) and material jetting (PolyJet). Both additive manufacturing methods deposit the material layer-by-layer on a platform. A) FDM is a printing method based on material extrusion. An extrusion head heats a thermopolymeric filament above its glass transition temperature and deposits the material through a nozzle. In this study, no support material was used. B) Material jetting is a printing method based on photopolymerization. A printhead with many nozzles deposits small droplets of photo-reactive polymers as three-dimensional voxels and cures the material with light (UV). For material jetting, the support material is obligatory. The figure was adapted from [32] under a Creative Commons license open access CC BY 4.0.

Comparative studies of FDM and PolyJet printing have mainly focused on printing components made of solid materials. The result of said solid material studies tend to favor PolyJet printing, noting that it offers very high accuracy and resolution (50 μm) for even complicated printed geometries. These studies involving solid materials also concede that it also has low robustness and high material and production costs [33, 34]. However, application-related comparative studies of FDM and PolyJet showed that both processes deliver similarly good results in terms of clinical relevance (<1 mm) [35, 36]. Comparisons of 3D printing methods in a soft robotic context have so far been based on a detailed review of the 3D printing methods used for soft robots [25,

26, 37]. The comparison was made by comparing the results of individual studies with different actuator designs (not specifically focusing on bending actuators). The present work is a first step in filling the lack of studies comparing 3D printing processes by an identical flexible actuator design. We compare a widespread and popular 3D printing method (FDM) and a high-resolution method with a wide selection of flexible materials (PolyJet) in an application-oriented soft robotic approach. Therefore, we designed and characterized a bending actuator as a test object that can be printed equivalently with both methods, which allows the characterization of the individual strengths and weaknesses of both manufacturing techniques. The main goal of this study is to identify whether the two types of 3D printing would be equally suitable for the fabrication of pneumatic bending actuators or whether one of the techniques should be preferred for specific applications in the future.

2 Materials and Methods

In order to practically compare the two 3D printing processes (FDM and PolyJet) in regards to their suitability for fabricating pneumatic actuators, we developed a bending actuator which was adapted to the methodological requirements of both processes. To ensure that the selected materials were as comparable as possible, the available flexible materials were tested for their Shore hardness and tensile properties after printing.

2.1 Printing and Materials

We used the customized FDM multi-material printer by Conrad et al. (2021) [31] for the fabrication of pneumatic actuators. The base frame for this printer was a model FT-5 R2 from Folger Technologies LLC with an E3D Hemera extruder as print head and customized software and post-processing scripts. The filament flow rate was 1.5 mm^3/s, and the extruder ran at a speed of 10 mm/s. Ten bottom and top layers each were printed with an infill of 50%. For overhangs, the extrusion rate was reduced to 0.8 mm^3/s to achieve sufficient base tension of the bridging material.

A soft material reduces the needed pneumatic pressure and thereby energy consumption of a pneumatic actuator. The softest elastomer filament we can currently use for pneumatic actuators is Filaflex Ultra-Soft A70 from Recreus, a thermoplastic polyurethane (TPU) with a specified Shore hardness of A70. This material was thus set for the FDM printed version of the actuator. For printing, the print bed was heated to a temperature of 60 °C, and the TPU was printed at 230 °C.

The material jetting printer used was an Objet260 Connex 3, PolyJet from Stratasys. In contrast to the FDM printer, the PolyJet printer has the ability to mix flexible with rigid materials giving a wide selection of soft materials within Shore hardness scale A. We had two possible flexible digital materials (DMs) at our disposal. In both cases, Agilus30™ Clear (Shore hardness A30–35) was the flexible component and either RGD720 or VeroClear was added in varying proportions to achieve the aimed Shore hardness. Since material properties can be significantly affected by print settings, we tested material samples of our prints for their actual Shore hardness and tensile properties. We validated the post-print Shore hardness specified by the material manufacturer according to the

DIN ISO 7619-1 test standard for elastomers. A solid infill type was chosen for the test specimen to mimic the solid actuator walls of the FDM prints. The specimens were tested after a 24 h resting period to ensure the full release of stresses after cooling down from the print. The measurements were performed at room temperature using the measuring device "Digital Shore Hardness Tester," Sauter HD (HD-BA-d-1723), version 2.3 (07/2017), from Sauter GmbH. The device's accuracy was specified as $\leq 1\%$, and the resolution was 0.1 Shore A. The device met the conditions of the DIN ISO 7619-1 standard and was calibrated according to the manufacturer's instructions (calibration on test block: nominal value $= 22.6 \pm 1$ Shore A, actual value $= 21.7$ Shore A). Each test specimen was measured five times with a prescribed minimum distance of ≥ 5 mm between the individual measurements and ≥ 12 mm to the edges.

Table 1. Material properties obtained from Shore hardness and uniaxial tensile tests for the used FDM filament (Filaflex A70) and a selection of digital PolyJet materials (DM). DMs with two different material compounds (FLX46: Agilus30™ + Rigur; FLX99: Agilus30™ + VeroClear) were tested for a manufacturer-specified Shore hardness of A60 and A70 respectively. Post printing Shore hardness was tested according to the DIN ISO 7619-1 test standard for elastomers with a sample size of $n = 5$ each. The data of measured Shore hardness for FLX9960 were non-parametric. Therefore, all Shore hardness values are given as median and IQR. The tensile strength σ_{max}, elongation at break ε_R, and stresses σ at an elongation of $\varepsilon = 20\%$ and $\varepsilon = 100\%$ are given as mean values with standard deviation. The tensile tests were performed according to DIN 53504. Only minimum values are given for Filaflex A70 since the specimens could not be made to crack in the used tensile setup. Invalid measurements caused differing sample sizes n. Only for specimens that reached an elongation of $\varepsilon = 100\%$ could the stress at that strain be calculated (sample size is given in parentheses).

Material	Shore A (median (IQR))	n	Elongation at break ε_R [%]	Tensile strength σ_{max} [MPa]	Stress σ at [MPa]	
					$\varepsilon = 20\%$	$\varepsilon = 100\%$
FLX4660	61.6 (4.6)	9	117.4 ± 5.02	2.9 ± 0.1	0.4 ± 0	2.4 ± 0.1
FLX9960	60.5 (0.3)	9	122.6 ± 7.24	2.7 ± 0.1	0.4 ± 0	2.1 ± 0.2
Filaflex A70	**75.2 (1.2)**	**9**	**> 728 ± 26**	**> 14.8 ± 0.4**	**1.7 ± 0.1**	**3.2 ± 0.1**
FLX4670	69.8 (0.9)	7 (3)	98.7 ± 5.5	3.6 ± 0.2	0.6 ± 0.1	3.5 ± 0.1
FLX9970	68.2 (1.4)	8 (2)	98.6 ± 6.4	3.6 ± 0.2	0.7 ± 0.1	3.4 ± 0.2

The Shore hardness (Table 1) of all tested PolyJet materials was significantly different from the Filaflex A70, which was used for FDM (Wilcoxon-Mann-Whitney test for FLX9960-DM; two-sided t-test for all other materials, Table 2). The measured values of the PolyJet materials deviated less than 5% from the manufacturer's specifications. However, this did not apply to Filaflex A70 with a median Shore hardness measurement of A75.2 (IQR: 1.2). We measured the closest Shore hardness median to Filaflex A70 for FLX4670-DM (69.8 (IQR: 0.9) Shore A) and FLX9970-DM (68.2 (IQR: 1.4) Shore A). Two different DMs showed no significant differences in measured Shore hardness among the same manufacturer-defined Shore hardness level ($p \geq 0.05$, Table 2). Further, we performed uniaxial tensile tests according to the DIN 53504 standard for rubber and elastomers with a universal testing machine (Hegewald & Peschke, Inspect Table 5 kN-1; equipment: AU31301 (testing machine with accessories), AU33056 (temperature cabinet T56LN2) accuracy: 1%). The tensile tests were performed at room temperature with a preload of 0.1 MPa and a feed rate of 200 mm/min. To compare the digital materials to the Filaflex A70, the tensile strength σ_{max}, elongation at break ε_R, and stresses σ at an elongation of $\varepsilon = 20\%$ and $\varepsilon = 100\%$ were calculated (Table 1). Exceeding requirements of the industrial standard, we manufactured and tested nine samples instead of three for each material. Previous studies have shown that the light-sensitive photopolymers which the PolyJet uses are particularly susceptible to changing mechanical properties over time due to exposure to air, light, and aging [38]. To reduce this risk, the specimens were tested within a time span of 24–48 h after printing.

Table 2. Statistical comparison (p-values) of the measured post-printing Shore hardness of the used FDM filament (Filaflex A70, TPU) and a selection of flexible digital PolyJet materials with close specified Shore hardness. The last two digits of the material names reflect the Shore hardness specified by the manufacturer. A two-tailed t-test was performed for the group comparisons of parametric data. The only non-parametric data of FLX9960 (Shapiro-Wilk test, $p = 0.011$) were compared to the other materials by a Wilcoxon-Mann-Whitney test. The level of statistical significance is defined as: n.s: $p \geq 0.05$ (not significant); *: $0.01 \leq p < 0.05$ (significant); **: $0.001 \leq p < 0.01$ (high significant); ***: $p < 0.001$ (highest significant)

Material	FLX9960	FLX4660	FLX4670	FLX9970
Filaflex A70	< 0.001 (***)	< 0.001 (***)	< 0.001 (***)	< 0.001 (***)
FLX9970	0.021 (*)	0.378 (n.s.)	0.121 (n.s.)	
FLX4670	0.012 (*)	0.191 (n.s.)		
FLX4660	0.834 (n.s.)			

The material tests showed that the measured Shore hardness of the DMs with the same specified value of A70 is significantly different (FLX4670: $p < 0.001$; FLX9970: $p < 0.001$) but still most similar to Filaflex A70 compared to DMs with other Shore hardness. The tensile tests showed that Filaflex A70 generally has a comparatively high tensile strength and elongation at break. Whereas the higher the Shore hardness of a DM, the lower its elongation at break and the higher the tensile strength. Since the actuator's function is based on elongation, the DM with the highest measured elongation at break, rather than the one with the most similar Shore hardness, was selected for the comparative study, i.e., FLX9960-DM with a specified Shore hardness of A60 was chosen.

2.2 Actuator Design

The aim of this study was to perform an application-oriented comparison of the suitability of two state-of-the-art 3D printing processes (FDM and PolyJet) for flexible material for the printing of pneumatic actuators. For this purpose, we developed a test actuator whose design met the methodological requirements of both printers.

The actuator had to be printable with the FDM printer without support material. Meanwhile it also had to have air chambers and openings large enough to mechanically remove the obligatory support material in material jetting (PolyJet) from the inside. The result was a 70 mm × 12 mm × 21 mm (length × width × high, without fixation part) large bending actuator (Fig. 2). The actuator walls are 2 mm thick and exclude a particular strain-limiting layer or distinct membranes. Thus bending occurs by the geometry itself. Three angled, abutting protrusions of the main pressure chamber on the top side expand with an increase in applied air pressure and cause the actuator to bend. The air chambers and opening at the actuator base were designed to not contain any bottlenecks or complicated branches that would hinder the removal of PolyJet support material. Additionally, a two-piece rigid adapter (PolyJet printed from VeroClear) that clamps the base part and closes the opening airtight was developed, allowing for firm fixation of the flexible actuator and a secure air supply.

Beyond incorporating the requirements of both methods into the basic design, we also made individual adjustments to the design for each method. These individual adjustments did not affect the basic design. For the PolyJet variant, the edges were rounded to reduce the tendency of material tearing. In preliminary tests, sharp edges were observed to cause this tendency due to the low tensile strength. In addition, the removal of support material necessitated a second closable opening in the tip of the actuator, thus lowering the risk of damaging the actuator during cleaning (Fig. 2A). The lid was press-fitted and provided an airtight sealing without any glue. This airtight sealing was maintained until the air pressure became high enough to squeeze the lid out. This happened whenever the air pressure was so high that it led to material failure in tests with a glued lid (ca. >1 bar). It was thus able to act as a pressure relief valve, protecting the actuator. In both variants, the actuator was printed lying on the right side. This is actually a requirement in the FDM method to reduce the complexity of the overhangs to the simplest shape possible, i.e., a flat surface (the sidewall). In this orientation, the walls that form the complex shape of the silhouette stand perpendicular to the printing plate and thus support themselves during printing. Nevertheless, the sidewall is too large of an overhang for FDM printing to perform airtight printing without any support. Therefore, we solved this issue by separately printing a support inlay from PVOH filament and inserting it during the stopped printing process (Fig. 2B). It supported the top layers and could be pre-dissolved by water. After which it could then be pulled out from the finished actuator with a handle.

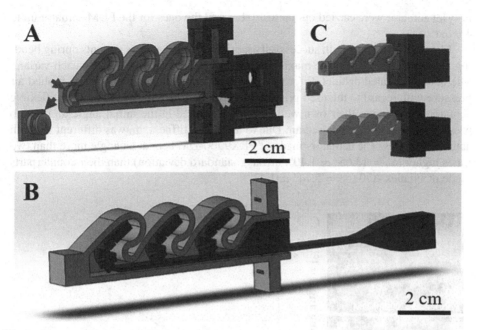

Fig. 2. Test actuator models for both used printing methods (A: PolyJet, green; B: FDM, grey). The basic design: Three angled, abutting protrusions of the main pressure chamber on the top side expanded when air pressure increased and caused the actuator to bend. The actuator is printed from flexible material lying on its right side as one part. A PolyJet printed rigid adapter (blue) clamped at the actuator base closed the main opening (grey arrow). This adapter provided an airtight seal and allowed fixation and air supply during testing. The walls were constantly 2 mm thick and excluded a strain-limiting layer. For each printing method, individual adjustments had to be made that did not affect the basic design. **A:** Longitudinal section of the actuator model (green) with assembled adapter (dark blue) for PolyJet printing. Adjustments were: rounded edges to prevent material tearing, and a second opening that was closable without extra gluing with a lid (red arrows) for removal of the support material. **B:** Longitudinal section of the actuator model (grey) with inserted support inlay (red). The inlay, which was separately printed from PVOH filament, was inserted during the stopped printing process. It supported the top layer overhangs and could be pre-dissolved by water and pulled out from the finished actuator by the handle. **C:** Exterior view of both models with the assembled adapter.

3 Results

Once we successfully printed the test actuators from Filaflex A70 (FDM) and FLX9960 (PolyJet), we characterized their bending behavior by bending angle (Fig. 3) and tip force (Fig. 4). Within these characterizations, the actuators showed a difference in bending behavior depending on which material was used. The PolyJet material variant could be safely actuated up to 1.0 bar. When compressed air was applied at a pressure greater than 1.0 bar, the material and thus the actuator failed. The same was observed in prolonged static actuation of the PolyJet actuator. In contrast, the FDM printed actuator could be actuated statically for prolonged periods and up to at least 4.0 bar without material failure or signs of plastic deformation. Accordingly, the measurement series for the

PolyJet actuator were carried out up to 1.0 bar and the ones for the FDM actuator up to 4.0 bar.

Fig. 3A and B show both successfully fabricated test actuators variants during bending angle measurement at the maximum applied air pressure suitable for each variant. The results revealed distinct differences in their bending angle response to applied air pressure with regard to the used printing process. In horizontal orientation, the flexible actuators bent due to their own weight, which resulted in the initial angle α_0 prior to pressurization with compressed air. Due to different stiffness, α_0 was different for both actuator variants. The actuators made of FLX9960-DM bent at an angle more than two times higher ($\alpha_0 = 13.65° \pm 1.40°$, mean $\pm$ standard deviation) than their counterparts made of Filaflex A70 ($\alpha_0 = 5.74° \pm 1.47°$).

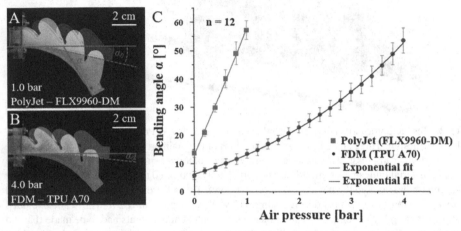

Fig. 3. Bending angles of the test actuator printed with both 3D printing processes. **A** and **B** show how the bending angle was defined by the example of actuator images in un-actuated state (initial angle α_0, transparent silhouette) and with maximum applied air pressure (bending angel α, highlighted in the foreground). **A:** PolyJet printed actuator (FLX9960-DM). **B:** FDM printed actuator (Filaflex TPU A70). **C:** Mean bending angles with standard deviation for PolyJet (red squares) and FDM (black circles) printed actuators. Due to the weight of the flexible actuators, α_0 was greater than zero. The bending angle was measured in 0.2 bar increments up until the maximum air pressure that the actuators could safely withstand without material failing. PolyJet actuators failed above 1.0 bar, while FDM printed actuators withstood at least 4.0 bar applied air pressure. Three actuators were tested four times each, and the data were pooled ($n = 12$, tested for variance homogeneity). An exponential fit (model: ExpDec1, OriginPro 2021b) was performed for both test series: PolyJet, FLX9960-DM ($R2 = 0.99698$); FDM, Filaflex A70 ($R2 = 0.99932$).

At 1.0 bar, the PolyJet actuators bent on average $57.19° \pm 3.33°$, already four times more than its FDM printed counterpart made of Filaflex A70. The bending angle of the latter increased with a significantly lower increase per unit of air pressure and only reached a similarly high maximum bending angle α_{max} of $53.52° \pm 4.46°$ at 4.0 bar.

On average, the generated torque of both actuator types was up to 1.0 bar without a significant difference (Fig. 4). However, beyond 1.0 bar, at which the PolyJet printed actuators failed, the FDM printed actuators generated significantly higher torque, indicating lower sensitivity but much higher robustness and performance.

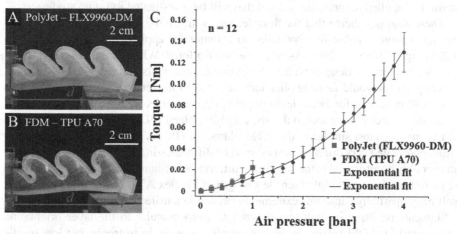

Fig. 4. Tip force, shown as torque, of the test actuator printed with both 3D printing processes. **A** (PolyJet) and **B** (FDM) show how the tip force was measured with a hemispherical adapter transmitting the force from the tip to the surface of a flat FlexiForce® sensor. The torque was calculated from the tip force and the distance d. **C:** Mean torque with standard deviation for PolyJet (red squares) and FDM (black circles) printed actuators. The tip force was measured in 0.2 bar increments up to the maximum air pressure that the actuators could safely withstand without the material failing. PolyJet actuators failed above 1.0 bar, while FDM printed actuators withstood at least 4.0 bar applied air pressure. Three actuators were tested four times each, and the data were pooled ($n = 12$, tested for variance homogeneity). An exponential fit (model: ExpDec1, OriginPro 2021b) was performed for both test series: PolyJet, FLX9960-DM ($R^2 = 0.99213$); FDM, Filaflex A70 ($R^2 = 0.99825$).

4 Conclusion and Outlook

This study took a practical approach of comparing PolyJet and FDM 3D printers using a test bending actuator, which can be printed equally with both additive manufacturing processes. In doing so we were able yield novel aspects of the methodological properties. Moreover, we encountered novel advantages and disadvantages of both processes in the production of bending actuators. The design of the test actuator already provided valuable insights into the advantages and limitations of each printing process. Some design characteristics of both printing methods interfered with each other and required adjusted solutions. Such as the separately printed support inlay that had to be inserted during FDM printing to support the large overhangs necessary for PolyJet.

The comparative characterization of the two actuator variants showed that the FDM printed actuator required relatively high air pressure and thus more energy input for actuation. However, it also showed high robustness to the applied air pressure. In contrast, the PolyJet actuators were more sensitive to applied air pressure and more prone to failure under high air pressure. As Zatopa et al. (2018) mentioned, this behavior is probably due to unfavorable material properties like "low compliance and robustness under fatigue" [39]. The low robustness of PolyJet printed actuators seems also to correlate with the duration of applied air pressure, a point that will be investigated in future studies.

These results indicate that for flexible, mono-material 3D printed actuators, FDM printing is more suitable for producing an actuator for applications demanding comparable high stiffness, robustness, and absolute tip force. Whereas the PolyJet printing process can fabricate designs with high volume air chambers and extended or complex overhangs. This would favor applications targeted to low-energy actuation as well as highly soft materials, for example, in gripping delicate objects.

Based on preliminary material tests, a PolyJet blend (FLX9960-DM) was selected with properties most similar to the FDM filament (TPU, A70), however the resulting actuators revealed very different properties. The difference in the actuator characteristics can probably be attributed to the significant difference in Shore hardness ($p < 0.001$) and the more than five times higher tensile strength of Filaflex A70. The printing principles itself might partially cause this extreme difference in tensile strength. Namely, deposal of filaments resulting in high tensile strength perpendicular to the layer orientation (anisotropy) for FDM versus deposal of voxels resulting, in isotropic, but low tensile strength for PolyJet. However, the significant difference in Shore hardness is probably more prominently connected to the available material types for each method.

What is important to note, are the evermore advancements in the fabrication of filament materials with lower Shore hardness, which could drastically reduce the required energy input for FDM printed actuators. For example, a TPU filament with a softer Shore hardness of A60 is available but, so far, challenging to use for printing airtight air chambers. While PolyJet, as a proven multi-material printing technology, offers the possibility to compensate for the limited properties of its very flexible but less robust materials with clever multi-material designs to reduce stress [40, 41].

As mentioned above, previous evaluations of 3D printing processes such as FDM or PolyJet mainly were done individually and, when compared, were based on solid components' print quality. This study is to our knowledge the first to compare both printing processes on a functional basis by an entirely flexible bending actuator, which was tailored to be printed and compared by both methods. The study results will form the basis to translate new inspirations from biological elastic movements into future designs of bioinspired low-energy actuators and gripper systems by fully exploiting the advantages of each additive manufacturing method.

Funding. Funded by the Deutsche Forschungsgemeinschaft (DFG, German Research Foundation) under Germany's Excellence Strategy – EXC-2193/1-390951807.

References

1. Kovacs, G., Düring, L., Michel, S., Terrasi, G.: Stacked dielectric elastomer actuator for tensile force transmission. Sens. Actuators, A **155**, 299–307 (2009). https://doi.org/10.1016/j.sna.2009.08.027

2. Wani, O.M., Zeng, H., Priimagi, A.: A light-driven artificial flytrap. Nat. Commun. **8**, 15546 (2017). https://doi.org/10.1038/ncomms15546
3. Kim, S., Laschi, C., Trimmer, B.: Soft robotics: a bioinspired evolution in robotics. Trends Biotechnol. **31**(5), 287–294 (2013). https://doi.org/10.1016/j.tibtech.2013.03.002
4. Wei, Y., et al.: A novel, variable stiffness robotic gripper based on integrated soft actuating and particle jamming. Soft Rob. **3**(3), 134–143 (2016). https://doi.org/10.1089/soro.2016.0027
5. Sun, Y., Liu, Y., Lueth, T.C.: Optimization of stress distribution in tendon-driven continuum robots using fish-tail-inspired method. IEEE Robot. Autom. Lett. **7**(2), 3380–3387 (2022). https://doi.org/10.1109/LRA.2022.3147456
6. Wehner, M., et al.: An integrated design and fabrication strategy for entirely soft, autonomous robots. Nature **536**(7617), 451–455 (2016). https://doi.org/10.1038/nature19100
7. Gorissen, B., Reynaerts, D., Konishi, S., Yoshida, K., Kim, J.-W., Volder, M.: Elastic inflatable actuators for soft robotic applications. Adv. Mater. **29**, 1604977 (2017). https://doi.org/10.1002/adma.201604977
8. Sun, T., Chen, Y., Han, T., Jiao, C., Lian, B., Song, Y.: A soft gripper with variable stiffness inspired by pangolin scales, toothed pneumatic actuator and autonomous controller. Robot. Comput. Integr. Manuf. **61**(2020), 101848 (2020). https://doi.org/10.1016/j.rcim.2019.101848
9. Esser, F., Steger, T., Bach, D., Masselter, T., Speck, T.: Development of novel foam-based soft robotic ring actuators for a biomimetic peristaltic pumping system. In: Mangan, M., Cutkosky, M., Mura, A., Verschure, P.F.M.J., Prescott, T., Lepora, N. (eds.) Living Machines 2017. LNCS (LNAI), vol. 10384, pp. 138–147. Springer, Cham (2017). https://doi.org/10.1007/978-3-319-63537-8_12
10. Esser, F., Krüger, F., Masselter, T., Speck, T.: Development and characterization of a novel biomimetic peristaltic pumping system with flexible silicone-based soft robotic ring actuators. In: Vouloutsi, V., Halloy, J., Mura, A., Mangan, M., Lepora, N., Prescott, T.J., Verschure, P.F.M.J. (eds.) Living Machines 2018. LNCS (LNAI), vol. 10928, pp. 157–167. Springer, Cham (2018). https://doi.org/10.1007/978-3-319-95972-6_17
11. Esser, F., Krüger, F., Masselter, T., Speck, T.: Characterization of biomimetic peristaltic pumping system based on flexible silicone soft robotic actuators as an alternative for technical pumps. In: Martinez-Hernandez, U., et al. (eds.) Biomimetic and Biohybrid Systems: 8th International Conference, Living Machines 2019, Nara, Japan, proceedings, vol. 11556, pp. 101–113. Springer, Cham (2019). https://doi.org/10.1007/978-3-030-24741-6_9
12. Agerholm, M., Lord, A.: The "artificial muscle" of McKibben. The Lancet **277**(7178), 660–661 (1961). https://doi.org/10.1016/S0140-6736(61)91676-2
13. Schulte, Jr. H.F.: The characteristics of the McKibben artificial muscle. The application of external power in prosthetics and orthotics, pp. 94–115. National Academy of Sciences - National Research Council, Washington, DC (1961)
14. Temirel, M., Yenilmez, B., Knowlton, S., Walker, J., Joshi, A., Tasoglu, S.: Three-dimensional-printed carnivorous plant with snap trap. 3D Printing Addit. Manuf. **3**(4), 244–251 (2016). https://doi.org/10.1089/3dp.2016.0036
15. Schaffner, M., Faber, J.A., Pianegonda, L., Rühs, P.A., Coulter, F., Studart, A.R.: 3D printing of robotic soft actuators with programmable bioinspired architectures. Nat. Commun. **9**(1), 878 (2018). https://doi.org/10.1038/s41467-018-03216-w
16. Geer, R., Iannucci, S., Li, S.: Pneumatic coiling actuator inspired by the awns of *Erodium cicutarium*. Front. Robot. AI **7**(7), 17 (2020). https://doi.org/10.3389/frobt.2020.00017
17. Ilievski, F., Mazzeo, A.D., Shepherd, R.F., Chen, X., Whitesides, G.M.: Soft robotics for chemists. Angew. Chem. **123**(8), 1930–1935 (2011). https://doi.org/10.1002/ange.201006464
18. Demir, K.G., Zhang, Z., Yang, J., Gu, G.X.: Computational and experimental design exploration of 3D-printed soft pneumatic actuators. Adv. Intell. Syst. **2**(7), 2070072 (2020). https://doi.org/10.1002/aisy.202070072

19. Polygerinos, P., et al.: Towards a soft pneumatic glove for hand rehabilitation. In: 2013 IEEE/RSJ International Conference on Intelligent Robots and Systems, pp. 1512–1517. IEEE, Tokyo, Japan (2013). https://doi.org/10.1109/IROS.2013.6696549

20. Herianto, W.I., Ritonga, A.S., Prastowo, A.: Design and fabrication in the loop of soft pneumatic actuators using fused deposition modelling. Sens. Actuator A Phys. **298**, 111556 (2019). https://doi.org/10.1016/j.sna.2019.111556

21. Hu, W., Alici, G.: Bioinspired three-dimensional-printed helical soft pneumatic actuators and their characterization. Soft Rob. **7**(3), 267–282 (2020). https://doi.org/10.1089/soro.2019.0015

22. Moseley, P., Florez, J.M., Sonar, H.A., Agarwal, G., Curtin, W., Paik, J.: Modeling, design, and development of soft pneumatic actuators with finite element method. Adv. Eng. Mater. **18**(6), 978–988 (2016). https://doi.org/10.1002/adem.201500503

23. Sun, Y., Song, Y.S., Paik, J.: Characterization of silicone rubber based soft pneumatic actuators. In: 2013 IEEE/RSJ International Conference on Intelligent Robots and Systems, pp. 4446–4453. IEEE (2013). https://doi.org/10.1109/IROS.2013.6696995

24. Sun, Y., et al.: Stiffness customization and patterning for property modulation of silicone-based soft pneumatic actuators. Soft Rob. **4**(3), 251–260 (2017). https://doi.org/10.1089/soro.2016.0047

25. Rus, D., Tolley, M.T.: Design, fabrication and control of soft robots. Nature **521**(7553), 467–475 (2015). https://doi.org/10.1038/nature14543

26. Wallin, T.J., Pikul, J., Shepherd, R.F.: 3D printing of soft robotic systems. Nat. Rev. Mater. **3**(6), 84–100 (2018). https://doi.org/10.1038/s41578-018-0002-2

27. Keneth, E.S., Kamyshny, A., Totaro, M., Beccai, L., Magdassi, S.: 3D Printing materials for soft robotics. Adv. Mater. Spec. Issue: Soft Robot. **33**(19), 2003387 (2021). https://doi.org/10.1002/adma.202003387

28. Tebyani, M., et al.: 3D Printing an assembled biomimetic robotic finger. In: 2020 17th International Conference on Ubiquitous Robots (UR), pp. 526–532. IEEE (2020). https://doi.org/10.1109/UR49135.2020.9144774

29. Shih, B., et al.: Design considerations for 3D printed, soft, multimaterial resistive sensors for soft robotics. Front. Robot. AI **6**, 30 (2019). https://doi.org/10.3389/frobt.2019.00030

30. Conrad, S., Speck, T., Tauber, F.J.: Multi-material 3D-printer for rapid prototyping of bio-inspired soft robotic elements. In: Vouloutsi, V., Mura, A., Tauber, F.J., Speck, T., Prescott, T.J., Verschure, P.F.M.J. (eds.) Biomimetic and Biohybrid Systems: Living Machines 2020. Lecture Notes in Computer Science(), vol. 12413, pp. 46–54. Springer, Cham. (2020). https://doi.org/10.1007/978-3-030-64313-3_6

31. Conrad, S., Speck, T., Tauber, F.J.: Tool changing 3D printer for rapid prototyping of advanced soft robotic elements. Bioinspir. Biomim. **16**(5), 055010 (2021). https://doi.org/10.1088/1748-3190/ac095a

32. Low, Z.-X., Chua, Y.T., Ray, B.M., Mattia, D., Metcalfe, I.S., Patterson, D.A.: Perspective on 3D printing of separation membranes and comparison to related unconventional fabrication techniques. J. Membr. Sci. **523**, 596–613 (2017). https://doi.org/10.1016/j.memsci.2016.10.006

33. Kluska, E., Gruda, P., Majca-Nowak, N.: The Accuracy and the printing resolution comparison of different 3D printing technologies. Trans. Aerosp. Res. **3**(252), 69–86 (2018). https://doi.org/10.2478/tar-2018-0023

34. Maurya, N.K., Rastogi, V., Singh, P.: Comparative study and measurement of form errors for the component printed by FDM and PolyJet process. Instrum. Mesure Métrologie **18**(4), 353–359 (2019). https://doi.org/10.18280/i2m.180404

35. Lee, K.-Y., et al.: Accuracy of three-dimensional printing for manufacturing replica teeth. Korean J. Orthod. **45**(5), 217–225 (2015). https://doi.org/10.4041/kjod.2015.45.5.217

36. Dorweiler, B., Baqué, P.E., Chaban, R., Ghazy, A., Salem, O.: Quality control in 3D printing: accuracy analysis of 3D-printed models of patient-specific anatomy. Materials **14**(4), 1021 (2021). https://doi.org/10.3390/ma14041021
37. Yap, Y.L., Sing, S.L., Yeong, W.Y.: A review of 3D printing processes and materials for soft robotics. RPJ **26**(8), 1345–1361 (2020). https://doi.org/10.1108/RPJ-11-2019-0302
38. Bass, L., Meisel, N.A., Williams, C.B.: Exploring variability of orientation and aging effects in material properties of multi-material jetting parts. Rapid Prototyping J. **22**, 826–834 (2016). https://doi.org/10.1108/RPJ-11-2015-0169
39. Zatopa, A., Walker, S., Menguc, Y.: Fully soft 3D-printed electroactive fluidic valve for soft hydraulic robots. Soft Rob. **5**(3), 258–271 (2018). https://doi.org/10.1089/soro.2017.0019
40. Bartlett, N.W., et al.: A 3D-printed, functionally graded soft robot powered by combustion. Science **349**(6244), 161–165 (2015). https://doi.org/10.1126/science.aab0129
41. Zhang, Y.-F., et al.: Fast-response, stiffness-tunable soft actuator by hybrid multimaterial 3D printing. Adv. Func. Mater. **29**(15), 1806698 (2019). https://doi.org/10.1002/adfm.201 806698

Integrating Spiking Neural Networks and Deep Learning Algorithms on the Neurorobotics Platform

Rachael Stentiford[1]($\boxtimes$) , Thomas C. Knowles[1] , Benedikt Feldotto[2] ,
Deniz Ergene[2] , Fabrice O. Morin[2] , and Martin J. Pearson[1]

[1] Bristol Robotics Laboratory, University of the West of England, Bristol, UK
{rachael.stentiford,tom.knowles,martin.pearson}@uwe.ac.uk
[2] Department of Informatics, Technical University of Munich,
85748 Munich, Germany
{morinf,feldotto,ergene}@in.tum.de

Abstract. We present a neurorobotic model that can associate self motion (odometry) with vision to correct for drift in a spiking neural network model of head direction based closely on known rodent neurophysiology. We use a deep predictive coding network to learn the generative model of representations of head direction from the spiking neural network to views of naturalistic scenery from a simulated mobile robot. This model has been deployed onto the Neurorobotics Platform of the Human Brain Project which allows full closed loop experiments with spiking neural network models simulated using NEST, a biomimetic robot platform called WhiskEye in Gazebo robot simulator, and a Deep Predictive Coding network implemented in Tensorflow.

Keywords: Neurorobotics platform · Predictive coding · Spiking neural network · pyNEST · NRP · WhiskEye · Head direction

1 Introduction

Neurorobotics is a discipline that works toward building embodied, bio-plausible models of animal neurology often with a view to improving our understanding of living neural systems. Modelling approaches include, but are not limited to, machine learning [13], bio- and neuromorphic hardware [9], functional subnetworks [18], layered control architectures [14] and spiking neural networks [1]. It is particularly well suited to addressing neuroscience questions for which conventional approaches are not ethically viable thus directly supporting one of the pillars of the NC3Rs: Replacement, by using advanced tools to address neuroscience questions without the use of animals [12]. Neurorobotics also allows us to perform experiments that alleviate the technical difficulties of animal behavioural experiments through the embodiment of models and their closed-loop interaction with either physical or real environmental stimuli.

The original version of this chapter was revised: The name of the author Benedikt Feldotto has been corrected. The correction to this chapter is available at https://doi.org/10.1007/978-3-031-20470-8_39

© The Author(s), under exclusive license to Springer Nature Switzerland AG 2022, corrected publication 2022
A. Hunt et al. (Eds.): Living Machines 2022, LNAI 13548, pp. 68–79, 2022.
https://doi.org/10.1007/978-3-031-20470-8_7

The Neurorobotics Platform is a tool developed as part of the Human Brain Project for conducting embodied robotics experiments with embedded bioinspired brain and control systems [4]. It provides synchronisation between Spiking Neural Network (SNN) simulators such as NEST, robot control and simulation tools such as ROS and Gazebo, as well as other popular libraries. Robot behaviours can be specified using the ROS framework and all run time data can be captured and exported after the experiment for analysis.

In this article we present the use of the Neurorobotics Platform (NRP) to integrate and coordinate an online model of the rodent head direction system. We model the rodent head direction cell system as an SNN which estimates the current head angle of a simulated robot based on self-motion (ideothetic) cues, and provides environmental (allothetic) information to the network using a Predictive Coding Network (PCN) implemented in Tensorflow. The model was developed offline in prior works [17] to explore the bidirectional learning that exists between self-motion cues serving as a scaffold for initial learning of change in pose, followed by corrective input from associated allocentrically anchored visual cues after learning. We had found that both discriminative Convolutional Neural Networks (CNN) and generative PCN approaches were appropriate for learning this association but that PCNs were more robust in applying corrective input to the SNN when visual allothetic cues were unreliable [17]. We explore this further in this article by correlating the prediction error generated by the PCN at its lowest layer as a proxy for the reliability of allothetic cues. We contend that this provides a biologically plausible signal which an animal may use to delineate trust in ideothetic or allothetic sensory cues for the update and representation of its estimate of head direction. The experiments presented to support this contention were made possible only through the closed loop integration provided by the NRP.

1.1 Background

Although the rodent head direction system works in the absence of vision, relying on self-motion (ideothetic) information to track head direction, the signal is subject to accumulated error (drift) [7,8,15,19,21,22]. Rodents use allothetic information such as vision, to counter this drift in head direction estimate [19]. This requires forming learned associations between visual scenes and the current head angle, so that the estimated head angle can be corrected when this visual scene is experienced again. This visual control of head direction begins at the Lateral Mammillary Nuclei (LMN) [20], stabilising the head direction signal at its origin. The head direction is thought to originate in the reciprocal connections between the LMN and dorsal tegmental nuclei (DTN) [2,3]. We model the head direction system as a continuous attractor network, exploiting the excitatory and inhibitory connections between these two regions.

To learn associations between heading and the visual scene we employ a generative paradigm that aims to learn to generate appropriate data samples like the training data in the appropriate contexts. The Predictive Coding Network (PCN) based on MultiPredNet [13], was re-purposed to receive head direction and vision information rather than vision and tactile. The PCN works by outputting a prediction from its latent layer that passes through the nodes of the hidden layers (if any) to the input later of each modality. At each layer, the prediction from the layer above is compared to the activity at the current layer and the difference (error) calculated. Weights between layers are then updated locally according to their prediction errors. For a full description of both the PCN and the SNN see [17].

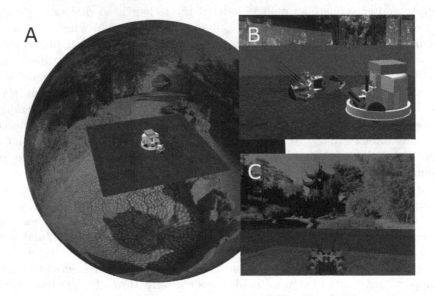

Fig. 1. Illustration showing the Chinese garden environment projected onto a sphere. (A) WhiskEye robot on a floating platform. (B) Image of the WhiskEye robot in the environment. (C) Image from a camera mounted on the WhiskEye robot.

2 Method

2.1 Neurorobotics Platform

We use a local copy of the NRP version 3.2.0. The NRP is a complete neurorobotics experiment platform that builds upon many *de facto* standard open source software for robotics and physics simulation. Specific components used in this paper include ROS (Noetic) [16], Gazebo (11.3) [11] and NEST (2.18) [6]. Gazebo and its integrated ODE physics engine supports the use of robot model files describing joints, actuators and sensors, which can be imported alongside meshes and textures to simulate moving, sensing, 3D models of robots with rigid body interactions inside a 3D virtual world. This often involves creating a virtual simulacrum of a real robot, such as the WhiskEye [10] robot, originally built physically at the BRL and later built in simulation for the NRP. This is then extended further by linking Gazebo to NEST and ensuring timely delivery of

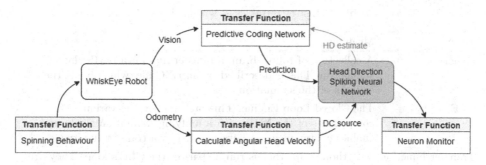

Fig. 2. Diagram showing the structure of the experiment in the NRP. The simulated WhiskEye robot turns on the spot as described by a transfer function. The pose of the robot is sent to a transfer function which calculates angular head velocity and converts it to current inputs to the conjunctive cells of the spiking neural network (SNN). The camera feed from the robot is passed to the trained Predictive Coding Network (PCN) in a transfer function and used to produce predictions which are converted to current input to each of the Head Direction cells in the SNN. The head direction estimate from the SNN, taken as the average of the active cells since the last prediction, is also passed to the PCN to measure prediction error.

messages between them (such as sensory data from the virtual environment, or spiking output from NEST) via the Closed-Loop Engine (CLE). The CLE is the heart of the NRP, providing a framework for all supported tools to communicate to each other using ROS Messages and transfer functions in the form of Python scripts. Such congruence between real and simulated robots allows for experimental results to be compared and serves as a valid substitute for working with physical robots. This is all assisted by a web portal GUI that allows for the environment to be altered, robots to be added on the fly and transfer functions to be created, enabled, disabled and deleted as needed. A summary of NRP-specific terms are summarised in Table 1.

Integrating Tensorflow. To avoid compatibility issues, Tensorflow 2.3 was installed into a separate Python virtual environment and imported via the Brain File. Though intended to set up NEST models, the Brain File also blocks simulation setup whilst it is running, making ideal for any heavy computations that need to be run once. Tensorflow code included defining the Predictive Coding model itself, creating a new session, and loading trained weights from file. Access to the Tensorflow model within transfer functions was achieved by assigning the model to a Brain File variable, which stay in memory for the duration of the simulation. Inference can then be done 'on the fly' as the robot explores the environment. This allows us to close the loop, producing head direction predictions from virtual camera images as the simulation runs, and passing these predictions as current input to the brain model to track and correct drift in the estimated head angle in real time. The PCN can also receive live input from the NEST model, with each tick of the CLE retrieving the activity of the NEST devices

Table 1. List of terms used within the NRP

Term	Meaning
Experiment	A collection of robot, brain and asset files for a particular simulation. This is described by an EXC file, which holds the settings of the simulation
CLE	The Closed Loop Engine. This orchestrates the various components of the NRP with a unifying simulation clock, and enables communication between them via transfer functions
Transfer Function	A Python script that is run as part of the CLE's loop. They are decorated with @Robot2Neuron or @Neuron2Robot accordingly
Brain File	A Python file that describes the NEST model to be loaded

that form its own ideothetic prediction of head direction. This provides both a target for causal inference for the PCN and allows error between the PCN and NEST estimates to be calculated, both which would be impossible without the synchronised execution of Tensorflow and NEST that the NRP supports. The flow diagram shown in Fig. 2 describes the interplay between major components of the experiment.

2.2 WhiskEye

WhiskEye in the NRP is a simulated version of a rat-inspired omnidrive robot with RGB cameras in place of eyes and active whisker-like tactile sensors reported previously (see Fig. 1). WhiskEye was integrated into the Human Brain Project's Neurorobotics Platform as part of prior work [10,13]. ROS topics including body angle, neck position, camera feeds published related to the robot are subscribed to in transfer functions and these data passed to the PCN or SNN, see below. Camera feeds must be deserialised and converted into the flattened RGB format that the PCN expects; this is accomplished by the PCN Inference transfer function.

2.3 Environment

Within the NRP we situate a sphere mesh onto which a background image is projected, enclosing a central suspended platform with grey stone texture for WhiskEye to move on. The sphere is large enough that translation within the bounds of the platform lead to no perceptible changes to the visual scene. This ensures the robot nominally observes the same scene when it returns to that head angle, analogous to rodents observing distal environmental cues.

2.4   Brain Model

The brain model is a pyNEST (2.18) SNN. Using a network structure supported by experimental observations, we define four populations each of 180 standard leaky integrate-and-fire neurons (iaf_psc_alpha) which use alpha-function shaped synaptic currents. These populations represent head direction cells in the Lateral Mammillary nuclei (LMN) and Dorsal Tegmental nuclei (DTN); and two conjunctive head direction by asymmetric angular head velocity populations [2]. LNM cells have constant current input of 450 pA that maintains spontaneous firing at a rate of 50 spikes per second prior to inhibitory input from the DTN.

Reciprocal connections between the LMN and DTN have been shown to be essential for generating the head direction signal [3]. A single stationary bump of activity is produced by providing inhibitory input to all cells surrounding the most active LMN cell. Excitatory connections from LMN neurons to the DTN with declining synaptic strength as a function of distance, inhibition is returned from DTN cells with synaptic strength decreasing as a function of distance offset by a constant (μ).

Conjunctive cells are connected one to one with LMN cells offset by one cell either clockwise or anticlockwise. Conjunctive cells require both AHV and HD input to fire, and shift the bump around the ring. AHV input is provided by a transfer function. For further description of the spiking neural network structure see [17].

2.5   Transfer Functions

In the NRP transfer functions are used to coordinate interactions between the various component simulators and libraries that make up an experiment. Table 2 summarises the transfer functions used in this study.

2.6   Predictive Coding Network

We use a multimodal predictive coding network, based on the previously proposed MultiPredNet [13], that attempts to reconstruct each pair of inputs - images of visual scenes and head direction - from a multimodal latent space. Prior work [13,17] has shown this network's effectiveness at predicting pose and head direction from natural scenes using its bio-plausible local learning rules. Having been trained in an offline setting on at least one full rotation of views from the same environment, these weights are loaded into the network during setup. This enables it to produce robust predictions of head direction based on the allothetic cues of the visual scene. These predictions are 180 elements in width at each update step, matching the number of HD cells. The prediction values are injected as current into the network via 180 dc_source devices connected one to one with the LMN population. To prevent negative current injections, any negative values in the prediction are set to 0.

Table 2. List of transfer functions supporting the experiment

Name	Function
AHV Input	The head velocity is cached using a Brain File variable, enabling Angular Head Velocity (AHV) to be calculated in each time step. Any changes in AHV are passed to the NEST model and injected into the conjunctive cell population
Spinning	Head angle is varied continuously by sending z-axis angular velocity commands to WhiskEye
PCN Inference	The PCN model is passed the current camera state as input, with influence from head direction input disabled. It then generates an inference of the current head direction based on its prediction of the camera state, which is then converted into a current value and passed to the NEST model
Neuron Monitor	LMN head direction cell population spikes are collected using a *spike_recorder device*, and written to a CSV using a *CSVRecorder*. Recorded spikes are also displayed in the spike train window

2.7   Spike Analysis

The most active cell in 40 ms bins is identified and assumed to be the current most active cell and the peak of the bump. Converting the cell number to a value between π and $-\pi$, these values are then compared to the ground truth head angle. The difference between the estimated and ground truth head angle indicates accumulation of drift over time, with total error measured as Root Mean Squared Error (RMSE).

3   Results

3.1   Head Angle Estimated by the SNN Follows Ground Truth

The bump of activity in the SNN is centred on the current estimate of head angle. Movement of the bump is driven by Direct Current (DC) input to the conjunctive layers which are connected one cell clockwise or anticlockwise around the ring. In the absence of corrective input from the PCN, the bump, driven by ideothetic input only, is subject to drift (Fig. 3A blue), as the model for transferring AHV to current is not optimal. The difference between the ground truth head angle and the estimated head angle increases over time (Fig. 3B blue), resulting in a total error of 2.42 rad (1.263 RMSE), after 3 min of simulation.

When the PCN transfer function is active, it produces predictions of the current head angle based on the current visual scene observed by the robot's cameras. These predictions are converted to DC and injected into the head direction cells as corrective input. As seen in our previous work [17], this corrective signal reduced the drift resulting in total error of 0.43 rad (82.23% reduction; 0.370 RMSE).

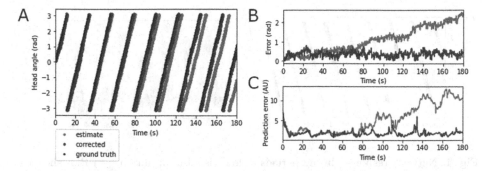

Fig. 3. Estimated head angle from the spiking neural network (SNN). (A) Plot showing estimated head angle with ideothetic drive only (blue), the corrected estimated head angle (red) which is updated using predictions from the predictive coding network (PCN), and ground truth head angle (black). (B) Error measured as the difference between the estimate and the ground truth is shown. Allothetic input from the PCN results in minimised drift and the corrected estimate and ground truth are almost indistinguishable. (C) Plot showing the prediction error at each time point when the head direction estimate is passed back to the PCN, when the predictions are used to correct for drift (red) or not (blue). (Color figure online)

3.2   PCN Prediction Error Increases with Drift

Until this point we have measured the drift in the SNN by directly comparing the HD estimate to the ground truth. However, rodents do not have access to this ground truth information in order to evaluate the confidence of the HD estimate. As part of its inference process, the PCN produces a prediction error between the expected head angle and its reconstruction, which may be a suitable alternative. The NRP allows both the SNN and the PCN to run synchronously as the robot moves. This makes it possible to send continuous feedback between the two models. The predictions from the PCN can be used to update the SNN estimate, and in return the current HD estimate supplied to the PCN to be compared to the prediction generated based on the visual data. By passing the current head angle to the PCN, the prediction error between the presented head angle and the reconstruction is calculated. When the predictions are used to correct for error in the HD estimate, the prediction error remains low (Fig. 3C red) with small peaks representing small inconsistencies that remain in the corrected head direction estimate. If we generate the predictions but do not feed these to the SNN, the head direction estimate drifts, resulting in an overall gradual increase in error (Fig. 3C blue). The prediction error in the drifting case correlates strongly with the calculated error (Fig. 3B,C blue; 0.929 Pearson correlation coefficient). When the predictions are used to correct for error in the HD estimate, the prediction error reflects the reconstruction quality for each of the head angles (Fig. 3C red). The oscillation in the prediction error indicates the prediction quality is not equal across all head angles.

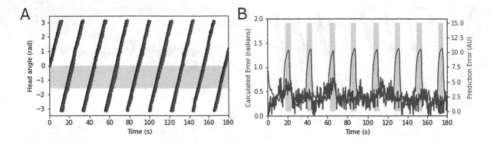

Fig. 4. Network response during periods of low visual information. (A) Plot showing the corrected estimated head angle (red) which is updated using predictions from the predictive coding network (PCN), and ground truth head angle (black). Visual information is obscured in the region shaded blue. (B) Plot showing the calculated error (red) between the ground truth and the estimate, and the prediction error from the PCN (red). Visual information is obscured in the regions shaded blue. (Color figure online)

3.3   Ideothetic Information Drives Network in Periods of Darkness

During periods of darkness or when distal visual information is not available because it is obscured by proximal objects, animals must rely upon ideothetic information to keep track of their head direction. To observe the response of the network to ambiguous visual information we obscured a 90 s°C portion of the visual scene (Fig. 4 A blue shaded region). During this period the predictions produced by the PCN became close to a flat line, and very little current was injected into the network. Figure 4A shows ideothetic information driving the bump during the dark period with minimal drift. Figure 4B shows while the calculated error between the ground truth and the estimated head angle remains low (red), the prediction error (green) from the PCN shows peaks not visible in the calculated error which match up the periods of darkness. This is a strong signal that the predictions are inaccurate, and in future experiments could be used to trigger learning after extended periods of poor prediction.

4   Discussion

This work demonstrates the use of using machine learning and spiking neural networks in a closed loop, embodied, and situated model on the Neurorobotics platform (NRP). We have replicated the results of our previous work reducing drift in a Spiking Neural Network (SNN) model of the head direction system using head angle predictions inferred by a Predictive Coding Network (PCN). The NRP allowed us to close the loop, with the SNN and the PCN running synchronously as the robot moves, controlled by the Closed-Loop Engine of the NRP. Closing the loop has enabled new avenues for reciprocal information transfer between the PCN and the SNN to be explored that were not possible before NRP integration. As the prediction error produced by the PCN reflects drift in the network, it could serve as a parsimonious indicator of poor predictions. In novel environments or in the dark, where visual information is unreliable, we would expect this error to increase and the SNN to drift, as the PCN would be unable to reconstruct the head angle associated with a novel visual scene. This highlights, at least at a functional level of description, a biologically plausible error signal that could be used to drive learning as required. Furthermore, this error signal can act as a proxy for confidence in a particular modality, allowing the agent to dynamically apportion its reliance on allothetic vs ideothetic cues when estimating head direction.

Currently the simulation inside the NRP runs slower than real time. The NRP allows this by blocking processes, such as transfer functions (including the PCN) and the brain model, until the current process is complete. As the online NRP currently utilises CPUs only, we have restricted our work to CPUs, however Tensorflow is suited to using GPUs and as NEST is CPU intensive, a combination of the two will lead to faster simulation. Further, by working with SNN invites the future integration of SpiNNaker based neuromorphic hardware [5] via the NRP and ultimately leading toward real-time, embedded physical robot deployment. Using these methods and tools enable new neuroscience questions to be explored which in turn inspires new questions for experimental studies to be generated. We anticipate similar experiments will encourage collaboration between experimental and computational neuroscientists or roboticists, working towards the principles of Replacement and Reduction of animal research set out by the NC3Rs.

The use of the NRP presented in this paper centres around rat navigation. Though the hippocampal formation has been clearly linked to navigation in mammals, there are competing models of how the various sub-problems of navigation - integrating position and head direction, incorporating external sensory cues, dealing with unreliable sensors - are solved in the brain. This paper's solution is consistent with available neuroscience data and theory; a ring attractor network formed by reciprocal LMN-DTN connections, driven by angular head velocity input from the supragenual nucleus, with a deep predictive coding model of sensory cortices feeding corrective inputs via the postsubiculum. Our contribution in this space being that one of the intrinsic network components of the predictive coding approach to learning can be used as a useful proxy for determining confidence in associating sensory stimuli to head directions. This is turn could be used to drive further learning or initiate changes in behaviour to accommodate the sensory ambiguity.

Acknowledgements. This research has received funding from the European Union's Horizon 2020 Framework Programme for Research and Innovation under the Specific Grant Agreement No. 945539 (Human Brain Project SGA3). Chinese Garden in Stuttgart panorama taken and released under CC0 license by Andreas Mitchok.

References

1. Aljalbout, E., Walter, F., Röhrbein, F., Knoll, A.: Task-independent spiking central pattern generator: A learning-based approach. Neural Process. Lett. **51**(3), 2751–2764 (2020)
2. Bassett, J.P., Taube, J.S.: Neural correlates for angular head velocity in the rat dorsal tegmental nucleus. J. Neurosci. **21**, 5740–5751 (2001)
3. Blair, H.T., Cho, J., Sharp, P.E.: The anterior thalamic head-direction signal is abolished by bilateral but not unilateral lesions of the lateral mammillary nucleus. J. Neurosci. **19**, 6673–6683 (1999)
4. Falotico, E., et al.: Connecting artificial brains to robots in a comprehensive simulation framework: the neurorobotics platform. Front. Neurorobot. **11**, 2 (2017). https://doi.org/10.3389/fnbot.2017.00002
5. Furber, S., Galluppi, F., Temple, S., Plana, L.: The spinnaker project. Proc. IEEE **102**, 652–665 (2014). https://doi.org/10.1109/JPROC.2014.2304638
6. Gewaltig, M.O., Diesmann, M.: Nest (neural simulation tool). Scholarpedia **2**(4), 1430 (2007)
7. Goodridge, J.P., Taube, J.S.: Preferential use of the landmark navigational system by head direction cells in rats. Behav. Neurosci. **109**, 49–61 (1995). https://doi.org/10.1037/0735-7044.109.1.49
8. Goodridge, J.P., Dudchenko, P.A., Worboys, K.A., Golob, E.J., Taube, J.S.: Cue control and head direction cells. Behav. Neurosci. **112**, 749–761 (1998). https://doi.org/10.1037/0735-7044.112.4.749
9. Hunt, A., Szczecinski, N., Quinn, R.: Development and training of a neural controller for hind leg walking in a dog robot. Front. Neurorobot. **11** (2017)
10. Knowles, T.C., Stentiford, R., Pearson, M.J.: WhiskEye: a biomimetic model of multisensory spatial memory based on sensory reconstruction. In: Fox, C., Gao, J., Ghalamzan Esfahani, A., Saaj, M., Hanheide, M., Parsons, S. (eds.) TAROS 2021. LNCS (LNAI), vol. 13054, pp. 408–418. Springer, Cham (2021). https://doi.org/10.1007/978-3-030-89177-0_43
11. Koenig, N., Howard, A.: Design and use paradigms for gazebo, an open-source multi-robot simulator. In: 2004 IEEE/RSJ International Conference on Intelligent Robots and Systems (IROS) (IEEE Cat. No. 04CH37566). vol. 3, pp. 2149–2154 (2004). https://doi.org/10.1109/IROS.2004.1389727
12. NC3Rs: The 3rs. https://www.nc3rs.org.uk/who-we-are/3rs
13. Pearson, M.J., et al.:Multimodal representation learning for place recognition using deep hebbian predictive coding. Front. Robot. AI **8** (2021). https://doi.org/10.3389/frobt.2021.732023
14. Prescott, T.J., Redgrave, P., Gurney, K.: Layered control architectures in robots and vertebrates. Adapt. Behav. **7**(1), 99–127 (1999)
15. Stackman, R.W., Golob, E.J., Bassett, J.P., Taube, J.S.: Passive transport disrupts directional path integration by rat head direction cells. J. Neurophysiol. **90**, 2862–2874 (2003). https://doi.org/10.1152/JN.00346.2003
16. Stanford Artificial Intelligence Laboratory et al.: Robotic operating system https://www.ros.org
17. Stentiford, R., Knowles, T.C., Pearson, M.J.: A spiking neural network model of rodent head direction calibrated with landmark free learning. Front. Neurorobot. **16** (2022). https://doi.org/10.3389/fnbot.2022.867019, https://www.frontiersin.org/article/10.3389/fnbot.2022.867019

18. Szczecinski, N.S., Hunt, A.J., Quinn, R.D.: Design process and tools for dynamic neuromechanical models and robot controllers. Biol. Cybern. **111**(1), 105–127 (2017). https://doi.org/10.1007/s00422-017-0711-4
19. Taube, J.S., Burton, H.L.: Head direction cell activity monitored in a novel environment and during a cue conflict situation. J. Neurophysiol. **74**, 1953–1971 (1995). https://doi.org/10.1152/JN.1995.74.5.1953
20. Yoder, R.M., Peck, J.R., Taube, J.S.: Visual landmark information gains control of the head direction signal at the lateral mammillary nuclei. J. Neurosci. **35**, 1354–1367 (2015). https://doi.org/10.1523/JNEUROSCI.1418-14.2015
21. Yoder, R.M., Taube, J.S.: Head direction cell activity in mice: robust directional signal depends on intact otolith organs. J. Neurosci. **29**, 1061–1076 (2009). https://doi.org/10.1523/JNEUROSCI.1679-08.2009
22. Yoder, R.M., Taube, J.S.: The vestibular contribution to the head direction signal and navigation. Front. Integr. Neurosci, **8**(32) (2014). https://doi.org/10.3389/fnint.2014.00032

Quasi-static Modeling of Feeding Behavior in *Aplysia Californica*

Bidisha Kundu$^{(\boxtimes)}$ (ID), Stephen M. Rogers (ID), and Gregory P. Sutton (ID)

School of Life Sciences, University of Lincoln, Lincoln LN6 7TS, UK
{bkundu,sterogers}@lincoln.ac.uk, RScealai@gmail.com

Abstract. Behaviors that are produced solely through geometrically complex three-dimensional interactions of soft-tissue muscular elements, and which do not move rigid articulated skeletal elements, are a challenge to mechanically model. This complexity often leads to simulations requiring substantial computational time. We discuss how using a quasi-static approach can greatly reduce the computational time required to model slow-moving soft-tissue structures, and then demonstrate our technique using the biomechanics of feeding behavior by the marine mollusc, *Aplysia californica*. We used a conventional 2nd order (from Newton's equations), forward dynamic model, which required 14 s to simulate 1 s of feeding behavior. We then used a quasi-static reformulation of the same model, which only required 0.35 s to perform the same task (a 40-fold improvement in computation speed). Lastly, we re-coded the quasi-static model in Python to further increase computation speed another 3-fold, creating a model that required just 0.12 s to model 1 s of feeding behavior. Both quasi-static models produce results that are nearly indistinguishable from the original 2nd order model, showing that quasi-static formulations can greatly increase the computation speed without sacrificing model accuracy.

Keywords: *Aplysia Californica* · Biomechanics · Equilibrium point

1 Introduction

Understanding the neural control of behavior requires understanding both the nervous system and the muscles that it controls [1]. This often is facilitated by combining models of the nervous system [5] with forward kinetic models of the body [16]. A widely used model for such research has been the feeding apparatus of the marine mollusc, *Aplysia californica*, which has an experimentally tractable nervous system, composed of relatively few, large neurons, combined with a musculature that is easily experimented upon. These features have made

This work was funded by UKRI Grant Number (MR/T046619/1), part of the NSF/CIHR/DFG/FRQ/UKRI-MRC Next Generation Networks for Neuroscience Program. Also, there was additional supports to G.P.S. provided by the Royal Society (UF130507) and US Army Research Office (W911NF-15-038).

© The Author(s), under exclusive license to Springer Nature Switzerland AG 2022
A. Hunt et al. (Eds.): Living Machines 2022, LNAI 13548, pp. 80–90, 2022.
https://doi.org/10.1007/978-3-031-20470-8_8

it a frequently used model system for the study of neural control [4]. Computer models of complex systems can greatly assist in understanding their fundamental properties, but a problem has arisen because of a major difference in the simulation times required to run models of neuronal function compared to those simulating the musculature: for example, the neuronal models of Li et al. [6] and Webster-Wood et al. [14] require 0.1 s of computation time to simulate 1 s of activity. In contrast, a commensurate model of the biomechanics of the buccal mass [12] requires 14 s of computation time to simulate the mechanics of that 1 s of behavior. These large computational requirements of the mechanical models have provided a substantial impediment to any research that involves evolutionary algorithms, machine learning, or any iterative technique that require running models large numbers of times. We have refined the 2nd order kinetic biomechanical model of [12] into a 0th order quasi-static form by using an algebraic reformulation, which reduces the computational time of the model by over 40 fold, thus making the entire model more compatible for research techniques that require large numbers of iterations. This algebraic refomulation technique is applicable for any slow-moving system.

Our biomechanical model system is the feeding apparatus of the marine mollusc, *Aplysia californica* [2,12]. This feeding apparatus is called 'the buccal mass', and has four key anatomical components. First, there is a spherical grasping structure, the "radula odontophore", which is moved toward the mouth (protraction), grasps food, and then moves back toward the esophagus (retraction) to deposit food (hereafter referred to as the 'odontophore'). Second, there is a sheet of muscle, the "I2", posterior to the odontophore, which, when activated, moves the odontophore forward. Third, there is a large circular muscle anterior to the odontophore, the "I3", which squeezes around the circumference of the odontophore. And fourth, there is a muscular structure called "the hinge" which anchors the ventral-most part of the odontophore to the surrounding tissue of the head. This acts to pull the odontophore back toward the esophagus. These four parts of the buccal mass were modeled using a 2nd order Newtonian formulation in [12].

2   Model

We have re-formulated the kinetic model of [12]. In this model [12], the four components of the *Aplysia* buccal mass are modeled as follows (Fig. 1): (1) odontophore is a sphere, (2) the I2 muscle is a sheet posterior to the odontophore, (3) the I3 muscle is a torus through which the odontophore passes and which can deliver either a forward or backwards force depending on the odontophore's position, and (4) the hinge is an elastic attachment connecting the odontophore to an external anchor. These three forcing agents generate the main forces in translation on the odontophore for grasping food and passing it back to the esophagus. The tensions in the I2 and I3 muscles are modeled as Hill type muscles with non-linear activation [10,12,15] with identical parameters as [12]. The hinge is modeled using both Maxwell and Kelvin visco-elastic elements in parallel, following the method of [11,12]. The complete mechanical system is shown schematically in Fig.1.

2.1   Odontophore and I2, I3 Muscles

The odontophore is represented by a sphere of radius R, with mass M. The I2 muscle lies posterior to the odontophore and is modeled as hemispherical object with sheet-like extensions Fig. 1(b). In the 2D cross-sectional view Fig.(1a), the I2 muscle is the combination of AH (sheet like structure), HH' (hemispherical part), and $H'A'$ (sheet like structure). I3 muscle is modeled as a torus anterior to I2 with mass m and cross-sectional radius r (see Fig. 1).

2.2   Assumptions

The center of the toroidal muscle I3 is the origin O of our coordinate system. The horizontal (anterior-posterior) direction is the X axis, and the Y axis is orthogonal to this passing through O. The location center of the odontophore, E, is constrained to move only along the X axis Fig. 1. The mechanics of the rest of the system are subsequently derived from the following assumptions.

– The I3 torus volume is constant, i.e., $V = 2\pi^2 y(t) r^2(t) = Constant$
– All the muscles and the odontophore remain in contact throughout. Contact condition: $x^2(t) + y^2(t) = (R + r(t))^2$
– The line AG connecting the center G of the minor radius of the torus and the contact point A of the I2 muscle to the I3 muscle is always parallel to X axis.

The force from I2 and the hinge both act directly on the odontophore, moving it horizontally, and thus these two forces can be summed (the sum of these forces will be referred to as 'F_1' in the subsequent equation of motion). The constraint on I3's position causes force from the I3 to act vertically, with the angle of contact (θ) between the I3 and the odontophore acting to mediate the resultant force. Consequently, the I3 force on the odontophore is calculated independently and called 'F_2'.

2.3   Governing Equations

This geometry leads to the fundamental equation of motion for the entire system (Eq. 1), from [12], Eq. 3 we have

$$(m\ddot{y} + F_2)cos(\theta) = (M\ddot{x} - F_1)sin(\theta) \tag{1}$$

where F_1 is the force on the odontophore caused by I2 and the hinge, while F_2 is the force on the odontophore caused by I3. $F_1(x,t)$ and $F_2(x,t)$ can be solved in terms of the muscle geometry: θ, y, x, and r are then calculated for the each timestep, which then yields the linear acceleration of the odontophore, $\ddot{x}$. The acceleration is then integrated twice to calculate the position of the odontophore, $x(t)$. Details and full model can be found in [12].

2.4   Reformulation

In simulations of buccal mass feeding behavior [12], the majority of the mechanical energy generated by the muscles is stored by elastic and visco-elastic elements of the hinge.

The kinetic energy ($\frac{1}{2}$ mass × velocity^2) due to the motion of the system is very low, with a maximum value of 2.66703×10^{-8} J. The dissipation of energy due to viscous fluid drag surrounding the odontophore ($\frac{1}{2}$ Coefficient of drag×density of water ×(velocity)^2× area × displacement) is, at most, 4.13178×10^{-9} J. In contrast, the elastic energy of the system ($\frac{1}{2}$ elastic constant × displacement^2) has a maximum of 5.50×10^{-4} J, over 4 orders of magnitude higher than the kinetic energy or viscous damping(parameters taken from [12]). Less than 0.1% of the energy in the system is kinetic or dissipated by damping (damping coefficient × velocity × displacement). We thus propose the following reformulation of (Eq. 1), where we approximate $\ddot{x}$ and $\ddot{y}$ with 0. This is an example of a 'quasi-static' approximation [7–9] - and reduces the 2nd order differential equation to a much simpler equation of static equilibrium (Eq. 2):

$$0 = F_2 \, Cot(\theta) + F_1 \tag{2}$$

Within the expressions of F_1 and F_2, however, there are velocity dependent terms for the Force-Velocity properties of the I2 and the I3 muscles [12, 16], which do affect the elastic energy in the system and thus cannot be removed. To show where these velocity terms occur, we expand Eq. (2) as follows

$$2\pi T_{I2}(x, y, \dot{x}, r, activation)Cos(\phi) + 2\pi T_{I3}(x, y, \dot{x}, r, activation)Cot(\theta) - Hinge force = 0 \tag{3}$$

where T_{I2} and T_{I3} are the muscle tensions for the I2 and I3 muscles, respectively and $\angle AHQ = \phi$ (Fig. 1).

We make one final substitution to bring these equations down to a zeroth order formulation. To produce a purely position-dependent equation (i.e., x, y, and r dependent only), the velocity terms ($\dot{x}$) are approximated at each timestep as $\dot{x} = \frac{x - x_{previous}}{\Delta t}$. Then Eq. (3) can be expressed as

$$2\pi T_{I2}(x, y, \frac{x - x_{previous}}{\Delta t}, r, activation)Cos(\phi) + 2\pi T_{I3}(x, y, \frac{x - x_{previous}}{\Delta t}, r, activation)Cot(\theta) - Hinge force = 0. \quad (4)$$

The equation of motion of the odontophore is Equation (4) with the added constraints that I3 is iso-volumetric ($V = 2\pi^2 y(t)r^2(t)$ =Constant) and that I3 must be in contact with the odontophore ($x^2 + y^2 = (R + r)^2$)). This produces a system where one variable (x) can be solved for its static equilibrium position.

At each time step we summed all of the forces that protracted the odontophore (positive), and all the forces that retracted the odontophore (negative), to find the equilibrium point where these forces are equal; i.e. the position where the sum of the forces on the odontophore is zero Fig. 2. The position of these equilibrium points varied as a function of muscle activation, and tracking the movement of these equilibrium points over time resulted in an approximation for odontophore position x. These equilibrium points were found numerically using Newton's method. In the Python formulation, these equations were solved using a Gauss-Newton algorithm with gradient descent (fsolve command) [13].

3 Results and Discussion

We simulated the complete 2nd order model [12] in Mathematica (Wolfram) [3] using the semi-implicit Euler method [14] for 60 s of odontophore motion. We set the initial position at $t = 0$ as $x = -5$mm. At the beginning of the simulation the odontophore moves from its initial position to its resting equilibrium state. We activated I2 to protract the odontophore, and then let I2 relax, which resulted in a retraction of the odontophore Fig. 3. It required 14s of computer processing time to simulate 1 s of behavior Fig. 3. Next, we simulated the same equations using our quasi-static formulation, which required only 0.13 s of computer processing time to simulate 1 s of behavior; a 107 times increase in computational speed Fig. 5. The results closely resemble results obtained from the original 2nd order formulation Fig. 3 with the maximum difference in position observed at the end of retraction Fig. 3c. This was the result of the rapid loss of muscle tension causing the odontophore to move at a relatively high velocity. There was a small temporal disparity between models, which translated into a brief spike of increased positional difference. The system time constant is 2.45 s [12] and this spike of discrepancy lasts for less than 0.01 s, which is too short a period for the muscles to react or change behavior.

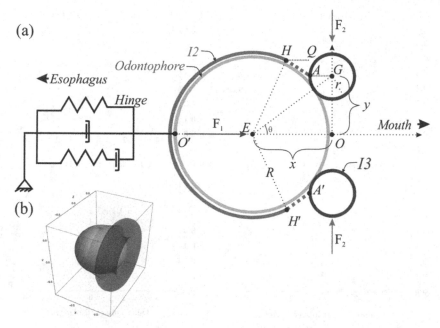

Fig. 1. a) Schematic figure of a 2D mid-sagittal view of the buccal mass system. Grey sphere, the odontophore; cyan, the I2 muscle comprised of hemispherical (solid line) and sheet-like (dotted line) elements; blue, section through the toroidal I3 muscle. The hinge is a passive elastic element anchoring the odontophore to the back of the head. See text for full details. b) Schematic 3D construction of the buccal mass: the odontophore (grey sphere) is surrounded by the hemispherical I2 muscle (cyan) which attaches anteriorly to the I3 ring muscle (blue). (Color figure online)

The majority of this computational speed increase (Fig. 5) was because the quasi-static formulation was numerically stable for step sizes of 0.01 s, while the 2nd order model required a step size of 0.0008 s. As the inertia term is present in the 2nd order model, it takes step size of 0.0008 s to accurately follow acceleration in the system. This step size is required because the mechanical resonant-frequency of the odontophore-hinge system is of the order 1000 Hz, requiring a very small step size to stably model it using the 2nd order system. This vibration is not biologically relevant to the system which is why the quasi-static model (which disregards this vibration) accurately reflects movements despite a much larger step size.

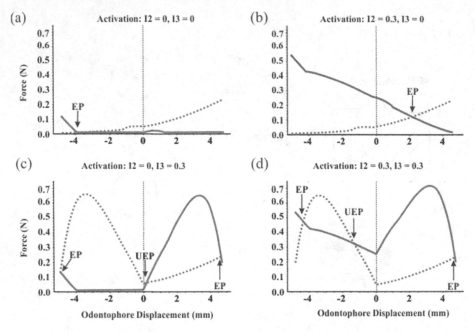

Fig. 2. The locations of equilibrium points, where the resultants of all the forces are zero. The red lines represent the positive and magenta dotted lines represent the negative parts of the resultant force. a) the profile of the forces when no muscles are active; passive forces within I2 and the hinge create a stable equilibrium point (EP) at an odontophore displacement of −4 mm. b) Profile of the forces when I2 is 30% activated. This results in a stable equilibrium point occurring at +2 mm. c) Profile of the forces when I3 is 30% activated. This results in an unstable equilibrium point (UEP) at a displacement of 0 mm (the location at which the I3 is squeezing directly on the central axis of the odontophore). There is a stable equilibrium point at a displacement of +5 mm where I3 force is equal and opposite to the force of the hinge. There is a second a stable equilibrium point at −5 mm, where the I3 force is equal and opposite to the passive forces of I2. d) Profile of the forces when both I2 and I3 are 30% activated. There is an unstable equilibrium at a displacement of −1.5 mm, which occurs when the hinge and I3 forces are equal to the force of the active I2. There are two stable equilibrium points, one at +5.5 mm where I3 and I2 forces are equal and opposite to the hinge, and at −4.5 mm where I3 force is equal and opposite to I2 force.

We simulated a second behavior where both I2 and I3 muscles were activated Fig. 4. The computation time for this simulation was the same as the simulation where only the I2 muscle was activated. As with the previous simulation, the quasi-static model and 2nd order model generated very similar output for odontophore position Fig. 4 with the quasi-static model requiring less than 5% of the computer processing time than the 2nd order model. This demonstrates that our quasi-static reformulation holds for more complex simulations of *Aplysia* feeding behavior.

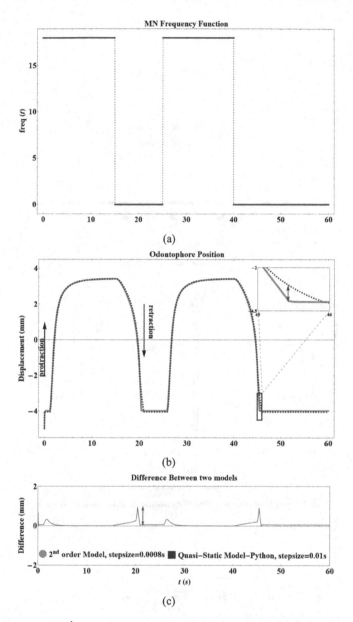

Fig. 3. Examples of 2nd order and quasi-static simulations of activating I2 within the buccal mass. a) Firing frequency function of motor neurons (MN) driving I2 where $freq(t) = 18$ Hz for $0\,s \le t \le 15\,s$, $25\,s \le t \le 40\,s$ or otherwise 0. b) The resulting displacement of the odontophore (x) as simulated by the 2nd order (teal, solid line) and quasi-static (green, dotted line) models. The initial rapid displacement to -4 mm at the beginning of the simulation corresponds to the stable equilibrium that arises from purely passive forces in the buccal mass as shown in Fig. 2a. (c) The difference between the numerical values of solution x using the two models. The inset in (b) shows a magnified-version of the difference in the time interval $[45\,s, 46\,s]$. (Color figure online)

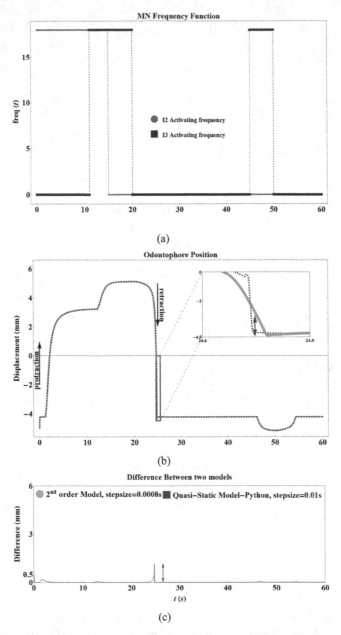

Fig. 4. Examples of 2nd order and quasi-static simulations of activating both I2 and I3 within the buccal mass. a) Firing frequency function of motor neurons (MN) driving I2 (orange) where $freq(t) = 18$ Hz for $0\,s \le t \le 15\,s$, $25\,s \le t \le 40\,s$ or otherwise 0 and driving I3 (red) where $freq(t) = 18$ Hz for $11\,s \le t \le 20\,s$, $45\,s \le t \le 50\,s$ or otherwise 0. b) The resulting displacement of the odontophore (x) as simulated by the 2nd order (teal, solid line) and quasi-static (green, dotted line) models. (c) The difference between the numerical values of solution x using the two models. The inset in (b) shows a magnified-version of the difference in the time interval [24.6 s, 24.9 s]. (Color figure online)

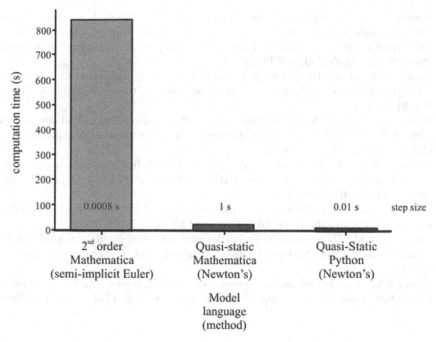

Fig. 5. Bar chart comparison of computation time of different models calculated using Mathematica and Python languages.

References

1. Chiel, H.J., Beer, R.D.: The brain has a body: adaptive behavior emerges from interactions of nervous system, body and environment. Trends Neurosci. **20**(12), 553–557 (1997)
2. Howells, H.: The structure and function of the alimentary canal of Aplysia punctata. J. Cell Sci. **2**(331), 357–397 (1942)
3. Inc., W.R.: Mathematica, Version 13.1. Champaign (2022). https://www.wolfram.com/mathematica
4. Kandel, E.R.: Behavioral Biology of Aplysia. A Contribution to the Comparative Study of opisthobranch molluscs 463 (1979)
5. Kandel, E.R., et al.: Principles of Neural Science, vol. 4. McGraw-hill, New York (2000)
6. Li, Y., et al.: Using Synthetic Nervous Systems to Model the Multifunctional and Adaptive Feeding Behavior of Aplysia californica, vol. P962.02. Society for Neuroscience (2021)
7. Peshkin, M.A., Sanderson, A.C.: A variational Principle for Quasistatic Mechanics. Carnegie-Mellon University, Robotics Institute (1986)
8. Peshkin, M.A., Sanderson, A.C.: Minimization of energy in quasistatic manipulation. In: Proceedings. 1988 IEEE International Conference on Robotics and Automation, pp. 421–426. IEEE (1988)
9. Ruina, A.L.: Friction laws and instabilities: a quasistatic analysis of some dry frictional behavior. Ph.D. thesis, Brown University (1981)

10. Snyder, V.A.: Analysis of the biomechanics and neural control of two kinetic models of the buccal mass of Aplysia. Case Western Reserve University (Health Sciences) (2005), https://www.proquest.com/docview/305390183/abstract/B303E6FBC4924763PQ/1
11. Sutton, G.P., et al.: Passive hinge forces in the feeding apparatus of Aplysia aid retraction during biting but not during swallowing. J. Comp. Physiol. A **190**(6), 501–514 (2004)
12. Sutton, G.P., et al.: Neural control exploits changing mechanical advantage and context dependence to generate different feeding responses in Aplysia. Biol. Cybern. **91**(5), 333–345 (2004)
13. Virtanen, P., et al.: SciPy 1.0 Contributors: SciPy 1.0: fundamental algorithms for scientific computing in python. Nat. Methods **17**, 261–272 (2020). https://doi.org/10.1038/s41592-019-0686-2
14. Webster-Wood, et al.: Control for multifunctionality: bioinspired control based on feeding in Aplysia californica. Biol. Cybern. **114**(6), 557–588 (2020)
15. Yu, S.N., et al.: Biomechanical properties and a kinetic simulation model of the smooth muscle I2 in the buccal mass of Aplysia. Biol. Cybern. **81**(5), 505–513 (1999)
16. Zajac, F.E.: Muscle and tendon: properties, models, scaling, and application to biomechanics and motor control. Crit. Rev. Biomed. Eng. **17**(4), 359–411 (1989)

Conversion of Elastic Energy Stored in the Legs of a Hexapod Robot into Propulsive Force

Atsushi Kaneko[1(✉)] , Masahiro Shimizu[2] , and Takuya Umedachi[1]

[1] Faculty of Textile Science and Technology, Shinshu University,
3-15-1 Tokida, Ueda City, Nagano 386-8567, Japan
{21fs309a,umedachi}@shinshu-u.ac.jp
[2] Department of Systems Innovation, Graduate School of Engineering Science,
Osaka University, 1-2 Machikaneyama-machi, Toyonaka, Osaka 560-0043, Japan
shimizu@sys.es.osaka-u.ac.jp
http://umedachi-lab.com/

Abstract. The conversion of elastic energy due to ground reaction force into propulsive force can help increase the locomotion speed of a legged robot. Many legged robots inspired by animals have been developed, which utilize the elasticity of their legs to increase the efficiency of locomotion. An example is RHex, a hexapod robot that has C-shaped legs. These robots are designed using the spring loaded inverted pendulum (SLIP) model. In contrast, we proposed a new leg design (i.e., D-shaped leg) and an optimization method in which the speed can be increased by kicking the ground strongly in the opposite direction of locomotion due to the elastic force accumulated in the legs. An experiment with a hexapod robot demonstrated that the walking speed could be increased by up to 89% compared to the speed obtained by C-shaped legs. This result can be applied to the design of hands, grippers, and robot bodies to store external force in the flexible body, introduce new functions, and improve performance.

Keywords: Soft robotics · Flexible material · Elastic energy · Legged robot · Optimization

1 Introduction

Many legged robots with flexible and elastic legs, which have been inspired by animals, have been designed to achieve efficient locomotion [1,2]. During the first half of the stance phase of the locomotion of animals, the kinetic and gravitational potential energy are transformed into elastic energy and stored in the legs (especially in their muscles and tendons). In the latter half of the stance phase, this energy is reconverted to the kinetic and gravitational potential energy to accelerate their bodies and generate locomotion efficiently [3]. Many design methods have

---

Supplementary Information The online version contains supplementary material available at https://doi.org/10.1007/978-3-031-20470-8_9.

© The Author(s), under exclusive license to Springer Nature Switzerland AG 2022
A. Hunt et al. (Eds.): Living Machines 2022, LNAI 13548, pp. 91–102, 2022.
https://doi.org/10.1007/978-3-031-20470-8_9

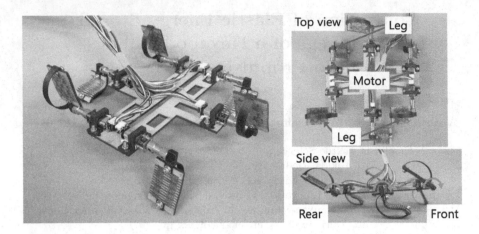

Fig. 1. Prototype (hexapod robot) with the proposed D-shaped legs. The green arrows indicate the direction of the leg rotation when the prototype moves forward. (Color figure online)

been developed and investigated to mimic this efficient mechanism (Sect. 2.1 in [1] and [2]). In these methods, the robot's body is simplified as a mass point and the whole leg as a spring. This simplified model is called the spring loaded inverted pendulum (SLIP) model [4–6] (Fig. 2(d–f)). Here, the spring constant is as stiff as that of an animal's leg of the same mass. RHex [1] and DASH [2] are pioneering examples of the robots designed using the method. It is suggested that these robots can move efficiently by exploiting elastic energy in the legs.

Expeditious advances in rapid prototyping, including 3D printers, have reduced the cost and technical barriers to design and fabricate flexible and complex robotic systems (e.g., robot legs) [7]. Major traditional robotic systems have been composed of rigid mechanical elements. As a result, deformation of the mechanical systems is limited to a few degrees of freedom, such as joints. In contrast, the body parts of living creatures, such as elephant trunks and octopus arms, are composed of flexible materials with complex shapes that deform continuously [8]. By taking advantage of their soft bodies and shapes, living creatures can produce a variety of adaptive behaviors that are difficult for rigid-bodied robotic systems [9]. For example, animals can move over uneven terrain or confined spaces by bending, stretching, or twisting their bodies significantly. It can also grasp objects and the environment with a surface instead of a few contact points. As a result, attempts to employ such flexible and complex mechanical elements in robots have been prevalent in soft robotics [10,11].

This study proposes a novel leg design method to increase the speed of legged robots further using flexible materials. The leg designed by the proposed method is unique because it can convert the elastic energy stored in the leg under normal force into propulsive force. The pioneering SLIP model and the hexapod robot RHex [1] were used as references. However, our proposed method differs from the previous methods because our proposed leg *deforms to produce a greater propulsive force*. We compare the walking performance of the proposed method with the existing method with a prototype. The experimental results show that the proposed method can accelerate locomotion by up to 89%. Furthermore, it is considered to have the potential to be applied to various soft robot parts such as hand, gripper, and body design and is not limited to only legs. The proposed method converts the externally obtained force once into an elastic force and uses it for the desired function.

2 Related Works

A typical model of locomotion in animals is the SLIP model [4–6] (see Fig. 2(d–f)). Studies on various animals [6] have shown that the stiffness of the leg spring tends to be proportional to the 0.67 power of the body mass. Animals can use the elasticity of the leg for efficient locomotion.

Inspired by this biological finding, some studies have suggested that appropriately designing a robot's leg spring stiffness can help improve its performance in terms of locomotion efficiency and suppression of disturbances from the ground during locomotion [12,13]. The robots in [1,2,14] are excellent examples of adjusting the stiffness of the leg spring to improve locomotion performance.

Existing pioneering research that attempts to improve mobility performance by utilizing soft parts in robots and excellent jumping robots that use elastic energy are described. Mahkam et al. [15] showed that when the robot uses compliant backbones and legs, the locomotion speed is improved compared to that when rigid ones are used. Spröwitz et al. [16] reported that attaching compliant elements to the robot's toes increased its maximum speed. Brown et al. [17] developed the Bow Leg that can move with low power consumption. The behavior during locomotion is different from our robot because this leg is used for hopping, and the driving mechanism is different; however, the shape of the Bow Leg is similar to that of our leg proposed in this study. In [18], Mochiyama et al. described the mechanism of generating instantaneous force by buckling for jumping. In contrast, in this study, the propulsive force is increased by utilizing the energy stored in the legs and simply releasing it.

3 Proposed Method

The concept of our proposed model is shown in Fig. 2(a–c). This study proposes to add a torsion spring in the leg model (SLIP model in Fig. 2(d–f)) to increase the propulsive force by designing these stiffnesses appropriately. In this paper, the newly-added torsion spring is called "leg torsion spring", and the spring inherited from the SLIP model is called "leg linear spring".

3.1 D-Shaped Leg

We propose a D-shaped leg that converts elastic energy stored by the normal force from the ground into propulsive force. If a robot's legs can kick the ground

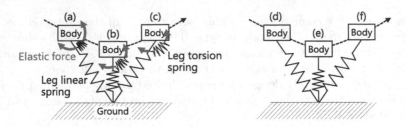

Fig. 2. Concept of the proposed model and the different interaction with the ground between the proposed and existing SLIP models during the locomotion. This figure shows the two models moving to the right. (a–c) show a new model with a torsion spring added to the SLIP model. In (a), the leg touches the ground, the torsion spring is compressed, and elastic energy is stored in the torsion spring. In (b, c), the elastic energy stored in the torsion spring is released, and the body is pushed forward. The linear spring is drawn assuming that it deforms similarly as in the SLIP model. (d–f) show the SLIP model [4–6].

strongly in the opposite direction of locomotion due to elastic force, it can achieve a large propulsive force that increases its speed. For this, the legs must store a large amount of elastic energy just before they kick the ground. The direction of the elastic force generated by the legs is also essential. If the legs are deformed in such a way that the toes project forward (as in Fig. 3(a–c)) just before the legs kick the ground, the elastic force acts to push the body forward. The greater the protrusion, the more effectively the legs push the body forward. The D-shaped leg is based on the C-shaped leg in the previous study (Sect. 3.4 of [1]) and combines a C-shaped component with an I-shape beam (see Fig. 3(d, e)). Each D-shaped leg has a rubber pad on the toe to increase friction with the ground.

The D-shaped leg is designed by a combination of physical simulation and optimization with the following two policies:

i) To maximize the elastic energy stored in the leg just before kicking the ground
ii) To adjust the stiffness of the leg linear spring based on the mass of the robot as in the previous study (Sect. 2.1 of [1])

Like the C-shaped leg, the D-shaped leg rolls as the robot locomotes, so the point of contact with the ground changes from the hip side to the toe (see Fig. 3(a–c)). In this study, a static simulation is performed for the state just before the leg kicks the ground. As described below (see Sect. 3.3), each D-shaped leg is composed largely of a material with a relatively low damping coefficient; therefore, static simulation could be used. Then, in Sect. 4, the performances of the D-shaped legs and the C-shaped legs fabricated based on the design method of the previous study (Sect. 2.1 of [1]) were compared. For a fair comparison, the stiffnesses of the leg linear spring of the two legs should be the same; therefore, ii) was included in the design policies.

For physical simulation, entire D-shaped leg is modeled as springs and torsion springs (see Fig. 3(f)). This is a two-dimensional simplified version of a D-shaped leg, focusing on the deformation in the case viewed from the side. As shown in Fig. 3(f), the D-shaped leg is divided into a C-shaped and an I-shaped part. The stiffnesses of the torsion springs in each C-shaped and I-shaped section are used as variables in the optimization. The torsion springs were varied uniformly in each of the two parts. The range of possible values for the torsion spring's stiffness variables and the adopted linear spring's stiffness are shown in Table 1. After making samples of each part and ascertaining the range of stiffnesses that could be fabricated, the range of variables was determined. The stiffnesses of the linear springs are set to the values obtained when the legs are fabricated by the manufacturing method described below.

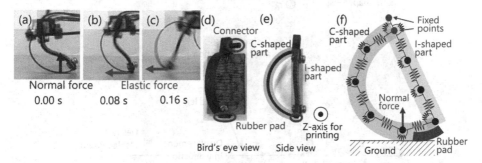

Fig. 3. (a–c) show the deformation of the D-shaped leg during locomotion. At (a), the D-shaped leg touches the ground, and the normal force from the ground deforms the leg forward. In (b, c), the elastic force of the leg acts as a propulsive force. (d, e) show the fabricated D-shaped leg. We attached a 2 mm long rubber pad to toe of the D-shaped leg. We connect the leg to the motor with the connector part on the top. (f) shows the simulation model of the D-shaped leg. The leg is fixed at the orange point at the top, and 0.7 N (i.e., the weight of the robot divided by the number of supporting legs (3)) is applied to the edge of the C-shaped part of the rubber pad as the normal force.

We used the above simulation model to perform a static simulation that reproduces the state just before the leg kicks the ground. In the prototype, the leg is connected to the body at the upper part (i.e., connector in Fig. 3(d)). Thus, in the simulation, the leg is fixed at the same point as shown in Fig. 3(f). The forces actually applied to the leg are the normal force from the ground, the friction force, and the force from the connection with the body. The normal force is applied in the direction and at the force point as shown in Fig. 3(f), taking into account the inclination of the leg at this moment. The magnitude of the force is the weight of the robot per leg (i.e., the weight of the robot divided by the number of supporting legs (3), 0.7 N). The friction force from the ground is not considered in this optimization design because the objective is to design the D-shaped leg so that the normal force generated by the robot's weight can be converted into a force to kick the ground.

3.2   Optimization of D-Shaped Leg

To perform the above simulation and optimization, we used Rhinoceros 6, a 3D CAD system, and its plug-in, Grasshopper, which includes a physical simulator.

Table 1. Simulation settings.

Parameter	Value
Range of torsion spring's stiffness in the C-shaped part	20–50000 N · mm/rad
Range of torsion spring's stiffness in the I-shaped part	5–50000 N · mm/rad
Stiffness of the C-shaped part's linear springs	530 N/mm
Stiffness of the I-shaped part's linear springs	66000 N/mm

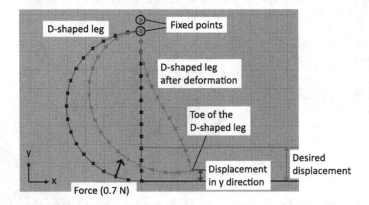

Fig. 4. Deformation of the D-shaped leg (simulated in Rhinoceros) and explanation of the optimization design. As shown in Fig. 3(f), a model of the D-shaped leg has been created, but no spring is shown in this figure. The leg was fixed at the top two points and the force of the thick black arrow was applied. The plots in red and green show the D-shaped leg before and after deformation, respectively. (Color figure online)

Figure 4 shows the deformation of the simulation model of the D-shaped leg in Rhinoceros during the static simulation as described above.

We set up two objective functions corresponding to the design policies i) and ii) and performed a multi-objective optimization. The objective function for i) was set to maximize the elastic energy stored in the leg after deformation, whereas the objective function for ii) was set to minimize the difference between the y-direction displacement of the toe of the D-shaped leg (see Fig. 4) and the desired displacement as described below. The elastic energy stored in the leg after deformation is obtained by the following equation.

$$E = \sum \frac{1}{2} k_\theta \Delta\theta^2 + \sum \frac{1}{2} k_l \Delta l^2 \qquad (1)$$

E is the sum of the elastic energy stored in the leg, k_θ is the stiffness of the torsion spring, $\Delta\theta$ is the angular displacement of each torsion spring, k_l is the stiffness of the linear spring, and Δl is the change in the length of each linear spring. The objective function of ii) is

$$f(y) = |y - y_{target}| \qquad (2)$$

Table 2. Optimization parameters.

Parameter	Value
Population size	100
Mutation rate	0.9
Mutation probability	0.2
Crossover rate	0.8
Max generation	25
Elitism	0.7

Table 3. Optimization results.

Parameter	Value
Stiffnesses of the C-shaped part's torsion springs	$476.50 \text{ N} \cdot \text{mm/rad}$
Flexural rigidity of the C-shaped part	$529 \text{ N} \cdot \text{mm}^2$
Stiffnesses of the I-shaped part's torsion springs	$49.81 \text{ N} \cdot \text{mm/rad}$
Flexural rigidity of the I-shaped part	$38 \text{ N} \cdot \text{mm}^2$

where y is the displacement of the toe in the y-direction after deformation, and y_{target} is the desired displacement required to achieve the appropriate stiffness of the leg linear spring (These can be displayed on the Rhinoceros screen as shown in Fig. 4). The appropriate stiffness of the leg linear spring is obtained from Fig. 3C of [6], and the mass of the prototype (0.21 kg). The appropriate stiffness of the leg linear spring for this mass is 230 N/m. From the number of supporting legs (3) and the normal force applied to the leg during locomotion (0.70 N), the required leg displacement y_{target} can be obtained by the following equation.

$$y_{target} = \frac{0.70}{\frac{230}{3}} = 0.0091 \tag{3}$$

From this equation, y_{target} is 9.1 mm. The optimization was performed using a genetic algorithm (named Octopus[1] as a Grasshopper plug-in). We chose genetic algorithms as they are versatile. Octopus performed a multiobjective evolutionary algorithm called HypE [19]. The parameters related to the optimization are shown in Table 2. From the optimization, the stiffnesses of the torsion springs of the C-shaped and I-shaped parts were obtained. The bending stiffness values of each part were obtained from these stiffnesses using the Rhinoceros simulation. The results are shown in Table 3.

3.3 Fabrication of the Leg

The C-shaped and I-shaped parts were fabricated to achieve the bending stiffness obtained from the simulation, respectively. The C-shaped part was fabricated by

---

[1] Octopus, a Grasshopper plug-in: https://www.food4rhino.com/en/app/octopus.

Table 4. Parameters of the prototype.

Body mass			210 g
Body		Length	165 mm
		Width	138 mm
Length of both the D-shaped leg and C-shaped leg			50 mm
D-shaped leg	I-shaped part (2D repetitive slit pattern)	Length	41 mm
		Width	28 mm
		Thickness	2.5 mm
	C-shaped part	Width	7 mm
		Thickness	0.7 mm
C-shaped leg		Width	15 mm
		Thickness	0.7 mm

a 3D printer (MarkTwo, Markforged) using a nylon-based filament (Onyx) at 100% fill rate. The z-axis for 3D printing of the C-shaped part is displayed in Fig. 3(e). The I-shaped part was comprised of a 2D repetitive slit pattern cut [20] from a 2.5 mm thick MDF (fiberboard made of wood) by a laser cutting machine (VLS6.60, Universal Laser Systems). We used this method because the slit can significantly reduce the bending stiffness, and the bending stiffness can be varied by changing the number of slits [20].

4   Experiment

4.1   Fabrication of the Prototype

We fabricated the prototype to compare the locomotion performances of the D-shaped legs proposed in this study and the C-shaped legs fabricated by the design method proposed in Sect. 2.1 of [1]. The comparison was made by changing the legs attached to the prototype. Six DC motors (model number 3043, gear ratio 210:1, Pololu) were fixed to the body as shown in Fig. 1. Each leg is rotated by one motor to realize locomotion with six legs, similar to RHex [1]. The rotation of each motor that drives the legs was sensed by rotary encoders (model number 4760, Pololu) and controlled by microcontrollers (LPC1768, NXP). Power was supplied to the motors via motor drivers (TB6612FNG, Toshiba) with a 12.0 V input. The body was composed of a 2.5 mm thick MDF, which is relatively light and rigid. The mass and dimensions of the prototype are specified in Table 4.

The C-shaped leg is designed similarly as in Sect. 2.1 of [1], i.e., the stiffness of the leg linear spring should be appropriate for the mass of the robot. The appropriate stiffness for the prototype is 230 N/m from Sect. 3.2. From Castigliano's theorem, the displacement of the tip of a curved bar when a force is applied to it can be determined (Sect. 80 of [21] provides more details). Therefore, when we consider the C-shaped leg as a curved bar, the stiffness of the leg linear spring

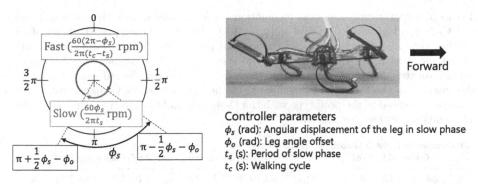

Fig. 5. Rotation of the right leg of the robot when the robot moves forward toward the right side. The angle of the transition from fast phase to slow phase, the angle of the transition from slow phase to fast phase, and the rotation speed of the motor in each phase are written. This control is based on [22,23].

can be obtained based on the relationship between the force applied to the toe and the displacement of the toe. In this way, we adjusted the dimensions of the C-shaped leg appropriately and fabricated the leg with Onyx using the above mentioned 3D printer. We attached a rubber pad to each toe.

4.2 Control of the Prototype

The controller parameters of previous studies [22,23] are used as a reference for control of the prototype (see Fig. 5). This is because the prototype, similar to RHex, moves by repeatedly rotating its legs. From the previous study [22], it can be determined that there are four essential controller parameters when using C-shaped legs and moving forward with a tripod gait, as shown in Fig. 5.

When starting locomotion, the desired angle of each leg is first calculated from the four parameters as shown in Fig. 5. Then, the PD control of the motor is performed so that the encoder value is close to the calculated value. The walking cycle is t_c [s]. As shown in Fig. 5, there are two phases in the cycle, the "fast phase" and "slow phase". In the fast phase, the motor rotates the leg by $2\pi - \phi_s$ [rad] during $t_c - t_s$ [s]. In the slow phase, the motor rotates the leg by ϕ_s [rad] during t_s [s]. When ϕ_o is 0, the range from $\pi - \frac{1}{2}\phi_s$ to $\pi + \frac{1}{2}\phi_s$ corresponds to the slow phase. Otherwise, the angle of the slow phase is shifted by ϕ_o as shown in Fig. 5. This process is repeated during the locomotion.

The six legs are divided into two sets, each synchronized separately. One set is right front, right rear, and left middle, and the other is left front, left rear, and right middle. The former three legs are 180° out of phase with the latter three legs. The details are described in previous studies [22,23].

4.3 Experimental Results

We measured and compared the locomotion speed of the robot with the D-shaped legs proposed in Sect. 3.1 and the C-shaped legs described in Sect. 4.1.

Table 5. Experimental results of locomotion speeds obtained with the D-shaped legs and C-shaped legs when $t_s = 0.38$ and $t_c = 0.76$. Crosses indicate that the body often touched the ground and the experiment was not performed. (a) The ratio (in percent) of the speed with the D-shaped leg to the speed with the C-shaped leg. A ratio of 100% indicates that the two speeds are the same. The deeper the red color, the faster the speed with the D-shaped leg compared to the speed with the C-shaped leg. (b, c) Locomotion speed of the prototype with the D-shaped and C-shaped legs, respectively. The units are meters per second.

(a) Comparison of the D-shaped legs and C-shaped legs [%]

$\phi_o \backslash \phi_s$	0.4	0.8	1.2	1.6	
0.8	×	×	×	×	200
0.4	189	163	132	×	150
0.0	120	148	144	122	100
-0.4	136	125	122	×	50
-0.8	×	×	×	×	0

(b) Locomotion speed with the D-shaped legs [m/s]

$\phi_o \backslash \phi_s$	0.4	0.8	1.2	1.6
0.8	×	×	×	×
0.4	0.18	0.19	0.20	×
0.0	0.073	0.14	0.21	0.25
-0.4	0.16	0.21	0.24	×
-0.8	×	×	×	×

(c) Locomotion speed with the C-shaped legs [m/s]

$\phi_o \backslash \phi_s$	0.4	0.8	1.2	1.6	
0.8	×	×	×	×	0.25
0.4	0.10	0.11	0.15	×	0.20
0.0	0.061	0.093	0.15	0.20	0.15
-0.4	0.12	0.17	0.20	×	0.10
-0.8	×	×	×	×	0.05
					0.00

The prototype moved for five periods, the distance traveled was measured, and the speed was calculated. Since the robot has a relatively small mass, the average speed was obtained by dividing the distance traveled by the elapsed time without considering the time for acceleration or deceleration. We experimented with different motor controller parameters ϕ_s and ϕ_o as described in Sect. 4.1. We varied these parameters to the extent that the body did not touch the ground and the body was not dragged. The remaining parameters, t_s and t_c, were set as 0.38 s and 0.76 s, respectively. First, we repeated the locomotion three times with each parameter setting and obtained the average value. The velocities of the prototypes with the D-shaped legs and C-shaped legs are shown in Table 5.

The results (Table 5) show that the locomotion speed is up to 1.89 times greater when using the D-shaped legs than when using the C-shaped legs. The

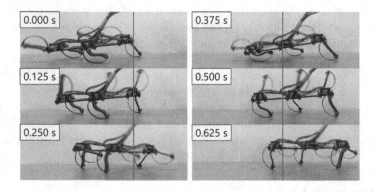

Fig. 6. Snapshots of the prototype with D-shaped legs during locomotion ($\phi_s = 1.6$, $\phi_o = 0.0$). The snapshots show that the legs are deformed as in the simulation, and the legs kick the ground. The red line denotes the position of the head of the prototype at 0.000 s (Color figure online).

difference depends on the controller parameters ϕ_s and ϕ_o. As shown in Fig. 6, the D-shaped legs are deformed in such a way that the toes project forward during the stance phase. The increase in speed is thought to be due to the utilization of the elastic force generated by the deformation to kick the ground.

5 Conclusion

We demonstrated a method of designing legs that can increase locomotion speed by utilizing the elastic force of the legs to produce a propulsive force. In this design method, a new leg model with a "leg torsion spring" added to the SLIP model is considered, and the propulsive force is increased according to the design of an appropriate stiffness of the entire leg. In this study, a D-shaped leg is proposed to effectively convert elastic force into propulsive force when it is subjected to normal force. Physical simulations and optimization of the D-shaped leg were carried out to obtain a strong propulsive force. C-shaped and I-shaped parts were fabricated to match the bending stiffness obtained from the simulation. D-shaped legs were fabricated by combining these two parts. We compared the locomotion speed of the prototype with the D-shaped legs and that with the C-shaped legs fabricated by a design method of a previous study [1]. The experimental results show that the locomotion speed of the D-shaped legs is faster than that of the C-shaped legs, and the locomotion speed increases up to 1.89 times. In the case of the D-shaped leg, it was confirmed that the toe projected forward in the stance phase, as intended in the design phase (as in Fig. 3(a–c)).

In a further study, we will perform simulations and optimizations of the D-shaped leg, including the stiffnesses of the linear springs, as variables. In this study, we added a restriction so that the stiffnesses of the torsion springs could be uniform. We believe that by removing this restriction, we can further increase the elastic energy stored in the leg. We will also conduct an experiment to investigate the locomotion speed by rotating the legs at a higher speed, and we will compare the moving speed when t_s and t_c are changed.

Acknowledgement. Supported by KAKENHI Grant-in-Aid for Scientific Research on Innovative Areas "Science of Soft Robot" project funded by JSPS under Grant Number 18H05467, and Grant-in-Aid for Scientific Research (B) under Grant Number 21H01289.

References

1. Moore, E.Z.: Leg design and stair climbing control for the RHex robotic hexapod. Masters thesis (2002)
2. Birkmeyer, P., Peterson, K., Fearing, R.S.: DASH: a dynamic 16g hexapedal robot. In: 2009 IEEE/RSJ International Conference on Intelligent Robots and Systems, pp. 2683–2689 (2009)
3. Dickinson, M.H., Farley, C.T., Full, R.J., Koehl, M.A.R., Kram, R., Lehman, S.: How animals move: an integrative view. Science **288**, 100–106 (2000)

4. Blickhan, R.: The spring-mass model for running and hopping. J. Biomech. **22**, 1217–1227 (1989)
5. Hubicki, C., et al.: ATRIAS: design and validation of a tether-free 3D-capable spring-mass bipedal robot. Int. J. Robot. Res. **35**, 1497–1521 (2016)
6. Farley, C.T., Glasheen, J., McMahon, T.A.: Running springs: speed and animal size. J. Exp. Biol. **185**, 71–86 (1993)
7. Rus, D., Tolley, M.T.: Design, fabrication and control of soft robots. Nature **521**, 467–475 (2015)
8. Trivedi, D., Rahn, C.D., Kier, W.M., Walker, I.D.: Soft robotics: biological inspiration, state of the art, and future research. Appl. Bionics Biomech. **5**, 99–117 (2008)
9. Kim, S., Laschi, C., Trimmer, B.: Soft robotics: a bioinspired evolution in robotics. Trends Biotechnol. **31**, 287–294 (2013)
10. Pfeifer, R., Lungarella, M., Iida, F.: The challenges ahead for bio-inspired "soft" robotics. Commun. ACM **55**, 76–87 (2012)
11. Laschi, C., Cianchetti, M., Mazzolai, B., Margheri, L., Follador, M., Dario, P.: Soft robot arm inspired by the octopus. Adv. Robot. **26**, 709–727 (2012)
12. Calisti, M., Picardi, G., Laschi, C.: Fundamentals of soft robot locomotion. J. Roy. Soc. Interface **14**, 1–2 (2017)
13. Galloway, K.C., Clark, J.E., Koditschek, D.E.: Variable stiffness legs for robust, efficient, and stable dynamic running. J. Mech. Robot. **5**, 011009 (2013)
14. Galloway, K.C., Clark, J.E., Yim, M., Koditschek, D.E.: Experimental investigations into the role of passive variable compliant legs for dynamic robotic locomotion. In: 2011 IEEE International Conference on Robotics and Automation, pp. 1243–1249 (2011)
15. Mahkam, N., Yilmaz, T.B., Ozcan, O.: Smooth and inclined surface locomotion and obstacle scaling of a C-legged miniature modular robot. In: 2021 IEEE 4th International Conference on Soft Robotics (RoboSoft), pp. 9–14 (2021)
16. Spröwitz, A., Tuleu, A., Vespignani, M., Ajallooeian, M., Badri, E., Ijspeert, A.J.: Towards dynamic trot gait locomotion: design, control, and experiments with Cheetah-cub, a compliant quadruped robot. Int. J. Robot. Res. **32**, 932–950 (2013)
17. Brown, B., Zeglin, G.: The bow leg hopping robot. In: Proceedings of the 1998 IEEE International Conference on Robotics and Automation, pp. 781–786 (1998)
18. Tsuda, T., Mochiyama, H., Fujimoto, H.: Quick stair-climbing using snap-through buckling of closed elastica. In: 2012 International Symposium on Micro-NanoMechatronics and Human Science (MHS), pp. 368–373 (2012)
19. Bader, J., Zitzler, E.: HypE: an algorithm for fast hypervolume-based many-objective optimization. Evol. Comput. **19**, 45–76 (2011)
20. Ohshima, T., Tachi, T., Yamaguchi, Y.: Analysis and design of elastic materials formed using 2D repetitive slit pattern. In: Proceedings of the International Association for Shell and Spatial Structures Symposium, IASS 2015, pp. 526418:1–526418:12 (2015)
21. Timoshenko, S.: Strength of Materials, Vol. I : Elementary Theory and Problems (English Edition). CBS Publishers & Distributors Pvt Ltd. (2004)
22. Saranli, U., Buehler, M., Koditschek, D.E.: RHex: a simple and highly mobile hexapod robot. Int. J. Robot. Res. **20**, 616–631 (2001)
23. Weingarten, J.D., Lopes, G.A.D., Buehler, M., Groff, R.E., Koditschek, D.E.: Automated gait adaptation for legged robots. In: Proceedings - IEEE International Conference on Robotics and Automation, pp. 2153–2158 (2004)

The Shaker: A Platform for Active Perturbations in Neuromechanical Studies of Small Animals

Emanuel Andrada[1]([✉]) [iD], Andreas Karguth[2], and Martin S. Fischer[1]

[1] Institute of Zoology and Evolutionary Research, Friedrich-Schiller University, Jena, Germany
emanuel.andrada@uni-jena.de
[2] GentleRobotics, Tüttleben, Germany

Abstract. In this paper, we inform about the development of a three degrees of freedom active platform for neuromechanical experiments. This platform, termed 'the shaker', generates single or combined horizontal, vertical, and tilting perturbations with a payload up to 1 kg. It can produce horizontal and vertical perturbations with amplitudes up to 1 cm at oscillation frequencies up to 10 Hz. The tilting motions were constrained to 15°/s. The shaker can measure single ground reaction forces (GRF) using up to four custom-build force plates mounted on the platform. Preliminary experiments with rats combining X-ray fluoroscopy, and three dimensional GRF during active perturbations were performed. They indicate that the shaker may play a key role in determining motor-control strategies in response to active perturbations during posture and locomotion in small animals.

Keywords: Active perturbations · Locomotion · Neuromechanics

1 Introduction

In the last years, spinal sensorimotor systems have been studied extensively. Canonical mammalian spinal circuits were organized in Ia, reciprocal inhibitory system, Renshaw cells, Ib, and group II neurons e.g., [1]. Other works have focused on the pattern generating networks responsible for locomotion e.g., [2]. Despite important advances in the understanding of the organization of spinal motor systems, many aspects of spinal sensorimotor function remain unclear. For example, less is known about the descending systems in the brainstem and how they interact with spinal circuits [3, 4]. In addition, how do these systems ensure stable motor performance across unexpected changes in the environment? Or how do descending systems from the brainstem interact with spinal sensorimotor systems to produce flexible motor function? Understanding those questions requires a multidisciplinary approach. In the Neuronex project (C3NS) [5], we combine behavioral, neurophysiological, computational, and robotic experiments to understand how mechanical scale and task demands determine the function of low-level control centers in the spinal cord and their interactions with high level control centers in the brainstem in small mammals.

To infer the neuromechanical control strategies implemented by any animal, it is necessary to characterize how it responds to external perturbations. In the literature,

© The Author(s), under exclusive license to Springer Nature Switzerland AG 2022
A. Hunt et al. (Eds.): Living Machines 2022, LNAI 13548, pp. 103–106, 2022.
https://doi.org/10.1007/978-3-031-20470-8_10

biomechanists used "passive" perturbations, e.g., sudden drops [6, 7] or steps [8] to mimick, as far as possible, animal locomotion on rough terrains. We think, however, that to infer the interactions between spinal-reflex control and higher locomotor centers, reproducible "active" perturbations are necessary. They can help to search, for example, for the existence of a perturbation threshold at which spinal-reflex loop need to be helped by higher centers. In such a case we expect a sudden change in the kinematics, kinetics, and muscle activations.

In this paper, we mainly inform about a novel platform for neuromechanical experiments that we termed 'the shaker'. We also present shortly ongoing preliminary locomotion experiments on rats. The paper closes with the introduction of more complex experiments that will be undertaken to determine control strategies in response to perturbations during posture/locomotion in small animals.

2   The Shaker: A Three Degrees of Freedom Active Perturbation Platform

The shaker was designed for neuromechanical behavioral experiments during posture and locomotion of small animals (e.g., small mammals like rats or small terrestrial birds like the quail). Our design goal was that the shaker generates single or combined horizontal, vertical, and tilting perturbations with a payload up to 1 kg. During terrestrial locomotion, small animals exhibit contact times ranging between 0.1 s and 0.2 s depending on locomotion's speed. Therefore, every active perturbation applied by the shaker needs to be achieved in a time below 0.1 s. To fulfill the requirements during striding locomotion, the shaker was conceived to generate horizontal and vertical perturbations with amplitudes up to 1 cm at oscillation frequencies up to 10 Hz (repeat accuracy < 0.1 mm). Tilting perturbations are aimed only for posture experiments and therefore do not need to satisfy such higher oscillations rates. To permit the collection of single leg ground reaction forces (GRF) before, during and after the active perturbations, up to four force plates (like those presented in [9]) can be integrated into the platform. In our posture/locomotion experiments we use biplanar high-speed X-ray fluoroscopy to infer bones kinematics in three dimensions. Therefore, the active platform of the shaker was designed to be, as far as possible, X-ray transparent.

In Fig. 1A, the CAD design of the saker is shown. The support platform consists of two carbon plates with an elastomer in between (thickness = 6 mm) and two or three carbon tubes (external diameter $\phi = 25$ mm, wall thickness = 1mm). On the support platform, a ring made of Polyoxymethylene (POM) was rigged to permit the mounting of up to four ATI-Nano 17® force/torque sensors. Four plates made of acrylic glass (10 cm × 10 cm × 0.5 cm) were used as a platform for collecting GRFs and center of pressure (CoP) (see Fig. 1B).

The vertical oscillations of the platform (z-axis) are produced by two linear servomotors (Beckhoff, mod. AL8042). The horizontal ones (x-axis) by one linear servomotor (Beckhoff, mod. AL8040). Those linear motors are controlled by digital compact servo drives (Beckhoff, mod. AX5206, respectively Beckhoff, mod AX5106). Maximal translation amplitude ratio is 2 cm in 0.05 s. The tilting motions of the platform (about the y-axis) are produced by two stepper motors Nanotec (mod. LA421S14-B-UIEV) controlled by a Beckhoff motor controller (mod. EL7031–0030). Maximal angular displacement ratio is around 15°/ s. GUI and control programs were written in Beckhoff own software-environment (Beckhoff TwinCAT). Time dependent perturbation profiles can be freely designed using coma separated values (csv. File). Perturbation's release can be achieved manually or by means of a photoelectric sensor. The shaker was developed and constructed by H&S Robotics, Ilmenau, Germany.

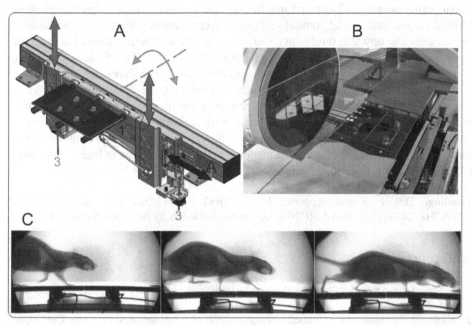

Fig. 1. The shaker and preliminary experiments. A) CAD image of the shaker indicating the motors and degrees of freedom: (1) one linear servomotor, horizontal motion along x-axis (red), (2) two linear servomotors, vertical motions along z-axis (blue), (3) stepper motors, tilting motions about y-axis (green). B) Platform with force plates and walking track. C) Pictures from X-ray video (600 f/s) showing a sudden drop of the platform of 10 mm in 0.05 s.

3   Preliminary and Coming Experiments

Two adult rats (*Rattus Norvegicus*) displaying a weight of 250 g and 340 g moved across a 2.3 m walking track, constructed around the shaker, at their preferred speeds. Body and limb kinematics were collected by using a biplanar high-speed X-ray fluoroscope (Neurostar, Siemens, Erlangen, Germany) and two synchronized standard light high-speed cameras (SpeedCam Visario g2, Weinberger, Erlangen, Germany). One plane of the X-ray machine recorded the motions of the rat on the sagittal plane (see Fig. 1B and C). The second plane, which normally records from above the animal, was rotated 30° form the vertical position to minimize interference with the force/torque sensors and to improve the recognition of the tantalum beans after motion's capture. The X-ray machine parameters were 55 kV and 40 mA, and a sampling frequency of 600 Hz. GRFs were collected at 1.2 kHz and force and X-ray data synchronized electronically (post-trigger). Onset of perturbation and force data were synchronized using a visual signal integrated in the shaker, which was captured by the light high-speed cameras. This synchronization is necessary to subtract the forces induced by accelerations (measured without payload) to those collected during posture/locomotion experiments.

In the preliminary phase of our experiments (Fig. 1C), we applied only one-way linear perturbations of 10 mm or 5 mm in 0.05 s during locomotion. Perturbations were termed cranial and caudal, ventral and dorsal (representing forward and backwards, downwards and upwards directions). Combination of those perturbations are expected to be used in the future. The Committee for Animal Research of the State of Thuringia, Germany, approved the animal care and all experimental procedures (registry number: 02-060/16). In coming experiments, we aim to combine three-dimensional bone kinematics with three-dimensional GRFs, and recordings of muscle activation during active perturbations. For this, rats will be implanted with tantalum beads (diameter: 0.5 mm) and EMG electrodes. We expect that by measuring motor responses to a range of perturbations, we can define the functional mapping between deviations in limb state, center of mass dynamics, and muscle activations.

Funding. This work was supported by the DFG FI 410/16-1 grant as part of the NSF/CIHR/DFG/FRQ/UKRI-MRC Next Generation Networks for Neuroscience Program.

References

1. Jankowska, E.: Spinal interneuronal networks in the cat: elementary components. Brain Res. Rev. **57**(1), 46–55 (2008)
2. Kiehn, O.: Development and functional organization of spinal locomotor circuits. Curr. Opin. Neurobiol. **21**(1), 100–109 (2011)
3. Brownstone, R.M., Chopek, J.W.: Reticulospinal systems for tuning motor commands. Front. Neural Circuits. **12**, 1–10 (2018)
4. LaPallo, B.K., et al.: Crossed activation of thoracic trunk motoneurons by medullary reticulospinal neurons. J. Neurophysiol. **122**, 2601–2613 (2019). https://doi.org/10.1152/jn.00194.2019
5. C3NS Homepage (2022). https://c3ns.org. Accessed 30 Mar 2022
6. Daley, M.A., Biewener, A.A.: Running over rough terrain reveals limb control for intrinsic stability. Proc. Nat. Acad. Sci. **103**, 15681–15686 (2006)
7. Wildau, J., et al.: A 3D-neuromechanical study of disturbed locomotion in rats. J. Morphol. **280**, 238 (2019)
8. Andrada, E., et al.: Limb, joint and pelvic kinematic control in the quail coping with steps upwards and downwards. Sci. Rep. **12**(1), 1–17 (2022)
9. Andrada, E., et al.: Adjustments of global and local hindlimb properties during terrestrial locomotion of the common quail (Coturnix coturnix). J. Exp. Biol. **216**, 3906–3916 (2013)

The Modelling of Different Dog Breeds on the Basis of a Validated Model

Heiko Stark$^{(\boxtimes)}$ ⓘ, Martin S. Fischer, and Emanuel Andrada ⓘ

Institute for Zoology and Evolutionary Research, Friedrich-Schiller-University Jena, 07743 Jena, Germany
heiko@starkrats.de
https://starkrats.de

Abstract. Based on our existing musculoskeletal models of the dog (Beagle & German Shepard) we have developed two additional ones. We have chosen the Dachshund and the Great Dane because they represent extreme body size values along dog breeds. Models for the French Bulldog, the Whippet, and Malinois will follow. We are confident that our models will advance the analysis of the influence of body size, physique and mobility on locomotion and joint dynamics.

Keywords: Neuromechanical models · Dachshund · Beagle · German shepard · Great dane

1 Introduction

The domestic dog (*canis lupus* f. familiaris) is the only animal species with more than 400 breeds recognized worldwide [1]. Therefore, it represents an interesting study group due to its great variability in body size, body mass and physique. In recent years, the number of clinical studies on the musculoskeletal system of dogs has increased [2,3]. However, the relationship between body structure and joint loading during locomotion, as well as between joint loading and degenerative musculoskeletal diseases (e.g. dysplasia) and their effects on neural control, has not yet been adequately elucidated [4]. A combination of experiments, detailed musculoskeletal models, finite element modelling (FEM), neuromechanical models and bioinspired robotics can help to analyze these interactions. For this purpose, a flexible modular software kit has been designed that can be used to create canine models ranging from individual leg segments to a complete musculoskeletal model [4]. In addition, this building kit can be used to create different models for different breeds to understand the influence of morphological parameters on e.g., locomotion or joint dynamics and control.

2 Material and Methods

From the publication of Stark et al. [4] we had a validated three-dimensional model of a beagle at our availability. This model was based on a German Shepard

© The Author(s), under exclusive license to Springer Nature Switzerland AG 2022
A. Hunt et al. (Eds.): Living Machines 2022, LNAI 13548, pp. 107–110, 2022.
https://doi.org/10.1007/978-3-031-20470-8_11

dataset, so that the scaling algorithms (for e.g., mass, lengths, muscle parameters) were existent. To build new models, we used the scaling function of Open-Sim [5,6]. It is implemented in the tool "Scale" and with it the individual segment masses, inertia, lengths, and muscle parameters, can be scaled uniformly or individually for all three axes. This made it easy to adapt the model to the different proportions of the dog breeds. However, the availability of the morphometric parameters is important.

We obtained these data from Fischer and Lilje [7]. For the different breeds, body lengths, wither heights and leg segment lengths in proportion to the leg length are there given. Note that the moments of inertia must be recomputed if the segment masses differ. The maximal muscle force must be manually scaled as well. For this, we used the relationships published by Stark et al. [4]. To generate the musculoskeletal models presented in this work, we selected the Dachshund and the Great Dane (see Fig. 1), They represent two extreme values of body size and the ratio between body length/wither height.

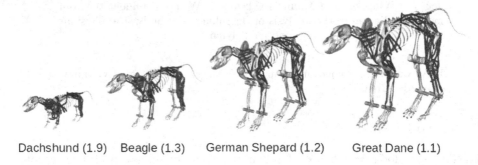

Dachshund (1.9)   Beagle (1.3)   German Shepard (1.2)   Great Dane (1.1)

Fig. 1. Perspective view of the four modelled breeds (body length/withers height) for the simulation tool OpenSim [5,6]. The segments (bones) are shown in gray, the musculature in red and the joint constraints in cyan. (Color figure online)

3   Results and Discussion

The models presented here represent extreme values among dog breeds. The Great Dane is in average 3.3 times larger than the Dachshund. It is well known that body length and height influences life span and the occurrence of degenerative musculoskeletal deceases. The average life span for the Great Dane is quite low (median: 6 years) [8]. Despite the short life span, it shows a high relative frequency within musculoskeletal disease as the cause of deaths (0.217) [9]. As well as for other large breeds: the Saint Bernard (0.262), Great Pyrenees (0.255), Irish Wolfhound (0.221), and Greyhound (0.214). In contrast, the Dachshund has a longer lifespan (median: 13.5 years) but is in the group with the highest relative frequency for neurologic disease as the cause of death (0.404) [9]. This can also be shown for other small breeds: Miniature Dachshund (0.397), Dutch Pug (0.274), Miniature Pinscher (0.223), and Boston Terrier (0.222). In addition, several small dog breeds also show an increase in the incidence of medial patellar luxation (MPL) [10]. Both models thus represent two important groups for the study of degenerative disease affecting locomotion.

The scaling presented here represent a first step towards a tool for the analysis of dog locomotion/health. Further steps are necessary. For example, the joint actuators must be optimized for every model. In addition, muscle geometry and parameters must be adapted to the different breeds (extremes: Whippet vs. Boxer [7]). Simulations will require additional data regarding ground reaction forces and kinematics for the individual breeds, as shown in [11]. The combination of morphological and experimental data with our models will make be possible the comparison of joint loads among breeds. We hypothesize that morphological changes might induce differing muscle activation or even changes in muscles synergies. Further trade-offs will be analyzed by scaling our Beagle model for Whippets (built for speed) and French bulldogs (built for strength). We are confident that these additional models will help to improve the analysis of the influence of body size, physique, mobility and disease on neural control and joint loading during locomotion in dogs.

Data availability

The data that support the findings of this study are available from the authors on reasonable request. The OpenSim model can be downloaded https://simtk. org/projects/dogmodel.

Funding. This work was supported by the DFG FI 410/16-1 grant as part of the NSF/CIHR/DFG/FRQ/UKRI-MRC Next Generation Networks for Neuroscience Program.

References

1. Ostrander, E.A., et al.: Dog10K: an international sequencing effort to advance studies of canine domestication, phenotypes and health. Natl. Sci. Rev. **6**(4), 810–824 (2019)
2. Spinella, G., Arcamone, G., Valentini, S.: Cranial cruciate ligament rupture in dogs: review on biomechanics, etiopathogenetic factors and rehabilitation. Vet. Sci. **8**(9), 186 (2021)
3. Witsberger, T.H., Villamil, J.A., Schultz, L.G., Hahn, A.W., Cook, J.L.: Prevalence of and risk factors for hip dysplasia and cranial cruciate ligament deficiency in dogs. J. Am. Vet. Med. Assoc. **232**(12), 1818–1824 (2008)
4. Stark, H., Fischer, M.S., Hunt, A., Young, F., Quinn, R., Andrada, E.: A three-dimensional musculoskeletal model of the dog. Sci. Rep. **11**(1), 1–13 (2021)
5. OpenSim Core Team: OpenSim is a freely available software system that allows you to build, exchange, and analyse musculoskeletal models and dynamic simulations of movement (V3.3). http://opensim.stanford.edu/
6. Delp, S.L., et al.: OpenSim: open-source software to create and analyze dynamic simulations of movement. IEEE Trans. Biomed. Eng. **54**(11), 1940–1950 (2007)

7. Fischer, M.S., Lilje, K.E.: Dogs in Motion. VDH/KOSMOS, 1st edn. (2011)
8. O'neill, D.G., Church, D.B., McGreevy, P.D., Thomson, P.C., Brodbelt, D.C.: Longevity and mortality of owned dogs in England. Vet. J. **198**(3), 638–643 (2013)
9. Fleming, J.M., Creevy, K.E., Promislow, D.E.L.: Mortality in North American dogs from 1984 to 2004: an investigation into age-, size-, and breed-related causes of death. J. Vet. Intern. Med. **25**(2), 187–198 (2011)
10. Lehmann, S.V., Andrada, E., Taszus, R., Koch, D., Fischer, M.S.: Three-dimensional motion of the patella in French bulldogs with and without medial patellar luxation. BMC Vet. Res. **17**(1), 1–12 (2021)
11. Andrada, E., Reinhardt, L., Lucas, K., Fischer, M.S.: Three-dimensional inverse dynamics of the forelimb of Beagles at a walk and trot. Am. J. Vet. Res. **78**(7), 804–817 (2017)

Analyzing 3D Limb Kinematics of *Drosophila Melanogaster* for Robotic Platform Development

Clarissa A. Goldsmith[1]([✉]), Moritz Haustein[2], Till Bockemühl[2], Ansgar Büschges[2], and Nicholas S. Szczecinski[1]

[1] Department of Mechanical and Aerospace Engineering, West Virginia University, Morgantown, WV, USA
clarissa@goldsmithgroup.org
[2] Institute of Zoology, University of Cologne, Cologne, Germany

Abstract. Recent work in insect-inspired robotics has highlighted the benefits of closely aligning the degrees of freedom (DoF) of a robotic platform with those of the target animal. However, to actualize this approach, the kinematics of the animal must be closely examined and balanced with considerations unique to a robotic counterpart. To inform the development of a robot inspired by *Drosophila melanogaster*, we collected 3D pose estimation data from the insect and analyzed the kinematics of the middle and hind limb pairs to find combinations of three DoF that best approximate animal motion. For our analysis, we simulated a baseline kinematic leg chain comprised of seven DoF for each frame of the motion capture data. We then fixed certain DoF and found a 'best fit' configuration relative to the animal. In these configurations, we analyzed the positional error of each joint's midpoints, as well as the angle of the leg plane from vertical. We found that using a three DoF combination of CTr elevation/depression, TrF pronation/supination, and FTi flexion/extension, we are able to closely approximate the motions of the insect while balancing necessary robotic platform considerations.

Keywords: *Drosophila melanogaster* · Drosophibot · DeepLabCut · Kinematic analysis

1 Introduction

In the context of legged locomotion, animals and robots can both be considered machines attempting to solve similar problems. In each case, a central controller dictates motor commands based on limb kinematics and dynamics and subject to modification from sensory feedback. While the consequences may vary, failure and success can be defined with similar criteria (e.g. remaining upright, making stable ground contact, adapting to dynamic terrain). Considering these criteria, animals currently have far greater walking capability than robots. However, the similarities between the two systems and their goals make it possible to

© The Author(s), under exclusive license to Springer Nature Switzerland AG 2022
A. Hunt et al. (Eds.): Living Machines 2022, LNAI 13548, pp. 111–122, 2022.
https://doi.org/10.1007/978-3-031-20470-8_12

improve robotic walking capabilities through close investigation of animal loco-motion. Many previous successful walking robots have been developed following this approach to varying degrees [10,12]. Additionally, a walking robot with a high degree of biological accuracy can be used as a test platform for biologi-cal hypotheses [3,4]. Such fidelity is key when using robots to investigate the animal nervous system, as the interplay between an organism's nervous system and mechanics is not presently understood. Highly bio-mimetic robots minimize controller-structure mismatch, ensuring greater neuroscientific applicability to data collected on the platform [9]. Such data can potentially be applied to more generic legged robot control, this continually expanding both fields.

Mimicking biology with a robotic platform presents challenges, however, such as actuation. While both animals and robots possess multi-jointed legs with actu-ators that control each joint, the design of robot legs is subject to different con-straints than those of animals. Robotic systems are inherently limited by techno-logical state-of-the-art, often a far cry from biological system capability. However, robot designs can be specialized in ways an animal's structure cannot without exis-tential consequences. One common issue in this vein is muscles are considerably more compact and lightweight than conventional electric actuators, making it dif-ficult to include all biological degrees of freedom (DoF) on a robotic counterpart without making the robot too heavy to stand. This constraint has often necessi-tated reducing the animal's various DoF to just three, the minimum DoF needed to position the chain's end effector at any arbitrary point in 3D space [14].

For certain groups of target animals, similar simplifications for leg DoF on robotic platforms have arisen over time. For example, many insect inspired robots follow a similar leg template of protraction/retraction with a thorax-coxa (ThC) joint, levation/depression with a coxa-trochanter (CTr) joint, and flex-ion/extension with a femur-tibia (FTi) joint [12]. Recently, however, Billeschou et al. highlighted the benefits of choosing specialized DoF based closely on the target animal's kinematics [3]. We wish to apply this methodology to our target animal, *Drosophila melanogaster*, in order to produce an updated version of our previous *Drosophila* inspired robot, Drosophibot, that more closely matches the animal's DoF [7].

In this work, we collect 3D pose estimation data from *Drosophila melanogaster* and conduct kinematic analysis on the middle and hind limb pairs to identify the three DoF that best approximate insect movement. We begin by constructing a simulated kinematic leg chain for each leg pair, then fix different DoF in the chain and attempt to construct a 'best fit' configuration to each frame of an animal data trial. We then investigate the effect these DoF fixations have on each joint's loca-tion in space and the angle of the leg plane to the vertical. In our analysis, fixing our hypothesized trochanter-femur (TrF) joint introduces high average error in the tip of the leg chain, as well as an inability to achieve animal-like leg plane angles. Meanwhile, fixing the ThC with a mobile TrF produces smaller positional error and maintains animal-like leg plane angles. We discuss the implications of these findings for understanding *Drosophila* leg kinematics, as well as our future goals to apply this analysis to the construction of a *Drosophila*-inspired robot.

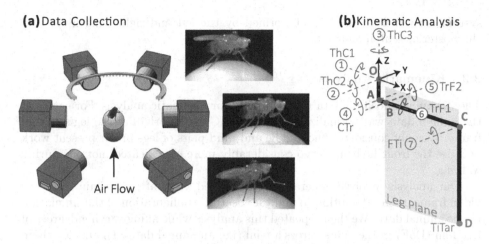

Fig. 1. (a) The spherical treadmill setup for acquiring 3D motion capture footage. (b) The DoF in our simulated leg chain, presented in the 'zero configuration' of the leg.

2 Methods

2.1 Data Collection

All experiments were performed with 3-to-8 days-old adult male and female Bolt-GAL4>UAS-CsChrimson *Drosophila melanogaster* flies [2]. This allowed opto-genetic initiation of sustained, fast forward walking using a red laser (658·nm) targeting the animal's head. Animals were reared on a semi-synthetic agar standard medium soaked with 50 μl of a 100 mmol L^{-1} all-trans-Retinal solution at 25 °C and 65% humidity in the dark.

Tethered flies walked on a spherical treadmill [1] and leg movements were recorded with six synchronised high-speed cameras (Basler acA1300-200um with Kowa LM50JC1MS 50 mm lenses) surrounding the animal (Fig. 1a). Cameras were arranged such that either body side was recorded simultaneously by three cameras providing a front, side, and hind aspect. Videos were recorded 400 Hz · and a resolution of 896 by 540 pixels. In each video, the flies stepped at frequencies between 5–13 Hz, corresponding to 30 to 80 postures per step cycle. We tracked the spatial position of six features on each leg: the thorax-coxa (ThC) joint, coxa-trochanter (CTr) joint, trochanter-femur (TrF) joint, femur-tibia (FTi) joint, tibia-tarsus (TiTar) joint, and the tarsus tip. We also tracked the position of the posterior scutellum apex on the thorax, the wing hinge, and the antennae. Tracking was done automatically using the DeepLabCut toolbox [13], which we used to train three independent ResNet-50 networks (training sets: 630 frames for each network) for the front, side, and hind camera groups. Cameras were calibrated by using a custom-made checkerboard pattern (7 × 6 squares with size 400 μm × 400 μm per square). For triangulation of 3D feature positions, a singular value decomposition algorithm was applied [8]. 3D positions of the tracked features were transformed to a body-centered coordinate system derived from the triangle formed by the left and right wing hinge and the posterior scutellum apex.

2.2 Kinematic Analysis

The 3D animal position data was then used for kinematic analysis. For each leg, the animal data was normalized with the ThC as the origin of the leg's spatial frame. We only considered the middle and hind pairs of legs in our present work because the front limbs undergo considerably more complicated motions during walking.

Our analysis involved generating a simulated kinematic leg chain for every video frame, then attempting to find the 'best fit' configuration of the simulation to the animal data. We then repeated this analysis while fixing varying degrees of freedom (DoF) in the joints across a trial (i.e. an animal dataset). Our leg chain contains seven total DoF in the fully mobile case. Figure 1b shows the DoF of each joint in our 'zero configuration' for the leg. In the zero configuration, each DoF's axes of rotation are a direct translation of the spatial frame's axes: (1–3) ThC protraction/retraction around the X axis (ThC1), levation/depression around the Y axis (ThC2), and rotation around the Z axis (ThC3); (4) CTr flexion/extension around the Y axis; (4–5) TrF flexion/extension around the X axis (TrF1) and rotation around the Y axis (TrF2); and (7) FTi flexion/extension around the Y axis [16]. The TiTar joint serves as the end effector of our leg chain. Historically, the TrF of *Drosophila* has been considered fixed [15]. However, findings of musculature and motor-neuronal innervation in the trochanter [5,16], as well as the necessity of a 'CTr roll' in Lobato Ríos et al. 2021 [11] to most closely match animal kinematic replay raise questions regarding this claim, so we included a mobile TrF in our chain to test both cases.

Using this baseline leg structure, we created a function that uses product of exponentials to generate the simulated forward kinematic leg chain using the segment lengths for the present frame of animal data. Our calculation method uses the initial position of a point in the spatial frame, $\vec{p}_{sim}(\vec{0})$, as well as the deflection of each DoF from their zero configuration, $\theta_1, \theta_2 ... \theta_7$, to calculate the updated position of the joint in the spatial frame, $\vec{p}_{sim}(\vec{\theta})$ [14]:

$$\vec{p}_{sim}(\vec{\theta}) = e^{\hat{\zeta}_1 \theta_1} e^{\hat{\zeta}_2 \theta_2} ... e^{\hat{\zeta}_7 \theta_7} \vec{p}_{sim}(\vec{0}) \tag{1}$$

Each exponential term in Eq. 1 describes the twist of a single DoF's joint axes in space dictated by the frame's twist matrix, $\hat{\zeta}$:

$$e^{\hat{\zeta}\theta} = \begin{bmatrix} e^{\hat{\omega}\theta} & (I - e^{\hat{\omega}\theta})\hat{\omega}\vec{v} + \vec{\omega}\vec{\omega}^T \vec{v}\theta \\ 0 & 1 \end{bmatrix}, \tag{2}$$

where $\hat{\omega}$ is the skew-symmetric matrix of the DoF axis of rotation, $\vec{\omega}$, and $\vec{v}$ is the zero-configuration location of the DoF frame's origin in the spatial frame.

We then embedded $\vec{p}_{sim}(\vec{\theta})$ in an error function for the ith joint, $e_i(\vec{\theta})$:

$$e_i(\vec{\theta}) = \frac{w_i}{l_i} \|\vec{p}_{sim,i}(\vec{\theta}) - \vec{p}_{fly,i}\|. \tag{3}$$

This function calculates the magnitude of the error between the simulated position of a joint (labeled A–D in Fig. 1) for a certain vector of joint angles, $\vec{p}_{sim,i}(\vec{\theta})$, and the point position from the animal, $\vec{p}_{fly,i}$, normalized by the length of the joint's proximal leg segment, l_i, and scaled by a weighting, w_i. Segment lengths are re-calculated from the animal data for each frame in order to minimize the effect of point tracking errors on the positional error between animal and simulated leg chains. We prioritized fit toward the end of the chain in our simulations by setting the weights $w_A, w_B, w_D = 1$ and $w_C = 3$.

Each of these error functions were then combined into an error vector, $\vec{E}(\vec{\theta})$. For each frame of the target leg's positional data, we minimized the vector norm of $E(\vec{\theta})$ to construct a 'best fit' configuration of our simulated leg with the least overall euclidean distance of each tracked point to the animal points. The fixed joint's angles were set as constants based on their average value in the fully mobile case. Once we found the best fit configuration, we stored the unweighted positional errors normalized to each joint's proximal segment. We also calculated the angle of the leg plane, a plane containing the femur and tibia (grey plane in Fig. 1b), from the vertical for both the animal and simulation. This process was repeated for every frame of a trial.

For choosing joint fixations, we primarily focused on the ThC and the TrF. The CTr and FTi have proven innervation and noticeable angular movement during stepping, so they were left mobile in all cases [15,16]. The ThC has similar evidence, but the difficulty of creating an electrically actuated 3 DoF joint at our scale motivated us to attempt to eliminate ThC DoF if possible. As the mobility of the TrF is presently debated, fixing TrF DoF also proved a natural choice.

3   Results

Figures 2 and 3 show the average spatial error over each trial of each of the simulated limb pairs' joints compared to the animal data for five different leg 'structures': 'all joints mobile', 'ThC1, ThC2 fixed', 'ThC1, ThC2, TrF2 fixed', 'ThC Fully Fixed, TrF2 Fixed', and 'ThC1, ThC2 Fixed, TrF Fully Fixed'. In the error plots, each symbol and color combination represents a different fly. Of the pair, the filled symbol represents the fly's right limb, and the unfilled symbol the left limb. Because we normalized the errors of each point to the length of the proximal segment, the average values are presented as a fraction of the proximal segment's length.

In the 'all joints mobile' case for the middle legs (Fig. 2a), the errors in the FTi and TiTar positions are relatively small, signifying a good match to the animal's foot trajectories. The errors for the CTr and TrF spatial position are slightly higher (nearly 0.1 coxa lengths of average CTr error), likely due to

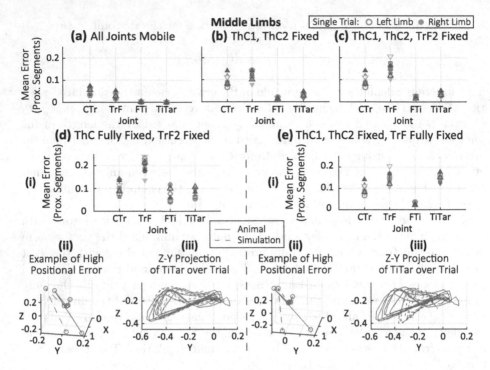

Fig. 2. Fixing TrF rotation greatly impacts the middle leg's ability to capture animal-like positions of tracked points on the animal. Each symbol/color represents a different fly. A filled symbol represents a right limb, an unfilled symbol a left limb. The error is normalized in terms of a fraction of the joint's proximal segment length. The mean normalized errors in the middle limbs are plotted for: (a) all joints mobile; (b) the ThC1 and ThC2 fixed; (c) the ThC1, ThC2, and TrF2 fixed; (di) the ThC fully fixed and the TrF2 fixed; and (ei) the ThC1 and ThC2 fixed and the TrF fully fixed. The leg chains for the animal (solid blue) and the simulation (dashed red) are plotted for the latter two cases (dii, eii) in a frame of high error, as well as the Z-Y projection of the TiTar over a single trial (diii, eiii). (Color figure online)

motion capture artifacts and video resolution limitations making it harder to pinpoint joint locations close to the thorax. Additionally, because the coxa and trochanter are relatively short segments in the limb, the error is inflated by our normalization. As seen in dii and eii of Fig. 2, these errors do not end up creating significant positional deviations from the animal data.

When the ThC1 and ThC2 are fixed in the middle limbs as in Fig. 2b, the average error in each segment slightly increases. However, the error at the end of the leg chain still remains low. This trend continues as we additionally fix the TrF2 (Fig. 2c).

Fixing the ThC3 to fully fix the ThC, in contrast, greatly increases average FTi and TiTar joint point error in the middle limbs (Fig. 2di). In this case, the FTi and TiTar points experience errors 2–5 times larger than the errors from the previous case in Fig. 2c. Figure 2dii shows the animal and simulation leg chains during a frame of high positional error to highlight this discrepancy. During such frames, the FTi and TiTar points do not fully match the positions of the animal data. However, the leg does achieve a similar angle of the leg plane. Additionally, the Z-Y projection of the simulated limb's TiTar position over the trial (red dashed line, Fig. 2diii) is still able to follow a similar path as the animal's. The major discrepancies occur at the transitional periods between leg stance and swing.

Fully fixing the TrF and mobilizing the ThC3 (Fig. 2e), by contrast, produces a more drastic effect. As shown in Fig. 2ei, fixing the TrF1 decreased the average error of the FTi point from the ThC3-fixed case, but also greatly increased the average error of the TiTar point. Looking at a frame of high error (Fig. 2eii), the simulated limb chain more accurately captures the FTi joint point than with the ThC3 fixed. However, the simulated leg plane's angle deviates greatly from the animal's, causing large TiTar point error. This error causes large discrepancies in the trajectories of the TiTar point projected on the Z-Y plane between animal and simulation (Fig. 2eiii). Overall, completely fixing the TrF joint in the middle limbs greatly diminished our simulation's ability to accurately capture the limb movements of the animal.

Analysis of the hind legs revealed similar patterns as in the middle legs (Fig. 3). The fit of the hind limb with all joints mobile (Fig. 3a) had similar errors as the middle limb, which we attributed to resolution limitations and motion capture artifacts. The hind limbs also showed minimal increase in end effector error when fixing the ThC1, ThC2, and TrF2 (Fig. 3b–c). Fully fixing the ThC (Fig. 3di) resulted in increased error for all points, particularly in the FTi and TiTar. The leg chains in a position of high error in Fig. 3dii show a similar behavior as the middle limbs in this case: the simulated FTi and TiTar are not able to achieve the same positioning as the animal, but the overall angle of the leg plane appears similar. The simulated hind limb is also able to complete a similar TiTar Z-Y trajectory as the animal, albeit with less overall protraction and retraction (Fig. 3diii).

The major difference between the middle and hind limb behavior appears when the TrF is fully fixed and the ThC3 is made mobile (Fig. 3e). The average error of the FTi and TiTar points both decrease (Fig. 3ei), signifying an improved fit. Plotting the leg chains supports this idea (Fig. 3eii); the simulated limb is still not fully able to achieve the position of the animal data, but the spatial distance between the two chains is shorter. The position of the TiTar over time further shows a closer fit between the two datasets (Fig. 3eiii).

To further elucidate the differences between fully fixing the ThC vs. the TrF, we also calculated the angle of the leg plane from vertical, shown in Fig. 3. Similar to the error plots, fixing the ThC1, ThC2, and TrF2 in (a–c) causes minimal increases («5 °C in most cases) in the angle errors (Fig. 3a). The range of leg plane angles over the trial also remains similar (Fig. 3b).

The angle data for combinations (d–e) in the middle limb also seems to align with the error data. The highest average angle error occurs when the TrF is fully

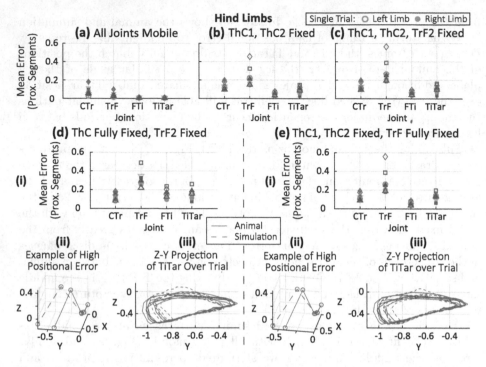

Fig. 3. Fixing the ThC3 or the TrF1 in the hind limbs does not produce as stark of a difference in point positional error as fixing them in the middle limbs. Each symbol/color represents a different fly. A filled symbol represents a right limb, an unfilled symbol a left limb. The error is normalized in terms of a fraction of the joint's proximal segment length. The mean normalized errors are plotted for: (a) all joints mobile; (b) the ThC1 and ThC2 fixed; (c) the ThC1, ThC2, and TrF2 fixed; (di) the ThC fully fixed and the TrF2 fixed; and (ei) the ThC1 and ThC2 fixed and the TrF fully fixed. The leg chains for the animal (solid blue) and the simulation (dashed red) are plotted for the latter two cases (dii, eii) in a frame of high error, as well as the Z-Y projection of the TiTar over a single trial (diii, eiii). (Color figure online)

fixed, as shown in Fig. 3ai. The total range of angles is also much lower with the TrF fixed (Fig. 3bi). The ThC being fully fixed, meanwhile, produces less average error and a much closer range of angles over the trials. Figure 3ci, showing typical angles over a trial, highlights the difference between the two ranges. While fully fixing the ThC causes the simulation (red dashed line) to overshoot the animal's (blue solid line) peak angles slightly, the overall waveform follows the animal's. With the TrF fixed, however, the simulated leg is unable to achieve angles close to those of the animal.

The data in Fig. 3 also helps elucidate the key DoF in the hind limbs. Figure 3aii shows that the average leg plane angle error is highest with the ThC fully fixed. With the ThC3 mobile instead, the error shifts closer to baseline levels. Fully fixing the ThC also produces much higher angle ranges (Fig. 3bii),

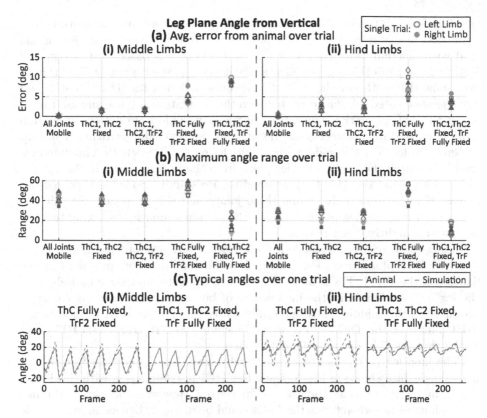

Fig. 4. Investigating tibia angles from vertical for various limb structures helps further illuminate movement differences. Each symbol/color represents a different fly. A filled symbol represents a right limb, an unfilled symbol a left limb. (a) The average error between the simulation and the animal over a trial for the middle (i) and hind (ii) limbs for various DoF structures. (b) The maximum range of angles over a trial for the simulated middle (i) and hind (ii) limbs. (c) Typical angles over a trial for the animal (blue solid) and simulation (red dashed) while the ThC and TrF2 were fixed, and the TrF, ThC1, and ThC2 were fixed. Data is included in both configurations for the middle (i) and hind (ii) limbs. (Color figure online)

similar to the middle limbs. However, the baseline range for the hind limbs is about half that of the middle limbs, so the higher ranges cause an increased overall error. Figure 3cii highlights how the modified ranges affect the fit to the animal data over a trial (Fig. 4).

4   Discussion

In this work, we analyzed the kinematics of the middle and hind limbs of *Drosophila melanogaster* from 3D pose estimation data, with the aim of determining the three most crucial degrees of freedom (DoF) to include on the corresponding limbs of a fruit fly inspired robot. We constructed a kinematic chain of the limb for each frame of the data and attempted to determine a 'best-fit' configuration to the animal data. This process was repeated over an entire animal trial with different DoF fixed. Our kinematic chain was based on five reported DoF in *Drosophila* [15,16], as well as a mobile TrF joint with two DoF. Our findings show that with our chosen DoF orientations, fixing the ThC1, ThC2, and TrF2 joints created minimal error between the simulation and the animal. Fixing either the ThC3 or TrF1 joints, both of which provide a pronation/supination motion, created much larger errors throughout the leg chain, particularly toward the end effector. For the middle limbs, fully fixing the TrF left the simulated leg unable to match the angle of the leg plane from the vertical found in the animal. Meanwhile, fixing the ThC fully retained the leg's ability to achieve animal-like angles. For the hind limbs, fixing these joints had similar results, but due to the smaller range of leg plane angles in the animal's hind limbs, fixing the TrF produced a slightly closer match.

Using these results, we made a final determination about the limbs of our updated *Drosophila* robot. For both limb pairs, the low errors produced by the fixation of the ThC1, ThC2, and TrF2 joints allow us to omit them entirely from the leg designs. Similarly, the high degree of both positional and angular error produced in the middle limbs upon fully fixing the TrF leads us to include the TrF1 joint over the ThC3. Thus, we will include the CTr, TrF1, and FTi joints as the three DoF in our robotic middle limb.

The hind leg pair presents a less straightforward decision. Based on the leg plane angle data shown in Fig. 3, fixing the TrF1 in conjunction with the ThC1, ThC2, and TrF2 provides the least angular error. However, the increased range of leg plane angles when fixing the ThC3 could be uniquely beneficial to a robotic platform. In stance phase, an organism's body weight produces a vertical ground reaction force (GRF) at the foot, producing moments in the frontal plane on the proximal end of each leg segment. Components of these moments aligned with the joint axis must be counteracted by the actuator, while the rest are passively resisted by the joint structure. Thus, a larger leg plane angle results in lower actuator torques than a vertical plane. Billeschou et al. demonstrated as such by creating an angle in the leg planes of their dung beetle robot, which better distributed the torques required to support the body among all the actuators of the leg [3]. Zill et al. similarly found that the force profiles encoded by the stick insect's trochanteral campaniform sensilla were highly dependent on the orientation of the leg plane [17]. This redistribution of torque could provide a further factor of safety for our robot. Additionally, it is presently unclear how the hind limb motions are affected by walking on a curved surface vs. a flat surface. As shown in Figs. 2d and 3d, during stance the hind TiTar moves along a path approx. twice as steep as the middle TiTar. As such, hind limb motions may be more similar to the middle limbs on flat ground. For these reasons we conclude that including the CTr, TrF1, and FTi joints in our robot's hind limbs is most beneficial to our present purposes.

We found it curious that with our investigated DoF we could not achieve animal-like limb movements without a mobile TrF, despite no conclusive evidence of the joint's mobility in *Drosophila*. Other *Drosophila* studies have found similar results: adding 'CTr roll' decreased kinematic replay error in Lobato Ríos et al. 2021, creating pronation/supination motion added similar to our TrF [11]. Studies of larger species within *Diptera* during flight have reported pronation/supination in the CTr of the unloaded middle limbs [6]; however, this joint movement has not been observed during loaded walking. No final determination can be made about this pronation/supination or the mobility of the TrF in *Drosophila* without the identification of condyles or specific neuronal innervation. However, we believe our data contributes to a growing call to more closely examine the mobility of *Drosophila's* legs.

Our work presently targets only a small subset of fly leg behaviors. In addition to forward walking, flies can walk in curves, walk backward, and turn in place, in addition to behaviors such as searching, cleaning, mating, etc. The apparent overactuation of insect legs could serve the need to perform such varying functions. It is unclear how well our proposed simplified leg structures can emulate non-walking movements, but such behaviors are outside of our present scope. We plan to apply our present methodology to omni-directional walking in future work.

We also do not address the tarsal segment of *Drosophila*, a common simplification for insect-inspired robots. However, biologically the tarsus comprises a large portion of the leg length and plays an important role in managing ground interactions [12]. We aim to further explore the role of the tarsal segment in future work.

For robot design, our future work will first involve analysis of the fly's front limbs. We believe our present methodology can be directly applied, though more than three DoF will likely be needed to capture the greater movement complexity. We will then conduct dynamical analysis of the proposed robot design through a dynamic simulation of the robot. The simulation will allow us to test leg movements corresponding to forward, backward, and curved walking on a flat surface in lieu of biological motion capture. We will use the calculated forces and torques to inform final mechatronic design (e.g. actuator selection). With the resulting robot, we seek to expand our work developing synthetic nervous system controllers like the controller developed for our previous robot, Drosophibot [7]. We also plan to explore how the campaniform sensilla discharge in insect limbs is influenced by leg movements [18].

Acknowledgements. Many thanks to Sasha Zill for his comments and insight while preparing this manuscript. This work was supported by NSF DBI 2015317 as part of the NSF/CIHR/DFG/FRQ/UKRI-MRC Next Generation Networks for Neuroscience Program.

References

1. Berendes, V., Zill, S.N., Büschges, A., Bockemühl, T.: Speed-dependent interplay between local pattern-generating activity and sensory signals during walking in Drosophila. J. Exp. Biol. **219**(23), 3781–3793 (2016)
2. Bidaye, S.S., et al.: Two brain pathways initiate distinct forward walking programs in Drosophila. Neuron **108**, 469–485 (2020)
3. Billeschou, P., Bijma, N.N., Larsen, L.B., Gorb, S.N., Larsen, J.C., Manoonpong, P.: Framework for developing bio-inspired morphologies for walking robots. Appl. Sci. **10**(19), 6986 (2020)
4. Buschmann, T., Ewald, A., von Twickel, A., Büschges, A.: Controlling legs for locomotion-insights from robotics and neurobiology. Bioinspir. Biomim. **10**(4), 41001 (2015)
5. Enriquez, J., Venkatasubramanian, L., Baek, M., Peterson, M., Aghayeva, U., Mann, R.: Specification of individual adult motor neuron morphologies by combinatorial transcription factor codes. Neuron **86**(4), 955–970 (2015)
6. Frantsevich, L.: Biomechanics of the multisclerite middle coxa in flies (Diptera). Arthropod Struct. Dev. **29**(2), 147–161 (2000)
7. Goldsmith, C.A., Szczecinski, N.S., Quinn, R.D.: Neurodynamic modeling of the fruit fly Drosophila melanogaster. Bioinspir. Biomim. **15**, 065003 (2020)
8. Hartley, R.I., Zisserman, A.: Multiple View Geometry in Computer Vision, 2nd edn. Cambridge University Press, Cambridge (2003)
9. Hooper, S.L.: Body size and the neural control of movement. Curr. Biol. **22**(9), R318–R322 (2012)
10. Ijspeert, A.J.: Biorobotics: using robots to emulate and investigate agile locomotion. Science **346**(6206), 196–203 (2014)
11. Lobato Ríos, V., et al.: NeuroMechFly, a neuromechanical model of adult Drosophila melanogaster. bioRxiv (2021). https://doi.org/10.1101/2021.04.17.440214
12. Manoonpong, P., et al.: Insect-inspired robots: bridging biological and artificial systems. Sensors **21**(22), 1–44 (2021)
13. Mathis, A., et al.: DeepLabCut: markerless pose estimation of user-defined body parts with deep learning. Nat. Neurosci. **21**(9), 1281–1289 (2018)
14. Murray, R., Li, Z., Sastry, S.: A Mathematical Introduction to Robotic Manipulation, 1st edn. CRC Press, Boca Raton (2017)
15. Sink, H.: Muscle Development in Drosophila, 1st edn. Springer, New York (2006). https://doi.org/10.1007/0-387-32963-3
16. Soler, C., Daczewska, M., Da Ponte, J.P., Dastugue, B., Jagla, K.: Coordinated development of muscles and tendons of the Drosophila leg. Development **131**(24), 6041–6051 (2004)
17. Zill, S.N., Schmitz, J., Chaudhry, S., Büschges, A.: Force encoding in stick insect legs delineates a reference frame for motor control. J. Neurophysiol. **108**(5), 1453–1472 (2012)
18. Zyhowski, W., Zill, S., Szczecinski, N.: Load feedback from a dynamically scaled robotic model of Carausius Morosus middle leg. In: Verschure, M. (ed.) Living Machines 2022. LNAI, vol. 13548, pp. 128–139. Springer, Cham (2022)

Gut Feelings: Towards Robotic Personality Generation with Microbial Fuel Cells

Hemma Philamore[1], Martin Garrad[1]($\boxtimes$), Martin Grao[1], and Max Jones[2]

[1] Softlab, University of Bristol, Bristol, UK
{hemma.philamore,m.garrad}@bristol.ac.uk
[2] Department of Philosophy, University of Bristol, Bristol, UK

Abstract. We present a new paradigm of bio-hybrid generation of robot personalities inspired by the gut-brain axis. We combine information from user interaction and microbial fuel cells (MFCs), a bioelectrical source of power, to generate personalities. We evaluate our system by investigating its capacity for generating varied personalities, incorporating history-dependence, and balancing interpretability with unexpectedness. To the best of our knowledge, this work represents the first exploration of bio-hybrid personality generation for robotic systems.

Keywords: Robot personality · Human-robot interaction · Bio-hybrid

1 Introduction

Humans anthropomorphise robots, assigning them personalities, which affect acceptance and trust [1]. Here, we explore a novel aspect of robot personality: the process of personality generation. Our hypothesis is that by integrating a bioelectrical signal into the generation process, humans interacting with the robot are more likely to accept and trust robot companions. Figure 1 shows a conceptual diagram of our proposed bio-hybrid personality generation system.

2 Background

Personality "represents those characteristics of the person that account for consistent patterns of feeling, thinking and behaving" [5]. In this work we adopt a widely used approach for categorising personality, the *Big Five personality traits*. These are openness to experience, conscientiousness, extraversion/introversion, agreeableness and neuroticism.

Prior work into robot personality has investigated expression of robotic personalities via voice and movement [4]. However, a key facet of human personality is variation. This can be achieved in a robot by selecting behaviour from a probability distribution over potential behaviours, with different distributions

© The Author(s), under exclusive license to Springer Nature Switzerland AG 2022
A. Hunt et al. (Eds.): Living Machines 2022, LNAI 13548, pp. 123–127, 2022.
https://doi.org/10.1007/978-3-031-20470-8_13

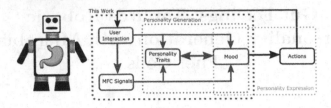

Fig. 1. Bio-hybrid personality generation concept: robot personality is influenced by interaction with users and a bioelectric signal.

corresponding to different personalities. One approach to generating personalities is to randomly modify these distributions. Our hypothesis is that using living organisms to modify personality may render the variation in the robot's behaviour more genuine, since the emergent personality traits will be sensitive to the robot's perceived physiological requirements.

This approach takes inspiration from the gut-brain axis, a bidirectional neural communication channel, which links emotional and cognitive centres of the brain with gut behaviour [7]. The connection between the robot's behaviour and its internal metabolic state provides a first step towards a homeostatic robot with emergent behaviours that can be perceived as genuinely meaningful [3]. Interactivity has also been observed to play a key role in personal attachment to companion robots [2], suggesting that using metabolism to influence robot personality may have a functional role in improving acceptability of robots.

To derive a biolectrical signal we use a microbial fuel cell (MFC) as the robot's 'artificial gut'. An MFC generates a voltage from anaerobic respiration by electrogenic microbes feeding on organic matter [6].

3 Methods

We consider a social robot (Fig. 1) that interacts with a user. The answers to the robot's questions (*answers*) and orders given by the user (*orders*) are converted to numeric scores using sentiment analysis. These scores indicate the quality of interaction and range 0 (least positive) to 1 (most positive). In this study, we focus on the integration of the bioelectric signal and so keep orders and answers constant at 0.5. Additionally, the robot has an MFC 'artificial gut', that outputs a voltage that increases with the energy level of the MFC. The MFC voltage time series (22.4 days) was synthesized by concatenating four periods (each 5.6 days) of empirical data from previous MFC experiments.

Algorithm 1 shows our personality generation model. At time steps of 2 min the MFC voltage, *answers* score and *orders* score are sampled. At regular intervals (10.7 mins) the robot's history-dependent personality is updated. This involves first calculating happiness and stability scores based on the MFC voltage. These scores are combined with the *answers* and *orders* scores to calculate the robot's *personality*, which is represented as values in the range 0 to 1 for each of the Big Five personality traits (O, C, E, A, N). In this work, we use simple additive combinations of happiness, stability, order and answers scores to calculate the OCEAN values to maintain interpretability of the generation process.

Algorithm 1. Robot personality generation shown in pseudocode

---

1: **define empty arrays:** Data, Delta, Answers, Orders

2: **define functions:** mean, std: returns mean and standard deviation respectively

3: **variables equal to 0:** a, b, c, d, e, f, g, h, H, S, Delta[0], μ_{Dat}, σ_{Dat}, μ_{Del}, σ_{Del}

4: **for** i ← 0 to n **do**

5:   **read** voltage, order, answer   ▷ Read new empirical data and add to time series

6:   Data[i] ← voltage, Answers[i] ← answer, Orders[i] ← order

7:   **if** i ≠ 0 **then**

8:     Delta[i] ← (Data[i] - Data[i-1])

9:   **if** Data[i] > $(\mu_{Dat} + \sigma_{Dat})$ **then** ▷ Sort into bins a to d

10:     $a \leftarrow a + 1$

11:   **else if** $(\mu_{Dat} + \sigma_{Dat}) \geq$ Data[i] > μ_{Dat} **then**

12:     $b \leftarrow b + 1$

13:   **else if** $\mu_{Dat} \geq$ Data[i] > $(\mu_{Dat} - \sigma_{Dat})$ **then**

14:     $c \leftarrow c + 1$

15:   **else**

16:     $d \leftarrow d + 1$

17:   **if** Delta[i] > $(\mu_{Del} + \sigma_{Del})$ **then** ▷ Sort into bins e to h

18:     $e \leftarrow e + 1$

19:   **else if** $(\mu_{Del} + \sigma_{Del}) \geq$ Delta[i] > μ_{Del} **then**

20:     $f \leftarrow f + 1$

21:   **else if** $\mu_{Del} \geq$ Delta[i] > $(\mu_{Del} - \sigma_{Del})$ **then**

22:     $g \leftarrow g + 1$

23:   **else**

24:     $h \leftarrow h + 1$

25:   **if** i % interval = 1 **then**

26:     $H \leftarrow \frac{2a+b}{2a+b+c+2d}$, $S \leftarrow \frac{g+2h}{2e+f+g+2h}$ ▷ Happiness (mood) and Stability scores

27:     Ans ← mean(Answers), Ord ← mean (Orders)

28:     $O \leftarrow \frac{1}{3}H + \frac{2}{3}$Ans ▷ 'Big Five' traits (personality)

29:     $C \leftarrow S$

30:     $E \leftarrow \frac{2}{3}H + \frac{1}{3}$Ans

31:     $A \leftarrow \frac{1}{3}H + \frac{2}{3}$Ord

32:     $N \leftarrow \frac{2}{3}(1 - H) + \frac{1}{3}(1\text{-Ord})$

33:     $\mu_{Dat} \leftarrow$ mean(Data), $\mu_{Del} \leftarrow$ mean(Delta) ▷ Update time series mean

34:     $\sigma_{Dat} \leftarrow$ std(Data), $\sigma_{Del} \leftarrow$ std(Delta) ▷ Update time series std

---

4 Results and Discussion

We argue that the following features are desirable: (1) believable and varied personalities (2) predictable and unexpected behaviour, and (3) history-dependant personalities that are neither static, nor rapidly varying.

While full evaluation of our model is beyond the scope of this work, we believe our preliminary results demonstrate the potential of our approach. The MFC signal gives both an interpretable and unpredictable response to human interaction (feature 2). The voltage peaks in Fig. 2a correspond to the times at which the MFC fuel was replenished, but vary noticeably in amplitude. History-dependence (feature 3) can be seen in the evolution of voltage bands a, b, c, d.

The increasing voltage range covered by bands b and c reduces the likelihood that data points fall into bands a or d leading to variation in the early-phase of the generation process and convergence during the latter stages (Fig. 2b). The model output can be interpreted as generating a *believable* personality (feature 1) in that is distributed across the Big Five personality traits [5].

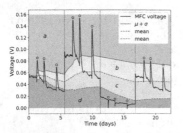

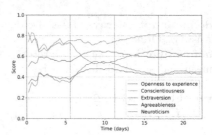

(a) MFC voltage data used to cal-   (b) Evolution of Big Five personality traits.
culate happiness, H.

Fig. 2. Time series of a) MFC data input to, and b) personality data output by, the model. Concatenated empirical data sets are distinguished by vertical lines.

Future work will extend our model by including explicit representation of metabolic state (mimicking the role of the brain in the gut-brain axis) and using sentiment analysis to score verbal interactions. We will also explore alternative representations of personality and translate these representations into embodied behaviours, closing the loop on the human-robot-interaction (Fig. 1).

5   Conclusion

This study shows for the first time, biohybrid robotic personality generation by translating a bioelectrical signal into a temporally evolving robotic personality. We believe our exploration of bio-hybrid systems and robot behaviour is a step towards wider acceptance of robots in the home, the workplace, and society.

References

1. Goetz, J., Kiesler, S.: Cooperation with a robotic assistant. In: CHI 2002 Extended Abstracts on Human Factors in Computing Systems, pp. 578–579 (2002)
2. Kusahara, M.: The art of creating subjective reality: an analysis of Japanese digital pets. Leonardo **34**(4), 299–302 (2001)
3. Man, K., Damasio, A.: Homeostasis and soft robotics in the design of feeling machines. Nat. Mach. Intell. **1**, 446–452 (2019)
4. Mou, Y., Shi, C., Shen, T., Xu, K.: A systematic review of the personality of robot: mapping its conceptualization, operationalization, contextualization and effects. Int. J. Hum.-Comput. Interact. **36**(6), 591–605 (2020)
5. Pervin, L.A., John, O.P.: Handbook of Personality. Theory and Research 2 (1999)

6. Philamore, H., Rossiter, J., Stinchcombe, A., Ieropoulos, I.: Row-bot: an energetically autonomous artificial water boatman. In: 2015 IEEE/RSJ International Conference on Intelligent Robots and Systems (IROS), pp. 3888–3893. IEEE (2015)
7. Johnson, K.V.A.: Gut microbiome composition and diversity are related to human personality traits. Hum. Microbiome J. **15**, 100069 (2020)

Load Feedback from a Dynamically Scaled Robotic Model of *Carausius Morosus* Middle Leg

William P. Zyhowski[1](✉), Sasha N. Zill[2], and Nicholas S. Szczecinski[1]

[1] West Virginia University, Morgantown, WV 26506, USA
wz00007@mix.wvu.edu
[2] Marshall University, Huntington, WV 25755, USA

Abstract. Load sensing is critical for walking behavior in animals, who have evolved a number of sensory organs and neural systems to improve their agility. In particular, insects measure load on their legs using campaniform sensilla (CS), sensory neurons in the cuticle of high-stress portions of the leg. Extracellular recordings from these sensors in a behaving animal are difficult to collect due to interference from muscle potentials, and some CS groups are largely inaccessible due to their placement on the leg. To better understand what loads the insect leg experiences and what sensory feedback the nervous system may receive during walking, we constructed a dynamically-scaled robotic model of the leg of the stick insect *Carausius morosus*. We affixed strain gauges in the same positions and orientations as the major CS groups on the leg, i.e., 3, 4, 6A, and 6B. The robotic leg was mounted to a vertically-sliding linear guide and stepped on a treadmill to simulate walking. Data from the strain gauges was run through a dynamic model of CS discharge developed in a previous study. Our experiments reveal stereotypical loading patterns experienced by the leg, even as its weight and joint stiffness is altered. Furthermore, our simulated CS strongly signal the beginning and end of stance phase, two key events in the coordination of walking.

Keywords: Campaniform sensilla · Insects · Dynamic scaling · Strain gauges · Legged locomotion · Robotics

1 Introduction

Locomotion is fundamentally an interaction with the environment, which is a challenge for animals and robots alike. Animals have evolved a wide array of sensory organs and neural control systems that give them an innate ability to solve this problem [1–3]. Robots, on the other hand, need to be meticulously designed to accomplish these feats. By constructing robotic models of animals, it may be possible to better understand how their sensors and nervous systems function and simultaneously build robots that leverage biological mechanisms to maneuver more capably.

Load sensing is critical for walking animals [1, 4]. Insects measure this load using campaniform sensilla (CS). CS are not simple sensors; in fact, they measure force in a highly dynamic way [5]. Due to their dynamics, CS are very sensitive to changes in force,

© The Author(s), under exclusive license to Springer Nature Switzerland AG 2022
A. Hunt et al. (Eds.): Living Machines 2022, LNAI 13548, pp. 128–139, 2022.
https://doi.org/10.1007/978-3-031-20470-8_14

including transient changes in the effect of body weight [6], movements of the substrate under their feet [7], and small variations in bending moments on each leg segment that naturally occur over the course of a step [5]. In a previous study, we made a CS model of how the forces on the leg are transduced into neural signals [8]. Related CS models describe how forces on the halteres of dipterans are transduced into signals [3]. Such models give insight into what neural signals the nervous system may receive due to the dynamic forces experienced as the animal moves through its environment.

Despite many insect-like robots having been built in the past few decades, few robots directly incorporate insect-like load sensing [9]. Some robots such as Octavio have applied animal-like walking control networks to drive walking through a combination of sensory feedback and central pattern generators [10]. Despite the success of this study, the robot had only rudimentary ground contact sensing via a toggle switch, meaning that the robot could not measure the dynamics of force over the course of the step. In contrast, other robots such as Hubodog2 [11] and Drosophibot [12] have implemented animal-like load sensing in the legs by mounting strain gauges to the leg segments. However, it can be difficult to tune the bias of the amplifiers to set a threshold to determine ground contact white ensuring the load signal does not saturate. We hypothesize that using our dynamic CS model as a filter for strain measurements in a robot will alleviate both of these issues. The model is very sensitive to changing loads, enhancing transitions between stance and swing, and its model adapts its output in response to a constant load, meaning that amplifier bias may be canceled out over time.

In this study, we investigate what dynamic load feedback the nervous system may experience while the leg makes contact with the ground, supports and propels the body, and then breaks contact with the ground. We hypothesize that the dynamics of the CS will accentuate increases in load at the initiation of stance while eliminating the others. We also hypothesize that these features are robust to changes in sensor configuration. For example, weight can be added to the leg and the servomotor's P gain can be changed without greatly affecting responses to increasing and decreasing load.

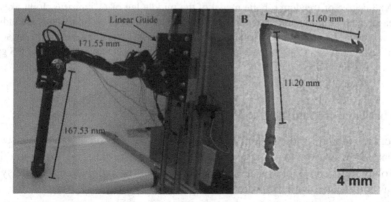

Fig. 1. A) Robotic model of the middle leg of *Carausius morosus* attached to linear guide. The linear guide can only move in the vertical direction (Z axis). As the leg steps on the treadmill, the linear guide is free to move, meaning that the leg must support its weight when stepping. B) A *Carausius morosus* middle leg for comparison to its biological counterpart.

2 Methods

2.1 Robotic Leg Construction

The robotic leg in Fig. 1 consists of three MX-28 dynamixel servomotors along with 3D printed parts, which were used to construct a 14.79:1 scale model with the same segmental proportions as the middle leg of the stick insect *Carausius morosus* (*C. morosus*) [13, 14]. Figure 2 shows the leg with the thorax-coxa (ThC), coxa-trochanter (CTr), and femur-tibia (FTi) joint axes labeled. The proximal servomotor (ThC) is attached to a linear guide to simulate the weight and movement of the insect body. Two strain gauge rosettes on the leg capture the strain data and are connected to operational amplifiers to boost the signal. Each rosette measures the transversal and axial strain of the leg segment. The location and orientation of the rosettes is comparable to the location and orientation of major CS groups on the stick insect leg: the proximal femur rosette measures axial (CS group 3) and transversal (CS group 4) strain, and the proximal tibia rosette measures axial (CS group 6B) and transversal (CS group 6A) strain [2, 7]. An OpenCM 9.04 microcontroller converts the analog amplified strain signal into a 12-bit digital signal that is sent to the control computer over a serial connection.

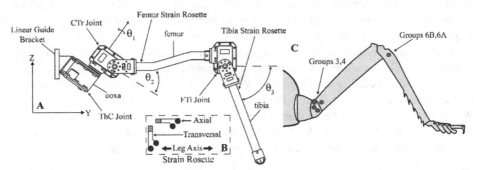

Fig. 2. A) 3 degree of freedom robotic model of the middle leg of *C. morosus*. Joint axes, joint angle measurements, and leg segments are labeled. The locations of strain rosettes are indicated. B) The inset shows the orientation of each strain rosette relative to the long axis of the leg segment on which it is mounted. C) An illustration of a *C. morosus* leg indicating locations of CS groups.

2.2 Robot Forward and Inverse Kinematics

The kinematic model for the system has the same degrees of freedom as the insect [13, 14]. Great care was taken to properly scale the kinematics of the *C. morosus* middle leg for the robot (values in Table 1). The kinematic spatial (i.e., global coordinate system) chain was constructed with the product of exponentials,

$$g_d = e^{\hat{\xi}_1 \theta_1} e^{\hat{\xi}_2 \theta_2} e^{\hat{\xi}_3 \theta_3} g_{st} \tag{1}$$

where θ_1 is the angle of the ThC joint, θ_2 is the angle of the CTr joint, and θ_3 is the angle of the FTi joint [15]. The matrix exponentials produce the augmented 4×4 matrix g_d,

, which contains the rotation matrix and coordinates of the end effector (i.e., the foot) in relation to the spatial reference frame. $g_{st}(0)$ describes the end effector in the leg's zero configuration, that is, when the leg is in its neutral posture. Each joint's impact on the end effector's position and orientation is described by the augmented matrix $e^{\hat{\xi}_n \theta_n}$. $\hat{\xi}_n$ represents the axis of rotation for the nth joint.

Table 1. Vectors of model parameters in zero configuration. ω is a unit vector in direction of twist, q is point on the axis of rotation (mm)

Zero Configuration Vectors			
	x	y	z
ω_1	0	$-\sin(37°)$	$-\cos(37°)$
ω_2	1	0	0
ω_3	1	0	0
q_1	0	63.35	17.30
q_2	0	91.39	19.62
q_3	0	228.41	-83.62
q_{end}	0	360.69	-183.28

The footpath was modeled and scaled after that of *C. morosus* [13]. To calculate the inverse kinematics, Newton-Raphson determined the necessary angles to achieve the footpath in Fig. 3. Because the leg has 3 non-parallel joint axes, there is a unique set of joint angles that places the foot in any particular 3D position in space.

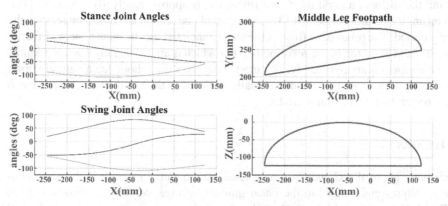

Fig. 3. Left graphs show stance and swing angles of robotic *C. morosus* middle leg (ThC upper, CTr middle, FTi lower) plotted against the x-coordinate of the foot in space as in [13]. The swing phase and stance phase each last 2 s. The right graphs show the projected scaled footpath of the *C. morosus*. The upper right graph is projected in the y-x plane, the lower right graph is projected in the z-x plane.

2.3 Robotic Control

Data was collected using a MATLAB script to command servomotor angles through the OpenCM 9.04 microcontroller acting as an intermediary. On a desktop computer, the MATLAB script solved the inverse kinematics problem to calculate angle commands for the servomotors that would generate the desired foot path. The script sent the angle commands over a serial connection to the OpenCM 9.04 microcontroller. The OpenCM broadcasted the angle commands to the servomotors in the leg, and then returned the current servomotor angles and strain gauge readings, converted from analog to a 12-bit digital value, to the desktop computer.

2.4 Treadmill and Dynamic Scaling

The robotic leg stepped on a treadmill to simulate pushing the body forward. Because the ThC servomotor was mounted to a linear guide which is a vertically-sliding carriage, the leg also supported the carriage's weight during each stance phase. The treadmill's speed was matched to the stepping of the leg. The treadmill speed was synced with the use of a calibrated tachometer.

To ensure that the robot is dynamically scaled to the insect, that is, that it experiences a similar balance of inertial, viscous, elastic, and gravitational forces, the stepping cycle of the robot must be scaled to its dynamics in the same way as the animal's. In particular, the cycle period needs to be proportional to the natural frequency of the leg oscillation in both the animal and the robot. Insects are quite small, and gravity does not affect them considerably; similarly, when the robot is powered on, the leg is supported against gravity. This means that the leg does not act like a pendulum, but like a spring and mass. As a result, the natural frequency depends on the elastic stiffness of the joints and the moment of inertia of their limbs. A *C. morosus* leg is approximately a 11 mg [13] slender rod and the stiffness around the femur tibia joint is approximately 10^{-6} Nm/rad [19]. This means the natural period is 0.132 s, so a step of one second is 6 times longer than the natural period. The robotic leg follows the same characteristic. Its main source of inertia is the moment of inertia of the servomotor rotor which is approximately 1×10^{-2} kgm^2, and the stiffness is approximately 1 Nm/rad. This gives the robotic leg a natural period of 0.63 s, so four seconds is the dynamically scaled step time of the robotic leg, also 6 times longer than the natural period.

3 Results

The robotic leg of the *C. morosus* completed 50 sequential steps in its baseline configuration (no weight added to the linear guide's carriage, default servomotor P gain) for Fig. 4. Data collected from each of the two strain gauge rosettes gave the axial and transversal strain of the femur and tibia. The geometry of the leg and orientation of the strain sensors gave a great deal of information about each other. The axial strain of the femur is the largest because this segment primarily supports the weight of the body, and it continues to increase after stance begins as it aligns the plane of the leg with gravity. As it rotates past the vertical orientation, the signal decreases. The transversal strain has about 1/3 the amplitude and the opposite sign of the axial strain, consistent with the Poisson's ratio of typical solid materials.

The model output in Fig. 5 shows that the responds of the femur axial CS (Group 3) greatly increased at the onset of stance. Once stance was half completed and strain began do decrease, Group3's response was silenced. The same situation was seen with tibia axial CS (Group 6B) and tibia transversal CS (Group6A), albeit on a smaller scale as strain is smaller for the tibia [14]. Note the peak CS discharges at the beginning and end of stance phase.

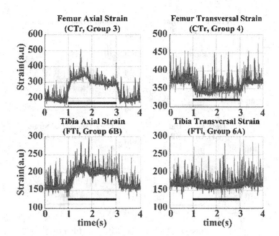

Fig. 4. Raw strain data from every strain gauge from 50 robot steps, with the average overlaid in red and stance phase represented by the black bar. Positive changes in values indicate compression; negative changes in values indicate tension. The Y axis has arbitrary units of strain (Color figure online).

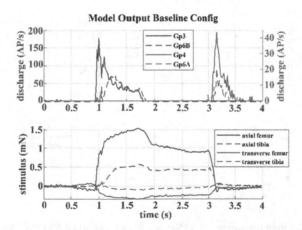

Fig. 5. Model CS output for mean of 50 steps in baseline configuration.

In Fig. 6, the leg walked 50 steps, with the linear guide weighed down with an extra 500 g. The shape of the strain for both the femur and tibia remained relatively unchanged from Fig. 4, except the amplitude increased. The model CS data in Fig. 7 also reflects what was seen in Fig. 5, with strong signaling at the beginning and end of stance phase. Group 3 was activated on the onset of stance then deactivated halfway through stance once the leg plane flipped orientation. Group 4 increased once the leg was unloaded, signaling that the stance phase had ended. Group 6B shows a similar pattern, with Group 6A activating at the end of stance. It should also be noted that the model response had a better signal-to-noise ratio as the strain increased. This was particularly evident in Groups 6A and 6B because the strain was relatively small compared to Groups 3 and 4.

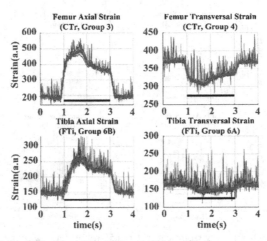

Fig. 6. Raw strain data of 50 steps with additional 500 g, with the average overlaid in red. Stance phase is represented by a black bar. Positive change in values indicate compression, negative change in values indicate tension. Y axis has arbitrary units of strain (Color figure online).

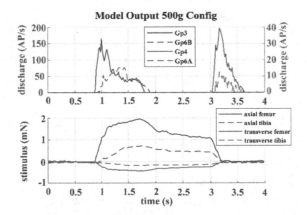

Fig. 7. Model CS output for a mean of 50 Steps with an additional 500 g (Color figure online).

Figure 8 includes an additional 50 leg steps but with 1000 g of extra weight. The amplitude of the strain on the tibia and femur increased further compared to previous loading conditions. The shape of the strain response remained approximately unchanged despite the large increase in weight. While the model CS responses in Fig. 9 are generally similar to past trials, the exception is Group 3, whose responses show large fluctuations in discharge over time. This is because the "ripple" in the load signal is amplified under larger weight, and the CS model is sensitive to changing loads.

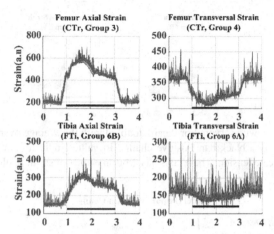

Fig. 8. Raw Strain data of 50 steps with additional 1000 g, with the overlay of average in red; stance phase is represented by a black bar; Positive change in values indicate compression, negative change in values indicate tension; Y axis has arbitrary units to signify strain (Color figure online).

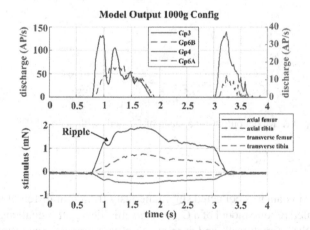

Fig. 9. Model output for mean of 50 Steps and an additional 1000 g

Data in Fig. 10 was collected after doubling the servomotor P gain, which approximately doubled the stiffness of the leg. No additional weight was added. Like the other configurations, Fig. 11 shows Group 3 activates at the start of stance and deactivates once the load decreases. Group 4 did the opposite. Group 6A and 6B followed suit, but at lower strain levels. It should also be noted that the increased stiffness helped reduce the bounce of the leg upon impact.

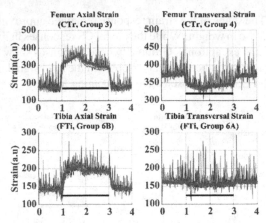

Fig. 10. Raw stain data with servomotor P gain doubled with the average overlaid in red. Stance phase is represented by a black bar. Positive change in values indicate compression; negative change in values indicate tension. The Y axis has arbitrary units of strain (Color figure online).

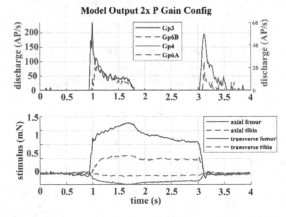

Fig. 11. Model output for a mean of 50 steps with doubled P gain

4 Discussion

In this study, strain data was collected simultaneously from four different locations on a dynamically scaled robotic model of a *C. morosus* middle leg. It is challenging to collect such data from the animal itself, and even successful attempts at recording from CS in behaving animals have been limited in scope [6, 7, 17]. With this robotic model, we can estimate the sensory signals that the nervous system may receive from all over the leg.

We applied a dynamic CS model [5] to filter the average strain data. This filter accentuates the dynamic changes in force that occur when stance phase begins and ends. These are critical events to the timing of stepping across the legs [18, 19]. Since the timing of load is so important to the coordination of the stepping of an insect's multiple legs [1, 4, 18, 19], a robot that employs such filtering may have improved coordination compared to a robot that does not. We will explore this idea in future studies by implementing this dynamic CS model in a closed-loop walking controller for a six-legged robot. We hypothesize that dynamic load sensing will produce interleg coordination that is robust to changes in body weight or actuator properties.

Our study has several limitations. For example, in Fig. 5 the tibia transversal strain was quite small, resulting in a poor signal-to-noise ratio. However, this is unsurprising because the tibia is nearly aligned with gravity during walking, meaning that it experiences very little bending moment. Furthermore, due to the Poisson Effect, the transversal sensor only experiences about 1/3 the strain of the axial sensor [7]. Another complication was the bouncing of the leg at the start of stance phase for the baseline configuration. It seems unlikely that the animal would experience similar bouncing, because it actively grips the substrate. Changing the weight of the body or stiffness of the servomotors greatly reduced the bounce, suggesting that this bounce was due to resonance in the leg's mechanics. In the future, we plan to add an active tarsus with which to grip the substrate, which may reduce bounce. We also plan to further explore the effects of the leg's material properties on the sensory signals.

4.1 Comparison to Biomechanics and Neurophysiology

The linear guide was a critical part of the experiment because it allowed for the recording of the leg strain due to the leg's and linear guide's weight and not the strain of the leg pushing against a fixed bracket. As a result, the posture of the leg could change but the applied force was nearly constant, just as in walking. Preliminary experiments in stick insects suggest that CS respond differently between the controlled force, uncontrolled posture condition as we tested in this study and the constrained posture, uncontrolled force condition that is typical for experiments characterizing CS responses [5, 20–22]. Despite our robot only being one leg, we may be capturing important features of leg loading, that is, controlling the force but not constraining the posture.

The model could reliably distinguish the start and end of stance phase. This is evidenced by high-amplitude discharge from Groups 3 and 6B at the start of stance with relatively invariant amplitude and silencing when the force decreased. Groups 4 and 6A showed the opposite trend, with high-amplitude discharge at the start of swing and silencing by the end of swing. These results mimic the active signaling of unloading that has been described in insect CS [1, 6].

It is important to note that our model emulates the characteristics of the larger CS rather than the smaller, more tonic CS. In ramp and hold tests, tonic receptors show more prolonged discharges and incomplete adaptation to sustained loads [20, 21]. This could produce discharges throughout the stance phase, unlike Groups 3 and 6B in our robotic model. In addition, the discharges of receptors of opposite orientations (i.e., Group 3 vs. Group 4, Group 6B vs. 6A) are completely reciprocal in tests using ramp and hold force application and release in the leg plane. Similar reciprocal patterns of activity are seen both in the model simulations and in biological experiments in partially restrained animals showing "single leg stepping" [22].

The results of the robotic leg and model suggest new experiments in the biological system that could test this interpretation. Although technically challenging, it would be beneficial to examine the responses of the tibial sensilla to forces applied to the leg using the waveforms of strain seen in the present study, including those obtained when additional loads must be supported.

4.2 Application to Robotics

The type of dynamic sensing presented in this study may improve the practicality of strain gauges in legged robots by making it easier to calibrate the sensors. This is important because simplifying calibration may reduce the burden of designing robots with many redundant sensors as seen in animals [9, 13]. We hypothesize that robots would be more graceful if they utilized more sensory feedback from additional modalities, as animals do [13, 23]. More robust sensory filtering may eliminate the need for careful calibration, removing one engineering hurdle to building robots with orders of magnitude more sensors.

Acknowledgments. This work was supported by NSF IIS 2113028 as part of the Collaborative Research in Computational Neuroscience Program. A special thanks to Clarissa Goldsmith for providing the necessary experimental data on the MX-28 dynamixel servomotors.

References

1. Zill, S.N., Schmitz, J., Büschges, A.: Load sensing and control of posture and locomotion. Arthropod Struct. Dev. **33**, 273–286 (2004). https://doi.org/10.1016/j.asd.2004.05.005
2. Delcomyn, F., Nelson, M.E., Cocatre-Zilgien, J.H.: Sense organs of insect legs and the selection of sensors for agile walking robots. Int. J. Rob. Res. **15**, 113–127 (1996). https://doi.org/10.1177/027836499601500201
3. Mohren, T.L., Daniel, T.L., Eberle, A.L., Reinhall, P.G., Fox, J.L.: Coriolis and centrifugal forces drive haltere deformations and influence spike timing. J. R. Soc. Interface **16**(153), 20190035 (2019). https://doi.org/10.1098/rsif.2019.0035
4. Duysens, J., Clarac, F., Cruse, H.: Load-regulating mechanisms in gait and posture: comparative aspects. Physiol. Rev. **80**, 83–133 (2000)
5. Zill, S.N., Dallmann, C.J., Szczecinski, N., Büschges, A., Schmitz, J.: Evaluation of force feedback in walking using joint torques as "naturalistic" stimuli. J. Neurophysiol. **126**, 227–248 (2021). https://doi.org/10.1152/jn.00120.2021
6. Keller, B.R., Duke, E.R., Amer, A.S., Zill, S.N.: Tuning posture to body load: Decreases in load produce discrete sensory signals in the legs of freely standing cockroaches. J. Comp. Physiol. A. **193**(8), 881–891 (2007). https://doi.org/10.1007/s00359-007-0241-y
7. Ridgel, A., Frazier, F., Zill, S.: Dynamic responses of tibial campaniform sensilla studied by substrate displacement in freely moving cockroaches. J. Comp. Physiol. A **187**(5), 405–420 (2001). https://doi.org/10.1007/s003590100213
8. Szczecinski, N.S., Dallmann, C.J., Quinn, R.D., Zill, S.N.: A computational model of insect campaniform sensilla predicts encoding of forces during walking. Bioinspir. Biomim. **16**, 065001 (2021). https://doi.org/10.1088/1748-3190/ac1ced
9. Manoonpong, P., et al.: Insect-inspired robots: bridging biological and artificial systems. Sensors **21**(22), 7609 (2021). https://doi.org/10.3390/s21227609
10. von Twickel, A., Hild, M., Siedel, T., Patel, V., Pasemann, F.: Neural control of a modular multi-legged walking machine: Simulation and hardware. Robot. Auton. Syst. **60**(2), 227–241 (2012). https://doi.org/10.1016/j.robot.2011.10.006

11. Sim, O., Jung, T., Lee, K.K., Oh, J., Oh, J.-H.: Position/torque hybrid control of a rigid, high-gear ratio quadruped robot. Adv. Robot. **32**(18), 969–983 (2018). https://doi.org/10.1080/016 91864.2018.1516162
12. Goldsmith, C.A., Szczecinski, N.S., Quinn, R.D.: Neurodynamic modeling of the fruit fly Drosophila melanogaster. Bioinspir. Biomim. **15**(6), 065003 (2020). https://doi.org/10.1088/ 1748-3190/ab9e52
13. Cruse, H., Bartling, C.: Movement of joint angles in the legs of a walking insect, *Carausius morosus*. J. Insect Physiol. **41**, 761–771 (1995). https://doi.org/10.1016/0022-1910(95)000 32-P
14. Theunissen, L.M., Bekemeier, H.H., Dürr, V.: Comparative whole-body kinematics of closely related insect species with different body morphology. J. Exp. Biol. **218**, 340–352 (2015). https://doi.org/10.1242/jeb.114173
15. Lynch, K.M., Park, F.C.: Modern Robotics: Mechanics, Planning, and Control, 1st edn. Cambridge University Press, USA (2017)
16. Hooper, S.L., et al.: Neural control of unloaded leg posture and of leg swing in stick insect, cockroach, and mouse differs from that in larger animals. J. Neurosci. **29**(13), 4109–4119 (2009). https://doi.org/10.1523/JNEUROSCI.5510-08.2009
17. Noah, J.A., Quimby, L., Frazier, S.F., Zill, S.N.: Sensing the effect of body load in legs: Responses of tibial campaniform sensilla to forces applied to the thorax in freely standing cockroaches. J. Comp. Physiol. A **190**(3), 201–215 (2004). https://doi.org/10.1007/s00359-003-0487-y
18. Cruse, H.: What mechanisms coordinate leg movement in walking arthropods? Trends Neurosci. **13**, 15–21 (1990). https://doi.org/10.1016/0166-2236(90)90057-H
19. Dallmann, C.J., Hoinville, T., Du, V., Schmitz, J.: A load-based mechanism for inter-leg coordination in insects. **284** (2017). https://doi.org/10.1098/rspb.2017.1755
20. Zill, S., Büschges, A., Schmitz, J.: Encoding of force increases and decreases by tibial campaniform sensilla in the stick insect, *Carausius morosus*. J. Comp. Physiol. A **197**, 851–867 (2011)
21. Zill, S., Schmitz, J., Chaudhry, S., Büschges, A.: Force encoding in stick insect legs delineates a reference frame for motor control. J. Neurophysiol. **108**, 1453–1472 (2012)
22. Zill, S., Chaudhry, S., Büschges, A., Schmitz, J.: Directional specificity and encoding of muscle forces and loads by stick insect tibial campaniform sensilla, including receptors with round cuticular caps. Arthr. Struct. Dev. **42**, 455–467 (2013)
23. Dallmann, C.J., Karashchuk, P., Brunton, B.W., Tuthill, J.C.: A leg to stand on: computational models of proprioception. Curr. Opin. Physiol. **22**, 100426 (2021). https://doi.org/10.1016/j. cophys.2021.03.001

A Computational Approach for Contactless Muscle Force and Strain Estimations in Distributed Actuation Biohybrid Mesh Constructs

Saul Schaffer$^{(\boxtimes)}$ ⓘ, Janice Seungyeon Lee, Lameck Beni,
and Victoria A. Webster-Wood ⓘ

Carnegie Mellon University, 5000 Forbes Ave, Pittsburgh, PA 15213, USA
biorobot@cmu.edu, vwebster@andrew.cmu.edu
http://engineering.cmu.edu/borg

Abstract. Biological muscle tissue can adapt to mechanical stimuli such as strain and become stronger. While this property has been explored for single, independent muscle actuators, it is still not well understood for more complex, distributed actuation architectures, which are needed for more complex biohybrid robotic systems. This study presents a computational approach for contactless methods to estimate individual muscle actuator strains and individual muscle forces on a distributed-actuator biohybrid mesh substrate. The methods presented in this work estimate the strain each muscle experiences as the substrate is stretched by creating a finite element model of our distributed muscle actuator biohybrid mesh, taking 79.8±51.9 s to compute. Additionally, two contactless methods for muscle force estimation based on patterned substrate deformation are presented and compared: 1) Response Surface optimization, and 2) Direct Optimization. Both force estimation methods extract distributed muscle forces based on global substrate deformations. The Response Surface optimization resulted in a prediction error of $321 \pm 219 \,\mu m$ with a runtime after model creation of 26 ± 1.3 s. The Direct Optimization method resulted in a prediction error of $0 \,\mu m$ but took a long, highly-variable runtime of 663.4 ± 918.5 s. Directions for further improvement are discussed. Towards experimental validation of the outlined computational tools, a biaxial stretcher was constructed, and the ability to command desired displacements with the apparatus was characterized. The biaxial stretching platform achieved an average precision error of $3.10 \pm 5.92\%$ and $5.34 \pm 2.38\%$ for the x- and y-bars, respectively. Our methods aim to fill a critical gap in the design and analysis capabilities available to biohybrid robotics researchers. These preliminary estimation methods indicate the feasibility of our contactless muscle strain and muscle force estimation paradigm, which will be used to inform future *in vitro* experiments.

Keywords: Biohybrid · Distributed actuation · Mesh · Biohybrid muscle training · Computational tool

ⓒ The Author(s), under exclusive license to Springer Nature Switzerland AG 2022
A. Hunt et al. (Eds.): Living Machines 2022, LNAI 13548, pp. 140–151, 2022.
https://doi.org/10.1007/978-3-031-20470-8_15

1   Introduction

Soft robots with bioinspired distributed actuation schemes show great promise for tasks that require navigating tight spaces. Using their high number of degrees of freedom, systems like the MIT Meshworm [25] and the CWRU Meshworm [6, 13] are able to contort their structures to squeeze through otherwise inaccessible spaces, with promising use cases in pipe inspection [10] as well as search and rescue and medicine. However, robots built with traditional materials are limited in how far they can be scaled down, as there is a lack of soft microactuators available to drive sufficiently small, soft systems [23,30].

Fortunately, biological muscle actuators are able to operate at significantly smaller scales than those achievable with current synthetic actuators [23]. Additionally, muscle actuators can endow robotic systems with desirable capabilities such as high compliance [16,30], self-healing [21], and biocompatibility [23,30]. Using muscle tissue as an actuator, researchers have demonstrated inchworm locomotion [7,28], jellyfish [19], ray-like [17], and fish swimming [14], as well as rudimentary manipulation [16]. Using a biohybrid paradigm, researchers could develop trainable, behaviorally flexible, biocompatible systems that could adapt to dynamic environments beyond the lab. Long-term applications of such systems include medical applications, such as robotic stents (Fig. 1d–e) that are able to travel inside a patient's blood vessels with earthworm-inspired peristaltic locomotion and deploy themselves at the site of arterial blockages.

While impressive, the capabilities of biohybrid robots—those that leverage both living and synthetic materials—remain much less sophisticated than traditional robots. One reason for this is that muscle actuators adapt to their environment, which means they will change their properties during use. Such adaptation makes the modeling and design of complex biohybrid systems quite challenging [23,30]. One such example of adaptation is seen when muscle actuators experience tensile strain either through activation or external stretching. Under such loading, muscles become stronger, producing more force [8,11,15,18,20,22,26]. While this property of muscle is well known, this relationship between the strain the muscle experiences and the resulting increase in force they are able to produce in distributed multi-actuator systems is not well understood and has led to the state-of-the-art in biohybrid robotics being low degree-of-freedom, lab-chained devices [16,23,30]. However, just as in synthetic robots, distributed actuation in biohybrid robots has great promise for future applications.

Mesh-based biohybrid architectures (Fig. 1a–c) can serve as a platform to study muscle adaptability in distributed actuation biohybrid systems, an important step in the development of more functional, complex biohybrid systems. However, the strains muscle actuators would experience in a distributed architecture, like the mesh substrate illustrated in Fig. 1, are challenging to measure directly, as are the forces the muscle actuators produce. These challenges arise from the fragility of the muscle actuators, their low force output, and their adaptation to the mechanical stimulus present in the muscle's environment [23].

To study the effects of exercise in biohybrid distributed actuation architectures, there is a need to know the strains individual muscles experience on a

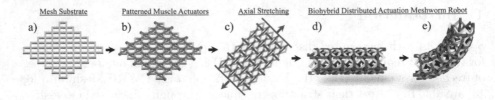

Fig. 1. Concept of distributed actuation biohybrid meshworm. **a)** Mesh substrate. **b)** Muscles patterned on the substrate, forming a 2D biohybrid distributed actuation construct. **c)** Biohybrid construct subjected to strain exercise training. **d)** 2D construct is wrapped into biohybrid meshworm robot. **e)** Biohybrid meshworm robot bending through selective activation of the muscle actuators patterned on the substrate.

stretched mesh (Fig. 1c). Due to the mesh's anisotropic deformation and loading conditions, individual muscles on the same mesh will experience different amounts of strain depending on where they are located. Previous studies have shown muscle maturation is sensitive to this strain, with muscles that experience more strain becoming stronger as a result [20]. Therefore, understanding the experienced strain of each muscle on the mesh substrate is critical for elucidating the effects of strain loading on muscle force development.

A second critical factor for studying the effects of exercise on a biohybrid distributed actuation system is the output force of individual muscles. The computational estimation methods presented here are designed to enable future *in vitro* experiments investigating the relationship between muscle strain and muscle force. As such, the material models, geometries, and boundary conditions are all reflections of what will be embodied in those experiments. It is also important that these computational tools be efficient and accurate so that they can be used to aid future researchers in designing more complex biohybrid systems.

This work presents a set of computational tools for estimating strains experienced and forces produced by distributed muscle actuators patterned on a biohybrid mesh substrate. The first section details a contactless method for estimating muscle strain on a stretched mesh. The second section details and compares two approaches to contactless force estimation, which will equip future *in vitro* experiments with the ability to characterize the relationship between experienced muscle strain during maturation and increased mature muscle force production. Lastly, we showcase preliminary work towards physical experiments validating our computational tools in the form of characterizing a biaxial stretcher.

2   Methods

To address the need for contactless strain and force estimation for distributed actuator biohybrid mesh-based systems (Fig. 2a), a suite of computational methods were developed. These methods were created to supplement future *in vitro* experiments by quantifying the relationship between muscle strain and muscle force on a distributed actuation system using optimization tools in ANSYS

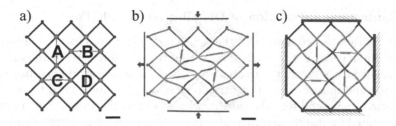

Fig. 2. a) Mesh substrate *(blue)* with patterned muscle actuators A-D *(grey springs)* connecting adjacent nodes *(green dots)* of the mesh. **b)** Loading conditions for mesh substrate when stretched, implemented in strain estimation method. Mesh deforms from external stretching loads. **c)** Loading conditions for force estimation methods. Mesh construct deforms under action of the muscles contracting, mesh is fixed on all sides. All mesh deformations are to scale, and all scale bars are 5 mm. (Color figure online)

Workbench 2021 R2 (Canonsburg, PA, USA). For this preliminary study, the mesh substrate is assigned an elastic modulus of 250 kPa and a Poisson's ratio of 0.499, as an idealized linear elastic model of collagen, a common structural biomaterial [12] used in biohybrid robotics [29]. Furthermore, a mesh convergence study was conducted, resulting in the selection of an element size of 400 μm (13,441 elements). Subsequently, the finite element mesh was automatically generated in ANSYS using Program Controlled element order and triangular surface mesher. Simulations were performed with Large Deflections enabled and Solver Type set to "Direct".

2.1 Contactless Estimation of Distributed Muscle Strain

To understand the effect of muscle strain on muscle force, it is critical to quantify the strain experienced by muscles as the substrate on which they are patterned is stretched (Fig. 2b). The stretch loading conditions of the construct were determined by the capabilities of a modified open-source biaxial stretcher [26]. We hypothesized that the strain experienced by the muscles is not a constant scalar multiple of the stretch imposed on the mesh. Instead, we posit that the strains experienced by the patterned muscles depend not only on the stretch imposed on the mesh but also on the muscle alignment to the stretch orientation, as well as the distance the muscles are placed from the center of the mesh. To test this hypothesis, a finite element model that tracks the relative displacement between mesh nodes (Fig. 2a) corresponding to muscle attachment points was developed. As the construct was subjected to a prescribed external displacement load (Fig. 2b), the muscles stretched and shrank depending on their location and orientation on the substrate. The strain estimations for each potential muscle actuator was implemented by estimating the strain of negligibly soft springs ($k_{spring} < 10^{-14}\,\mu\text{N/mm}$) attached between these nodes. As the nodes moved relative to each other, these virtual strain gauges enabled tracking of the strain a muscle actuator would have experienced if patterned between those nodes.

2.2 Contactless Estimation of Distributed Muscle Force

Equipped with a tool to determine the strain individual muscles experience on a stretched mesh construct, a method for estimating the forces those muscles produce is needed to ascertain the relationship between muscle strain loading during maturation and muscle force. Potential force estimation tools need to meet two key criteria to be useful for this endeavor. First, the method should estimate the force generated by distributed muscle actuators *in vitro* without physically contacting the muscles. This is because removing the muscles from the environment in which they are grown to measure their force has the chance to damage the muscle and/or change how the muscle might have performed if left *in situ*. Furthermore, any additional mechanical contact with the mesh during culture may alter the loading condition experienced by the muscles. Secondly, a useful force estimation method needs to allow for multiple muscle forces to be estimated simultaneously, especially when these muscles are mechanically coupled, as in a distributed actuation mesh (Fig. 1a–c). One such approach to estimating muscle forces that satisfies these criteria is to have the substrate on which the muscles are patterned act as a force gauge. By optically quantifying the deformation of the substrate under the action of the muscles patterned on it, we hypothesize that we can estimate the forces those patterned muscles are producing. Presented here are two computational methods based on this approach, namely Response Surface Optimization and Direct Optimization. All the mesh deformations described here were generated from a finite element model of the system with assumed muscle forces. However, in an experimental setup, mesh deformation estimations would be found by taking optical images of the biohybrid construct and using digital image correlation methods [27] to estimate the mesh deformation under the action of the muscles. The possible muscle forces used for each actuator was 0–8,000 μN, which is within the range of actuator forces expected from the literature from a muscle of 0.4 mm thick and 5 mm wide [7,9,18,21,24]. As the goal of these estimation methods is to become fast and accurate tools for distributed actuation biohybrid robot design and analysis, computational runtime was recorded for all methods, both in method setup or training and method implementation.

Response Surface Optimization Force Estimation. The first method tested for estimating muscle forces from mesh deformation was centered around creating a continuous response surface mapping from patterned muscle forces to mesh deformation (Fig. 3). Once the response surface was established, a multi-objective optimization problem was set up that searches on the response surface for a muscle force set that produces a mesh deformation closest to a specific input mesh deformation. With this approach, mesh deformations were input to the Response Surface optimization method, which would output its optimal estimation for the corresponding muscle forces. The response surface was trained with 200 sets of input muscle forces for muscles A–D (Fig. 2a) and generated using the Genetic Aggregation algorithm available in the ANSYS DesignXplorer suite [2]. In brief, Genetic Aggregation uses a genetic algorithm to configure, generate, evaluate, and evolve populations of response surfaces, drawing from the

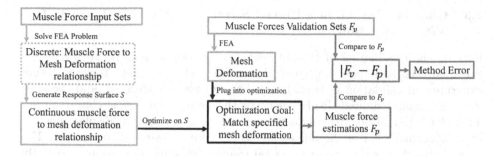

Fig. 3. Flow diagrams for Response Surface Optimization method: Generate response surface *(yellow)*, search *(black)* for optimal muscle forceS given a deformation *(green)*. (Color figure online)

set of response surface types available in ANSYS (e.g. Full 2nd-Order Polynomials, Non-Parametric Regression, and Kriging). The fitness of a given response surface was determined in part by the fidelity of the response surface to data it is representing. Genetic Aggregation was selected as it is more reliable than the other response surface generation algorithms, while taking more time [5]. Once the response surface was generated, the Multi-Objective Genetic Algorithm (MOGA) was selected as the goal-driven optimization method to find muscle force estimation sets. This method generates populations of muscle force sets and evaluates their outputs on the response surface with a fitness function [3], iteratively improving the muscle force set estimations by subsequently generating evolved populations through cross-over and mutation of the fittest estimations [4]. MOGA converged when the mean and standard deviation of the output parameters of successive populations were within 2%.

Direct Optimization Force Estimation. An alternate approach to the Response Surface method is to perform Direct Optimization (Fig. 4). Rather than generating a response surface, Direct Optimization directly implements MOGA, solving the finite element problem for guesses of muscle force sets that iteratively reducing the error between the input mesh deformation and the finite element solution mesh deformation. MOGA for Direct Optimization also converged when the mean and standard deviation of the output parameters of successive populations were within 2%.

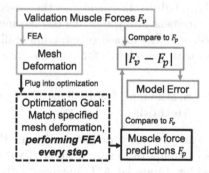

Fig. 4. Direct optimization method: search *(black)* for muscle force values given a deformation *(green)*. Method error is quantified *(blue)*. The dashed block is the most computationally expensive. (Color figure online)

2.3   Characterization of a Biaxial Stretching Platform Towards *In Vitro* Validation

Experimental validation of the outlined computational tools requires a physical apparatus to impose known strains on a mesh construct. Towards future experimental validation, a biaxial stretcher [26] was constructed, and the ability to command desired displacements with the apparatus was characterized. This characterization was conducted by analyzing the actual displacement of each attachment bar of the biaxial stretcher given a desired displacement. The biaxial stretcher is attached to a metal frame with a camera mounted directly above the stretcher (Fig. 7a). This biaxial stretcher has four attachment bars, two that move in the x-axis and two in the y-axis (Fig. 7b). These bars move an equal distance away or towards each other, creating a stretching or contracting motion. The stretcher is controlled by gcode on a Duet WiFi board (Duet3D). During operation, the camera records 15 s of the bar oscillations for a given displacement. Five commanded displacement were tested: 5, 10, 15, and 20 mm. To facilitate motion tracking, labeled dots were mounted on each attachment bar. The actual displacements of each bar were then determined using the "Tracker" software [1]. It was noted that the displacements commanded in gcode differed from the displacements achieved by the bars of the apparatus. Thus, we developed a method of generating adjustment ratios to achieve the desired displacements. Two adjustment ratios approaches were tested, uniform and displacement-specific ratio values. The uniform ratio was found using the polyfit() function from MATLAB (MathWorks, Natick, MA, USA) with $n = 1$ for each of the four attachment bars and averaging for x- and y-axis independently. The displacement-specific ratio was found by averaging the value from each of the two bars in the x- and y-axis, respectively. We adjusted the input displacement values by dividing the identified ratio value when writing the gcode that commands the biaxial stretcher. The difference in the actual displacement and desired displacement was then used to adjust the gcode to match the input displacement and the actual displacement. The remaining deviation at each displacement was measured experimentally using both adjustment ratios, and the ratio with lower error for each displacement was determined for further use.

2.4   Statistical Analysis of Contactless Force and Strain Estimation Methods

For each muscle force estimation method, performance was calculated for 10 sets of computationally generated validation muscle force sets, where each set considered muscles A–D independently (Fig. 2a). A one-way ANOVA was conducted to determine if there was a difference in force estimation error between individual muscles (A, B, C, D) for the Response Surface method. Additionally, a one-way ANOVA was conducted to compare the force estimation error between the Response Surface and Direct Optimization methods, aggregating muscle force estimation errors across muscles. Statistical significance was determined by $p < 0.001$. All analysis was performed in MATLAB.

3 Results and Discussion

3.1 Muscle Strain Estimation

As hypothesized, the muscle strain estimation method showed a relationship between *i)* the muscle orientation relative to stretch direction and *ii)* muscle placement on the muscle strain. For each muscle, maximum strain was achieved when maximum positive stretch was applied in the direction of the muscle's orientation and maximum compressive displacement – 'negative stretch' – was applied perpendicular to that orientation (Fig. 5). In future *in vitro* experiments, this negative stretch would result in the unloading of those muscles. Additionally, we found that muscles placed in the center of the mesh would experience more strain than elsewhere. Each muscle strain estimation took 79.8±51.9 s to simulate a set of four muscles, with $n = 10$.

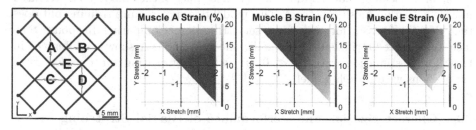

Fig. 5. Strain experienced by individual muscle actuators subjected to biaxial stretching, where positive stretch indicates tension. Plots for Muscles A and B (shown) are the same as Muscles D and C (not shown), respectively. Maximum strain values for Muscles A, B, C, D and E are 19.48%, 19.47%, 19.60%, 19.52%, and 28.13%, respectively. Color bar unit is percent strain.

3.2 Muscle Force Estimation

To evaluate the performance of the muscle force estimation methods, we generated mesh deformations from validation muscle force sets that were not used in Response Surface generation. The force estimation methods were used to estimate what forces were required to generate those deformations. Force estimation method error was calculated for 10 sets of muscle forces by taking the magnitude of the difference between the force estimations and the

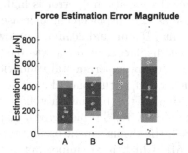

Fig. 6. Force estimation error for four muscle actuators on a substrate. Error is the absolute value of the difference of the model's force estimations and force value of the validation point. Mean value *(red line)*, one standard deviation from the mean *(dark grey region)*, 95% t-interval for mean *(light grey)*. (Color figure online)

forces originally used for the validation simulations.

Response Surface Performance. The Response Surface method had an error of 321 ± 219 µN and a maximum error of 913 µN (Fig. 6). One-way ANOVA showed no statistically significant difference between the force estimation error of different muscles ($p = 0.555$). This model takes days to train on 200 force input sets, but 79.8 ± 51.9 s for each force set estimation, with four muscles per set.

Direction Optimization Performance. The Direct Optimization method had an average and maximum error of 0 µN. This occurred because the method could keep updating its estimation of muscle forces until the resulting mesh deformation matched the input mesh deformation exactly. If this model were evaluated on *in vitro* measurements of mesh deformation, we would expect it to have some error arising from the discrepancies between the mechanics captured in the finite element model and the actual mechanics of the embodied distributed muscle actuation mesh construct. This model does not require training but does take 663.4 ± 918.5 s for each force set estimation. Comparing Response Surface and Direct Optimization methods, one-way ANOVA shows a difference in their force estimation error ($p \ll 0.001$) when aggregating the muscles' force estimations within each model.

3.3   Characterization and Performance of Biaxial Stretching Platform

Using the experimentally identified adjustment ratio to more closely achieve desired displacements, our biaxial stretching platform achieved an average positioning error of $3.10 \pm 5.92\%$ and $5.34 \pm 2.38\%$ for the x- and y-axis, respectively. The uniform adjustment value was used for short displacements (5, 10) and the displacement-specific adjustment was used for longer displacements (15, 20). The average relative positioning error is higher for shorter displacements and tends to decrease as the displacement increases (Fig. 7c). The error value for higher displacements, 15 mm and 20 mm, had low displacement error, of less than 2.5%. The highest displacement error was 0.64 mm for the y-bar at 20 mm displacement. Since future experimental validations involve using displacements values in this higher range, the biaxial stretching platform performance is promising. The precision of the biaxial stretcher was also characterized, as it is important to know how repeatable a given displacement can be achieved. Over a ten second trial, the displacement oscillation maintains a consistent movement profile (Fig. 7d), which is an important requirement for future validation of the computational tools. Table 1 details this repeatability, showcasing low standard deviations for the system across all commanded displacements.

Table 1. Mean ± standard deviation of measured displacements for four commanded displacements.

Commanded (mm)	Measured (mm, x-bars)	Measured (mm, y-bars)
5 mm	4.75 ± 0.17	5.03 ± 0.10
10 mm	10.22 ± 0.34	10.53 ± 0.14
15 mm	15.08 ± 0.33	14.87 ± 0.18
20 mm	19.78 ± 0.12	19.84 ± 0.37

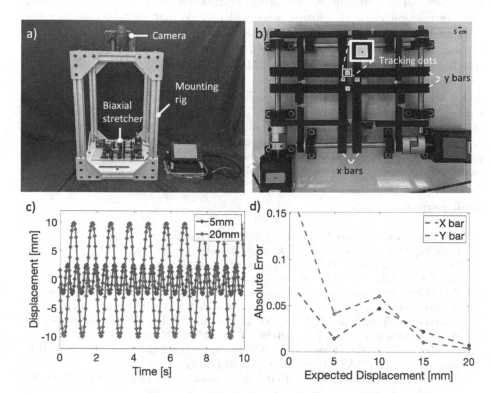

Fig. 7. a) Mounting rig housing biaxial stretcher and camera. **b)** Four tracked points on each attachment bar of the biaxial stretcher. **c)** Representative plots of displacement vs time for biaxial stretcher y-bar. **d)** Plot of the absolute error ratio vs displacement for x- and y-bars.

4   Conclusion

The work presented here suggests that our computational tools can achieve contactless strain and force estimation of distributed muscle actuators patterned on a mesh substrate based on mesh deformation. We show that the placement and orientation of muscle actuators on a stretched mesh substrate affect the strain those muscles experience. We also present two methods for extracting force estimations from distributed muscle actuators patterned on a mesh substrate. The first method, Response Surface Optimization, outputs force estimations quickly after model training, but has high error between its estimations and the computationally generated validation force sets. The second method, Direct Optimization, generates force estimations approximately 8 times slower, but provides more precise estimations. Towards validation of the estimation approaches, an experimental platform was constructed that can apply known deformations to a polymer mesh and will feature known forces applied by springs as analogs for muscle forces. To improve the strain estimation method—as well as both force estimation methods—future work will include materials testing to refine the material model of the mesh substrate to be more representative of collagen. Following validation, these methods will support *in vitro* experiments towards the design and fabrication of a biohybrid meshworm robot.

Acknowledgements. This material is based on work supported by a Carnegie Mellon University (CMU) Dean's Fellowship as well as National Science Foundation Graduate Research Fellowship Program under grant No. DGE1745016 and by the National Science Foundation CAREER award program (grant no. ECCS-2044785). The authors would also like to acknowledge Ian Turner for his work on design and assembly of the camera mounting rig and Brian Bock for helpful comments on the manuscript.

References

1. Tracker Video Analysis Tool. https://physlets.org/tracker/
2. Designxplorer user guide (2019). https://ansyshelp.ansys.com/
3. Genetic aggregation (2020). https://ansyshelp.ansys.com/
4. MOGA Workflow MOGA Steps to Generate a New Population (2020)
5. Ben Salem, M., Roustant, O., Gamboa, F., Tomaso, L.: Universal prediction distribution for surrogate models. Soc. Ind. Appl. Math. **5**, 1086–1109 (2017)
6. Boxerbaum, A.S., Shaw, K.M., Chiel, H.J., Quinn, R.D.: Continuous wave peristaltic motion in a robot. Int. J. Robot. Res. **31**(3), 302–318 (2012)
7. Cvetkovic, C., et al.: Three-dimensionally printed biological machines powered by skeletal muscle. PNAS **11**(28), 10125–10130 (2014)
8. Donnelly, K., Khodabukus, A., Philp, A., Deldicque, L., Dennis, R.G., Baar, K.: A novel bioreactor for stimulating skeletal muscle in vitro. Tissue Eng. Part C Methods **16**(4), 711–718 (2010)
9. Hinds, S., Bian, W., Dennis, R.G., Bursac, N.: The role of extracellular matrix composition in structure and function of bioengineered skeletal muscle. Biomaterials **32**(14), 3575–3583 (2011)
10. Horchler, A.D., et al.: Peristaltic locomotion of a modular mesh-based worm robot: precision, compliance, and friction. Soft Robot. **2**(4), 135–145 (2015)
11. Ingber, D.E.: Cellular mechanotransduction: putting all the pieces together again. FASEB J. **20**(8), 811–827 (2006)
12. Islam, A., Chapin, K., Younesi, M., Akkus, O.: Computer aided biomanufacturing of mechanically robust pure collagen meshes with controlled macroporosity. Biofabrication **7**(3), 035005 (2015)
13. Kandhari, A., Wang, Y., Chiel, H.J., Daltorio, K.A.: Turning in worm-like robots: the geometry of slip elimination suggests nonperiodic waves. Soft Robot. **6**(4), 560–577 (2019)

14. Lee, K.Y., et al.: An autonomously swimming biohybrid fish designed with human cardiac biophysics. Science **375**(6581), 639–647 (2022)
15. Mammoto, T., Mammoto, A., Ingber, D.E.: Mechanobiology and developmental control. Annu. Rev. Cell Dev. Biol. **29**(1), 27–61 (2013)
16. Morimoto, Y., Onoe, H., Takeuchi, S.: Biohybrid robot powered by an antagonistic pair of skeletal muscle tissues. Sci. Robot. **3** (2018)
17. Nawroth, J.C., et al.: A tissue-engineered jellyfish with biomimetic propulsion. Nat. Biotechnol. **30**(8), 792–797 (2012)
18. Pagan-Diaz, G.J., et al.: Simulation and fabrication of stronger, larger, and faster walking biohybrid machines. Adv. Func. Mater. **28**(23), 1–13 (2018)
19. Park, S.J., et al.: Phototactic guidance of a tissue-engineered soft-robotic ray. Science **353**(6295), 158–162 (2016)
20. Powell, C.A., Smiley, B.L., Mills, J., Vandenburgh, H.H.: Mechanical stimulation improves tissue-engineered human skeletal muscle. Am. J. Physiol. Cell Physiol. **283**(5), 1557–1565 (2002)
21. Raman, R., et al.: SI: damage, healing, and remodeling in optogenetic skeletal muscle bioactuators. Adv. Healthc. Mater. **6**(12) (2017)
22. Rangarajan, S., Madden, L., Bursac, N.: Use of flow, electrical, and mechanical stimulation to promote engineering of striated muscles. Ann. Biomed. Eng. **42**(7), 1391–1405 (2014). https://doi.org/10.1007/s10439-013-0966-4
23. Ricotti, L., et al.: Biohybrid actuators for robotics: a review of devices actuated by living cells. Sci. Robot. **2** (2017)
24. Selman Sakar, M., et al.: Formation and optogenetic control of engineered 3D skeletal muscle bioactuators. Lab Chip **23**, 4976–4985 (2012)
25. Seok, S., Onal, C.D., Cho, K.J., Wood, R.J., Rus, D., Kim, S.: Meshworm: a peristaltic soft robot with antagonistic nickel titanium coil actuators. IEEE/ASME Trans. Mechatron. **18**(5), 1485–1497 (2013)
26. Shiwarski, D.J., Tashman, J.W., Eaton, A.F., Apodaca, G., Feinberg, A.W.: 3D printed biaxial stretcher compatible with live fluorescence microscopy. HardwareX **7**, e00095 (2020)
27. Turner, D.Z.: Digital image correlation engine (DICe) reference manual, Sandia report, SAND2015-10606 O. Technical report, Sandia report (2015). https://github.com/dicengine/dice
28. Webster, V.A., et al.: *Aplysia Californica* as a novel source of material for biohybrid robots and organic machines. In: Lepora, N.F.F., Mura, A., Mangan, M., Verschure, P.F.M.J.F.M.J., Desmulliez, M., Prescott, T.J.J. (eds.) Living Machines 2016. LNCS (LNAI), vol. 9793, pp. 365–374. Springer, Cham (2016). https://doi.org/10.1007/978-3-319-42417-0_33
29. Webster, V.A., Hawley, E.L., Akkus, O., Chiel, H.J., Quinn, R.D.: Effect of actuating cell source on locomotion of organic living machines with electrocompacted collagen skeleton. Bioinspiration Biomimetics **11**(3), 036012 (2016)
30. Webster-Wood, V.A., Akkus, O., Gurkan, U.A., Chiel, H.J., Quinn, R.D.: Organismal engineering: toward a robotic taxonomic key for devices using organic materials. Sci. Robot. **2**(12), 1–19 (2017)

Development and Characterization of a Soft Bending Actuator

Armin Jamali[✉], Robert Knoerlein, Frank Goldschmidtboeing, and Peter Woias

Department for Microsystems Engineering (IMTEK), University of Freiburg, Freiburg, Germany
armin.jamali@imtek.uni-freiburg.de

Abstract. Artificial muscles, made of soft and compliant materials, are one the main components of soft robots. In any case, and independent from the type and design of such actuators, the choice of material and fabrication process plays a critical role for their performance. Dielectric Elastomer Actuators (DEAs), also known as a subset of artificial muscles, are made of thin elastomer layers embedded between two layers of soft electrodes. In the journey of finding a suitable elastomer material with relatively low elastic modulus, high relative permittivity, and high dielectric breakdown strength, we found the ECOFLEX$^{\text{TM}}_{00\text{-}10}$ mixed with SILICONE THINNER™ as a promising candidate. In this paper, first we investigate into the mechanical and electrical properties of this silicone-based elastomer. Then, we explain the fabrication method of these soft actuators. Finally, after describing how the implementation of rigid poly(methyl methacrylate) (PMMA) structure makes the actuator bend, we present a bending actuator.

Keywords: Dielectric elastomer actuators · Soft robotics · Soft grippers · Artificial muscles · Electroactive polymers

1 Introduction

Artificial muscles are implemented in a variety of fields such as soft robotics, medical tools, and haptics [1]. DEAs, made of soft smart materials, respond to electrical stimulations and change in dimensions. The actuation of DEAs is basically by transducing the electrical energy into mechanical work.

$$p = \varepsilon_r \cdot \varepsilon_0 \cdot E^2 \tag{1}$$

$$Sz = -\frac{p}{Y} = -\left(\frac{\varepsilon_r \cdot \varepsilon_0}{Y}\right)\left(\frac{U}{z}\right)^2 \tag{2}$$

DEAs, in principle, are made of a soft dielectric elastomer layer between two compliant and conductive electrode layers. The layers of elastomers and electrodes could be stacked on top of each other resulting in a so-called multi-stack to gain a better mechanical stress and elongation. Equations (1) and (2) state the role of material properties in the relation between the mechanical strain and the input voltage, where p is known as

© The Author(s), under exclusive license to Springer Nature Switzerland AG 2022
A. Hunt et al. (Eds.): Living Machines 2022, LNAI 13548, pp. 152–156, 2022.
https://doi.org/10.1007/978-3-031-20470-8_16

Maxwell stress, ε_0 is the permittivity of free space, ε_r is the relative permittivity of the elastomer, z is the thickness of the elastomer, E is the electric field, S_z is the mechanical strain in the direction of elastomer thickness, and Y is the Young's modulus of the elastomer [2]. In this research, we investigated into these mechanical and electrical properties of ECOFLEX^{TM}$_{00-10}$, a silicone-based elastomer, mixed with 10% SILICONE THINNER^{TM} (both from Smooth-On Inc., USA). For ease of referencing, we call this compound Ecoflex10T. The index 00–10 after the name of ECOFLEX shows the shore hardness of the material. There are other available types of ECOFLEX such as 00–20, 00–30, and 00–50, nevertheless, the softness of 00–10 is an advantage.

2 Material Characterization

A suitable choice of material as well as an optimized fabrication process result in unique properties of DEAs, which make them good candidates for artificial muscles: flexibility, low mass density, simplicity, scalability, no acoustic noise, and low material and fabrication costs [1]. Hence, here as the first step, we measured electrical breakdown strength, dielectric constant, density, and Young's modulus of Ecoflex10T.

2.1 Electrical Breakdown Strength

To measure the electrical breakdown strength, a layer of Ecoflex10T with the known thickness of $z = 271 \pm 6$ μm was placed between two electrodes. The thickness values were measured under the microscope (Axio Scope.A1, Carl Zeiss Microscopy GmbH, Germany) to achieve a micron precision. Then, a high voltage signal from a high-voltage power supply (10HVA24-P1, HVP High Voltage Products GmbH, Germany) was applied through the electrodes. The voltage was incrementally increased from 0 V by $U_{step} = 10$ V per second until the material broke down. Then, the electrodes were moved to another arbitrary measuring point on the elastomer. The measurement was repeated 15 times and resulted in a breakdown voltage $U_{BD} = 5.9 \pm 0.3$ kV, which concludes in a breakdown field strength $E_{BD} = 21.9 \pm 0.8$ V μm^{-1}.

2.2 Dielectric Constant

To determine the relative permittivity of Ecoflex10T, a plate capacitor was built with a defined active circular area with 30 mm diameter and dielectric layer thickness of 3 mm. The capacitances were measured with an LCR-meter (Programmable LCR Bridge HM8118, Rohde & Schwarz, Germany). 10 measurements per specimen were taken and resulted in $C = 9.2 \pm 0.4$ pF @ 20 Hz which concludes in $\varepsilon_r = 4.4 \pm 0.1$ @ 20 Hz. It is important to mention that the relative permittivity for the ECOFLEX^{TM}$_{00-10}$ without the thinner was measured 3.5 ± 0.1 @ 20 Hz, which means the silicone thinner has a positive impact on the dielectric constant.

2.3 Density and Viscosity

For the layer-deposition, we chose the approach of spin-coating the uncured Ecoflex10T onto the substrate wafer. According to the method presented by Lee, Kim et al. [3], the density and the viscosity of the uncured elastomer as well as the rotation speed and duration of the spin-coating machine define the layer thickness. To measure the density of Ecoflex10T, 0.05 mL of the uncured Ecoflex10T was filled incrementally into a mixing cup, placed on a precision scale. The measurements resulted in the density $\rho_{Ecoflex10T}$ = 987 ± 2 kg m^{-3}. Moreover, the viscosity of the Ecoflex10T was estimated to 7 Pa s according to the datasheet of the thinner. Since the viscosity is indeed dependent on the pot life, we prepared a fresh mixture for every layer before spin-coating.

2.4 Elastic Behavior

To measure the Young's modulus of Ecoflex10T, the material was cured into a "dog-bone" mold, fulfilling the requirements of ISO 37:2017–11 [4]. The cured specimens were fixed into a stress-strain machine (Inspekt table, Hegewald & Peschke, Germany). The measurements resulted in $Y_{Ecoflex10T}$ = 0.052 MPa (R^2 = 0.9789) for strains higher than 500% and 0.010 MPa (R^2 = 0.9601) for strains lower than 300% (Fig. 1).

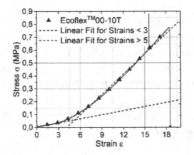

Fig. 1. Stress-strain curve of Ecoflex10T

3 Bending Actuator

For fabricating a bending actuator, first we made a simple DEA by spin-coating the elastomer and patterning carbon powder directly onto the elastomer with a soft dry brush [5]. Then, we introduced a stiff back-bone structure made of 0.5 mm thick PMMA sheets onto the last layer of the actuator (Fig. 2) which causes an asymmetric planar elongation, resulting in a bending motion. The actuator had dimensions of 40 × 25 × 1.95 mm with two active layers of elastomer (600 ± 30 μm each). Figure 3 depicts the bending actuator with maximum bending angle (α) of 18.3°, 48.7°, and 67.9° respectively for the actuation voltage of 5 kV, 7 kV, and 8 kV (ramp-up in 3 s).

PDMS passive layer → | → PMMA back bones
Elastomer → | → Electrode
PDMS passive layer → | → Active elastomer

Fig. 2. Cross-sectional view of the bending actuator stack [6]

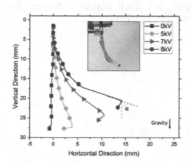

Fig. 3. The bending line for a 2-layered actuator (2.30 g) under voltages up to 8 kV. The bending lines are captured by a laser camera (scanCONTROL 3002–25/BL, Micro-Epsilon, Germany).

4 Conclusion and Outlook

In this paper, we characterized bending actuators made of Ecoflex10T. We characterized the elastomer electrically and mechanically and received $E_{BD} = 21.87$ V.μm^{-1} (determining how much voltage is allowed to be applied considering the thickness of elastomer layer), $\varepsilon_r = 4.39$ @ 20 Hz, $\rho = 987$ kg.m^{-3}, and $Y = 0.052$ MPa for strains higher than 500% and 0.010 MPa for strains lower than 300%. Here, we also refer to the work of Vaicekauskaite, Mazurek et al. [7] to compare these values to other materials. Then we presented the free-hanging actuator (mass = 2.30 g) bending up to 67.9° under 8 kV. For the future work, the bending actuator can get miniaturized, and thinner active layers may be deposited to achieve the same performance driven by lower voltages. For that, the other aforementioned spin-coating parameters should also be characterized.

Acknowledgement. Funded by the Deutsche Forschungsgemeinschaft (German Research Foundation) under Germany's Excellence Strategy – EXC-2193/1 – 390951807.

References

1. Carpi, Federico (ed.): Electromechanically Active Polymers: A Concise Reference. Springer International Publishing, Cham (2016). https://doi.org/10.1007/978-3-319-31767-0
2. Carpi, F. (ed.): Dielectric Elastomers as Electromechanical Transducers: Fundamentals, Materials, Devices, Models and Applications of an Emerging Electroactive Polymer Technology. Elsevier, Amsterdam (2008)
3. Lee, U.G., Kim, W.-B., Han, D.H., Chung, H.S.: A Modified equation for thickness of the film fabricated by spin coating. Symmetry **11**(9), 1183 (2019)
4. ISO 37:2017-11: Rubber, vulcanized or thermoplastic – Determination of tensile stress-strain properties

5. Shigemune, H., et al.: Dielectric elastomer actuators with carbon nanotube electrodes painted with a soft brush. Actuators **7**(3), 51 (2018)
6. Jamali, A., Knoerlein, R., Goldschmidtboeing, F., Woias, P.: Development of a Scalable Soft Finger Gripper for Soft Robots. Accepted for Hilton Head Workshop 2022, Hilton Head, USA
7. Vaicekauskaite, J., Mazurek, P., Vudayagiri, S., Skov, A.L.: Mapping the mechanical and electrical properties of commercial silicone elastomer formulations for stretchable transducers. J. Mater. Chem. C **8**(4), 1273–1279 (2020)

Evaluation of Gait Generation in Quadrupedal Legged Locomotion with Changing Anterior/Posterior Extreme Positions

Kodai Kodono$^{(\boxtimes)}$ and Hiroshi Kimura

Kyoto Institute of Technology, Sakyo-ku Matssugasaki, Kyoto 606-8585, Japan
d1821004@edu.kit.ac.jp, kimura61@kit.ac.jp
http://www.robotlocomotion.kit.ac.jp

Abstract. In an attempt to understand the gait generation of decerebrate cats, several studies have conducted locomotion experiments using a quadrupedal robot. However, studies on understanding the mechanisms focusing on the changing leg trajectory, such as touch-down and lift-off positions, are scarce. In our previous study, we proposed the spinal and thalamic cat model to understand a split-belt adaptation constructively. The current study attempted to propose the gait generation mechanism, focusing on the walk, trot, and pace gait generation mechanisms at the spinal level with the spinal cat model. That aim was to clarify the relationship between gait generation, forward movement, and touch-down/lift-off positions. Subsequently, the gait generation mechanism was considered from the perspective of the sensory-motor level using the spinal cat model. The dynamic simulation results revealed that the anterior extreme position (AEP) and posterior extreme position (PEP) in the leg trajectory were closely related to the walk/ trot/pace gait generation. In addition, when PEP distance increased in middle AEP distances, the generated gait changed from walk to trot with higher forward movement. Thus, we concluded that only increasing AEP and PEP distances may lead to the gait generation from walk to trot using the spinal cat model.

Keywords: Gait generation · Spinal cat model · Quadrupedal forward movement

1 Introduction

Decerebrate cats[1] can generate different gaits according to the surrounding environment. For example, a mesencephalic cat can change its gait according to the

---

[1] A cat disconnected from upper central nerves with remaining locomotor regions at the sub-thalamic (SLR), cerebellum (CLR), and mesencephalic (MLR) is called a "thalamic cat." A cat disconnected from upper central nerves, including SLR but remaining CLR and MLR, is called a "mesencephalic cat." In contrast, a cat disconnected from the upper central nerves, including the cerebellum and brain stem, is called a "spinal cat.".

Supported by JSPS KAKENHI Grant Number JP19K12169 and JP21J23064.

© The Author(s), under exclusive license to Springer Nature Switzerland AG 2022
A. Hunt et al. (Eds.): Living Machines 2022, LNAI 13548, pp. 157–168, 2022.
https://doi.org/10.1007/978-3-031-20470-8_17

belt speed on the treadmill [1]. However, these gait generation mechanisms for transitions remain largely unknown.

The gait generation mechanism of decerebrate cats can be understood by understanding how a low-central nervous system generates its gait. Several studies have conducted locomotion experiments using quadrupedal robots for a constructive understanding of gait generation and transition. Aoi et al. proposed a central pattern generator (CPG) model that could realize a walk-trot transition [2]. The controller utilized a phase resetting based on a non-linear dynamic system and mathematically addressed the dynamics of relative phases between the legs. Therefore, the model could be described as a non-linear dynamic system. Fukuoka et al. [3] and Owaki et al. [4] also proposed a CPG model that could realize a walk-trot-gallop transition. The authors have aimed to propose a model based on biological knowledge to understand the gait transition and adaptation of decerebrate cats at the sensory-motor level constructively. In our previous study [5], the spinal and the thalamic cat models capable of partially realizing split-belt adaptation were proposed using a quadrupedal robot. However, these models did not realize the gait transition. The current study considered specific knowledge needed to realize the gait transition and to understand it at the sensory-motor level. Therefore, we used the spinal cat model to investigate how the spinal cord generates different gaits at the sensory-motor level.

The spinal cat model was based on Frigon's spinal leg phase transition model [6]. In Frigon's model, sensory information such as leg loading and hip joint flexion/extension was fed back to the spinal cord, which then determined the leg phase based on the sensor information. As mentioned above, a mesencephalic cat changed their gait according to the belt speed of the treadmill. That is, sensory information about how far the leg was stretched by the belt and where it lifted off was very important. Therefore, sensor information of the hip joint flexion/extension had closely related to the gait generation and transition. Considering hip joint flexion/extension in legged locomotion, we concluded that the touch-down (TD) and lift-off (LO) positions were important factors for the gait generation in this study.

Here, we show previous studies discussing the relationship between the TD/LO positions and gait generation. Adachi et al. analyzed the equation of motion with a 3-D quadrupedal model and reported that the region of the periodic solution of trot/pace gaits was divided by TD position [7]. However, few studies exist on changing the TD and LO positions with a quadrupedal robot or a dynamic simulation to realize the different gait generations. In our previous study [8], quadrupedal symmetrical gaits, trot/pace/bound, were simulated using the spinal cat model based on Frigon's leg phase transition model. However, walk gait generation and the extent to which the model moved forward were not discussed. To realize the walk–trot gait transition with a quadrupedal robot, the conditions wherein a walk gait was likely to be generated or the forward distance at each gait must be considered. This study aimed to constructively understand the relationship between changing the TD/LO positions, gait generation, and the model moving forward. Further, dynamic simulations of locomotion were performed by changing the anterior extreme position (AEP) and posterior extreme position (PEP) in the leg trajectory. In addition, to investigate the model moving forward capacity, the forward distance was defined which was evaluated in each trial. The effect of AEP/PEP change on gait generation and forward distance was discussed.

The hat ^, tilde ~, and bar ‾ symbols represent the nominal, desired, and measured values of a single variable.

2   Spinal Cat Model

The spinal cat model is used to constructively understand the split-belt adaptation in decerebrate cats [5]. It is based on the leg controller (LC) [9] integrated with Frigon's leg phase transition model of a spinal cat [6].

2.1   Leg Controller

LC (Fig. 1) [9] is a quadrupedal robot controller modeled on a CPG. Each leg is actuated by the leg controller, as shown in Fig. 1, having two leg phases: swing (sw) and stance (st). Sensory information such as leg loading regulates the transfer of activity between swing and stance phases. Each LC is associated with a simple oscillator with variable phase ϕ^i of constant angular velocity $\dot{\phi}^i$, where i is the leg index ($i \in \{LF,\ RF,\ LH,\ RH\}^2$).

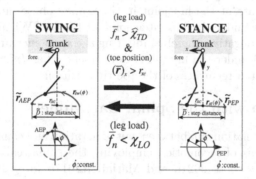

Fig. 1. Leg controller [9] for quadrupedal locomotion. The toe tip r moves along phase-dependent leg trajectory $r_{sw}(\phi)$ and $r_{st}(\phi)$. The leg controller transits a leg phase utilizing the measured leg loading $\bar{f}_n$ and toe tip position $(\bar{r})_x$.

Leg phase transition is initiated using the measured leg loading $\bar{f}_n^i$ and the measured x component of the toe tip position $(\bar{r})_x^i$ with force and toe position thresholds ($\hat{\chi}_{TD}$ and r_{xc}, respectively, Fig. 1) for touch-down. Similarly, using the threshold χ_{LO}^i for the lift-off.

---

^{2} Denote a left fore leg, right fore leg, left hind leg, and right hind leg as LF, RF, LH, and RH, respectively, for short.

2.2   Trajectory Planning

The foot position is determined by the leg trajectory, which depends on the phase ϕ^i. The foot positions at the sw-to-st and st-to-sw transitions are referred to as the AEP and PEP, respectively. In this study, the swing leg trajectory is a cubic spline curve and the stance leg trajectory is a line with constant velocity. The calculations for these trajectories are based on AEP and PEP. Therefore, the AEP and PEP can be arbitrarily changed when the trajectories are provided. Distance from AEP to a vertical axis through the hip joint is defined as "AEP distance $(|(\boldsymbol{r}_{AEP})_x|)$," and that from PEP to the vertical axis through the hip joint as "PEP distance $(-(\boldsymbol{r}_{PEP})_x|)$." Furthermore, $\tilde{D}$ (Fig. 1) indicates desired step distance, while the following equation holds.

$$\tilde{D} = |(\tilde{\boldsymbol{r}}_{AEP})_x| + |(\tilde{\boldsymbol{r}}_{PEP})_x| \tag{1}$$

2.3   Phase Transition from the Stance to the Swing

The spinal cat model integrates the LC and Frigon's leg phase transition model [6]. Threshold χ_{LO}^i for the st-to-sw-transition is defined as follows:

$$\chi_{LO}^i = \begin{cases} \hat{\chi}_{LO} \cdot (r_{xc} - (\bar{r})_x^i)/(\tilde{D}/2) & \text{(if } lp^{cntr} = st) \\ -5 & \text{(otherwise)} \end{cases} \tag{2}$$

where $\hat{\chi}_{LO}$ and $\tilde{D}$ are the nominal leg loading threshold (5 [N]) for the st-to-sw transition and the step distance in Fig. 1, respectively. On the other hand as shown in Fig. 1, $(\bar{r}_{st}^i)_x$ is the x component of the measured toe tip position in the x-y coordinate at the hip joint in the stance phase, and $r_{xc}(=0)$ is the x component right under the hip pitch joint of the leg. When $lp^{cntr} = st$, the threshold becomes negative, thereby inhibiting the st-to-sw transition, unless the toe tip is extended under the hip joint. Conversely, when $lp^{cntr} = sw$, st-to-sw transition is inhibited regardless of the toe tip position.

3   Simulation with the Spinal Cat Model

To investigate the relationship between gait generation and change in AEP/PEP, dynamic simulations of locomotion employing the spinal cat model were conducted. We used Webots 2021b and Matlab R2017b for gait simulation and evaluation, respectively.

3.1   Methods

Dynamic locomotion simulation was performed using the spinal cat model. A simulation model (Fig. 2) was constructed based on "Kotetsu." Furthermore, AEP and PEP distances were set in the range of 0.5 to 8 [cm], respectively. Because the step width was set to 0.5 [cm], the number of trials was $(16 \times 16 =)$ 256. The remaining simulation conditions were identical.

The simulation model (Fig. 2-(A)) was equipped with force, encoder, IMU, and GPS sensors, which measured the leg loading, toe tip position, body Euler angles, and body position in world coordinate systems, respectively.

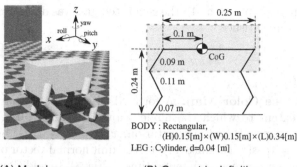

(A) Model appearance   (B) Geometric definition

Fig. 2. (A) Model appearance and definition of coordinate system. Toe tips are spherical and grounded at point. (B) Geometric definition based on a quadrupedal robot, "Kotetsu." The mass of each component is the default value of Webots 2021b. Center of gravity is set close to the center of body.

3.2   Color Maps for Evaluations

To analyze the generated gait and degree of forward movement of the model, two color maps were created: the gait color and forward distance color maps.

Gait Color Map. Following previous research [10], the gait color map was used to determine the type of gait generated in each trial. First, the averages of relative phases $\Delta\phi_{ij}$ were calculated for initial t_0 ($= 25$ [s]) to the end t_1 ($= 30$ [s]). This study adopted the relative phase based on the lift-off of the LF, represented it as $\Delta\phi_j$, $j \in \{RF, LH, RH\}$. Subsequently, the gait color map was created, where the RGB values $(R_g, G_g, B_g) \in [0, 1]$ were defined as follows:

$$(R_g, G_g, B_g) = \left(\frac{1 - \cos(\Delta\phi_{RF})}{2}, \frac{1 - \cos(\Delta\phi_{LH})}{2}, \frac{1 - \cos(\Delta\phi_{RH})}{2} \right) \quad (3)$$

For generated gait being bound, trot, and pace, the colors were red, green, and blue, respectively. In addition, to classify the walk gait, the generated gait was categorized as follows:

$$gait = \begin{cases} bound & (\text{if } R_g > B_g, \ G_g) \\ walk & (\text{else if } |B_g - 1/2| < \frac{1}{2\sqrt{2}} \ \& \ |G_g - 1/2| < \frac{1}{2\sqrt{2}}) \\ trot & (\text{else if } G_g > B_g) \\ pace & (\text{otherwise}) \end{cases} \quad (4)$$

For the discriminant expression (4), the generated gait was determined as follows: $\Delta\phi_{LH}$, $\Delta\phi_{RH}$ were satisfied[3]:

$$-\frac{3\pi}{4} \leq \Delta\phi_{LH} \leq -\frac{\pi}{4}, \frac{\pi}{4} \leq \Delta\phi_{RH} \leq \frac{3\pi}{4} \tag{5}$$

Forward Distance Color Map. A forward distance color map was used to determine the extent to which the model moved forward. First, consider the forward distance. Let $\psi(t)$ be the orientation, $\boldsymbol{x}(t) = (x(t), y(t))$ be the position vector, and $\boldsymbol{n}(t) = (\cos(\psi(t)), \sin(\psi(t)))$ be the unit normal vector of the model in the horizontal plane at the experimental time t (Fig. 3). In addition, let $\boldsymbol{\Delta x}(t) = \boldsymbol{x}(t+\Delta t) - \boldsymbol{x}(t)$ be the displacement after Δt. A model was then defined to move forward when the following equation was satisfied:

$$\langle \boldsymbol{\Delta x}(t), \boldsymbol{n}(t)\rangle > 0 \tag{6}$$

We referred to this inner product as the forward distance.

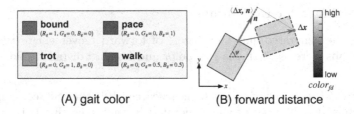

(A) gait color   (B) forward distance

Fig. 3. (A) Examples of gait colors. R_g, G_g, and B_g are determined by $\Delta\phi_j$ and Eq. (3). Generated gaits are classified by Eq. (4). (B) Definition of the forward distance. $\psi, \boldsymbol{\Delta x}$, and $\boldsymbol{n}$ mean the orientation, displacement vector, and unit normal vector in the horizontal plane, respectively. When the model moves from a solid to dotted line, the green line $\langle \boldsymbol{\Delta x}, \boldsymbol{n}\rangle$ is equivalent to the forward distance. The sum of the forward distance Σ_{fd} is higher, $color_{fd}$ becomes whiter. (Color figure online)

Next, a forward distance color map was created, where the sum of the forward- distance is represented in $t \in [t_0, t_1]$ as Σ_{fd} $(= \sum\langle\boldsymbol{\Delta x}(t), \boldsymbol{n}(t)\rangle)$. The RGB values $(R_f, G_f, B_f) \in [0, 1]$ were defined as follows:

$$R_f = G_f = B_f = color_{fd} \tag{7}$$

$$color_{fd} = \min\{(1, \max(g \cdot \Sigma_{fd}, 0)\} \tag{8}$$

where g $(= 2)$ was the gain to adjust the shade of the color. When the model did not move forward ($\Sigma_{fd} \leq 0$ [m]), the color became black. The larger the forward distance, the whiter the color.

---

[3] In this study, straight and reverse walks are collectively considered as a walk gait. During straight walk, the hind leg lifts off before the ipsilateral fore leg in a one-step cycle. Whereas, during reverse walk, the hind leg lifts off after the ipsilateral fore leg.

3.3   Stability Analysis Using Potential Function

One of the stability analysis methods of generated gaits was to calculate a potential functions based on the return map [2]. When we used this method, we could investigate which gait was more likely to be generated by changing AEP or PEP distances numerically. In this paper, we investigated which gaits were generated by changing PEP distances in the middle AEP distances ($4 \leq |(\hat{r}_{AEP})_x| \leq 5$ [cm]). We plotted the data with normalized PEP on the x-axis, $\cos(\phi_j(n))$ on the y-axis, and $\cos(\phi_j(n+1))$ on the z-axis. Then, we calculated an approximate surface [8].

$$\cos(\Delta\phi_j(n+1)) = \sum_{s=1}^{N}\sum_{t=1}^{M} \alpha_{st} \cdot |(\hat{r}_{PEP})_x|^{s-1} \cdot \cos^{t-1}(\Delta\phi_j(n)) \qquad (9)$$

where α_{st} was a coefficient determined by the least-square method. N, M were constants to determine the dimension of the approximate surface. $|(\hat{r}_{PEP})_x|$ was a PEP distance. When we fixed $|(\hat{r}_{PEP})_x|$ in Eq. (9), we could obtain an approximate curve at each PEP distance. Then, following the proposed method [2], we could also obtain an potential function of the generated gaits and evaluated the relationship between a PEP distance and gait generation.

3.4   Results

Figures 4, 5, 6 and 7 show the results of locomotion simulation.

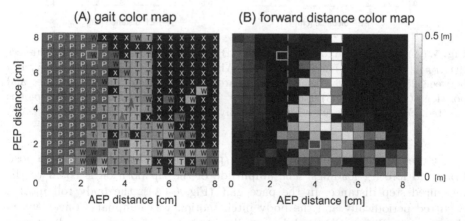

Fig. 4. (A) Gait and (B) forward distance color maps ($25 \leq t \leq 30$ [s]). The horizontal and vertical axes refer to AEP and PEP distances, respectively. In the gait color map, the green box and the letter 'T' in the box indicate gait classification as a trot. Further, the blue box and the letter 'P' indicate pace, while the letter 'W' and 'X' indicate walk and that the model has fallen, respectively. In the forward distance color map, lighter colors mean the model had moved more forward movement. (Color figure online)

Figure 4 shows the generated gait and forward distance in each trial. At first, we classified the AEP distances into the following: low AEP distances ($|(\hat{r}_{AEP})_x| \le 2.5$ [cm]), middle AEP distances ($3 \le |(\hat{r}_{AEP})_x| \le 5$ [cm]), and high AEP distances ($5.5 \le |(\hat{r}_{AEP})_x|$ [cm]). From Fig. 4-(A), we found the following: In the low AEP distances, almost pace gaits was generated. In the middle PEP distances, almost trot gait was generated. Some walk gait was also generated. In the high PEP distances, some walk gait was generated, but the model fell in most trials.

Figure 5 shows the toe tip speed and forward speed of the model in the low and middle AEP distances. The former was calculated from TD & LO times and positions in stance phase. The latter was calculated from the forward distance (Fig. 4-(B)). We found that as the step distance increased, the toe tip speed also increased linearly (Fig. 5-(A)). In addition, almost forward speed was increased by increasing PEP distance (Fig. 5-(B)). However, because of unstable locomotion, forward speed was small in some trials. These were more likely to be seen at high PEP distances.

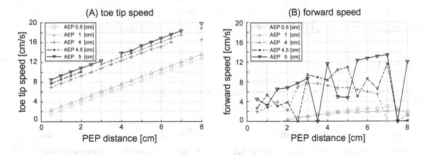

Fig. 5. (A) Average of all toe tip speeds and (B) forward speed in the low AEP distances ($|(r_{AEP})_x| = 0.5, 1$ [cm]) and in the middle AEP distances ($|(r_{AEP})_x| = 4, 4.5, 5$ [cm]) between $25 \le t \le 30$ [s]. Toe tip speeds are calculated from TD & LO times and positions ($|(\bar{r}_{LO})_x - (\bar{r}_{TD})_x)/(t_{LO} - t_{TD})|$). When the model has fallen, the plot is omitted. Forward speeds are calculated by dividing $|\Sigma_{fd}/(t_1 - t_0)|$.

Figure 6 shows the gait diagrams, roll/pitch angles of the body, toe tip position, and fore leg loadings. The amplitude of the tip position is equal to the measured step distance. In the pace gait (Fig. 6-(A)), the body roll motion occurred periodically and the body pitch motion was minimal. Conversely, in the trot gait (Fig. 6-(B)), both body roll and pitch motion occurred, albeit with small amplitudes. In addition, the measured step distances in the trot were larger than those for the pace. Figure 6-(C), (D) represent the reverse walk gaits. (C) was not forward and (D) was forward (Fig. 4-(B)). Although both roll motions of (C) & (D) occurred periodically, their waveforms were different. In addition, the pitch motion between the front and back occurred only in (D). Moreover, the measured step distances and stance durations of the fore legs in (C) were larger than those in (D). The variation in the RF loading of (D) was smaller than that of (C). That is, the weight shift in the stance phase was smaller in (D) than in (C).

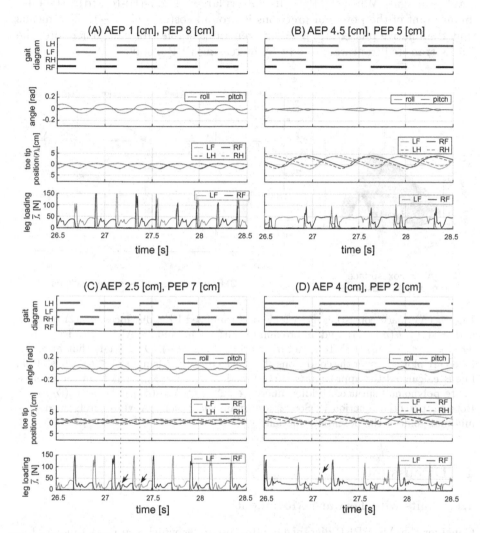

Fig. 6. The detail results of simulations. (A) Pace gait & (B) trot gait are equivalent to the red box in Fig. 4, and (C) & (D) the reverse walk gaits are equivalent to the orange box in Fig. 4. Top: Gait diagram calculated from the leg controller measurements. Second from top: Body angle measured by the IMU sensor. Third from the top: Toe tip position of each leg measured by the encoder. Bottom: Leg loading measured by the force sensor. (Color figure online)

For the analysis of gait stability, we see the potential functions in the middle AEP distances (Fig. 7, $N = 4$, $M = 4$). When the PEP distance is small (Fig. 7-(B)-(a), (b)), the minimum point of the potential functions is around $\cos(\Delta\phi_{LH}) = 0$. This means that the relative phase: $\Delta\phi_{LH} = \pm\pi/2$, generates stable walk gait. When the PEP distance is larger (Fig. 7-(B)-(c), (d)), the minimum point of the potential functions is around $\cos(\Delta\phi_{LH}) = -1$. This means that the relative phase: $\Delta\phi_{LH} = \pm\pi$, generates stable trot gait. Therefore, the gait is transited from walk to trot by increasing PEP distance.

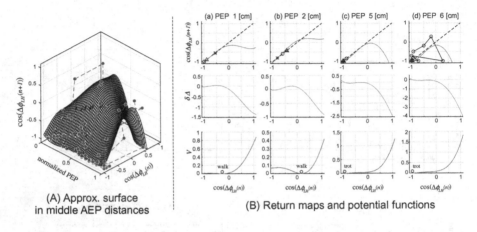

(A) Approx. surface
in middle AEP distances

(B) Return maps and potential functions

Fig. 7. (A) Space consisting of variable of normalized PEP distances, $\cos(\Delta\phi_{LH}(n))$, and $\cos(\Delta\phi_{LH}(n + 1))$ and approximate surface in middle AEP distances ($4 \leq |(r_{AEP})_x| \leq 5$ [cm]). (B) Top: Return map of $\cos(\Delta\phi_{LH})$. Only trials that have not fallen are plotted under the conditions of $4 \leq |(r_{AEP})_x| \leq 5$ [cm] in $25 \leq t \leq 30$ [s]. Bold line is calculated the approximate curve function $P(\Delta\cos(\phi_{LH}(n)))$ from the approximate polynomial surface. Middle: difference $\delta\Delta = P(\Delta\cos(\phi_{LH}(n))) - \cos(\phi_{LH}(n))$. Bottom: potential function V. See [2] for detail calculations. A white circle means the minimal point of the potential function.

4   Discussions

4.1   Gaits with Forward Movement

Consider the AEP/PEP distance conditions under which the model moved forward. First, consider the low AEP distance ($|(r_{AEP})_x| \leq 2.5$ [cm]), wherein the model generated pace gait. From Figs. 4-(B) and 5, the model moved increasingly forward with increase in the PEP distance. Because the nominal duty ratio and step cycle were under the same conditions, an increase in the PEP distance led to an increase in the step distance and speed of the toe tip (Fig. 5-(A)). Therefore, it was concluded that the forward speed of the model also increased (Fig. 5-(B)). However, while the AEP distance increased, the forward distance decreased, and eventually, the model stopped moving forward. Considering the gait shown in Fig. 6-(C), because an increase in AEP distance caused weight shift between the ipsilateral legs in stance phase [8], the leg loading of the fore legs decreased after the hind leg touched down (Fig. 6-(C), arrows); that is, the center of gravity moved backward in the forelimb stance phase and decelerated the model. Additionally, we found the stance phase period was short (approx. 0.2 [s]) in the gait diagram. Therefore, it was difficult for the model to move forward with.

Next, consider the middle AEP distance ($3 \leq |(r_{AEP})_x| \leq 5$ [cm]) wherein the model generated walk or trot gaits. As evident from the gait shown in Fig. 6-(D), leg loading of the LF kept high even when the LH touched down (Fig. 6-(D), arrow). Additionally, the stance phase period was long (approx. 0.5 [s]), and the duration that the legs moved the body was also long. Therefore, the model moved forward, unlike the gait shown in Fig. 6-(C). Similarly, because the variation of leg loading was small and the stance periods was long, the trot gait also moved forward (Fig. 6-(B)). Finally, consider the high AEP distances ($|(r_{AEP})_x| \geq 5.5$ [cm]) wherein the model did not move forward. Because the toe tip speed was too high, the posture became unstable. To control posture under the high speed of the toe tip, another controller which a model can leap may be needed.

4.2   Walk-Trot Transition Mechanism

We focus on the walk gaits in higher PEP (Fig. 6-(C)) and lower PEP (Fig. 6-(D)) distances. A step distance and toe tip speed were higher in the former than in the latter. However, the former was not forward and the latter gait was forward. In addition, as a mesencephalic cat transitioned from walk to trot by increasing the belt speed [1], the toe tip speed in walk gait should be smaller than that in trot gait. From this view point, the lower PEP distance was better suited for walk in the gait transition than the higher PEP distance. Therefore, we proposed one walk-trot transition mechanism by changing the leg trajectory as follows:

When a cat walks on the treadmill, the AEP distance is middle and the PEP distance is low (Fig. 6-(D)). When the belt speed increases, the toe tip speed is also increases; that is, the PEP distance is larger. At this time, the gait generated from walk to trot stable (Fig. 7). Thus, only a larger PEP distance could generate a trot gait (Fig. 4-(A), dotted line arrow). Alternatively, to avoid generating an unstable gait or pace gait, the AEP distance may be increased (Fig. 4-(A), solid line arrow). In any case, we consider that a cat can transition to a trot gait by changing the AEP and PEP distances (Fig. 6-(D) to (B)).

Details of the proposed mechanism should be studied using a transition simulation and quadrupedal robot experiment. We also need to compare the other robot experiments of gait transition and biological knowledge. In addition, the cat did not generate a reverse walk, but a straight walk. Thus, future work will include an examination of these differences and comparisons with the results of cat and robot experiments.

5   Conclusion

To evaluate the gait generation and forward movement of the spinal cat model by changing the touch-down and lift-off, a dynamic simulation of quadrupedal locomotion was performed. For low AEP distance, pace gait was generated, and the model moved more forward with increasing PEP distance. Further, for middle AEP distance, walk and trot gaits were generated. The forward distance in the trot gait was larger than that in the walk gait because of the increasing speed of the toe tip. When the PEP distance became too high, however, the gait became unstable owing to the too high speed of the toe tip.

Based on the results, we proposed a walk-trot transition mechanism that changed the AEP and PEP distances triggering an increasing speed of the toe tip. However, the dynamic simulation differed from real world environments in many aspects, such as the fully inelastic collisions and high torque motors for creating an ideal physical environment. In addition, locomotion experiments based only on dynamic simulations had limitations because computational errors cannot be ignored. Therefore, we need locomotion experiments with quadrupedal robot to evaluate these concepts definitively.

References

1. Orlovsky, G., Deliagina, T.G., Grillner, S.: Neuronal Control of Locomotion: From Mollusc to Man. Oxford University Press, Oxford (1999)
2. Aoi, S., et al.: A stability-based mechanism for hysteresis in the walk- trot transition in quadruped locomotion. J. R. Soc. Interface **10**, 20120908 (2013)
3. Fukuoka, Y., Habu, Y., Fukui, T.: A simple rule for quadrupedal gait generation determined by leg loading feedback: a modeling study. Sci. Rep. **5**, 8169 (2015)
4. Owaki, D., Ishiguro, A.: A quadruped robot exhibiting spontaneous gait transitions from walking to trotting to galloping. Sci. Rep. **7**, 277 (2017)
5. Kodono, K., Kimura, H.: Split-belt adaptation model of a decerebrate cat using a quadruped robot with learning. In: Vouloutsi, V., Mura, A., Tauber, F., Speck, T., Prescott, T.J., Verschure, P.F.M.J. (eds.) Living Machines 2020. LNCS (LNAI), vol. 12413, pp. 217–229. Springer, Cham (2020). https://doi.org/10.1007/978-3-030-64313-3_21
6. Frigon, A., Desrochers, É., Thibaudier, Y., Hurteau, M.F., Dambreville, C.: Left-right coordination from simple to extreme conditions during split- belt locomotion in the chronic spinal adult cat. J. Physiol. **595**(1), 341–361 (2017)
7. Adachi, M., Kamimura, T., Matsuno, F.: Dynamical analysis of pace and trot gait using a 3D quadrupedal model. Syst. Control Inf. **31**(12), 428–436 (2018). (in Japanese)
8. Kodono, K., Kimura, H.: Constructive understanding of quadrupedal symmetrical gait generation with changing nominal touch-down and/or lift-off positions. In: SICE DAS Symposium, vol. 34, 1C3-3 (2022). (in Japanese)
9. Maufroy, C., Kimura, H., Takase, K.: Integration of posture and rhythmic motion controls in quadrupedal dynamic walking using phase modulations based on leg loading/unloading. Auto. Robot. **28**, 331–353 (2010). https://doi.org/10.1007/s10514-009-9172-5
10. Suzuki, S., Owaki, D., Fukuhara, K., Kano, T., Ishiguro, A.: CPG-based control for quadruped robot that exploits head motion. SICE in Touhoku Chapter Research Gathering, vol. 314, 314-4 (2018). (in Japanese)

Active Inference for Artificial Touch: A Biologically-Plausible Tactile Control Method

Pernilla Craig[1]([✉]), Laurence Aitchison[2], and Nathan F. Lepora[1,3]

[1] Bristol Robotics Laboratory, University of Bristol and University of the West of England, Bristol, UK
pc17701@bristol.ac.uk
[2] Department of Computer Science, University of Bristol, Bristol, UK
[3] Department of Engineering Mathematics, University of Bristol, Bristol, UK

Abstract. This work presents a proof of concept implementation of an active inference based control mechanism for tactile sensing systems. Active inference is a theory developed in neuroscience to model decision making in the human brain. Here, we use an active inference framework to successfully complete a localisation task using a biomimetic optical tactile sensor mounted on a robotic arm and tactile stimulus as the environment. The system demonstrated optimal control strategies for action selection and achieved a high degree of accuracy.

Keywords: Perceptual inference · Tactile sensing · Localisation

1 Introduction

Touch is an integral part of how humans interact with the world. It allows us to sense temperature, texture, pressure, and we are able to modulate grip strength and identify objects through tactile feedback alone [1]. When our sense of touch is limited we lose much of our ability to complete fine motor tasks [2]. Its importance to the human experience is highlighted as lack of tactile feedback is a significant reason for prosthetic limb rejection [3] and when included it increases prostheses functionality [4,5]. As touch plays such an important role for humans we should consider it when designing dexterous robotic systems.

This research uses active inference as the basis for developing a control mechanism for purely tactile-based robotic systems. Active inference was developed in neuroscience to model the human brain and decision making [6]. It proposes that humans make decisions to minimise statistical free energy, equivalent to minimising the difference between an expected and subsequently observed outcome. It is a biologically plausible method with the steps involved in decision making able to be mapped to the physical structure of the brain [7,8]. Given this, it presents a novel opportunity for recreating more human-like intelligent behaviour within the field of robotics.

© The Author(s), under exclusive license to Springer Nature Switzerland AG 2022
A. Hunt et al. (Eds.): Living Machines 2022, LNAI 13548, pp. 169–181, 2022.
https://doi.org/10.1007/978-3-031-20470-8_18

We present a proof of concept implementation of an active inference-based control system for tactile sensing. It successfully completed a localisation task in a known environment to a high degree of accuracy. The system was robust to incorrectly classified sensory observations and able to produce optimal control strategies without introducing human bias into the decision making framework.

1.1 Background and Related Work

Active inference was developed in neuroscience as a model of the human brain and has been used to investigate decision making in neurological disorders, such as schizophrenia and Parkinson's [9,10]. It has been presented as a unified brain theory [11] and is capable of explaining a wide variety of phenomena including habit formation, reward-seeking [12], and the interaction of decision making with attention and learning [13–15].

Recent years have shown an increase in research into using active inference-based methods of control for different robotic systems. Research has given positive results in trajectory planning of simulated robotic arms [16,17], navigation of a mobile robot in a known warehouse system [18], and also with goal-directed light seeking behaviour for a simulated robot [19]. Success has also been shown in using an active inference-based setup to complete a pick and place task using a 7 degree of freedom robot arm [20].

Most research into using active inference-based control systems uses the sensory modalities of vision and proprioception. Recently, research has shown success using an active inference framework to perform reaching and head tracking behaviours on a humanoid robot, using a touch modality in the form of pressure sensors to act as a stop trigger once the robot made contact with the goal [21].

2 Methodology

2.1 Experimental Setup

The experimental setup consists of a TacTip biomimetic optical tactile sensor [22] mounted on a DOBOT 4 degree of freedom robotic arm and a cylindrical stimulus as the known environment, as shown in Fig. 1. The TacTip has an array of 127 pins on the internal surface of a soft deformable shell, mimicking the papillae pins found in the fingertip. Tactile observations take the form of a tap, where the sensor comes into contact with a stimulus, deforms, and the sensor camera takes an image of the pin array from which the x and y deviations of the pins are extracted.

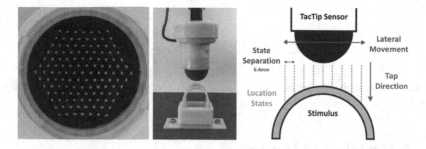

Fig. 1. Left: Internal structure of the TacTip, showing pin distribution. Centre: TacTip mounted on the DOBOT arm and the cylindrical stimulus. Right: Illustration of the environment, outlining movement axes of the sensor and the state definitions.

The cylindrical stimulus is chosen to allow for easy comparison to previous work using active perception [23–26]. We define position states across its cross section with a total of 61 states spaced at 0.4mm intervals, spanning a total distance of 24 mm and allowing for the greatest number of states. This constrains the localisation problem to one dimension.

Robotic movement is restricted to two dimensions: lateral movement allows for transition between states, and vertical movement allows the sensor to tap the stimulus. The sensor is initialised 2 mm above the stimulus surface at the cross section midpoint, and each tap corresponds to a 6.25 mm movement from this height to make contact with the stimulus. A histogram classifier is used to define the states. Here, a tactile observation is taken at each position state and the deflections of the sensor pins are used to construct a histogram representation of that state. The model consists of a full set of these histograms, one for each state. Incoming sensory observations are then analysed and compared to the model histograms using a dissimilarity measure to find the closest match. Further information on this classifier is available in previous work [26, 27].

2.2 Task Overview

We use an active localisation task as the basis for testing the active inference control system, hereby referred to as the *agent*. The aim is for the agent to determine its location in a known environment after being placed in a random unknown starting state. The agent is allowed to explore its environment by selecting a series of actions and gathering tactile observations from the stimulus, it has access to no other senses. It is considered to be localised once its belief about its position reaches a pre-set decision threshold. We define a set of simple actions for the agent to select from to move around the environment, these being:

u_1 - Move down one state/remain in the lowest state.

u_2 - Move up one state/remain in the highest state.

u_3 - Do not move/remain in the same state.

The state transitions that accompany these actions, for a system with n states ranging from s_0 to s_n, are illustrated in Fig. 2.

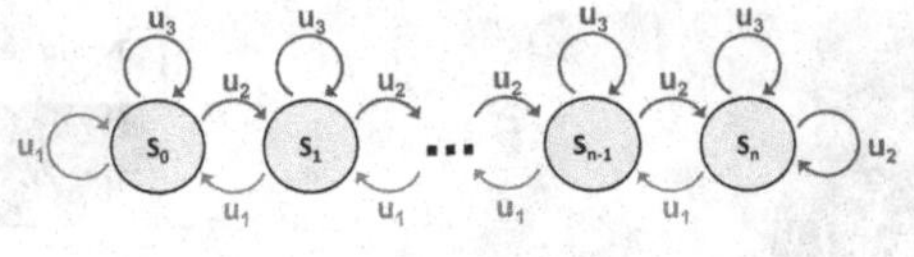

Fig. 2. State transitions for actions u_1 (green), u_2 (red), and u_3 (blue). (Color figure online)

2.3 Active Inference Framework

Active inference proposes that humans make decisions to minimise statistical free energy. This is functionally equivalent to minimising prediction error or the difference between an expected outcome, as calculated by the controlling agent, and the actually observed outcome. It is a predictive method whereby the agent uses its knowledge of how informative states are and how desirable the achievable future states are to determine which actions to take to reach the most favourable end result. To do this, the agent is equipped with an understanding of how its actions will affect future states of the world. This knowledge and understanding is encoded in a set of matrices which the agent has access to, the form of these matrices and the overall decision making process is outlined as follows.

We begin by defining the position states s to represent the ground truth state the agent is in and observations o, generated by passing gathered sensory data through the classification model, to act as a proxy for the real world. These represent the agent's understanding of its state, with each observational state o_i corresponding to a true state s_i, where i the state index.

The agent can control its position by undertaking one of the three defined actions: u_1, u_2, u_3. After each action it takes a tactile observation and classifies it into an observational state. We use finite horizon iterations that consist of an initial observation followed by 3 action and observation pairs, as initial simulation results indicate this is best. Each iteration therefore consists of four time steps, from $t = 0$ for the initial observation up to $t = 3$ for the final action and observation. A set of policies are generated for the agent to choose between, with each policy π corresponding to a sequence of allowable actions. Every permutation of actions is allowed so as to avoid biasing the agent towards selecting policies that appear favourable to an outside observer. The agent updates its beliefs at each time step and if its belief level in its state location reaches a pre-set decision threshold, it declares itself localised and ends the trial. If it does not localise within a single iteration, these beliefs are consolidated and used as the basis for a new iteration, using the final tactile observation as the initial observation of the next trial. The specific decision threshold is manually set at the beginning of the experiment.

The agent's overall decision making process is presented in Fig. 3.

The set of matrices that allow the agent to understand its environment and how its actions affect its position are summarised in Table 1. These matrices are used to drive the behaviour of the agent and their specific forms are presented in Sect. 2.4.

The agent's set of beliefs regarding its state location is defined as the probability of being in state s at time point τ under each policy π, denoted by

$$x_{\pi,s,\tau} = P(s_\tau = s | o_{0...\tau}, \pi). \tag{1}$$

At each time point the agent uses its sensory observations to update its beliefs about its state location at all time points: past, present, and predictions for its future states under each allowable policy.

The basis of the active inference framework is that the agent aims to minimise its total variational free energy. The current free energy is calculated for each policy π, such that at time τ the free energy $F_{\pi,\tau}$ is [9]

$$F_{\pi,\tau} = \sum_s x_{\pi,s,\tau} \log \left(\frac{x_{\pi,s,\tau}}{P(o_\tau | s_\tau = s) \sum_{s'} P(s_\tau = s | s_{\tau-1} = s', u_{\tau,\pi}) x_{\pi,s',\tau-1}} \right). \tag{2}$$

Table 1. The different quantities passed to the agent, the symbols they are denoted by, and their purposes.

Name	Symbol	Purpose
Confusion matrix	$P(o|s)$	The probability of getting a tactile observation o given that the robot is in a specific state s
Transition matrices	$P(s_t|s_{t-1}, u_{t,\pi})$	The probability of being in state s_t at time t given that it was in state s_{t-1} at time $t-1$ and action $u_{t,\pi}$ has been followed according to the policy under consideration π and the time t
Utility of states	$U(o|t = T)$	The desirability of achieving outcome o at the final time point T
Prior beliefs	$P(s|t = 0)$	The probability of being in state s at time $t = 0$. This is used to give the agent any pre-determined information

The agent also calculates expected free energy in the future for each policy π, denoted by $Q_{\pi,\tau}$. This expected free energy is defined with regards to the agent's prior beliefs about future outcomes as set out in both the confusion matrix, which encodes the information quality of each state, and in the utility matrix, which encodes the desirability of states. The agent uses its expected free energy to direct its goals as it is based on the agent's understanding of the system itself. This means that changes to the confusion matrix and the utility matrix should result in different patterns of behaviour. For further details on the active inference framework see [9].

Overall, the decision making process comes down to the agent selecting policy π with the lowest total free energy, calculated by combining $F_\pi = \sum_\tau F_{\pi,\tau}$ and $Q_\pi = \sum_\tau Q_{\pi,\tau}$.

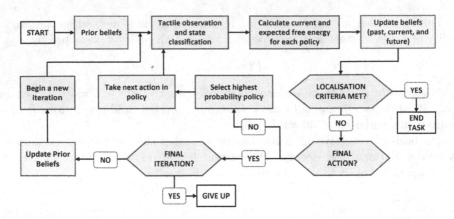

Fig. 3. Flowchart showing the active inference decision making process. Green boxes relate specifically to the agent's beliefs, blue boxes represent physical actions, purple boxes represent calculations and decision selection, and red boxes represent criteria triggers that direct the decision making flow. (Color figure online)

2.4   Experimental Conditions

The agent's decision making process is driven by two main quantities: its confusion matrix $P(o|s)$ and its utility matrix $U(o|t = T)$. The agent aims to minimise its total free energy by seeking out informative states, as encoded in the confusion matrix, and by seeking out desirable states, as encoded in the utility matrix. We aim to determine whether an active inference-based control system is capable of successfully completing the localisation task, as well as investigating how different methods of driving behaviour affect the end results. We consider two forms of confusion matrix and two forms of utility matrix.

For the confusion matrix we use a model confusion matrix and a Gaussian smoothed confusion matrix. The model confusion matrix is generated by testing the histogram classification model against 50 test data sets. The Gaussian smoothed confusion matrix is generated as part of a deeper investigation into model trends. We average the confusion of 9 different classification models tested against 100 test data sets, as shown in Fig. 4. We then generate a Gaussian smoothed confusion matrix such that the amplitude along the diagonal matches the best fit for the average confusion level. This smoothing generalises the confusion between neighbouring states, removing local confusion minima that may prevent the agent from exploring, and creates a model independent matrix.

For the utility matrix we use a flat utility matrix and a Gaussian smoothed utility matrix. For the flat utility matrix all states are designated as being equally desirable such that the observed behaviour will be entirely driven by the confusion matrix. The Gaussian smoothed utility matrix is generated using the diagonal from the Gaussian smoothed confusion matrix. The formula used to create this utility matrix is

$$U(o|t = \tau) = n_{\text{states}}(P(o|s) - \min(P(o|s))) + 1 \,, \tag{3}$$

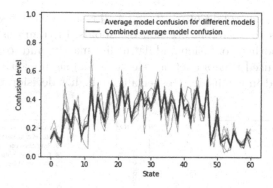

Fig. 4. Average confusion level for states (blue) calculated using the average confusion levels of 9 different model sets (grey) tested against 100 test data sets. (Color figure online)

where n_{states} is the total number of states. We use a +1 shift to ensure no states have a utility of zero. By creating the utility matrix in this manner it allows us to amplify the information content contained within the model and use it to further drive behaviour without introducing any form of human bias.

Overall, we define five sets of experimental conditions to investigate the effects these different matrix setups will have on behaviour and well as adding a random choice action selection option to act as a baseline. These conditions are structured as follows:

1. Model confusion matrix and flat utility matrix
2. Model confusion matrix and Gaussian smoothed utility matrix
3. Gaussian smoothed confusion matrix and flat utility matrix
4. Gaussian smoothed confusion matrix and Gaussian smoothed utility matrix
5. Random choice action selection

We test each condition at five decision thresholds, corresponding to 75%, 80%, 85%, 90%, and 95% certainty in state location, and set prior probability $P(s|t = 0)$ equal for all states as the initial state is unknown to the agent.

3   Results

3.1   Localisation and Error

Figure 5 shows the percentage of trials from each experimental condition in which the agent localised and the percentage of those localisations that were incorrect. These results show a decrease in the number of trials that localise incorrectly as we increase the decision threshold and trials use more sensory observations to gather information, which is consistent across all experimental conditions. We also begin to see a decrease in the number of trials that reach the decision threshold as the required belief level to localise is considerably higher and the agent times out before reaching it.

Overall we see that conditions 1, 2, and 4 all result in very high levels of trial localisation across the different decision thresholds. In comparison condition 3, that used the smoothed confusion and flat utility matrix, and to a greater extent condition 5, that used random action selection, had significantly lower levels of trials that resulted in localisation, especially at higher decision thresholds.

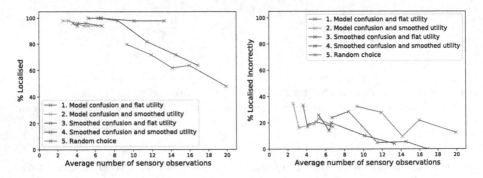

Fig. 5. Left: Total percentage of trials from each set of experimental conditions that localised. Right: The percentage of those trials that localised incorrectly.

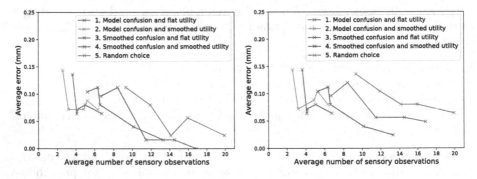

Fig. 6. Average position error in mm for (left) localised trials and (right) all trials, for each set of experimental conditions.

There are different trial lengths for different experimental conditions. Conditions 1 and 2 localised significantly faster, using the fewest sensory observations, followed by conditions 3 and 4 with condition 5 taking the longest. There were similar levels of incorrectly classified trials, though where conditions 1 and 2 reach a plateau at approximately 20% incorrect independent of decision threshold, conditions 3, 4, and 5 all demonstrate a continued decrease as we increase the decision threshold. This indicates a level of flexibility within the setup and a speed accuracy trade off that can be exploited differently based upon situation.

Figure 6 shows the average position error for localised trials as well as average position error for all trials including those that did not reach a conclusion. The highest error that we see if for the lowest decision thresholds of conditions 1 and 2, with a position error of 0.144mm, which is still on par with results achieved on similar tasks using active perception-based control methods [23–26].

All active inference-based experimental conditions significantly outperformed random choice action selection. Random choice consistently results in longer trials, lower levels of localisation, and greater position error at equal trial length compared to those achieved using active inference-based control.

Overall, these results indicate that the best setup for an active inference-based control system would be with condition 4, using the smoothed confusion matrix and smoothed utility matrix. These results show consistently high levels of localisation, at all decision thresholds tested, as well as some of the lowest levels of position error for the number of sensory observations required to localise. The trials are longer than those achieved using conditions 1 and 2; however, the ability to fine tune trial length with decision threshold to achieve more accurate results demonstrates greater flexibility.

3.2 Belief Updating

Over the course of each trial the agent uses sensory observations to inform and update its beliefs regarding its state location. Figure 7 shows this belief updating process, specifically for a trial from the 95% decision threshold experiment run using condition 4, smoothed confusion and smoothed utility matrices.

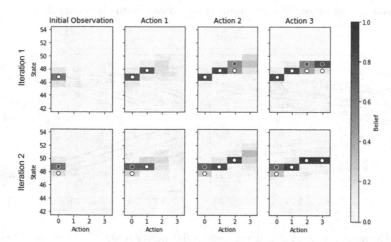

Fig. 7. Belief updating from an experiment trial using experiment condition 4 and decision threshold 95%. The agent took two iterations to localise, the top row shows the agent's belief levels in each state for the first iteration and the second row shows the second iteration. The red circles identify incorrectly classified states, and the white circles identify the ground truth state of the robot. (Color figure online)

This test highlights the agent's ability to overcome incorrectly classified sensory observations and demonstrates what happens when the agent's understanding of how its movements affect its state location comes into direct opposition with its sensory observations. The trial has two incorrectly classified data points, corresponding to the final two observations in the first iteration. The observation at the second action time point remains confused as the information gained from the previous and subsequent states are in direct contradiction with each other. Knowing that it has not moved since observing state 48 the agent believes that it should still be in state 48, in direct opposition to its observation of state 49 at that and the final time point. As such, the agent is unable to determine which of its observations is more reliable. When the beliefs are carried over to the next iteration, the subsequent series of correctly classified observations results in an increased belief level for the true position the agent was in at the start of the second iteration. By the end of the second iteration the agent is able to successfully localise despite carrying over confusion from the previous iteration.

3.3 Behaviour

The smoothed confusion matrix shows consistently high levels of confusion at the centre of the stimulus where it more closely resembles a flat surface. In contrast, the states at the edge of the stimulus have consistently lower levels of confusion as there is a more significant change in gradient between neighbouring states. This means that the difference between contact locations are more pronounced which is reflected in the pin deflections. As the agent's decision making process is driven by a desire for high information, low confusion states we expect it to move towards the edges of the stimulus and away from the central states.

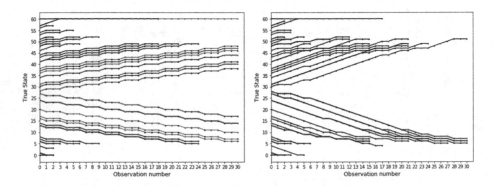

Fig. 8. The agent's trajectories using (left) a flat utility matrix, and (right) the Gaussian smoothed utility matrix. Black lines are correctly localised trials, green lines are undecided trials where the best guess is correct, blue lines are incorrectly localised trials one state away from true. Red circles are incorrectly classified observations. (Color figure online)

Figure 8 presents the trajectories achieved using conditions 3 and 4 when using a 95% decision threshold. Higher decision thresholds result in longer trials, allowing us to investigate long term trends. Overall, we see that the agent consistently selects sequences of actions that will move its position towards the high information states at the edges of the stimulus, and that the trials are generally shorter when the starting location is already near an edge.

We see a considerable difference in behaviour for different experimental conditions. Both demonstrate advantageous trajectories, however it is far more pronounced when using condition 4. We conclude that whilst using a smoothed confusion matrix alone does encourage movement to high information states, the magnification in differences between neighbouring states provided by the smoothed utility matrix does encourage larger movements. This also results in decreased trial lengths, from an average of 16.86, using condition 3, to 13.30 observations using condition 4.

4   Discussion

This research presented an active inference-based control mechanism for a tactile sensing system and demonstrated its success at an active localisation task in a known environment. The system had a high accuracy and was robust in the face of incorrectly classified data.

The movement trajectories displayed by the agent showed an emergent behavioural trend, following paths towards more informative states without hard coding this behaviour or introducing human bias. This agent outperformed random choice decision making, in terms of the number of successful trials and average trial length. Our results are comparable with those achieved for similar localisation tasks that use active perception-based control. We achieve lower error for the same task [25], and are able to show comparable trial lengths on similar localisation tasks using a range of tactile sensors [23–26].

We demonstrate that using Gaussian smoothed confusion matrices results in a more accurate and flexible controlling agent but that using a model confusion matrix results in faster localisation. The localisation error for using model confusion matrices plateaus at $\approx$ 20%, even with a decision threshold of 95%. In contrast, the Gaussian smoothed confusion matrix gives localisation errors effectively on par with the decision threshold, achieving 95–100% accuracy at a 95% decision threshold. This ability to trade off between accuracy and trial length means that despite having longer trials overall the Gaussian smoothed confusion matrix offers more versatility to the agent. We also show that using a smoothed utility matrix significantly decreases trial length without compromising on accuracy independent of the type of confusion matrix being used. These smoothed matrices offer flexibility that can be tuned through the decision threshold, offering significant advantage as we move to more complex environments and tasks.

This localisation task represents a useful toy scenario, giving a proof of concept for active inference control for tactile robotics. We expect that this work can be extended to unstructured environments by defining generalised position states that represent physical structures such flat surfaces and edges rather than specific position related states. This will allow the framework to complete tasks independent of stimulus shape and also allow for easy switching between tasks.

In future work we also look to use deep networks which estimate confidence to give the agent the ability to differentiate between informative and confusing observations on a case by case basis rather than relying on general trends. Overall, our work shows that active inference-based control is able to generate advantageous control policies and we expect that introducing more sophisticated models will allow for robust interactions in unknown environments in the future.

References

1. Kandel, E.R., Schwartz, J.H., Jessell, T.M., Siegelbaum, S., Hudspeth, A.J., Mack, S. (eds.): Principles of Neural Science, vol. 4. McGraw-Hill, New York (2000)
2. Westling, G., Johansson, R.S.: Factors influencing the force control during precision grip. Exp. Brain Res. **53**(2), 277–284 (1984)
3. Smail, L.C., Neal, C., Wilkins, C., Packham, T.L.: Comfort and function remain key factors in upper limb prosthetic abandonment: findings of a scoping review. Disabil. Rehabil. Assist. Technol. **16**(8), 821–830 (2021)
4. Schiefer, M., Tan, D., Sidek, S.M., Tyler, D.J.: Sensory feedback by peripheral nerve stimulation improves task performance in individuals with upper limb loss using a myoelectric prosthesis. J. Neural Eng. **13**(1), 016001 (2015)
5. Graczyk, E.L., Resnik, L., Schiefer, M.A., Schmitt, M.S., Tyler, D.J.: Home use of a neural-connected sensory prosthesis provides the functional and psychosocial experience of having a hand again. Sci. Rep. **8**(1), 1–17 (2018)
6. Friston, K., Kilner, J., Harrison, L.: A free energy principle for the brain. J. Physiol.-Paris **100**(1), 70–87 (2006)
7. Buckley, C.L., Kim, C.S., McGregor, S., Seth, A.K.: The free energy principle for action and perception: a mathematical review. J. Math. Psychol. **81**, 55–79 (2017)
8. Parr, T., Friston, K.J.: The anatomy of inference: generative models and brain structure. Front. Comput. Neurosci. **12** (2018)
9. Friston, K., FitzGerald, T., Rigoli, F., Schwartenbeck, P., Pezzulo, G.: Active inference: a process theory. Neural Comput. **29**, 1–49 (2017)
10. FitzGerald, T., Schwartenbeck, P., Moutoussis, M., Dolan, R.J., Friston, K.: Active inference, evidence accumulation, and the urn task. Neural Comput. **27**(2), 306–328 (2015)
11. Friston, K.: The free-energy principle: a unified brain theory? Nat. Rev. Neurosci. **11**(2), 127–138 (2010)
12. Friston, K., FitzGerald, T., Rigoli, F., Schwartenbeck, P., O'Doherty, J., Pezzulo, G.: Active inference and learning. Neurosci. Biobehav. Rev. **68**, 862–879 (2016)
13. Friston, K.: Learning and inference in the brain. Neural Netw. **16**(9), 1325 1252 (2003)
14. Parr, T., Friston, K.J.: Working memory, attention, and salience in active inference. Sci. Rep. **7**(1), 1–21 (2017)
15. Hohwy, J.: The Predictive Mind. Oxford University Press, Oxford (2014)
16. Lanillos, P., Cheng, G.: Active inference with function learning for robot body perception. In: International Workshop on Continual Unsupervised Sensorimotor Learning (2018)
17. Pio-Lopez, L., Nizard, A., Friston, K., Pezzulo, G.: Active inference and robot control: a case study. J. R. Soc. Interface **13**(122), 20160616 (2016)
18. Çatal, O., Verbelen, T., Van de Maele, T., Dhoedt, B., Safron, A.: Robot navigation as hierarchical active inference. Neural Netw. **142**, 192–204 (2021)

19. Baltieri, M., Buckley, C.L.: An active inference implementation of phototaxis. In: ECAL 2017, the Fourteenth European Conference on Artificial Life (2017). https://doi.org/10.1162/isal_a_011

20. Pezzato, C., Ferrari, R., Corbato, C.H.: A novel adaptive controller for robot manipulators based on active inference. IEEE Robot. Autom. Lett. **5**(2), 2973–2980 (2020)

21. Oliver, G., Lanillos, P., Cheng, G.: An empirical study of active inference on a humanoid robot. IEEE Trans. Cogn. Dev. Syst. (2021). https://doi.org/10.1109/TCDS.2021.3049907

22. Ward-Cherrier, B., et al.: The TacTip family: soft optical tactile sensors with 3d-printed biomimetic morphologies. Soft Rob. **5**(2), 216–227 (2018)

23. Lepora, N.F., Sullivan, J.C., Mitchinson, B., Pearson, M., Gurney, K., Prescott, T.J.: Brain-inspired Bayesian perception for biomimetic robot touch. In: 2012 IEEE International Conference on Robotics and Automation, pp. 5111–5116. IEEE (2012). https://doi.org/10.1109/ICRA.2012.6224815

24. Lepora, N.F., Martinez-Hernandez, U., Prescott, T.: Active Bayesian perception for simultaneous object localization and identification. In: Robotics: Science and Systems (RSS) (2013)

25. Lepora, N.F., Ward-Cherrier, B.: Superresolution with an optical tactile sensor. In: 2015 IEEE/RSJ International Conference on Intelligent Robots and Systems (IROS), pp. 2686–2691 (2015). https://doi.org/10.1109/IROS.2015.7353744

26. Lepora, N.F.: Biomimetic active touch with fingertips and whiskers. IEEE Trans. Haptics **9**(2), 170–183 (2016)

27. Lepora, N.F., Fox, C.W., Evans, M.H., Diamond, M.E., Gurney, K., Prescott, T.J.: Optimal decision-making in mammals: insights from a robot study of rodent texture discrimination. J. R. Soc. Interface **9**(72), 1517–1528 (2012)

SLUGBOT, an *Aplysia*-Inspired Robotic Grasper for Studying Control

Kevin Dai[1] , Ravesh Sukhnandan[2] , Michael Bennington[1] ,
Karen Whirley[1] , Ryan Bao[1] , Lu Li[4] , Jeffrey P. Gill[5] ,
Hillel J. Chiel[5,6,7] , and Victoria A. Webster-Wood[1,2,3(✉)]

[1] Department of Mechanical Engineering, Carnegie Mellon University,
Pittsburgh, PA, USA
`vwebster@andrew.cmu.edu`
[2] Department of Biomedical Engineering, Carnegie Mellon University,
Pittsburgh, PA, USA
[3] McGowan Institute for Regenerative Medicine, Carnegie Mellon University,
Pittsburgh, PA, USA
[4] Robotics Institute, Carnegie Mellon University, Pittsburgh, PA, USA
[5] Department of Biology, Case Western Reserve University,
Cleveland, OH, USA
[6] Department of Neurosciences, Case Western Reserve University,
Cleveland, OH, USA
[7] Department of Biomedical Engineering, Case Western Reserve University,
Cleveland, OH, USA

Abstract. Living systems can use a single periphery to perform a variety of tasks and adapt to a dynamic environment. This multifunctionality is achieved through the use of neural circuitry that adaptively controls the reconfigurable musculature. Current robotic systems struggle to flexibly adapt to unstructured environments. Through mimicry of the neuromechanical coupling seen in living organisms, robotic systems could potentially achieve greater autonomy. The tractable neuromechanics of the sea slug *Aplysia californica's* feeding apparatus, or buccal mass, make it an ideal candidate for applying neuromechanical principles to the control of a soft robot. In this work, a robotic grasper was designed to mimic specific morphology of the *Aplysia* feeding apparatus. These include the use of soft actuators akin to biological muscle, a deformable grasping surface, and a similar muscular architecture. A previously developed Boolean neural controller was then adapted for the control of this soft robotic system. The robot was capable of qualitatively replicating swallowing behavior by cyclically ingesting a plastic tube. The robot's normalized translational and rotational kinematics of the odontophore

K. Dai, R. Sukhnandan, M. Bennington—These authors contributed equally to the work.
This work was supported by NSF DBI2015317 as part of the NSF/CIHR/DFG/FRQ/
UKRI-MRC Next Generation Networks for Neuroscience Program and by the NSF
Research Fellowship Program under Grant No. DGE1745016. Any opinions, findings,
and conclusions or recommendations expressed in this material are those of the authors
and do not necessarily reflect the views of the National Science Foundation.

© The Author(s), under exclusive license to Springer Nature Switzerland AG 2022
A. Hunt et al. (Eds.): Living Machines 2022, LNAI 13548, pp. 182–194, 2022.
https://doi.org/10.1007/978-3-031-20470-8_19

followed profiles observed *in vivo* despite morphological differences. This brings *Aplysia*-inspired control *in roboto* one step closer to multifunctional neural control schema *in vivo* and *in silico*. Future additions may improve SLUGBOT's viability as a neuromechanical research platform.

Keywords: Bio-inspired robot · *Aplysia* · Boolean neural control

1 Introduction

Robots have typically struggled to replicate the innate behavioral flexibility of animals to act in unstructured environments [21, 24]. Animals can fluidly adapt to their changing environment by exploiting the close coupling of their neural and muscular systems [9, 16]. This behavioral flexibility is driven in part by the multifunctionality of limbs and appendages, which can achieve different tasks by enacting new motor control strategies or leveraging changing mechanical advantages [9, 16]. One bioinspired method specifically integrates knowledge of an organism's neuromechanics to improve robotic performance in tasks such as locomotion and grasping [10, 16]. Here, knowledge of the model animal is used in the design of the robot's morphology and control. These bio-inspired robots may also serve as a platform for testing biological hypotheses and validating neuromechanical simulation since such robots must solve real physical problems [16, 19].

Determining the right level of biological detail to capture in bioinspired and biomimetic robotics for neuromechanical research remains an ongoing challenge [20]. In addition to the difficulties in matching the mechanical properties of muscles and tissues, replicating the complex neural circuits that control the periphery for robotic control is often impossible as such circuits are not known in their entirety [20]. The neural circuitry governing the feeding behavior of the marine mollusk *Aplysia californica* has been extensively studied [25], which makes it an ideal model organism for investigating the level of biomimicry needed to create a robotic platform for neuromechanical research. In this work, we present the real-time control of a soft-robotic Slug-Like Uniaxial Grasper roBOT (SLUGBOT) inspired by the morphology and control of *Aplysia's* feeding apparatus (buccal mass, Fig. 1a). The grasper is controlled by a modified version of Webster-Wood et al.'s hybrid Boolean model of *Aplysia* neuromechanics [25], and can qualitatively replicate *Aplysia* swallowing behavior. This robot may serve as a platform for testing future hypotheses related to *Aplysia's* neuromechanics, as well as for elucidating techniques for generating multifunctional grasping behavior.

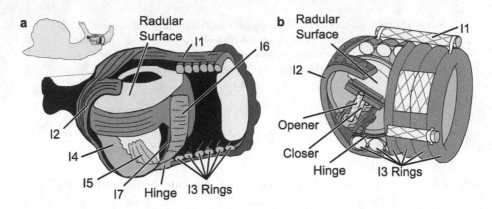

Fig. 1. Cutaway views of a) *Aplysia* buccal mass anatomy located in the animal (modified with permission [5]) and b) SLUGBOT, showing key muscle groups and features.

1.1 Feeding Behavior in *Aplysia* and Prior Work

Aplysia moves food through its buccal mass primarily by means of a grasper composed of a layer of flexible cartilage covered with very fine teeth (radula) that covers a muscular structure (odontophore) [8]. The grasper closes to grasp food and opens to release it, and can either protract (pivot and translate towards the animal's jaws) or retract (pivot and translate towards the esophagus and crop) [6]. *Aplysia* is capable of generating multifunctional behavior by varying the timing of the activation of muscles responsible for protraction, retraction, and opening and closing of the grasper [13,15]. In the ingestive behaviors of biting and swallowing, the grasper is closed during retraction to bring food into the esophagus and crop [6].

The previous state-of-the-art in *Aplysia* inspired robot was developed by Mangan et al., who created a pneumatically actuated soft-robotic gripper inspired by *Aplysia's* feeding apparatus morphology [10]. The device consisted of McKibben actuators that activated to peristaltically protract or retract a rubber ellipsoid. The rubber ellipsoid grasped objects by pressurizing McKibben actuators that served as inflatable "lips". Although this robot included the I3 retractor muscle, it did not include several key muscles involved in feeding behavior in the animal, namely the I2 muscle, which is the main driver of protraction [28], the I1 muscle, and separate opener and closer muscles for the radular surface [8].

The peristaltic sequence used to protract and retract Mangan et al.'s grasper did not incorporate a neural controller based on the established neural circuitry of *Aplysia*. It also did not include real time sensory feedback to trigger multifunctional behavior based on changing stimuli. Our robot addresses this gap by implementing real time control of the robot's actuators based on the Boolean model of *Aplysia*'s neuromechanics by Webster-Wood et al. [25]. The Boolean model uses simplified biomechanics and an on/off representation for neuronal activity [25], which allows faster than real time simulation of the model. These properties make it suitable for real-time control of the robotic grasper.

2 Methods

SLUGBOT is a robotic representation of the buccal mass of *Aplysia*. We represent the odontophore and a portion of surrounding musculature including the I1, I2 and I3 muscles (Fig. 1b). The hinge is represented by an elastic band.

2.1 Fabricating McKibben Artificial Muscles

The I1 muscles (125 mm-long), and the odontophore opener and closer muscles (45 mm-long, see Sect. 2.3) were represented by linear McKibben actuators, while the I3 muscle was represented by a series of unsegmented, toroidal McKibben actuators (295 mm circumference). Both types of McKibbens share a similar fabrication scheme (Fig. 2a). The inner bladder of the McKibben consisted of a latex balloon attached to plastic fittings. The linear McKibbens required one barbed 3.18 mm to 1.59 mm reducer fitting and one 3.18 mm plug fitting, whereas the toroidal McKibbens required two barbed reducers. The latex balloon was held onto the fittings with two Kevlar thread slipknots to create an airtight seal. A soapy water test was performed on the inner bladder to ensure it was sealed before adding the outer mesh. A 9.53 mm overexpanded braided sleeving (Flexo®️ PET) was heated at both ends to prevent unravelling of the mesh, and then held in place over the latex bladder using Kevlar slipknots and 6 mm-long rings of latex balloons, which were placed between the mesh and the Kevlar thread to increase friction and prevent slipping. To complete the linear McKibben actuators, cyanoacrylate (CA) adhesive (Loctite Gel) was used to adhere the ends

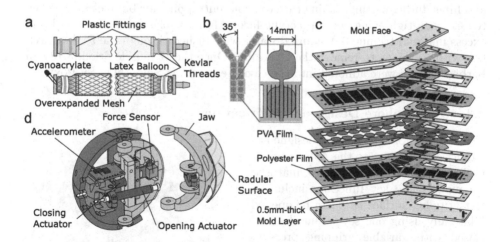

Fig. 2. Fabrication of SLUGBOT actuators and grasper. a) Construction of McKibben actuators with internal layer (upper) and external layer (lower), b) Y-shaped I2 muscle geometry with PVA film dimensions and PET reinforcing film, c) I2 FPAM mold and material layup during casting process, and d) cutaway view with partial exploded view of odontophore grasper geometry.

of the braided sleeve to the fittings and the latex bladder. To form the circular shape of the toroidal muscles, the two barbed reducers were also connected by 12 mm lengths of tubing to a 1.59 mm Y-fitting.

2.2 Fabricating Flat Artificial Muscles

The I2 muscle was represented by a 2 mm-thick, Y-shaped assembly of flat pneumatic artificial muscles (FPAMs) containing two series of 20 mm-wide FPAM cells (Fig. 2b) [18,26,27]. The FPAMs were structured with 25.4 μm-thick polyester (PET) reinforcing films on each side of a polyvinyl alcohol masking film (PVA, Sulky Ultra Solvy), separated by 0.5 mm-thick layers of elastomer (Smooth-On Dragonskin 10 Slow). The films were cut using a Silhouette Portrait 2. Creases in the PVA film were smoothed out prior to cutting by annealing the film under tension with a heat gun, taking care to avoid warping the PVA film. The PET reinforcing film was wiped after cutting with isopropyl alcohol and DOWSIL 1200 OS primer, which was allowed to cure for 60–90 min prior to elastomer casting. For forming the elastomer, two laser-cut pieces of acrylic formed the top and bottom faces of a mold along with four 0.5 mm-thick Y-shaped outlines 3D-printed with polylactic acid (PLA) to form a Y-shaped cavity when placed between the mold's acrylic faces. The FPAMs were fabricated by sequentially (1) assembling the mold in 0.5 mm layer increments on the bottom acrylic plate, (2) casting liquid elastomer into the mold, (3) smoothing elastomer using a wooden mixing stick, and (4) adding reinforcing or masking films onto the elastomer as necessary, and (5) repeating these steps until the casting reached a total thickness of 2 mm (Fig. 2c). M3 fasteners indexed the assembly of the mold and films during casting, taking care to avoid entrapping air bubbles in the elastomer when tightening the top acrylic face. After the elastomer was cured and excess material trimmed, de-ionized water was flushed through the FPAM cavities with a syringe to remove the PVA film. Once the I2 muscle dried, 3.18 mm barbed fittings were adhered into the cavity ends using SmoothOn Sil-Poxy.

2.3 Odontophore Design and Fabrication

The odontophore grasper was designed as a functional analogy to the *Aplysia* odontophore instead of as a direct anatomical model. The key functions include a soft gripping surface that can be opened bilaterally using one set of muscles and closed with variable gripping pressure using antagonist muscles (Fig. 2d). The grasper consisted of a rigid PLA outer shell fabricated by 3D printing, two 3D printed radular halves, and a cast rubber surface. The radular halves pivoted freely

Fig. 3. SLUGBOT experimental setup showing the odontophore in the forward position and the laser time-of-flight sensor positioned at the rear of the robot.

about two M3 bolts at the shell's poles. The grasper was actuated by three linear McKibben actuators forming one antagonistic pair. Two of the muscles shared an air inlet and actuated together to open the grasper. These muscles were attached to the internal edge of the radular halves and to the back of the shell. The third McKibben was placed in the middle of the grasper and attached to the internal edge of the soft surface with a 3D printed clamp. When activated, this muscle pulled the surface further into the grasper and pulled the radular halves together to generate closing pressure.

The soft gripping surface was fabricated by casting rubber (SmoothOn Vytaflex 30) into a 3D printed mold lined with circumferential Kevlar threads, creating an inextensible surface in the closer muscle's pulling direction. The surface was attached to the radular halves using CA glue applied only at the edge distal to the opening, which allowed the surface to lift away from the radula when the closer muscle was inactive but remained taut with an activated closer muscle.

The grasper was fitted with two sensors: 1) a 9-degree of freedom inertial measurement unit (BNO055) to sense absolute orientation of the grasper, and 2) a Hall-effect-based soft magnetic force sensor [4,7] to measure the grasper's closing pressure. A laser time-of-flight sensor (VL53L5CX, SparkFun®) was mounted externally and pointed at the odontophore outer shell to obtain positional feedback. Retroreflective tape was applied to the external surface of the shell where the laser was expected to coincide. The remainder of the shell was coated with 76.2 μm-thick Ultra-High Molecular Weight tape to reduce friction.

2.4   Robot Assembly

The actuators representing the I1, I2, and I3 muscles were assembled using a nylon spandex sheath. Two sheets of spandex fabric were sewn together with 300 mm-long, parallel seams separated by 20 mm, which formed six channels for housing the I3 toroidal actuators. The linear I1 actuators were attached on the outside of the sheath with 6.35 mm-wide elastic straps over fittings at each end of each actuator. The straps were positioned to avoid constricting the actuator when inflated. The I2 actuator was attached at each corner to the posterior portion of the spandex sheath with thread. Sil-Poxy was applied to the thread contacting the I2 actuator to avoid tear-out of the silicone actuator. A 6.35 mm-wide elastic band representing the hinge was attached at one end to the posterior I3 ring using a hook-and-loop fastener, and attached to the odontophore at the other end using a sewn loop of kevlar thread that wrapped around a pole bolt.

2.5 Robot Control

To qualitatively compare the robot's movements to those of the published hybrid Boolean model [25], we prepared the robot to accept simulated Boolean neural commands (Figs. 3 and 4). The neural commands were generated by one microcontroller and sent to a second microcontroller that integrated the neural command signals into muscle activations and controlled the pressure within each actuator. Prior to each experiment, the odontophore was placed in the posterior of the robot touching the I2 muscle, with

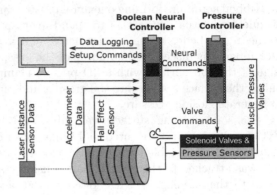

Fig. 4. SLUGBOT control schema. Behavioral stimuli and sensor feedback are input to the neural controller, which outputs neural signals to the pressure controller. The pressure controller integrates neural signals into muscle activation pressures.

radula facing upwards. Behavioral movement was initialized by pushbuttons corresponding to seaweed-inspired stimuli.

Boolean Neural Controller. A modified version of the Boolean neural network presented by Webster-Wood et al. [25] was implemented on a microcontroller (Teensy 3.6) to determine the muscle activation patterns in real time. This model represents bursting neural activity as discrete Boolean variables and the neural interactions are captured in logical calculations.

Additional neurons and connections were added (Table 1) to the existing model to activate muscles that were included in the robot but not in the previous biomechanical model [25]. Motor neurons were needed for the I1 muscles, the odontophore opener, and the individual segments of I3. Note that these additional interneuron connections are based on phenomenological connections and may not reflect the true neural connections. For I1, motor neurons B43 and B45 were selected [1], and an excitatory connection with B64 was hypothesized to synchronize firing with retraction. The odontophore opener had behavior-dependent excitation from B48 (ingestive, firing during retraction) and B44 (egestive, firing during protraction) [3]. As the opener is a single muscle, these neurons were lumped together and excited by B64 to mark retraction and by CBI-3 to indicate ingestion or egestion. The I3 required a decohered B3/B6/B9 motor pool to produce peristalsis, which was complicated by reports of different firing patterns in intracellular recordings [2,6]. For generating peristalsis in SLUGBOT, we introduced fixed time delays between the sequential firings for three functional retractor motor units that may not reflect true firing patterns of B3, B6, and B9 *in vivo*. Finally, the context-dependent role of I3 as a protractor [23] was incorporated into the design, so additional innervation to the posterior of I3 was

Table 1. Modifications to Hybrid Boolean Model for SLUGBOT

Motor unit	Activated actuator group	Activation logic
RU1	Anterior/medial I3	Same as B3/B6/B9 motor pool in [25]
RU2/RU3	Medial/posterior I3	Fixed time delays after Retractor Unit 1 fires to generate peristalsis
B10	Medial/posterior I3	Fixed time delay after B31/32
B44/B48	Odontophore Opener	On for protraction in biting/swallowing
		On for retraction in rejection
B43/B45	I1	On for retraction in all behaviors

performed by B10 [1] near the end of protraction [12], activated by a fixed time delay after the firing of B31/B32. The activation of each I3 ring was set as a weighted sum of three Retractor Units (RU1/RU2/RU3), B10, and B38 (responsible for pinching in the anterior I3 [11]) based on the regional innervation [1]. The weights were experimentally tuned to produce peristalsis.

During experimentation, the neural signals were calculated in real time on one Teensy 3.6, and then passed to the pressure microcontroller via UART. The neural controller collected the proprioceptive feedback from the integrated sensors, calculated the Boolean neural signals, and logged the neural and sensors signals to a PC. Different SLUGBOT behaviors could be set by changing the states of sensory feedback neurons (related to mechanical stimulus at the lips, chemical stimulus at the lips, and mechanical stimulus at the grasper) as well as the general arousal of the grasper via push buttons. During swallowing, tape strips or plastic tubing were placed in the grasper's radula to represent seaweed.

Muscle Pressure Controller. The Boolean neuron signals were received from the neural microcontroller and integrated by a muscle pressure microcontroller (Teensy 3.6). These activations were scaled and used as pressure set points. For each actuator, pressurization was controlled through bang-bang actuation of two electromechanical valves (KOGANEI GA101HE1) with feedback from a 30 psig pressure sensor (ELVH-030G-HAND-C-PSA4). One valve acted as an inlet leading to the pressure supply line (15 psig) and another valve acted as relief leading to ambient pressure. Pressure information from each of the ten actuators was collected serially, with actuation done in parallel through three daisy-chained shift-register low-side switches (TPIC6595). A 0.4-psig tolerance band was added around the pressure setpoint to further improve stability.

3   Results

SLUGBOT qualitatively demonstrated swallowing behavior when presented with the corresponding stimuli (Figs. 5 and 6). The data are time shifted to align peak retraction with peak retraction reported in [14]. Multiple cycles ($n = 8$) were time normalized and averaged together, using the activation of B31/B32 to determine the normalization period. Due to this averaging, some robot neural signals show values within the range of 0 to 1, rather than Boolean values of 0 and 1. The additional neurons from the robot controller were implemented in the original Boolean model framework for comparison but do not affect the *in silico* biomechanics. For most neural signals, activation and deactivation triggered at similar points in the cycle, with a range of 13.3% of cycle length

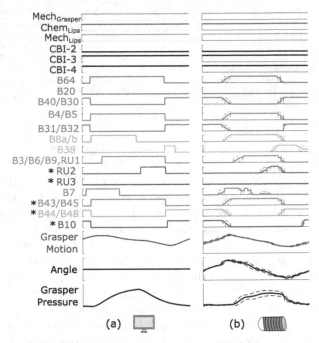

Fig. 5. SLUGBOT qualitatively replicates the *in silico* [25] neural signals, kinematics, and grasper pressure. SLUGBOT data is normalized to cycle length and averaged over multiple cycles, with dashed lines indicating standard deviation. a) Boolean model, swallowing; b) SLUGBOT, swallowing ($n = 8$). Asterisks indicate neural signals modified from the hybrid Boolean model. Retractor Unit 1 follows the same activation logic as B3/B6/B9. Mech$_i$ indicates mechanical stimulus at location i (either the grasper or lips, and Chem$_{Lips}$ indicates chemical stimulus at the lips.

for swallowing. In both models, a third retractor unit, RU3, was implemented but did not fire because the fixed time delay after RU1 fired was longer than the retraction time.

In comparison to the *in vivo* kinematics of *Aplysia's* odontophore measured by Neustadter et al. [14], SLUGBOT reproduces the main characterisitics of the odontophore's translation and rotation during swallowing. For both *in vivo* and *in roboto* swallows, the forward translation of the odontophore during protraction is accompanied by simultaneous rotation. The radula rotate approximately 90 °C during protraction, with the radula facing the dorsal surface at the start of the cycle and then facing outwards from the lumen at peak protraction [15]. The odontophore then retracts by translating towards the posterior to bring the grasped food into the lumen and towards the esophagus. This is accompanied by an approximately 90° rotation of the odontophore such that the radula are facing the dorsal surface of the buccal mass, as with the start of protraction.

4 Discussion

4.1 Morphological Differences Between SLUGBOT and *Aplysia*

SLUGBOT qualitatively replicated key features of the translational and rotational kinematics of the *Aplysia's* odontophore measured during *in vivo* swallowing experiments. Once the parameters for the Boolean controller were tuned, the range and timing of the odontophore's translations and rotations were repeatable during the cyclic protraction and retraction during swallowing.

However, there exists a number of key morphological features present in the animal which are essential for successful feeding behavior but were not captured in SLUGBOT. In the animal, the anterior portion of the I3 musculature near the jaws tightens and clamps together, holding food in place during swallowing [11]. The toroidal McKibben actuators that constituted SLUGBOT's I3 musculature were not capable of sufficient radial expansion to clamp onto the narrow plastic tubing representing food. As a consequence, the plastic tubing needed to be held in place by methods external to the robot, which is not needed *in vivo*.

In vivo, the odontophore is capable of a total range of posterior rotation beyond 90° during swallowing [14,17]. This additional rotation was utilized by Mangan et al. to translocate an object through their *Aplysia*-inspired grasper [10]. SLUGBOT's inability to rotate beyond 90° may have contributed to inconsistent swallowing behavior because the radular surface was not tilted towards the esophagus as in *Aplysia*. Plastic tubing released at the end of retraction tended to fall directly back onto the radular surface instead of being deposited posterior to the robot. *In vivo*, both active and passive hinge forces play an important role in assisting retraction [22]. Modification of the hinge's mechanical properties and adding active control may enable more biomimetic motion.

The deformation of the soft structures and musculature of the buccal mass plays an important role *in vivo* that can improve SLUGBOT's biomimicry and feeding performance in the future. For instance, the movement of the radular stalk into the odontophore both increases posterior rotation during the loss of the Γ shape and also changes the effective shape of the odontophore [17]. The shape of the odontophore during retraction increases the mechanical advantage and effective force from the I1/I3 complex, enhancing retraction [17]. The I2 muscle likewise benefits from mechanical reconfiguration to enhance protraction during rejection and biting [17]. SLUGBOT is not currently capable of taking advantage of such mechanical reconfiguration because (1) the odontophore is a rigid sphere and (2) there is no analogue to the radular stalk. Using softer materials and incorporating a radular stalk-like mechanism can help address this gap. The context-dependent enhancement of the effective force on the odontophore could reduce the impacts of friction and poor mechanical advantage during movement.

4.2 Neuronal Controller

By implementing a biomimetic neuronal controller using Boolean logic to control SLUGBOT, we were able to demonstrate swallowing. Qualitatively, the behavior resembled that of the previously developed *in silico* Boolean model [25] when comparing the neural signals, grasper motion, and grasping force. Repeatability between cycles and comparable motion profiles suggest that bioinspired control of *Aplysia*-inspired robotic structures is possible even with simplified neural mechanics and a smaller number of controlling neurons than in the animal. Both the *in silico* and *in roboto* models are qualitative models of the grasper motion and are not fit to animal data. As the appropriate *in vivo* data is collected, the robot can be further tuned to match the observed behaviors, such as with the different activation patterns of B3, B6 and B9 neurons recorded *in vivo* [2,6].

5 Conclusion

SLUGBOT - a soft robotic grasper inspired by the buccal mass of *Aplysia californica* - demonstrates robotic control via Boolean logic to replicate swallowing behavior exhibited by the model animal. The robot's grasp-

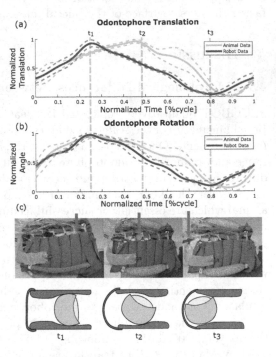

Fig. 6. Kinematic comparison with MRI data from behaving animals. (a) Odontophore translation. (b) Odontophore rotation. (c) Frames from swallowing video with corresponding cartoon representation showing the retraction phase and the "ingestion" of a tube. The time-normalized swallowing kinematics are compared between the robot and the behaving animal data taken from MRI images, presented in [14]. Three time points in the retraction phase (peak protraction, mid retraction, and peak retraction) are indicated in the data, and corresponding images and cartoon are shown. A small tube (highlighted in green) was fed to the robot and successfully transferred to the rear of the robot. The tip of the tube is indicated with an arrow. (Color figure online)

ing motion and force profiles qualitatively resemble that of the previously developed *in silico* Boolean model. Future iterations of SLUGBOT can improve its feeding performance by incorporating additional biomimetic elements that are not present in the current version. Of particular importance are the anterior pinch of the I3 musculature to hold food in place, mechanical reconfiguration of the shape of the odontophore and better matching of the hinge and I2 properties to those measured *in vivo*. Further developments could also improve SLUG-BOT's viability as a platform for neuromechanical research by enabling behavorial switching and integration with more complex neural models. This brings *Aplysia*-mimetic control *in roboto* one step closer to multifunctional neural control schema *in vivo* and *in silico*.

Acknowledgment. We thank Jesse Grupper (Harvard University) and Al Turney (KOGANEI International America, Inc.) for help in developing the pneumatic controller.

References

1. Church, P.J., Lloyd, P.E.: Expression of diverse neuropeptide cotransmitters by identified motor neurons in Aplysia. J. Neurosci. **11**(3), 618–625 (1991). https://doi.org/10.1523/jneurosci.11-03-00618.1991
2. Church, P.J., Lloyd, P.E.: Activity of multiple identified motor neurons recorded intracellularly during evoked feedinglike motor programs in Aplysia. J. Neurophys. **72**(4), 1794–1809 (1994). https://doi.org/10.1152/jn.1994.72.4.1794
3. Cropper, E.C., Jing, J., Weiss, K.R.: The Feeding Network of Aplysia. Oxford University Press, Oxford (2019). https://doi.org/10.1093/oxfordhb/9780190456757.013.19
4. Dai, K., et al.: Design of a biomimetic tactile sensor for material classification. In: International Conference on Robotics and Automation. IEEE (2022)
5. Drushel, R.F., Neustadter, D.M., Hurwitz, I., Crago, P.E., Chiel, H.J.: Kinematic models of the buccal mass of Aplysia Californica. J. Exp. Biol. **201**(10), 1563–1583 (1998). https://doi.org/10.1242/jeb.201.10.1563
6. Gill, J.P., Chiel, H.J.: Rapid adaptation to changing mechanical load by ordered recruitment of identified motor neurons. eNeuro **7**(3) (2020). https://doi.org/10.1523/ENEURO.0016-20.2020
7. Harber, E., Schindewolf, E., Webster-Wood, V., Choset, H., Li, L.: A tunable magnet-based tactile sensor framework. In: 2020 IEEE Sensors. IEEE (2020). https://doi.org/10.1109/SENSORS47125.2020.9278634
8. Kehl, C.E., et al.: Soft-surface grasping: radular opening in Aplysia Californica. J. Exp. Biol. **222**(16) (2019). https://doi.org/10.1242/jeb.191254
9. Lyttle, D.N., Gill, J.P., Shaw, K.M., Thomas, P.J., Chiel, H.J.: Robustness, flexibility, and sensitivity in a multifunctional motor control model. Biol. Cybern. **111**(1), 25–47 (2016). https://doi.org/10.1007/s00422-016-0704-8
10. Mangan, E.V., Kingsley, D.A., Quinn, R.D., Sutton, G.P., Mansour, J.M., Chiel, H.J.: A biologically inspired gripping device. Ind. Robot. (2005). https://doi.org/10.1108/01439910510573291
11. McManus, J.M., Lu, H., Cullins, M.J., Chiel, H.J.: Differential activation of an identified motor neuron and neuromodulation provide Aplysia's retractor muscle an additional function. J. Neurophysiol. **112**(4), 778–791 (2014). https://doi.org/10.1152/jn.00148.2014
12. Morton, D.W., Chiel, H.J.: The timing of activity in motor neurons that produce radula movements distinguishes ingestion from rejection in Aplysia. J. Comp. Physiol. **173**(5), 519–536 (1993). https://doi.org/10.1007/BF00197761

13. Morton, D., Chiel, H.: In vivo buccal nerve activity that distinguishes ingestion from rejection can be used to predict behavioral transitions in Aplysia. J. Comp. Physiol. **172**(1), 17–32 (1993). https://doi.org/10.1007/BF00214712

14. Neustadter, D.M., Drushel, R.F., Crago, P.E., Adams, B.W., Chiel, H.J.: A kinematic model of swallowing in Aplysia californica based on radula/odontophore kinematics and in vivo magnetic resonance images. J. Exp. Biol. **205**(20), 3177–3206 (2002). https://doi.org/10.1242/jeb.205.20.3177

15. Neustadter, D.M., Herman, R.L., Drushel, R.F., Chestek, D.W., Chiel, H.J.: The kinematics of multifunctionality: comparisons of biting and swallowing in Aplysia californica. J. Exp. Biol. **210**(2), 238–260 (2007). https://doi.org/10.1242/jeb.02654

16. Nishikawa, K., et al.: Neuromechanics: an integrative approach for understanding motor control. Integr. Comp. Biol. **47**(1), 16–54 (2007). https://doi.org/10.1093/icb/icm024

17. Novakovic, V.A., Sutton, G.P., Neustadter, D.M., Beer, R.D., Chiel, H.J.: Mechanical reconfiguration mediates swallowing and rejection in Aplysia californica. J. Comp. Physiol. **192**(8), 857–870 (2006). https://doi.org/10.1007/s00359-006-0124-7

18. Park, C., et al.: An organosynthetic dynamic heart model with enhanced biomimicry guided by cardiac diffusion tensor imaging. Sci. Robot. **5**(38) (2020). https://doi.org/10.1126/scirobotics.aay9106

19. Pfeifer, R., Bongard, J., Grand, S.: How the Body Shapes the Way We Think: A New View of Intelligence. MIT Press, Cambridge (2006). https://doi.org/10.7551/mitpress/3585.001.0001

20. Ritzmann, R.E., Quinn, R.D., Fischer, M.S.: Convergent evolution and locomotion through complex terrain by insects, vertebrates and robots. Arthropod Struct. Dev. **33**(3), 361–379 (2004). https://doi.org/10.1016/j.asd.2004.05.001

21. Royakkers, L., van Est, R.: A literature review on new robotics: automation from love to war. Int. J. Soc. Robot. **7**(5), 549–570 (2015). https://doi.org/10.1007/s12369-015-0295-x

22. Sutton, G.P., et al.: Passive hinge forces in the feeding apparatus of Aplysia aid retraction during biting but not during swallowing. J. Comp. Physiol. **190**(6), 501–514 (2004). https://doi.org/10.1007/s00359-004-0517-4

23. Sutton, G.P., Mangan, E.V., Neustadter, D.M., Beer, R.D., Crago, P.E., Chiel, H.J.: Neural control exploits changing mechanical advantage and context dependence to generate different feeding responses in Aplysia. Biol. Cybern. **91**(5), 333–345 (2004). https://doi.org/10.1007/s00422-004-0517-z

24. Valero-Cuevas, F.J., Santello, M.: On neuromechanical approaches for the study of biological and robotic grasp and manipulation. J. Neuroeng. Rehabil. **14**(1), 101 (2017). https://doi.org/10.1186/s12984-017-0305-3

25. Webster-Wood, V.A., Gill, J.P., Thomas, P.J., Chiel, H.J.: Control for multifunctionality: bioinspired control based on feeding in *Aplysia californica*. Biol. Cybern. **114**(6), 557–588 (2020). https://doi.org/10.1007/s00422-020-00851-9

26. Wirekoh, J., Park, Y.L.: Design of flat pneumatic artificial muscles. Smart Materi. Struct. **26**(3), 035009 (2017). https://doi.org/10.1088/1361-665X/aa5496

27. Wirekoh, J., Valle, L., Pol, N., Park, Y.L.: Sensorized, flat, pneumatic artificial muscle embedded with biomimetic microfluidic sensors for proprioceptive feedback. Soft Robot. **6**(6), 768–777 (2019). https://doi.org/10.1089/soro.2018.0110

28. Yu, S.N., Crago, P.E., Chiel, H.J.: Biomechanical properties and a kinetic simulation model of the smooth muscle I2 in the buccal mass of Aplysia. Biol. Cybern. **81**(5–6), 505–513 (1999). https://doi.org/10.1007/s004220050579

Robotic Platform for Testing a Simple Stereopsis Network

Shamil S. Patel[1]($\boxtimes$), Jenny C. A. Read[2] (iD), Vivek Nityananda[2] (iD),
and Nicholas S. Szczecinski[1] (iD)

[1] Department of Mechanical and Aerospace Engineering, West Virginia University,
Morgantown, WV 26505, USA
ssp0006@mix.wvu.edu
[2] Faculty of Medical Sciences, Biosciences Institute, Newcastle University,
Newcastle Upon Tyne NE2 4HH, UK

Abstract. To better understand how insects use stereopsis to discern the proximity of objects, we previously developed a stereopsis algorithm that was tested in simulation. In the present study, we have begun to implement this algorithm as part of a robot controller. This includes building a small mobile robot, characterizing its cameras, and building a test arena. Implementing the stereopsis algorithm on a robot will test whether the algorithm performs as intended in real-world scenarios and will enable a robot to determine the proximity of objects in its field of view with a low power algorithm.

Keywords: Stereopsis · Stereoscopic vision · Depth cues · Binocular vision · Robotics · Insect vision

1 Introduction

The computational demands of performing stereopsis for mobile robots are very high and may require an impractical amount of computing power. Despite this challenge, vision is a key functionality for many unmanned mobile robots [1, 9]. Robotic vision necessitates real-time operation, meaning that outputs such as object detection, segmentation, and 3D reconstruction must be performed in real-time or faster [10]. One way that engineers try to cope with the complexities of these applications is to train deep neural networks that can replicate these operations, then deploy them onboard robots [1]. However, deploying such networks may require specialized hardware such as large CPUs, GPUs, and batteries that may require space and energy that mobile robots cannot provide [4]. Such limitations require that performance be sacrificed for mobile operation, often resulting in less refined and capable robots [2].

Insects can be used as inspiration for solutions that address these challenges. Insect visual systems possess high temporal resolution while only using low spatial resolution

This work was supported by NSF DBI 2015317 as part of the NSF/CIHR/DFG/FRQ/ UKRI-MRC Next Generation Networks for Neuroscience Program.

© The Author(s), under exclusive license to Springer Nature Switzerland AG 2022
A. Hunt et al. (Eds.): Living Machines 2022, LNAI 13548, pp. 195–198, 2022.
https://doi.org/10.1007/978-3-031-20470-8_20

allowing for the rapid detection of colors, polarized light, and geometric patterns [7]. Some insects, such as the praying mantis, have eyes with overlapping fields of view, which has been shown to underlie stereopsis to discern distance of objects from the insect [3]. Furthermore, due to their low spatial resolution and the hardiness of insects, their visual systems are more experimentally accessible than those of other living beings such as mammals.

Modeling of insect vision has been conducted to emulate the neural capabilities of insects [7]. The success of robots such as the Beebot Quadcopter has shown that insect-inspired visual processing is a promising approach for real-time visual processing [8]. However, processing may be too computationally demanding to be performed online, requiring the robot to send video to an offline server, process the data, then send the result back to the robot, which is susceptible to network interruptions.

To move toward a computationally inexpensive way to locate the closest object to a robot using stereopsis, we have begun to embody a model of insect stereopsis in a mobile robot. We designed a robot and a testing arena and show that our hardware measures disparity between its eyes. Our approach differs from previous studies in that it utilizes a simple correspondence-free algorithm which doesn't need to explicitly match pixels between cameras but rather has as "intuitive" understanding of the distance of objects [5]. We discuss how the algorithm will be implemented onboard the robot in the future.

2 Methods

2.1 Robot and Cameras

We built a small mobile robot with which to test the stereopsis algorithm (Fig. 1A). The robot is a Zumo chassis with a Raspberry Pi 3B and two Pixy2 cameras [6] (Fig. 1B) mounted on top. These components are attached via a custom 3D-printed body. Each Pixy2 has wide-angle lens with 87° field of vision and an integrated filtering system that locates specific color hues within the field of view. The Pixy2s are mounted on the robot 3.825 cm apart and 10.9 cm above the arena floor, facing straight forward, resulting in 87° of overlap between each camera's field of view. The Raspberry Pi serves as the "brain" of the robot by receiving visual input and directing behavior by issuing motor commands to the Zumo's Arduino microcontroller. To simplify validation, we constructed a controlled visual environment (CVE) with a uniform background (Fig. 1C). The usable volume of the CVE is 87.6 cm × 87.6 cm × 30.5 cm constructed using a series ten 80/20 framework and 6.35 mm-thick white acrylic sheets. The floor of the CVE has a black border approximately three centimeters from the walls, which the robot detects to avoid collision with the walls.

Fig. 1. A) Zumo Robot with attached Arduino R3, B) PixyCam2 with wide-angle lens, C) Controlled visual environment with Zumo Robot, D) "Prey" Targets

2.2 Neural Network

The visual data collected by each individual Pixy2 will be inputted into a neural network that determines the location of the closest landmark in the visual field [6] (Fig. 2A). The network has a winner-take-all (WTA) structure that maps the landmark coordinates from each eye to the azimuthal position of the closest landmark (Fig. 2B). The network's function is the result of its spatially-correlated synaptic weights (Fig. 2C), which in effect solve the correspondence problem [7].

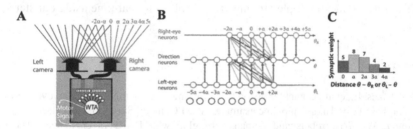

Fig. 2. A) Robotic platform with field of view broken into bins, B) Corresponding links between the two camera bins, C) Synaptic weights generated from links

3 Preliminary Results and Discussion

3.1 Camera Binocular Images

Figure 3 shows two images of variable height targets at varying distances taken from each of the robot's eyes. These images demonstrate that there is noticeable binocular disparity between the cameras, suggesting our camera configuration is sufficient for use with the stereopsis algorithm in question [7].

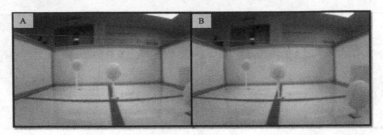

Fig. 3. A) Image captured by "left eye", B) Image captured by "right eye"

3.2 Future Work

With a robot and arena constructed and a control network that functions in simulation [7], our next step is to integrate the network with the robot and evaluate how well the network performs when confronted by real-world conditions, e.g., limited bandwidth and self-motion. The neural network's number of inputs and synaptic weights will be updated to reflect the robot's cameras' resolution, field of view, and interocular distance. The network will be implemented on the Raspberry Pi 3B and will receive input from the Pixy2 cameras. The output of the network will drive saccades of the body to orient the robot toward the closest "prey" target. In the future, we plan to test the "predator" robot's ability to track multiple moving "prey" robots in real-time using our stereopsis model.

References

1. Kakaletisis, E., et al.: Computer vision for autonomous UAV flight safety: an overview and a vision-based safe landing pipeline example. ACM Comput. Surv. (9), 1–37 (Dec 2021)
2. Knight, W.: Why robots and humans struggled with DARPA's challenge. MIT Technol. Rev. https://www.technologyreview.com/2015/06/09/110342/why-robots-and-humans-struggled-with-darpas-challenge/. 2 Apr 2020
3. Giurfa, M., Menzel, R.: Insect visual perception: complex abilities of simple nervous systems. Curr. Opin. Neurobiol. **7**(4), 505–513 (1997)
4. Martin, J.F., Chiang, L.: Low cost vision system for an educational platform in artificial intelligence and robotics. Comput. Appl. Eng. Educ. **10**(4), 238–248 (2002)
5. O'Keeffe, J., Yap, S.H., Llamas-Cornejo, I., Nityananda, V., Read, J.C.A.: A computational model of stereoscopic prey capture in praying mantises. PLoS Comput. Biol. **18**(5), e1009666 (2022). https://doi.org/10.1371/journal.pcbi.1009666
6. Pixy Is the Easiest Way to Add Vision to Your Robot!. PixyCam. https://pixycam.com/
7. Read, J.C.A.: Binocular vision and stereopsis across the animal kingdom. Annu. Rev. Vis. Sci. **7**(1), 389–415 (2021)
8. Sabo, C., et al.: A lightweight, inexpensive robotic system for insect vision. Arthropod Struct. Dev. **46**(5), 689–702 (2017)
9. Susnea, I., et al.: Machine vision for autonomous vehicles – potential and limitations. a literature review. Annals of the University Dunarea de Jos of Galati Fascicle III: Electrotechnics, Electronics, Automatic Control and Informatics **41**(2), 24–30 (2018)
10. Sünderhauf, N., et al.: The limits and potentials of deep learning for robotics. Int. J. Rob. Res. **37**(4–5), 405–420 (2018)

A Scalable Soft Robotic Cellbot

Ridhi Bansal[1,3]([⊠]) [iD], Helmut Hauser[2,3] [iD], and Jonathan Rossiter[2,3] [iD]

[1] Department of Aerospace Engineering, University of Bristol, Bristol, UK
[2] Department of Engineering Mathematics, University of Bristol, Bristol, UK
[3] SoftLab, Bristol Robotics Laboratory, University of Bristol and University of the West of England, Bristol, UK
`{ridhi.bansal,helmut.hauser,jonathan.rossiter}@bristol.ac.uk`

Abstract. In nature, cells combine into different structures to perform the task at hand. Taking inspiration from cells, we present a proof-of-concept and a prototype of a soft modular cellbot composed of simple spherical elements (cells). Locomotion is achieved by establishing and exploiting frictional asymmetries in the interaction of cells and the terrain. We explore the effect of friction coefficient, actuation forcing function, number of cells and axial robot orientation on robot movement, using both simulation model and physical robot. The robot was built using multiple inflatable balls to represent cells connected by linear actuators. The structure, softness, compliance and the ability to deflate the structure for transporting are designed to enhance robustness, fault tolerance and cost effectiveness for disaster affected areas, nuclear sites, and outer space applications. The trend of displacement versus number of cells varies for different friction values. For a surface with mid-to-high static and kinetic friction coefficient, increasing the number of cells stabilises the robot on the ground, increasing the necessary frictional asymmetry and reducing slipping. This helps the designer exploit friction conditions by specifying the robot with suitable structural materials. Understanding the effect of these parameters will help to maximise robot movement by choosing an optimal configuration with respect to orientation or by merging or splitting the cellbot, based on the frictional properties of terrain.

Keywords: Cellular robots · Surface friction · Soft robotics · Bio-inspiration

1 Introduction

In hazardous and unapproachable environments, such as outer space, nuclear, or disaster affected areas, there are high degrees of uncertainty and time delays in communication between robots and the operator. These require robots to autonomously and efficiently manoeuvre over a variety of uneven topographies. Understanding optimal robot morphologies and number of connected units for different robot parameters, such as orientation and environmental conditions such as friction, will help to build future robots, where the robot can autonomously choose a suitable shape based on the encountered terrain. This would help in applications such as disaster recovery where there are unknown and diverse terrains. Various solutions have been proposed, e.g., tensegrity structures that self-modify to pass through tight spaces and traverse different terrains

© The Author(s), under exclusive license to Springer Nature Switzerland AG 2022
A. Hunt et al. (Eds.): Living Machines 2022, LNAI 13548, pp. 199–211, 2022.
https://doi.org/10.1007/978-3-031-20470-8_21

[1,2]. While tensegrity structures show potential for lightweight pop-up robots, they employ rigid elements (beams) which limit the range of morphologies they can adopt and the environments they can operate in. Recent research on polygon-shaped robots has shown capabilities to adapt morphology based on the encountered surface undulation [3]. However, due to the connection of all joints to form a polygon, the shapes that could be achieved were highly constrained.

Modular robots could provide an effective solution for these varied and challenging environments. Post et al. [4] recently discussed the advantages of using modular robotics in outer space applications, highlighting different modular robots being developed for in-orbit servicing, space exploration and Mars habitat building. Recent experiments by Carillo et al. [5] showed that swarms can efficiently change their morphology. These studies showed the ability of morphological robots to adapt their shape according to the encountered obstacle on their path, but in most of these cases robots were not attached to each other. Using soft materials allows individual units to easily change shape upon actuation and to passively deform according to the roughness of the terrain through a soft-hard interaction. This permits the system to accommodate some degree of error or noise, increasing robustness. Recently, Suzuki et al. [6] investigated swarm robots, where each unit could change its morphology using a linear actuator. However, the agents were not attached and morphology change was restricted to individual agents and not the whole robot.

Other works have investigated evolving different types of soft robots such as origami robots [7], snake robots [8], and robots made of soft cubic units termed voxels [9] with the help of simulation software, aiming to efficiently manoeuvre across a range of terrains. These experiments were only conducted in simulation environments. With a single non-evolving robot used to evaluate the principles [9]. In a related study, Hawkes et al. [10] showed how a soft robot with the capability to grow in length can navigate through constrained environments.

In nature, cells combine into shapes to carry out a task. In this paper, we take inspiration from cells to develop a multi-cell soft modular robot made by connecting a series of inflated balls termed 'cells'. The aim is to find the most suitable robot shape so that the robot can be adapted to achieve maximum robot locomotion for different frictional surfaces. The cells can be deflated for transport to reduce volume and transportation costs. The soft modular robot is driven by a series of linear actuators which connect the cells. Joey et al. [11] presented an earthworm inspired locomotion method, where the movement was felicitated by anchoring one of the ends and inflating/deflating the middle part. Here, we use a similar locomotion strategy but instead of using an anchoring and release method, we use the contact of the stationary cells with the ground to provide a force to anchor the robot to the ground. The robot's movement is caused by exploiting frictional asymmetry and using a controlled sequence of actuation. We explore the effect of friction coefficient, number of units, robot orientation about its axis, and actuation force function in order to explore the optimal robot configuration and most effective actuation for locomotion.

We first investigate movement using a 3-cell-in-line simulation model with different friction coefficients and actuation forces. The number of cells n in the simulation is then changed for $n = 2, 3,...,7$, while keeping the actuation function the same to explore the effect of friction coefficients with change in n. A series of physical robots with $n = 2, 3$ and 4 in linear arrangement were fabricated and tested on two different surfaces (high friction and low friction) to validate our simulation results.

2   Concept of Robot Movement

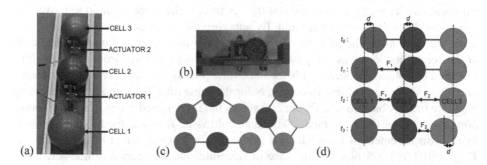

Fig. 1. (a) The 3-cellbot (3 cell robot), showing cells and actuators. (b) Image of actuator without its cover lid, showing its internal working principle. (c) Some possible 2D shapes for 3- and 4-cellbots. (d) 3-cellbot movement for one actuation cycle (t_0–t_3), d shows the displacement of a cell and F_1 and F_2 represent the forces of actuators 1 and 2 respectively.

A simulation model of a 3-cell-in-line (3-cellbot) force-driven robot with rigid connections was programmed in Matlab Simscape. Here, one cell is moved at a time, forming a simple gait cycle inspired by the Golestanian swimmer [12] (Sect. 3). Keeping all the cells stationary, except one, helps to anchor the model to the ground, reducing backward slipping. Figure 1(d) shows the movement of a 3-cell model for one actuation cycle. Here F_1 denotes the force generated by actuator 1, fixed between cell 1 and cell 2, and F_2 denotes the force from actuator 2, located between the cell 2 and cell 3. Initially at t_0, all forces are zero, i.e., $F_1 = F_2 = 0$. F_1 is then increased to move cell 1 (at time step t_1), then simultaneously F_1 is decreased and F_2 is increased to move cell 2 (t_2). Finally, F_2 is reduced to move cell 3 (t_3). Figure 1(d) represents the displacement of a cell in one actuation cycle. This model is later extended to a robot with n cells in a row for $n = 2$ to 7 (see Sects. 4 and 5). The robot design allows more cells to be easily added to make larger and more complex versions of the robot in future. Figure 1(c) shows some of the possible 2D shapes for 3- and 4-cellbots.

3   Simulation Results for 3-Cell Model

A 3-cell linear arrangement was simulated using Simscape. For the sake of simplicity, the three point masses were all defined as 1kg each. The frictional interaction with the ground was simulated using Matlab's 'Loaded-Contact Translational Friction' block. The actuators were simulated by combining a spring and damper system in parallel with a force block to capture the underlying compliance. A family of forcing functions (actuator force) was defined, see Fig. 2(a), where the maximal force was held for different durations. This affects the time that the net force – the force required to move the robot – is above the friction threshold. By applying this set of actuation profiles to the robot we determined the ideal forcing function for a particular friction surface. Each of the force functions was composed of a linear increase of force from 0 to 1 N (N), followed by holding the force at 1 N for some time (i.e., T_{hold}), then a reduction in force linearly to -1 N, then holding force at -1 N for the same time T_{hold}, and finally increase the force linearly back to 0 N. Figure 2(a) shows the investigated group of forcing functions used to drive the 3-cell model. The same hold value T_{hold} was used for both F_1 and F_2. The displacement of the model was evaluated for seven different hold values, i.e., $T_{hold} = [0, 1, 2, 3, 4, 5, 6]$ s. For the sake of simplification, the period of one actuation cycle was kept the same for all tests. Positive and negative actuation forces correspond to the expansion and contraction of the actuators as shown in Fig. 1(d).

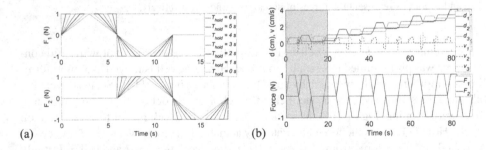

(a)   (b)

Fig. 2. (a) Actuation force family with different hold values T_{hold} with respect to time, F_1 and F_2 represent actuation force of actuator 1 and 2 respectively. (b) Displacements (d_1, d_2, d_3) and velocities (v_1, v_2, v_3) of the cell 1, 2, 3 respectively for a 3-cell model as shown in Fig. 1(d) with respect to time, for an actuation force with $T_{hold} = 3$ s, static friction coefficient $\mu_s = 0.4$ and kinetic friction coefficient $\mu_k = 0.3$; Grey box represents the model settling time.

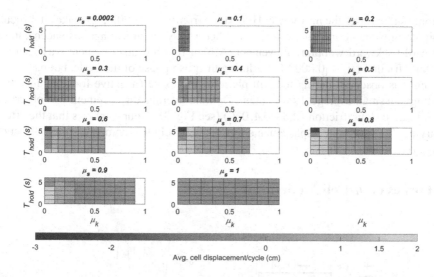

Fig. 3. Simulated robot displacement per cycle. Colour represents the average displacement (in cm) of the 3-cell model over a range of kinetic (μ_k) and static (μ_s) friction and actuation force hold times (T_{hold}). In all of the subplots, results are calculated for 10 different μ_k, where $\mu_k \in (0, \mu_s)$. (Color figure online)

Figure 2(b) shows that the simulation model requires some time (shaded in gray) to reach a steady-state cyclic movement, i.e. its characteristic gait. A settling time was defined to capture only the achieved displacement during its characteristic locomotion (i.e. without the settling time). The model is defined to have achieved a steady-state cyclic gait if the difference between the displacements achieved during an actuation cycle for any two cells becomes negligible (< 0.1 cm), which is 5% of the maximum relative displacement between any two cells in the simulation study. The simulation was run for the 3-cell model for different values of static friction coefficients (μ_s) and kinetic friction coefficients (μ_k), and for each forcing function. Figure 2(b) shows an example of the average displacement and velocity of each of the three cells of the 3-cell model with respect to time, for an actuation force with $T_{hold} = 3$ s, $\mu_s = 0.4$ and $\mu_k = 0.3$. Figure 3 shows the average displacement of the model for different values of T_{hold} and for different friction values μ_s and μ_k, the average displacement was calculated by first finding an average for the displacement for each cell for all actuation cycles after the settle time, and then taking the mean of these values. When an actuator is turned on, it pushes the front part of robot forward and at the same time pushes the rear part backwards. The negative force in Fig. 2(b) shows this backward push during which a backward slip was observed for the corresponding cell. If the model operates under the condition of zero friction, it generates zero net average displacement. In the case where the kinetic friction was small but not zero (e.g., $\mu_k = 0.0001$) the model slipped significantly for low values of static friction ($\mu_s \in [0.0002, 0.5]$). In this friction range, the robot moved in the opposite direction to the intended direction, as can be seen by the blue squares in first column of subplots in Fig. 3. For $\mu_k > 0.0001$, the model moved forward. In general, the average model displacement is inversely proportional to the kinetic friction, as it opposes the movement. High static friction ($\mu_s \in [0.8, 1]$) makes it difficult to initiate movement and this resulted in either a very small average displacement, or a forward-backward wobbling movement. A high forward displacement was seen for low static friction ($\mu_s \in [0.0002, 0.3]$) during the push phase of the cycle, but backward slipping was observed during the pull phase of the cycle (negative forcing function), resulting in a small average displacement. Optimal average displacement was observed for mid-range static friction ($\mu_s \in [0.4, 0.7]$) (see Fig. 3). Figure 3 shows that the effect of varying T_{hold} on robot displacements was qualitatively less compared to the effect of change of frictional values.

4   Forces on n-Cell Model

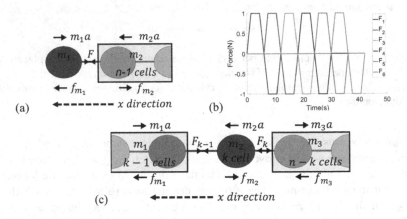

(a)

(b)

(c)

Fig. 4. (a) Force diagram for a 2-cell model or an end cell in an n-cell array, where, f_{m_1} and f_{m_2} represent friction forces on m_1 and m_2 respectively. (b) Actuation forces for 7-cell model for one actuation cycle for T_{hold}=3s. (c) Force diagram for a 3-cell model or an arbitrary k^{th} cell in an n-cell array, where, f_{m_1}, f_{m_2}, and f_{m_3} represent friction forces on m_1, m_2, and m_3 respectively and F_k represents the force of the actuator between cell $k-1$ and k.

The length of the simulation model can be easily extended by attaching more cells. This section shows the generalisation to a linear n-cell model. All masses are assumed to be 1 kg to simplify notation. Furthermore, we assume rigid connections between the cells and x is the desired direction of motion, see Fig. 4(a). The force profile for an n-cell model resembles a travelling wave, as shown in Fig. 4(b). The net force of all $n-1$ actuators summed over one actuation cycle is zero, $\sum_{i=1}^{n-1} F_i = 0$. In order to initiate a movement, the force applied to move a cell needs to be greater than the maximum static friction value (threshold friction), since static friction μ_s always exceeds kinetic friction μ_k. The force on a 2-cell model or on the end cell in an n-cell array is defined in Fig. 4(a), where m_1 is the mass of the first cell and m_2 is the mass of second cell or the combined mass of all the other $n-1$ cells for an n cell model ($m_2 = n-1$ kg), and F represents the actuator force. The movement can be summarised by the following three cases:

Case 1 - Stationary condition, where neither m_1 nor m_2 move because the actuator force is below the threshold friction force.

$$F < m_1 g \mu_s, \quad F < m_2 g \mu_s. \tag{1}$$

Case 2 - One of the masses moves. For example, m_1 moves and m_2 remains stationary. Once the mass begins to move, the friction force transitions from static μ_s to kinetic friction μ_k.

$$F = m_1 a_1 - m_1 g \mu_k, \quad F < m_2 g \mu_s. \tag{2}$$

Case 3 - Both of the masses move, because forces on both cells exceed their respective friction forces.

$$F = m_1 a_1 - m_1 g \mu_k = m_2 a - m_2 g \mu_k. \tag{3}$$

We can extend this analysis to the forces that exist within a 3-cell model or for an arbitrary k^{th} cell in an n-cell array, with $k - 1$ and $n - k$ cells to the left and right of kth cell respectively (see Fig. 4(c)). For an n-cell model, the masses m_1 and m_3 are simply equal to $(k - 1)$ kg and $(n - k)$ kg respectively. During the movement of the kth cell, where the actuator before it contracts and the actuator after it expands to make it move forward, cells on either side are pushed in the negative x direction, i.e. opposite to the intended direction of motion. For the n-cell case, eight cases emerge, which are summarised in Table 1.

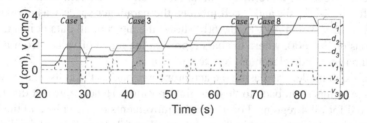

Fig. 5. Effect of forces on cell displacement and velocity for some of the cases mentioned in Table 1, for the 3-cell model with $T_{hold} = 3$ s, $\mu_s = 0.4$ and $\mu_k = 0.3$.

Table 1. Forces on a 3-cell model or an arbitrary k^{th} cell in an n-cell array (Fig. 4(c)), where, ● represents a stationary cell and ○ represents a moving cell

Case	m_1	m_2	m_3	Force Equations
1	●	●	●	$F_{k-1} < m_1 g \mu_s,\ F_{k-1} + F_k < m_2 g \mu_s,\ F_k < m_3 g \mu_s$
2	○	●	●	$F_{k-1} = m_1 a_1 - m_1 g \mu_k,\ F_{k-1} + F_k < m_2 g \mu_s,\ F_k < m_3 g \mu_s$
3	●	○	●	$F_{k-1} < m_1 g \mu_s,\ F_{k-1} + F_k = m_2 a_2 - m_2 g \mu_k,\ F_k < m_3 g \mu_s$
4	●	●	○	$F_{k-1} < m_1 g \mu_s,\ F_{k-1} + F_k < m_2 g \mu_s,\ F_k = m_3 a_3 - m_3 g \mu_k$
5	○	○	●	$F_{k-1} = m_1 a_1 - m_1 g \mu_k,\ F_{k-1} + F_k = m_2 a_2 - m_2 g \mu_k,\ F_k < m_3 g$
6	○	●	○	$F_{k-1} = m_1 a_1 - m_1 g \mu_k,\ F_{k-1} + F_k < m_2 g \mu_s,\ F_k = m_3 a_3 - m_3 g \mu_k$
7	●	○	○	$F_{k-1} < m_1 g \mu_s,\ F_{k-1} + F_k = m_2 a_2 - m_2 g \mu_k,\ F_k = m_3 a_3 - m_3 g \mu_k$
8	○	○	○	$F_{k-1} = m_1 a_1 - m_1 g \mu_k,\ F_{k-1} + F_k = m_2 a_2 - m_2 g \mu_k,\ F_k = m_3 a_3 - m_3 g \mu_k$

The threshold friction value will depend on the number of cells and the position of the moving cell. The predominance of each case in Table 1 will depend on the mass and number of cells, the actuator forces, and the static and kinetic friction coefficients. To achieve efficient locomotion in the robot, transitions are desired only between the cases 2, 3, and 4, as all other cases represent a loss of energy. Figure 5 highlights four cases (1, 3, 7, and 8) mentioned in Table 1 for the movement of 3-cell model for the cell trajectories shown in Fig. 2(b). In the next section we show examples of the emergence of these cases in our n-cell simulation.

5   Simulation Results for n-Cell Model

The previous simulation model from Sect. 3 was extended to explore the effects of the number of connected cells on robot locomotion. The 3-cell model (Sect. 3) showed that the effect of T_{hold} on robot performance was not significant. Hence, a value of $T_{hold} = 3$ s was chosen for all simulations in this section, Fig. 4(b) shows actuation forces for a 7-cell model. Figure 6(a) shows the average displacement for models with different number of cells, n. The model shows different displacement trends for different μ_s and μ_k values. For example, Figure 6(c) shows the displacement trend plot extracted from all subplots, for $\mu_s = 0.8$. The figure shows that the trends are heavily dependent on n, as illustrated by the different trends in plot of $n = 3$ and $n = 5$. Future work will investigate these different trends in more detail. Here, based on the different behavioural trends observed for 3-, 4-, 5-, 6-, and 7-cell models, the parameter space was divided into 4 regions (A1, A2, A3, and A4). Figure 6(b) shows the mean of all data points in each of the 4 regions of Fig. 6(a), where the bars represent the range of values from minimum to maximum average displacement for each region.

For the 2-cell model, increasing the actuator force pushes the cells apart and reversing the force brings them back to their original position. Hence, zero net displacement was observed for all 4 regions. For $n > 3$, the movements of the cells and the trend of displacement versus n observed in these regions (Fig. 6(b)) can be explained using the model discussed in Sect. 4:

Region A1 - In this region, the kinetic friction on the model is very small ($\mu_k \approx 0.0001$), hence the cells remain in a sliding motion once the threshold of static friction has been exceeded. Moving from the low to high values of static friction ($\mu_s = 0.1$ to $= 1$) in region A1 corresponds to increase in the slip transition friction threshold value. Hence, a general decrease in displacement can be observed moving from low to high μ_s. For the same friction values, as n increases, the number of times a cell could be pushed in the backward direction during the actuation cycle increases. Hence a decrease in displacement is observed with increasing n. Low friction results in high backward slipping, causing net negative displacement in some cases, shown by dark blue in Fig. 6(a).

Region A2 - This is defined as the region with low friction coefficients ($\mu_s \in [0.1, 0.6], \mu_k = [0.1, 0.3]$), hence, the friction threshold could easily be exceeded even for large values of n. With increasing n, there is an increase in the number of times a cell is pushed backwards due to the movement of other cells. Hence, this region shows decrease in average displacement with the increase in number of cells.

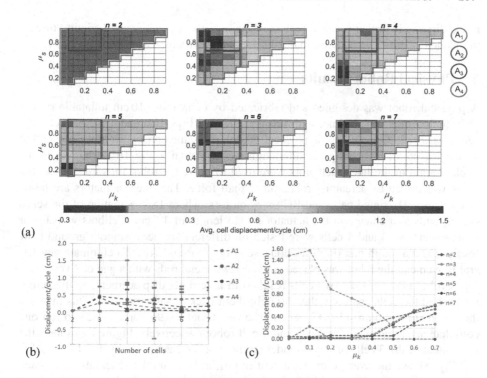

Fig. 6. (a) Average displacement (in cm) of simulation models with different number of cells (*n*) over a range of kinetic ($\mu_k \in [0.0001, 0.9]$) and static ($\mu_s \in [0.1, 1]$) friction coefficient values. Regions A1, A2, A3, and A4 (see colour codes on top right) show the different behavioural trends observed in the model. (b) Average displacement per cycle (in cm) for cell models with different number of cells (*n*), bars are drawn between the minimum and maximum average displacement for each region of Fig. 6(a). (c) Average displacement (in cm) vs kinetic friction (μ_k) for different number of cells connected, for $\mu_s = 0.8$, showing one of displacement trend plots for values shown in Fig. 6(a). (Color figure online)

Region A3 - This region is defined by high μ_s and low μ_k values ($\mu_s \in [0.7, 1]$, $\mu_k \in [0.1, 0.3]$). High static friction makes it difficult to initiate movement due to an increased friction threshold value. However, once the threshold has been exceeded, the model experiences low kinetic friction and maintains movement for a longer period. The net displacements, however, are low due to backward slipping. For the 3-cell model, a large forward displacement was observed as a result of a low friction threshold value and less backward pushes due to the small number of cells. For $n > 3$, the overall displacement was not significantly affected by the number of cells, as the increase in backward movement due to low kinetic friction in this region is countered by the increase in static friction threshold, with the increase in cell count.

Region A4 - This region represents mid-high μ_s and μ_k values ($\mu_s \in [0.4, 1]$, $\mu_k \in [0.4, 0.9]$). Similar to A2, movement does not readily emerge due to high friction threshold values, but in this region the model experiences more kinetic friction during its movement. The slipping back of cells is reduced due to increase in kinetic friction.

Back slipping is further reduced with increase in cells due to increased friction threshold values, resulting in increase in net displacement with increase in n from 2 to 7.

6 Physical Robot Results

A physical robot was designed and fabricated by connecting 10 cm inflatable rubber balls (cells) in a straight line, with linear actuators (Figs. 1(a) and 1(b)) between the cells, for $n = 2$, 3, and 4. In the physical model, the same concept to move one cell at a time was used, replicating the simulation model shown in Fig. 1(d). Changes in the stroke length of the linear actuators were used to move the robot forward. Hence, the robot was driven by actuator stroke, rather than force. The linear actuators are fabricated using 3D printed parts and RC servo motors, where 180° actuation of the servo corresponds to a change in the actuator stroke length of 1.5 cm. Cellbots with linear arrangements of 3 and 4 cells were tested on different surfaces; smooth ground (low friction) and a rough mat (high friction), see Figs. 7(a) and 7(b). To eliminate any lateral movement, the robot was placed between two metal rods with a gap of 13 cm.

A robot made of only two cells resulted in a zero net displacement, as the actuator pushed the cells apart and then brought them back to same position. This matches the 2-cell simulation results (Fig. 6(a)). The robot took 10.96 s and 14.62 s to run one complete actuation cycle for 3-cell and 4-cell robot respectively. Figure 7(e) shows the movement of the 3 cells of 3-cell model on the mat for 2 actuation cycles. Figures 7(f) and 7(g) shows the average displacement in cm in 3 min for 10 observations of each condition: floor, mat, R0, and R90, for the 3- and 4-cellbots. A higher robot displacement was observed on smooth ground in comparison to the displacement on the rough mat for both, 3- and 4-cell configurations, as higher friction on the mat leads to larger resistance to robot movement (Fig. 7(f)). A significant increase in displacement can be observed with an increase in n from 3 to 4 for high friction coefficient region in both simulation model (A_4) and physical robot (floor), see Figs. 6 (b), 7(f), and 7(g).

In our robot prototype, the orientation of the robot about its central axis affects the position of the servo motor – which was mounted slightly off-axis – which in turn affects the centre of mass of the robot. The weight of the servo motor positioned to one side of centre axis shifts the centre of mass of the whole robot. We define the rotational orientation of the robot with respect to rest as R0, i.e. when the servo motor is oriented downward (Fig. 7(c)). When the axis is rotated 90 °C, termed R90 (Fig. 7(d)), the servo motor lies off the centreline, causing a slight displacement of the centre of mass of robot to one side. This misalignment of the center of mass from the axis imposed an additional torque on the robot in R90 orientation, as the actuator force does not pass through the centre of the cell. This caused the robot to hit the metal bars on the sides (Fig. 7). Hence, the interplay between the forces of the bars and the friction from the ground impacts robot movement. The imbalance caused slipping in the 3-cell robot and a reduction in motion of the 1st cell in the 4-cell robot, resulting in higher displacements for R0 compared to R90 orientation for both robots (Fig. 7(g)). The reduction in the p-value for statistical test between R0 and R90 orientation from 1.12×10^{-5} for 3-cellbot to 2.92×10^{-6} for 4-cellbot shows that the effect of axial orientation on model becomes less significant as n increases from 3 to 4 cells. Future work will explore this in more depth for larger numbers of connected cells.

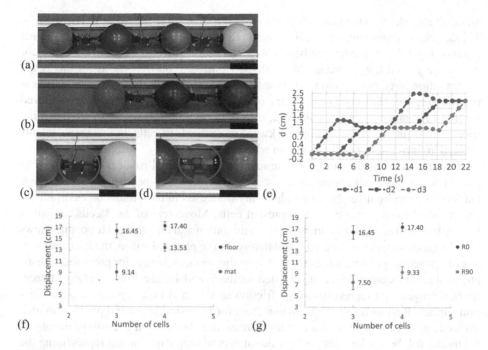

Fig. 7. (a) 4-cell robot on smooth floor (low friction). (b) 3-cell robot on rough mat (high friction). (c) Zoomed image showing the actuator in R0 orientation (servo axis rotated 0 °C). (d) Zoomed image showing the actuator in R90 orientation (servo axis positioned at 90 °C). Black scale bar at bottom of figures (a), (b), (c), and (d) represents 10 cm. (e) Displacement (in cm) of the 3 cells of a 3-cellbot on mat, for 2 actuation cycles; d_1, d_2, d_3 correspond to 1st (red cell), 2nd (blue cell), 3rd (green cell) respectively. Average displacement (in cm) for robots with 3 and 4 cells in 3 min, for 10 observations of each condition- (f) for different friction surfaces (high friction surface – mat, lower friction surface – floor) for R0 orientation. (g) for different axial orientations (servo axis positioned at 0 °C, R0 and servo axis rotated 90 °C, R90) on smooth floor; Error bars represent one standard deviation. (Color figure online)

7 Conclusions and Future Work

In this work, we designed and fabricated a multi-cell modular soft robot prototype. In comparison to other models discussed in Sect. 1, we present a simulation model and physical robot, made out of soft simple units making it possible to adapt it to large range of robot configurations. Robot uses a simple low-cost and low-complexity locomotion mechanism, allowing control parameters to be easily altered for different surfaces with different frictions. This makes it advantageous for applications with low human interventions such as, outer space. The model was programmed to move one cell at a time, to maximise stationary contact with ground and to reduce slipping. Different actuation force functions were used to drive a 3-cell simulation model to understand the effect of actuation force on robot displacement, over a range of μ_s and μ_k values which mimic different terrains. Results showed that the effect of different actuation forces were less significant compared to the effect of different friction coefficients on robot displacement. The model was then extended to an n-cell model for $n = 2, 3, ..., 7$. The trend of displacement versus number of cells connected in a line varied for different frictional regions. For a 3-cell model, the best robot locomotion performance was observed for mid range μ_s and low μ_k values ($\mu_s \in [0.4, 0.7]$, $\mu_k \in [0.0001, 0.4]$), as for this range the actuation force can overcome friction to move forward but there was still sufficient friction to reduce slipping. For $n > 3$, the most optimal robot performance was achieved for mid-high range μ_s and μ_k values ($\mu_s \in [0.4, 1]$, $\mu_k \in [0.4, 0.9]$), as a high threshold friction value in this range reduced backward movements of cells. In this range, results showed an increase in net displacement with increase in n.

For simplicity of the model, the simulation and physical robot were modelled to have a force and a displacement-based actuation model respectively. Also, a point mass of 1kg and lightweight deformable balls were used in the simulation environment and physical robot respectively to represent cells. Movement of the 3 cells, shown in Figs. 2(b) and 7(e) was quite similar for the simulation and the physical robot this shows that the models can be compared qualitatively. In the physical world, the frictional values of surfaces depend on interaction between the surfaces, hence, for preliminary tests, physical robot locomotion is demonstrated for the 3- and 4-cell robots over two different friction ranges, mat representing high friction surface and floor representing low friction surface. Results for the high friction case, for both simulation and physical model, showed an increase in performance with increase in n. In future, the results of the physical model will be used to create a high-fidelity simulation environment representing the physical system more closely. The effect of robot orientation about its axis (R0, $0\,^{\circ}$C and R90, $90\,^{\circ}$C) was found to be less significant with increase in n.

Understanding the effect of friction coefficients on displacement for different n-cell in-line simulation models helps to build more robust physical robots by adapting them to the frictional region for maximum locomotion range (Figs. 6(a) and 6(b)). This can be done by using material for the cells with suitable frictional properties based on the frictional properties of the terrain and for the number of cells in the model. In other instances it may be better to change the number of cells connected in-line, based on the frictional properties of the material used for cells and the surface. The results from simulation and physical robot help to understand the effects of environmental conditions and robot parameters on robot displacement, and are important for building robust future robots comprising larger 1, 2 and 3D arrays of cells and more complex structures. Future experiments will look at increasing the softness of the model and using pneumatic actuation. This would be beneficial for low pressure environments such as outer space where only a small pressure would be required for robot movement, hence, reducing the associated cost. The future tests would explore more terrains, such as sand and regolith, which resembles more closely to real environments. Subsequently, intelligent behavior can be added where multiple individual cells can autonomously merge or break-off from the main robot to structurally reconfigure into an optimal shape and orientation based on the encountered terrain.

References

1. Bruce, J., et al.: Superball: exploring tensegrities for planetary probes. In: 12th International Symposium on Artificial Intelligence, Robotics and Automation in Space (i-SAIRAS) (2014)
2. Usevitch, N., Hammond, Z., Schwager, M., Okamura, A., Hawkes, E., Follmer, S.: An untethered isoperimetric soft robot. Sci. Robot. 5(40), 1–36 (2020)
3. Zhang, F., Yang, Yu., Wang, Q., Zeng, X., Niu, H.: A terrain-adaptive robot prototype designed for bumpy-surface exploration. Mech. Mach. Theory 141, 213–225 (2019)
4. Post, M.A., Yan, X.-T., Letier, P.: Modularity for the future in space robotics: a review. Acta Astronautica 189, 530–547 (2021)
5. Carrillo-Zapata, D., Sharpe, J., Winfield, A.F.T., Giuggioli, L., Hauert, S.: Toward controllable morphogenesis in large robot swarms. IEEE Robot. Autom. Lett. 4(4), 3386–3393 (2019)
6. Suzuki, R., et al.: ShapeBots: shape-changing swarm robots. In: Proceedings of the 32nd Annual ACM Symposium on User Interface Software and Technology, pp. 493–505 (2019)
7. Auerbach, J.E., Bongard, J.C.: Environmental influence on the evolution of morphological complexity in machines. PLoS Comput. Biol. 10(1), e1003399 (2014)
8. Kano, T., Yoshizawa, R., Ishiguro, A.: Tegotae-based decentralised control scheme for autonomous gait transition of snake-like robots. Bioinspir. Biomimet. 12(4), 046009 (2017)
9. Ogawa, J.: Evolutionary multi-objective optimization for evolving soft robots in different environments. In: Compagnoni, A., Casey, W., Cai, Y., Mishra, B. (eds.) BICT 2019. LNICST, vol. 289, pp. 112–131. Springer, Cham (2019). https://doi.org/10.1007/978-3-030-24202-2_9
10. Hawkes, E.W., Blumenschein, L.H., Greer, J.D., Okamura, A.M.: A soft robot that navigates its environment through growth. Sci. Robot. 2(8), eaan3028 (2017)
11. Ge Joey, Z., Calderón, A.A., Chang, L., Pérez-Arancibia, N.O.: An earthworm-inspired friction-controlled soft robot capable of bidirectional locomotion. Bioinspir. Biomimet. 14(3), 036004 (2019)
12. Golestanian, R., Ajdari, A.: Analytic results for the three-sphere swimmer at low Reynolds number. Phys. Rev. E 77, 036308 (2008)

A Real-World Implementation
of Neurally-Based Magnetic Reception
and Navigation

Andrew Harvey[ID] and Brian K. Taylor[✉][ID]

The University of North Carolina at Chapel Hill, Chapel Hill, NC 27599, USA
{aj,brian.taylor}@unc.edu

Abstract. The Earth's magnetic field provides a signal that animals
and man-made systems can leverage for navigation across long-distances
(e.g., continents and oceans). Despite ongoing research in animal magnetoreception, the underlying magnetoreceptors, neural processing, and
strategies that ultimately drive behavior are still not well understood.
One hypothesis is that animals might use unique or rare combinations
of magnetic field properties as a magnetic signature to denote specific
locations or regions. While biological observations have provided evidence of this navigation strategy, both the strategy and its underpinnings
remain unconfirmed. Software simulations have demonstrated the feasibility of this type of navigation strategy, and a nervous system's ability to
execute it. However, software simulations are limited in the phenomena
they are able to properly capture. In this study, expanding on previous
work, we implement a magnetic signatures-based navigation strategy in a
laboratory-based robotic system. The system consists of a robotic rotary
motion platform that serves as a proxy for a navigating animal, a magnetometer for magnetic field sensing, and a computer-controlled magnetic
coil system. The system uses neural fields to process magnetic information in a neurally relevant way. The findings demonstrate that nervous
system-based processing can successfully enable navigation using magnetic signatures. This lends further credence to the concept of animals
using magnetic signatures to navigate, and can provide inspiration for the
development of novel man-made navigation and sensor-fusion systems.

Keywords: Magnetoreception · Neural fields · Navigation

1 Introduction

The Earth's magnetic field serves as an omnipresent signal that both animals
and man-made systems can use to navigate within an environment ([1, 2], Fig. 1).
From an animal perspective, detection of the magnetic field (i.e., magnetoreception) enables long range navigation across continents and oceans. While

Supported in part by a grant from the Air Force Office of Scientific Research (FA9550-
20-1-0399).

© The Author(s), under exclusive license to Springer Nature Switzerland AG 2022
A. Hunt et al. (Eds.): Living Machines 2022, LNAI 13548, pp. 212–223, 2022.
https://doi.org/10.1007/978-3-031-20470-8_22

magnetoreception has been demonstrated in numerous species, the associated receptors, neural processing, and navigation strategies at play remain mysterious [3]. With respect to navigation strategies, one possible strategy that animals may use relies on using unique or rare combinations of magnetic field properties as navigational markers. We refer to this strategy as using *magnetic signatures*. A magnetic signature could direct an animal to move towards a specific location, or prevent it from drifting into an undesirable area. This strategy has been discussed in reference to long-distance migrants such as sea turtles [4], salmon [5], and eels [6]. With respect to sensing and neural processing, the physics of various hypothesized mechanisms suggests that magnetoreception may not be accomplished within a single organ, but instead within a volume of tissue through a distributed array of sensors (i.e., distributed sensing). Magnetoreceptors have not conclusively been located in any animal besides magnetotactic bacteria [1].

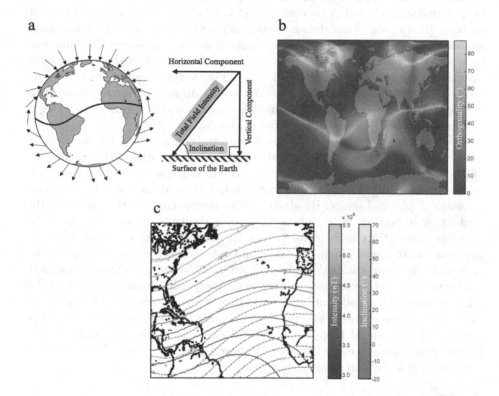

Fig. 1. Panel **a**: Illustration of the magnetic field around Earth, including magnetic inclination and intensity. Panel **b**: Heatmap of the orthogonality of lines of constant inclination and intensity. Panel **c**: Lines of constant intensity and inclination in the North Atlantic Ocean. (Color figure online)

From an engineering perspective, understanding animal magnetoreception is potentially useful for the development of novel navigation systems. Modern systems rely on satellite-based positioning for navigation, such as the United States' Global Positioning System (GPS) and other Global Navigation Satellite Systems (GNSS). Such systems are vulnerable to both natural and intentional compromise [7], are unavailable underwater [8], and are expensive to deploy and maintain [9]. The magnetic field presents a naturally occurring navigation aid that can surmount these issues. Because animals can navigate long distances without relying on satellite-based navigation or other pre-deployed systems, understanding animal navigation may help to reveal principles that can aid the development of novel engineered navigation systems with reduced satellite dependence.

In [10], a computational model was presented in which processing that is based on the dynamics of real-world nervous systems [13] is used with an array of distributed magnetoreceptors to complete closed-circuit migrations in a simulated magnetic environment under a variety of conditions. Combining previous studies that used 1) agent-based simulations to explore navigation based on magnetic signatures [11] and 2) processing that is based on the dynamics of nervous systems [12,13], the study demonstrated that neurally relevant processing can enable a magnetic signatures-based navigation strategy to successfully navigate to a series of points. However, this study was purely executed in a computer simulation, so it is unclear how well this navigation strategy or its underlying processing would translate to a physical system. Motion and sensing errors that are difficult to properly capture in models can cause algorithms and strategies that perform well in simulations to fail in the real world.

To determine whether magnetic signatures and neural processing can enable a physical system to navigate in the real world, our present study extends the work of [10] by investigating the performance of the model in a system with real-world motion and sensing. This system allows the model to further be explored in the presence of physical errors. By studying the performance of the model in this context, it is possible to 1) validate its applicability to real-world conditions, 2) support its utility as a research tool for animal navigation, and 3) garner principles that might aid in the development of novel engineered navigation systems. The computational model was adapted to include physical magnetic field generation via a computer controlled magnetic coil system, physical sensing via a magnetometer, and simplistic motion control via a robotic turntable (i.e., a rate table). These elements effectively incorporated physical sensing and motion errors into the control loop of the simulation. The results demonstrate that magnetic signatures powered by neurally-based processing can enable successful navigation in a physical system.

2   Methods

We first highlight the study presented in [10] to provide a context and baseline for our current work. We then describe our expansion of this work, specifically: 1) the coil system that generates the physical magnetic fields, 2) the robotic rate table system, and 3) the sensor that is used to measure generated fields and how it is mapped into a neural framework. We conclude this section by describing the experiments that were conducted.

2.1 Summary of Earlier Work: Simulation Baseline

The model presented in [10] includes three primary components: 1) a simulated magnetic environment, 2) a simulated agent that navigates within the magnetic environment, and 3) a neural processing system that collects and processes information from the environment to provide the agent with motion commands. The simulated magnetic environment is a simplified magnetic field that does not represent any specific location on Earth, but contains the same gross features as the real-world magnetic field while being easier to adjust and modify for experimental purposes. In particular, the simplified field 1) contains a singularity that serves as a magnetic anomaly, 2) has contour lines that serve as proxy's for lines of constant magnetic intensity (i.e., magnitude of the magnetic field) and inclination (i.e., the angle the field makes with the horizontal) (Fig. 1a), 3) can be made to be curvilinear (the real magnetic field is nonlinear) (Fig. 1c), and 4) can be altered so that lines of constant inclination and intensity are not orthogonal to each other (Fig. 1b). We have used this approach in several studies to better understand how a navigation strategy works before implementing the strategy in a more realistic environment where success and failure mechanisms may be harder to identify [11]. The simplified magnetic field consists of two field properties, β (corresponding to inclination angle) and γ (corresponding to intensity). Both properties vary along gradients specified by Eqs. 1 and 2.

$$\beta = (V_\infty)(x)\left(1 + \frac{R^2}{x^2 + y^2}\right) - \frac{\Gamma_E}{2\pi}\arctan\left(\frac{y}{x}\right) \tag{1}$$

$$\gamma = (V_\infty)(-x\sin(\lambda) + y\cos(\lambda))\left(1 - \frac{R^2}{x^2 + y^2}\right) + \frac{\Gamma_E}{2\pi}\ln\left(\frac{\sqrt{x^2 + y^2}}{R}\right). \tag{2}$$

The variables x and y are spatial positions within the environment. R and V_∞ (set to 1 in this study) are parameters that define lines of constant β and γ. The parameters λ and Γ_E respectively specify the nonorthogonality and curvilinearity of lines of constant β and γ. Four goal points are present in the environment, one in each quadrant about the origin. The agent migrates in a closed loop clockwise from one goal point to the next, traveling at a constant speed. At each time step, the agent detects the magnetic field at its current location and is given the magnetic field at the current goal point. These values are passed to the neural field model, which simulates perception at an array of distributed sensors in an ellipse around the agent and generates an updated bearing angle for the agent to take at the next time step. Example illustrations of this environment with various parameter combinations are shown in Fig. 2.

For a set of distributed magnetic sensors, a perceived direction from the current magnetic coordinates that have been corrupted by noise $(\tilde{\beta}, \tilde{\gamma})$ to the goal magnetic coordinates (β_g, γ_g) is computed as follows (see [10] for details).

$$d_i = \begin{bmatrix} \beta_g - \tilde{\beta} \\ \gamma_g - \tilde{\gamma} \end{bmatrix} \tag{3}$$

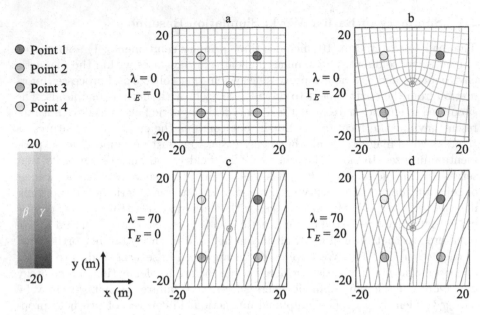

Fig. 2. Illustration of the magnetic environment used with different levels of rotation λ, and curvilinearity Γ_E. Contour lines are plotted for β (green) and γ (purple). This environment can resemble a rectilinear grid (**a**), a curvilinear grid that is orthogonal at all points (**b**), a nonorthogonal grid (**c**), or a nonorthogonal curvilinear grid (**d**). In this and all similar figures, shaded circles are goal points that the agent seeks. The points are located at ($x = 10, y = 10 \rightarrow$ point 1), ($x = 10, y = -10 \rightarrow$ point 2), ($x = -10, y = -10 \rightarrow$ point 3), and ($x = -10, y = 10 \rightarrow$ point 4). The agent is initially located at point 4, and migrates to points 1 through 4 in ascending order. Values of $\lambda = \{0, 20\}$ and $\Gamma_E = \{0, 70\}$ were used in this study to mirror parameters that were used in [10] (Color figure online)

$$d_i = |\boldsymbol{d_i}| \tag{4}$$

$$\theta_i = \arccos\left(\frac{\boldsymbol{u} \cdot \boldsymbol{d_i}}{|\boldsymbol{u}||\boldsymbol{d_i}|}\right). \tag{5}$$

In these equations, $\boldsymbol{d_i}$ is the perceived direction to the target based on the magnetic field at the ith sensor. $\boldsymbol{u}$ is the vector that denotes the spatial agent's orientation in the world, and θ_i is the angle between the ith sensor and the agent's orientation vector.

The computational neural model used by [10] is based on the formulation presented by [13]. In this model, a set of neural subpopulations are connected to each other by synapses (i.e., weights) that are either excitatory or inhibitory (i.e., W). Each population has a preferred direction of excitation Ω that generates a maximal level of neural activity R_Ω in response to input E. Using the magnetic field detected in Eqs. 3–5, the equations for the neural model are given as

$$E_\Omega = \sum_{i=1}^{n} d_i cos(\Omega - \theta_i) - C \tag{6}$$

$$\tau \frac{dR_\Omega}{dt} = -R_\Omega + (E_\Omega - W * R_\Omega)_+. \tag{7}$$

The "+" in Eq. 7 indicates that the parenthesis only has a nonzero value if its argument is greater than zero. Also, "$*$" in Eq. 7 denotes convolution. τ (set to 1 in this study) is the time-constant for the system's neural processing. Viewed as a ring, a population excites its nearest neighbors while simultaneously inhibiting more distant neighbors (Fig. 3 and [13]).

Using Eqs. 3–7, the agent can sense the magnetic field, process it in a manner that is similar to the dynamics of a real nervous system, and use the resulting neural output to generate motion commands that allow the agent to successfully navigate from point to point (see [10] for details).

2.2 Current Study: Magnetic Coil System, Robotic Rate Table, and Physical Sensing

To generate real-world magnetic fields, we employ a triaxial magnetic coil system that is designed to produce uniform magnetic fields ([14], Fig. 4a). This type of system has been used in the past for behavioral magnetoreception experiments with animals such as loggerhead sea-turtles [4]. The system works by running electrical current through each of three orthogonal coils, which generates a magnetic field. By controlling the currents with a computer, the resulting physical field can be made to mimic simulated fields from any point in the magnetic environment. A linear transformation was used to map between corresponding physical and simulated field components. During a trial, the generated magnetic field is updated at the beginning of each time step to mirror the simulated field at the agent's location. Once the electrical currents for each coil have achieved their target values, the field is sensed with a magnetometer. As the simulated agent makes migration progress, this process effectively allows the agent to move through and sense a continually changing magnetic field.

In the current study, rather than simulating agent orientation changes purely in software, we use a nontranslating rotary robotic platform (i.e., a rate table) to rotate the magnetometer to match the simulated agent's orientation at each time step. Specifically, we use the Ideal Aerosmith 1291BL rate table system as our rotary platform (Fig. 4b, bottom). By introducing translation in software on top of the physical platform's rotation, this setup executes simplified planar real-world motion control. This motion is subject to errors based on errors in the orientation of the table. Motion errors can also arise due to sensor errors associated with rotation of the magnetometer used to sense the magnetic environment. The rate table was allowed to reach its target orientation and come to a full stop before the field was sensed for each time step.

The Sparton AHRS-8 Attitude Heading Reference System (AHRS-8) was used as a magnetometer to perform sensing (Fig. 4b, top). For each measurement, a single field sample is collected and passed as input to each subpopulation in the distributed sensing array. We elected to use one magnetometer to sense the magnetic field for this study to reduce complexity in the setup, and to establish a baseline for future work. Each neural subpopulation has its own preferred direction. Therefore, when a given magnetic field is applied across all populations, each subpopulation responds differently despite all of them receiving the same magnetic field input. This allows us to explore the efficacy of using distributed sensing to navigate even though we only employ a single sensor. Using multiple physical sensors would 1) allow us to quantify how well the neural field performs when data that is fed to one of the subpopulations becomes corrupted or unavailable and 2) introduce physical sensing error from multiple discrete sensors, bringing the simulation closer to the theoretically ideal state of incorporating sensing error separately for each sensor in the distributed array. These are both topics that we will explore in future studies (see Sect. 5).

2.3   Current Study: Experiments

The experiments conducted for this research included three experimental setups: one software-only setup that illustrates the behavior of the model as it was developed in [10] for comparison, and two hardware setups that incorporated physical error. In the software-only setup, noise (described in [10]) was introduced so that comparisons could be drawn between navigation results in the presence of software-generated random noise, and noise that arises from physical sensing and motion. The first hardware setup incorporated actuation of the magnetic coil system and sensing with the magnetometer, but did not include rotation of

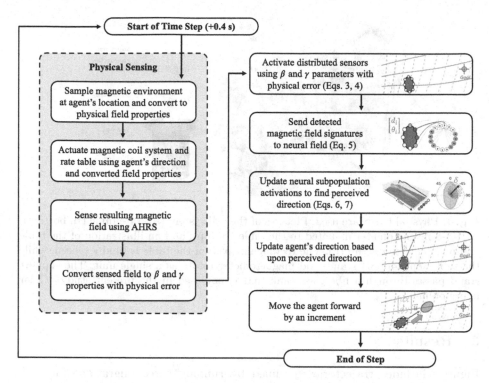

Fig. 3. Flowchart outlining the steps that are taken each time step to incorporate physical error into the model. The magnetic field at the agent's position in the simulation is used to actuate the coil system and, optionally, the agent's orientation is used to position the rate table. The AHRS-8 is then used to sense the resulting physical magnetic field. This information is used to update the neural field model and simulate motion by the agent (blue oval) through its environment. The blue and white dots surrounding the agent represent the array of distributed sensors. Once the agent comes within 1 m of its current goal point, the next point in the set of goal points is targeted. (Color figure online)

the magnetometer with the rate table. For these trials, the rate table was present and maintained a fixed orientation during the migrations. The second hardware setup also incorporated the coil system and magnetometer as in the first hardware setup. However, the rate table was used to rotate the magnetometer at each time step to match the agent's orientation, introducing another source of actuation and sensing error and providing another degree of realism to validate the model's performance.

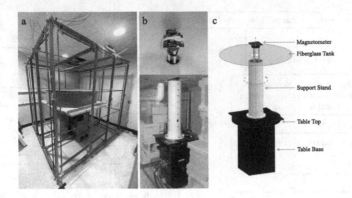

Fig. 4. Physical hardware used. Pictures of the coil system (**a**), rate table (**b**, bottom), AHRS-8 magnetometer mounted to the table (**b**, top), and an illustration of the table and magnetometer setup (**c**). The rectangular base of the table is rigidly placed, while the table top, support stand, and magnetometer rotate as a single unit. The support stand passes through a fiberglass tank that is not used in the present study. (Color figure online)

3   Results

Figure 5 includes trajectories obtained by running three migrations for each experimental setup across two combinations of magnetic environment parameters, $(\lambda = 0, \Gamma_E = 0)$ and $(\lambda = 70, \Gamma_E = 20)$. The trajectories generated by the software-only simulation (Fig. 5a) are nearly identical to the corresponding trajectories presented in [10] that use the same combinations of λ, Γ_E, and noise. This was expected, as the time step value was the only parameter that differed between corresponding simulations.

The trajectories obtained from the hardware simulations (Figs. 5b and 5c) are qualitatively similar to those from the software-only simulation, with the setup that included rate table rotation showing the greatest deviation. The deviation in these trials is consistent across replicate migrations, indicating the presence of systematic error in the rotation and sensing for this setup. This error may be the result of limitations in the experimental setup, such as nonparallelism between the vertical axis of the coil system and the rate table's axis of rotation, magnetic interference by the rate table, nonorthogonality in the axes of the magnetometer and coil system, and nonuniformity in the field around the magnetometer, or may be a natural component of the noise present when sensing magnetic fields from a rotating frame of reference. If the latter is true, the software model could be improved by quantifying this noise and integrating it into the simulation to enhance its applicability to real-world conditions and bolster its utility as a research tool.

Based upon the variation among replicate migrations, the scale of random noise in field sensing appears to be similar between the software-only and hardware setups. Of the two hardware setups, the configuration that included the rate table showed the most variation between migrations. Unexpectedly, this variation was not the same across both magnetic environment parameter sets, but was greater in the trial with the orthogonal rectilinear field (Fig. 5a, top), indicating that the magnetic environment may have an impact on the stability of trajectories in the presence of physical noise and that stability may improve in more curvilinear or nonorthogonal environments. For each of the hardware trials, the agent was able to complete all migrations without any failures or substantial excursions relative to the software-only simulations.

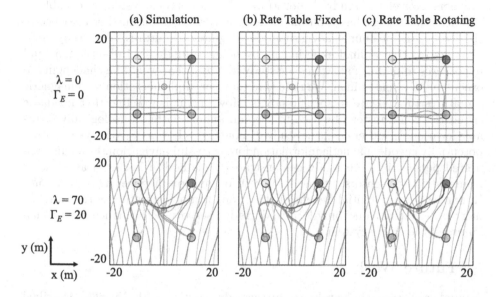

Fig. 5. Example trajectory plots in environments with parameter combinations ($\lambda = 0$, $\Gamma_E = 0$) and ($\lambda = 70$, $\Gamma_E = 20$) across the three experimental setups. Goal points and β and γ contour lines are plotted as described for Fig. 2. The trajectory of the agent is plotted as a dotted line with line color matching that of the goal point being targeted during each portion of the migration. A time step value (Δt in [10]) of $0.4s$ was used for each trial. Setup **a** consisted of a software-only simulation like that described in [10]. Zero-mean normally distributed noise with a standard deviation of 1 was used for both magnetic properties. Setup **b** used the hardware setup consisting of only the magnetic coil system and magnetometer. Setup **c** used the hardware setup with all components including the magnetic coil system, rate table, and magnetometer. The noise was set to 0 for setups **b** and **c** and all noise in these simulations was introduced through error in physical actuation and sensing by the hardware devices. (Color figure online)

4   Discussion and Conclusion

The results of our current study further validate the simulated results obtained in [10]. In particular, the results from our robotic studies demonstrate that 1) magnetic signatures are a viable navigation signal for animals, 2) that magnetic signatures can be successfully processed in a neurally relevant way, and 3) that the combination of magnetic signatures and neural processing can in fact be executed by a physical system. Taken together, our study demonstrates sensation, processing, and navigation in an end-to-end manner. From a biological perspective, the study demonstrates that a nervous system is capable of executing a strategy based on magnetic signatures, lending further credence to the hypothesis of animal navigation via magnetic signatures. The study compliments existing animal experiments by using animal-based observations and hypotheses to perform a parametric study in a way that would be challenging to execute with a real animal. We note here that our implementation uses magnetic signatures to navigate to specific points. However, it is possible that magnetic signatures could instead be used to keep an animal within a geologically favorable location. In either case, the study demonstrates how a nervous system could potentially encode magnetic information for successful navigation. From an engineered perspective, this study demonstrates a method of fusing measurements from distributed sensors, a topic of interest for multiple engineering applications. In particular, a potential benefit of this type of implementation is that impairment of one sensor may only lead to degraded sensory performance rather than failure of the entire system.

5   Future Work

A number of steps can be taken to further advance this work. First, as described previously, this work only uses data from one sensor that is passed to each input in the neural array. We are currently working on incorporating several sensors into our system so that sensing can be done with an array of physical sensors. Second, the magnetic environment used here is abstract in that, while it contains several real-world magnetic features, it does not represent any particular location on Earth. In the future, we will run this system in a magnetic environment that resembles a real-world location such as the North Atlantic Ocean. We have successfully demonstrated this strategy in behavioral implementations with no neural processing [11]. Successful replication of our current study in a more realistic environment would lend further credence to the hypothesis that magnetic signatures can enable animals such as sea-turtles to navigate and migrate over long distances. Third, we would like to repeat these experiments with a larger variety of noise (i.e., standard deviations > 1, similar to experiments presented in [11]). Fourth, we would like to expand the number of sensor modalities in our system so that we may fuse magnetic data with other sensory data (e.g., vision, audition, mechanoreception). Both biological and engineered systems typically use data from multiple types of sensors, so incorporating multiple sensor modalities would enable more representative biological studies and potentially present novel methods of data integration. In the long term, we would like to compare results from our computational-neuroscience-based method of processing to more traditionally engineered approaches (e.g., Kalman and Particle filters) to explore the similarities and differences between these methods, and where they might diverge or could potentially be fused with one another.

References

1. Johnsen, S., Lohmann, K.J.: Magnetoreception in animals. Phys. Today **61**(3), 29–35 (2008). https://doi.org/10.1063/1.2897947
2. Lee, T.N., Canciani, A.J.: MagSLAM: aerial simultaneous localization and mapping using Earth's magnetic anomaly field. Navigation **67**(1), 95–107 (2020). https://doi.org/10.1002/navi.352
3. Putman, N.F.: Magnetosensation. J. Comp. Physiol. A. **208**, 1–7 (2022). https://doi.org/10.1007/s00359-021-01538-7
4. Lohmann, K.J., Putman, N.F., Lohmann, C.M.F.: The magnetic map of hatchling loggerhead sea turtles. Curr. Opin. Neurobiol. **22**(2), 336–342 (2012). https://doi.org/10.1016/j.conb.2011.11.005
5. Putman, N.F., et al.: An inherited magnetic map guides ocean navigation in juvenile Pacific salmon. Curr. Biol. **24**, 446–450 (2014). https://doi.org/10.1016/j.cub.2014.01.017
6. Naisbett-Jones, L.C., Putman, N.F., Stephenson, J.F., Ladak, S., Young, K.A.: A magnetic map leads juvenile European eels to the Gulf Stream. Curr. Biol. **27**, 1236–1240 (2017). https://doi.org/10.1016/j.cub.2017.03.015
7. Tucker, P.: The Air Force's latest GPS alternative: earth's magnetic fields. https://www.defenseone.com/technology/2020/07/air-forces-latest-gps-alternative-earths-magnetic-fields/167387/ (2020). Accessed 22 Nov 2020
8. Hidalgo, F., Bräunl, T.: Review of underwater SLAM techniques. In: 6th International Conference on Automation, Robotics and Applications (ICARA), Massey University, 17–19 February 2015. https://doi.org/10.1109/icara.2015.7081165
9. GPS program funding (2021). https://www.gps.gov/policy/funding/. Accessed 30 Oct 2021
10. Nichols, S., Havens, L., Taylor, B.: Sensation to navigation: a computational neuroscience approach to magnetic field navigation. J. Comp. Physiol. A. **2208**, 167–176 (2022). https://doi.org/10.1007/s00359-021-01535-w
11. Pizzuti, S., et al.: Uncovering how animals use combinations of magnetic field properties to navigate: a computational approach. J. Comp. Physiol. A. **208**, 155–166 (2022). https://doi.org/10.1007/s00359-021-01523-0
12. Taylor, B.K., Johnsen, S., Lohmann, K.J.: Detection of magnetic field properties using distributed sensing: a computational neuroscience approach. Bioinspir. Biomim. **12**(3), 036013 (2017). https://doi.org/10.1088/1748-3190/aa6ccd
13. Wilson, H.R.: Spikes, Decisions, and Actions: The Dynamical Foundations of Neuroscience. Oxford University Press, Oxford (1999). http://cvr-archive.apps01.yorku.ca/webpages/spikes.pdf
14. Alldred, J.C., Scollar, I.: Square cross section coils for the production of uniform magnetic fields. J. Sci. Instrum. **44**(9), 755–760 (1967). https://doi.org/10.1088/0950-7671/44/9/327

Design of a Biomolecular Neuristor Circuit for Bioinspired Control

Ahmed S. Mohamed[1], Ashlee S. Liao[2], Yongjie Jessica Zhang[2,3],
Victoria A. Webster-Wood[2,3,4(✉)], and Joseph S. Najem[1(✉)]

[1] Department of Mechanical Engineering, The Pennsylvania State University,
315 Reber Building, University Park, PA 16802, USA
jsn5211@psu.edu
[2] Department of Mechanical Engineering, Carnegie Mellon University,
Pittsburgh, USA
vwebster@andrew.cmu.edu
[3] Department of Biomedical Engineering, Carnegie Mellon University,
5000 Forbes Ave, Pittsburgh, PA 15213, USA
[4] McGowan Institute for Regenerative Medicine, University of Pittsburgh,
4200 Fifth Ave, Pittsburgh, PA 15260, USA
http://engineering.cmu.edu/borg,
https://www.meche.engineering.cmu.edu/faculty/zhang-computational-bio-modeling-lab.html, https://sites.psu.edu/najemlab/

Abstract. The nervous system serves as an inspiration for control and processing systems but can be difficult to replicate or directly implement using biological neurons in bioinspired and biohybrid systems. An alternative path is to use synthetic biomolecular neuristors that are inspired by biological neurons and can closely mimic their spiking behavior. A neuristor is built using two dynamical lipid-bilayer-based devices that exhibit volatile memory and negative differential resistance arising from the dynamics of voltage-gated ion channels and the ion gradients across the lipid membranes. The firing pattern and frequency can be easily tuned by engineering the composition of each neuristor. To investigate the viability of using biomolecular neuristors to design neural control circuits, a neuristor computational model was implemented and compared to that of the Izhikevich neuron model. Both models were assessed for individual cells and then arranged to form mutually inhibitory circuits, as central pattern generators commonly found in motor control circuits. Both models can replicate the alternating firing behavior, but further parameter tuning is needed for the neuristor model to better match the firing frequency of the biological neuron model.

Keywords: Neuristor · Izhikevich neurons · Central-pattern generator · Bio-inspired · Memristor · Droplet interface bilayer

---

A. S. Mohamed and A. S. Liao—These authors contributed equally to this work.

© The Author(s), under exclusive license to Springer Nature Switzerland AG 2022
A. Hunt et al. (Eds.): Living Machines 2022, LNAI 13548, pp. 224–235, 2022.
https://doi.org/10.1007/978-3-031-20470-8_23

1   Introduction

Biological neural mechanisms have commonly been used as inspiration for control and processing systems [2,8,9,22]. For example, while maintaining a much smaller scale and energy consumption than traditional control strategies, the nervous system can exhibit control over complex motions and demonstrate behavioral flexibility in response to a dynamic environment [2,22]. These abilities result from various neuronal functions, which include exerting control over muscle force responses during orderly recruitment [16]. For bioactuators and biohybrid robots that use muscle tissue, the inclusion of neural tissue can enhance muscle contractility [1]. However, culturing neurons and creating specific neural circuits *in vitro* can be challenging. The growth of *in vitro* neurons is complex and dependent on a combination of intra- and extracellular signaling to influence the neurite development for circuit formation [13,14,20]. Furthermore, biological neurons must be cultured in patterned environments to achieve specific network connections, often requiring access to clean-room facilities, and be carefully maintained to ensure cell viability and function. To overcome these limitations, biological neurons can be replaced by neuron-inspired, biomolecular neuristors that closely emulate biological firing behaviors to create designer circuits *in vitro* while being easier to fabricate, maintain, and scale-up than cultured neurons.

Biomolecular neuristors are synthetic devices that emulate important neural functions (Fig. 1), including all-or-nothing spiking at different frequencies. Each neuristor comprises two synthetic lipid membranes connected in parallel and hosting voltage-activated ion channels [17] that exhibit different switching thresholds and memory timescales (Fig. 1B). These highly modular neuristors can provide a variety of biomimetic spiking behaviors by modifying the compositions of the lipid membranes and ion channel concentration [17]. Therefore, if these neuristors are to be used in place of neurons to create custom control circuits *in vitro*, several neuristor characteristics can be tuned to better match the behavioral profile of a given neuron or neural circuit, thus improving the performance of the controller. Computational models are needed to test the viability of using biomolecular neuristors in neural-inspired control circuits and determine how altering the neuristor parameters impacts the controller's performance.

To meet this need, this work presents a computational model of a biomolecular neuristor and a multi-neuristor circuit tuned to qualitatively match the behavior of a central pattern generator (CPG) [6,9,15]. The neuristor model is inspired by the Hodgkin-Huxley (HH) model [7], as it comprises two locally-active Alamethicin (Alm)-doped, lipid-bilayer-based memristors with intrinsic bilayer capacitance, electrochemical gradient, and leakage resistance [4,17]. The behavior of this neuristor circuit model is compared with that of a simplified HH neuron model presented by Izhikevich [10–12] for qualitative functional evaluation. A single-cell configuration and a mutually-inhibitory CPG circuit configuration are used as test cases for the comparison. Parameters from the neuristor models can inform conditions, such as peptide concentration and lipid and salt types, needed to experimentally reproduce biologically similar behaviors in a laboratory. Thus, this modeling framework can guide the development

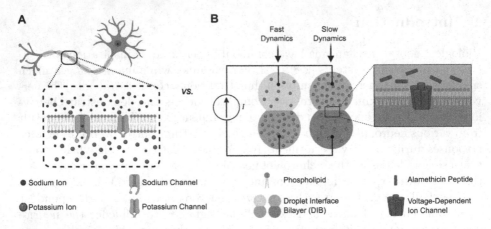

Fig. 1. Neuristors exhibit voltage-gated properties similar to biological neurons. (A) Neuron dynamics are dependent on the balance of sodium and potassium ions. (B) Neuristor dynamics are dependent on the interactions between depolarizing and hyperpolarizing memristors that act similarly to the biological sodium and potassium channels, respectively. Individual memristor properties depend on the voltage threshold and the rate of insertion and withdrawal of Alm peptides into the lipid bilayer.

of biomolecular neuristors that can produce neuron-like signals and to design neuristor circuits that mimic the behavior of *in vitro* or *in vivo* neural circuits.

2   Methods

To compare the dynamics of a biomolecular neuristor to a biological neuron, computational models were used. The behavior of a single neuristor was compared with that of a single model neuron cell under a constant stimulation. Once the neuristor parameters were tuned to qualitatively mimic the behavior of a neuron, the performance of the neuristor circuit model was compared with that of the Izhikevich neuron model in a mutually inhibitory circuit configuration, which is a common central pattern generator (CPG) for motor control [6,9,15].

2.1   Biological Neuron Model

To represent realistic neurons, the Izhikevich spiking neuron model with tonic bursting parameters (Table 1) was simulated using forward Euler in the Brian2 simulator [10–12,21]. The neuron dynamics were represented using membrane voltage (v) and recovery current (u), which were calculated as [10–12]:

$$C\frac{dv}{dt} = k(v - v_r)(v - v_t) - u + I \qquad (1)$$

$$\frac{du}{dt} = a\big(b(v - v_r) - u\big) \qquad (2)$$

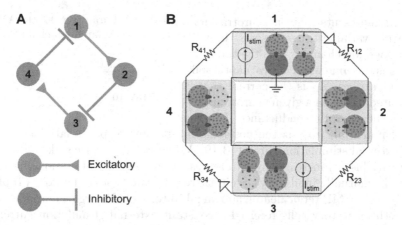

Fig. 2. The neuron and neuristor CPG model configurations. (A) The neurons are arranged in a mutually inhibitory circuit where the firing activity of Cell 1 will inhibit Cell 3 and vice versa. (B) The neuristors are arranged to mirror the mutually inhibitory neural circuit where the activity of Neuristor 1 will inhibit Neuristor 3 and vice versa.

Table 1. Parameters for modeling tonic bursting neuronal dynamics [11,12].

C (pF)	k (nS/mV)	v_r (mV)	v_t (mV)	v_p (mV)	a (1/s)	b (nS)	c (mV)	d (pA)
50	1.5	−60	−40	25	30	1	−40	150

where C is the membrane capacitance, t is time, v_r is the resting potential, v_t is the instantaneous threshold potential, I is the current, a is the recovery time, and k and b collectively represent the cell's rheobase and input resistance [10–12]. To induce spiking, v and u were modified as follows:

$$if\ v \geq v_{peak},\ then \begin{cases} v \leftarrow c \\ u \leftarrow u + d \end{cases} \tag{3}$$

where v_p is the peak membrane potential, c is the after-spike voltage, and d is the current activated by a spike event [10–12].

The Izhikevich neurons were stimulated with a current input (I). For the single neuron case, I was kept constant at 600 pA. In the mutually inhibitory circuit, the spiking behavior from a presynaptic neuron affected the current coming into the postsynaptic neuron using the following synaptic equations:

$$\frac{ds_{nt}}{dt} = -\frac{s_{nt}}{\tau_{nt}} + \sum_k \delta(t - t_k) \tag{4}$$

$$I_{nt} = g_{nt}s_{nt}(E_{nt} - v_{post}) \tag{5}$$

$$I = I_{ext} + \sum_{nt}(I_{nt}) \tag{6}$$

where nt represents a given neurotransmitter, gating variable (s) represents the fraction of open ion channels, τ is the time constant, t_k is the time when a presynaptic spiking input arrives, I_{nt} is the current that is contributed based on a given neurotransmitter, g is the synaptic conductance, E is the

Table 2. Parameters for the AMPA- and GABA-gated ion channels [19].

nt	g_{nt} (nS)	E_{nt} (mV)	τ_{nt} (ms)
AMPA	10	0	2
GABA	10	−80	10

reversal potential, v_{post} is the postsynaptic membrane potential, I_{ext} is additional external stimulation current [3,19]. When a presynaptic spike occurs, the gating variable (s) increases by 1 to represent the opening of the ion channels.

For the mutually inhibitory circuit, there were two types of neurons (Table 2): an excitatory, AMPAergic neuron and an inhibitory, GABAergic neuron. In addition, both excitatory cells received a constant external stimulation current of 600 pA, but Neuron 3 (Fig. 2A) experienced a 5 ms delay.

2.2   Neuristor Model

Taking inspiration from the Hodgkin-Huxley neuron model [7], neuristor dynamics are governed by the transmembrane potential (v_m) relative to a resting potential and two voltage-dependent state variables, $N_d(v_m), N_h(v_m)$, which quantify the number of Alm channels in the membrane. The d and h represent memristors with fast, depolarizing dynamics and slow, hyperpolarizing dynamics, respectively. In neuristors, memristors are fabricated using the droplet interface bilayer (DIB) method to form a lipid membrane between lipid-encased droplets of water in oil. The Alm peptides are in the aqueous phases and driven into the membrane to create channels by applying a voltage larger than their insertion threshold [17]. The current passing through a memristor [17] was calculated as:

$$I_{M(d,h)} = g_{u(d,h)} N_{(d,h)}(v_m) A_{m(d,h)}(v_m - E_{(d,h)}) \tag{7}$$

$$\frac{dN_{(d,h)}}{dt} = \frac{1}{\tau_{0(d,h)} e^{|v_m|/v_{\tau(d,h)}}}(N_{0(d,h)} e^{|v_m|/v_{e(d,h)}} - N_{(d,h)}) \tag{8}$$

where g_u is the mean conductance of a single Alm channel, A_m is the measured lipid bilayer area [17], E is the reversal potential of the memristors formed by imposing a salt concentration gradient in the DIB, τ_0 is the time constant for

Table 3. Parameters for modeling the neuristor model.

Dynamics	I_{stim} (A)	g_u (S)	A_m (m^2)	E (mV)	τ_0 (s)	v_τ (mV)
Depolarization	50×10^{-9}	5×10^{-9}	5.99×10^{-8}	150	1×10^{-3}	400
Hyperpolarization	50×10^{-9}	5×10^{-9}	5.99×10^{-8}	−30	4×10^{-3}	200
Dynamics	N_0 (pores/m^2)	v_e (mV)	c_m (F/m^2)	C_m (F)	R_m (Ω)	$R_{i,i+1}$ (Ω)
Depolarization	0.526×10^{-3}	4	7×10^{-3}	$c_m A_{mp}$	10×10^9	20×10^4
Hyperpolarization	5×10^{-6}	3.7	7×10^{-3}	$c_m A_{mn}$	10×10^9	20×10^4

channel withdrawal from the membrane at zero potential, v_τ the voltage required to drive an e-fold increase in the pore closure time constant ($\tau = \tau_0 e^{|v_m|/v_\tau}$), N_0 is the number of inserted channels at zero potential, v_e is the voltage required to drive an e-fold increase in the number of open pores (at steady-state $N_\infty = N_0 e^{|v_m|/v_e}$). Assuming a constant current stimulation (I_{stim}), the transmembrane potential state was calculated in terms of the capacitive current as:

$$C_m \frac{dv_m}{dt} = I_{stim} - (I_{Md} + I_{Mh} + v_m/R_m) \tag{9}$$

where C_m and R_m are the combined bilayer capacitance and leakage resistance of both memristors, respectively. Equations (7,8,9) were solved using the parameters shown in Table 3. The neuristor circuit (Fig. 2B) had four neuristors serially coupled via coupling resistors ($R_{i,i+1}$, where $i \in [1,3]$). The current flowing between resistors was computed implicitly using Ohm's law:

$$I_{i,i+1} = (v_{m,i} - v_{m,i+1})/(R_{i,i+1}) \tag{10}$$

The coupling current direction was reversed (Fig. 2(B)) between Neuristors 1 and 2 and Neuristors 3 and 4. Injecting negative, hyperpolarizing currents into the inhibitory neuristors yielded a negative spike, which suppressed the subsequent neuristor to enable mutual inhibition.

3   Results and Discussion

To assess the viability of using a neuristor circuit as a neural controller, computational models of both biological neurons and synthetic, biomolecular neuristors were used to tune neuristor model parameters and conduct a qualitative comparison. Like biological neurons where the membrane potential is dictated by the interplay between sodium and potassium permeabilities [7], a neuristor membrane potential (v_m) is governed by depolarizing and hyperpolarizing currents. The underlying mechanisms influencing the magnitudes and directions of these memristive currents were analyzed to assess the impact of each of the neuristor model parameters on the memristive currents' behavior. Understanding each parameter's effect on the memristive currents, and therefore the membrane potential, serves as a neuristor design tool as it enables targeted parameters tuning to achieve a desired neuristor oscillatory pattern and frequency.

The behavior of a single neuristor was compared with that of a single neuron (Fig. 3A). Based on parameters previously reported by Najem et al. for two lipid-based memristors [17] with the addition of an ionic gradient of either 90mV and −90 mV, the simulated neuristor model oscillated at 1.28 Hz, which is much lower than either the firing frequency or bursting frequency observed in the single neuron model (Fig. 3A, top). Therefore, the neuristor parameters were independently adjusted (Table 3) to achieve activity oscillation frequencies similar to the bursting frequency from the model of a single tonic bursting neuron (40 Hz as shown in Fig. 3A), while maintaining their experimental feasibility. To qualitatively match the activity period of a neuron (Fig. 3A, top), the parameters values for $v_{\tau(d,h)}$ in Table 3 were selected based on a minimized period, a maximized peak-to-peak amplitude, and experimental feasibility (Fig. 3B, red circles and triangles). For the remaining 9 parameters in Table 3, an identical selection process can be independently implemented to achieve desired oscillation patterns and frequencies while maintaining experimental realizability.

To match neuron's behavior, the neuristor model was used as a design tool to identify relevant experimental parameters based on six events that occur during a single spike (Fig. 3C). To instigate an action potential, an external stimulus injects (I_{stim}) current into the capacitive bilayers of both memristors, thus raising the membrane potential (v_m) linearly (Event 1, Fig. 3C). The rate at which v_m varies is reliant on the magnitudes of the injected current (I_{stim}), combined membrane capacitance (C_m), and combined membrane resistance (R_m). Identifying primary parameters driving Event 1 informs the design to alter the slope of this event, which can be realized experimentally by varying the droplet size to change the interfacial bilayer area (A_m), thus the capacitance (C_m) [17].

As v_m increases past the insertion threshold of the depolarizing memristor, Alm peptides in the depolarizing memristor rapidly insert into the membrane as evidenced by the exponential increase in N_d (Event 2, Fig. 3C). Peptide insertion and channel formation allow the discharge of ions from the extracellular to the intracellular droplet due to the enforced ion gradient across the membrane. The insertion threshold can be tuned only by altering the parameters $N_{0(d,h)}$ and $g_{u(d,h)}$ because $v_{e(d,h)}$ is invariant and only slightly pH dependent [18]. This tuning is experimentally achievable by changing the concentration of the Alm peptides and the salt [5,17]. For faster insertion and a lowered insertion threshold for the depolarizing memristor, a larger value for N_{0d} or g_{ud} is favorable, thus requiring a higher concentration of peptides and a smaller cation salt [5].

After Event 2, v_m rises nonlinearly due to the fast memristor's depolarizing current and eventually reaches the slow hyperpolarizing memristor threshold, triggering the increase in N_h (Event 3, Fig. 3C). Due to the enforcement of an opposing ion gradient, the increase in the number of open pores in the hyperpolarizing memristor results in an increase in a hyperpolarizing current (Event 3 of Fig. 3C). As v_m approaches the reversal potential of the depolarizing memristor ($E_d = 150\,\text{mV}$), hence minimizing the depolarizing current, the hyperpolarizing current starts to predominantly drive a decay in v_m. During this decay, although the hyperpolarizing memristor threshold is reached before the depolarizing fast memristor threshold, the time constant of pore closure τ_{0h} for the hyperpolarizing memristor is tailored to be much larger than τ_{0d} of the depolarizing memristor. The speed of insertion in either memristors is dominated by the parameters τ_0 and v_τ, which mainly correspond experimentally to the concentration of peptides and lipid type. A sufficient difference between the two decay times constants can cause the neuristor to be driven to a membrane potential lower than $v_m(t = 0)$, thus creating a refractory period similar to that of a neuron. The time constants can be predominantly controlled experimentally by changing the lipid type or the peptide concentration [5,17]. Assuming that the neuristor is still being stimulated by I_{stim}, the charging of the membrane

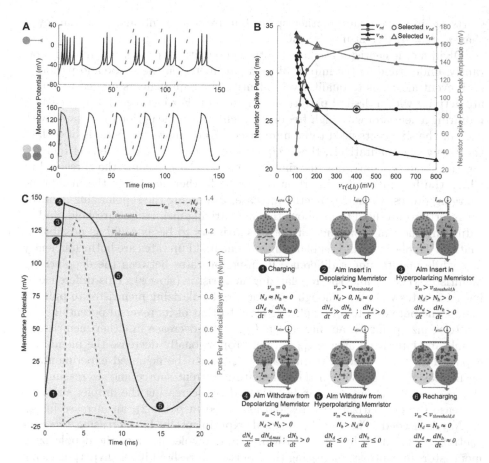

Fig. 3. (A) Single unit behavior for a bursting excitatory neuron (top) and a neuristor (bottom). The dashed lines indicate that the neuron bursting activity period is qualitatively similar to the neuristor oscillation period. (B) To modify the neuristor oscillation profile and match the neuron burst frequency, several model parameters were tuned, of which v_τ had the greatest influence on the neuristor spike period (black lines) and peak-to-peak amplitude (gray lines). The results in (A) were produced using the v_τ circled by the red circles and triangles for the depolarizing and hyperpolarizing memristors, respectively. (C) Our computational model can be used to tune neuristor models based on key events in the activity profile of a single oscillation (shaded region in A). All neuristor spikes have 6 major constituent events that involve the interplay between the depolarizing (right, pink memristor) and the hyperpolarizing (left, purple memristor) memristors: (1) Membrane Charging, (2) Fast insertion of Alm peptides in the depolarizing memristor, (3) Slow insertion of Alm peptides in the hyperpolarizing memristor, (4) Peaking of the neuristor membrane potential due to equilibrium of depolarizing and hyperpolarizing currents. Hyperpolarization then triggers the fast withdrawal of Alm peptides in the depolarizing memristor (5) The slow withdrawal of peptides from the membrane in the hyperpolarizing memristor, and finally (6) the recharging of the neuristor membrane potential by the stimulus current (I_{stim}). (Color figure online)

starts again to generate another spike, but from a membrane potential lower than $v_m(t = 0)$ (Event 6 in Fig. 3C).

Dividing the neuristor oscillation into six constituent events and, more importantly, understanding the impact of each parameter on the shape and period of each event allows us to qualitatively identify the requirements needed to generate activity with a desired pattern and frequency. For instance, for applications requiring a neuristor with high-frequency oscillations, the periods associated with each of the six events need to be minimized. To optimize the periods of each of the six events qualitatively, these requirements need to be satisfied: 1) Increasing the slope of membrane charging at event 1, 2) Decreasing the threshold at which the fast memristor insertion occurs to further accelerate the membrane charging process to an exponential increase, 3) Forcing the repolarizing memristor insertion threshold to be above the depolarizing memristor threshold, and 4) Adjusting the time constants of both memristors to be as rapid as possible so that the depolarizing and repolarizing current build up rates are both sufficiently fast while maintaining a difference in insertion rates between the depolarizing memristor (faster) and the repolarizing memristor (slower). This difference in insertion rates will allow enough time for the depolarizing memristor to pull the membrane potential to an amplitude close to that of its reversal potential.

To realize point 1), an increase in I_{stim} or a decrease in either memristors' membrane interfacial area $A_{m(d,h)}$ (will proportionally decrease the membrane capacitance C_m) is required. Increasing I_{stim} can be achieved experimentally by increasing the activity of the stimulating current source and decreasing the $A_{m(d,h)}$ and, therefore, C_m can be achieved by decreasing the droplet sizes. To decrease the depolarization threshold as stated in point 2), an increase in g_{ud} or N_{0d} is needed. This can be realized experimentally by increasing the concentration of Alm or by adding crowding macromolecules into the depolarizing memristor. In contrast, increasing the insertion threshold in the hyperpolarizing memristor can be attained by decreasing the value of g_{uh} or N_{0h}, which experimentally corresponds to decreasing the concentration of Alm in the hyperpolarizing memristor. Finally, to satisfy point 4), the magnitudes of time constant-related parameters ($\tau_{0(d,h)}$ and $v_{\tau(d,h)}$) should be carefully selected to maintain the difference in rates between the two memristors, where small $\tau_{0(d,h)}$ and large $v_{\tau(d,h)}$ values will increase the memristor insertion rate and vice versa.

Even with preliminary manual tuning, the oscillation rate of the neuristor model still varies from the firing and bursting rates of the neuron models after our initial tuning (dashed reference lines in Fig. 3A). These results highlight the need for further tuning and optimization of the neuristor parameters. However, such tuning will need to be accompanied by experimental fabrication to ensure that the resulting neuristor parameters are still achievable in the lab. In addition, by adjusting key neuristor parameters (droplet size, lipid type, salt type, peptide concentration, and salt concentration), the neuristors could be tuned to better mimic neuron behavior in future studies, both *in silico* and *in vitro*.

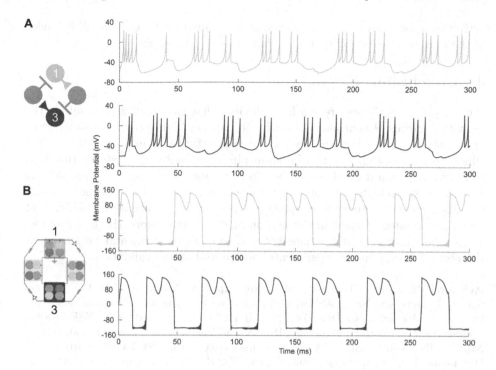

Fig. 4. The mutually inhibitory circuit configuration affects the membrane potential behavior of both the neurons (A) and the neuristors (B). Activity from neurons/neuristors 1 (light blue) and 3 (dark blue) are shown in response to a chronic stimulating current. Both the modeled biological neuron CPG and the neuristor CPG result in alternating activity patterns qualitatively characteristic of biological central pattern generators. However, the frequency of the periods of excitation is higher in the neuristor model than when using experimentally reported parameters [17] (Color figure online)

In addition to the single-unit case, our modeling tool indicates that neuristors can be combined to create biologically-inspired control circuits with qualitatively similar behavior to analogous neural circuit models (Fig. 4). When arranged in a mutually inhibitory configuration, both the neuristor and the neuron models demonstrate that their excitatory units alternate between periods of excitability and quiescence (Fig. 4). This pattern has a different frequency of activity as compared to the single-unit activity (Fig. 3A). For both the single-unit and mutually inhibitory cases, the duration of the periods of excitability and spiking profiles vary between the neuristor and neuron models. However, the ability to achieve the characteristic alternating activity pattern seen in biological CPGs is a promising result for the neuristor circuits presented here. Since this alternating pattern is important to the control of cyclical behavior in many animals, applications of such circuits may include biohybrid or soft robotics, where actuators acting as a low-pass filters will be primarily influenced by the overall behavior of the periods of excitability, rather than individual spikes.

4 Conclusion

Biomolecular neuristors are synthetic devices that can qualitatively mimic the activity patterns of neurons. The ability to capture bioinspired control patterns makes them potential candidates for creating artificial neural circuits *in vitro*, which have control applications in bio-inspired and biohybrid systems. However, to fully replicate a desired neuron behavior in fabricated neuristors, parameters for future experiments must be tuned. The computational model of the neuristor circuits presented here achieved qualitatively similar periods of excitability that was demonstrated by the bursting neuron model. Furthermore, this tool provides insight into how relevant parameters may impact experimental performance, thereby informing future experimental design and model validation.

Acknowledgements. This material is based upon work supported by the National Science Foundation (NSF). ASL was supported by the Graduate Research Fellowship Program under Grant No. DGE1745016, and YJZ was supported by the NSF Leading Engineering for America's Prosperity, Health, and Infrastructure program under Grant No. CMMI-1953323. ASL and VAW were supported by the NSF Faculty Early Career Development Program under Grant No. ECCS-2044785. Any opinions, findings, and conclusions or recommendations expressed in this material are those of the author(s) and do not necessarily reflect the views of the NSF. ASL was also supported by the Carnegie Mellon University Jean-Francois and Catherine Heitz Scholarship. ASL, YJZ, and VAW were also supported by a Pennsylvania Infrastructure Technology Alliance grant and a Pennsylvania Manufacturing Fellows Initiative grant.

Figs. 1, 2B, portions of the right panel of Fig. 3C, and portions of Fig. 4 were created with BioRender.com.

References

1. Aydin, O., et al.: Development of 3D neuromuscular bioactuators. APL Bioeng. **4**(1), 016107 (2020). https://doi.org/10.1063/1.5134477
2. Bing, Z., Meschede, C., Röhrbein, F., Huang, K., Knoll, A.C.: A survey of robotics control based on learning-inspired spiking neural networks. Front. Neurorobot. **12**, 35 (2018). https://doi.org/10.3389/fnbot.2018.00035
3. Brunel, N., Wang, X.J.: Effects of neuromodulation in a cortical network model of object working memory dominated by recurrent inhibition. J. Comput. Neurosci. **11**(1), 63–85 (2001). https://doi.org/10.1023/A:1011204814320
4. Chua, L.O.: Local activity is the origin of complexity. Int. J. Bifurc. Chaos. **15**(11), 3435–3456 (2005). https://doi.org/10.1142/S0218127405014337
5. Eisenberg, M., Hall, J.E., Mead, C.A.: The nature of the voltage-dependent conductance induced by Alamethicin in black lipid membranes. J. Membr. Biol. **14**(1), 143–176 (1973). https://doi.org/10.1007/BF01868075
6. Friesen, W.O.: Reciprocal inhibition: a mechanism underlying oscillatory animal movements. Neurosci. Biobehav. Rev. **18**(4), 547–553 (1994). https://doi.org/10.1016/0149-7634(94)90010-8

7. Hodgkin, A.L., Huxley, A.F.: A quantitative description of membrane current and its application to conduction and excitation in nerve. J. Physiol. **117**(4), 500–544 (1952). https://doi.org/10.1113/jphysiol.1952.sp004764

8. Ijspeert, A.J.: Biorobotics: using robots to emulate and investigate agile locomotion. Science. **346**(6206), 196–203 (2014). https://doi.org/10.1126/science.1254486

9. Ijspeert, A.J.: Central pattern generators for locomotion control in animals and robots: a review. Neural Netw. (2008). https://doi.org/10.1016/j.neunet.2008.03.014

10. Izhikevich, E.: Simple model of spiking neurons. IEEE Trans. Neural Netw. **14**(6), 1569–1572 (2003). https://doi.org/10.1109/TNN.2003.820440

11. Izhikevich, E.: Which model to use for cortical spiking neurons? IEEE Trans. Neural Netw. **15**(5), 1063–1070 (2004). https://doi.org/10.1109/TNN.2004.832719

12. Izhikevich, E.M.: Dynamical Systems in Neuroscience. The MIT Press, Cambridge (2006). https://doi.org/10.7551/mitpress/2526.001.0001

13. Liao, A., Cui, W., Zhang, Y.J., Webster-Wood, V.: Quantitative evaluation of neuron developmental morphology in vitro using the change-point test. Neuroinformatics (Under Review, PREPRINT at Research Square) (2022). https://doi.org/10.21203/rs.3.rs-1527309/v1

14. Liao, A.S., Webster-Wood, V.A., Zhang, Y.J.: Quantification of neuron morphological development using the change-point test. In: 2021 Summer Biomechanics, Bioengineering and Biotransport Conference (2021)

15. Marder, E., Bucher, D.: Central pattern generators and the control of rhythmic movements. Current Biol. **11**(23), R986–R996 (2001). https://doi.org/10.1016/S0960-9822(01)00581-4

16. Mendell, L.M.: The size principle: a rule describing the recruitment of motoneurons. J. Neurophysiol. **93**(6), 3024–3026 (2005). https://doi.org/10.1152/classicessays.00025.2005

17. Najem, J.S., et al.: Memristive ion channel-doped biomembranes as synaptic mimics. ACS Nano. **12**(5), 4702–4711 (2018). https://doi.org/10.1021/acsnano.8b01282

18. Okazaki, T., Sakoh, M., Nagaoka, Y., Asami, K.: Ion channels of alamethicin dimer n-terminally linked by disulfide bond. Biophys. J. **85**(1), 267–273 (2003). https://doi.org/10.1016/S0006-3495(03)74472-5

19. Pham, T., Haas, J.S.: Electrical synapses regulate both subthreshold integration and population activity of principal cells in response to transient inputs within canonical feedforward circuits. PLOS Comput. Biol. **15**(2), e1006440 (2019). https://doi.org/10.1371/journal.pcbi.1006440

20. Qian, K., et al.: Modeling neuron growth using isogeometric collocation based phase field method. Sci. Rep. (Under Review) (2022)

21. Stimberg, M., Brette, R., Goodman, D.F.: Brian 2, an intuitive and efficient neural simulator. eLife. **8**, e47314 (2019). https://doi.org/10.7554/eLife.47314

22. Webster-Wood, V.A., Akkus, O., Gurkan, U.A., Chiel, H.J., Quinn, R.D.: Organismal engineering: toward a robotic taxonomic key for devices using organic materials. Sci. Robot. **2**(12), eaap9281 (2017). https://doi.org/10.1126/scirobotics.aap9281

GymSlug: Deep Reinforcement Learning Toward Bio-inspired Control Based on *Aplysia californica* Feeding

Wenhuan Sun[1]([envelope])[iD], Mengdi Xu[1][iD], Jeffrey P. Gill[2][iD], Peter J. Thomas[2][iD], Hillel J. Chiel[2][iD], and Victoria A. Webster-Wood[1][iD]

[1] Carnegie Mellon University, Pittsburgh, PA 15213, USA
wenhuans@andrew.cmu.edu, vwebster@andrew.cmu.edu
[2] Case Western Reserve University, Cleveland, OH, USA

Abstract. Developing robots with animal-like flexibility, adaptability, and robustness remains challenging. However, the neuromuscular system of animals can provide bioinspiration for robotic controller design. In this work, we have developed a bio-inspired simulation environment, Gym-Slug, for reinforcement learning of motor control sequences based on our prior models of feeding behavior in the marine mollusk *Aplysia californica*. Using a range of model-free deep reinforcement learning algorithms, we train agents capable of producing motor neural control sequences, muscle activities, and feeding apparatus behavior that are qualitatively similar to behaviors observed in the animal during swallowing of unbreakable seaweed. The robustness of the trained agent is demonstrated by its ability to adapt to a previously unseen environment with breakable seaweed of varying strength. In addition, the environment can be easily reconfigured to train agents for additional tasks, including effective egestion of inedible objects. Our extensible simulation environment provides a platform for developing novel controllers to test biological hypotheses, learn control policies for neurorobotic models, and develop new approaches for soft robotic grasping control inspired by *Aplysia*.

Keywords: Deep reinforcement learning · *Aplysia Californica*

1 Introduction

Living systems exhibit remarkable flexibility, adaptability, and robustness of control during the interaction with their environment. For example, the marine mollusk *Aplysia californica* robustly adapts to efficiently ingest food with varying mechanical strengths [1–3]. Achieving such capabilities in robotics remains challenging. One strategy to develop robotic controllers is to build simulated robots that map the known animal neural circuitry and biomechanics of the musculature onto a computational model [4–7]. Such models help facilitate the fast

This work was supported by NSF DBI 2015317 as part of the NSF/CIHR/DFG/FRQ/UKRI-MRC Next Generation Networks for Neuroscience Program.

© The Author(s), under exclusive license to Springer Nature Switzerland AG 2022
A. Hunt et al. (Eds.): Living Machines 2022, LNAI 13548, pp. 236–248, 2022.
https://doi.org/10.1007/978-3-031-20470-8_24

prototyping, design iteration, and testing of robotic control policies. Members of our group recently reported a computationally efficient, biologically relevant model for simulating feeding behavior in *Aplysia* [8], which provides a testbed for designing and testing robotic controllers for *Aplysia* feeding control. The present work builds on this prior work by creating an *Aplysia* feeding simulation environment for reinforcement learning (RL), which can be used to develop and test RL algorithms toward effective robotic controllers and prediction of neuromechanical control signals.

Advances in deep reinforcement learning have expanded the application of RL control policy generation for robotic control. Specifically, the Deep Q-Network (DQN) and its extensions, a type of model-free algorithm that uses deep neural networks to approximate the value (Q) function of state and action, may be particularly relevant to neural control [9]. In addition to DQNs, successful robotic control has also been achieved using policy optimization methods, including Proximal Policy Optimization (PPO) and Trust Region Policy Optimization (TRPO) [10,11]. These algorithms contribute to a powerful toolbox for the development of robotic control architecture in simulated hybrid animal models.

In this work, we adapt the model reported in [8] to create a custom OpenAI gym RL simulation environment for *Aplysia* feeding behavior control policy learning, termed GymSlug. We use Deep RL to create bio-inspired control policies where the policy represents a motor control sequence that can produce functional behavior in a biomechanical model of an animal. Such motor control sequences resemble the way in which animals control muscle groups via orchestrated motor neuron activities. We use representative Q-learning (DQN) and policy optimization (TRPO) methods to train a control policy in a GymSlug environment where the simulated animal learns to swallow unbreakable seaweed. The trained agent demonstrates expert-level performance, as measured relative to our original model [8], and generates behavior qualitatively similar to *Aplysia* swallowing. Furthermore, we demonstrate the robustness of the trained agent by exposing it to a novel environment with breakable seaweed, where it shows adaptive ingestion of seaweed with varying strengths. We also successfully reconfigure the GymSlug and use DQN to train an agent to respond to a novel problem, egesting inedible material.

2   Methods

2.1   Hybrid Biomechanical Model of the Musculature and Boolean Network Model of Known Motor Neurons

During feeding, *Aplysia* ingests food, i.e. seaweed, through cyclic movement of the feeding apparatus by recruiting head muscles, including the I2, I3, I4, and hinge muscles (Fig. 1A). In this work, the feeding behavior of *Aplysia* was modeled using a bottom-up modeling approach as outlined in [8]. Briefly, the seaweed is attached to a fixed force transducer and a user-defined force threshold is implemented to represent the tensile strength of the seaweed (Fig. 1B). During feeding,

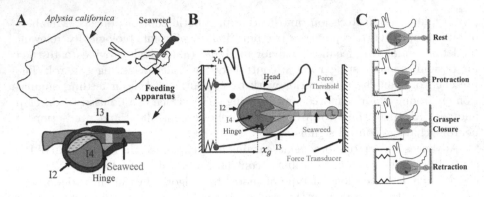

Fig. 1. A biomechanical model of *Aplysia* feeding. **A** A schematic showing positions of the body (red), food (green), and feeding apparatus (black) during feeding with a schematic of key muscles (I2, I3, I4, and hinge) involved. **B** A schematic of the biomechanical model in which the seaweed is attached to a fixed force transducer. The model constrains motion of the head and grasper to the x axis and object masses are considered negligible. **C** A schematic of the model in one swallowing cycle. The seaweed is swallowed during retraction when the grasper is closed. Modified from [8] ©Springer Nature with permission (Color figure online)

the seaweed remains intact until the tensile load exceeds the force threshold. Due to the quasi-static nature of *Aplysia* muscle activity [6], the mass of the components are neglected. For modeling simplicity and computational efficiency, the movement and force elements are constrained to the x-axis. A characteristic swallowing cycle of the feeding apparatus is illustrated in Fig. 1C, which consists of the protraction, grasper closure, retraction, and rest phases. The seaweed is ingested in the retraction phase during which the grasper closes and retracts relative to the head. It is worth noting that as long as the seaweed does not break, the head is pulled toward the food during the retraction phase and slips back in the rest phase which is when the grasper opens. Detailed implementation of the biomechanical model can be found in [8].

Each of the four muscles are controlled by a corresponding motor neuron/group, which forms a simplified Boolean logic statement in the Boolean network model (Fig. 2). In the Boolean representation, the burst activity observed in the animal neural recording data is approximated by the *on* state. For example, the protraction phase is driven by the I2 muscle activated by the B31/B32 neurons, which pushes the grasper towards the food. Then, exciting the B8a/b neurons activates the I4 muscle that closes the grasper on the food. In the retraction phase, the hinge and I3 muscles work in synergy, controlled by the B7 and B6/B9/B3 motor neurons, respectively. In the rest phase, an intermediate state between retraction and subsequent protraction, the anterior region of the I3 muscle pinches on the food to prevent slipping, activated by the B38 neuron.

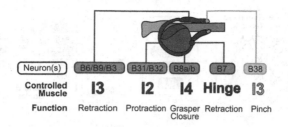

Fig. 2. A schematic of the motor neurons responsible for muscle control during feeding with corresponding controlled muscle and function indicated

2.2 GymSlug Reinforcement Learning Environment

We implemented the RL environment as a registered OpenAI gym environment [12] (available at https://github.com/CMU-BORG/GymSlug.git).

Action Space: The action at time step t, $a_t = (\text{B6/B9/B3}, \text{B31/B32}, \text{B8a/b},$ $\text{B7}, \text{B38})$, is one frame of the control signal for the motor neuron layer with five neurons. Due to the Boolean nature of the acceptable input of each neuron, there are 32 (2^5) discrete choices of actions at each step. The action from the policy network is fed into the hybrid model to update the corresponding muscle activity, the forces, and the location of the corresponding components for the next step $t + 1$. The control frequency 20 Hz.

State Space: The state S_t at time step t consists of 7 elements: $S_t = (x_h, x_g, F_o, P_g, P_j, e, f_g)$ (Fig. 3). The first two elements denote the position of the head and grasper, respectively. F_o represents the nominal total axial force exerted on the object. P_g and P_j indicate the transverse pressure exerted by the grasper and jaw muscles, respectively. e is a Boolean element representing the edibility of the object (e.g., 1 for seaweed, and 0 for polyethylene tube). f_g is a Boolean element representing the type of friction on the object: 1 indicates static friction where the grasper motion is identical with the object motion, while 0 indicates kinetic friction where the grasper slips along the object. During environment reset in each episode, all state elements except e and f_g are randomly sampled from a uniform distribution $U(0, 0.05)$.

Goal: The goal is to learn a policy that is capable of performing bio-inspired control while interacting with the environment. Specifically, the learned policy should achieve similar or higher cumulative episode reward when compared to the original *Aplysia* model presented in [8], which is referred to as the expert. In addition to cumulative reward, a successful agent should also exhibit similar neural control signals/actions and muscle activities.

Reward Function: The reward function is designed to encourage ingestion of edible food or egestion (the process of discharging unusable material from an organism) of inedible objects over a given time. The unit-less reward at time step $t + 1$ is calculated based on the nominal relative grasper motion if static

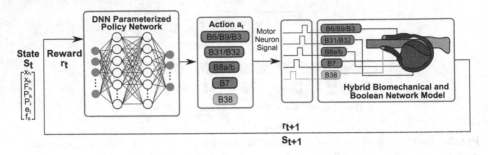

Fig. 3. A schematic of the reinforcement learning setup. The state space consists of the positions of the head (x_{h}) and grasper (x_{g}), force on object/food F_o, grasper pressure P_{g}, jaw pressure P_{j}, object edibility e, and grasper-object friction state f_{g}. For the current state frame, S_t, the policy network outputs an action set a_t with 5 discrete elements to control the five motor neurons. The environment model subsequently takes a_t and outputs the updated state S_{t+1} and the reward r_{t+1} is calculated.

friction is present or based on the nominal axial force on the seaweed if static friction is not present as:

$$r_{t+1} = (1-2e_{t+1})\{f_{\mathrm{g}t+1}\Delta_{\mathrm{gm}t+1}+(1-f_{\mathrm{g}t+1})\frac{F_{ot+1}}{100}[(\Delta_{\mathrm{gm}t+1} > 0)\wedge(F_{ot+1} < 0)]\} \tag{1}$$

where the relative grasper motion $\Delta_{\mathrm{gm}t+1}$ is calculated from:

$$\Delta_{\mathrm{gm}t+1} = (x_{\mathrm{g}t+1} - x_{\mathrm{h}t+1}) - (x_{\mathrm{g}t} - x_{\mathrm{h}t}) \tag{2}$$

In this context, $\wedge$ is a logical AND operation. Under static friction conditions with an edible object ($f_{\mathrm{g}t+1} = 1$, $e_{t+1} = 1$), $r_{t+1} = -\Delta_{\mathrm{gm}t+1}$, which assigns high positive reward to significant negative grasper motion when the grasper holds onto the food without slipping and moves toward the head. In comparison, under a condition of kinetic friction ($f_{\mathrm{g}t+1} = 0$), edible object ($e_{t+1} = 1$), and the grasper moving away from the body ($\Delta_{\mathrm{gm}t+1} > 0$), while applying compressive load to the object ($F_{ot+1} < 0$), the updated reward is given by $r_{t+1} = \frac{F_{ot+1}}{100}$, which penalizes the agent for significant compressive load that tends to push edible seaweed out of the feeding apparatus. When the object is inedible ($e_{t+1} = 0$), the sign of the reward function is reversed.

2.3   Learning Model and Training Setup

The reinforcement agent's policy network was parameterized by a deep neural network composed of 2 layers containing 64 neurons each, and including 22,979 trainable parameters. A standard, sequential decision making process commonly used in RL was adopted in this study, where at time step t, the agent observed a frame of the environment S_t and picked an action a_t from a discrete set of 32 actions. The simulated environment then provided an updated state S_{t+1} and reward r_{t+1}. The goal of RL algorithms is to maximize the expected future discounted return $\mathbb{E}[R_t]$ at time step t, where $R_t = \sum_{\tau=t}^{T} \gamma^{\tau-t} r_\tau$. Here $\gamma \in [0, 1]$ is a discount factor that trades-off the importance of rewards from immediate and future steps, T is the episode end step. Using a policy π (mapping from state to action) and starting from state $s_t = s$, action $a_t = a$, such a goal can be expressed as a state-action value function (Q function): $Q^\pi(s, a) = \mathbb{E}[R_t | s_t = s, a_t = a, \pi]$, and its optimum can be defined as $Q^*(s, a) = \max_\pi Q^\pi(s, a)$ [13]. Given $Q^*(s, a)$, the optimal policy can be given: $a = \pi(s) = \max_a Q^*(s, a)$.

To demonstrate that our simulation environment can fully integrate with existing OpenAI RL algorithms, we used the Deep Q-Network (DQN) [13] and Trust Region Policy Optimization (TRPO) [14] algorithms to train agents for 500,000 steps. **DQN** is a model free, off-policy algorithm that uses a deep Q-network to approximate the Q function [13]. Unlike DQN, **TRPO** is an on-policy, policy gradient algorithm that directly learns the policy function. For both DQN and TRPO, we used the OpenAI baseline implementation for training [15]. DQN was found to be more successful in agent training, and therefore subsequent tests of agent robustness were performed with DQN-trained agents.

3 Results

3.1 Deep Reinforcement Learning Achieves Effective Motor Neuron Control on the Hybrid Simulation Environment

To obtain the expert action/motor neuron control sequence, the original hybrid model [8] was run for 1200 steps (60 s), where the original hybrid model contains more complex neural circuitry, including buccal interneurons and cerebral interneurons for sensor data processing and motor neuron regulation. The resultant motor neuron control sequence (Fig. 4A) was fed into a GymSlug environment and run for 10 episodes (1000 steps per episode), where the agent actions were sequentially taken from the expert action and the muscle activities (Fig. 4B, C) and performance (Fig. 4D) were monitored. These coordinated muscle activations result in cyclic swallowing of food, leading to a unit-less averaged cumulative episode reward of 132.84±3.58 (mean±s.d.). This expert performance establishes a strong baseline and benchmark for RL agent training.

Swallowing of Unbreakable Seaweed: RL agents were trained in the unbreakable seaweed environment ($e = 1$, seaweed strength $= \infty$) using the DQN and TRPO algorithms with the agent performance checked every 500 steps for 250,000 training steps, which corresponds to 6.94 h of interaction with the simulation environment (Fig. 5A). We used averaged episode reward as the evaluation metric where the agent interacted with the environment for five episodes and the averaged episode reward was computed. For RL, this metric can be very noisy because minor updates to the neural network weights can lead to significant changes to the agent trajectory [13]. This is observed in the agent episode reward plots for both DQN and TRPO training (Fig. 5A). As shown in the best agent performance progress (yellow tracing) of both algorithms, the

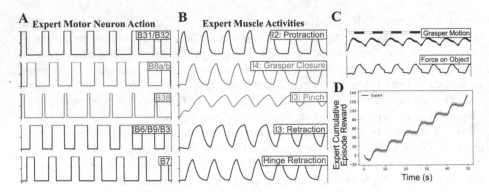

Fig. 4. Expert performance plot. **A** Color coded plots of the expert motor neuron actions taken from the original hybrid model. **B** Simulation of the expert muscle activities as a result of the actions. **C** (Top) Grasper motion plot. Thick regions denote static friction is present ($f_g = 1$, no relative movement between grasper and the object). Black and white bars represent retraction and protraction phases, respectively. (Bottom) Plot of the total axial force exerted on the object. **D** Plot of the cumulative episode reward as a function of time. Shaded area denotes one standard deviation. The variability is resulted from the random sampling of initial conditions for the state space. (Color figure online)

agents showed relatively fast performance improvement in the first 250,000 training steps where the performance gap between agent and expert was large. At the end of the training session, both DQN and TRPO trained agents' performance converges to the expert-level performance in terms of averaged episode reward. The DQN and TRPO training trials were repeated for 10 times each using maximum episode reward as the evaluation metric and the results indicate that DQN algorithm has better training stability than TRPO in the GymSlug environment (Fig. 5B). In addition, trained agents with three different performance levels (13.77, 75.37, and 133.29) were re-evaluated by running them in a new GymSlug environment for 10 episodes with the mean and standard deviation plotted (Fig. 5C). Agents started with an initial policy that output random actions. At early training stages (averaged cumulative reward (ACR) = 13.77), the agent starts to exhibit cyclic feeding behavior that leads to a slow but cyclic increase of reward. As the training advances, the period of agent reward starts to converge to the expert (ACR = 75.37) although the reward-per-cycle is still lower than the expert. When the agent reaches expert-level performance (ACR = 133.29±0.84), it shows similar reward patterns to the expert with small variance, indicating consistent agent behavior across different runs.

In addition to reward comparisons, the motor neuron activity, muscle activities, grasper motion, and axial force on the object were examined qualitatively. The force on the object shows good agreement in period and magnitude between the expert and the trained agent with expert-level performance (Fig. 6D). In addition, the agent exhibits good agreement in grasper motion magnitude and period (Fig. 6C). However, within each cycle, the trained agent spends a longer time performing retraction and less on protraction. This similarity in grasper

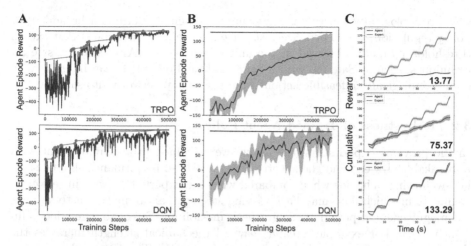

Fig. 5. Training progress graphs and characteristic agent performance plots. **A** The agent episode reward plots as a function of training steps of the TRPO (Top) and DQN (Bottom) training algorithms (blue tracing shows a typical agent's performance throughout the training process). The overlaid yellow tracing indicates the progress of the agent's best performance. The red horizontal line indicates the expert performance. **B** Plots of the average and standard deviation of reward from 10 training trials using TRPO (Top) and DQN (Bottom). **C** A set of plots of agent-expert cumulative reward comparison when the agents reached three performance checkpoints: (Top) 13.77, (Middle) 75.37, (Bottom) 133.29. Shaded areas indicate one standard deviation (Color figure online)

motion and force output between the agent and expert can be explained by the comparison of the muscle activities (Fig. 6B). The agent exhibits good agreement with the expert for I2 (for protraction) and I4 (for grasper closure) muscle activities. The pinch force activity in both the agent and expert simulations show similar periods, although the agent produces a higher pinch force. Activities of the two muscles for retraction (I3 and hinge muscles) show different patterns with similar period, which explains the difference in retraction grasper motion.

Similarities and differences in the observed muscle activities can be explained by the motor neuron actions (Fig. 6A), because the duration of Booleanized neuron activation affects the force magnitude. For example, the B31/B32 and the B8a/b neurons show good agreement in period and *on-off* ratio, which explains the observed similarity in I2 and I4 muscle activities. The B38 neuron activity of the expert and agent is similar in period, yet the agent shows longer *on* duration, which explains the comparatively higher I3 pinching force. These findings confirm that the agent learned a motor neuron control policy and corresponding muscle activities that lead to similar feeding apparatus behaviors with the expert. In the current setting, it is possible that the agent learns a policy that is functionally different from the expert model while still achieving a similar or better reward. To promote functional resemblance between the learned policy and the expert model, the reward function can be modified to penalize policies that are biologically infeasible. For example, a penalty term can be added for policy regulation, which penalizes excessive muscle force and speed that exceed thresholds normally observed in the animal's behavior. Alternatively, safe AI techniques, such as Safe RL with a Safety Editor Policy [16], can be utilized to modify biologically infeasible actions from the policy network into safe ones.

3.2   Robustness of Trained Agent Policy

In the previous experiments, the agents were trained in an environment with unbreakable seaweed and the agent with expert-level performance showed similar swallowing behavior when compared with the expert. However, in real environments in which food may have varying strength, an animal robustly adjusts the magnitude and period of the grasper's motion and forces to ingest food efficiently [1–3]. For example, greater seaweed mechanical strength increases the duration of swallowing in the animal experiments [1]. Therefore, robustness to varying food mechanical strength is a desirable property for the feeding behavior controller and should be included in the metric for performance evaluation.

To examine the trained agent's robustness in response to varying seaweed strength (breakable seaweed), we deployed an agent that was trained with unbreakable seaweed in new test environments with breakable seaweed of varying strengths. Specifically, the agent was tested in four environments with increasing seaweed strength by specifying a force threshold (0.2, 0.3, 0.4, and ∞). When the seaweed strength increases (Fig. 7A), the agent was able to adapt to the increasing force threshold by increasing the overall period of swallowing motion, as seen in the animal. Such dynamic, environment-dependent policy showcases the

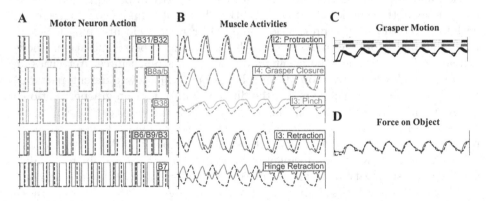

Fig. 6. Plots of agent-expert performance comparisons. **A** Overlaid plot of motor neuron actions of the expert (dashed lines) and the agent with expert-level performance (solid lines). **B** Overlaid plot of muscle activities of the expert (dashed lines) and the agent (solid lines) **C** Overlaid grasper motion plot of the expert (solid blue line) and the agent (line with partial transparency). Thickening of the grasper motion shows regions with static friction between the grasper and the object. **D** Overlaid plots of total axial force on the object of the expert (dashed line) and the agent (solid line) (Color figure online)

learned model's adaptability in a novel environment, a fundamental capability that contributes to the animal's success in the natural environment.

In addition to episode-to-episode robustness assessment, we examined the adaptability of the agent within one episode by running the agent in a test environment where the seaweed strength was a function of time (Fig. 7B). The agent was able to adapt to varying seaweed strength by adopting different strategies. When the seaweed strength increased from 0.2 to ∞, the agent automatically increased the duration of retraction phase (as indicated by the extended black bars in Fig. 7B) and exerted higher force to facilitate seaweed ingestion. It shifted to another behavior with shorter retraction duration when the seaweed strength decreased to 0.3, as shown in the video. These findings confirm that the trained agent shows robustness and adaptability against novel, varying environments to facilitate effective motor neuron control.

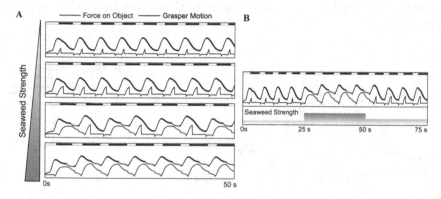

Fig. 7. Agent behavior (grasper motion and total axial force on object) in a new environment with varying seaweed strength. **A** Agent behavior in four environments with increasing seaweed strength (top to bottom: 0.2, 0.3, 0.4, ∞/unbreakable). Thickening of the grasper motion trace indicates the regions where static friction between the grasper and seaweed is present. Black and white bars represent retraction and protraction movement regions, respectively. **B** (Top) Agent behavior in an environment where the seaweed strength is a step function of time (0–25 s: 0.2, 25–50 s: ∞, 50–75 s: 0.3). (Bottom) Visual illustration of the varying seaweed strength in one run.

3.3 Egestion Behavior Training

Following ingestion behavior training, we next used DQN to train an agent for egestion behavior. The expert egestion action sequence was obtained by running the original hybrid model with the functional characteristics of *Aplysia californica* egestion behavior [8] for 1200 steps (60 s). The resultant motor neuron control sequence was fed into a GymSlug environment and run for 10 episodes, where the agent actions were sequentially taken from the expert action.

The trained agent was able to learn an egestion policy with higher performance than the expert (Fig. 8A). The agent with the best performance was

tested after training and it shows faster, more efficient reward growth over time
(Fig. 8A). This improved performance can be explained by the grasper motion
and total axial force on object comparison between the expert and the trained
agent (Fig. 8B): the agent is capable of performing faster grasper retraction which
leads to more cycles of egestion in the same amount of time. Compared with the
ingestion behavior training, the egestion environment allowed the agent to learn
a policy that is better than the expert in less time. This phenomena may be
partially explained by the difference in nature between ingestion and egestion.
Unlike the ingestion environment, in which the grasper needs to overcome resistance to swallow objects, the egestion of objects does not require significant
grasper or total axial force on the object. This relaxation may impose a lower
learning threshold or lower difficulty for deep reinforcement learning. It is also
possible that the expert was not as well tuned for egestion as it was for ingestion. Another possibility is that the actual animal has relatively slow muscles,
and that it may not be easy to speed them up to the rate that was used by the
RL trained agent.

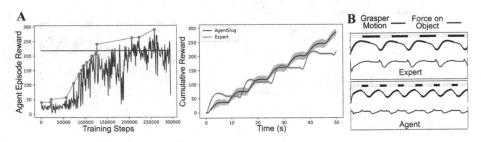

Fig. 8. Plots of egestion training progress using DQN and agent-expert performance
comparison. **A** (Left) A training progress plot. Blue trace indicates the averaged episode
reward as a function of training for a typical agent. The yellow tracing indicates the
progress of best agent performance over time. The red trace is the expert performance.
(Right) The averaged cumulative episode reward of the expert and a trained agent
with better than expert performance. Shaded areas indicate one standard deviation.
B Plots of grasper motion and total axial force on object. Thickening of the grasper
motion tracing indicates regions with static friction between the grasper and object.
Black and white bars indicate retraction and protraction phases, respectively (Color
figure online)

4   Conclusion

To our knowledge, this paper is the first to demonstrate the application of
reinforcement learning to create bio-inspired motor neuron control policies for
control of effective object ingestion and egestion behavior. In this work, we
introduced a custom OpenAI gym simulation environment for *Aplysia californica* feeding behavior learning, termed GymSlug, which is based on a hybrid
model of a simplified biomechanical model of the *Aplysia* feeding musculature

and a Boolean network model of the motor neuron circuitry that was directly responsible for the control of the feeding musculature. This environment is easily configurable to simulate different feeding scenarios, such as food with varying mechanical strength and edibility. For the food ingestion environment with unbreakable seaweed, we used the Deep Q-Network (DQN) and the Trust Region Policy Optimization (TRPO) algorithms to train agents that achieve expert-level performance by producing effective motor neuronal control sequences. The trained agent exhibits strong robustness to novel, breakable seaweed with varying mechanical strength. In addition, the agent achieves better than expert performance in the object egestion environment training. The modeling framework of GymSlug can be adapted for other bio-inspired control problems with appropriate update of problem-specific muscle mechanics, neuron functions, and reward structure. Future directions include 1) expanding the complexity of the current simplified hybrid model to account for geometric shape of muscles during feeding and higher levels of neuron circuitry, such as interneurons or the sensory neurons that detect chemical cues in the environment; 2) including the operation of a physical soft robotic feeding apparatus in the training and testing.

References

1. Gill, J.P., Chiel, H.J.: Rapid adaptation to changing mechanical load by ordered recruitment of identified motor neurons. eNeuro. 7, 1–18 (2020)
2. Lyttle, D.N., Gill, J.P., Shaw, K.M., Thomas, P.J., Chiel, H.J.: Robustness, flexibility, and sensitivity in a multifunctional motor control model. Biol. Cybern. 111(1), 25–47 (2017)
3. Shaw, K.M., et al.: The significance of dynamical architecture for adaptive responses to mechanical loads during rhythmic behavior. J. Comput. NeuroSci. 38, 25–51 (2015)
4. Szczecinski, N.S., et al.: Introducing MantisBot: hexapod robot controlled by a high-fidelity, real-time neural simulation. IEEE Int. Conf. Intell. Robots Syst. 2015, 3875–3881 (2015)
5. Szczecinski, N.S., Quinn, R.D.: Leg-local neural mechanisms for searching and learning enhance robotic locomotion. Biol. Cybern. 112(1–2), 99–112 (2018)
6. Sutton, G.P., Mangan, E.V., Neustadter, D.M., Beer, R.D., Crago, P.E., Chiel, H.J.: Neural control exploits changing mechanical advantage and context dependence to generate different feeding responses in Aplysia. Biol. Cybern. 91(5), 333–345 (2004)
7. Hunt, A., Szczecinski, N., Quinn, R.: Development and training of a neural controller for hind leg walking in a dog robot. Front. Neurorobot. 11, 1–16 (2017)
8. Webster-Wood, V.A., Gill, J.P., Thomas, P.J., Chiel, H.J.: Control for multifunctionality: bioinspired control based on feeding in Aplysia californica. Biol. Cybern. 114(6), 557–588 (2020)
9. Mitchell, B.A., Petzold, L.R.: Control of neural systems at multiple scales using model-free, deep reinforcement learning. Sci. Rep. 8, 1–12 (2018)
10. Li, Z., et al.: Reinforcement Learning for Robust Parameterized Locomotion Control of Bipedal Robots (2021)
11. Song, S., et al.: Deep reinforcement learning for modeling human locomotion control in neuromechanical simulation. J. NeuroEng. Rehabil. 18, 126 (2020)

12. Brockman, G., et al.: OpenAI Gym. arXiv:1606.01540, pp. 1–4 (2016)
13. Mnih, V., et al.: Playing Atari with Deep Reinforcement Learning. arXiv:1312.5602v1, pp. 1–9 (2013)
14. Schulman, J., Levine, S., Moritz, P., Jordan, M., Abbeel, P.: Trust region policy optimization. In: 32nd International Conference on Machine Learning, ICML 2015, vol. 3, pp. 1889–1897 (2015)
15. Hill, A., et al.: Stable Baselines (2018). https://github.com/hill-a/stable-baselines
16. Yu, H., Xu, W., Zhang, H.: Towards Safe Reinforcement Learning with a Safety Editor Policy (2022)

A Synthetic Nervous System
with Coupled Oscillators Controls
Peristaltic Locomotion

Shane Riddle[1]([✉])(iD), William R. P. Nourse[2](iD), Zhuojun Yu[3](iD),
Peter J. Thomas[2,3](iD), and Roger D. Quinn[1](iD)

[1] Department of Mechanical and Aerospace Engineering, Case Western Reserve
University, Cleveland, OH 44106, USA
shane.riddle@case.edu
[2] Department of Electrical, Computer, and Systems Engineering, Case Western
Reserve University, Cleveland, OH 44106, USA
[3] Department of Mathematics, Applied Mathematics, and Statistics, Case Western
Reserve University, Cleveland, OH 44106, USA

Abstract. This paper details the development and analysis of a computational neuroscience model, known as a Synthetic Nervous System, for the control of a simulated worm robot. Using a Synthetic Nervous System controller allows for adaptability of the network with minimal changes to the system. The worm robot kinematics are inspired by earthworm peristalsis which relies on the hydrostatic properties of the worm's body to produce soft-bodied locomotion. In this paper the hydrostatic worm body is approximated as a chain of two dimensional rhombus shaped segments. Each segment has rigid side lengths, joints at the vertices, and a linear actuator to control the segment geometry. The control network is composed of non-spiking neuron and synapse models. It utilizes central pattern generators, coupled via interneurons and sensory feedback, to coordinate segment contractions and produce a peristaltic waveform that propagates down the body of the robot. A direct perturbation Floquet multiplier analysis was performed to analyze the stability of the peristaltic wave's limit cycle.

Keywords: Synthetic nervous system · Central pattern generator ·
Peristalsis · Functional subnetwork · Motor control · Worm robot

1 Introduction

Worms move via a process known as peristaltic locomotion, in which the muscles contract and relax in wavelike patterns propagating down the body [16]. The pattern of muscle activation propels the worm forward or backward depending

This work was supported by NSF PIRE Award 1743475, NIH BRAIN Initiative grant R01 NS118606, and NSF DBI 2015317 as part of the NSF/CIHR/DFG/FRQ/UKRI-MRC Next Generation Networks for Neuroscience Program.

© The Author(s), under exclusive license to Springer Nature Switzerland AG 2022
A. Hunt et al. (Eds.): Living Machines 2022, LNAI 13548, pp. 249–261, 2022.
https://doi.org/10.1007/978-3-031-20470-8_25

on the direction of the wave, a process made possible by the hydrostatic properties of the worm body. Hydrostats maintain a constant volume due to the incompressibility of fluids within the body. A worm body can be approximated as a series of hydrostatic cylinders known as segments, each of which has longitudinal and circumferential muscles. When the circumferential muscles contract, the segment diameter decreases, which necessitates an increase in length to maintain the volume of the segment. Similarly, contraction of the longitudinal muscles causes a shortening of the segment, which necessitates an expansion of the diameter. Stringing a series of these segments together forms an analogous worm body. Many worm-like robots have been constructed following geometric approximations of this motion [5,8,11].

A Synthetic Nervous System (SNS) is a dynamical network composed of biologically-inspired neuron and synapse models [13]. An SNS can be differentiated from artificial neural networks by its use of conductance-based synapses, rather than weight-based synapses, and the use of the Functional Subnetwork Approach (FSA) [13]. The FSA is a method that allows for direct analytical tuning of small dynamical networks so they may perform specific operations in a larger network without resorting to global optimization methods. These functional subnetworks can be made to perform such actions as addition, subtraction, multiplication, division, differentiation, and integration of incoming signals. The subnetworks can then be assembled to form an SNS for the control of biologically inspired robots [2,5,6,8,14].

The wave-like nature of peristalsis implies periodic behavior in the nervous system. Oscillator networks called central pattern generators (CPGs) are believed to control rhythmic behaviors like breathing, walking, flying, and swimming [9]. CPGs produce periodic outputs without requiring periodic inputs. For peristalsis, CPGs can be used to control the muscle contraction cycles of each segment [7]. This paper develops an SNS neural controller for peristaltic locomotion of a model of a worm-like robot. We hypothesize that coupled oscillators can be used to produce peristaltic waveforms for use in worm-like locomotion.

2   Simplified Worm Robot Kinematic Model

For the purposes of this work, the worm robot segment model is simplified using rhombuses with hinge joint vertices [8]. This model operates similarly to the hydrostat cylinder model but in two dimensions instead of three. The worm body segments consist of rhombuses linked corner to corner with joints at all vertices. It is assumed that the sides of these rhombuses are rigid and that the angle between adjacent sides can change via joints placed at each vertex. Pushing two opposing corners together results in an outward displacement of the other two corners in the rhombus (Fig. 1a). This is akin to the hydrostat longitudinal contraction. Pulling the other two corners together similarly displaces the first pair of vertices (Fig. 1b). This is akin to the hydrostat circumferential contraction. Just as in the hydrostat model these are antagonistic actions that can propagate down a worm body in a peristaltic wave. The relationship between rhombus height (w) and length (l) for a given side length (l_s) is $l^2 + w^2 = 4l_s^2$.

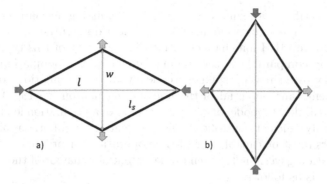

Fig. 1. Rhombus segment at two states: a) fully contracted and expanding, b) fully expanded and contracting.

The robot discussed in this paper is simulated but was loosely modelled after an existing robot presented in [4]. The physical robot uses servo motors connected to cords wrapped around the circumference of a cylinder composed of flexible rhombuses. For a visual of this robot, refer to Fig. 3 of [4]. Spooling and unwinding the cord directly changes the heights of the rhombuses resulting in segment contraction and expansion, respectively. While the motor is only able to provide contracting tension to the cord, longitudinally oriented springs provide return force allowing for control of both directions of movement. The simulation in this work models the motors as linear actuators. Each rhombus segment has one such actuator spanning between its top and bottom vertices.

These motors use proportional control, whereby the actuator velocity (v) is determined by the difference between the current height (w_i) and target height (w_targ). The subscript i indicates the simulation time step and w_targ is set by the CPG neurons as detailed in Sect. 3.1. The equation governing the actuator velocity is $v = k * (w_\mathrm{targ} - w_i)$, where k is a gain that can be tuned to achieve a desired actuation behavior. For the purposes of this paper k was set to 0.0091. The height updates at each time step (of size dt) following the equation $w_i = w_{i-1} + v * dt$. The velocity also updates so the actuation speed decreases as the segment height approaches w_targ. The segment length is calculated at each time step via the geometric relationship $l_i = \sqrt{4l_s^2 - w_i^2}$. Maximum and minimum height limits ($w_\mathrm{max} = 11\mathrm{cm}$, $w_\mathrm{min} = 6.5\mathrm{cm}$) were set to reflect the physical limits of the robot in [4], however the limits are arbitrary so long as they do not violate the geometry. At these limits the actuator velocity is set to zero.

3   Methods

3.1   Mathematical Models

Neurons and Synapses: As stated previously, the SNS is composed of neurons and synapses. Non-spiking, leaky integrator neurons were chosen for this network. The leaky-integrator dynamics convey ion channel gating without expressing action potentials generated by Hodgkin-Huxley (H-H) fast transient sodium and delayed rectifier potassium currents [3,13]. Omitting action potentials simplifies the neuron model by removing the non-linear differential equations needed to properly convey H-H ion channel gating. The activity of this type of neuron is qualitatively comparable to the spiking frequency of a population of spiking neurons, whereby increasing spiking frequency in the population correlates to increasing membrane potential in the non-spiking neuron [15,18]. The simpler equations and ability to model one neuron instead of a population leads to a more computationally efficient controller. This is essential for robotic applications as the controllers must be capable of real-time operation for practical use. The differential equation governing the membrane potential behavior of the non-spiking neuron model is as follows:

$$C_m \frac{dV}{dt} = G_m(E_r - V) + \sum_{j=1}^{n} G_{\mathrm{syn},j}(E_{\mathrm{syn},j} - V) + I_{\mathrm{app}} \tag{1}$$

C_m is the membrane capacitance, V is the membrane potential, G_m is the membrane conductance, and E_r is the cell's resting potential. E_{syn} is the synaptic reversal potential, n is the number of presynaptic neurons, and I_{app} is any current applied directly to the neuron. G_{syn} is the synaptic conductance through which presynaptic neuron j influences the postsynaptic neuron. Non-spiking conductance-based synapses were chosen for this network [13]. These are synapses which only influence the post-synaptic neuron if the presynaptic neuron is excited. Unlike the leak term (G_m) the synaptic conductance depends on the presynaptic neuron potential. In biological models this relationship, known as the synaptic conductance curve, can be represented by any monotonic function that saturates, like a sigmoid. For this SNS a piecewise linear approximation is used [13]. This allows for precise tuning of the network (shown in Sect. 3.2) and reduces the complexity of the math involved. The synaptic conductance curve is defined by the following:

$$G_{\mathrm{syn},i} = \begin{cases} 0 & \text{when } V_{\mathrm{pre}} < E_{\mathrm{lo}} \\ g_{\mathrm{syn},i} \dfrac{V_{\mathrm{pre}} - E_{\mathrm{lo}}}{E_{\mathrm{hi}} - E_{\mathrm{lo}}} & \text{when } E_{\mathrm{lo}} \leq V_{\mathrm{pre}} \leq E_{\mathrm{hi}} \\ g_{\mathrm{syn},i} & \text{when } V_{\mathrm{pre}} > E_{\mathrm{hi}} \end{cases} \tag{2}$$

E_{hi} and E_{lo} are the upper and lower threshold potentials of the synapse and their difference is known as the "operating range" R $(R = E_{\mathrm{hi}} - E_{\mathrm{lo}})$. From Eq. 2 we can see that this means the synapse is essentially off when E_{lo} is reached and saturates at its maximum conductance (g_{syn}) when E_{hi} is reached. To simplify this equation the actual membrane potential of the cell is normalized to be 0mV at rest. The normalized potential is represented by the variable U which is the neuron activation level above resting potential $(U = V - E_r)$. Assuming the synaptic potentials stay within the operating range $(0, R)$ we can substitute U and R into Eq. 2 to reduce the piecewise linear relationship to just $g_{\mathrm{syn},i} \frac{U_{\mathrm{pre}}}{R}$. Since the membrane potential was normalized to U, the synaptic reversal potential must also be corrected ($\Delta E_{syn} = E_{syn} - E_r$). Substituting these parameters into Eq. 1 produces the following:

$$C_m \frac{dU}{dt} = -G_m U + \sum_{j=1}^{n} g_{syn,j} \frac{U}{R}(E_{syn,j} - U) + I_{app} \tag{3}$$

This ordinary differential equation can be solved using the forward Euler numerical method of approximation. In this method the time differential components are calculated at each time step i and build off the state of the neuron at the previous time step $i - 1$. When converted into this format and solved for U, the differential equation takes the following form:

$$U_i = U_{i-1} + \frac{dt}{C_m}(-G_m U_{i-1} + \sum_{j=1}^{n} g_{syn,j} \frac{U_{i-1}}{R}(E_{syn,j} - U_{i-1}) + I_{app}) \tag{4}$$

Central Pattern Generators: The driving components of the SNS controller are the CPGs [10,12]. Each segment has one CPG composed of two neurons: one encouraging segment contraction (U_1), the other segment expansion (U_2). The activation levels of the CPG neurons directly control the actuator's target position. The target position is set by subtracting the membrane potential of the contracting neuron from that of the expanding neuron. Each CPG neuron's operating range is between 0 and R, meaning the total range of values for this operation is $[-R, R]$. This range is mapped to the range of heights the segments are capable of achieving $[w_{min}, w_{max}]$. When the contraction neuron is more strongly activated the actuator decreases the segment height (not exceeding w_{min}). When the expansion neuron is more strongly activated the segment height increases (not exceeding w_{max}).

The CPG neurons use the same non-spiking model but now incorporate voltage-gated sodium ion channels [12]. This allows for additional temporal dynamics that enable pattern generation. The ion channels are modeled using fast m gates and slow h gates, like those in the H-H model [3]. The m and h gating variable behaviors are modeled using the following functions:

$$h_\infty(U) = \frac{1}{1 + 0.5e^{s_h*(U)}} \tag{5}$$

$$m_\infty(U) = \frac{1}{1 + e^{s_m*(U-R)}} \tag{6}$$

$$\tau_h(U)\frac{dh}{dt} = h_\infty(U) - h \longrightarrow \tau_h(U) = \tau_{h,max}\frac{\sqrt{0.5e^{s_h*(U)}}}{h_\infty(U)} \tag{7}$$

The s values are the slopes of the sigmoids dictating the behaviors of m and h while τ_h is the time constant that determines how fast the h gates close. The m gates are much faster than the h gates which means τ_m is significantly smaller than τ_h. This allows us to ignore τ_m.

The sodium channel current presents as $G_{Na}m_\infty(U)h(U)*(\Delta E_{Na}-U)$ in the neuron model. G_{Na} is the sodium conductance that allows the U_1 CPG neuron's steady state potential to be R at equilibrium when the other neuron's potential U_2 is at 0. Analyzing the sodium conductance in this state lets us find G_{Na} using the following calculation instead of solving a four-dimensional system.

$$G_{Na} = \frac{G_m R}{m_\infty(R) h_\infty(R) * (\Delta E_{Na} - R)} \tag{8}$$

The CPG structure is composed of two of these neurons mutually inhibiting each other, known as the half-center model [1]. The mutual inhibition paired with the sodium channel behavior allows the neurons to switch back and forth between excited and inhibited states in a catch-and-release fashion. When the excited neuron's potential drops below the necessary threshold the inhibition of the other neuron lets up just enough for the fast m gates to start opening. This results in the cascading effect which quickly depolarizes the neuron and simultaneously inhibits/ hyperpolarizes the previously excited neuron. This cycle continues indefinitely unless halted by an outside force such as an applied current.

Sensors: Each segment is equipped with a stretch sensor oriented longitudinally between the middle vertices of the rhombus (see Fig. 3 of [4]). The signal from the stretch sensor is approximated as a piecewise function such that it sends a current directly to the CPG command neuron (U_3 of the SNS diagram in Fig. 2) only when the segment reaches its minimum length/maximum height (fully expanded state). This function is shown below.

$$I_{sens} = \begin{cases} R & \text{when } l \leq l_{min} \\ 0 & \text{when } l \geq l_{min} \end{cases} \tag{9}$$

The applied current value of R was chosen to keep the math simple when tuning the network.

3.2   Functional Subnetwork Tuning

The worm robot's Synthetic Nervous System (Fig. 2) was developed using the neuroscientific models described in Sect. 3.1. The SNS is split up into subnetworks corresponding to the "physical" worm segments. As such there are N CPGs, stretch sensors, command neurons (U_3), and inter-segment neurons (U_4) where N is the number of worm segments in the model (any integer of value 3 or greater works for peristalsis). The order of operations within each segment is broken down in the flowchart in Fig. 3. Each synapse is tuned by taking the parameter values of the relevant pre and postsynaptic neurons at a given point in the cycle outlined in the flowchart and applying these to the following equation (where n signifies the number of presynaptic neurons influencing the postsynaptic neuron).

$$U^* = \frac{\sum_{j=1}^{n} g_{syn,j} \dfrac{U_{j,pre}}{R} E_{syn,j} + I_{app}}{G_m + \sum_{j=1}^{n} g_{syn,j} \dfrac{U_{j,pre}}{R}} \tag{10}$$

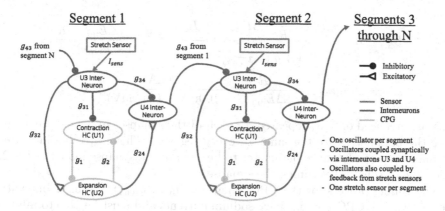

Fig. 2. Synthetic Nervous System controller diagram for a simulated worm robot

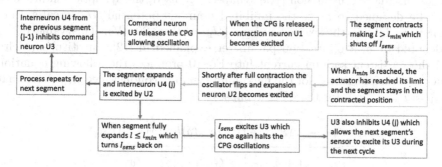

Fig. 3. Flowchart explaining the SNS diagram operations in order

This equation is the key for direct analytical tuning of transmission synapses via the FSA as presented in [13]. U^* here is the desired steady state potential of the postsynaptic neuron for a given set of presynaptic potentials. For this network $G_m = 1\,\mu S$, $C_m = 5\,nF$, $E_r = -60\,mV$, and $R = 20\,mV$ or nA depending on the parameter. All inhibitory synaptic reversal potentials (E_{inh}) were taken to be $-100\,mV$. All excitatory reversal potentials (E_{ex}) were taken to be $134\,mV$, the reversal potential of an excitatory calcium neurotransmitter found in some organisms [13]. Relevant earthworm nervous system data was not readily available to use for this SNS. As such these parameters were chosen somewhat arbitrarily but all values were kept within the realm of biological plausibility (mV, nA, and μS scales) and follow the guidelines laid out in [13].

The tuning of the synapse between neurons $U_{4,j-1}$ and $U_{3,j}$ (g_{syn43}) will be used to demonstrate the design process. This synapse will be evaluated when $U_{4,j-1}$ is inhibiting $U_{3,j}$ while the sensor is still providing current (just before the CPG restarts). At this point in time $U_{3,j}^* = 0\,mV$ since it is inhibited, $I_{\text{sens}} = R = 20\text{nA}$ since the segment has not yet contracted, and $U_{4,j-1} = R = 20\,mV$ since it is excited. When plugged into Eq. 10, the only remaining unknown is g_{syn43} which can now be solved for:

$$U_{3,j}^* = 0 = \frac{g_{\text{syn43}}\dfrac{U_{4,j-1}}{R}\Delta E_{\text{syn43}} + I_{\text{sens}}}{1 + g_{\text{syn43}}\dfrac{U_{4,j-1}}{R}} = \frac{g_{\text{syn43}}\Delta E_{\text{inh}} + R}{1 + g_{\text{syn43}}} \tag{11}$$

$$\longrightarrow g_{\text{syn43}} = \frac{-R}{\Delta E_{\text{inh}}} = \frac{-20\text{nA}}{-100\text{mV} - (-60\text{mV})} = 0.5\mu\text{S}$$

This process need only be repeated for each of the synapses in a single segment since the parameters are the same for every segment. This g_{syn} value indicates the maximum conductance parameter to be used in the synapse model in Eq. 2. Finding g_{syn} constitutes tuning the synapse.

The tuning process for the CPG synapses (g_{syn1}, g_{syn2}) is similar but with one caveat. The CPG neurons have sodium currents and must be able to inhibit each other in such a way that allows their membrane potentials to oscillate back and forth. Since transmission type synapses are used, the synaptic conductance must be designed to make the inhibited neuron's potential (U_2) greater than 0 for it to inhibit the excited neuron ($U_1 = R = 20\,\text{mV}$). This value of U_2 is denoted by δ, a bifurcation parameter explained in [12]. Substituting delta and the persistent sodium current into Eq. 10 produces the following equation which can then be solved for the maximum synaptic conductance g_{syn}. Note that $g_{\text{syn1}} = g_{\text{syn2}} = g_{\text{syn}}$ for the CPG synapses.

$$\delta = \frac{g_{\text{syn}}\dfrac{U_1}{R}\Delta E_{\text{syn}} + G_{\text{Na}}m_\infty(\delta)h_\infty(\delta) * (\Delta E_{\text{Na}})}{1 + g_{\text{syn}}\dfrac{U_1}{R} + G_{\text{Na}}m_\infty(\delta)h_\infty(\delta)} \tag{12}$$

$$\longrightarrow g_{\text{syn}} = \frac{-\delta - G_{\text{Na}}m_\infty(\delta)h_\infty(\delta)(\delta - \Delta E_{\text{Na}})}{\delta - \Delta E_{\text{Na}}}$$

E_{Na} was set to $50\,\text{mV}$, a typical value for the sodium reversal potential in a neuron, and $\Delta E_{\text{Na}} = E_{\text{Na}} - E_r$. Other parameter values used for these calculations were $\tau_{h,\text{max}} = 300\,\text{ms}$, $s = 0.05$, and $\delta = 0.01$. Using these parameters to tune the CPG synapses results in a continuous pattern of oscillation between the neuron potentials U_1 and U_2.

Since the CPG relies on the neuron potentials just barely crossing their thresholds to induce oscillation, it is possible to halt the CPG by applying current to the neurons. This can be done directly or through a synaptic connection from a command neuron. By exciting the expansion CPG neuron while it is already excited, and inhibiting the contraction CPG neuron when it is inhibited, the command neuron (U_3) is able to push their potentials away from the thresholds thus halting oscillation. When the command neuron is inhibited this influence is released allowing oscillation to resume.

3.3   Stability Analysis

For the parameters used in this work, the simulated robot with $N = 6$ segments exhibits a stable limit cycle with a period $T \approx 5250\text{ms}$. That is, there is a unique periodic orbit that attracts nearby trajectories. In order to confirm the stability of the orbit we performed a direct Floquet multiplier analysis as follows. There are seven variables per segment: four neuron potentials, two "h" gating variables, and the segment height. Thus there are 42 variables for a robot with six segments. Given a base point $\mathbf{x}_0 \in \mathbb{R}^{42}$, we consider 42 different trajectories with perturbed initial conditions $\mathbf{x}_i(0) = \mathbf{x}_0 + \epsilon\,\mathbf{e}_i$, where $\mathbf{e}_i \in \mathbb{R}^{42}$ is the ith standard unit vector, and $|\epsilon| \ll 1$. We construct an approximation to the Monodromy matrix M, defined with the ith column M_i given by

$$M_i = \lim_{\epsilon \to 0} \frac{\mathbf{x}_i(T) - \mathbf{x}_0}{\epsilon},$$

where $\mathbf{x}_i(T)$ is the point on the perturbed trajectory after one period evolution. The periodic orbit is linearly stable if and only if the eigenvalues of M, the Floquet multipliers, may be ordered such that

$$\lambda_1 \equiv 1 > |\Re(\lambda_2)| \geq |\Re(\lambda_3)| \geq \ldots \geq |\Re(\lambda_{42})|.$$

The Monodromy matrix M obtained depends on the choice of base point $\mathbf{x}_0$; in theory the eigenvalues of M are independent of $\mathbf{x}_0$. For the specific base point used here, see the code available at https://github.com/sriddle97/SNS-Controlled-Peristalsis.git.

4   Results

4.1   SNS Simulation

Running the simulation with all the parameters set, neurons modelled, and synapses tuned as described in Sect. 3 produced the results in Fig. 4. N was chosen to be 3 for these plots for the purposes of legibility. $N = 6$ was still used for the stability analysis.

Figure 4 shows that the SNS network does induce sequential CPG activity from segment to segment down the worm body. As intended, the CPGs halt when their sensor detects full re-expansion of the segment thus applying current to the command neuron U_3 which inhibits U_1 and excites U_2. The CPG begins oscillating once more when the previous segment's U_4 neuron inhibits the U_3 command neuron, thus removing its effect on the CPG. In this way the CPGs are effectively coupled via the U_4 inter-segment neuron and the stretch sensors. The height plots in Fig. 4 show that this coupling allows the propagation of a peristaltic waveform when the CPG potentials are mapped to the actuator model to produce segment motion. Close inspection of the neuron potential and height plots reveals that the segment height decreases when it's corresponding CPG neuron U_1 is excited. This makes sense since U_1 encourages segment contraction. Likewise, when the expansion CPG neuron U_2 is excited, the segment height increases. Since U_2 excites the inter-segment neuron U_4 which then starts the oscillation of the following segment, the wave is able to propagate down the worm from segment to segment in a peristaltic fashion.

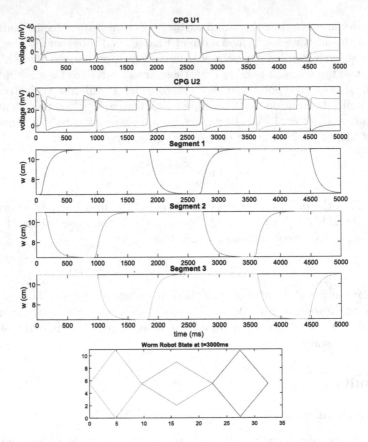

Fig. 4. Plot of the CPG neuron membrane potentials and segment heights over time, as well as a snapshot of the simulation at t=3000 ms, color coded by segment. (Color figure online)

4.2   Stability

We obtained the Monodromy matrix M via direct estimation, using a perturbation of $\epsilon = 0.001$. When a height variable is on the upper threshold $h = h_{max}$, linear disturbances are automatically rejected. Thus, linear order, small perturbations in the height lead to no perturbation of the limit cycle when the perturbed variable is pressed against a hard boundary. That is, the system has a limit cycle with a sliding component [17]. The corresponding columns of M are thus identically equal to zero, meaning that if j variables are thus constrained at the reference point $\mathbf{x}_0$ anchoring the Floquet analysis, the 42×42 matrix M necessarily has rank $\leq 42 - j$. Consequently at least j of the multipliers are identically zero, indicating the presence of "superstable" directions at $\mathbf{x}_0$. Using the direct analysis, we obtained that the leading Floquet multipliers are

$$\lambda_1 = 0.9945 \approx 1, \quad \lambda_2 = 0.0081, \quad \lambda_3 = -0.0001,$$

and the remaining multipliers are either identically zero or else negligibly small. The nontrivial Floquet multipliers are less than 1 in magnitude, indicating that the periodic orbit of our model is linearly stable. For the full Monodromy matrix and list of Floquet multipliers see the code linked in Sect. 3.3.

5   Discussion and Future Work

We hypothesized that coupled oscillators can form peristaltic waves in a worm robot model. The results in Sect. 4 indicate that it is indeed possible, thus confirming the hypothesis. The CPGs coupled via the inter-segment neurons U_4 and the stretch sensors are capable of propagating a signal from segment to segment. The CPGs themselves are also effective in controlling the pattern of segment contraction and expansion that translates this signal into peristaltic locomotion. Thus, the SNS described in this paper is capable of controlling a simple worm-like robot model. Direct evaluation of the Floquet multipliers for the periodic orbit suggested that the periodic motions of the neural and mechanical elements together indeed produce a linearly stable limit cycle.

While the simple worm-robot model described in this paper could be controlled via a state machine or conventional artificial neural network (ANN), the SNS controller has advantages. Adding complexity to the mechanical model to make it more realistic may require a full re-design of a state machine controller. An SNS may only require a few additional neurons or a subnetwork to account for the changes [10,13]. Additionally, SNSs do not require large amounts of computational power or training data for global optimization methods (such as genetic algorithms) unlike ANNs [13]. The direct analytical tuning of an SNS also makes it tractable unlike the black box controllers produced by global optimization.

In its present state the kinematic model does not sufficiently capture the detailed movements of a physical robot. As such, both the model and the SNS controller designed in this paper need alteration before use in a real-world context. Most of this alteration could be accomplished by re-designing the model to include forces and compliant mechanical coupling between segments, making it a kinetic model. This would allow the application of friction force which must be accounted for to mitigate segment slip and to accurately portray contact with the robot's environment [4]. Incorporating a more complex motor controller would also allow the motors to have a wider range of actuation patterns/behaviors which could enable more efficient locomotion [8]. Lastly, more research on earthworm nervous systems could be performed. Some parts of the SNS structure, like the back-to-front synaptic connection between segment N and segment 1, were included to make the system functional but are not necessarily features grounded in neuroscience literature. Further study could reveal neural architectures and properties that could be used to make the SNS even more biologically relevant.

References

1. Brown, T.G.: On the nature of the fundamental activity of the nervous centres; together with an analysis of the conditioning of rhythmic activity in progression, and a theory of the evolution of function in the nervous system. J. Physiol. **48**(1), 18–46 (1914)
2. Goldsmith, C.A., Szczecinski, N.S., Quinn, R.D.: Neurodynamic modeling of the fruit fly drosophila melanogaster. Bioinspiration Biomimetics **15**(6), 065003 (2020)
3. Hodgkin, A.L., Huxley, A.F.: A quantitative description of membrane current and its application to conduction and excitation in nerve. J. Physiol. **117**(4), 500–544 (1952)
4. Horchler, A.D., et al.: Peristaltic locomotion of a modular mesh-based worm robot: Precision, compliance, and friction. Soft Rob. **2**(4), 135–145 (2015)
5. Huang, Y., Kandhari, A., Chiel, H.J., Quinn, R.D., Daltorio, K.A.: Mathematical modeling to improve control of mesh body for peristaltic locomotion. In: Mangan, M., Cutkosky, M., Mura, A., Verschure, P.F.M.J., Prescott, T., Lepora, N. (eds.) Living Machines 2017. LNCS (LNAI), vol. 10384, pp. 193–203. Springer, Cham (2017). https://doi.org/10.1007/978-3-319-63537-8_17
6. Hunt, A., Szczecinski, N., Quinn, R.: Development and training of a neural controller for hind leg walking in a dog robot. Front. Neurorobot. **11**, 18 (2017)
7. Ijspeert, A.J.: Central pattern generators for locomotion control in animals and robots: a review. Neural Netw. Robot. Neurosci. **21**(4), 642–653 (2008)
8. Kandhari, A., Wang, Y., Chiel, H.J., Quinn, R.D., Daltorio, K.A.: An analysis of peristaltic locomotion for maximizing velocity or minimizing cost of transport of earthworm-like robots. Soft Rob. **8**(4), 485–505 (2021)
9. Marder, E., Bucher, D.: Central pattern generators and the control of rhythmic movements. Curr. Biol. **11**(23), 986–996 (2001)
10. Nourse, W., Quinn, R.D., Szczecinski, N.S.: An adaptive frequency central pattern generator for synthetic nervous systems. In: Vouloutsi, V., Halloy, J., Mura, A., Mangan, M., Lepora, N., Prescott, T.J., Verschure, P.F.M.J. (eds.) Living Machines 2018. LNCS (LNAI), vol. 10928, pp. 361–364. Springer, Cham (2018). https://doi.org/10.1007/978-3-319-95972-6_38
11. Seok, S., Onal, C.D., Cho, K.J., Wood, R.J., Rus, D., Kim, S.: Meshworm: Aa peristaltic soft robot with antagonistic nickel titanium coil actuators. IEEE/ASME Trans. Mechatron. **18**(5), 1485–1497 (2013)
12. Szczecinski, N.S., Hunt, A.J., Quinn, R.D.: Design process and tools for dynamic neuromechanical models and robot controllers. Biol. Cybern. **111**(1), 105–127 (2017). https://doi.org/10.1007/s00422-017-0711-4
13. Szczecinski, N.S., Hunt, A.J., Quinn, R.D.: A functional subnetwork approach to designing synthetic nervous systems that control legged robot locomotion. Front. Neurorobot. **11**, 37 (2017)
14. Szczecinski, N.S., Quinn, R.D.: Template for the neural control of directed stepping generalized to all legs of MantisBot. Bioinspiration Biomimetics **12**(4), 045001 (2017)
15. Szczecinski, N.S., Quinn, R.D., Hunt, A.J.: Extending the functional subnetwork approach to a generalized linear integrate-and-fire neuron model. Front. Neurorobot. **14**, 577804 (2020)
16. Tanaka, Y., Ito, K., Nakagaki, T., Kobayashi, R.: Mechanics of peristaltic locomotion and role of anchoring. J. R. Soc. Interface **9**(67), 222–233 (2012)

17. Wang, Y., Gill, J.P., Chiel, H.J., Thomas, P.J.: Shape versus timing: linear responses of a limit cycle with hard boundaries under instantaneous and static perturbation. SIAM J. Appl. Dyn. Syst. **20**(2), 701–744 (2021)
18. Wilson, H.R., Cowan, J.D.: Excitatory and inhibitory interactions in localized populations of model neurons. Biophys. J . **12**(1), 1–24 (1972)

Simple Reactive Head Motion Control Enhances Adaptability to Rough Terrain in Centipede Walking

Kotaro Yasui[1,2(✉)], Shunsuke Takano[2,3], Takeshi Kano[2], and Akio Ishiguro[2]

[1] Frontier Research Institute for Interdisciplinary Sciences, Tohoku University, Sendai, Japan
k.yasui@riec.tohoku.ac.jp
[2] Research Institute of Electrical Communication, Tohoku University, Sendai, Japan
[3] Graduate School of Engineering, Tohoku University, Sendai, Japan

Abstract. Multi-legged animals such as myriapods exhibit highly adaptive and effective locomotion on rough terrain. They achieve this locomotor performance by coordinating their flexible bodies and legs in response to the environmental situation. To capture the essential motor control mechanisms in centipedes, we have constructed mathematical models based on behavioral findings. Although our latest model succeeded in producing adaptive centipede walking on irregular terrain, the simulated centipede sometimes became stuck because of head collision with an obstacle in front. To overcome this limitation, in this paper, we added a simple reactive head motion control in which a few anterior body segments actively bend to keep the head section from becoming stuck. Through simulation experiment, we verified that the proposed head motion control improves the centipede-like robot's ability to traverse rough terrain with many gaps.

Keywords: Decentralized control · Multi-legged walking · Head motion

1 Introduction

Myriapods (*i.e.*, centipedes and millipedes) can walk effectively on rough terrain. They achieve this remarkable locomotor performance by coordinating their flexible bodies and legs in response to changes in the environment [1]. Therefore, clarifying the adaptive motor control mechanisms underlying myriapod walking will benefit the development of multi-legged robots that can navigate on complex terrain such as disaster areas and unexplored space environments. Bio-inspired roboticists have investigated myriapod locomotor mechanics and control mechanisms [2,3]. However, the essential control mechanism for the adaptive body and leg movement, especially on rough terrain, remains mostly unclear.

To address this issue, we have constructed mathematical models based on the results of behavioral experiments and tested the hypothesized control mechanisms via simulations and robots [4–6]. For rough terrain walking, our latest

© The Author(s), under exclusive license to Springer Nature Switzerland AG 2022
A. Hunt et al. (Eds.): Living Machines 2022, LNAI 13548, pp. 262–266, 2022.
https://doi.org/10.1007/978-3-031-20470-8_26

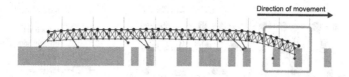

Fig. 1. Snapshot of the simulated centipede walking on irregular terrain with many gaps using the control scheme previously proposed in [6]. The green square indicates the head collision with the ground. (Color figure online)

model successfully produced adaptive centipede-like gaits owing to the synergetic coupling between decentralized leg control and flexible body dynamics [6]. However, the simulated centipede sometimes became stuck when walking on irregular terrain with many gaps because the head collided with an obstacle in front (Fig. 1). To solve this problem, in this study, we extended our previous model by adding simple reactive head motion control. Specifically, we implemented a control rule that a few anterior body segments actively bend when the head detects collision with the obstacle in front. In simulation, we found that the reactive head motion control improves the robot's ability to traverse rough terrain. Thus, we expect our model to provide new insight into the control mechanisms underlying centipede walking as well as the controller design of multi-legged robots.

2   Model

In this section, we first briefly introduce our previously proposed model [6]. Thereafter, we propose a simple reactive control for head movement to overcome the limitation of the previous model.

Previous Model [6]. We constructed a two-dimensional physical model of a centipede based on a mass–spring–damper system (Fig. 2A). Each leg base is connected to the body trunk with a rotational actuator to generate swing motion in a forward–backward direction, and a linear actuator is implemented at the distal part of the leg to generate lifting and lowering motions. Owing to the passive mechanics implemented in the body trunk and legs, the model can reproduce the flexible body and leg movements of a centipede in response to the environmental situation.

For each leg motion, we proposed the decentralized control scheme illustrated in Fig. 2B. The leg can enter four states, and the state transitions occur according to the leg positions and the ground contact signals at the leg tip and ventral body surface. Specifically, when the leg touches the ground, it swings backward and kicks the ground (State 1). In contrast, when the leg loses ground contact, it lifts off the ground and swings forward (State 2). Then, when the leg has swung forward enough and its anterior leg touches the ground, it moves to the ground contact point of its anterior leg (State 3). Furthermore, when the abdomen touches the ground, the leg extends to contact the ground (State 4).

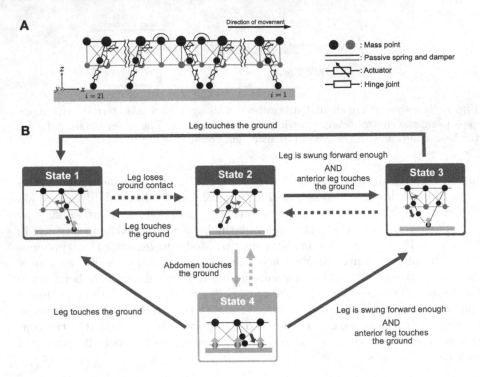

Fig. 2. Previously proposed model. (A) Physical model, (B) decentralized leg control algorithm. The figures were adapted from [6].

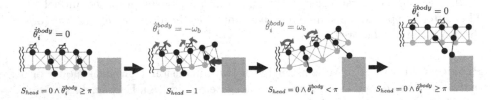

Fig. 3. Proposed reactive head motion control. The blue arrow indicates the reaction force from the obstacle. (Color figure online)

Proposed Reactive Head Motion Control. To overcome the problem of the head becoming stuck during walking on irregular terrain with gaps (Fig. 1), we here extend the previous model by adding simple reactive head motion control (Fig. 3). Specifically, we implemented rotational actuators instead of passive torsional springs on the dorsal side of the body trunk in the first four segments from the head ($i = 1, 2, 3, 4$), and their target angular velocities ($\dot{\bar{\theta}}_i^{body}$) are controlled as follows:

$$\dot{\bar{\theta}}_i^{body} = \begin{cases} -\omega_b & (S_{head} = 1) \\ \omega_b & (S_{head} = 0 \wedge \bar{\theta}_i^{body} < \pi) \\ 0 & (S_{head} = 0 \wedge \bar{\theta}_i^{body} \geq \pi), \end{cases} \tag{1}$$

where ω_b is the positive constant and S_{head} denotes the binary signal indicating head collision with an obstacle in front. According to Eq. (1), when the head is pushed against an obstacle in front, the anterior four body segments are raised by active bending (Fig. 3). Then, when the head collision is resolved, the anterior body segments start to bend in the opposite direction until the target angles for a straight posture ($\bar{\theta}_i^{body} = \pi$).

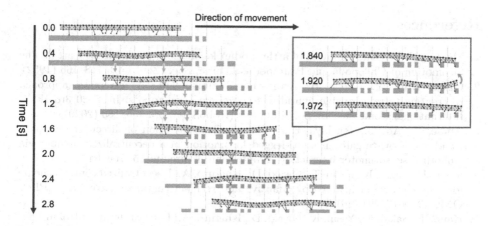

Fig. 4. Snapshots of the simulation result using the proposed model. Orange arrows indicate the ground contact points of the legs also used by the posterior legs. (Color figure online)

3   Result

To validate our extended model with reactive head motion control, we performed a simulation experiment on irregular terrain with many gaps. The initial leg positions were randomly set, ω_b was set to 3.0 rad/s, and the other model parameters were the same as in our previous study [6]. The simulated centipede exhibited an adaptive gait similar to that of real centipedes, where each leg roughly moves to the ground contact point of its nearest anterior leg (Fig. 4). Furthermore, we found that it could avoid becoming stuck by resolving the head collision using the reactive head motion control (see the period 1.840–1.972 s).

4　Conclusion and Future Work

In this paper, we proposed a simple reactive head motion control to keep a walking centipede from becoming stuck and showed that the control scheme improved the terrain adaptability of our previous model [6]. In future, we would like to evaluate the walking performance of our proposed model using a multi-legged robot in the real-world environment.

Acknowledgements. This work was supported by the JSPS KAKENHI (Grant Number JP21K14177) and the research fund from the Frontier Research Institute for Interdisciplinary Sciences, Tohoku University.

References

1. Manton, S. M.: The evolution of arthropodan locomotory mechanisms. Part 3. The locomotion of Chilopoda and Pauropoda. J. Linn. Soc. (Zool.) **42**, 118–166 (1952)
2. Ozkan-Aydin, Y., Chong, B., Aydin, E., Goldman, D.I.: A systematic approach to creating terrain-capable hybrid soft/hard myriapod robots. In: 2020 3rd IEEE International Conference on Soft Robotics (RoboSoft), pp. 156–163 (2020)
3. Ambe, Y., Aoi, S., Tsuchiya, K., Matsuno, F.: Generation of direct-, retrograde-, and source-wave gaits in multi-legged locomotion in a decentralized manner via embodied sensorimotor interaction. Front. Neural Circuits **15**, 706064 (2021)
4. Yasui, K., Sakai, K., Kano, T., Owaki, D., Ishiguro, A.: Decentralized control scheme for myriapod robot inspired by adaptive and resilient centipede locomotion. PLoS ONE **12**, e0171421 (2017)
5. Kano, T., Sakai, K., Yasui, K., Owaki, D., Ishiguro, A.: Decentralized control mechanism underlying interlimb coordination of millipedes. Bioinspir. Biomim. **12**, 036007 (2017)
6. Yasui, K., Takano, S., Kano, T., Ishiguro, A.: Adaptive centipede walking via synergetic coupling between decentralized control and flexible body dynamics. Front. Robot. AI **9**, 797566 (2022)

Surrogate Modeling for Optimizing the Wing Design of a Hawk Moth Inspired Flapping-Wing Micro Air Vehicle

Wei Huang[✉], Roger D. Quinn, Bryan E. Schmidt, and Kenneth C. Moses

Case Western Reserve University, Cleveland, OH 44106, USA
wei.huang12@case.edu

Abstract. Proving the feasibility and overall efficiency of Flapping-Wing Micro Air Vehicles (FWMAVs) over other types of MAVs is vital for their advancement. Due to their complex aerodynamics and the difficulty of building accurate models of the flying animal, assessing the flight performance and efficiency of animals and FWMAVs mimicking those animals can be a challenging task. This paper investigates the hawk moth (*Manduca sexta L.*) forewing as inspiration for designing an optimal wing for a moth-scale FWMAV. Through a process of decoupling the flapping-wing kinematics from the aerodynamics, an experiment is designed to assess the variation in aerodynamic lift-to-drag ratio due to variations in the wing geometry parameters (i.e., wingspan, chord length, cross sectional geometry). Using the data from the experiments, a surrogate model is trained and serves as an optimization solution for determining a wing geometry configuration that maximizes the lift-to-drag ratio. The resulting trained surrogate model is a computationally inexpensive model that can rapidly evaluate the aerodynamic efficiency based on the wing geometry input parameters, thus identifying local extrema within the design space.

Keywords: Hawk moth · Flapping-wing kinematics · Computational fluid dynamics · Airfoil · Surrogate modeling · Optimization

1 Introduction

The contribution from nature's flyers to the development of modern-day flying robots have motivated researchers to investigate the hawk moth (*Manduca sexta L.*) as an inspiration for Flapping-Wing Micro Air Vehicle (FWMAV) design. Research has characterized the physical properties [1], structural dynamics [2], and flapping kinematics [3] of the moth forewing. Furthermore, Computational Fluid Dynamics (CFD) [4] studies on flapping wing aerodynamics have advanced our current understanding of the moth. Compared to fixed-wing and rotary-wing flight, flapping-wing flight takes greater advantage of unsteady airflow to generate lift and thrust. However, due to the complexity of

Supplementary Information The online version contains supplementary material available at https://doi.org/10.1007/978-3-031-20470-8_27.

© The Author(s), under exclusive license to Springer Nature Switzerland AG 2022
A. Hunt et al. (Eds.): Living Machines 2022, LNAI 13548, pp. 267–278, 2022.
https://doi.org/10.1007/978-3-031-20470-8_27

the aerodynamics and the variety of biomechanical design hawk moth, modeling and predicting the flight efficiency and performance of such vehicles are difficult.

Aerodynamic optimization commonly utilizes the surrogate modeling approach as a rapid design optimization technique. Surrogate modeling is a computationally inexpensive method that is based on data from expensive to run wind tunnel or CFD experiments. Although CFD-based optimization is inexpensive compared to wind tunnel testing, convergence can take hours for complex simulations such as those involving flapping-wing aerodynamics. For rapid airfoil design optimization, neural network based surrogate models have been used to predict CFD simulation results in less than a few seconds [5]. Ensembles of machine learning models have shown promising results compared to methods using one base model to determine the sensitivity of varied kinematic parameters in flapping-wing flight [6].

This paper describes a surrogate modeling design approach as an optimization solution for designing the wing of a hawk moth inspired FWMAV. In particular, this research investigates the effects of the variation in wing geometry on the flight efficiency of the vehicle. A process, shown in Fig. 1, that incorporates biological wing data from [1] and flapping kinematic data from [3] is designed to work alongside a CFD model to assess the variation in aerodynamic efficiency from varying the wing geometry. From the geometry input parameters and CFD output data, a surrogate model is trained using machine learning, and the model can be evaluated at any point within the design space. The trained surrogate models are generalized models that can estimate lift-to-drag ratio based on the input parameters that describe the geometry of the flapping-wing without the need to run numerous CFD simulations. With this approach, an inexpensive model of the CFD experiment is designed to assess areas of maximum lift-to-drag ratio within the design space of the wing.

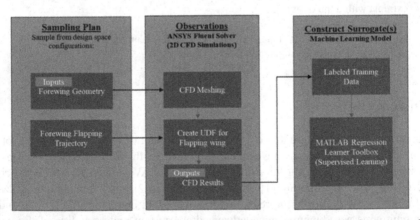

Fig. 1. Diagram showing the designed experiment for obtaining training data for constructing a surrogate model. The experiment starts by sampling a configuration of parameters that define the geometry of the moth wing (i.e., wingspan, chord length, and wing cross section parameters) and ends with an observation of the CFD results.

2 Method

2.1 Wing Geometry Modeling

Contemporary research characterizing the aerodynamics of flapping-wing flight within a CFD simulation uses simple models for the cross section of the wing such as a flat plate or other types of symmetrical cross section geometry. However, the cross section of the moth forewing more closely resembles that of an asymmetric airfoil. With the thickest venation near the leading edge of the forewing and a camber line, the cross-sectional geometry of the forewing is parameterized as a NACA 4-digit airfoil. A 3D wing geometry is modeled using data collected in [1] that characterized a sample of 30 hawk moth forewings by their wingspan, chord length, centroid location, and camber profile, among others. With the data in [1] and the NACA airfoil model, the design space for the wing consists of the wingspan R, chord length C, thickness rate of change along the wingspan $\frac{dT}{dR}$, and the 3 parameters that describe the geometry of a NACA airfoil.

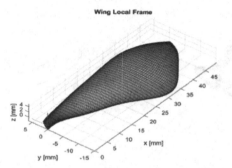

Fig. 2. 3D geometry of the Manduca sexta L. forewing, designed based on the geometric parameters discussed in this section. R = 48.3 mm, C = 22.6 mm, $\frac{dT}{dR}$ = 0.06, NACA 2406

2.2 Flapping Kinematics

The kinematics of the wing are defined by 4 coordinate variables that describe the wingtip trajectory and the wing orientation relative to the inertial frame. From the moth data obtained from [3], the trajectory of any airfoil element on the wing can be described using its stroke plane angle β, sweep angle ϕ, elevation angle θ, and rotation angle α. The rotation angle α describes the orientation of the wing about the wingtip vector. The maximum sweep angle indicates a rotation angle at pronation while the minimum sweep angle indicates a wing supination. For the wing local frame as defined in Fig. 2, the wingtip vector points in the same direction as the local x-axis and has a magnitude of the wingspan. The origin of the wing local frame is located at the root of the wing. A transformation between this local frame and the global inertial frame can be defined by the coordinate transform below.

$$\vec{r}_{I,i} = [R_1(\beta(t))][R_2(\phi(t))][R_3(\theta(t))][R_1(\alpha(t))] \, \vec{r}_{w,i} \tag{1}$$

In the equation, $[R_k(x(t))]$ is the rotation matrix about the kth axis defined by the time dependent variable $x(t)$. The vector, $\vec{r}_{I,i}$ is the coordinate of the ith element on the wing in the global frame. Finally, the vector $\vec{r}_{w,i}$ is the coordinate of the same i^{th} element of the wing in the local wing frame. Suppose the 2D wing element that is being investigated in the CFD simulation is located at a length of n percent of the whole wingspan. Assuming the wing is a rigid body, the trajectory of any element along the wingspan can be described with the following set of equations for wing position in the global frame (Fig. 3).

$$
\vec{r}_{I,n} = \frac{n}{100}R\begin{bmatrix} \cos(\theta)\cos(\phi) \\ \sin(\theta)\cos(\beta) + \cos(\theta)\sin(\phi)\sin(\beta) \\ \sin(\theta)\sin(\beta) - \cos(\theta)\sin(\phi)\cos(\beta) \end{bmatrix} \tag{2}
$$

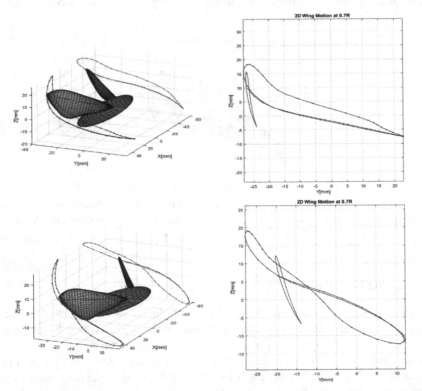

Fig. 3. The wingtip trajectory depicted here in the global inertial frame was produced using biological data gathered in [3] of a hawk moth in hovering flight (top image) and forward flight at 2.1 m/s (bottom image). The airfoil geometry being investigated for this sample is located at 70% of the wingspan, and the trajectory was created using Eq. (2).

For the purpose of investigating the aerodynamics at a specified cross-sectional geometry, the position vector is simplified to a 2D vector in the y-z global frame at n

percent of the length from the origin to the wingtip. Although the aerodynamics around a three-dimensional (3D) geometry can be investigated with the motion presented in Eq. (2) and the geometry created in Fig. 2, a 3D CFD simulation is beyond the scope of this paper. The 3D geometry created in Fig. 2, however remain a critical step in parametrizing the 2D geometry because parameters such as wingspan and wing thickness variation along the wingspan will affect the 2D geometry being tested in the CFD simulation.

Results from the work done in [3] indicate that the hawk moth showed a tendency to increase its stroke plane angle, β as its forward flight velocity increased. For hovering flight, the stroke plane angle ranged between 10° and 30°, whereas this angle ranged between 50° and 60° for the highest measured forward flight speed of 5 m/s. The wing velocity in the global frame is derived under the assumption that the wingtip trajectory is at a constant stroke plane angle for constant forward flight velocities. The stroke plane angles in the kinematic model described in this paper are defined as the average of the measured stroke plane angles among each moth specimen in [3] for different forward flight velocities.

With the two simplifications of the forewing kinematics described above, the velocity of any 2D wing geometry of the forewing in the global frame can be modeled as

$$\vec{v}_n = \frac{n}{100} R \begin{bmatrix} \dot{\theta}(\cos(\theta)\cos(\beta) - \sin(\theta)\sin(\phi)\sin(\beta)) + \dot{\phi}\cos(\theta)\cos(\phi)\sin(\beta) \\ \dot{\theta}(\cos(\theta)\sin(\beta) + \sin(\theta)\sin(\phi)\cos(\beta)) - \dot{\phi}\cos(\theta)\cos(\phi)\cos(\beta) \end{bmatrix} + \begin{bmatrix} v \\ 0 \end{bmatrix} \quad (3)$$

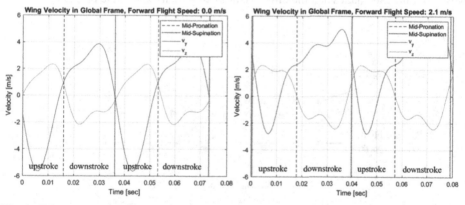

Fig. 4. Wing velocity results for hovering flight and forward flight velocity of 2.1 m/s. Lines indicating mid-pronation and mid-supination separate the upstroke and downstroke trajectories. The plots show velocity components near 0 m/s for hovering flight and 2.1 m/s for forward flight during mid-pronation and mid-supination. The mid-pronation and mid-supination points are defined as the point of maximum and minimum sweep angle respectively.

Equation (3) models the velocity of the wing at an airfoil element located $n\%$ down the wingspan R measured from the origin by taking the first derivative of Eq. (2) with respect to time and adding the forward flight velocity, v in the positive y direction. The stroke plane angle β is constant for a constant forward flight velocity of v. Additionally, θ, $\dot{\theta}$, ϕ, and $\dot{\phi}$ are the elevation and sweep angles measured in [3], and their respective time rates of change. The wing velocity results calculated using Eq. (3) for hovering flight and forward flight at 2.1 m/s are shown in Fig. 4. From the results in Fig. 4, initial intuitions about the velocity of the wing are validated. As the wing trajectory transitions from upstroke to downstroke and vice versa, the speed of the wing is expected to approach 0 m/s or the forward flight speed. This is evident in the hovering flight plot as mid-supination and mid-pronation occurs at points where the y and z velocity components intersect, and the point of intersection is near 0 m/s as there is no forward flight velocity. For a forward flight velocity of 2.1 m/s, this trend is not as evident because the intersection points do not occur during mid-pronation and mid-supination. However, the transition between upstroke and downstroke does occur when the wing velocity is near 2.1 m/s. This is a consequence of the asymmetric shape of the flapping trajectory and where the mid-supination and mid-pronation points are defined in the trajectory.

The equations for the wing velocity in the global frame aid in defining the airflow conditions for the CFD simulation. The effective airflow velocity relative to a stationary local wing is a velocity vector in the opposite direction of the wing velocity in the global frame, and the effective angle of attack can be determined using the components of the wing velocity and the rotation angle of the wing as defined in the equation:

$$\alpha_{eff} = \alpha - \tan^{-1} \frac{v_{n,z}}{v_{n,y}} \tag{4}$$

In Eq. (4) α is the rotation angle of the wing relative in the global frame, and $v_{n,y}$ and $v_{n,z}$ are the y and z components of the wing velocity. Figure 5 depicts the relation between wing kinematics and the effective airflow velocity and angle of attack.

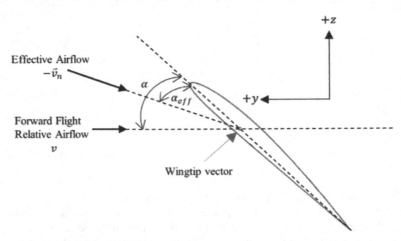

Fig. 5. Diagram of the wing cross-sectional geometry and the relation between the wing kinematic and the airflow for the CFD simulation (Effective Angle of Attack and Effective Airflow).

2.3 Computational Aerodynamic Simulations

The governing equations solved in the CFD simulation are the 2D incompressible, unsteady, Navier-Stokes equations. They are written in the y-z components as the continuity equation (Eq. 5) and the fluid momentum equations (Eq. 6 and Eq. 7.)

$$\frac{\partial v}{\partial y} + \frac{\partial w}{\partial z} = 0 \tag{5}$$

$$\rho\left(\frac{\partial v}{\partial t} + v\frac{\partial v}{\partial y} + w\frac{\partial v}{\partial z}\right) = -\frac{\partial p}{\partial y} + \mu\left(\frac{\partial^2 v}{\partial y^2} + \frac{\partial^2 v}{\partial z^2}\right) \tag{6}$$

$$\rho\left(\frac{\partial w}{\partial t} + v\frac{\partial w}{\partial y} + w\frac{\partial w}{\partial z}\right) = -\frac{\partial p}{\partial y} + \rho g_z + \mu\left(\frac{\partial^2 w}{\partial y^2} + \frac{\partial^2 w}{\partial z^2}\right) \tag{7}$$

In the above equations, v and w are the flow velocities in the y and z directions, respectively. ρ is the constant airflow density at 1.225 kg/m^3, μ is the dynamic viscosity of the fluid (1.789 $\times$ 10^{-5} Pa * s), p is the flow pressure, g_z is the gravitational acceleration, and finally t is time. Using the Ansys Fluent pressure-based solver and a dynamic meshing method on triangle mesh structures, transient time CFD simulations are utilized to determine the aerodynamic mechanisms responsible for the vertical and horizontal forces on a 2D flapping wing. The 2D wing cross section geometry depicted in Fig. 3 is imported into the Ansys workflow and an optimal mesh structure consisting of 8.8E4 cells is generated around the geometry. This resolution for the mesh was chosen after conducting a grid sensitivity study on three different mesh structures with varying resolutions.

The Fluent solver used in this research is a pressure-based coupled algorithm that simultaneously solves for the system of momentum and pressure-based continuity equations at each cell. After the simulation is initialized and Eq. 5 to Eq. 7 are solved, the mass flux of the airflow is updated at each cell, and the convergence criteria are checked at each iteration. The flow properties are updated at each iteration until the convergence criteria are met. Afterwards, the mesh structure updates according to the dynamic meshing function defined by the flapping kinematics modeled in Sect. 2.2. The simulation is considered converged at each time step if the residual reaches a value less than 1E-5.

Results in [3] on the aerodynamic lift mechanisms of the Manduca Sexta forewing identify three lift enhancing mechanisms for flapping flight. During downstroke, delayed stall generates leading edge vortices on the upper surface of the wing to create a pressure differential between the lower and upper surface. Following mid-downstroke, the wing aggressively transitions its rotation angle to generate rotational lift before entering upstroke. Finally, during upstroke, wake capture occurs where the wing switches directions to collide with the previously shed wake. At certain angles of rotation, the moth can take advantage of wake capture to enhance lift and even propel itself forward. The study done in [3] concluded that the moth utilized unsteady flow for all flight speeds with flow visualization results even showing larger leading-edge vortices during higher flight speeds compared to hovering flight.

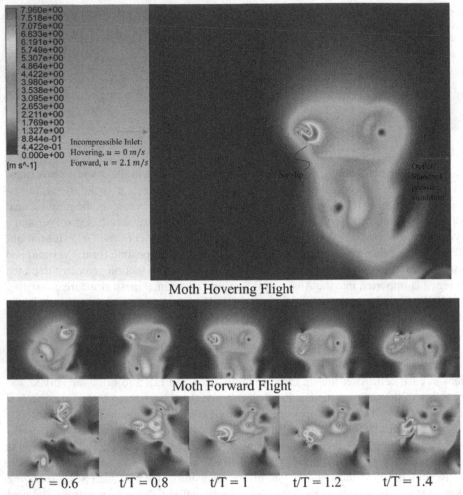

Fig. 6. Transient CFD simulations ran using dynamic meshing functions defined by the hovering and forward flight flapping kinematics. The boundary conditions are identified in the figure as a no slip boundary condition at the wing, zero gauge pressure at the outlet, and an incompressible inlet with flow velocity equivalent to the forward flight velocity of the moth.

The top frame in the CFD simulation depicted in Fig. 6, shows the wing section in mid-supination during hovering flight. Boundary conditions are defined for each flapping case and the simulation ran for 4 flapping cycles. The sequence of frames depicted at the bottom of Fig. 6 show the wing going into downstroke, supination, and then upstroke during both hovering and forward flight. The resulting aerodynamics show a leading-edge vortex forming on the upper surface of the wing during downstroke ($t/T = 0.6$, $t/T = 0.8$). The wing then rotates during supination to generate rotational lift ($t/T = 1$ and $t/T = 1.2$). Finally, during upstroke, the wing collides with the wake created during downstroke ($t/T = 1.4$) and additional lift is generated during the upstroke phase. The leading-edge vortex creates a region of high velocity and low pressure on the upper surface of the wing while lower surface pressure remains relatively high, hence this pressure gradient creates the main lifting force on the moth during both types of flapping. Additionally, a comparison of the CFD results show larger regions of unsteady flow in forward flight compared to hovering flight. Validating the observations in [3], a larger leading-edge vortex is formed at supination in the forward flight case.

Aerodynamic force results from the CFD simulations are calculated as net force components in the positive y and z directions defined in Fig. 5. The time-varying 2D horizontal and vertical forces are calculated as the sum of the pressure and viscous forces acting on the wing.

$$f_V(t) = \left(\vec{f}_p(t) + \vec{f}_v(t) \right) \hat{z} \tag{8}$$

$$f_H(t) = \left(\vec{f}_p(t) + \vec{f}_v(t) \right) \hat{y} \tag{9}$$

In Eq. 8 and Eq. 9, $f_V(t)$ and $f_H(t)$ are the time-varying z and y components of the aerodynamic forces and $\vec{f}_p(t)$ and $\vec{f}_v(t)$ are the time-varying pressure and viscous force vectors on the 2D wing. Units for the 2D aerodynamic forces are in Newtons per unit meter span (N/m). The approximated total aerodynamic forces are calculated for two 3D wings under the assumption of uniform chord length along the span. The total vertical and horizontal forces are calculated as $F_V(t) = 2f_V(t)R$ and $F_H(t) = 2f_H(t)R$.

3   Results and Discussion

The modeled flapping kinematics are used to calculate effective velocity and angle of attack in Fig. 7. For a hovering flight frequency of 25.4 Hz, one flapping cycle is completed by the moth in approximately 0.03 s. The maximum effective velocity of 5.84 m/s is reached in mid-upstroke and the minimum occurs during mid-supination at 0.58 m/s. For a forward flight speed of 2.1 m/s, the maximum effective velocity of 5.37 m/s occurs at mid-downstroke and the minimum occurs during mid-upstroke at 1.91 m/s. Additionally, a comparison of the two data sets shows a greater downstroke velocity and smaller upstroke velocity for forward flight, and a greater upstroke velocity and smaller downstroke velocity for hovering flight. The range of effective angle of attack at hovering flight is also much larger than that of the forward flight wing trajectory. For both cases, the effective angle of attack remains positive during downstroke. The upstroke effective angle of attack for hovering flight remains negative, whereas in forward flight, the wing's effective angle of attack transitions from positive to negative and then negative to positive during upstroke, aligning with an increase in effective velocity during negative angles of attack. Observation of the horizontal force results from the CFD simulation suggests this is the main thrusting mechanism utilized by the moth during forward flight. As the wing transitions from a positive to negative angle of attack at increasing effective velocities, a maximum horizontal force in the positive y-direction is experienced by the moth.

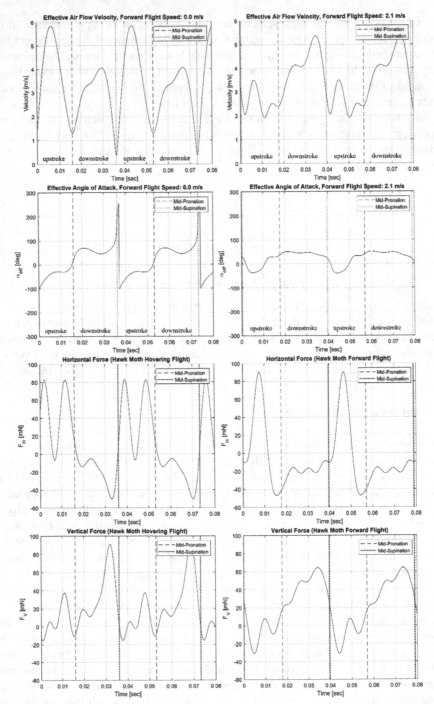

Fig. 7. Plots of effective air flow velocity magnitude, angle of attack, and total aerodynamic forces for the two flapping cases.

For both flapping cases, the simulations ran for 4 flapping cycles, and the wing section and fluid around it start at rest. The steady trends in the aerodynamic forces seen in Fig. 7 were not observed until the beginning of the 3rd flapping cycle. This is because the first two flapping cycles served as initial wake formation cycles in the simulation for wake interaction during the 3rd and 4th cycle.

The aerodynamic forces shown in Fig. 7 for hovering flight reveal a trend in the vertical force data that indicate where lifting mechanisms take effect. During the beginning of the upstroke phase, the wing is pitched down relative to the airflow, hence aggressively increasing the effective angle of attack during mid-supination induced a Magnus effect on the wing. While the wing is at a negative effective angle of attack, rapidly pitching the wing up in a clockwise direction creates a region of high velocity on the trailing edge and low velocity on the leading edge because the trailing rotates in the direction of flow and the leading opposes. As effective velocity continued to increase during upstroke, the angle of attack begins to level off before it reaches mid-supination. This creates an interaction between the wing and the fluid wake from the previous stroke, which created a vertical lift force as indicated by the second peak after mid-supination. During the end of the upstroke phase, a leading-edge vortex is formed underneath the wing as it enters stroke reversal. At this point, the vertical lift force decreases as the effective velocity decrease and the pressure above the wing start to become greater than the pressure below. The first peak in the vertical force plot after mid-pronation is created from the rotational lift as the effective angle of attack increases again. Finally, the greatest vertical force is created during downstroke. CFD results show a larger leading-edge vortex being formed in downstroke than in upstroke. This results in a larger pressure differential on the upper surface compared to the lower surface, hence creating a greater lift force during downstroke.

The time-averaged vertical and horizontal forces are calculated for hovering flight and the results are compared to the work done in [4]. The research done in [4] also investigated the hovering flight on a hawk moth in a 3D transient, Fluid Structure Interaction simulation. In that study, the kinematic variables ϕ and α are sinusoidal functions of time and elevation angle θ is 0. The range of ϕ and α are approximately equal to those in this paper, and the main difference between the hovering flight kinematic model in [4] and in this paper is the elevation angle θ. Compared to the rigid wing case in [4], the trends in the vertical force data are consistent, but horizontal force trends are significantly different. The average vertical force from Fig. 7 is calculated to be 21.2 mN whereas the reported average vertical force from [4] is 19.2 mN for the rigid wing case. The average horizontal forces are significantly different. The reported force from [4] is 5.7 [mN] while the average horizontal force from Fig. 7 is calculated to be 10.6 [mN]. The average lift results for hovering flight are further validated with wind tunnel test results in [3]. The reported mean lift coefficient for hovering flight in [3] ranged between 1.5 and 2 for three moth specimens with asymmetric wingtip trajectories, whereas the calculated mean lift coefficient here is 1.72. From this comparison, it appears that the 2D CFD model used in this paper is effective in estimating the lift forces on the moth in hovering flight, but drag and thrust forces require further consideration of 3D aerodynamics.

The continuation of this work involves testing various wing section geometries modeled using the method in Sect. 2.1. The aerodynamics around the wing sections are investigated for hovering flight and the results are compared to the control group geometry presented in this paper. The design of experiments used Latin hypercube sampling to obtain 20 wing geometry configurations. Each sample geometry is tested in CFD simulations similar to the one discussed in this paper for hovering flight. Results are compared against the control group sample and a surrogate model is trained through supervised learning to estimate the lift-to-drag ratio from the simulation. Finally, the surrogate model is tested with a new set of geometry inputs and the results are compared against CFD simulations on the test set. Once surrogate model results can be successfully validated with CFD results, the surrogate model can be evaluated to identify local extrema in the design space of the wing, hence finding a solution to optimal wing designs.

References

1. O'Hara, R.P., Palazotto, A.N.: The morphological characterization of the forewing of the *Manduca sexta* species for the application of biomimetic flapping wing micro air vehicles. Bioinspir. Biomim. **7**(4), 046011 (2012)
2. Sims, T.W., Palazotto, A.N., Norris, A.: A structural dynamic analysis of a *Manduca sexta* forewing. Int. J. Micro Air Vehic. **2**(3), 119–140 (2010)
3. Willmott, A.P., Ellington, C.P.: The mechanics of flight in the hawk moth *Manduca sexta* 2. Aerodynamic consequences of kinematic and morphological variation. The J. Exp. Biol. **200**(21), 2723–2745 (1997)
4. Nakata, T., Liu, H.: Aerodynamic performance of a hovering hawk moth with flexible wings: a computational approach. In: Proceedings of the Royal Society B: Biological Sciences, pp. 722–731, (2011)
5. Du, X., He, P., Martins, J.R.R.A.: Rapid airfoil design optimization via neural networks-based parameterization and surrogate modeling. Aerosp. Sci. Technol. **113**, 106701 (2021)
6. Trizila, P., Kang, C., Visbal, M., Shyy, W.: A surrogate model approach in 2D versus 3D flapping wing aerodynamic analysis. In: 12th AIAA/ISSMO Multidisciplinary Analysis and Optimization Conference, pp. 5914–5947, Canada (2008)
7. Forrester, A.I.J., Keane, A., Sobester, A.: Engineering Design via Surrogate Modeling: A Practical Guide, 1st edn. John Wiley & Sons Ltd., United Kingdom (2008)
8. Moses, K., Willis, M., Quinn, R.: Biomimicry of the hawk moth, *Manduca sexta* (L.), produces an improved flapping-wing mechanism. Biomimetics **5**(2), 25–46 (2020)
9. Sun, G., Wang, S.: A review of the artificial neural network surrogate modeling in aerodynamic design. In: Proceedings of the Institution of Mechanical Engineers, Part G: Journal of Aerospace Engineering, pp. 5863–5872 (2019)
10. Forrester, A.I.J., Bressloff N.W., Keane, A.J.: Optimization using surrogate models and partially converged computational fluid dynamics simulations. In: Proceedings of the Royal Society A: Mathematical, Physical, and Engineering Sciences, pp. 2177–2204 (2017)

A Novel Multi-vision Sensor Dataset for Insect-Inspired Outdoor Autonomous Navigation

Jan K. N. Verheyen[✉], Julien Dupeyroux, and Guido C. H. E. de Croon

Micro Air Vehicle Laboratory, Department of Control and Simulation Faculty
of Aerospace Engineering, Delft University of Technology,
2629HS Delft, The Netherlands
jan.verheyen@protonmail.com, g.c.h.e.decroon@tudelft.nl

Abstract. Insects have—over millions of years of evolution—perfected many of the systems that roboticists aim to achieve; they can swiftly and robustly navigate through different environments under various conditions while at the same time being highly energy efficient. To reach this level of performance and efficiency, one might want to look at and take inspiration from how these insects achieve their feats. Currently, no dataset exists that allows bio-inspired navigation models to be evaluated over long >100 m real-life routes. We present a novel dataset containing omnidirectional event vision, frame-based vision, depth frames, inertial measurement (IMU) readings, and centimeter-accurate GNSS positioning over kilometer long stretches in and around the TUDelft campus. The dataset is used to evaluate familiarity-based insect-inspired neural navigation models on their performance over longer sequences. It demonstrates that current scene familiarity models are not suited for long-ranged navigation, at least not in their current form.

Keywords: Long-range navigation · Neuromorphic systems · Event-based camera · RGB Camera · GPS · GNSS

1 Introduction

To date, some insect-inspired aerial robots have been developed [9,19] which mimic the flight capabilities of insects and while basic navigating capabilities have already been shown on board such limited platforms [26], their navigational performance falls short compared to their biological counterparts. Recent neural insect-inspired navigational models [2,3,11,36] show promising results over short distances, but lack the capacity for long-ranged (>100 m) navigation. This could be overcome by chaining local navigation strategies [10], although the difficulty here lies in where to transition from one local navigation strategy into the other. One of the major hurdles still holding back high-performance navigation onboard robots is energy-efficient visual processing. Insects' visual system is event-based, where photosensitive cells react *independently* from each other to changes in light intensity and subsequently generate spikes that propagate

© The Author(s), under exclusive license to Springer Nature Switzerland AG 2022
A. Hunt et al. (Eds.): Living Machines 2022, LNAI 13548, pp. 279–291, 2022.
https://doi.org/10.1007/978-3-031-20470-8_28

through the visual system to be processed in their miniature brains. Event cameras are *neuromorphic* vision sensors that mimic that process. Here, pixels take the role of the photosensitive cells and generate events asynchronously. Visual information is thus captured in a stream of events opposed to synchronous frames as taken by traditional cameras. This allows neuromorphic cameras to operate at very high temporal resolution and low latency (in the order of microseconds), very high dynamic range (140 dB compared to 60 dB of standard cameras), high pixel bandwidth (in the order of kHz), and low power consumption (order of mW) [14]. Processing such information requires novel methods to be developed. Biologically plausible methods involve the use of spiking neural networks (SNNs) since they are biologically more similar to networks of neurons found in animal nervous systems than regular artificial neural networks (ANNs). Implemented on neuromorphic processors such as Intel's Loihi and IBM's Truenorth, SNNs can deliver highly powerful computing at a fraction of the power budget of traditional hardware (CPUs, GPUs), making them promising candidates for implementation on robots.

Datasets form an important part of training and evaluating such novel methods. Currently, there are several event-based vision datasets focusing on navigation, covering applications in visual odometry, depth reconstruction, and SLAM, but little focusing on insect-inspired navigation. Images, events, optic flow, 3D camera motion, and scene depth in static scenes using a mobile robotic platform are provided in [4]. A large automotive dataset containing over 250000 human-labeled box annotations of cars and pedestrians is presented by [31]. The dataset provided by [35] includes synchronized stereo event data, augmented with grayscale images, and inertial measurement unit (IMU) readings. Ground truth pose and depth images are provided through a combination of a LiDAR system, IMU, indoor and outdoor motion capture, and GPS. The DDD20 [17] dataset consists of an extensive automotive dataset with events, frames, and vehicle human control data collected from 4000 km of mixed highway and urban driving. However, most insects have compound eyes that cover an almost panoramic FOV and this plays an important role in insects' navigational dexterity [15]. Additionally, insects fuse various sensory inputs from their environment together during navigation [13], making datasets that combine sensors valuable sources for training and evaluating such methods in e.g. multimodal navigation such as [16, 30]. None of the datasets above provide event data captured through an omnidirectional lens enhanced with additional sensors over long distances.

This paper presents two main contributions. First, a dataset containing omnidirectional event camera and IMU data, forward-facing high-resolution footage, and centimeter-level accurate GPS data along with a software package to load, process and manipulate the dataset. The dataset, including the software package, will be made available at https://github.com/tudelft/NavDataset. Secondly, an evaluation is presented of three different familiarity-based insect-inspired navigation models from the literature [2,3,36] with respect to their performance in long-ranged navigation.

2   The Biological Principles in Insect Navigation

2.1   Visual Perception

Insects' compound eyes consist of small individual hexagonally-shaped photoreceptive units, called *ommatidia*, which are arranged to form a faceted surface, capable of covering an almost panoramic field of view. Each such ommatidium receives light only from a small angle in the visual field, constricting the visual *acuity* of the insect's visual system. When excited by photons, these photoreceptive cells generate electric signals encoding the amount of light it absorbs, which downstream neurons turn into *spikes* that are passed through to the underlying optic lobes [25]. This low resolution but often almost panoramic vision from insects plays a crucial role in the success of their visual navigation's neural implementations.

2.2   Insect Visual Navigation Models

Insects are adept navigators capable of maneuvering through cluttered environments and memorizing long routes. Cartwright and Collett's [8] seminal snapshot model presented some of the first work that studied and modeled the visual navigation feats of honeybees. It hypothesized that honeybees store a single retinotopic *snapshot* of the place that they later want to navigate back to. Other methods include the Average Landmark Vector (ALV) model [21], image warping [12], and rotationally invariant panoramic methods that utilize Fourier-transformed [29] images or other frequency-domain-based methods [28].

The area surrounding the stored snapshot from which agents can successfully return is categorized as the *catchment area*. The extent of the catchment area changes depending on various factors such as the deployed navigation technique and the complexity and texture of the environment [34]. Insects therefore implement different visual navigation strategies, depending on whether they are on an already familiar route or find themselves in unfamiliar surroundings, respectively switching between route-following and visual homing behaviors [33].

Route-following methods commonly exploit the fact that generally, in natural scenes, the root-mean-square difference between the stored panoramic snapshot and another panoramic snapshot (also called the *image difference*) changes smoothly in correlation with the distance from the stored snapshot, where it terminates in a sharp minimum [34]. Visual route following methods include the Descent in Image Difference (DID) methods, which follows the declining gradient in image difference towards the stored snapshot [23]. Later, more biologically plausible DID models employed an ANN-based approach. In the scene familiarity model [3], a route is learned through training a 2-layer feedforward network to memorize snapshots along a route. An SNN-based scene familiarity model, modeled after the mushroom bodies (MBs) of ants was later formulated by [2]. Other work looked at integrating various cues in a multimodal decentralized neural model, combining input from the Central Complex (CX), the MB and the Path Integration (PI) centers [30].

2.3   Neuromorphic Processing

Event-Based Vision Sensors. Event cameras are vision sensors that take inspiration from the working principle of the biological retina. Each pixel reacts asynchronously to changes in light intensity. The sensor logs the pixel's location, time (in microsecond resolution), and polarity ('ON' or 'OFF'), and sends it over a digital bus in an Address-event Representation (AER) format [14]. Because event cameras only react to small *changes* in light intensity at individual pixels, visual information is more efficiently conveyed compared to frame-based cameras.

Spiking Neural Networks. Analogous to their biological counterparts, artificial neurons in SNNs generate a spike (action potential) if their membrane potential reaches a certain threshold after receiving a series of excitatory spikes from upstream neurons over their synaptic connections. After firing, the neuron lowers its internal voltage to a resting state. For a short time (the so-called refractory period) the neuron will not react to any incoming signals anymore. Various computational models of biological neurons exist to replicate this behavior. The most used neuronal models in artificial spiking neural networks nowadays are the Leaky Integrate-and-Fire (LIF) [27], Spike Response Model (SRM) [20], and the Izhikevich [18] model. The LIF neuron model in Eq. 1 shows how presynaptic spikes $s_j(t)$ arriving from neurons in layer $l-1$ increase (or decrease)—depending on weight matrix $W_{i,j}$, denoting its synaptic connectivity—the neuron's membrane potential $v_i(t)$ (scaled with the time constant λ_v) after which it decays to its resting potential v_{rest} if no more signals arrive. If enough excitatory presynaptic spikes arrive in short succession, the membrane potential will reach a certain internal threshold after which the neuron spikes ($s_i(t)$), resets its membrane potential, and enters a refractory period. Inhibiting presynaptic spikes have the opposite effect and will lower the membrane potential.

$$\lambda_v \frac{dv_i(t)}{dt} = -(v_i(t) - v_{\text{rest}}) + \sum_{j=1}^{n^{l-1}} \left(W_{i,j} s_j^{l-1}(t - \tau_d) \right) \tag{1}$$

Information in SNNs can be encoded in several different manners including position, temporal, rate coding, and subsequent combinations thereof. Learning in SNNs thus takes place in these domains, traditionally with much focus on a mechanism called Spike-Timing-Dependent Plasticity (STDP) [7]. STDP is a (biological) form of Hebbian learning that changes the synaptic strength of neuron connections dependent on their relative spike timing.

3   Dataset Design

The following section presents the utilized sensors and how the dataset was collected. The dataset was collected in both rural and urban environments in and around the TUDelft campus (Delft, The Netherlands). It mainly consists of events and IMU readings captured by a DAVIS240 event camera (as a more biologically accurate source of visual data) and video from a GoPro Hero 8 Black along with RTK GNSS positioning data. Video was collected in HEVC encoded MP4 and ROS bag files for the rest. The dataset also provides the same raw data in HDF5 containers. The DAVIS240 sensor was fitted with an omnidirectional lens to more accurately represent insects' vision, and its benefits in visual route following. Section 3.1 gives an overview of the dataset collection platform and the acquisition environment. A Python3 package will be made available for converting the bag and HDF5 files to and from various formats, as well as performing the data (pre)processing as elaborated upon in Sect. 3.2.

3.1 Sensors and Data Acquisition

Sensors. Table 1 provides an overview of the sensors with their characteristics. The complete logistical overview of the dataset acquisition platform can be seen in Fig. 1A and B. The dataset junction box forms the housing holding the various sensors as well as the Intel Up board computation platform. The Intel Up board runs ROS Kinetic and is responsible for collecting and time synchronizing the data from the various sensors which are connected over USB2/3 buses. The GNSS antenna was mounted at the back of the bike to minimize interference from the USB3 controllers. A mobile phone with cellular was connected to the Intel Up board by connecting to the phone's wifi hotspot. This allowed for running commands on the Intel Up board over ssh as well as provided the Intel Up board with internet access. This was needed for RTK GNSS positioning; RTCM messages were sent to the ublox ZED-F9P GNSS receiver by connecting to the EUREF-IP network ntrip server allowing for up to centimeter-accurate positioning. The DAVIS240 camera was mounted to an omnidirectional catadioptric lens to achieve omnidirectional vision. The GoPro camera was manually operated, thus a small gap exists between its timing and the rest of the sensors; this has been manually compensated for in the post-processing of the data. An external portable SSD was utilized to offload the collected data after every single run as the internal storage of the Intel Up board was limited. The dataset box was then mounted to a bike (Fig. 1B).

Sequences. The dataset consists of 12 routes traversed by bike from and to the start point (Fig. 2). The runs cover both rural and urban environments in and around the TUDelft campus. The dataset was collected over two days in April in the afternoon with similar partially clouded sunny weather conditions. Each bike run was travelled at about 18 km/h on primarily bike lanes.

3.2 Data Processing

Central to this dataset is the data provided by the DAVIS240 equipped with the omnidirectional catadioptric lens. As can be seen in Fig. 3, the omnidirectional lens projects its light on a circular region on the DAVIS240 sensor. In Fig. 3A the direction of the view with respect to the bike's heading is annotated. The

Table 1. Dataset collected data

Type	Sensor	Characteristics	Container
Visual	DAVIS240	240 × 180 pixel DVS AER	ROS bag/HDF5
Visual	GoPro Hero 8 Black	1920 × 1080 pixel 60 fps	mp4 (HEVC)
Visual	Intel Realsense d435i	720 × 1280 pixel depth 30 fps 16UC1	ROS bag
Positioning	Ublox ZED-F9P GNSS	NavPVT 5 Hz capture rate Position Accuracy 1.3 cm CEP	ROS bag/HDF5

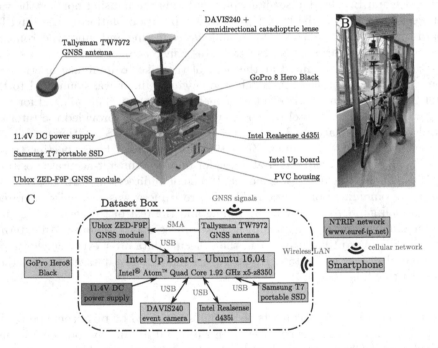

Fig. 1. Dataset acquisition hardware. **A** shows an overview of the various sensors mounted on the dataset box. **B** shows the full setup—the dataset box mounted on a bike to cover the long distances. **C** shows the data flow diagram between the sensors and the central computers.

approximate location of the capture can be seen in Fig. 3B. This circular projection can easily be masked as it stays fixed with respect to the sensor, subsequent unwrapping (in this case unwrapping is simply performed by mapping the polar coordinates of view Fig. 3A directly to image coordinates) results in the view presented by Fig. 3C.

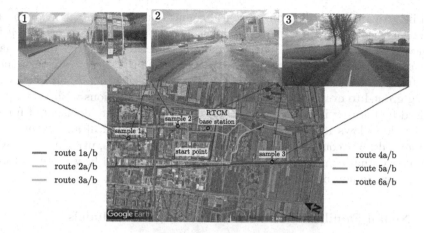

Fig. 2. Map of the routes covered by the dataset. Route 'a' indicates runs away from the start point, 'b' towards the start point. Samples are shown in 1–3.

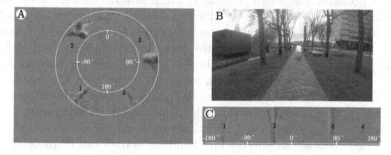

Fig. 3. Example of the omnidirectional events captured by the DAVIS240 and subsequent preprocessing. **A** shows an accumulated event frame as captured by the omnidirectional system, the two concentric circles show the boundaries of the visible field. **B** shows a frame from the GoPro footage, the left snapshot coincides with the camera position in the frame. **C** shows the event stream after masking and unwrapping the events.

4   Experimental Study: Evaluating Familiarity-Based Neural Insect Navigation Models

The following section presents the use of the dataset to investigate a few recent neural insect-inspired familiarity-based navigational models. The experiments compare three neural familiarity-based insect navigation models in terms of their performance for long-ranged navigation, namely [3]'s scene familiarity neural network, [2]'s Mushroom Body (MB) model, and [36]'s MB model. The mushroom bodies are relatively large structures in the insect brain that consist of large parallel arrangements of neurons, called Kenyon Cells (KCs), which are sampled by a relatively small amount of extrinsic neurons, also called Mushroom Body Output Neurons (MBONs). The mushroom bodies' role in visual learning has been investigated, revealing direct neural connections between the medulla and mushroom bodies [32]. Recent research has shown that MBs are *necessary* for learned visual navigation [6]. The aforementioned scene-familiarity models have been mostly tested in either simulated environments [2,3] or over very short distances in a controlled environment [36]. This dataset provides an interesting testing ground to evaluate these methods in real-life conditions with visual data inspired by the way insects perceive their environment. The inclusion of frame-based video allows for comparison between frame-based [2,3] and event-based [36] methods, but could also be used for multimodal models, utilizing the GNSS data as a virtual compass. We are specifically interested in how these methods hold up over longer distances.

4.1 Neural Familiarity-Based Insect Navigation Models

Baddeley et al.'s Scene Familiarity Model. The (frame-based) scene familiarity model of [3] consists of an input layer with the same dimensions as the number of pixels in the acquired images, which is fully connected by feedforward connections to a novelty layer which consists of tanh activation functions. The information about the input presented by the novelty layer is maximized through weight adaptation following the Information-Maximization (infomax) principle [5]. The infomax principle adjusts the weights of the network in such a way as to maximize the information about the input that the novelty layer presents. This is performed by following the gradient of mutual information [3]. By maximization of information through weight adaptation, the output of the novelty layer units is decorrelated, effectively reducing the network's output for sequences that have already been seen. 'Familiar' frames can be discerned after a single training run.

Ardin et al.'s Mushroom Body Model. The (frame-based) SNN MB model presented by [2] consists of 360 visual projection neurons (vPNs) that are sparsely connected to 20000 KCs which connect to a single MBON. Each such vPN can thus activate only a handful of KCs, representing a sparse encoding of information. Learning is performed by lowering the synaptic weights (Long-Term Depression (LTD)) between the KCs and the MBON through STDP. As a result, after training, the MBON's spike rate is lower for familiar views opposed to novel ones. Due to solely applying LTD, these connections are permanently weakened. This limits the model's capacity to memorize long sequences to the amount of depletable weights and the sparseness of the connections.

Zhu et al.'s Mushroom Body Model. The model presented by [36] (event-based) adapts Ardin et al.'s [2] model based on the finding that 60% of the input synapses of KCs come from other KCs. Instead of performing learning on the weights connecting the KCs to the MBON; when a KC spikes, it inhibits its connection to downstream KCs that spike at a later time based on an STDP rule. The KCs are split up into two groups of 5000 neurons to speed up learning; each solely acting within its group. Additionally, an anterior paired lateral (APL) [1] neuron is included that inhibits the activity of the KC layer.

4.2 Setup

The aforementioned neural networks were trained on sequences of 8, 16, 24, and 32 s from a 32-s section of route 1a (see Fig. 2). The respective networks were trained to 'memorize' that stretch of the route. Ensuing runs would result in a lower response from the network for already seen sequences, compared to unseen sequences. Ideally having a high (thus comparable to the untrained baseline run in orange) response for unfamiliar views and vice versa for familiar views. During the validation run, the same sequence was injected with unfamiliar views over stretches of 4 s and presented to the networks (gray bars in Fig. 4). The injected parts were sampled from sections of other routes in the dataset. For the event-based networks, the injected sequences were closely matched to the event rate of the original sequence, to maintain similar levels of activity in the network's layers. The frame-based models were presented with 28×8 pixel grayscale histogram equalized frames flattened to a 1D array. Input from the DAVIS240 sensor was max-pooled to 32×7 pixels before passing it to the network.

4.3 Results

The results of the experiment can be seen in Fig. 4. Inspired by [36]'s novelty index, we apply a performance index P

$$P = \frac{\sum s_{\text{unfamiliar}} - \sum s_{\text{familiar}}}{\sum s_{\text{total}}} \tag{2}$$

with s the response (familiarity index/spike rate) of the network, to evaluate the model's performance over increasingly longer test sequences ($P = 1$ is 'perfect' performance). The performance index captures the normalized relative difference in the response of the network between familiar and unfamiliar views. Its results are visualized in Fig. 4D. The Infomax scene familiarity [3] model's performance index decreased overall, while Ardin et al.'s [2] stabilized, but both these frame-based models maintain an adequate performance level to still separate familiar from unfamiliar views. This is in stark contrast with Zhu et al.'s [36] event-based model, which has depleted its 'memory' after about 16 s of learning (so not showing the full 32 s for visual clarity in Fig. 4). This deteriorating performance over longer distances is a result of the limited capacity of the networks, as synaptic connections' weights are depleted during training. This could be improved upon by a number of factors. First, the networks were trained with a constant learning rate, this could be tuned for longer distances, although at the cost of lower performance in general. Secondly, one could lower the number of presented frames 60 Hz to lower rates based on some metric of the input data. Further increases in the network's size by increasing the amount of KCs remains an option as well, although its computational increase would severely limit the

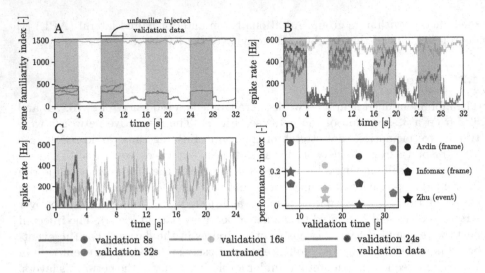

Fig. 4. Insect navigation models response to 8-, 16-, 24-, and 32-second sequences of a section of route 1a. **A** Infomax neural network [3] (frame-based). **B** Ardin et al.'s [2] MB model (frame-based). **C** Zhu et al.'s [36] MB model (event-based). **D** Performance index P (Eq. 2)

number of deployable robotic platforms. The frame-based method's more stable performance could be a consequence of them having more control over their input through well-established techniques such as normalization, which are less developed for event-based vision. Investigating intrinsically modulating mechanisms such as [24]'s adaptive LIF neuron could perhaps provide more fundamental solutions for this. Furthermore, it is known that insects perform a number of preprocessing steps (including elementary motion detection such as optic flow) in their optic lobes [25] as well as have mechanisms present that adjust the learning and forgetting of 'unnecessary' information [13], worth investigating.

5   Conclusion

The aforementioned navigational models have been evaluated on their capability to discriminate between familiar and unfamiliar views, which differs from closed-loop navigation evaluations as presented in e.g. [2,3]. Nonetheless, the experiments in Sect. 4 present some issues with how usable these networks are for memorizing longer sequences. Successful navigational methods could utilize different mechanisms to still obtain dependable navigational e.g. combining attractive and repulsive cues [22] or integrating several navigational cues [16,30]. This work aims to provide a valuable tool with which the further development of such neural insect-inspired long-range navigation methods can be accelerated.

References

1. Amin, H., Apostolopoulou, A.A., Suárez-Grimalt, R., Vrontou, E., Lin, A.C.: Localized inhibition in the Drosophila mushroom body. eLife 9 (2020). https://doi.org/10.7554/eLife.56954, https://elifesciences.org/articles/56954
2. Ardin, P., Peng, F., Mangan, M., Lagogiannis, K., Webb, B.: Using an insect mushroom body circuit to encode route memory in complex natural environments. PLOS Comput. Biol. **12**(2), e1004683 (2016). https://doi.org/10.1371/journal.pcbi.1004683, https://dx.plos.org/10.1371/journal.pcbi.1004683
3. Baddeley, B., Graham, P., Husbands, P., Philippides, A.: A Model of Ant Route Navigation Driven by Scene Familiarity. PLoS Computational Biology **8**(1), e1002336 (2012). https://doi.org/10.1371/journal.pcbi.1002336,https://dx.plos.org/10.1371/journal.pcbi.1002336
4. Barranco, F., Fermuller, C., Aloimonos, Y., Delbruck, T.: A dataset for visual navigation with neuromorphic methods. Front. Neurosci. **10**, 49 (2016). https://doi.org/10.3389/fnins.2016.00049, http://journal.frontiersin.org/Article/10.3389/fnins.2016.00049/abstract
5. Bell, A.J., Sejnowski, T.J.: An Information-Maximization Approach to Blind Separation and Blind Deconvolution. Neural Comput. **7**(6), 1129–1159 (1995). https://doi.org/10.1162/neco.1995.7.6.1129,http://www.mitpressjournals.org/doi/10.1162/neco.1995.7.6.1129
6. Buehlmann, C., Wozniak, B., Goulard, R., Webb, B., Graham, P., Niven, J.E.: Mushroom bodies are required for learned visual navigation, but not for innate visual behavior. Ants. Current Biol. **30**(17), 3438-3443.e2 (2020). https://doi.org/10.1016/j.cub.2020.07.013
7. Caporale, N., Dan, Y.: Spike timing-dependent plasticity: a Hebbian learning rule. Ann. Rev. Neurosci. **31**(1), 25–46 (2008). https://doi.org/10.1146/annurev.neuro.31.060407.125639, https://www.annualreviews.org/doi/10.1146/annurev.neuro.31.060407.125639
8. Cartwright, B.A., Collett, T.S.: Landmark learning in bees - Experiments and models. J. Comparat. Physiol. **151**(4), 521–543 (1983). https://doi.org/10.1007/BF00605469, http://link.springer.com/10.1007/BF00605469
9. de Croon, G., de Clercq, K., Ruijsink, R., Remes, B., de Wagter, C.: Design, aerodynamics, and vision-based control of the DelFly. Int. J. Micro Air Vehicles **1**(2), 71–97 (2009). https://doi.org/10.1260/175682909789498288, http://journals.sagepub.com/doi/10.1260/175682909789498288
10. Denuelle, A., Srinivasan, M.V.: A sparse snapshot-based navigation strategy for UAS guidance in natural environments. In: 2016 IEEE International Conference on Robotics and Automation (ICRA). vol. 2016-June, pp. 3455–3462. IEEE, May 2016. https://doi.org/10.1109/ICRA.2016.7487524, http://ieeexplore.ieee.org/document/7487524/
11. Dupeyroux, J., Serres, J.R., Viollet, S.: Antbot: a six-legged walking robot able to home like desert ants in outdoor environments. Sci. Robot. **4**(27), eaau0307 (2019)
12. Franz, M.O., Schölkopf, B., Mallot, H.A., Bülthoff, H.H.: Where did I take that snapshot? Scene-based homing by image matching. Biol. Cybern. **79**(3), 191–202 (1998). https://doi.org/10.1007/s004220050470, http://link.springer.com/10.1007/s004220050470
13. Freas, C.A., Schultheiss, P.: How to Navigate in Different Environments and Situations: Lessons From Ants. Front,. Psychol. **9**, 1–7 (2018). https://doi.org/10.3389/fpsyg.2018.00841, https://www.frontiersin.org/article/10.3389/fpsyg.2018.00841/full

14. Gallego, G., et al.: Event-based vision: a survey. IEEE Trans. Pattern Anal. Mach. Intell. **44**(1), 154–180 (2022). https://doi.org/10.1109/TPAMI.2020.3008413

15. Graham, P., Philippides, A.: Vision for navigation: what can we learn from ants? Arthropod Struct. Dev. **46**(5), 718–722 (2017). https://doi.org/10.1016/j.asd.2017.07.001, https://www.sciencedirect.com/science/article/pii/S1467803917300932

16. Hoinville, T., Wehner, R.: Optimal multiguidance integration in insect navigation. Proc. Natl. Acad. Sci. U.S.A. **115**(11), 2824–2829 (2018). https://doi.org/10.1073/pnas.1721668115

17. Hu, Y., Binas, J., Neil, D., Liu, S.C., Delbruck, T.: DDD20 end-to-end event camera driving dataset: fusing frames and events with deep learning for improved steering prediction. In: 2020 IEEE 23rd International Conference on Intelligent Transportation Systems (ITSC), pp. 1–6. IEEE, September 2020. https://doi.org/10.1109/ITSC45102.2020.9294515, https://ieeexplore.ieee.org/document/9294515/

18. Izhikevich, E.: Simple model of spiking neurons. IEEE Trans. Neural Networks **14**(6), 1569–1572 (2003). https://doi.org/10.1109/TNN.2003.820440, http://ieeexplore.ieee.org/document/1257420/

19. Jafferis, N.T., Helbling, E.F., Karpelson, M., Wood, R.J.: Untethered flight of an insect-sized flapping-wing microscale aerial vehicle. Nature **570**(7762), 491–495 (2019). https://doi.org/10.1038/s41586-019-1322-0, https://www.nature.com/articles/s41586-019-1322-0

20. Kistler, W.M., Gerstner, W., Hemmen, J.L.V.: Reduction of the hodgkin-huxley equations to a single-variable threshold model. Neural Comput. **9**(5), 1015–1045 (1997). https://doi.org/10.1162/neco.1997.9.5.1015, https://doi.org/10.1162/neco.1997.9.5.1015

21. Lambrinos, D., Möller, R., Pfeifer, R., Wehner, R.: Landmark navigation without snapshots: the average landmark vector model. In: Elsner, N., Wehner, R. (eds.) Proceedings of the Neurobiology Conference on Göttingen, p. 30a. Georg Thieme Verlag (1998). www.cs.cmu.edu/~motionplanning/papers/sbp_papers/integrated2/lambrinos_landmark_vector.pdf

22. Le Möel, F., Wystrach, A.: Opponent processes in visual memories: a model of attraction and repulsion in navigating insects' mushroom bodies. PLOS Computational Biology **16**(2), e1007631 (2020). https://doi.org/10.1371/journal.pcbi.1007631, https://dx.plos.org/10.1371/journal.pcbi.1007631

23. Möller, R., Vardy, A.: Local visual homing by matched-filter descent in image distances. Biol. Cybern. **95**(5), 413–430 (2006). https://doi.org/10.1007/s00422-006-0095-3, http://link.springer.com/10.1007/s00422-006-0095-3

24. Paredes-Valles, F., Scheper, K.Y.W., De Croon, G.C.H.E.: Unsupervised learning of a hierarchical spiking neural network for optical flow estimation: from events to global motion perception. IEEE Trans. Pattern Anal. Mach. Intell. **8828**(c), 1–1 (2019). https://doi.org/10.1109/TPAMI.2019.2903179, https://ieeexplore.ieee.org/document/8660483/

25. Sanes, J.R., Zipursky, S.L.: Design Principles of Insect and Vertebrate Visual Systems. Neuron **66**(1), 15–36 (2010). https://doi.org/10.1016/j.neuron.2010.01.018, https://linkinghub.elsevier.com/retrieve/pii/S0896627310000449

26. Scheper, K.Y., Karasek, M., De Wagter, C., Remes, B.D., De Croon, G.C.: First autonomous multi-room exploration with an insect-inspired flapping wing vehicle. In: 2018 IEEE International Conference on Robotics and Automation (ICRA), pp. 5546–5552. IEEE (2018). https://doi.org/10.1109/ICRA.2018.8460702, https://ieeexplore.ieee.org/document/8460702/

27. Stein, R.B.: A theoretical analysis of neuronal variability. Biophys. J. **5**(2), 173–194 (1965). https://doi.org/10.1016/S0006-3495(65)86709-1, https://www.sciencedirect.com/science/article/pii/S0006349565867091

28. Stone, T., Mangan, M., Wystrach, A., Webb, B.: Rotation invariant visual processing for spatial memory in insects. Interface Focus **8**(4), 20180010 (2018). https://doi.org/10.1098/rsfs.2018.0010, https://royalsocietypublishing.org/doi/10.1098/rsfs.2018.0010

29. Stürzl, W., Mallot, H.: Efficient visual homing based on Fourier transformed panoramic images. Robot. Auton. Syst. **54**(4), 300–313 (2006). https://doi.org/10.1016/j.robot.2005.12.001, https://linkinghub.elsevier.com/retrieve/pii/S0921889005002113

30. Sun, X., Yue, S., Mangan, M.: A decentralised neural model explaining optimal integration of navigational strategies in insects. eLife **9** (2020). https://doi.org/10.7554/eLife.54026, https://elifesciences.org/articles/54026

31. de Tournemire, P., Nitti, D., Perot, E., Migliore, D., Sironi, A.: A large scale event-based detection dataset for automotive. arXiv preprint (2020). http://arxiv.org/abs/2001.08499

32. Vogt, K., et al.: Direct neural pathways convey distinct visual information to Drosophila mushroom bodies. eLife **5**(APRIL2016), 1–13 (2016). https://doi.org/10.7554/eLife.14009, https://elifesciences.org/articles/14009

33. Wystrach, A., Beugnon, G., Cheng, K.: Ants might use different view-matching strategies on and off the route. J. Exp. Biol. **215**(1), 44–55 (2012). https://doi.org/10.1242/jeb.059584, https://doi.org/10.1242/jeb.059584

34. Zeil, J., Hofmann, M.I., Chahl, J.S.: Catchment areas of panoramic snapshots in outdoor scenes. J. Opt. Soc. Am. A **20**(3), 450 (2003). https://doi.org/10.1364/JOSAA.20.000450, https://www.osapublishing.org/abstract.cfm?URI=josaa-20-3-450

35. Zhu, A.Z., Thakur, D., Ozaslan, T., Pfrommer, B., Kumar, V., Daniilidis, K.: The multivehicle stereo event camera dataset: an event camera dataset for 3D perception. IEEE Robot. Autom. Lett. **3**(3), 2032–2039 (2018). https://doi.org/10.1109/LRA.2018.2800793, http://ieeexplore.ieee.org/document/8288670/

36. Zhu, L., Mangan, M., Webb, B.: Spatio-temporal memory for navigation in a mushroom body model. In: Living Machines 2020. LNCS (LNAI), vol. 12413, pp. 415–426. Springer, Cham (2020). https://doi.org/10.1007/978-3-030-64313-3_39 https://link.springer.com/10.1007/978-3-030-64313-3_39

Using DeepLabCut to Predict Locations of Subdermal Landmarks from Video

Diya Basrai[1]([✉]), Emanuel Andrada[2], Janina Weber[2], Martin S. Fischer[2], and Matthew Tresch[1,3]

[1] Department of Physiology, Northwestern University, Chicago, IL, USA
diyabasrai@gmail.com
[2] Institute of Zoology and Evolutionary Research, Friedrich-Schiller-University, Jena, Germany
[3] Shirley Ryan Ability Lab, Chicago, IL, USA

Abstract. Recent developments in markerless tracking software such as DeepLabCut (DLC) allow estimation of skin landmark positions during behavioral studies. However, studies that require highly accurate skeletal kinematics require estimation of 3D positions of subdermal landmarks such as joint centers of rotation or skeletal features. In many animals, significant slippage between the skin and underlying skeleton makes accurate tracking of skeletal configuration from skin landmarks difficult. While biplanar, high-speed X-ray acquisition cameras offer a way to measure accurate skeletal configuration using tantalum markers and XROMM, this technology is expensive, not widely available, and the manual annotation required is time-consuming. Here, we present an approach that utilizes DLC to estimate subdermal landmarks in a rat from video collected from two standard cameras. By simultaneously recording X-ray and live video of an animal, we train a DLC model to predict the skin locations representing the projected positions of subdermal landmarks obtained from X-ray data. Predicted skin locations from multiple camera views were triangulated to reconstruct depth-accurate positions of subdermal landmarks. We found that DLC was able to estimate skeletal landmarks with good 3D accuracy, suggesting that this might be an approach to provide accurate estimates of skeletal configuration using standard live video.

1 Introduction

DeepLabCut (DLC), an open-source markerless tracking software package, allows automated and robust position estimation of skin landmarks [1], and has been widely adopted for use in extracting kinematics from a wide range of animal behaviors. However, since muscles and tendons act directly on bones and joints, quantifying accurate kinematics often requires estimation of the skeletal structure itself, not the skin above [2].

X-ray reconstruction of moving morphology (XROMM) utilizes high-speed X-ray cameras to obtain accurate 3D estimates of subdermal landmarks, such as skeletal features or joint centers [3]. However, XROMM requires frame-by-frame manual annotation, and subdermal landmarks frequently need to be 'marked' with implanted tantalum beads to show up in X-ray videos. Moreover, because of their expense and complexity, XROMM systems are difficult to use widely across experimental setups.

© The Author(s), under exclusive license to Springer Nature Switzerland AG 2022
A. Hunt et al. (Eds.): Living Machines 2022, LNAI 13548, pp. 292–296, 2022.
https://doi.org/10.1007/978-3-031-20470-8_29

Here we present an approach that leverages DLC's ability to estimate skin land-marks to increase the throughput and reduce the labor when quantifying kinematics with XROMM. Instead of training DLC models with hand-annotated frames, we train DLC models with frames that are labeled by projecting the 3D positions of skeletal land-marks obtained with XROMM onto simultaneously obtained frames from live video. Thus, well-trained DLC models can learn to estimate the position of subdermal skeletal features using information present in the live video images. Predicted locations from multiple camera views can then be triangulated to reconstruct depth-accurate positions of subdermal landmarks.

In this paper, we demonstrate preliminary results evaluating this approach on the rat forelimb from an overground running task.

2 Methods

2.1 Data Collection

4 trials of a rat performing an overground running task were recorded by two standard video cameras and two high-speed X-ray acquisition cameras. 'Objective' 3D positions of skeletal features and implanted tantalum landmarks in the rat forelimb were manually annotated, using methods described elsewhere [4].

Training data for the DLC models was generated by projecting the 3D position of subdermal landmarks identified using XROMM onto views from the live camera. Each DLC model, one per camera, was trained with 20 equally spaced frames per trial, from 3 trials total. The fourth trial was held out for use in cross-validation of the method (Fig. 1).

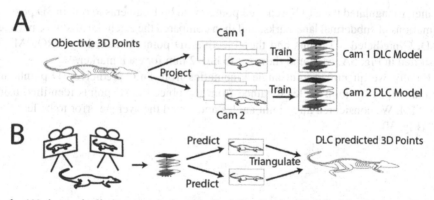

Fig. 1. (A) shows pipeline to generate frames of training data for DLC models. (B) shows pipeline of using trained DLC models to predict 3D positions.

3 Results

3.1 2D Estimation of Skeletal Landmarks

We first evaluated how well DLC models were able to predict the 2D positions of subdermal landmarks. We compared the Euclidian distance between the actual projected points and the DLC predicted points on a trial neither model was trained on. As illustrated in Fig. 2B, we found that errors from this reconstruction were small (~2 pixels).

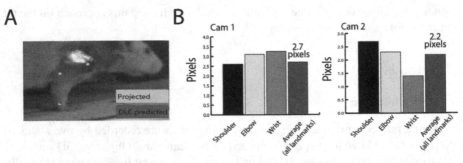

Fig. 2. (A) shows a zoomed in sample frame with projected positions and DLC predicted position. (B) Pixel error for DLC models for certain subdermal landmarks. Pixel error is Euclidean distance between predicted and projected.

3.2 3D Estimation of Skeletal Landmarks

We then triangulated the DLC-predicted points from both cameras to obtain 3D position estimations of subdermal landmarks, and then compared the Euclidian distance between the DLC-predicted 3D points and the objective 3D points obtained by XROMM. As illustrated in Fig. 3A, we found the error to be ~2 mm for each marker.

Finally, we quantified joint angle kinematics from DLC-predicted 3D points and compared those to joint angles obtained from the objective 3D points identified using XROMM. We considered three joint angles and found the average error to be less than ~ 4° (Fig. 3B).

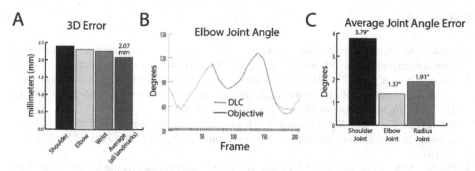

Fig. 3. (A) shows Euclidian distance between DLC triangulated 3D points and objective points. (B) Frame by frame joint angles calculated from DLC predicted landmarks (orange) and from objective (blue) landmarks identified using XROMM. The plot illustrates the joint angle between the shoulder marker, elbow marker, and wrist marker. (C) Average error over all frames for each calculated joint angle. Shoulder joint is calculated between scapular marker, shoulder marker, and wrist marker. Elbow joint is between shoulder marker, elbow marker, and wrist marker. Radius joint is calculated between humerus post marker, radius post landmark and wrist marker (Color figure online).

4 Discussion

Trained DLC models were able to estimate 3D positions of subdermal, skeletal landmarks with low error. At a minimum, this approach can increase the throughput of studies needing 3D position estimates of subdermal landmarks in experiments using XROMM data. DLC models can be trained on data from a small number of frames from each trial in a study, and then used to generate 3D positions with low error. However, for the purpose of reducing labor of analysis, it is debatable whether it might be more efficient to instead apply DLC directly to X-ray data to automate the manual annotation process.

Instead, the promise of the method presented here comes from its potential for generalizability to trials and experiments that do not use XROMM recordings. For instance, in this dataset, the field of view of the live video cameras was wider than the X-ray acquisition cameras, allowing the DLC models to predict frames that the X-ray cameras had no access to. Conceivably, a well-trained DLC model could estimate 3D positions for a specific animal across a wide range of experimental conditions, even tasks where there isn't training data from the X-ray acquisition cameras. Even more speculatively, it might be possible to standardize experimental conditions for a specific species across laboratories closely enough so that multiple investigators could estimate skeletal landmarks with accuracy levels close to those achieved using XROMM but using only standard, off-the-shelf, cameras. In future work, we will evaluate the generalizability of this approach, testing whether it would be possible to create a DLC model for a specific species that can be used across laboratories and experimental conditions to estimate accurate skeletal kinematics.

References

1. Mathis, A., Mamidanna, P., Cury, K.M., et al.: DeepLabCut: markerless pose estimation of user-defined body parts with deep learning. *Nat Neurosci* **21,** 1281–1289 (2018)
2. Bauman, J.M., Chang, Y.H.: High-speed X-ray video demonstrates significant skin movement errors with standard optical kinematics during rat locomotion. J. Neurosci. Methods. **186**(1), 18–24 (2010). https://doi.org/10.1016/j.jneumeth.2009.10.017
3. Brainerd, E.L., et al.: X-ray reconstruction of moving morphology (XROMM): precision, accuracy and applications in comparative biomechanics research. J. Exp. Zool. **313A**, 262–279 (2010)
4. Fischer, M.S., Lehmann, S.V., Andrada, E.: Three-dimensional kinematics of canine hind limbs: in vivo, biplanar, high-frequency fluoroscopic analysis of four breeds during walking and trotting. Sci. Rep. **8**, 16982 (2018). https://doi.org/10.1038/s41598-018-34310-010.1002/jez.589

Underwater Light Modulators: Iridescent Structures of the Seagrass *Posidonia Oceanica*

Fabian Meder[(✉)] [iD], Goffredo Giordano [iD], Serena Armiento [iD],
and Barbara Mazzolai[(✉)] [iD]

Bioinspired Soft Robotics, Istituto Italiano Di Tecnologia (IIT), Via Morego 30, 16163 Genova,
Italy
{fabian.meder,barbara.mazzolai}@iit.it

Abstract. Colors are crucial for animals and plants to interact with their environment and other organisms. Especially the bright, iridescent colors in nature often rely on micro- and nanoscale features made by organic materials. The occurrence and shape of these structures causing the colors is not only fascinating, but it is becoming increasingly important for biomimetics and bioinspired devices that imitate functional principles of living systems. Many plants developed structural colors based on photonic crystals, e.g., in the cuticle of fruits to attract animals. Here, we report the first time on the iridescent structures in the seagrass *Posidonia oceanica* and provide evidence that the resulting color likely relies on a multilayered 1D photonic crystal consisting of multiple liquid and organic layers. The structure evolves and changes throughout the leaf blade (from its base to the top) resulting in different light interactions on the same leaf. Photonic structures become increasingly important in bioinspired optical devices, also integrated in robots as sensors, as organism-machine interacting element, or photoprotection and the here described structures could be especially interesting as inspiration for developing light modulators for applications in underwater scenarios.

Keywords: Photonic structures · Iridescence · Bioinspired optics and sensors · Structural mechanochromism

1 Introduction

The capability of modulating light in living organisms represents a source of inspiration for designing innovative technologies in fields, from optics to robotics, especially soft robotics [1–4]. Structural colors result from an optical interference caused by material geometries that are in the wavelength-scale also known as natural photonic crystals rather than from a molecular or chemical origin like pigments [5]. Examples of biological photonic structures have been studied extensively in the animal kingdom [2, 3] and in the plant kingdom, in particular in flowers, fruits and some leaves and to less extent in aquatic photosynthetic organisms [5, 6]. Such biological photonic materials have been used to design structures for novel robotic applications increasing the functionality of

---

F. Meder and G. Giordano—Contributed equally to this work.

© The Author(s), under exclusive license to Springer Nature Switzerland AG 2022
A. Hunt et al. (Eds.): Living Machines 2022, LNAI 13548, pp. 297–308, 2022.
https://doi.org/10.1007/978-3-031-20470-8_30

artificial materials, e.g. by making it sensitive, or stimuli-responsive while actuating [4, 7–10].

How nature implements such structures is a crucial starting point for developing tunable structurally colored devices. Here, we aimed to characterize and reveal what causes the iridescence of *P. oceanica* to expand the yet limited portfolio of structures creating color underwater. *P. oceanica* is a widespread seagrass in the Mediterranean basin, which forms large meadows where numerous organisms like fishes and turtles find food and shelter [11] and it is one of the most effective underwater photosynthetic CO_2 fixators [12]. We show that the observed iridescence interestingly evolves along the leaf blade from its base to the apex and it occurs, preferentially in the lower leaf part. It is not caused by 3D grating-like cuticular structures but likely by a liquid/organic multilayer 1D photonic structure [13, 14]. Our analysis shows the interference of light within a multilayered structure localized between epidermis cells and the cuticle that changes its morphology and optical properties along the blade. The results extend the current examples of variable underwater light modulators and could be a source of inspiration for technical solutions that vary light interactions along the structure.

2 Materials and Methods

2.1 Plant Samples

Samples of the seagrass *Posidonia oceanica* were collected in the Mediterranean Sea in Livorno, Italy in the period September-October 2020 from meadows growing at a depth of about 2–3 m and at a distance of 20–30 m from the coast. The samples were kept in sea water at 4 °C for analysis and samples were replaced with freshly harvested leaves after 14 days.

2.2 Methods

Optical characterization. Reflection measurements were done with a reflectometer (NanoCalc-2000-UV-VIS-NIR, spectral resolution 0.1 nm, Ocean Optics, USA) and a goniometer to adjust the angle between detector and light source. Using 400 μm-diameter optical fibers, the UV-VIS-NIR light source was fixed at 0° and the detector moved at different angles. The leaf sample was fixed flat onto a glass container filled with sea water (filtered through a 0.2 μm pore size membrane to remove particulate matter) and the light source and detector were immersed under water during the analysis to avoid effects from the air-water interface. All measurements were repeated at least 3 to 10 times and results are representative.

Microscopy. Leaf surfaces and leaf sections were observed in a digital microscope (KH-8700, Hirox, Japan). Leaf sections were hand-cut using a razor blade. The cuticle in the leaf sections were stained with Sudan IV by exposure to a 0.1% (w/v) solution of Sudan IV in isopropyl alcohol diluted 1:1 in 0.2 μm pore size membrane-filtered sea water for 10 min followed by gentle washing in sea water. Scanning electron microscopy (SEM) was done in a Helios NanoLab 600i, ThermoFisher Scientific, Inc., USA. The samples were fixed with glutaraldehyde and dried using a critical point dryer (Autosamdri-931,

Tousimis, USA) using standard procedures. Layer thicknesses were measured from microscopy images using ImageJ (Version 1.51j8).

Photography. Photographs were taken using a digital camera (D7100, Nikon, Japan).

Modelling of the Photonic Structure. The theoretical modelling of the organic photonic crystal in the lower part of the leaf, was carried out using the Transfer Matrix Method (TMM) [15]. In particular, we modelled a planar (no curvature was considered) 1D photonic crystal using the software Wolfram Mathematica as reported earlier [16, 17]. We focused on the optical behavior of a multilayered structure in the lower part of the *P. Oceanica* leaf, in particular in the adaxial cuticle/epidermis layer as highlighted in the SEM micrograph in Fig. 2d and 2e. Several models replicate the complex optical behavior of plant leaves [18]. For our purposes, we adopted evidently simplifying assumptions to best highlight the role of the nanostructures, its emergent photonic stop band (PSB), and its angular dependency (i.e., iridescence). Specifically, the optical system was modelled along the z-axis from top to bottom as follows: a homogeneous cuticle layer (refractive index $n_{cuticle} = 1.45$ [19], thickness $d_{cuticle,homogenous} = 2$ μm), the multilayered lamellae structure (7 pairs of organic material likely from the cuticle, $n_{cuticle} = 1.45$, $d_{cuticle} = 134$ nm, and water-filled lamellar layers, $n_w(\lambda) + i*k_w(\lambda)$ [20], $k_w(\lambda)$ is the extinction coefficient dispersion, d_w spanning from 146 nm up to 220 nm), and the chloroplast-containing cellular system ($n_{chloroplast} = 1.415$ [21], $d_{chloroplast} >> 2$ μm). The dimensions were obtained from the SEM and digital microscope analyses (Fig. 2a and Fig. 2e, respectively in wet/dry condition). The simulated environment was aqueous to be consistent with the experimental data acquisition. The main hypothesis considers that in wet environment the invaginations were filled with water, and we deliberately spanned the water-filling layer thickness. We assumed the effective extinction coefficients of the cuticle and chloroplast coincident with the $k_w(\lambda)$. Indeed, Ref. [22] analyzed the water density in fresh leaves reporting the highest concentration in the upper leaf depths (0 μm - 40 μm). Consequently, for the uppermost layer of the leaf a multi-component homogeneous mixture of water and organic components was assumed.

Data Analysis. All measurements were, if not indicated otherwise, repeated at least 3 to 10 times and on up to 10 individual leaves and the results shown are representative. The data were analyzed and plotted in MATLAB (Version R2021b).

3 Results

3.1 *P. oceanica* Leaf Images and Leaf Structure-dependent Reflection

Figure 1A shows images of *P. oceanica* leaves collected in the Mediterranean Sea. Especially the lower part of the about 20–40 cm long and about 1 cm wide leaves show a yellow-golden light reflection not occurring on the upper leaf parts which have a dark-green color. The reflection is especially visible, when the leaf is rolled/folded. Figure 1b shows the gradual change of the optical properties along a whole leaf. The bottom part starts with a white base (base) with which the leaf is fixed in the shoot. The

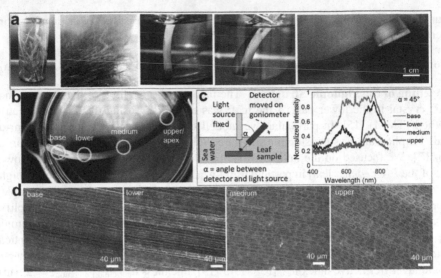

Fig. 1. Appearance, reflectance, and cellular structure of the leaf blade of *P. oceanica*. A) Images of some collected leaf samples in a glass container, an underwater image of part of a *P. oceanica* meadow, a single leaf in three different configurations showing its golden-greenish-reddish iridescence (from left to right). b) Single leaf blade with indications of the four zones (base, lower, medium, upper leaf parts) which show different optical properties that were analyzed in detail. c) Schematic of the measurement setup for "underwater" reflectance measurements and the reflectance spectra recorded from different positions along the leaf blade. d) Digital microscopy images (reflected light) from the base, lower, medium, and upper leaf part showing the arrangement of the epidermal cells.

base is typically not exposed to light, as it is burden in the shoot. A bright golden-green-reddish iridescent area (lower) follows which is the first part exposed from the shoot (not burden in the shoot and exposed to the environment) and it shows a strong light reflection. In the following leaf part (medium), the reflection decreases and a darker, greener color is observed. The leaf apex (upper) appears dark green and does not show light reflections. By measuring the wavelength-dependent leaf reflectance, we confirmed this behavior. Figure 1c shows the setup for reflection measurements that were performed submersing the light source and detector as well as the leaf sample under sea water to avoid a) reflections from the air-water interface and b) drying of the leaf outside its natural environment. The measurements show a location-dependent reflection spectrum with clear differences along the leaf structure. While the lower white base part of the leaf shows expectedly a broad reflection in the whole visible and near infrared (NIR) range, the lower visually iridescent leaf part bears two distinct reflection peaks at 580 nm (spanning from ~ 520 to 640 nm at FWHM) and a second at 760 nm (spanning from ~ 700 to 810 nm at FWHM). Instead, the dark green medium and upper leaf parts show a significantly smaller reflection peak at 570 nm and at 760 nm which may indicate that those reflections in the medium and upper leaf region are mostly originated in a pigmentary component (i.e., chlorophyll) rather than on a physical structure light-matter interaction. In addition, the digital microscopy images in Fig. 1d recorded show the reflected light and indicate the color gradient. Moreover, it can be clearly observed, that the cellular structure changes. The initially ~40 μm-diameter epidermis cells (base and lower leaf region) build a tightly packed cell layer. The cell structures become smaller in the medium and upper region reaching diameters of ~20–30 μm and appear more distant from each other.

3.2 Microscopy Analysis of the Leaf and Possible Photonic Structure

Figure 2A shows microscopy images of fresh leaf sections imaged in sea water. The outer leaf surface, the cuticle, was stained in red to better visualize the leaf's border. It can be seen that the epidermis cells in the base part of the leaf are directly attached to the cuticle, transparent, and absent of chloroplasts. In the iridescent lower leaf part, the epidermis cells begin to fill with the green-pigmented chloroplasts and the cells appear at a larger distance from the cuticle. Medium and upper leaf parts show further increasing chloroplast density corresponding to the dark green color and the cells again appear slightly

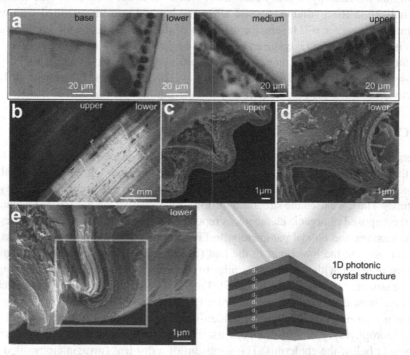

Fig. 2. Structural analysis of *P. oceanica* leaves. a) Digital transmission microscopy image of leaf sections (cuticle stained in red) at base, lower, medium, and upper leaf part showing the different structure, e.g., the distance of the epidermis from the cuticle and the increasing green chloroplast content. b) Digital microscopy image of the reflected light of the upper and lower part of the leaf placed side-by-side showing the different optical properties. c-e) SEM images of sections of leaves of the upper and lower leaf-parts showing differences in the micro- and nanostructure. In particular, the lower leaf part shows a characteristic multilayer structure which could cause the photonic structure illustrated in e). The square in e) highlights the multilayer structure with about 100 nm single organic layer thickness.

closer to the cuticle as compared to the lower part. The difference between the upper and lower leaf optical behavior is also visualized in direct comparison with the digital microscopy images of the reflected light (Fig. 2b). SEM analysis of glutaraldehyde-fixed leaf samples of the upper (Fig. 2c) and lower (Fig. 2d and 2e) leaf part from the region between cuticle and epidermis cells suggest that a layered structure could be responsible for the reflectance in the lower leaf part resembling typical properties of a 1D photonic crystal as illustrated in Fig. 2e. Indeed, the sub-epidermal layered structures have been observed only in the lower leaf region and not in the upper or medium region which do not show reflectance. An analysis of 46 layers (from images taken from 4 individual leaves of the same meadow) revealed an average layer thickness of 100 ± 30 nm (lower leaf region) which are typical dimensions found in stacked multilayered photonic crystals. On average, a stack of 6–7 layer were found. Our hypothesis is that the spaces between the organic (expectedly cellulose- and/or cutin-based) layers are filled with liquid, building the photonic structure displayed in Fig. 2e. Indeed, measuring the thickness between the epidermis cells and the cuticle in the leaf sections revealed a difference between wet (digital microscopy) and dry conditions (SEM) of about ~ 1.5 μm. This difference is an indication for a volume increase when the layered structure is filled with water. Assuming on average 6–7 layers, the thickness of the liquid layers between the organic layers is 220 ± 100 nm (average and standard deviation from 40 measurements).

Thus, the photonic structure could be a multilayer composed of alternating organic ($d_{organic} = 100 \pm 30$ nm) and liquid ($d_{liquid} = 220 \pm 100$ nm) layers with different refractive indices of the organic ($n_{organic}$) and the liquid layer (n_{liquid}).

3.3 Comparison with a Photonic Crystal Model

The emergent optical behavior of the lower part of the *P. oceanica* leaf originates likely from the cuticle and the intermediate layers above the epidermis cells. The structural data obtained from the SEM pictures (Fig. 2c, d, e) confirm the occurrence of multilayered structures. Thus, we used the structural information to model the behavior of a photonic crystal composed of organic elements, as reported in the Materials and Methods regarding dimensions and optical parameters. In Fig. 3a, the resulting theoretical reflectance spectra related to the lower part of the leaf (black and red) are plotted with a lamellar structure together with a structure similar to the upper leaf parts (orange) lacking the lamellar structure ($\alpha = 0°$). A first order PSB in the NIR optical spectrum (both in wet/dry condition) is evident. A slight second order PSB is also evident in the visible spectrum but it is not sufficient to explain the golden-green hue whose occurrence is likely due to the chlorophyll/pigmentary components, or to some other, yet not revealed structural component below the epidermis. The spectrum of a dry leaf (invaginations filled with air instead of water) was modelled with a multilayered lamellar structure of 7 pairs of cuticular ($d_{cuticle} = 134$ nm)/air ($d_{air} = 220$ nm) media, whose result is consistent with the literature [23]. However, the analytical model does not predict a structural chromatic behavior in the middle and upper part of the leaf with a reflectance spectrum almost neglected (orange line). It was modelled as a uniform organic and homogeneous element with thickness around 4 μm. Nonetheless, it appears green (Fig. 1b), thus showing a chromatic behavior likely dependent on the higher concentration of pigments rather than on a photonic micro/nanostructure.

Figure 3b shows how the PSB in the NIR varied due to a potential water-filling of the invaginations. An optimal 7 pairs composition of cuticular ($d_{cuticle}$ = 134 nm)/water (d_w = 152 nm) media resembles the angular iridescence behavior of the leaf (Fig. 3c). Indeed, varying the angle, a blue-shift of the first order PSB appears evident, and specifically the peak turned in the red range between 20°-35°. The model predicts what it is clearly visible in the leaf in Fig. 3d.

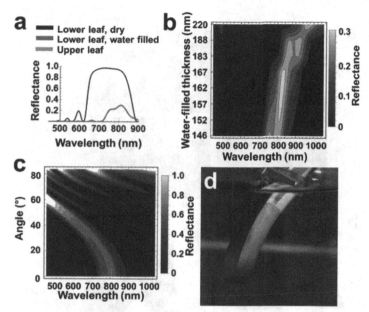

Fig. 3. Model of the photonic crystal structure. a) Simulated reflectance spectra in the vis-NIR region for dry (invaginations air-filled) nanostructured lower part of the *P. oceanica* leaf (black), wet (invagination water-filled) nanostructured lower part (red), and for the upper part of the *P. oceanica* (orange) lacking a nanostructured 1D organic photonic crystal and not showing any peak because there is no Bragg's interference pattern. b) Contour plot of the lower leaf part's photonic structure assuming it is water-filled. The y-axis shows variation of the dimension of the water-lamellae. The wet condition lowers the peak of the photonic stop band that red-shifts the higher the water content/water layer thickness is. c) Contour plot that highlights the iridescence phenomenon of the nanostructured 1D organic photonic crystal with d_w = 152 nm varying the angle of detection. d) Photograph of the *P. oceanica* leaf showing the golden-greenish-reddish hue.

3.4 Angular Resolved Reflectance Spectra

Further experimental analyses confirming the iridescent effect were done by measuring the angular-resolved reflectance spectra of the different leaf regions (Fig. 4a). The results are in agreement with the simplified analytical model and show that the maximum intensity of the reflected light is expectedly in the base and lower leaf parts. The angular dependency is clear and further shows an evident broadening of the second order PSB (yellowish/greenish region). In Fig. 4b we theoretically predicted this behavior considering the superposition of tilted planar nanostructured reflectors with the planar one previously analyzed (i.e., convolution of trapezoidal-shaped multilayered structures as reported in Fig. 2e). Further investigations are required to evaluate in detail the spectra outcomes' geometrical-dependency. The medium and upper leaf parts instead are dominated by the green pigmentation of the chloroplasts and do not show any significant structural reflectance, as predicted by the model.

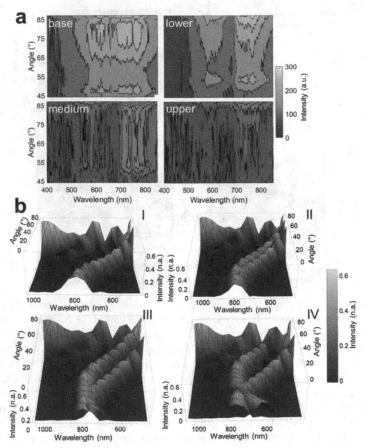

Fig. 4. Angular-resolved reflectance spectra from *P. oceanica* leaves. a) Measurements were performed at different positions along the leaf blade (base, lower, medium and upper parts) showing that the intensities of reflected light are angularly dependent as typical for structural chromism emerging from 1D photonic crystals and that the optical properties interestingly evolve along the leaf blade. b) Model-based convolution of two 1D photonic crystals in the lower part of the leaf blade resembling the trapezoidal-shape reported by the SEM images. (i) 3D plot of 1D planar reflector angularly dependent, (ii) convolution of a 1D planar reflector and a 12.5° tilted, (iii) the tilting angle raise up to 25°, and (iv) to 37.5° tilted. The convolution shows two PSB angularly dependent spanning from the NIR to the visible range.

4 Discussion

Here, we report on the iridescence properties of *P. oceanica* leaves and the possible structures causing a color change along the leaf blade. We believe that the occurrence of this structure in the seagrass may reveal interesting approaches both, at the biological and technological level for biomimetic or bioinspired layered photonic systems acting especially in underwater environments. At the technological level, the modulation of light by an abiotic multilayered photonic structure is extensively investigated in the field of optoelectronics and photonics, but nowadays an emerging interest exists also for bio-photonic devices to better understand the more intimate interaction between light and organic materials. Compliant light-modulators could help robots, buildings, smart actuators to visually interact with the external world while at the same time co-habit and interplay. Several techniques have been investigated to obtain synthetic organic dielectric mirrors. Inorganic, oxide-based dielectric mirrors are commonly fabricated by sputtering, chemical vapor deposition, electron-beam evaporation, molecular beam epitaxy techniques, etc., while organic, polymer-based ones can be obtained by spin coating, bar coating, self-assembly, roll-to-roll doctor blade, dip-coating, photolithography, co-extrusion [24, 25]. In robotics and soft robotics, photonic crystals are interesting as outer layer of actuators to change on-demand the optical appearance (i.e., as sensing elements) and for damage detecting-, photoprotection-, adornment-elements. Stretching the soft photonic structures can induce a reduction/increase of the thick layers and a modulation of the Bragg's interference pattern as it occurs along the *P. oceanica* leaf blade. Similarly, one could generate gradual structural colors along a device. Furthermore, recent advances are in the field of bioelectronics and biochemistry leading to manipulation of the emergent optical response of stretchable photonic crystals, acting on the proton/electron extraction at the protein level altering both thickness and refractive index of the innermost materials, going toward biohybrid systems. Hence, plant-inspired photonic structures fabricated with organic materials may enable biodegradable and environmental-respectful sensing/actuating elements in robotic/human-made platforms [26].

Our investigation resolved crucial structural parameters, dimensions, properties, and possible formation mechanism (i.e., water-filled organic multilayers) of the photonic structures in *P. oceanica* that could be resembled in an artificial device. However, to further detail the optical properties of the leaf-matter, further investigations could be useful. Yet, measuring absorption coefficients in leaves is extremely challenging due to the influence of multiple components on the optical properties (e.g., pigments, cellulose, chloroplasts, photosynthetic membranes, spherical diffusion elements, etc. [27, 28]). Evidently, some investigations are needed for more consistent assumptions at the model level. On the other hand, further opportunities may derive from better understanding the biological role of such structures in underwater plants. Yet, it remains indeed unclear which are the biological functions for the iridescence properties of *P. oceanica*. Speculative assumptions are for example the purpose of reflecting light towards the upper leaf parts, which have more chloroplasts and perform photosynthesis or for light trapping [29–31]. As suggested for algae, it could play a role in protection against radiation at certain wavelengths or for the complex and not yet understood seagrass-herbivore or

-fish interaction that, e.g., may provide nutrients from excrements among other potential functions [5, 32].

5 Conclusions

Structural colors are a fascinating phenomenon caused by the light-matter interaction at the micro/nanoscale. In addition, materials in animals and plants are able to modulate light for various purposes. We report for the first time a lamellar 1D photonic crystal structure in the underwater plant *P. oceanica* causing iridescence in a fraction of the leaf blade. The layered structure discovered in the lower part of the leaf, consisted of 6–7 alternating organic and liquid layers. This photonic structure was confirmed by microscopic and spectroscopic analyses and was predicted by a simplified analytical model. The results confirm the hypothesis that the layers found between the epidermis cells and the cuticle could cause the iridescence of the lower leaf parts that lead to a golden-greenish-reddish hue. The structures that vary along the leaf blade extend the database of biomimetic and organic photonic systems from which one could take inspiration for, e.g., artificial sensors, actuators, dielectric mirrors, that adaptively change their apparent coloration. In particular, for underwater applications new devices exploiting such multilayered structures in which water-filling modulates their appearance, could be developed for, e.g., communication with the environment, optical sensing feedback with organisms, or with other devices as detailed in the discussion.

References

1. Laschi, C., Mazzolai, B., Cianchetti, M.: Soft robotics: Technologies and systems pushing the boundaries of robot abilities. Sci Robot. **1**(1), eaah3690 (6 Dec 2016). https://doi.org/10.1126/scirobotics.aah3690
2. Kolle, M.: Photonic Structures Inspired by Nature, Springer Science & Business Media, http://www.springer.com/series/8790 (2011)
3. Giordano, G., Carlotti, M., Mazzolai, B.: A perspective on cephalopods mimicry and bioinspired technologies toward proprioceptive autonomous soft robots. Adv. Mater. Technol. 6, 2100437 (2021). https://doi.org/10.1002/admt.202100437
4. Pikul, J.H., Li, S., Bai, H., Hanlon, R.T., Cohen, I., Shepherd, R.F.: Stretchable surfaces with programmable 3D texture morphing for synthetic camouflaging skins. Science **1979**(358), 210–214 (2017). https://doi.org/10.1126/science.aan5627
5. Lopez-Garcia, M., et al.: Light-induced dynamic structural color by intracellular 3D photonic crystals in brown algae. Sci Adv. **4**(4), eaan8917 (11 Apr 2018). https://doi.org/10.1126/sciadv.aan8917
6. Vignolini, S., et al.: The flower of Hibiscus trionum is both visibly and measurably iridescent. New Phytol **205**, 97–101 (2015). https://doi.org/10.1111/nph.12958
7. Banisadr, S., Chen, J.: Infrared actuation-induced simultaneous reconfiguration of surface color and morphology for soft robotics. Scientific Reports 7, (2017). https://doi.org/10.1038/s41598-017-17904-y
8. Wang, Y., Cui, H., Zhao, Q., Du, X.: Chameleon-inspired structural-color actuators. Matter. 626–638 (2019). https://doi.org/10.1016/j.matt.2019.05.012
9. Sitti, M.: Physical intelligence as a new paradigm. Extreme Mech Lett. **46**, 101340 (2021). https://doi.org/10.1016/j.eml.2021.101340

10. Nojoomi, A., Arslan, H., Lee, K., Yum, K.: Bioinspired 3D structures with programmable morphologies and motions. Nat. Commun. **9**, 3705 (2018). https://doi.org/10.1038/s41467-018-05569-8

11. Montefalcone, M.: Ecosystem health assessment using the Mediterranean seagrass Posidonia oceanica: A review. Ecol. Ind. **9**, 595–604 (2009). https://doi.org/10.1016/j.ecolind.2008.09.013

12. Pergent-Martini, C., Pergent, G., Monnier, B., Boudouresque, C.-F., Mori, C., Valette-Sansevin, A.: Contribution of Posidonia oceanica meadows in the context of climate change mitigation in the Mediterranean Sea. Mar. Environ. Res. **165**, 105236 (2021). https://doi.org/10.1016/j.marenvres.2020.105236

13. Moyroud, E., et al.: Disorder in convergent floral nanostructures enhances signalling to bees. Nature **550**, 469–474 (2017). https://doi.org/10.1038/nature24285

14. Johansen, V.E., Onelli, O.D., Steiner, L.M., Vignolini, S.: Photonics in Nature: From Order to Disorder. In: Gorb, S.N., Gorb, E.V. (eds.) Functional Surfaces in Biology III. BS, vol. 10, pp. 53–89. Springer, Cham (2017). https://doi.org/10.1007/978-3-319-74144-4_3

15. Yeh, P.: Optical Waves in Layered Media, p. 416. Wiley, March 2005. ISBN 978-0-471-73192-4

16. Genco, A., et al.: High quality factor microcavity OLED employing metal-free electrically active Bragg mirrors. Org. Electron. **62**, 174–180 (2018). https://doi.org/10.1016/j.orgel.2018.07.034

17. Byrnes, S.J.: Multilayer optical calculations. arXiv: Computational Physics (2016). https://doi.org/10.48550/arXiv.1603.02720

18. Jacquemoud, S., Susan, U.: Comprehensive reviews of leaf optical properties models. In: Leaf Optical Properties. pp. 229–264. Cambridge University Press (2019). https://doi.org/10.1017/9781108686457

19. Seyfried, M., Fukshansky, L.: Light gradients in plant tissue. Appl. Opt. **22**, 1402 (1983). https://doi.org/10.1364/AO.22.001402

20. Segelstein, D.J.: The complex refractive index of water. PhD Thesis. University of Missouri, Kansas City (1981)

21. Charney, E., Brackett, F.S.: The spectral dependence of scattering from a spherical alga and its implications for the state of organization of the light-accepting pigments. Arch. Biochem. Biophys. **92**, 1–12 (1961). https://doi.org/10.1016/0003-9861(61)90210-7

22. Carter, G.A., McCain, D.C.: Relationship of leaf spectral reflectance to chloroplast water content determined using NMR microscopy. Remote Sens. Environ. **46**, 305–310 (1993). https://doi.org/10.1016/0034-4257(93)90050-8

23. Zygielbaum, A.I., Gitelson, A.A., Arkebauer, T.J., Rundquist, D.C.: Non-destructive detection of water stress and estimation of relative water content in maize. Geophys. Res. Lett. **36**, L12403 (2009). https://doi.org/10.1029/2009GL038906

24. Comoretto, D. (ed.): Organic and Hybrid Photonic Crystals. Springer, Cham (2015). https://doi.org/10.1007/978-3-319-16580-6

25. Lova, P., Manfredi, G., Comoretto, D.: Advances in Functional Solution Processed Planar 1D Photonic Crystals. Advanced Optical Materials. **6**, 1800730 (2018). https://doi.org/10.1002/adom.201800730

26. Mazzolai, B., Laschi, C.: A vision for future bioinspired and biohybrid robots. Sci Robot. **5**(38), eaba6893 (22 Jan 2020). https://doi.org/10.1126/scirobotics.aba6893

27. Paillotin, G., Leibl, W., Gapiński, J., Breton, J., Dobek, A.: Light Gradients in Spherical Photosynthetic Vesicles. Biophys. J. **75**, 124–133 (1998). https://doi.org/10.1016/S0006-3495(98)77500-9

28. Sultanova, N., Kasarova, S., Nikolovb, I.: Dispersion Properties of Optical Polymers. ACTA Physica Polonica 116 (2009). https://doi.org/10.12693/APhysPolA.116.585

29. Mandoli, D.F., Briggs, W.R.: Fiber-optic plant tissues: spectral dependence in dark-grown and green tissues. Photochem. Photobiol. **39**, 419–424 (1984). https://doi.org/10.1111/j.1751-1097.1984.tb08199.x
30. Vogelmann, T.C., Bjorn, L.O.: Measurement of light gradients and spectral regime in plant tissue with a fiber optic probe. Physiol. Plant. **60**, 361–368 (1984). https://doi.org/10.1111/j.1399-3054.1984.tb06076.x
31. Vogelmann, T.C., Bjorn, L.O.: Plants as light traps. Physiol. Plant. **68**, 704–708 (1986). https://doi.org/10.1111/j.1399-3054.1986.tb03421.x
32. Chandler, C.J., Wilts, B.D., Brodie, J., Vignolini, S.: Structural color in marine algae. Advanced Optical Materials 5 (2017). https://doi.org/10.1002/adom.201600646

Canonical Motor Microcircuit for Control of a Rat Hindlimb

Clayton Jackson[1]([☒])(iD), William R. P. Nourse[2](iD), C. J. Heckman[3](iD), Matthew Tresch[4](iD), and Roger D. Quinn[1](iD)

[1] Department of Mechanical and Aerospace Engineering, Case Western Reserve University, Cleveland, OH 44106-7222, USA
clayton.jackson@case.edu
[2] Department of Electrical, Computer, and Systems Engineering, Case Western Reserve University, Cleveland, OH 44106-7222, USA
[3] Department of Physical Therapy and Human Movement Sciences, Northwestern University, Evanston, IL 60208, USA
[4] Department of Biomedical Engineering, Northwestern University, Evanston, IL 60208, USA

Abstract. This work focuses on creating a controller for the hip joint of a rat using a canonical motor microcircuit. It is thought that this circuit acts to modulate motor neuron activity at the output stage. We first created a simplified biomechanical model of a rat hindlimb along with a neural model of the circuit in a software tool called Animatlab. The canonical motor microcircuit controller was then tuned such that the trajectory of the hip joint was similar to that of a rat during locomotion. This work describes a successful method for hand-tuning the various synaptic parameters and the influence of Ia feedback on motor neuron activity. The neuromechanical model will allow for further analysis of the circuit, specifically, the function and significance of Ia feedback and Renshaw cells.

Keywords: Canonical Motor Microcircuit · Renshaw cells · Neuromechanical simulation · Rat

1 Introduction

The neural circuit used for locomotion in mammals continues to be a topic of research. A prevailing theory is that central pattern generators (CPG's) drive the motor neurons to produce the repetitive, rhythmic joint motion for walking [11]. In addition to these CPG's, there are a variety of lower-level circuits which act to modulate motor neuron activity and include muscle feedback. An example of one of these was introduced by Hultborn et al. [5]. We have created a model which we call the Canonical Motor Microcircuit (CMM), which loosely resembles the Hultborn circuit but does not include gamma motoneurons for the sake of

This work was supported by NSF DBI 2015317 as part of the NSF/CIHR/DFG/ FRQ/UKRI-MRC Next Generation Networks for Neuroscience Program.

© The Author(s), under exclusive license to Springer Nature Switzerland AG 2022
A. Hunt et al. (Eds.): Living Machines 2022, LNAI 13548, pp. 309–320, 2022.
https://doi.org/10.1007/978-3-031-20470-8_31

simplicity [5]. The CMM is present in numerous models for mammalian locomotion but is typically driven by a CPG [8,12,16]. The current model of the CMM is meant to be a starting point, additional pathways will be added as the model expands. While the exact role of the CMM is unknown, it is replicated along the spinal cord and is thought to play a role in muscle control during locomotion. This circuit contains three types of neurons: alpha motor neurons, Ia inhibitory neurons, and Renshaw Cells and relies strongly on Ia feedback from the muscle spindles.

A study was conducted to examine the activity of a CMM in cats during fictive locomotion, showing that each of these three types of neurons are active during locomotion [14]. In addition, this study showed that the activity and timing of the Ia inhibitory neurons and Renshaw cells is directly tied to the alpha motor neurons. Although experiments such as these have been done to examine the CMM in animals, the function of this circuit, specifically the Renshaw cells, remains unclear. Due to the topology of the circuit, it can be seen that the Renshaw cells act to suppress excessive output from the motor neurons. Other theories include that the recurrent circuitry of the Renshaw cells acts as a variable gain regulator for the motor neurons [5]. However, the existence of some of these synaptic connections is controversial in itself.

2 Methods

2.1 Modeling

In order to examine the functionality of the CMM as well as the Renshaw cells and their connectivity, we created a model of a rat hindlimb and tuned a CMM to control a pair of flexor-extensor muscles for the hip joint. The hip joint was chosen as a starting point for this work, as the knee and ankle positions during walking are dependent on the position of the hip. Figure 1 shows a simplified model of a rat hindlimb created in Animatlab, which was adapted from Deng et al. [3,4]. The biomechanical model was simplified to only the pelvis, femurs, shins, feet and flexor-extensor muscle pairs modeled with a linear-Hill muscle model. Other models exist in the full musculoskeletal complexity of the rat hindlimb, this is a reduced biomechanical model used to evaluate the CMM [2,17]. For these experiments, the pelvis was fixed in place and the model performed air stepping.

The joint and muscle placement was modeled using data on rat hindlimbs [4, 7,10]. Figure 2 shows the CMM created in Animatlab which controls the muscles for one of the hip joints of the biomechanical model. The model shown in Fig. 2 was constructed using non-spiking leaky-integrator neural models:

$$C\frac{dV}{dt} = I_{app} - I_{leak} + \sum_{i=1}^{n} I_{syn_i} \tag{1}$$

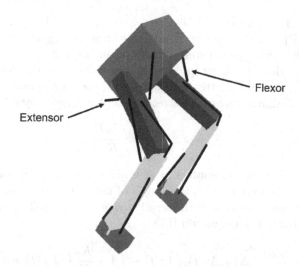

Fig. 1. Animatlab Biomechanical Model. Red: pelvis. Blue: femurs. Yellow: Shins. Pink: Feet. Black: Flexor and Extensor muscles. The flexor muscle pulls the leg forward while the extensor muscle pulls the leg backward. (Color figure online)

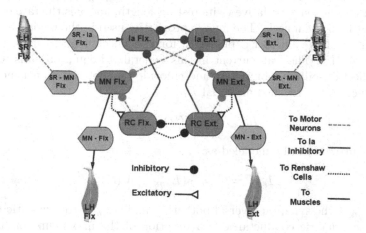

Fig. 2. CMM Neural Model in Animatlab. Ia: Ia inhibitory neuron. MN: alpha motor neuron. RC: Renshaw cell. LH: Left Hip. SR: stretch receptors for Ia type feedback. Grey Blocks: first order polynomial gains. (Color figure online)

where C is the membrane capacitance, V is the membrane voltage, I_{app} is an external applied current, I_{leak} is the membrane leak current, and I_{syn} are the synaptic currents. The inputs from the muscle stretch receptors were modeled as applied currents amplified by their respective gains, as implemented in Animatlab [3]:

$$I_{app_i} = S_i m_i + b_i \qquad (2)$$

where S_i is the discharge rate of the stretch receptor, and m_i and b_i are slope and intercept of polynomial curve which amplifies the signal. Note that based on the values for these parameters as shown in Table 2, the neurons receive tonic input from the stretch receptors. The tonic input a function of both the resting discharge rate of the stretch receptor and the corresponding parameters in Table 2. The discharge rate of the stretch receptor is given by the equation [3]:

$$S_i = a(x - x_1) = \frac{aT}{K_{SE}} \tag{3}$$

where a is the active tension applied by stimulation of the membrane potential, x is the length of the muscle, x_1 is the length of the serial spring in the muscle, T is the muscle tension, and K_{SE} is the serial spring constants. The muscle tension is given by the differential equation [15]:

$$\dot{T} = \frac{K_{SE}}{b}\left(K_{PE}\Delta x(t) + b\dot{x}(t) - \left(1 + \frac{K_{PE}}{K_{SE}}\right)T(t) + a \right) \tag{4}$$

where K_{SE} is the stiffness of the serial elastic component, K_{PE} is the stiffness of the parallel elastic component, b is the linear damping coefficient, Δx is the change in muscle length relative to its resting length, and $\dot{x}$ is the rate of change of the length off the muscle. The muscle properties used in the model were taken from Hunt et al. [7]. Further explanation for the muscle model can be found in Rubeo et al. [15]. The leak current in this generalized equation aims to model the net effect of sodium, potassium, and chloride channels with a net membrane conductance G and reversal potential E_R:

$$I_{leak} = G \cdot (V(t) - E_R). \tag{5}$$

Synaptic currents can be modeled as:

$$I_{syn_i} = G_{syn_i} \cdot (E_{syn_i} - V(t)) \tag{6}$$

where E_{syn} is the synaptic reversal potential, and G_{syn} is the synaptic conductance. The synaptic conductance is a function of the maximum conductance, g_{max_i}, the membrane potential of the pre-synaptic neuron, V_{pre}, and saturation and threshold parameters, E_{hi_i} and E_{lo_i}, which are properties of the pre-synaptic neuron:

$$G_{syn_i} = g_{max_i} \cdot \min\left(\max\left(\frac{V_{pre} - E_{lo_i}}{E_{hi_i} - E_{lo_i}}, 0 \right), 1 \right). \tag{7}$$

The advantage of using the non-spiking leaky-integrator model is that each neuron models the average activity of a population of spiking neurons [19]. These generalized equations were applied to each of the neurons in the CMM. For example, the equation for the motor neuron controlling the flexor muscle included a leak current term, an applied current modeling the input from the stretch receptor, and two synaptic current terms. This can be visualized by looking at the gold dashed lines attached to the flexor motor neuron in Fig. 2.

2.2   Tuning

The goal was to tune the parameters in the CMM such that the simulated hip angle resembles that of a rat walking. We used rat walking data to compare the outputs of the Animatlab simulation. This data for the hip trajectory of a rat walking on a treadmill was collected as described in Alessandro et al. and is not the focus of this work [1]. We predicted that the CMM network could be tuned to generate muscle activity for the hip joint of the rat hindlimb biomechanical model such that the angle of the hip joint in the simulation approximates that of a rat walking. We were confident in our ability to do so because of the abundance of inhibition in the network, which loosely resembles an oscillator. After successfully tuning the model, we then evaluated the relative strengths of the synaptic conductance's, specifically, the reciprocal inhibition between Renshaw cells.

We used two methods to tune the CMM. The first was done in a qualitative manner and aimed to produce oscillations in the network. The second method was a more quantitative approach, evaluating the oscillations in terms of a cost function comparing the simulated data to the animal data. There are a total of 72 parameters to tune in this network. These include synaptic properties, neural properties, and gain factors to and from muscles. We reduced the number of parameters by applying symmetry to the model. For example, on both the flexor and extensor side of the CMM there is a synapse going from the motor neuron to the Renshaw cell. Under this assumption, these synapses have the same reversal potential, saturation voltage, and threshold voltage, but may differ in terms of maximum synaptic conductance. Resting potentials for the motor neurons, Ia inhibitory neurons, and Renshaw cells were set to -62 mV, -60 mV, and -50.5 mV, respectively [9,13,20]. Lastly, in the experiments done on cats during fictive locomotion, it was found that Ia neurons were most active in phase with the motor neurons, while the Renshaw cells became excited after motor neurons and were maximally excited in the latter phases of motor neuron excitement [14]. While this may not provide a quantifiable value for any of the neural parameters, it does indicate that the time constants for the motor neurons and Ia inhibitory neurons are similar while the Renshaw cells have a significantly larger time constant. Time constants for the model neurons are functions of the membrane capacitance and conductance: $\tau = C/G$. Based on the modeling in Animatlab, we give each neuron a conductance of one microsiemen and membrane capacitance's of 5, 30, and 130 nanofarads milliseconds for the motor neurons, Ia inhibitory neurons, and Renshaw cells, respectively [3]. After applying these assumptions and incorporating biological data, the number of parameters to be tuned was decreased from 72 to 37.

In order to properly evaluate the simulation as it compares to the animal data, we first needed to find a set of parameters which induces oscillations in the hip joint. As previously stated, this was done in a qualitative sense which primarily consisted of evaluating the outputs of the motor neurons for a give simulation. For example, Fig. 3 shows the results of a simulation whose parameter set does not result in oscillation of the hip joint. In the motor neuron plots in fig.

3 there is an initial phase of oscillatory behavior, however, this quickly dies out as the flexor motor neuron is not able to escape and overcome the extensor motor neuron. Based on these results the strengths of the synapses were adjusted to decrease the inhibition to the flexor motor neuron. This was done by decreasing the maximum synaptic conductance for the synapse coming from the extensor Ia inhibitory neuron to the flexor motor neuron.

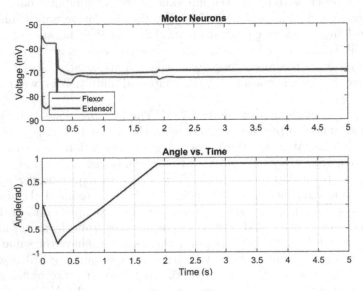

Fig. 3. Simulation results for a system with no oscillations. Top: Motor Neuron activity. Bottom: Hip joint activity.

Once a set of parameters was found which produced oscillatory behavior of the hip joint for the biomechanical model of the rat hindlimb, the tuning method switched to a quantitative analysis of the trajectory of the hip joint. This analysis was done by comparing the simulated hip joint vs. time to animal data. Note that the animal data is for the average hip trajectory of the rats during experiments, and may vary from step to step and animal to animal. The comparison was done in attempt to minimize a cost function, which was the sum of three equally weighted factors: the root means square error for a single stride, the frequency error, and the error in the swing/stance ratio. In the hip angle vs. time plots shown in Fig. 4, the stance and swing phases can be differentiated by the direction of motion. The stance phase corresponds to an increasing angle while the swing phase occurs while the angle is decreasing. The frequency and swing/stance ratio errors were taken in the form of percent error:

$$\%Error = \left| \frac{v_A - v_E}{v_E} \right| \tag{8}$$

where v_A is the observed value, in this case the simulated value, and v_E is the expected value, the value from the animal data. The values used for the simulated data were the averages over multiple gait cycles. Although this method was designed to provide a quantitative approach to the tuning of the CMM, the decisions on which parameters to change and how was largely based on knowledge gained during the tuning process.

3   Results

The CMM was successfully tuned such that the trajectory of the simulated hip joint matched the animal data. The oscillatory behavior is driven by the interplay between the fast Ia feedback from the muscles and the slow time constant of the Renshaw cells. Figure 4 shows the angle vs. time plots for the simulation and animal data for both a single and multiple gait cycles. The results from the simulation including neuron potentials and stretch receptor discharge rates can be found in Fig. 5. Note that the plot of the hip angle in Figs. 4 and 5 are the same data. Due to constraints in Animatlab, the joint angle begins at zero, Fig. 4 shows only the time period of oscillations, removing the initial descent into oscillatory behavior. The time axis was also shifted to remove this introductory period.

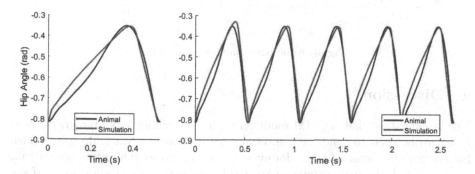

Fig. 4. Hip Angle vs. Time for simulated hindlimb and rat walking on a treadmill. Left: single gait cycle. Right: continuous oscillations. For the single gait cycle (left), transition from swing to stance occurs at 0.3582 s seconds for the animal data and 0.3807 s seconds for the simulated data.

The synaptic parameters in the simulation above can be found in Table 1. Notice that the strength of the synapse going from the extensor to the flexor Renshaw cell is zero. This indicates that, for this set of parameters, this synapse does not exist. Therefore, there is no reciprocal inhibition between the Renshaw cells. In addition to these synaptic parameters, the strength of the feedback from the stretch receptors had a significant impact on the behavior of the model. As shown in Eq. 2, this Ia type feedback is modeled as an applied current, Table 2 shows the values used to model this current. Table 2 also shows the amplification of the motor neuron output to the muscles.

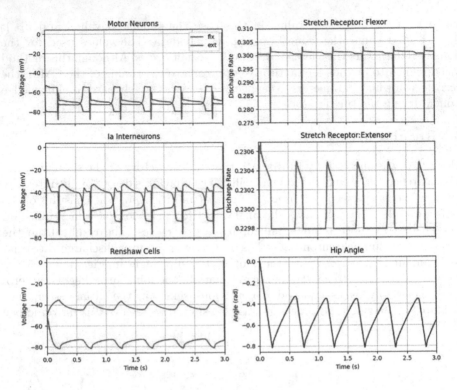

Fig. 5. Animatlab simulation outputs.

4   Discussion

The results show that a CMM modeled with non-spiking leaky-integrator neurons can be used to generate the oscillatory motion of a rat's hip joint which largely matches animal data. However, there is a noticeable difference in that the simulated hip angle rotates at relatively constant velocities for much of the stance and swing phases with a transition period between. Whereas the animal data shows a change in angular velocity throughout the stance and swing phases, as shown in Fig. 4. This is likely due to the simplified models of both the biomechanics and neural circuit in the simulation. For the given model, the hip joint is actuated by only two muscles forming an agonist-antagonist pair. In reality, the motion of a rat's hip joint is caused by the contraction of several muscles working together to cause a moment about the hip joint. The simplification to a single muscle lifting the leg vastly simplifies the forces acting on the joint. Additionally, each of the muscles in a rat may be activated by separate pools of motor neurons. The variation of motor neuron activity acting on different muscles would likely lead to a system with dynamics that more closely match the animal data. Although it is reasonable to assume that a more biologically accurate model would be able to fully capture the dynamics of the hip joint during locomotion, it is not a necessary step to evaluate the CMM. We also see that the error in the hip trajectory is larger in the stance phase than in the swing phase. This is likely due to the simulation being done with an air stepping model and lacks the external forces from the treadmill acting on the body. The simplified models were able to replicate the trajectory of a rat's hip joint during locomotion well with understandable discrepancies.

Table 1. Hand Tuned Synaptic parameters.

Synapse (from - to)	g_{max} (μS)	E_{syn} (mV)	E_{hi} (mV)	E_{lo} (mV)
Ia flx. – Ia ext.	2.5	-99.7	-40	-62
Ia ext. – Ia flx.	2.198	-99.7	-40	-62
Ia flx. – MN ext.	1.076	-100	-40	-62
Ia ext. – MN flx.	1.0	-100	-40	-62
MN flx. – RC flx.	0.6	0	-54.35	-78
MN ext. – RC ext.	0.5	0	-54.35	-78
RC ext. – Ia ext.	5.0	-70	-40	-60
RC flx. – Ia flx.	4.2	-70	-40	-60
RC ext. – MN ext.	0.55	-70	-40	-60
RC flx. – MN flx.	0.45	-70	-40	-60
RC flx. – RC ext.	1.8	-100	-40	-60
RC ext. – RC flx.	0.0	-100	-40	-60

Relatively little work has been done to provide quantifiable values for the strength of the synapses in the CMM circuit. It had been predicted that the strength of inhibition acting on the motor neurons from the Renshaw cells was much less than the inhibition of the Ia neurons by the Renshaw cells. The resulting parameters shown in Table 1 support this claim as the strength of these synapses, represented by g_{max}, differ by an order of magnitude. Table 1 also shows that there is no mutual inhibition between Renshaw cells in this system. Therefore, the issue of the Renshaw cells as a point of gain control is unclear at present because the Renshaw cells have modest effects, but strong actions on the motor neurons [5]. This would indicate that the primary function of the Renshaw cells in this CMM model is to regulate the potential of the corresponding motor neurons.

Table 2. Hand Tuned Gain parameters (as used in Eq. 2). SR: Stretch Receptor. MN: Motor Neuron

Connection	Slope (m)	y-intercept (b)
SR – Ia Flx	10.032 μ	-2.864 μ
SR – Ia Ext	10.04 μ	-2.234 μ
SR – MN Flx	2.04 μ	-0.599 μ
SR – MN Ext	1.002 μ	-0.227 μ
MN – Flx Muscle	0.965	0
MN – Ext Muscle	1.026	0

While this is true for the set of parameters found in Table 1, this set of parameters is by no means the only set that would produce similar results. Therefore, it would be difficult to make any conclusions on the functionality of Renshaw cells with much certainty. It is reasonable to assume that there is a larger family of possible solutions for the various parameters in the model. The method of hand-tuning parameters failed to find these other solution sets. Ongoing work is being conducted to implement a Bayesian/Monte Carlo/Markov Chain approach that will automate the parameter search of the network [18]. Ideally this approach would search a larger space than was done through hand-tuning the network and would provide sets of parameters which produce similar results to those shown in Fig. 4 as opposed to the single set found while hand tuning. We could then compare the strength of the mutual inhibition between Renshaw cells for multiple sets of parameters to create a clearer image of their impact on motor output.

While the simulation has shown that a CMM is able to produce the rhythmic, oscillatory motion required for locomotion, it is likely that this circuit receives input from a central pattern generator [8,12,14,16]. However, this work aimed to evaluate the oscillatory properties of the isolated CMM. In future works, the CMM network will be evaluated with the addition of a CPG as an input to both the motor neurons and Ia inhibitory neurons. We can then compare the results of the CPG-fed CMM control strategy to previous works such as a two-layer CPG and muscle synergy and the functional subnetwork approach to neural controllers [4,6]. In this way we can evaluate various neural control strategies for robotics. Perhaps the more interesting implications of this research is the insight gained on the neural system. Through simulations such as this we can test theories in neuroscience and evaluate the purpose of specific neurons and synapses. This will ultimately lead to a better understanding of the neural circuitry responsible for locomotion in humans and animals alike and may inform medical efforts to restore motor function after spinal cord injuries.

References

1. Alessandro, C., Rellinger, B.A., Barroso, F.O., Tresch, M.C.: Adaptation after vastus lateralis denervation in rats demonstrates neural regulation of joint stresses and strains. eLife **7**, e38215 (2018). https://doi.org/10.7554/eLife.38215
2. Charles, J.P., Cappellari, O., Spence, A.J., Wells, D.J., Hutchinson, J.R.: Muscle moment arms and sensitivity analysis of a mouse hindlimb musculoskeletal model. J. Anat. **229**(4), 514–535 (2016). https://doi.org/10.1111/joa.12461
3. Cofer, D., Cymbalyuk, G., Reid, J., Zhu, Y., Heitler, W.J., Edwards, D.H.: AnimatLab: a 3D graphics environment for neuromechanical simulations. J. Neurosci. Methods **187**(2), 280–288 (2010). https://doi.org/10.1016/j.jneumeth.2010.01.005
4. Deng, K., et al.: Neuromechanical model of rat hindlimb walking with two-layer CPGs. Biomimetics **4**(1), 21 (2019). https://doi.org/10.3390/biomimetics4010021
5. Hultborn, H., Lindström, S., Wigström, H.: On the function of recurrent inhibition in the spinal cord. Exp. Brain Res. **37**(2), 399–403 (1979). https://doi.org/10.1007/BF00237722
6. Hunt, A., Szczecinski, N., Quinn, R.: Development and training of a neural controller for hind leg walking in a dog robot. Front. Neurorobot. **11**, 18 (2017). https://doi.org/10.3389/fnbot.2017.00018
7. Hunt, A.J., Szczecinski, N.S., Andrada, E., Fischer, M., Quinn, R.D.: Using animal data and neural dynamics to reverse engineer a neuromechanical Rat model. In: Wilson, S.P., Verschure, P.F.M.J., Mura, A., Prescott, T.J. (eds.) LIVINGMACHINES 2015. LNCS (LNAI), vol. 9222, pp. 211–222. Springer, Cham (2015). https://doi.org/10.1007/978-3-319-22979-9_21
8. Ivashko, D., Prilutsky, B., Markin, S., Chapin, J., Rybak, I.: Modeling the spinal cord neural circuitry controlling cat hindlimb movement during locomotion. Neurocomputing **52–54**, 621–629 (2003). https://doi.org/10.1016/S0925-2312(02)00832-9
9. Jiang, M., Heckman, C.: In vitro sacral cord preparation and motoneuron recording from adult mice. J. Neurosci. Methods **156**(1–2), 31–36 (2006). https://doi.org/10.1016/j.jneumeth.2006.02.002
10. Johnson, W.L., Jindrich, D.L., Roy, R.R., Reggie Edgerton, V.: A three-dimensional model of the rat hindlimb: musculoskeletal geometry and muscle moment arms. J. Biomech. **41**(3), 610–619 (2008). https://doi.org/10.1016/j.jbiomech.2007.10.004
11. MacKay-Lyons, M.: Central pattern generation of locomotion: a review of the evidence. Phys. Ther. **82**(1), 69–83 (2002). https://doi.org/10.1093/ptj/82.1.69
12. McCrea, D.A., Rybak, I.A.: Organization of mammalian locomotor rhythm and pattern generation. Brain Res. Rev. **57**(1), 134–146 (2008). https://doi.org/10.1016/j.brainresrev.2007.08.006
13. Perry, S., et al.: Firing properties of Renshaw cells defined by Chrna2 are modulated by hyperpolarizing and small conductance ion currents I $_{handI_{sk}}$. Eur. J. Neurosci. **41**(7), 889–900 (2015). https://doi.org/10.1111/ejn.12852
14. Pratt, C.A., Jordan, L.M.: IA inhibitory interneurons and Renshaw cells as contributors to the spinal mechanisms of fictive locomotion. J. Neurophysiol. **57**(1), 56–71 (1987). https://doi.org/10.1152/jn.1987.57.1.56
15. Rubeo, S., Szczecinski, N., Quinn, R.: A synthetic nervous system controls a simulated cockroach. Appl. Sci. **8**(1), 6 (2017). https://doi.org/10.3390/app8010006

16. Rybak, I.A., Stecina, K., Shevtsova, N.A., McCrea, D.A.: Modelling spinal circuitry involved in locomotor pattern generation: insights from the effects of afferent stimulation: modelling afferent control of locomotor pattern generation. J. Physiol. **577**(2), 641–658 (2006). https://doi.org/10.1113/jphysiol.2006.118711

17. Ramalingasetty, S.T., et al.: A whole-body musculoskeletal model of the mouse. IEEE Access **9**, 163861–163881 (2021). https://doi.org/10.1109/ACCESS.2021.3133078

18. Wang, Y.C., et al.: Algorithmic parameter estimation and uncertainty quantification for Hodgkin-Huxley neuron models. preprint, Neuroscience (2021). https://doi.org/10.1101/2021.11.18.469189

19. Wilson, H.R., Cowan, J.D.: Excitatory and inhibitory interactions in localized populations of model neurons. Biophys. J. **12**(1), 1–24 (1972). https://doi.org/10.1016/S0006-3495(72)86068-5

20. Wilson, J.M., Blagovechtchenski, E., Brownstone, R.M.: Genetically defined inhibitory neurons in the mouse spinal cord dorsal horn: a possible source of rhythmic inhibition of motoneurons during fictive locomotion. J. Neurosci. **30**(3), 1137–1148 (2010). https://doi.org/10.1523/JNEUROSCI.1401-09.2010

Direct Assembly and Tuning of Dynamical Neural Networks for Kinematics

Chloe K. Guie$^{(\boxtimes)}$ and Nicholas S. Szczecinski(iD)

Department of Mechanical and Aerospace Engineering, West Virginia University, Morgantown, WV 26505, USA
ckg00003@mix.wvu.edu

Abstract. It is unknown precisely how the nervous system of invertebrates combines multiple sensory inputs to calculate more abstract quantities, e.g., combining the angle of multiple leg joints to calculate the position of the foot relative to the body. In this paper, we suggest that non-spiking interneurons (NSIs) in the nervous system could calculate such quantities and construct a neuromechanical model to support the claim. Range fractionated sensory inputs are modeled as multiple integrate-and-fire neurons. The NSI is modeled as a multi-compartment dendritic tree and one large somatic compartment. Each dendritic compartment receives synaptic input from one sensory neuron from the knee and one from the hip. Every dendritic compartment connects to the soma. The model is constructed within the Animatlab 2 software. The neural representation of the system accurately follows the true position of the foot. We also discuss motivation for future research, which includes modeling other hypothetical networks in the insect nervous system and integrating this model into task-level robot control.

Keywords: Non-spiking interneuron · Leaky integrator · Compartmental model · Synthetic nervous system · Functional subnetwork approach · Legged locomotion

1 Introduction

Sensory feedback is critical for the control of legged locomotion in vertebrates and arthropods alike [1]. One hypothesis for how higher-order quantities such as body posture is controlled by the action of many smaller units such as individual joints and muscles is 'task-level control', in which the nervous system presumably issues motor commands at the task level (e.g., a desired foot position in space) and must calculate task-level feedback for comparison [2]. Many mechanical states that would be valuable to control, e.g., the position of the foot in space, cannot be measured directly by the nervous system, and therefore must be calculated by the nervous system using local measurements (e.g., joint angles). However, it is not known how such calculations are performed.

In insects, we hypothesize that local non-spiking interneurons (NSIs) in the thoracic ganglia (ventral nerve cord) may facilitate the calculation of task-level quantities for motor control. Measurements such as joint angles are represented by the activity of many

© The Author(s), under exclusive license to Springer Nature Switzerland AG 2022
A. Hunt et al. (Eds.): Living Machines 2022, LNAI 13548, pp. 321–331, 2022.
https://doi.org/10.1007/978-3-031-20470-8_32

distributed sensory neurons, each of which is sensitive to a small range of joint motion, an organizational principle called "range fractionation" [3]. Range fractionation consists of sensory neurons measuring the same state (e.g., joint angle), each with varying firing thresholds for different stimuli intensities. In insects such as the stick insect and locust, these range fractionated afferent neurons synapse onto NSIs, which integrate sensory input from joint angle sensors such as the chordotonal organ (CO) and segment strain sensors such as campaniform sensilla (CS) from across the leg, then synapse onto the motor neurons to contribute to control of the leg [4]. Although it is unclear what task-level calculations each NSI encodes, each appears to act as an information "hourglass" in which information from many range-fractionated sensory neurons converges onto the NSI, then diverges due to NSI synapses onto multiple motor neurons throughout the leg. In this study, we use a neuromechanical model to demonstrate that the NSIs could calculate task-level quantities directly from range-fractionated sensory inputs.

The model we propose could also be used to calculate task-level quantities for robot control. In robotics, task-level quantities may be calculated by the direct application of forward kinematics equations, e.g., through the product of exponentials formulation [5]. More recently, Deep Neural Networks (DNNs) have been trained to compute complicated nonlinear forward kinematics equations [6, 7]. Although this approach has been successful, DNNs can be computationally expensive to tune, making them impractical for some applications. Furthermore, their dense connectivity may not model the structure of the peripheral nervous system, which is exquisitely structured; because we are interested in modeling the nervous system, we seek a system with more direct biological inspiration. These challenges inspire the assembly and tuning of dynamical networks that can mimic the structure and function of the nervous system to perform kinematic calculations.

The goal of this research is to better understand how insects compute task-level quantities by integrating range-fractionated sensory signals. To accomplish this goal, we constructed a biologically plausible model in which spiking afferents from two joints in a leg are integrated by one nonspiking neuron, modeled with many dendritic compartments and one somatic compartment. The voltage of the somatic compartment encodes the x-coordinate of the foot's position relative to the body. Conductances between the compartments are tuned using the Functional Subnetwork Approach (FSA) [8], which has been used in the past to construct and tune rate-coded networks. The current study is the first application of the FSA to construct and tune place-coded networks. Finally, we discuss future opportunities for applying this network structure to model the nervous system or as part of a robot control system.

2 Methods

2.1 Neuron Model

The neuron model was designed using our Synthetic Nervous System (SNS) philosophy. An SNS model is meant to capture as many biological details as possible while running as quickly as possible to facilitate implementation as a robot control system. Thus, the NSI model was constructed from leaky integrator compartments [8]. Spiking neurons were implemented as generalized leaky integrate-and-fire neurons with conductance-based synapses [9]. Simulation was performed through the neuromechanical simulator AnimatLab 2 [10].

The non-spiking interneuron (NSI) was modeled as 25 low-capacity dendrite compartments that connect to 1 high-capacity soma compartment. Each of the 25 compartments is modeled as a leaky integrator with the dynamics

$$C_{mem} \cdot \dot{U} = -G_{mem} \cdot U + \sum_{i=1}^{n} G_{syn}^i \cdot \left(E_{syn}^i - U\right) + I_{app}, \tag{1}$$

where U is the compartment's voltage, G_{mem} is the leak conductance of the cell membrane (we set $G_{mem} = 1\mu S$ in every case), C_{mem} is the membrane capacitance of that compartment, I_{app} is an optional applied current, n is the number of incoming synapses to that compartment, G_{syn}^i is the instantaneous conductance of the ith incoming synapse, and E_{syn}^i is the reversal potential of the ith incoming synapse relative to the compartment's rest potential. When all incoming synapses have a conductance of 0, the neuron has the time constant $\tau_{mem} = C_{mem}/G_{mem}$; because $G_{mem} = 1\mu S$ in every case, τ_{mem} is directly proportional to C_{mem}.

To simulate the conductance of current from the dendrite to the soma, the compartments were connected by graded-potential synapses, such that

$$G_{syn} = G_{max} \cdot \min(\max(U/R, 0), 1), \tag{2}$$

where G_{max} represents the maximal inter-compartment coupling and R is a constant voltage that represents the expected fluctuation of one compartment's voltage [8].

The joint angle-encoding afferent neurons were modeled as generalized leaky integrate-and-fire neurons. The voltage of each neuron follows the same dynamics as the nonspiking compartments, but with the additional consideration that when the membrane voltage U surpasses the spiking threshold θ, a spike occurs and U is set to 0 in the following time step.

Spiking synapses were modeled as first-order different equations, with the conductance following the dynamics

$$\tau_{syn} \cdot \dot{G}_{syn} = -G_{syn}, \tag{3}$$

where τ_{syn} is the decay time constant. When the presynaptic neuron spikes, G_{syn} is set to its maximum value, G_{max}.

2.2 Sensory Model

To demonstrate that the NSIs may compute task-level states of the leg despite being only one or two synaptic connections from the sensory neurons themselves, we constructed a simple kinematic model of a two-jointed planar leg based on the stick insect (Fig. 1A). This leg has a hip joint, which is connected to the origin of the coordinate system, and a knee, which connects the femur and tibia segments. Each segment is 10 cm long. Each joint is limited to rotate between 0.75 rad (43°) and -0.75 rad (-43°). At the distal end of the tibia is the foot, whose position is designated by the point $P = \left(P_x, P_y\right)$.

We wished for our test network to encode the x coordinate of the foot's position, P_x, in the voltage of the NSI soma (Fig. 1B). We assumed that each joint angle is represented in a range-fractionated manner by five sensory neurons, although single joint sensing organs may possess hundreds of sensory neurons [11]. Each neuron receives an applied current based on the instantaneous joint angle θ,

$$I_{app}(\theta) = R \cdot \exp\left(-c \cdot (\theta - b)^2\right), \tag{4}$$

where R is the amplitude, b is the mean value, and c controls the width of the Gaussian bell curve. In our model, R = 20 nA. In our model, each hip sensory neuron had a unique value of b, equally spaced between the minimum (-0.75 rad [-43°]) and maximum (0.75 rad [43°]) angles of the joint (see diagrams in Fig. 1B). The knee sensory neurons were configured in the same way. Finally, parameter c was varied logarithmically between values of 7.5 and 60 to test its effect on the network's encoding accuracy.

Each sensory neuron was designed such that its spiking frequency was proportional to the Gaussian applied current I_{app} using the methods in [9]. In short, given a maximum input current of 20 nA and a desired maximum spiking frequency of 100 Hz, the parameter values in Eq. 1 could be determined. In our model, $C_{mem} = 200$ nF, $G_{mem} = 1 \mu S$ (resulting in a time constant of 200 ms), $\theta = 1$ mV, and each neuron receives a tonic applied current of 0.5 nA in addition to I_{app} from Eq. 4.

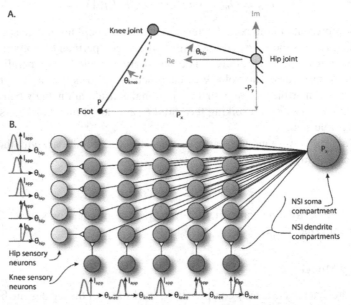

Fig. 1. (A) Schematic of a planar leg with a hip joint and a knee. The angle of rotation to the global real axis is defined by θ_{hip} or θ_{knee}. (B) Schematic of the sensory neurons from hip, the yellow circles, and knee, the green circles. One of each the hip and knee sensory neurons excites the NSI dendrite compartments in its row or column, respectively. Every NSI dendrite compartment, the smaller blue circles, then connects to the NSI soma compartment, the large blue circle, creating a unique conductance value that represents the diameter of each of the bell curves.

The network was structured such that each NSI dendrite compartment received excitatory synaptic input from exactly one hip sensory neuron and exactly one knee sensory neuron, reflected in the grid structure of Fig. 1B. Each dendrite compartment then made a connection to the soma with a unique conductance value. These varying conductance values represent the varying diameter of the dendritic structure of the NSI.

2.3 Tuning Parameters Within the Model

To tune the network parameter values, we first needed to calculate the ground-truth position to be encoded, P_x, the x coordinate of the foot's position. Because the leg model is planar, we can represent the position of the foot relative to the origin using complex number vector notation. Each vector is represented as a complex number, with the real component indicating the x coordinate and the imaginary component indicating the y coordinate. Rotations are performed by multiplying by $\exp(j\theta)$, in which $j = \sqrt{-1}$ and θ is the angle of rotation relative to the global real axis. Using this notation and the angles as defined in Fig. 1A,

$$P_x = \text{Re}\left(L \cdot \exp(j\theta_{hip}) + L \cdot \exp\left(j \cdot \left(\theta_{hip} + \theta_{knee} - \frac{\pi}{2}\right)\right)\right), \tag{5}$$

where Re is the real component of the result, L is the length of the femur and the tibia, θ_{hip} is the angle between the ground and the femur, and θ_{knee} is the angle between the femur and knee, with a $\pi/2$ radian offset. Plotting P_x versus θ_{hip} and θ_{knee} produces a surface of the foot position's dependence on the locally-measured joint angles that the network encodes (Fig. 2).

The lateral foot position P_x was mapped to the conductance values from each dendrite compartment to the soma. In this way, the soma voltage was driven to a value that reflected P_x simply due to the structure and tuning of the conductance values. Specifically, we applied the Functional Subnetwork Approach [8] by mapping the value of P_x for each pair of θ_{hip} and θ_{knee} values to the gain k of the conductance from the dendrite compartment to the soma compartment:

$$k = \frac{P_x - \min(P_x)}{\max(P_x) - \min(P_x)}. \tag{6}$$

Then, the corresponding conductance g could be calculated using R = 20 mV, the maximum expected membrane voltage above rest, and E = 70 mV, the reversal potential above the resting membrane potential,

$$g = \frac{k \cdot R}{E - k \cdot R}. \tag{7}$$

The resulting conductance value from each dendrite to the soma is plotted in Fig. 2. This conductance value surface is reminiscent of the lateral foot position surface but is ultimately different due to the difference in units and the nonlinear nature of Eq. 7.

To compare the membrane voltage of the soma to the actual foot position, we calculated the expected neural encoding of P_x as

$$U_{exp} = k \cdot R, \tag{8}$$

where k is defined in Eq. 6 and R = 20 mV.

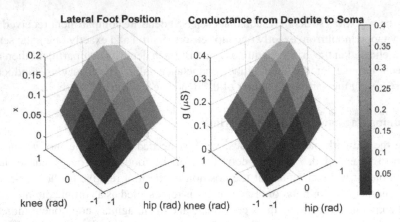

Fig. 2. From left to right respectively, a surface plot of the lateral foot position versus the knee and hip joint angles and a surface plot of the conductance from the dendrite to the soma versus the knee and hip joint angles.

3 Results

To test how well our model NSI could encode foot position, the hip and knee angles were cycled at different frequencies to sample many different combinations of angle

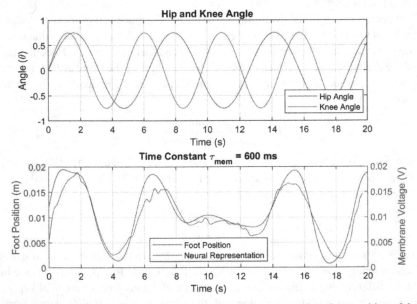

Fig. 3. Top, a plot of the hip and knee angles versus time. Bottom, a plot of the position of the foot and the neural representation versus time with the Gaussian function width $c = 15$ and the time constant $\tau_{mem} = 600$. Note that the neural representation has been advanced in time as calculated by cross-correlation between the curves.

values. Figure 3 compares the encoded foot position (U_{exp} in Eq. 8) and the neural representation of the foot position versus time during such a test. This plot shows that the neural representation tracks the position of the foot. The system works reasonably accurately with the Gaussian function width c = 15 for the sensory neurons and the soma's time constant τ_{mem} = 600ms (i.e., C_{mem} = 600 nF).

We sought to understand how the parameters within this network affect the accuracy and time lag of the neural representation of the foot position relative to the expected value. Altering the width c in the Gaussian function from Eq. 4 affected the offset of the soma's membrane voltage. Figure 4 shows that if each sensory neuron's response curve is too narrow, e.g., the width c = 30 in each Gaussian function, the soma's voltage level is lower than expected. This occurs because there are "dead zones" in which no sensory neurons are spiking as the joints rotate, and the dendrite and soma compartments leak their current. In contrast, Fig. 5 shows that if each sensory neuron's response curve is too wide, e.g., the width c = 7.5 in each Gaussian function, the soma's voltage level is higher than expected. This occurs because several sensory neurons are active at once, exciting many dendrite compartments and consequently overexciting the soma.

Altering the time constant of the soma (proportional to C_{mem} from Eq. 1) decreased the soma's response magnitude and introduced lag in the neural representation of the foot position. Figure 6 shows a case where c = 15 and τ = 6000 ms. The fluctuations in the neural representation lag behind the true foot position by almost 2 s, which is likely too long to be useful for closed-loop leg control. This motivates finding the lowest possible value for τ that preserves accurate encoding of the foot position.

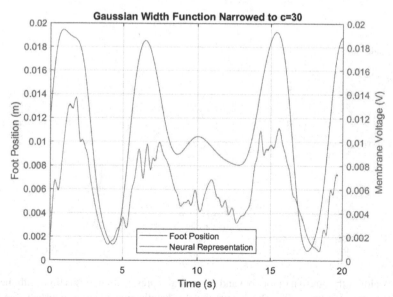

Fig. 4. A plot of the position of the foot and the neural representation versus time with the width 30 and the time constant 600 ms. This shows that by narrowing the width, the neural representation's amplitude decreases.

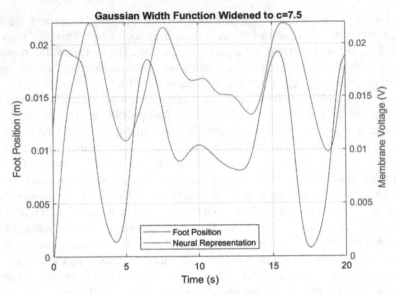

Fig. 5. A plot of the position of the foot and the neural representation versus time with the width 7.5 and the time constant 600 ms. This shows that by widening the width, the neural representation's amplitude decreases and its mean value is shifted upward.

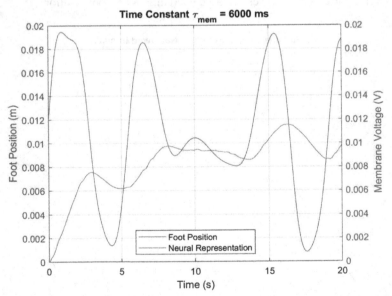

Fig. 6. A plot of the position of the foot and the neural representation versus time with the width 15 and the time constant 6000. This shows that by lengthening the time constant, the neural representation lags behind the foot position.

To better understand trends in the network performance as its parameter values change, we calculated the mean absolute error between the foot position and neural representation for multiple values of c, the width of the sensory encoding curve from Eq. 4. Figure 7 (A) plots mean absolute error between the expected and actual network activity throughout one trial *versus* the different widths, clearly demonstrating that for this leg motion, $c = 15$ minimizes the error of foot position encoding. We also calculated the lag of the neural representation relative to the foot position by finding the shift in time necessary to maximize the cross correlation between the signals. Figure 7 (B) plots the lag versus the time constant. The plot clearly shows that increasing the time constant increases the lag of the neural representation.

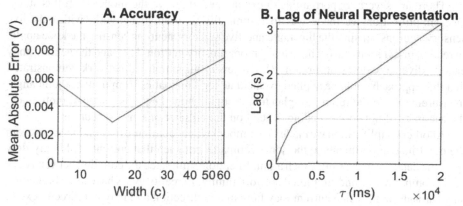

Fig. 7. A. A plot of the accuracy of the system. The system operates the most accurately when the width c = 15. When the width is changed in either direction, the system works less accurately. B. A plot of the lag of the system versus the time constant. This shows that the longer the time constant of the soma compartment, the longer the lag between the foot position and the soma's voltage. To decrease the lag, τ should be as small as possible.

4   Discussion

Although it is unknown, we discussed that higher-order quantities may be calculated by the nervous system through the use of many local measurements. We model how local NSIs of insects may calculate different quantities for motor control. In our model, range fractionated sensory inputs impinge onto multiple compartments that simulate the dendrite of the NSI. Each compartment is coupled to the soma with a different conductance value that reflects the mechanical quantity to be encoded (in this study, the x component of the foot's position in space). We modeled this using our Synthetic Nervous System philosophy to create and tune a dynamical network. For our system, we found parameter values for which the neuron's voltage encoded the position of the foot closely. We found that the performance of the network depended on the width of the sensory encoding curves (Eq. 4) and the time constant of the soma τ_{mem} (proportional to C_{mem} in Eq. 1).

We argue that models of nervous system processing of sensory information may be more accurate if they include range fractionated inputs. However, this is not commonly done. One study from Ache and Dürr demonstrated the power of range fractionated inputs by identifying and modeling descending interneurons (DINs) from the antennae to the thoracic networks of the stick insect *Carausius morosus* [12]. In their model, DINs integrated input from many range fractionated sensory neurons to calculate higher order "codings" of the antennae movement, e.g., their positions and velocities. Our study pursues a similar goal, to calculate the position of the foot from multiple range-fractionated measurements of several joints' angles. The diversity of DIN responses and the success of Ache and Dürr's model suggests that we can apply our method to calculate other features of leg motion, e.g., foot velocity, manipulator Jacobian of the leg.

There are several opportunities to expand and improve the model from this study. One simplification we made was to assume this is a small network, with only five sensory neurons sensing the hip angle and five sensory neurons sensing the knee angle. In reality, insect joint sensors have many more sensory neurons [11], and the neurons may encode diverse features of motion [3]. However, our simplified network demonstrated that this approach could be applied to calculate leg kinematics from multiple joint angle measurements. In the future, we plan to investigate how the joints' range of motion and the accuracy of network encoding depend on the number of sensory neurons.

Another simplification we made in our model was to configure the conductances from the dendrite compartments to the soma compartment such that current could only flow from the dendrite to the soma. Such a simplification eliminated the coupling between dendritic compartments and simplified network tuning. In reality, NSIs have large branching structures through which current may flow in any direction and may not directly excite the soma [13–15]. We have begun to apply the lessons learned from this study to construct more realistic NSI models, in which adjacent dendritic compartments are coupled and current can flow in any direction. We suspect that increasing the realism of our model will produce a computational unit whose function is highly resilient in the face of incomplete sensory feedback.

Another opportunity to expand this framework is to construct networks that calculate quantities other than forward kinematics for a simple leg model. To more broadly test the application of the Functional Subnetwork Approach to tuning models of this type (i.e., many-to-one mappings), we plan to build networks that calculate other quantities, such as the manipulator Jacobian, as noted above. Should this method prove broadly applicable, we plan to use it to construct transparent models of networks that incorporating the whole-limb and whole-body feedback for both leg-local control and ascending sensory signals to the brain.

Acknowledgements. This work was supported by NSF IIS 2113028 as part of the Collaborative Research in Computational Neuroscience Program. This work was also supported by NSF DBI 2015317 as part of the NSF/CIHR/DFG/FRQ/UKRI-MRC Next Generation Networks for Neuroscience Program.

References

1. Buschmann, T., Ewald, A., Twickel, A. von, Büschges, A.: Controlling legs for locomotion - Insights from robotics and neurobiology. Bioinspiration and Biomimetics. 10, (2015). https://doi.org/10.1088/1748-3190/10/4/041001
2. Safavynia, S.A., Ting, L.H.: Sensorimotor feedback based on task-relevant error robustly predicts temporal recruitment and multidirectional tuning of muscle synergies. J Neurophysiol. **109**, 31–45 (2013). https://doi.org/10.1152/jn.00684.2012.-We
3. Delcomyn, F., Nelson, M.E., Cocatre-Zilgien, J.H.: Sense organs of insect legs and the selection of sensors for agile walking robots. The International Journal of Robotics Research. **15**, 113–127 (1996). https://doi.org/10.1177/027836499601500201
4. Gebehart, C., Schmidt, J., Büschges, A.: Distributed processing of load and movement feedback in the premotor network controlling an insect leg joint. J Neurophysiol. **125**, 1800–1813 (2021). https://doi.org/10.1152/jn.00090.2021
5. Murray, R.M., Li, Z., Sastry, S.S.: A Mathematical Introduction to Robotic Manipulation. CRC Press (2017). https://doi.org/10.1201/9781315136370
6. Su, H., Qi, W., Yang, C., Aliverti, A., Ferrigno, G., de Momi, E.: Deep neural network approach in human-like redundancy optimization for anthropomorphic manipulators. IEEE Access. **7**, 124207–124216 (2019). https://doi.org/10.1109/ACCESS.2019.2937380
7. Sandbrink, K.J., Mamidanna, P., Michaelis, C., Mathis, M.W., Bethge, M., Mathis, A.: Task-driven hierarchical deep neural network models of the proprioceptive pathway. https://doi.org/10.1101/2020.05.06.081372
8. Szczecinski, N.S., Hunt, A.J., Quinn, R.D.: A functional subnetwork approach to designing synthetic nervous systems that control legged robot locomotion. Frontiers in Neurorobotics. 11 (2017). https://doi.org/10.3389/fnbot.2017.00037
9. Szczecinski, N.S., Quinn, R.D., Hunt, A.J.: Extending the functional subnetwork approach to a generalized linear integrate-and-fire neuron model. Frontiers in Neurorobotics. 14 (2020). https://doi.org/10.3389/fnbot.2020.577804
10. Cofer, D., Cymbalyuk, G., Reid, J., Zhu, Y., Heitler, W.J., Edwards, D.H.: AnimatLab: A 3D graphics environment for neuromechanical simulations. J. Neurosci. Methods **187**, 280–288 (2010). https://doi.org/10.1016/j.jneumeth.2010.01.005
11. Mamiya, A., Gurung, P., Tuthill, J.C.: Neural coding of leg proprioception in drosophila. Neuron **100**, 636-650.e6 (2018). https://doi.org/10.1016/j.neuron.2018.09.009
12. Ache, J.M., Dürr, V.: A computational model of a descending mechanosensory pathway involved in active tactile sensing. PLoS Computational Biology. 11 (2015). https://doi.org/10.1371/journal.pcbi.1004263
13. Burrows, M.: Inhibitory Interactions Between Spiking and Nonspiking Local Interneurons in the Locust (1987)
14. Pearson, K.G., Fourtner, C.R.: Nonspiking Interneurons in Walking System of the Cockroach
15. Smarandache-Wellmann, C.R.: Arthropod neurons and nervous system (2016). https://doi.org/10.1016/j.cub.2016.07.063

Homeostatic and Allostatic Principles for Behavioral Regulation in Desert Reptiles: A Robotic Evaluation

T. Ngo^(✉), O. Guerrero, I. T. Freire, and P. F. M. J. Verschure

Donders Centre for Neuroscience, 6525 AJ Nijmegen, The Netherlands
tue.ngo@donders.ru.nl

Abstract. Various recent studies have suggested homeostasis and allostasis as the explanatory fundamentals behind physiological and behavioral regulation. Both are endogenous processes responsible for stabilizing the internal states of organisms, in which allostasis orchestrates multiple homeostatic systems. We propose that allostasis can also help organisms adapt to unresolved fluctuations presented by an unstable environment without learning-based predictions. We upgraded a previous computational model of allostatic control by dynamically weighing the agents' motivational drives based on both situational interoceptive and exteroceptive signals. Our model was integrated as the control system of a simulated robot capturing thermoregulation and foraging as navigation profiles. Our results supported the re-organization of hierarchically-ordered drives as an essential feature of need-dependent adaptation that enhances internal stability.

Keywords: Allostatic control · Behavioral regulation · Biomimetic robotics

1 Introduction

The survival of animals is accomplished through behaviors being regulated not only in response to events in their ecological contexts but also to reduce their endogenous drives [1]. Those drives often arise due to an unbalanced, disturbed state of the living system's internal environment that includes several physiological conditions essential for viability. Homeostasis refers to any autonomic or somatic activity used to preserve the constancy of those physiological conditions [2, 3], and homeostatic imbalance is known in previous studies as the primary assessment that allows organisms to respond to their internal drives [4, 5]. At a meta-level, animals are driven to arbitrate between conflicting needs [6] and promote adaptation to stressors [7, 8]. Allostasis serves this purpose as it actively changes parameters of homeostatic control [3, 7] and maintains a dynamic equilibrium of multiple drives being satiated.

Homeostatic and allostatic adjustments apparently require frequent updates on the intensity of each motivational drive, i.e., the deviation between the actual and desired states of relevant physiological systems. In addition, Vouloutsi et al. [4, 5] suggested that the precedence of a certain drive plays an equally important role. Drives could be

© The Author(s), under exclusive license to Springer Nature Switzerland AG 2022
A. Hunt et al. (Eds.): Living Machines 2022, LNAI 13548, pp. 332–344, 2022.
https://doi.org/10.1007/978-3-031-20470-8_33

ordered hierarchically in a way that moderately matches Maslow's pyramid [9], where upper, less vital needs would only be considered if those at the base are fulfilled [6].

Previous works in allostatic control [10, 11] focus mainly on adjusting the desired values, i.e., the setpoints of homeostatic feedback systems. In this study, we aimed to examine the interactions between multiple regulatory loops by changing their weights instead. We enhanced a previous model of homeostatic control proposed by [6] with a reconfigurable hierarchy of internal drives. The relative positions of drives within the hierarchy, i.e., their weights, are regularly modified in response to either exteroceptive or interoceptive stressors. Our model was subsequently integrated into a robotic agent capturing essential properties of observed behaviors as navigation profiles. Our proof of concept was studied entirely through Gazebo robotic simulations. We specifically addressed whether such a dynamic weighing mechanism can permit better adaptation in comparison to a fixed order of weights. Furthermore, we analyzed the relevance of environmental settings during the whole adaptation process and how such information is used by agents. We defined the exteroceptive cue for adaptation as the likelihood of encountering a desired stimulus. Allostatic load – the accumulative burden of chronic exposure to unresolved homeostatic errors [3, 12] – was used as the interoceptive cue.

Thus, our concrete hypotheses are:

H1. The dynamic re-organization of hierarchically-ordered drives allows agents to achieve higher internal stability than a fixed order of constantly-weighted drives.

H2. An agent weighing its internal drives based on allostatic load can regulate its behaviors as sufficiently as one weighing its drives based on exteroceptive sensing.

2 Background

The Principles of Homeostasis and Allostasis. Hull (1943) coined the term "drive" as an unbalanced state that governs and affects behaviors [1]. His drive reduction theory was built around the notion of homeostasis in which essential physical and chemical conditions (e.g., body temperature, glucose level or pH) are kept within viable ranges [2]. Both the absence and excessive presence of environmental stimuli could result in internal fluctuations and create a tendency to react [4, 5]. An example of homeostasis can be observed through thermoregulatory behaviors of the Namib desert's lizards. Under extreme temperatures, the lizards engage in complex self-regulatory behaviors such as diving beneath the sand to maintain a desired body heat of 30 °C [13].

Computationally, each physiological property can be represented by a homeostatic controller which defines an ideal range and evaluates whether the actual condition is within that range (Fig. 1a). The state of an internal homeostatic system is classified as balanced when the actual value (aV) at a given time stays within the desired range (dVs). The agent only exhibits regulation when aV goes below the minimum dV or above the maximum dV, and the intensity of the tendency to bring aV back to balance is calculated by the distance from aV to the closest homeostatic bound. On top of the homeostatic assessment of each physiological system, there is an allostatic controller constantly monitoring the intensity of all generated drives and weighing them based on their priority levels. The end goal of this is to inform the animal about which need to fulfill foremost [6]. Figure 1b demonstrates how an organism selects its action based on described principles of intensity and priority.

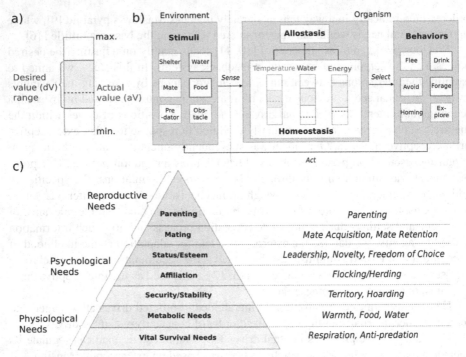

Fig. 1. a. An arbitrary homeostatic system. The *dV* range is determined by the blue lines. Reproduced from [6]. **b. Detailed diagram of drive-based behavior selection.** Homeostatic systems are arranged from left to right according to their descending precedence. When all homeostatic errors are equal, the system chooses actions that fulfill the drive with the highest priority. If a drive with a lower priority has an immense deviation, the corresponding action can be selected. **c. The renovated hierarchy of needs.** The activation of a drive-based goal will be triggered whenever relevant environmental cues are salient. Modified from [14].

Dynamic Hierarchy of Internal Drives. While the way we estimate the intensity of a certain drive seems to be apparent, how we could determine its relative importance remains unclear. We supported the idea from [4] that the priority levels of independent drives will likely form a pyramid approximating Maslow's hierarchy of needs [9]. In this hierarchical arrangement, some drives can take precedence over others.

A renewed hierarchy introduced in [14] was incorporated into our study (Fig. 1c) with two main modifications. First, each layer depicted in Fig. 1c contains needs with different priority values instead of having the same priority value for all needs within it. Furthermore, drives are goal-oriented, having their dynamics calibrated in response to situational threats and opportunities. Thus, the layers should be overlapped and the weights should be altered in accordance with immediate stressors [14].

Allostatic Load. Another potential extension of previous works in allostatic control [10, 11] could be the generalization of allostasis from simple corrections of already-sensed mismatches between desired and actual internal conditions to adaptations that inhibit erroneous outcomes from growing dangerously immense, especially in case of a capricious environment with limited observability of resources. Allostasis does not necessarily imply anticipating future needs through learning and preparing to fulfill needs before they arise. Instead, it can be retained as a reactive mechanism equivalent to the automatic responses orchestrated by homeostatic systems [15]. On this account, homeostasis is a collection of first-order negative feedback loops involving corrective reflexes constituted by the dynamic interplay of each system's inputs and outputs. If homeostasis fails to stabilize certain physiological variables within viable boundaries, allostasis intervenes to prioritize those homeostatic systems by weighing them more, and thus, promotes them to a higher rank within the above-mentioned hierarchy [15].

This adaptation mechanism embraced the role of allostatic load in coping strategies with hazards presented by an uncertain environment [3, 16]. Responses modulated by allostatic load are initiated by a stressor, sustain for an appropriate time interval, and then shut off when the stress is terminated. Many conditions might lead to increasing allostatic load, e.g., the lack of adaptation to frequent stress or inadequate responses that leads to unnecessary compensation from other mediating systems [12].

3 Proposed System

Distributed Adaptive Control Architecture. We decomposed our control system into modules representing fundamental functions of behavioral regulation. Such a layered structure is influenced by the Distributed Adaptive Control (DAC) framework [17]. Although our control system utilizes input categorization and goes beyond autonomic reflexes, it does not fully implemented DAC's adaptive layer. This is due to the lack of associative learning – which is considered a must-have of this second layer. Thus, we placed the allostatic module at the interface between reactive and adaptive layers instead of being merely reactive as in previous works [10, 11].

The cognitive modules proceed exteroceptive inputs from the environment as well as generate interoceptive signals. Those information are integrated and used to weigh motivational drives. The allostasis module retrieves information and makes changes to an internal hierarchical organization holding values of all weighting factors (k) of all drives. Drives are weighted and sent simultaneously to the action selection module which serves as a convergent bottleneck that transforms those enormous information into internal representations of behaviors and selects which action to trigger (Fig. 2).

Gradient and Non-gradient Homeostatic Systems. Previous works in allostatic control have represented homeostatic systems computationally in various directions.

Sanchez-Fibla et al. [10, 11] used vector fields, i.e., gradients, to compute the local perception of the robot, estimate the actual and desired values of homeostatic systems, and control the robotic agent's navigation. We followed this approach to construct the temperature gradient as a simple heat map. The agent will try to place itself at optimal distances to the highest peaks of the heat map. The left side of the gradient portrays higher temperatures while the right side represents cooler locales. We normalized and inverted the temperature from 50–27.5 °C to a value ranging from 0–1. The dV is 0.9, approximately equal to 30 °C. The agent's local view comprises four quadrants (upper-left, upper-right, lower-left, lower-right) with q^0, q^1, q^2, q^3 as mean temperature values of those four quadrants, and aV is calculated as the mean of the whole local view.

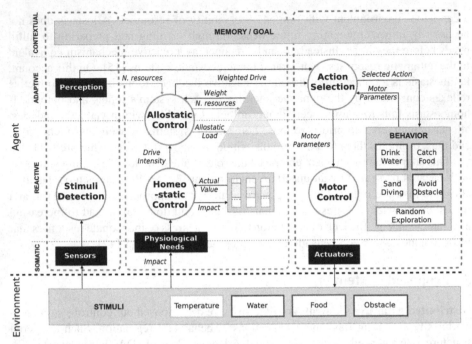

Fig. 2. The DAC framework. The left, blue column provides processed information from the environment. The middle, green column integrates, evaluates, and weighs internal variables. The right, red column chooses the most appropriate action based on the most salient stimulus and the most dominant drive, then executes that selected action. Orange arrows are performed only during exteroceptive adaptation, while the blue arrow is performed only during interoceptive adaptation. Memory and goal-based functions of the contextual layer are not elaborated in this study. Modified from [17].

In terms of navigation, h^{sign} controls the direction of the gradient i and AD^{sign} controls the direction between aV and dV:

$$h_i^{sign} = \begin{cases} 1 & \text{if } q_i^0 < q_i^l \\ -1 & \text{if } q_i^0 > q_i^l \\ 0 & \text{otherwise} \end{cases} \qquad AD_i^{sign} = \begin{cases} 1 & \text{if } aV_i < dV_i \\ -1 & \text{if } aV_i > dV_i \\ 0 & \text{otherwise} \end{cases} \qquad (1)$$

Gradients are particularly useful to optimize navigation due to faster identification of areas of interest. However, the agent was given the local perception of the constructed gradients instead of "sensing" data from equipped sensors. Thus, we decided to build the energy and water homeostatic systems without gradients and provided each with a decay factor b that can detract it. The symbolic representations of acquired data are "target" and "impact". The "target" entity informs the agent the type of resources it is in contact with and distance to those resources. "Impact" indicates changes that such resources make to the associated system after being consumed. Thus, given a timestep

t, a decay factor b, and an impact a, the aV of the system i will be updated as follows:

$$
aV_i^{t+1} = \begin{cases} aV_i^t + a_i - b_i & \text{if } a_i > 0 \\ aV_i^t - b_i & \text{otherwise} \end{cases}
\tag{2}
$$

Interoceptive and Exteroceptive Cues for Adaptation. We previously argued that the priority level, i.e., weighting factor k, is inconstant and could rather be modified based on either the chance of finding a certain resource or allostatic load.

In the first case of exteroceptive adaptation, the agent keeps track of all stimuli detected along its trajectory. This number of detected resources is inversely encoded as a value ranging from 0–1. This value is close to 1 when the agent barely spots any consumable target, and it approximates 0 when the agent perceives an abundance of resources. The weight k^0 is first initiated according to the hierarchy of drives in Fig. 1c. Given a timestep t, the initiated weight k^0, and the number n of detected resources:

$$
k_i^t = \begin{cases} k_i^0 \cdot \left(1 + \dfrac{1}{n_i^t}\right) & \text{if } n_i^t > 0 \\ k_i^0 & \text{otherwise} \end{cases}
\tag{3}
$$

In the second case of interoceptive adaptation, allostatic load was computed as the mean of accumulating drive intensities $|aV - dV|$ (all dVs $= 0.9$) during a predefined period. In this respect, given a timestep t and the allostatic load AL:

$$
k_i^t = k_i^0 \cdot (1 + AL_i^t)
\tag{4}
$$

All weighting factors of all drives are integrated into all drive intensities. The results – which we call "forces" – are the key criteria to determine the dominant drive as well as the increment factors applied to the agent's speed at the next timestep:

$$
f_i^t = 1 + k_i^t \cdot |aV_i^t - dV_i^t|
\tag{5}
$$

4 Method

To manipulate the robot and structure the interactions between cognitive modules, we used the open-source ROS framework [18]. The project comprises a simulated robot within a Gazebo environment – which we control using self-contained Python scripts. Visual detection is achieved using OpenCV [19].

We implemented three different types of agents and compared their performances within an open 2.2×2.7 m space with four walls. The first type of agent operates under a simple negative feedback mechanism with constant k factors. The second one allows agents to regulate k adaptively based on exteroceptive sensing of detected resources n. The third group promotes interoceptive agents configuring k based on allostatic load AL. After every 1,000 timesteps, the stored arrays of ALs and ns were reset. Each agent group was tested during 7 simulations. All simulations began with the same starting position and each of them includes 120,000 –150,000 timesteps.

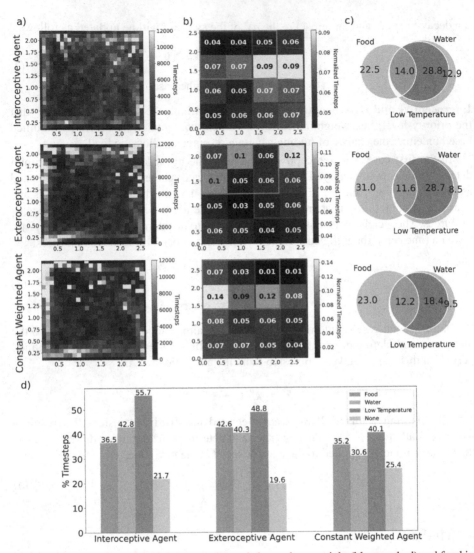

Fig. 3. A. Occupancy map of the arena. Water is located upper right (blue-marked) and food is located upper left (green-marked). The left side of the matrix represents high temperatures, and the other half represents cooler areas. Data were concatenated during all 7 simulations of each agent group. **b. Occupancy map with 4 × 4 grid.** Each cell contains a normalized number (0–1) of that area being visited. **c. Venn diagrams of timesteps spent at specific locations.** Numbers indicate the percentage of timesteps spent at certain locations. Green zone represents locations with food only, blue zone represents cool areas with both food and water resources, purple zone represents locations with water that has low temperature, and orange zone represents locations with cool temperatures and no resources. **d. Bar plots of timesteps spent at specific locations.** Numbers on top of bars indicate the percentage of timesteps spent at certain locations. Includes locations with food, water, low temperature and none of them.

Three homeostatic loops were implemented, namely thermoregulation, hunger, and thirst. Water and food resources were allocated within the robot's explorable space as green and blue spheres, respectively. Different types of spheres populated different corners of the arena. The probability to spawn resources was randomly distributed, and we expected to see the correlation between that and agents' internal states. The temperature gradient is represented as a matrix associated with the arena, being colder on the right side of the matrix and reaching the highest peak on the left side.

5 Results

Trajectories Analysis. By logging the robots' x, y coordinates within the experimental arena at every timestep, we could proceed to analyze behavioral trajectories of agents grouped by adaptation mechanism, and thus, evaluate their abilities to reach necessary entities within the open space (Fig. 3).

To visualize and quantify the agents' excursions, we built occupancy maps for each group of agents (Fig. 3a, 3b). We observed that both adaptive agents with dynamic weighing mechanisms were able to prioritize navigations towards the food and water sources. At the same time, they tended to visit the cooler areas of the arena frequently, while agents with constant weights generate trajectories that fail to avoid the highest peaks of temperature (Fig. 3b). In terms of occupancy at areas with low temperatures, the interoceptive agents slightly ameliorated their regulatory navigations since they're the only group achieving more than 50% of timesteps staying at cool locales (Fig. 3d).

In addition, both adaptive agents with dynamic weighing mechanisms were able to spend slightly more of their lifetime satisfying at least one of their needs. The exteroceptive agents spent 80.4% of their total lifetime successfully obtaining resources or avoiding high temperature peaks. This number is 78.3% for the interoceptive agents and 74.6% for agents with fixed order of drives (Fig. 3c, 3d).

However, we did not achieve any significant result regarding whether agents with dynamic weighing mechanisms can balance the trade-offs between conflicting needs. The interoceptive agents achieved a percentage of 42.9% of their lifetime staying at optimal locations where at least two resources occupied. This number is 40.9% for the exteroceptive agents and 42.1% for agents with constant weights (Fig. 3c).

Internal Stability Analysis. The objective of homeostatic and allostatic regulation is to stabilize physiological conditions within the living system and reduce erroneous deviations. We extracted the time series of aVs during a tracking session equivalent to the agent's predefined lifetime. Each homeostatic system supposes to keep aV higher than or equal to the minimum $dV = 0.9$. The organismic viability of an agent is fatally endangered whenever aV reaches the bottom of the graphs ($aV = 0.1$). The more the aVs stay within permissible homeostatic ranges, the more likely the agent has reached the appropriate stimulus, and the better homeostatic recovery the agent performs.

By analyzing these time series charts (Fig. 4a), we observed that interoceptive and exteroceptive agents could maintain aVs of energy and water around dVs with fewer deviations (i.e., fewer outliers and drastic shifts caused by either the lack of resources or insufficient responses). Besides, the interoceptive agents returned more quickly to cooler areas, considering these time series as a collapse of robot's trajectories into one dimension. Thus, we could see that both dynamically weighted agent groups had the tendency to achieve better stability than one with constant weights.

The interoceptive agents also achieved higher mean scores in both efficiency (0.84 compared to 0.80 and 0.74) and equality (0.94 compared to 0.91 and 0.90) (Fig. 4b). Efficiency of an agent during a simulation is the average value of all mean aVs from all homeostatic systems. On the other hand, equality is calculated by subtracting the discrepancy between aVs of the systems with the highest and lowest aVs from 1. This analysis gave an insight into how these agents can better distribute regulation efforts.

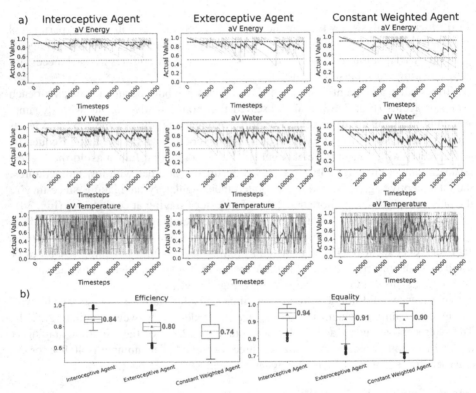

Fig. 4. A. Time series of actual values. Data were concatenated during 7 simulations of each agent group. Black dashed lines resemble dVs of the corresponding homeostatic systems. Grey dashed lines portray $aV = 0.5$ for all systems. Colored thick lines represent the mean aVs from all simulations, while each thin, dashed line comes from an individual simulation. **b. Box plots of efficiency and equality scores.** Green numbers indicate the mean scores of all simulations.

We carried out the same processes to achieve statistical results for drive intensities. The temporal component was eliminated to extract and plot data about which ranges of homeostatic deviations ($|aV - dV|$) each group falls within the most (Fig. 5a). We also ran Wilcoxon rank-sum and Levene's tests, getting p-values less than 7.2e–05 when comparing all ranges from each histogram. We noticed that the probability of achieving errors larger than 0.33 of the agents with fixed k is moderately higher than ones with dynamic weights. The mean error of each system can be found in Fig. 5b. Those results support our hypothesis that dynamic weighing mechanisms can permit agents to achieve higher viability than weighing internal drives in a static manner.

Correlation Analysis. Besides plotting how the weighting factor k was regulated in interoceptive and exteroceptive weighing mechanisms (Fig. 6a), a correlation analysis was done to quantify the relationship between several internal variables of the hunger and thirst homeostatic systems (Fig. 6b). The interoceptive agents exhibited a slight trend to have all variables negatively correlated with the number of detected resources n, especially the weighting factor k and the action force f.

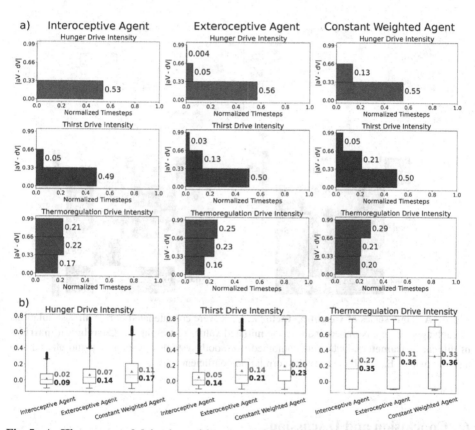

Fig. 5. A. Histograms of drive intensities grouped by agent types. The $|aV - dV|$ span are separated in 3 ranges: $0 \le 0.33 \le 0.66 \le 1$. The number next to a bar indicates the count of that particular range. **b. Box plots of drive intensities grouped by agent types.** Green numbers indicate mean values of drive intensities and black numbers indicate standard deviations.

On the other hand, we found the exteroceptive approach demonstrating correlation coefficients that point out the irrelevancy of the k factor in the reduction of drives. An example is the significant negative correlations between k and $|aV - dV|$ or allostatic load *AL*. Besides, the *k* factor and the force *f* are slightly negatively associated, which means the action selection was not considerably influenced by *k*. Likewise, there is a positive correlation between the number of resources detected *n* and the action force *f*, proving insufficient adaptation to resource availability. This does not mean storing the quantity of reached target is impractical, but future works could consider the couplets of state - action instead of simply inverting the detected number of resources into *k*.

Our results are not significant enough ($r < 0.3$) to establish any conclusion about how coherently interoceptive agents adapted to the fluctuating probability of stimuli, comparing to exteroceptive ones. Longer simulations or better techniques to tune the allostatic load could validate our suppositions about how allostatic load might play a key role in an intrinsic adaptive system.

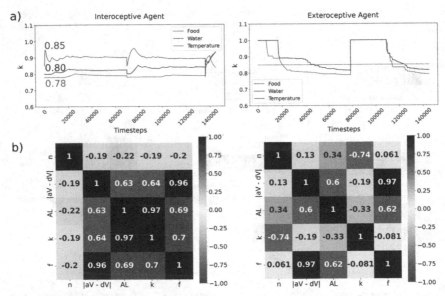

Fig. 6. A. Time series of weighting factor *k*. Data were concatenated during all 7 simulations of each agent group. Numbers indicate the initiated values of weights. **d. Correlation matrices of internal parameters.** Data were combined from both systems of each group and plotted into a single matrix. Each cell contains the correlation coefficient.

6   Conclusion and Discussion

In this research, we aimed to gain insights about how to improve the ability to reduce internal errors of an autonomous system while selecting proper actions during need-dependent behavioral regulation. We have addressed in which ways behaviors can be regulated based on complementary homeostatic and allostatic principles. The concept of a hierarchy of drives where their relative priorities are regularly reorganized was introduced. This dynamic weighing mechanism could offer finer matchings between the agent's internal states and threats or opportunities provided by its surroundings.

There is no predictive regulation carried out within our study. Our control system purely copes with immediate deviations that already occurred without forming any prior knowledge. Although previous external and internal fluctuations was utilized to follow a logic, the agents were unaware of upcoming events and lacked a heuristic to deal with environmental uncertainty. Future works should integrate our model into the full DAC architecture whose layers concurrently functioning for interfering purposes, i.e., habitual reflexes handling proximate triggers and goal-directed actions utilizing information from the past to make rewarding decisions for the future [20, 21].

Our model solves drive conflicts by ignoring less prioritized motivational drives, which results in the lack of multi-purpose behaviors such as ensuring an optimal path towards the location of resources that avoids high temperatures. A possible solution could be the integration of multiple gradients that can elicit multi-system navigation. Internally-defined and learned gradients influencing each other and forming a single observable behavior could underpin a more integrative arbitration process [22].

References

1. Hull, C.L.: Principles of behavior: an introduction to behavior theory. J. Philos. **40**(20), 558 (1943)
2. Cannon, W.B.: The Wisdom of the Body. W. W. Norton & Co., pp. 177–201 (1932)
3. McEwen, B.S., Wingfield, J.C.: The concept of allostasis in biology and bio-medicine. Hormones and Behavior **43**, pp. 2–15 (2003)
4. Vouloutsi, V., et al.: Towards the synthetic self: making others perceive me as an other. Journal of Behavioral Robotics (2015)
5. Vouloutsi, V., Lallée, S., Verschure, P.F.M.J.: Modulating behaviors using allostatic control. In: Conference on Biomimetic and Biohybrid Systems, pp. 287–298 (2013)
6. Guerrero, O., Verschure, P.F.M.J.: Robot regulatory behavior based on homeostatic and allostatic principles. In: Conference on Brain-Inspired Cognitive Architectures for Artificial Intelligence (2020)
7. Sterling, P., Eyer, J.: Allostasis: A new paradigm to explain arousal pathology. In: Handbook of life stress, cognition, and health (1988)
8. Ramsay, D.S., Woods, S.: C: clarifying the roles of homeostasis and allostasis in physiological regulation. Psychol. Rev. **121**(2), 225–247 (2014)
9. Maslow, A.: A theory of human motivation. Psychol. Rev. **50**(4), 370–396 (1943)
10. Sanchez-Fibla, M., et al.: Allostatic control for robot behavior regulation: a comparative rodent-robot study. Adv. Complex Syst. **13**(3), 377–403 (2010)
11. Sanchez-Fibla, M., Bernardet, U., Verschure, P.F.M.J.: Allostatic control for robot behavior regulation: An extension to path planning. In: IEEE/RSJ International Conference on Intelligent Robots and Systems, pp. 1935–1942 (2010)
12. McEwen, B.S.: Physiology and neurobiology of stress and adaptation: central role of the brain. Psychol. Rev. **87**(3), 873–904 (2007)
13. Houston, A., McFarland, D.: On the measurement of motivational variables. Animal Behavior **24**, pp. 459–475 (1976)
14. Kenrick, D.T., Griskevicius, V., Neuberg, S., Schaller, M.: Renovating the pyramid of needs: Contemporary extensions built upon ancient foundations. Perspect. Psychol. Sci. **5**(3), 292–314 (2010)
15. Corcoran, A.W., Hohwy, J.: Allostasis, interoception, and the free energy principle: Feeling our way forward. The interoceptive mind: From homeostasis to awareness **15**, 272–292 (2018)

16. Wingfield, J.C.: The concept of allostasis: Coping with a capricious environment. J. Mammal. **86**(2), 248–254 (2005)
17. Verschure, P.F.M.J., Duff, A.: Distributed Adaptive Control: Theory and Practice. Biologically Inspired Cognitive Architectures **1**, 55–72 (2012)
18. Stanford Artificial Intelligence Laboratory et al.: Robotic Operating System (2018)
19. Bradski, G.: The OpenCV Library. Dr. Dobb's Journal of Software Tools (2000)
20. Marcos, E., Sanchez-Fibla, M., Verschure, P.F.M.J.: The complementary roles of allostatic and contextual control systems in foraging tasks. Simulating Animal Behavior (SAB) LNCS Springer–Verlag (2010)
21. Freire, I.T., Amil, A.F., Vouloutsi, V., Verschure, P.F.M.J.: Towards sample-efficient policy learning with DAC-ML. Procedia Computer Science **190**, 256–262 (2021)
22. Wallraff, G.: Aviannavigation: pigeon homing as a paradigm. Springer–Verlag (2005)

Cognitive Architecture as a Service: Scaffolded Integration of Heterogeneous Models Through Event Streams

Alejandro Jimenez-Rodriguez[1,2]([⊠]) [ID], Julie Robillard[3] [ID],
and Tony Prescott[1,2] [ID]

[1] University of Sheffield, Sheffield, UK
{a.jimenez-rodriguez,t.j.prescott}@sheffield.ac.uk
[2] Sheffield Robotics, Sheffield, UK
[3] The University of British Columbia, Vancouver, BC, Canada

Abstract. The development of cognitive architectures for biomimetic robots can benefit from the seamless integration of computational models that capture some of the brain's capacity to co-ordinate adaptive behavior. Such integration could take advantage of recent advances in distributed systems technology to support the communication between models, however, a communication protocol general enough to allow for heterogeneity, yet, simple enough to be practical and widely used, remains elusive. In this work we propose a solution based on a scaffolded structure that provides constraints for the different models to satisfy. Within this paradigm, the models do not interact among themselves but communicate using event sourcing technology supported by the open source stream processing platform *Apache Kafka*. This design allows the integration of brain-based models without having to specify module-to-module interfaces. At the same time, the robot acts as a consumer and producer of events through the *Neurorobotic Platform* (NRP) (part of the Human Brain Project's *EBrains* platform), meaning that the cognitive architecture has the potential to integrate components provided by a growing community of computational neuroscientists, and to be integrated with different robot platforms. In this paper we present this approach, which we term *Cognitive architecture as a Service* (CaaS), which is further motivated by the goal of creating assistive robots for human care settings. We also describe some early results, based on the *MiRo-e* robot platform, aimed at the development and evaluation of brain-based control for applications in this setting.

Keywords: Cognitive architectures · Cognitive architectures as a Service · Distributed Systems · Brain-based robots · Socially-assistive robots

Supported by organization the Human Brain Project.

© The Author(s), under exclusive license to Springer Nature Switzerland AG 2022
A. Hunt et al. (Eds.): Living Machines 2022, LNAI 13548, pp. 345–353, 2022.
https://doi.org/10.1007/978-3-031-20470-8_34

1   Introduction

Socially assistive robots (SARs) are designed to support communication and interaction with people in human social and care settings, with the goal of supporting engaging and valued short- and long-term human-robot interactions, and to act as catalysts for human-human interaction. The potential value of social robots in care settings has been demonstrated in a variety of studies, both in pediatric populations [10,14] and in older adults [16]. Recent work also indicates the potential of social robots that integrate some of the affective components of human social interaction, based on their capacity to provide emotional support that can lead to improved feelings of self-worth [10,20]. The capacity of social robots to promote human-human interaction has also been demonstrated, for example, with the *Paro* animal-like robot which has been found to facilitate group interaction between adults with dementia [17,23].

In order to safely interact and effectively communicate with people, SARs must embed a control system, or 'cognitive architecture' [13], that includes many human-like functional capacities including verbal and non-verbal communication, person and object detection and recognition, scene analysis and world knowledge, action and interaction planning. Whilst existing SARas differ substantially in the design and configuration of this architecture, many have been directly inspired by human and animal psychology, and several have integrated ethologically-inspired or computational neuroscience models [5–8,15,18,19,24]. This prior work demonstrates the potential for robots with biomimetic control systems to be useful in care settings. Indeed, the capacity of brain-inspired control to generate life-like behavior could be an advantage in providing interactions that people find rewarding and engaging.

In order to provide the infrastructure for a biomimetic robot cognitive architecture that includes heterogenous components we propose a *Cognitive architecture as a Service* (CaaS) paradigm which leverages modern distributed systems methods. Specifically, the CaaS is designed to serve as an scaffold for the integration of both engineered and brain-inspired components such that they can interact to produce continuous and appropriate behaviour, despite operating on different time-scales, and with radically different forms of internal communication and representation.

Thanks to this approach, the cognitive architecture is brought to the foreground of the communication infrastructure, providing an unified interface for models to communicate based upon functional considerations. The concept of a scaffold allow us to constrain successful existing distributed technologies with domain specific design choices [9,27], therefore reducing the degrees of freedom available for the component models to communicate. The scaffold, in this case, is informed by the architecture of the mammalian brain [2].

The rest of the paper is structured as follows: in the next section we provide a conceptual description of the CaaS based upon the low level requirements of an autonomous SAR. We then provide a simple example that illustrates the main aspects of the architecture. Finally, we provide some conclusions and outlook.

2   The Architecture

Previous approaches for the integration of heterogenous models into cognitive architectures have used bespoke distributed systems technologies for message passing [1,4] between brain-inspired computational models. These particular architectural decisions constrain the design of the cognitive architecture itself. Particularly challenging is the fact that sometimes the input of one model comes from the output of another one, potentially developed in a different programming language, often using a different data representation.

In contrast, in the current work, the CaaS is designed using an event sourcing system based on open source *Apache Kafka* technology [12]. Kafka is an event stream platform that provides the necessary infrastructure for producing, consuming and storing events in distributed system. We also use the Neurorobotics platform (NRP) as part of the backbone [9]. The NRP consists of a set of *engines* that interact through a central core through the passing of messages or datapacks in order to execute simulations that control virtual or physical robots.

In using a set of event streams as the backbone of our architecture, we remove the need of the models to communicate with each other. Instead, the models produce and consume events in a set of predefined streams that are part of a pre-existing scaffold. This approach makes our system more flexible and extensible as it places fewer constraints on the design of interactions between modules. Figure 1 shows the design of the event stream of a first-generation CaaS inspired by the cognitive architecture of the mammalian brain. This CaaS builds on an earlier design developed for the MiRO-e animal-like robot an integrates a model of the vertebrate basal ganglia as a core action selection and conflict resolution mechanism [18]. The robot itself acts as a producer and consumer in the architecture.

The main conceptual aspects of this design are:

1. The raw perceptions enter the engine through datapacks that are collected and exposed as perception streams to be consumed and modified by the different models. Inspired by mammalian vision, perception splits into a "what" stream and a "where" stream where additional models can input object recognition, salience and location information. The streams are joined in the motivational controller which filters the perceptions according to the internal state of the robot [3]. This controller then selects between three phases of behaviour (seek, pursue, consume) according to the presence and distance to a goal. *Seek* will activate exploration sequences in the basal ganglia, *pursue* will activate approach or avoid actions and *consume* will execute predefined sequences like grasping.
2. The basal ganglia performs the actions selection based on the different motivational streams that are active in the robot, generally favouring one stream over the others, and produces to a stream of actions which represents the current action.
3. Part of the philosophy of Kafka is that the history of events that happened to the robot or the actions that it has performed are available (up to some

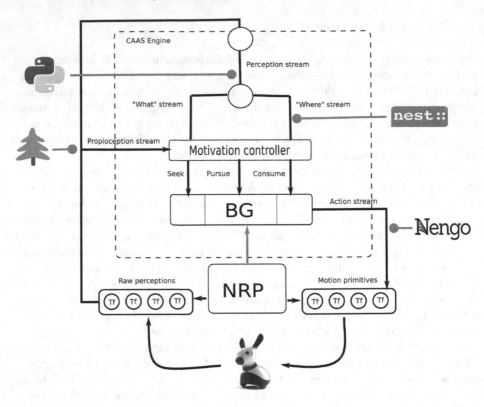

Fig. 1. CaaS scaffold architecture. The robot is modeled as a set of transfer functions that are fed the raw sensory streams and consume the action events. Each stream is fed by events generated by different models created in different simulators (for brain models, these might include models based on PyNN, NEST, Nengo, etc.). The set of streams shown in this particular figure is chosen as the minimal required to generate autonomous behaviour in MiRo.

time frontier) for the models to consume [27]. This acts as a very fine grained long term memory that can be processed and aggregated offline for future use depending upon the particular application needs.

4. The particular motor commands of the robot are consumers of the action stream as well; they control different aspects of the robot independently to develop approaching and avoiding behaviours, or specific gestures.
5. The Neurorobotics platform [9] orchestrates the execution of the CaaS along with the communications with the robot through the motor commands which are, effectively, transceiver functions.

3   Results

In order to illustrate the concepts of the previous section, we developed a toy
architecture with simple behaviours for the MiRo-e animal-like robot. The robot
will have a *green* motivational system that will care about green stimuli in the
field of vision and a *red* one which will do the same with the red stimuli. Possible
behaviours are approach green, approach red, and explore (Fig. 2).

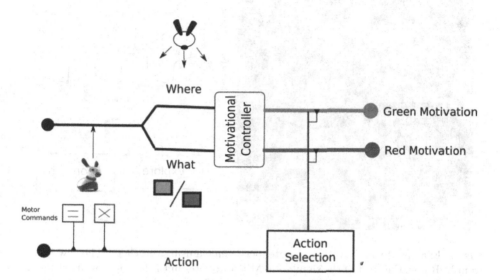

Fig. 2. Example application of the CaaS. The CaaS offers 7 streams the models can
produce events into and consume events from. The raw input from the camera is
consumed by basic detectors that generate *where* and *what* events. The events are consumed by simple NEST simulations that generate potential approach events onto the
motivational streams. The motivational controller modulates those actions according
to the internal state and generate additional *explore* commands. The final selection is
performed by a basal ganglia module. The patterns shown in the motor commands correspond to two different patterns of connections in Braitenberg vehicles. (Color figure
online)

When a frame from the cameras is available, the robot generates an event
in the raw input stream of the architecture. Two simple detectors consume the
camera stream and produce event in the *where* and *what* stream. The *where*
information is obtained by splitting MiRo's field of view in three equal parts and
scanning for the appropriate colors. Two simple NEST models, implemented as in
[25] take the *where* information, associated to each *what*, and generate approach
commands in the corresponding motivational stream (green/red in Fig. 2).

Afterwards, both motivational streams are transformed by the motivational
controller into two action streams corresponding to each motivation; each with
either an *explore* or an *approach* command. The motivational controller itself is

a switching dynamical system described elsewhere [3]. The basal ganglia selects the current action based upon the motivational state and the presence/absence of the stimuli. Finally, the commands are relayed to the transceiver functions which activate the wheels (Fig. 3)

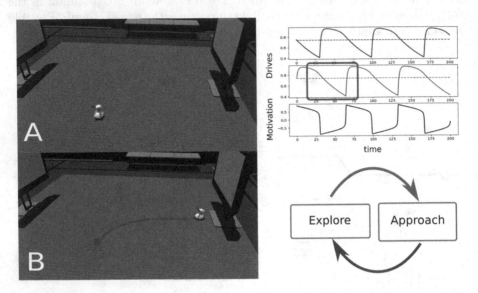

Fig. 3. Example two-motivations Braitenberg vehicle using the CaaS. The raw image from MiRo. At the start of the simulation MiRo explores until the appropriate stimulus is in the field of view. The motivational state (right) fluctuates between two motivations. When the need for red is low (square), the NEST simulation will be allowed to control the robot until the need is satisfied (being close enough to the stimulus). After that, a new cycle of exploration starts. (Color figure online)

4   Conclusions

We have presented a loosely coupled scaffold for Cognitive architectures we call CaaS, oriented towards the development of SARs within the Human Brain Project, and have demonstrated proof-of-concept for a simple model of motivated behaviour.

This technology presents three main advantages compared to alternative solutions.

Firstly, it avoids direct communication between models by defining a scaffold of streams with specific data formats that all the models have to comply to and that have semantic significance for the overall behaviour expected from the robot. In this way, we shift the focus from the particular technical aspects of the communication between models, towards the functional role a specific model should play in the behaviour.

Second, by using Kafka technology, the design automatically logs the history of past events that have happened to the robot, or to the environment, and makes this available for the different models to consume, allowing greater flexibility and increasing the potential for applications in which long-term analyses of event are necessary. Third, even when some models take longer that the time simulation time-step to deliver particular events, the architecture guaranties behaviour at each step and can be augmented by reflex mechanisms that will mitigate for undesirable delays.A potential disadvantage of this approach are its storage and computation requirements, however, we would advocate for a mixed solution in which both embedded systems and large (off-platform) databases could be employed.

Finally, this works's contribution to the HBP's Neurorobotics platform (NRP) allows modellers to create high-level cognitive architectures by combining lower-level models of brain regions and functions in a manner that is largely agnostic concerning specific model implementations or levels of description.

5 Future Work

As a further test case for the CaaS, and its digital twin potential, we plan to implement a modularised version of a more substantial cognitive architecture for the MiRo-e robot that integrates emotional expression and the capacity to align emotional state with that of the user (see [26]). MiRo-e is currently being evaluated as a potential therapy tool, with children and older adults, by the authors. We therefore hope that this extended brain-based cognitive architecture could be usefully applied for applications in hospitals, care homes, and other institutions where SARs could be deployed as therapy or emotional-support tools. A simulated version of MiRo-e has already been integrated with the NRP and will allow the usefulness of the device to be explored and assessed easily, freely, and without access to a physical robot, as well as easing further development of the robot's functionality. The NRP thus already functions as a robotic digital twin.

Acknowledgements. This work was supported by the EU H2020 Programme as part of the Human Brain Project (HBP-SGA3), and specifically, through the CATRA (Cognitive Architecture for Therapy Robots and Avatars) project which was supported by the EBRAINS Research Infrastructure Voucher Programme. We thank the anonymous reviewers for the useful comments on earlier versions of the paper.

Declaration of Interest. TJP is a director and shareholder of Consequential Robotics Ltd which develops the MiRo-e robot. The other authors have no competing interests.

References

1. Amoretti, M., Reggiani, M.: Architectural paradigms for robotics applications. Adv. Eng. Inform. **24**(1), 4–13 (2010)
2. Prescott, T.J., Redgrave, P., Gurney, K.: Layered control architectures in robots and vertebrates. Adapt. Behav. **7**(1), 99–127 (1999)

3. Jimenez-Rodriguez, A., Prescott, T.J., Schmidt, R., Wilson, S.: A framework for resolving motivational conflict via attractor dynamics. In: Living Machines 2020. LNCS (LNAI), vol. 12413, pp. 192–203. Springer, Cham (2020). https://doi.org/10.1007/978-3-030-64313-3_19

4. Mitchinson, B., et al.: BRAHMS: novel middleware for integrated systems computation. Adv. Eng. Inform. **24**(1), 49-61 (2010)

5. Arkin, R.C., et al.: An ethological and emotional basis for human-robot interaction. Robot. Auton. Syst. **42**(3), 191–201 (2003)

6. Asada, M., MacDorman, K.F., Ishiguro, H., et al.: Cognitive developmental robotics as a new paradigm for the design of humanoid robots. Robot. Auton. Syst. **37**(2), 185–193 (2001)

7. Cangelosi, A., Schlesinger, M., Smith, L.B.: Developmental robotics: from babies to robots. MIT Press, Cambridge, MA (2015)

8. Cross, E.S., Hortensius, R., Wykowska, A.: From social brains to social robots: applying neurocognitive insights to human-robot interaction. Philos. Trans. Roy. Soc. B: Biol. Sci. **374**(1771), 20180024 (2019)

9. Falotico, E., et al.: Connecting artificial brains to robots in a comprehensive simulation framework: the neurorobotics platform. Front. Neurorobot. **11**, 2 (2017)

10. Kabacińska, K., Prescott, T.J., Robillard, J.M.: Socially assistive robots as mental health interventions for children: a scoping review. Int. J. Soc. Robot. **13**, 919–935 (2020). https://doi.org/10.1007/s12369-020-00679-0

11. Kachouie, R., Sedighadeli, S., Abkenar, A.B.: The role of socially assistive robots in elderly wellbeing: a systematic review. In: Rau, P.-L.P. (ed.) Cross-Cultural Design 9th International Conference (2017)

12. Kreps, J., Narkhede, N., Rao, J.: Kafka: a distributed messaging system for log processing. In: Proceedings of the NetDB, vol. 11, pp. 1–7 (2011)

13. Kotseruba, I., Gonzalez, O.J.A., Tsotsos, J.K.: A review of 40 years of cognitive architecture research: focus on perception, attention, learning and applications. arXiv:1610.08602 (2016)

14. Logan, D.E., Breazeal, C., Goodwin, M.S., et al.: Social robots for hospitalized children. Pediatrics **144**(1), e20181511 (2019)

15. Lungarella, M., Metta, G., Pfeifer, R., et al.: Developmental robotics: a survey. Connect. Sci. **15**(4), 151–190 (2003)

16. Mann, J.A., et al.: People respond better to robots than computer tablets delivering healthcare instructions. Comput. Hum. Behav. **43**, 112–117 (2015)

17. Marti, P., et al.: Socially assistive robotics in the treatment of behavioural and psychological symptoms of dementia. In: The First IEEE/RAS-EMBS International Conference on Biomedical Robotics and Biomechatronics, pp. 483–488. BioRob (2006)

18. Mitchinson, B., Prescott, T.J.: MIRO: a robot "mammal" with a biomimetic brain-based control system. In: Lepora, N.F.F., Mura, A., Mangan, M., Verschure, P.F.M.J.F.M.J., Desmulliez, M., Prescott, T.J.J. (eds.) Living Machines 2016. LNCS (LNAI), vol. 9793, pp. 179–191. Springer, Cham (2016). https://doi.org/10.1007/978-3-319-42417-0_17

19. Prescott, T.J., Robillard, J.M.: Are friends electric? The benefits and risks of human-robot relationships. iScience **24**, 101993 (2021)

20. Ostrowski, A.K., DiPaola, D., Partridge, E., et al.: Older adults living with social robots: promoting social connectedness in long-term communities. IEEE Robot. Autom. Mag. **26**(2), 59–70 (2019)

21. Perugia, G., Díaz-Boladeras, M., Català-Mallofré, A., et al.: ENGAGE-DEM: a model of engagement of people with dementia. IEEE Trans. Affect. Comput. **PP**(99), 1 (2020). https://doi.org/10.1109/TAFFC.2020.2980275
22. Pu, L., Moyle, W., Jones, C., et al.: The effectiveness of social robots for older adults: a systematic review and meta-analysis of randomized controlled studies. Gerontologist **59**(1), e37–e51 (2018)
23. Shibata, T., Wada, K.: Robot therapy: a new approach for mental healthcare of the elderly - a mini-review. Gerontology **57**(4), 378–386 (2011)
24. Verschure, P.F.M.J.: The distributed adaptive control architecture of the mind, brain, body nexus. Biol. Inspired Cogn. Archit. - BICA **1**, 55–72 (2012)
25. Neurorobotics.net. 2022. Tutorial setup - HBP Neurorobotics Platform 3.2.0 documentation. https://neurorobotics.net/Documentation/latest/nrp/modules/CLE/hbp_nrp_cle/tutorials/setup.html. Accessed 4 July 2022
26. Robillard, J.M., Hoey, J.: Emotion and motivation in cognitive assistive technologies for dementia. Computer **51**(3), 24–34 (2018)
27. Apache Kafka. 2022. Apache Kafka. https://kafka.apache.org. Accessed 4 July 2022

A Synthetic Nervous System Controls a Biomechanical Model of *Aplysia* Feeding

Yanjun Li[1](✉) [ID], Victoria A. Webster-Wood[2] [ID], Jeffrey P. Gill[3] [ID],
Gregory P. Sutton[4] [ID], Hillel J. Chiel[3] [ID], and Roger D. Quinn[1]

[1] Department of Mechanical and Aerospace Engineering, Case Western Reserve University,
Cleveland, OH 44106-7222, USA
{yxl2259,rdq}@case.edu

[2] Department of Mechanical Engineering, Carnegie Mellon University, Pittsburgh, PA 15213,
USA
vwebster@andrew.cmu.edu

[3] Department of Biology, Case Western Reserve University, Cleveland, OH 44106-7080, USA
{jeff.gill,hjc}@case.edu

[4] Department of Life Sciences, University of Lincoln, Lincoln, UK
gsutton@lincoln.ac.uk

Abstract. Building an accurate computational model can clarify the basis of feeding behaviors in *Aplysia californica*. We introduce a specific circuitry model that emphasizes feedback integration. The circuitry uses a Synthetic Nervous System, a biologically plausible neural model, with motor neurons and buccal ganglion interneurons organized into 9 subnetworks realizing functions essential to feeding control during the protraction and retraction phases of feeding. These subnetworks are combined with a cerebral ganglion layer that controls transitions between feeding behaviors. This Synthetic Nervous System is connected to a simplified biomechanical model of *Aplysia* and afferent pathways provide proprioceptive and exteroceptive feedback to the controller. The feedback allows the model to coordinate and control its behaviors in response to the external environment. We find that the model can qualitatively reproduce multifunctional feeding behaviors. The kinematic and dynamic responses of the model also share similar features with experimental data. The results suggest that this neuromechanical model has predictive ability and could be used for generating or testing hypotheses about *Aplysia* feeding control.

Keywords: Multifunctionality · Computational neuroscience · *Aplysia* ·
Control · Synthetic nervous systems

1 Introduction

As a basic motor control task, feeding is extensively studied in animals [1]. *Aplysia californica*, a species of sea slug, is a good model system for studying feeding for a number of reasons. It generates multifunctional feeding behaviors including biting, swallowing and rejection [2]. It uses a relatively small neural network to achieve complex

© The Author(s), under exclusive license to Springer Nature Switzerland AG 2022
A. Hunt et al. (Eds.): Living Machines 2022, LNAI 13548, pp. 354–365, 2022.
https://doi.org/10.1007/978-3-031-20470-8_35

feeding control: its neural circuitry involved in feeding control contains about 2000 neurons. Additionally, the neurons can be uniquely identified across animals. With large and electrically compact soma, it is also possible to record or control neural activities through intracellular microelectrodes [3]. Fully understanding *Aplysia* feeding control could have significant impacts across various fields. For instance, it may be possible to discover how animals use a relatively small neural system to generate various behaviors adaptable to changes in environmental inputs and robust despite unpredictable variations in input, a critical capability for animals to survive in a changing environment [4]. Furthermore, the knowledge of *Aplysia* feeding control can be transferred to engineering, and could be used to design and control soft robotic graspers [5].

A computational model can enhance the understanding of *Aplysia* feeding control by providing a controlled platform to test hypotheses. Although the relatively small number and large size of neurons in *Aplysia*'s nervous system facilitate cell-level physiological studies, it is still difficult to experimentally test all neuronal biophysical properties and synaptic connections. For instance, both feedback pathways and pattern generators can be observed in the ganglia of *Aplysia* [2, 6], but the specific contributions of these mechanisms to feeding control remain unclear. Are pattern generators alone sufficient to generate multifunctional and robust feeding behaviors? Is the integration of feedback pathways into a small circuit sufficient for *Aplysia* feeding control? It is possible to address these questions using a computational model by running numerical simulations and comparing the results with animal data. Furthermore, predictions generated by models can lead to new hypotheses guiding future experiments [2].

Existing computational models of *Aplysia* feeding either lack essential neuromechanical elements or have limited biological plausibility. The model developed in [7] incorporates Hodgkin-Huxley-type neurons and complex synaptic dynamics to model key neurons in the buccal ganglion and CBI-2, a critical cerebral-buccal interneuron in the cerebral ganglion. It can generate ingestive-like motor patterns observed in isolated ganglia, but the lack of other cerebral-buccal interneurons (CBIs) prevents switching between different motor patterns. Moreover, the model does not consider the peripheral mechanics, so it cannot yet be used to study the effects of sensory feedback on neural activity and behavior. The complexity of Hodgkin-Huxley-type models also makes this approach challenging to scale to larger circuits. By employing a demand-driven approach, a neuromechanical model of *Aplysia* feeding was built in [2] using a Boolean neuron model. In this model, motor neurons and buccal interneurons are driven by proprioceptive feedback, and interneurons CBI-2, CBI-3, CBI-4 are responsible for coordinating biting, swallowing, and rejection based on exteroceptive feedback. The Boolean model can run several orders of magnitude faster than real-time, but its neurons only operate through logic operations, making the model less biologically plausible.

To meet the need for a scalable computational model to generate *Aplysia*-like kinematics, dynamics, and neural activities for multifunctional feeding behaviors, we developed an *Aplysia* neuromechanical model using a Synthetic Nervous Systems (SNSs) [8]. Like Hodgkin-Huxley-type neurons, the computational capability of an SNS comes from conductance-based mechanisms. SNSs can achieve a low computational complexity by locating all conductance within a single compartment and abstracting the spiking activity of individual neurons using a rate model. Our neuromechanical model generalizes the model in [2] with the Boolean circuits replaced with SNS circuits. In particular, the motor neurons and buccal interneurons receiving proprioceptive feedback are organized in nine subnetworks to control *Aplysia* feeding behavior *in silico*. In addition, three cerebral-buccal interneurons (CBIs) coordinate feeding behaviors according to exteroceptive feedback. The CBIs generate behavioral transitions by flexibly coordinating different subnetworks. We find that the SNS neural circuitry can generate different feeding behaviors, including biting, swallowing, and rejection. Comparisons between the model output and experimental data provides further support for the model's plausibility. These results support the hypothesis that integrating feedback and a relatively small neural network can control a model of *Aplysia* biomechanics and generate multifunctional and robust feeding behaviors in simulation.

2   Methods

We developed an *Aplysia californica* feeding model extending a previous Boolean model of the *Aplysia* neural system [2] to a Synthetic Nervous System with additional neurons and more biologically plausible neural dynamics. The SNS model is organized into nine functional subnetworks and a cerebral ganglion layer coordinating the feeding behaviors based on known neural circuitry reported in the literature.

2.1   Biomechanical Model

The biomechanical model receives motor commands from the neural circuitry model and returns proprioceptive feedback. This work adopts a simplified biomechanical model described in [2]. The peripheral mechanics represents a simplified *Aplysia* feeding system with two components connected by two translational degrees of freedom (DOFs) and actuated by four muscles. The components include the head and the grasper that are the main constituents of the feeding apparatus, also known as the buccal mass. Three muscle units, including the I2 protractor muscle, the I3 retractor muscle, and the hinge retractor muscle, actuate the head-grasper component. The remaining muscle unit, the I4 muscle, and the anterior portion of the I3 jaw muscle are responsible for grasper and jaw closure, respectively.

2.2   Synthetic Nervous System

The SNS is a rate model. A monotonically increasing activation function φ_i is used to represent the relationship between the activity y_i and the membrane potential U_i of the *i*th neuron $y_i = \varphi_i(U_i)$. A standard selection of φ_i is a piecewise linear function mapping the membrane potential to [0, 1]. Intuitively, y_i is an indicator of the temporal firing frequency of the corresponding neuron.

The dynamics of neurons in the SNS can be described as

$$I_{\mathrm{cap},i} = I_{\mathrm{leak},i} + I_{\mathrm{ion},i} + I_{\mathrm{syn},i} + I_{\mathrm{app},i}, \tag{1}$$

where $I_{\text{cap},i} = C_{\text{m},i}\,dU_i/dt$ and $I_{\text{leak},i} = G_{\text{m},i}\,(E_{\text{r},i} - U_i)$ are the capacitance current and leak current, respectively. $C_{\text{m},i}$ is the membrane capacitance, $G_{\text{m},i}$ is the membrane conductance, and $E_{\text{r},i}$ is the neuron's resting potential. $I_{\text{ion},i}$ represents the currents flowing through other voltage-gated ion channels responsible for strong nonlinear phenomena like plateau potentials and post-inhibitory rebound:

$$I_{\text{ion},i} = \sum_{j=1}^{r} g_{\text{p},j} A_j^{p_j} B_j (E_{\text{p},j} - U_i). \tag{2}$$

For the jth ion channel, $g_{\text{p},j}$ is the maximal conductance, $E_{\text{p},j}$ is its reversal potential, and A_j and B_j are the activation and inactivation variables, respectively. p_j, the activation exponent, is an integer parameter typically from the set $\{1, 2, 3, 4\}$. The transient responses of A_j and B_j are modeled as

$$\frac{dA_j}{dt} = \frac{A_{\infty,j} - A_j}{\tau_{A_j}}$$
$$\frac{dB_j}{dt} = \frac{B_{\infty,j} - B_j}{\tau_{B_j}}, \tag{3}$$

where $A(B)_{\infty,j}$ and $\tau_{A(B)j}$ denote the membrane-potential-dependent steady-state and relaxation time of $A(B)$.

In Eq. (1), $I_{\text{app},i}$ defines an optional applied external stimulus current. For example, feedback signals can be expressed as

$$I_{\text{app}} = \sum_{l=1}^{m} \xi_l \max(\varepsilon_l (x_l - S_l)\sigma_l, 0), \tag{4}$$

with ξ_l and S_l representing the feedback gain and the threshold of the lth feedback input x_l. $\sigma_l \in \{-1, 1\}$ indicates the corresponding direction of the feedback, while $\varepsilon_l \in \{-1, 1\}$ is the feedback polarization (excitatory if $\varepsilon_l = 1$, inhibitory if $\varepsilon_l = -1$). The remaining term, $I_{\text{syn},i}$, encompasses currents through both chemical and electrical synapses:

$$I_{\text{syn},i} = \sum_{j=1}^{n} G_{\text{s},ij} (E_{\text{s},ij} - U_i) + \sum_{k=1}^{m} G_{\text{e},ik} (U_{\text{pre},k} - U_i). \tag{5}$$

For the kth electrical synapse, $U_{\text{pre},k}$ is the membrane potential of the presynaptic neuron and $G_{\text{e},ik}$ is the electrotonic coupling conductance. For the jth chemical synapse, $E_{\text{s},ij}$ is the reversal potential. In the SNS, the synaptic conductance $G_{\text{s},ij}$ is written as $G_{\text{s},ij} = g_{\text{s},ij}\, r_{ij}$, where $g_{\text{s},ij}$ is the maximal conductance. R_{ij}, the activation of the synapse in $[0, 1]$, can be expressed as a cascade connection of two first-order linear systems:

$$\frac{ds_{ij}}{dt} = \frac{y_{\text{pre},j} - s_{ij}}{\tau_{\text{syn},ij1}}.$$
$$\frac{dr_{ij}}{dt} = \frac{s_{ij} - r_{ij}}{\tau_{\text{syn},ij2}} \tag{6}$$

In the above synaptic dynamics, $y_{\text{pre},j}$ is the activity of the jth presynaptic neuron, while s_{ij} represents the activation of presynaptic transmitter release of the jth synapse. $\tau_{\text{syn},ij1}$ and $\tau_{\text{syn},ij2}$ are two characteristic activation time constants.

2.3 Neural Control Circuitry

Using the SNS framework, we developed a neural circuitry model of *Aplysia* feeding control based on known synaptic connections while taking into account the feedback signals from the peripheral biomechanics (Fig. 1).

Motor Control Layer. The motor control layer consists of 5 known motor neurons innervating key musculature: B31 innervates the I2 Protractor muscle for protracting the grasper [9]; B6 innervates the I3 retractor muscle for retracting the grasper [10]; B8 innervates the I4 muscle for closing the grasper [10]; b38 innervates the anterior portion of the I3 muscle for pinching the jaws to hold onto food during the protraction phase of swallowing [11]; B7 innervates the hinge muscle for facilitating initial retraction [12]. Activations of the five motor neurons are mediated by the higher buccal interneuron layer and sensory feedback (B38 and B7 receive proprioceptive feedback on the position of the grasper within the head, x_{gh} [2]).

Buccal Ganglion Layer. IN the buccal ganglion layer model, we organized nine buccal interneurons into five subnetworks (B63/B31, B64/B52, B34/B40, B65/B30, B20/B4) based on their known functional roles in biting, swallowing, or rejection (Fig. 2). A subnetwork can accomplish its function by stimulating a specific set of motor neurons. To coordinate the behaviors, subnetworks receive commands from the higher layer, while some buccal interneurons also receive proprioceptive feedback on the grasper position, x_{gh}. In addition, activation of a subnetwork can modulate activations of other subnetworks to achieve appropriate functional timing.

Subnetwork B63/B31 (Fig. 2A) realizes grasper protraction through strong excitatory synaptic connections between B63 and motor neuron B31 [13]. Because B63 and B31 can be viewed as a single functional unit [14], we assign motor neuron B31 and interneuron B63 to the same subnetwork. In contrast, subnetwork B64/B52 (Fig. 2A) enables grasper retraction by a monosynaptic connection between B64 and the motor neuron B6 [15]. Due to the intrinsic slowly activating sodium channel and the slowly inactivating potassium channel, B64 can spontaneously generate a plateau potential some time after its activation [7]. Proprioceptive feedback to B64 can extend the duration of retraction, enabling feeding to adapt to external load [2]. B52 can demonstrate a post-inhibitory rebound (PIR) phenomenon due to a low threshold sodium channel [6]. PIR, together with the mutual inhibitory connections, ensures the termination of the retraction phase. The transition from the protraction phase to the retraction phase is realized by a slow excitatory synapse from B63 to B64 [7].

Subnetwork B34/B40 (Fig. 2B) and B65/B30 (Fig. 2C) are responsible for mediating variations in protraction durations and closing the grasper during the retraction phase. Their activation is in phase with protraction since both subnetworks are driven by B63/B31 and inhibited by B64 [16]. B34 and B40 make monosynaptic inhibitory connections with B64 [7], postponing the onset of B64 and promoting a longer protraction duration [17]. In contrast, B65 and B30 make fast inhibitory and slow excitatory connections with B64 [16], thus activating an earlier plateau potential in B64 and promoting a shorter protraction duration [17]. In addition, both B40 and B30 promote grasper closure during the retraction phase by slow excitatory synapses to B8 [16].

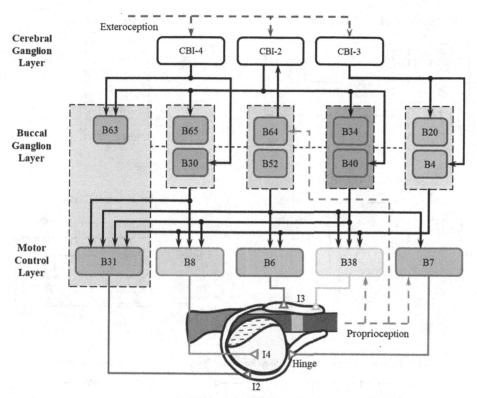

Fig. 1. Schematic of the neural circuitry model. In the motor control layer and buccal ganglion layer, we divided the neurons into nine subnetworks according to their functions. Neurons in the same subnetwork are indicated by the same color. The cerebral ganglion layer contains cerebral interneurons for behavior switching and coordination. Cross-layer synaptic connections are shown as bold black arrows. Dashed black lines represent intra-layer connections. Sensory signals, including proprioceptive and exteroceptive feedback, may be provided by additional sensory neurons or interneurons in the neural circuitry of the animal.

The last subnetwork modeled in this layer, B20/B4 (Fig. 2D), triggers grasper closure during the protraction phase and grasper relaxation during the retraction phase. B20 is excited by other protraction interneurons, indicating that it is activated in this phase [18]. Therefore, the excitatory synapse from B20 to B8 makes the grasper close during protraction. In addition, through the inhibitory synapse to B8, the hyperpolarization elicited by B4 can overcome the excitation produced by B40 or B30 during retraction.

Cerebral Ganglion Layer. The cerebral ganglion layer contains command-like neurons whose activation patterns encode which feeding behavior to generate. In this layer, the model incorporates the three critical cerebral-buccal interneurons, namely CBI-2, CBI-3, and CBI-4. CBI-3 strongly inhibits the B20/B4 subnetwork [18]. Thus, its activation determines the timing of grasper closure and differentiates between ingestive and egestive behaviors. CBI-2 and CBI-4 play a similar role in the rejection because they activate the protraction phase by exciting B63. However, their activations have different

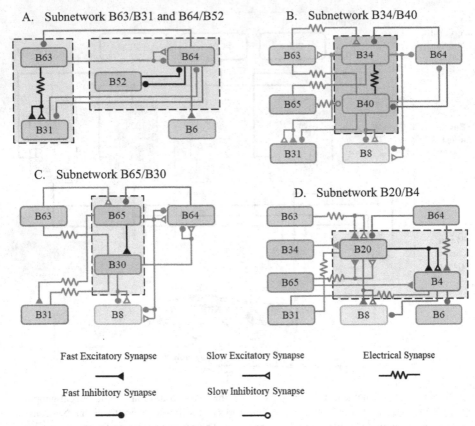

Fig. 2. Schematic of the buccal ganglion layer. This layer contains five subnetworks critical for multifunctional feeding control of *Aplysia*. A. Pathways of subnetworks B63/B31 and B64/B52. B. Pathways of subnetwork B34/B40. C. Pathways of subnetwork B65/B30. D. Pathways of B20/B4. Neurons in different subnetworks are highlighted in different colors, and each subnetwork is enclosed by a dashed and color-coded rectangle. The synaptic connections are color-coded according to their presynaptic neurons, with the exception that those within each subnetwork are black.

implications in terms of biting and swallowing. CBI-2 excites the B34/B40 subnetwork but inhibits B65 [17], leading to a longer protraction and biting-like pattern. CBI-4, by contrast, shortens the protraction phase by exciting B30 [16], making the pattern more like swallowing. The activations of CBIs are determined by the same feedback pathways in [2] so that they can coordinate behavioral switching based on exteroceptive stimuli.

2.4 Model Implementation

We implemented the neuromechanical model in the MATLAB Simulink/Multibody environment (R2021b). The parameters of the biomechanical model were taken from [2]. We referred to [7] to set the parameters governing the intrinsic dynamics of the neurons. We hand-tuned parameters to obtain realistic responses for those neurons that do not exist in [2] and for all chemical synapses. The simulation runs approximately two times faster than in real-time in accelerator mode on a 3.0 GHz CPU machine.

3 Results

3.1 Multifunctional Feeding Control

The model qualitatively generates multifunctional feeding behaviors of *Aplysia californica*, including biting, swallowing, and rejection (Fig. 3). Rhythmic biting patterns mediated by the SNS controller possess similar protraction duration and retraction duration, with weak grasper closure in-phase with retraction. As in the previously reported biomechanical model by Webster-Wood et al. [2], we neglect the interactions between the muscles and the environment during biting, so no force is experienced by the seaweed (Fig. 3A). The protraction duration is slightly shorter than the retraction duration during swallowing (Fig. 3B), as observed during swallowing behavior in the animal. A large positive (ingestive) force is exerted on the seaweed during retraction. The feedback pathways enable the model to adjust its retraction according to the external load, such that the period of high-load swallowing is longer than that of no-load biting (see below). The model can also successfully generate rejection-like behaviors (Fig. 3C). The period of rejection is much longer than ingestive patterns, and the force on the seaweed is negative (egestive) during the protraction phase, which is again similar to what is observed in the animal.

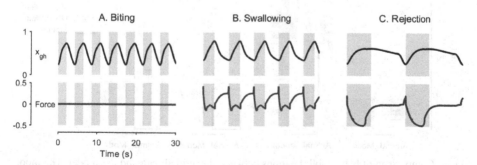

Fig. 3. The integration of the SNS model and simplified periphery is capable of producing kinematics (for biting) and both kinematics and kinetics (for swallowing and rejection) that are similar to those observed experimentally: A. Biting. B. Swallowing. C. Rejection. Shaded backgrounds indicate the protraction phase.

3.2 Comparison of Simulated Ingestive Behaviors with Animal Data

We quantitatively compared the model's behaviors to reported *Aplysia* experimental data (Fig. 4). The first data set is selected from [19] and compares ingestive motor pattern variability in intact animals (with sensory feedback) with variability in isolated ganglia (without sensory feedback) (Fig. 4A). *In vivo*, durations of biting are relatively short (4.26 ± 0.95 s), with similar mean values and variations (standard deviation) of the protraction phase (2.03 ± 0.62 s) and the retraction phase (2.17 ± 0.60 s). In contrast, the behavioral durations greatly increase when sensory feedback is removed (15.66 ± 7.34 s) (Fig. 4B). This increase in duration occurs mainly in protraction duration (10.40 ± 5.78 s), with a lesser increase in retraction duration (4.99 ± 3.28 s). The SNS model can generate similar biting behaviors with and without proprioceptive feedback (Fig. 4A, B). When the feedback signal of the grasper position (x_{gh}) is included, the duration of biting is 4.44 s. As in the animal data, the difference between the protraction duration (2.15 s) and the retraction duration (2.29 s) is minimal. When the proprioceptive feedback is removed in the model, the protraction duration significantly increases to 12.04 s, while the retraction duration (5.77 s) only experiences a moderate prolongation. The contrast between the durations with and without feedback illustrates the critical role proprioceptive pathways could play in normal biting behavior.

The second dataset from [20] compared the swallowing durations under different load conditions (Fig. 4C, D). When animals feed on unloaded seaweed (unloaded swallowing), the total cycle duration is 5.46 ± 0.76 s. When they attempt to ingest unbreakable seaweed (loaded swallowing), the addition of load slows down the behavior, increasing the total duration by about 30% (7.11 ± 0.9 s). In simulations, the unloaded condition can be implemented by removing the joint connecting the seaweed to the ground. When the joint is removed, the duration of swallowing generated by the model is 5.25 s, with a slightly shorter protraction duration (2.59 s) than the retraction duration (2.66 s) (Fig. 4C,

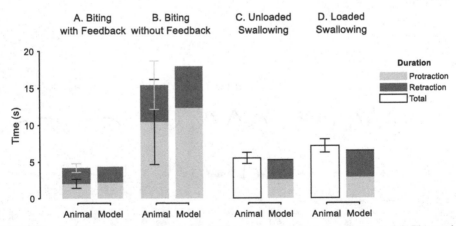

Fig. 4. Comparison of behavioral durations between the animal data and the model. The model was validated based on four experiments: A. *in vivo* biting [19]. B. Ingestive patterns generated by isolated ganglia [19]. C. Swallowing unloaded seaweed [20]. D. Swallowing unbreakable seaweed [20]. Error bars indicate standard deviations.

D). The restoration of the seaweed constraint increases the total duration by about 23% (6.45 s). Thus, the model data also follows the trend observed in the animal data that the increase of load results in longer ingestive durations.

4 Conclusions and Future Directions

We presented a Synthetic Nervous System that controls *Aplysia* feeding behaviors in simulation. The circuitry in the motor control layer and buccal ganglion layer is organized into nine subnetworks that generate activity patterns needed for biting, swallowing, and rejection. CBIs in the cerebral ganglion can coordinate feeding behaviors by modulating these subnetworks.

We then implemented the neural circuitry model in a simplified *Aplysia* biomechanical model. We found in simulations that this neuromechanical model is qualitatively sufficient to generate the three key feeding behaviors biting, swallowing, and rejection. Furthermore, by comparing the model's output with animal data, we demonstrated that the model produces similar outputs for *Aplysia* feeding behaviors under four different conditions (biting with feedback, biting without feedback, unloaded swallowing, loaded swallowing). Specifically, the integration of proprioceptive pathways considerably shortens the protraction phase during biting. Such variation in the protraction duration is due to the protraction-triggered excitatory feedback to B64 considered in our model. When the protraction of the grasper is strong enough (x_{gh} higher than a threshold), it tends to excite B64. The strength of the feedback is proportional to the difference between x_{gh} and the threshold in our model. Thus, incorporating it accelerates the termination of the protraction phase. If the feedback pathways are removed, the earlier onset of B64 also disappears. The intrinsic pattern generator will then produce a biting pattern featured with a long protraction phase. The feedback pathways influencing the termination of the B64 firing also exist in our model (retraction-triggered inhibitory feedback), indicating that a strong retraction of the grasper (x_{gh} lower than a threshold) tends to inhibit B64 and accelerates the termination of the retraction phase. However, the threshold of the pathways is set relatively low so that x_{gh} will not become much lower than the threshold before the termination of the retraction phase, while it can become much higher than the threshold before the termination of the protraction phase. Therefore, the retraction-triggered inhibitory feedback is generally weaker than protraction-triggered excitatory feedback in our model, and the variation in the retraction duration with and without feedback is less obvious than in the protraction phase. These results highlight the role of proprioceptive feedback in coordinating movements, and they suggest experimentally testable pathways by which robust responses to load are produced in the animal.

To further verify the predictive ability of the proposed model, we will compare its response with more animal data at both neural and behavioral levels. According to these results, we can tune the unknown parameters and determine whether it is necessary to include additional identified neurons and synaptic connections in the model. A good neural circuitry model should also generate robust control with uncertainties in the model parameters. Performing sensitivity analysis is critical to evaluate how much the variation in certain parameters will contribute to the variation in the model output.

Because the proposed computational model is rooted in neurobiology, it could serve as a guide in the experimental study of *Aplysia* feeding or as a platform for hypothesis testing. Furthermore, it is also possible to generalize the model for robotic control because the single-compartment and non-spiking neuron models in the SNS reduce the computational complexity and allows real-time implementation.

Acknowledgements. This work was supported by NSF DBI 2015317 as part of the NSF/CIHR/DFG/FRQ/UKRI-MRC Next Generation Networks for Neuroscience Program and NSF IIS1704436.

References

1. Chen, J.: Food oral processing - a review. Food Hydrocolloid. **23**(1), 1–25 (2009). https://doi.org/10.1016/j.foodhyd.2007.11.013
2. Webster-Wood, V.A., Gill, J.P., Thomas, P.J., Chiel, H.J.: Control for multifunctionality: bioinspired control based on feeding in *Aplysia californica*. Biol. Cybern. **114**(6), 557–588 (2020). https://doi.org/10.1007/s00422-020-00851-9
3. Huan, Y., et al.: Carbon fiber electrodes for intracellular recording and stimulation. J Neural Eng. **18**(6), 1–18 (2021). https://doi.org/10.1088/1741-2552/ac3dd7
4. Wolpert, D.M., Ghahramani, Z.: Computational principles of movement neuroscience. Nat Neurosci. **3**, 1212–1217 (2000). https://doi.org/10.1038/81497
5. Mangan, E.V., Kingsley, D.A., Quinn, R.D., Sutton, G.P., Mansour, J.M., Chiel, H.J.: A biologically inspired gripping device. Industrial Robot Int J. **32**, 49–54 (2005). https://doi.org/10.1108/01439910510573291
6. Cataldo, E., Byrne, J.H., Baxter, D.A.: Computational Model of a Central Pattern Generator. In: Priami, C. (ed.) CMSB 2006. LNCS, vol. 4210, pp. 242–256. Springer, Heidelberg (2006). https://doi.org/10.1007/11885191_17
7. Costa, R.M., Baxter, D.A., Byrne, J.H.: Computational model of the distributed representation of operant reward memory: combinatoric engagement of intrinsic and synaptic plasticity mechanisms. Learn Memory. **27**(6), 236–249 (2020). https://doi.org/10.1101/lm.051367.120
8. Szczecinski, N.S., Hunt, A.J., Quinn, R.D.: A functional subnetwork approach to designing synthetic nervous systems that control legged robot locomotion. Front Neurorobotics. **11**, 1–19 (2017). https://doi.org/10.3389/fnbot.2017.00037
9. Hurwitz, I., Neustadter, D., Morton, D.W., Chiel, H.J., Susswein, A.J.: Activity patterns of the B31/B32 pattern initiators innervating the I2 muscle of the buccal mass during normal feeding movements in *Aplysia californica*. J Neurophysiol. **75**(4), 1309–1326 (1996). https://doi.org/10.1152/jn.1996.75.4.1309
10. Morton, D.W., Chiel, H.J.: *In vivo* buccal nerve activity that distinguishes ingestion from rejection can be used to predict behavioral transitions in *Aplysia*. J Comp Physiology. **172**(1), 17–32 (1993). https://doi.org/10.1007/bf00214712
11. McManus, J.M., Lu, H., Cullins, M.J., Chiel, H.J.: Differential activation of an identified motor neuron and neuromodulation provide *Aplysia*'s retractor muscle an additional function. J Neurophysiol. **112**(4), 778–791 (2014). https://doi.org/10.1152/jn.00148.2014
12. Sutton, G.P., et al.: Passive hinge forces in the feeding apparatus of *Aplysia* aid retraction during biting but not during swallowing. J Comp Physiology. **190**(6), 501–514 (2004). https://doi.org/10.1007/s00359-004-0517-4
13. Hurwitz, I., Ophir, A., Korngreen, A., Koester, J., Susswein, A.J.: Currents contributing to decision making in neurons B31/B32 of *Aplysia*. J Neurophysiol. **99**(2), 814–830 (2008). https://doi.org/10.1152/jn.00972.2007

14. Hurwitz, I., Kupfermann, I., Susswein, A.J.: Different roles of neurons B63 and B34 that are active during the protraction phase of buccal motor programs in *Aplysia californica*. J Neurophysiol. **78**(3), 1305–1319 (1997). https://doi.org/10.1152/jn.1997.78.3.1305

15. Elliott, C.J.H., Susswein, A.J.: Comparative neuroethology of feeding control in molluscs. J Exp Biology. **205**, 877–896 (2002). https://doi.org/10.1242/jeb.205.7.877

16. Jing, J., Cropper, E.C., Hurwitz, I., Weiss, K.R.: The construction of movement with behavior-specific and behavior-independent modules. J Neurosci. **24**(28), 6315–6325 (2004). https://doi.org/10.1523/jneurosci.0965-04.2004

17. Jing, J., Weiss, K.R.: Generation of variants of a motor Act in a modular and hierarchical motor network. Curr Biol. **15**(19), 1712–1721 (2005). https://doi.org/10.1016/j.cub.2005.08.051

18. Jing, J., Weiss, K.R.: Neural mechanisms of motor program switching in *Aplysia*. J Neurosci. **21**(18), 7349–7362 (2001). https://doi.org/10.1523/jneurosci.21-18-07349.2001

19. Cullins, M.J., Gill, J.P., McManus, J.M., Lu, H., Shaw, K.M., Chiel, H.J.: Sensory feedback reduces individuality by increasing variability within subjects. Curr Biol. **25**(20), 2672–2676 (2015). https://doi.org/10.1016/j.cub.2015.08.044

20. Gill, J.P., Chiel, H.J.: Rapid Adaptation to Changing Mechanical Load by Ordered Recruitment of Identified Motor Neurons. ENEURO.0016-20.2020. **7**(3), 1–18 (2020). https://doi.org/10.1523/eneuro.0016-20.2020

Animal Acceptance of an Autonomous Pasture Sanitation Robot

Ian Adams[1]([✉]), Roger D. Quinn[1], Greg Lee[2], Alexandra Kroeger[3],
Rebecca Thompson[3], and Erica Feuerbacher[3]

[1] Department of Mechanical and Aerospace Engineering, Case Western Reserve
University, Cleveland, OH 44106-7222, USA
ija2@case.edu
[2] Department of Electrical Engineering and Computer Science, Case Western
Reserve University, Cleveland, OH 44106-7222, USA
[3] Department of Animal and Poultry Science, Virginia Tech,
Blacksburg, VA 24061, USA

Abstract. This work presents the collection and analysis of animal-robot
interaction in a pasture setting necessary to support the development of an
autonomous platform for maintenance of occupied pastures. Cows (*B. taurus*) and horses (*E. caballus*) were introduced to a teleoperated robot platform under differing modes of operation. Animal proximity to the robot,
the number of animals that came into contact with the robot, and the frequency of contact with the teleoperated robot platform were recorded. The
animal behavior data suggests that cows tend to flee at a regular distance
when approached, while horses flee inconsistent distances. Horses showed
a higher rate of interaction with the robot. Both species tended to interact with a stationary robot compared to a moving one. Outside of these
trends, animal behavior was highly variable and suggests a need to design
autonomous robot behaviors/algorithms in which robots should treat pasture inhabitants as unpredictable, but suggests that an autonomous pasture maintenance robot can operate in an occupied pasture.

Keywords: Autonomous robotics · Unmanned ground vehicle ·
Livestock management · Sanitation

1 Introduction

Greener Pastures is a project to automate the task of manure removal to support
improved management and sanitation of grazing pastures. Initial work focuses on
preliminary data collection of both animal behavior and platform performance
in pastures using an existing robot platform teleoperated within an inhabited
pasture. Animal behavior data are presented here.

Global farming, especially of ruminant animals, converts human-inedible
resources into human-edible protein [1]. While providing food resources, livestock farming also contributes significantly to greenhouse gas production, and
damage to local hydrological and nutritional systems [2,3]. Cows produce a disproportionate amount of greenhouse gas emissions, and waste runoff into water

© The Author(s), under exclusive license to Springer Nature Switzerland AG 2022
A. Hunt et al. (Eds.): Living Machines 2022, LNAI 13548, pp. 366–377, 2022.
https://doi.org/10.1007/978-3-031-20470-8_36

systems. Horses and cows both require large pastures. The current practice of manually searching for manure to collect within a pasture is time consuming as it can be difficult to even find the manure.

Cropland is generally flat and composed of highly homogenized topology and has seen significant leaps in automation, whereas, development of comparable pasture automation has lagged behind that crop farming automation [4]. Livestock pastures contain much more heterogeneous topology, contain greater botanical diversity, and can be much more hydrologically sensitive. The topology and vegetation can obscure manure and make manual retrieval more difficult. It is common for manure to not be removed from pastures because of the large amount of time required for the task. The fecal material can seep into ground water, or can be washed into surface waters during precipitation events. Coupling and improving existing animal sensor networks that can identify defecation events and report time and location with an automated ability to collect the manure will greatly reduce animal waste contaminating surface waters.

A significant complicating element, however, not present in autonomous crop maintenance is the presents of animals in the pasture. Larger livestock pose a physical danger to robots, and *vice versa*. Further, an autonomous vehicle in a pasture could induce stress upon pasture inhabitants. Such stress could have detrimental effects on the animals and must be prevented. The Greener Pastures project is collecting behavior data of animals interacting with a robot platform teleoperated in a pasture. Data is collected from two species of livestock: Cows (*B.taurus*) and horses(*E. caballus*). The understanding of the behavior of animals around an autonomous pasture maintenance robot will allow such a platform to effectively mitigate surface water contamination without inducing detrimental stress on the pasture inhabitants.

1.1   Robot Platform

The Pasture Sanitation Robot (PSR1) is an outdoor robot platform developed for high-load autonomous snowplowing and is shown in Fig. 1. The platform is an all wheel drive, skid-steer platform with four wheels driven by two electric motors. The platform is made from welded steel, has an overall footprint of approximately 1 m cubed, and a mass of approximately 90 kg. The relatively large mass, outdoor-rated sensors, and hardcase-enclosed control electronics of the robot yield a platform capable of sustaining little or no damage from rough contact by livestock. Skid-steer is not optimal for pasture operation as the skidding damages pasture vegetation much more than other platform configurations, but is acceptable for initial data collection.

The PSR1 has a low cost Ublox ZED-F9P Real-Time Kinematics (RTK) GPS module for localization and an Ouster OS-1-32 3D LIDAR for environment perception. The Ouster OS-1-32 was selected for its high scan rate, up to 120 m range, and 360° field of view. The high frame rate serves to better track motion of animals and features of the environment.

PSR1 uses the Robot Operating System (ROS) framework for communication, control and data collection. ROS is a commonly used framework in academic research for robot development that greatly facilitates combining existing robot technology with new advances and adaptations. It also facilitates the addition of new sensors and simplifies the development of communications for interacting with existing LoRa architecture in the pasture [6]. PSR1 leverages an extensive library of code developed in its previous applications and new code developed for the PSR1 will be easily reusable on subsequent platforms.

While the robot already has the ability to navigate autonomously between GPS waypoints, the robot is teleoperated when in the presence of animals at this time.

Fig. 1. The PSR1 platform is shown during data collection in a pasture at Virginia Tech. with a herd of cattle.

1.2   Animal Testing

In order to service the pasture, an autonomous pasture maintenance robot must safely coexist with the livestock. Animals can respond to new stressors, such as the introduction of a new piece of equipment, in unpredictable ways [7]. By modelling the interactions with stressors, optimal methods for robot-animal introduction can be developed, as well as robot behaviors that can minimize robot-animal interaction to minimize stress to the pasture inhabitants [8].

The Greener Pastures project is collecting animal behavior data from two livestock species: Cows (*B.taurus*) and horses(*E. caballus*) as they interact with the PSR1 in a pasture.

Measures recorded in pasture using the PSR1:

1. Minimum distance between animal and PSR1
2. Distance an animal flees from PSR1

3. Number of animals in the pasture that interact with PSR1 (interactors)
4. Number of total interactions between all animals in the pasture and PSR1 (interactions)

Closest approach distance describes the minimum distance between the PSR1 and any animal approaching it. This metric shows how animals might react to the robot sharing space. Larger closest approach distances reflect animals being wary or uninterested in the PSR1 in the pasture, while smaller values represent animals being more interested in approaching the PSR1. The flight distance is the minimum distance to which an animal flees when the robot approaches it. This represents the minimum distance an autonomous behavior should maintain while in typical operation to prevent inducing a stress behavior in the pasture animals. Lack of flight distance, or a flight distance 0 m, shows that an animal is unwilling to leave when a robot approaches. This could present a significant behavioral challenge for future autonomous behaviors.

For the purposes of this work, the term contact is used to refer to an animal approaching to within 25 cm of the robot, whether or not the animal actually physically touches the robot. The number of interactors describe the number of animals that come into contact with the robot. The number of interactions describes the total number of times any animals makes contact with the robot. These values give insight into the number of animals, and the volume of animal interactions a future autonomous platform might be expected to encounter.

2   Methods

2.1   Animal Testing

A four phase method for each pasture tested based on prior robot-animal tests were constructed to gauge animal response to the robot [7,9]. The four phases were selected to assess the responses of the animals to a moving and stationary robot, more typically used flight distance tests that are used with cattle [10] and horses [11,12], and a final phase to assess recovery after the flight distance test. The four phases were:

1. Introduce the robot to pasture and move with no predetermined path for 5 min.
2. Halt all robot motion for 10 min.
3. Maneuver the robot directly towards the animals, until either they begin to flee, or collision is imminent.
4. After the subjects have fled or failed to flee, halt all motion again for 5 min.

Each individual trial ran approximately 21 min with slight variations resulting from distance the robot would need to travel to induce a flight.

During the week of March 6–12, 2022, in Blacksburg, VA, cattle and horses were tested using the four phase process above. The data were collected over three days from two groups of cattle and three groups of horses.

The cattle were heifers and mainly Angus with a few Charolais in each herd. The two pastures of cattle were produced by splitting one large herd into two smaller herds; the larger home pasture was split into two pastures by adding an approximately 3 m aisle way using temporary fencing. The cattle were allowed to acclimate for three days prior to testing.

The horses were all mares of various breeds and ages. The horses were tested in their home pastures and the herds ranged from five to eight horses. These groups were separated into independent pastures, and given time to acclimate to their enclosures.

Each pasture was tested three times, once per day, with no more than one day between trials. For each round of trials for both species, the robot was introduced to the pasture from the same gate, and moved in the same regions of each pasture during each phase.

3   Results

3.1   Animal Testing

The results from the animal trial sequences are shown below in Figs. 2, 3, and 5a, b. Figure 2 shows the aggregate results for all trials separated by species. Figures 3, 5a, b show the group results for cows and horses, respectively. Figures 4a, b and 6a and b show the results of each animal group in a specific phase of motion versus trial number. These plots show trends which could demonstrate change in behavior towards the robot.

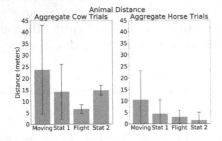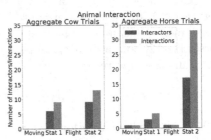

Fig. 2. The two left figures show the aggregate animal distances in each phase, sorted by species. Cows had a higher flight distance, and less interactivity. Horses show a higher variance in behavior and were on average more interactive than the cows.

The closest animal approach distance for each phase provides insight into how animals might respond to a robot working in the field.

Cows

For cattle, the animals had the highest average distance while the robot was in motion, with an average of 23.7 m from the robot. For both the initial motion sequence, and the flight sequence, the animals never interacted with the robot. While stationary, however, the cattle often came into closer proximity to with the robot with occasional contacts recorded.

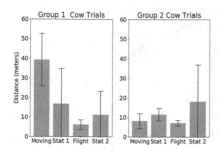 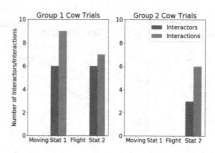

Fig. 3. The graphs show the individual cow group distances and interactions. The distance results for each phase in the trials are reported in the left two graphs, for groups 1 and 2 of cattle. On the right, the total interactors (blue) and interactions (orange) for each group are shown. (Color figure online)

Outside of the clear tendency to avoid the robot in motion, each group of cattle had different likelihoods of interacting with the robot. Cattle in group 1 had a high number of interactors and interactions. There were a total of 16 interactions across all three trials, split roughly evenly between the first and second stationary events. On the other hand, cattle in group 2 had far fewer with a total of 6 interactions, again limited to stationary phases.

The flight distance for cattle was between 6 and 7 m for both groups. Group 1 had an average of 6.1 m and group 2 had an average of 7.1 m.

Between the first and last trials for the Motion phase, both cow groups showed a general trend of increasing distance with trial instance. The flight distances for each group appeared consistent, both with respect to trial instance and with respect to the other group. Consistent behavior between the first and third trials indicates the flight distance may be stable across both groups and independent of the amount of previous exposure to the robot.

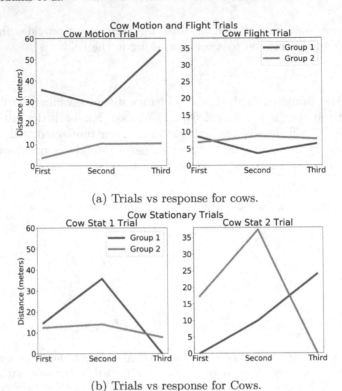

(a) Trials vs response for cows.

(b) Trials vs response for Cows.

Fig. 4. The cow trials by group, versus the trial number. (a) The minimum distance of both groups of cows in the Motion test and in the Flight test versus the trial instance are shown. In the Flight phase, both groups of cattle seemed to have similar flight distance regardless of trial. (b)The minimum distance during the first and secondary Stationary phase for each group versus the trial instance are shown. The number of interactions increases for each group in each trial.

With regards to the first stationary phase, both groups of cows tended to increase, and then decrease the distance to the robot. This could suggest the cows became more complacent or even curious about the robot. However, the behavior for each group in the second stationary phase was less consistent. In the secondary Stationary phases the groups showed mutually conflicting trends, and so no general trend should be supposed.

Horses

Horses had a higher average distance to robot during initial movement, of approximately 10.4 m. Similar to cattle, horses also more frequently interacted with the robot during stationary phases, especially the during the second stationary phase. Unlike cattle, however, horses interacted occasionally with the robot during motion. Horses showed a shorter flight distance as compared to cattle, with the average flight distance being just under 3 m. Horses had several non-flight results, significantly lowering the average flight distance. Horses were likely to not flee from an approaching robot but instead to approach and interact with it.

Table 1. Cow distance and interaction data summarized by phase.

Aggregate cow data summarized by phase				
Statistic	Motion	Flight	Stat 1	Stat 2
Average distance	23.70	14.13	6.5855	14.756
Std dev distance	19.22	11.92	1.89	14.56
Average interactors	0	1	0	1.5
Std dev interactors	0	2.45	0	2.51
Average interactions	0	1.5	0	2.17
Std dev interactions	0	4.02	0	3.58

The high variance indicates the different horse trial groups have especially different behavior patterns. Groups 1 and 2 both have high instances of interaction with the robot, and had several trials with no flights between them. Group 3 had more consistent behavior with an approximately 5.5 m flight distance average with no non-flight trials. This group also had the lowest rates of interactions for horses, with a total of 2 for the entire duration of testing.

For all three groups there is a trend of decreasing distance between animals and robot during the Motion phase. Based on group 3's willingness to approach the robot in the the stationary tests, it is possible the high value in trial 3 reflects apathy rather than aversion. In the flight phase, the horse trials seemed to trend similarly to the cow trials. The horse flight trials seem to be consistent with each other, and with the exception of group 1, they seem consistent across the trials. In the stationary trials, group 3 showed similar behavior in both stationary phases. It is unclear how groups 1 and 2 change, as both showed consistent curiosity to the robot during the second stationary phase, but inconsistent distance during the first stationary phase.

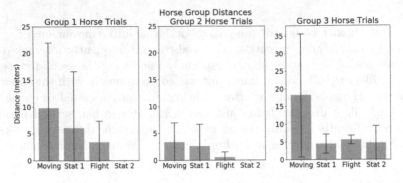

(a) Horse Group Distances.

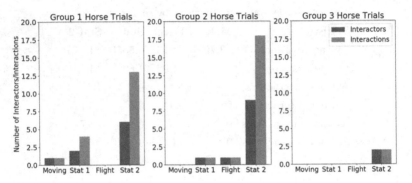

(b) Number of Horse Interactions.

Fig. 5. The horse trials by group, during each phase. (a) These are the approach and flight distances for each horse group at each phase. Groups 1 and 2 acted more consistent with each other than with group 3. Group 3 had a somewhat higher flight distance as well. In all cases, each group had highest distances during initial movement, and lesser distances during each of the stationary phases. (b) Horse interactors in blue, and interactions in orange. These are the total number for each group individually, summed over all trials. As with the distance trials, groups 1 and 2 acted more consistent with each other than with group 3. Groups 1 and 2 had high numbers of interactions with the robot, while group 3 had very limited interest. (Color figure Online)

The inconsistent patterns of behavior suggest that accurately predicting horse behavior will be more difficult than with cattle. This interaction variability and in many cases lack of flight distance suggest that the robot cannot count on horses moving away on approach, or on being left alone while in motion. Lastly, horses have a much higher rate of interaction with the robot compared to cattle. Therefor any model of autonomous behavior should expect horses to be more likely to interact with the robot, and to do so more frequently.

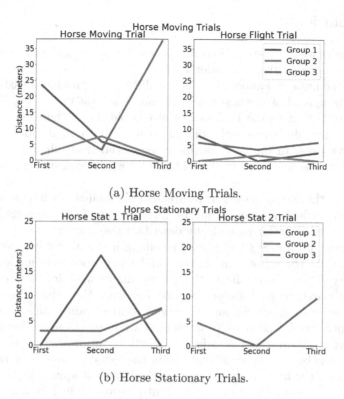

(a) Horse Moving Trials.

(b) Horse Stationary Trials.

Fig. 6. The horse trials by group, versus the trial number. (a) Trials vs response for horses. The two graphs show distance of all three groups of horses in the Motion test and in the Flight test versus the trial instance. While the Motion test showed a possible overall decrease as animals became more familiar with the robot, more sequential trials are needed to show this with certainty. The high distance on the third trial of group three may be reflective of apathy rather than avoidance. (b) The first and secondary stationary phase results for each group versus the trial instance. For the second stationary phase, groups 1 and 2 were both in contact at some point during each trial.

Table 2. Horse distance and interaction data summarized by phase.

Aggregate horse data summarized by phase				
Statistic	Motion	Flight	Stat 1	Stat 2
Average distance	10.44	4.38	2.99	1.58
Std dev distance	12.58	5.98	2.87	3.36
Average interactors	0.11	0.33	0.11	1.89
Std dev interactors	0.32	0.50	0.33	1.36
Average interactions	0.11	0.56	0.11	3.67
Std dev interactions	0.33	0.88	0.33	2.87

4 Conclusions

From this work we draw several general conclusions in service of the development of an autonomous pasture sanitation robot.

Due to the limited number of trials it is difficult to provide statistical significance to the spread of metrics analyzed, and more trials are planned to refine these values. Owing to the high degree of complexity of these trials it is also difficult to draw decisive conclusions as to how the animal-robot interaction changes over time. In future work, more sequential trials should be taken, to more accurately asses trends in animal behavior with increasing exposure to the robot.

Results of these tests show general trends in animal-robot interaction behavior by species, which inform the future development of autonomous behaviors, and future tests to better numerically describe these interactions.

Both cows and horses show general trends of interacting with the robot less frequently while the robot is in motion, and more frequently while the robot is stationary. These data indicate the general flight range for cows can be reasonably estimated to be between 6 m and 7 m from the robot. Based on that measurement, during autonomous behaviors, that distance, plus some margin, should be preserved if possible. Cows showed a uniform trend of fleeing from an approaching robot, and so it may be possible to count on them moving aside in the event the robot has to maneuver within the hypothesized flight range.

Meanwhile, the horse flight range is much shorter at approximately 3 m, but with greater variation. Horses less consistently moved or fled from an approaching robot, and were more likely to approach and interact with the robot even when the robot was in motion. This large uncertainty in behavior indicates that horses may be more unpredictable during autonomous operations. It is likely that behaviors in a pasture with horses will have to contend with more horse interaction compared to operation among cattle. These results suggest that interaction profiles may depend on species.

Regardless of uncertainty and some inconsistent data, a major finding of this work is that PSR1 was able to be introduced into a pasture with both cows and horses without inflicting undue stress upon them. Further data collection will help to quantify distances to maintain from the animals, but the current findings indicate an autonomous pasture maintenance robot is feasible and that animals can become habituated to the platform fairly quickly.

References

1. White, R.R., Hall, M.B.: Nutritional and greenhouse gas impacts of removing animals from US agriculture. Proc. Natl. Acad. Sci. **114**, 10301–10308 (2017)
2. Malik, P.K., Bhatta, R., Takahashi, J., Kohn, R., Prasad, C.S.: Livestock production and climate change. In: CABI (2015)
3. Food and Agriculture Organization of the United Nations: Tackling climate change through livestock: a global assessment of emissions and mitigation opportunities. (Food and Agriculture Organization (2013))

4. Precision agriculture technology for crop farming (2015). https://doi.org/10.1201/b19336

5. McKenzie, F.C., Williams, J.: Sustainable food production: constraints, challenges and choices by 2050. Food Security **7**(2), 221–233 (2015). https://doi.org/10.1007/s12571-015-0441-1

6. dos Reis, B.R., Easton, Z., White, R.R., Fuka, D.: A LoRa sensor network for monitoring pastured livestock location and activity. Transl. Animal Sci. **5**(2), txab010 (2021)

7. Ebertz, P., Krommweh, M.S., Büscher, W.: Feasibility study: improving floor cleanliness by using a robot scraper in group-housed pregnant sows and their reactions on the new device. Animals **9**, 185 (2019)

8. Thomas, B.L., Cutler, M., Novak, C.: A modified counterconditioning procedure prevents the renewal of conditioned fear in rats. Learn. Motiv. **43**, 24–34 (2012)

9. Doerfler, R.L., Lehermeier, C., Kliem, H., Möstl, E., Bernhardt, H.: Physiological and behavioral responses of dairy cattle to the introduction of robot scrapers. Front. Vet. Sci. **3**, 106 (2016)

10. Murphey, R.M., Duarte, F.A.M., Torres Penedo, M.C.: Responses of cattle to humans in open spaces: breed comparisons and approach-avoidance relationships. Behav. Genet. **11**, 37–48 (1981)

11. Lansade, L., Bouissou, M.-F., Erhard, H.: Fearfulness in horses: a temperament trait stable across time and situations. Appl. Anim. Behav. Sci. **115**, 182–200 (2008)

12. Austin, N.P., Rogers, L.J.: Asymmetry of flight and escape turning responses in horses. Laterality **12**, 464–474 (2007)

13. Kleinman, P.J.A., et al.: Managing agricultural phosphorus for water quality protection: principles for progress. Plant Soil **349**, 169–182 (2011)

14. Encyclopedia of energy, natural resource, and environmental economics. In: Newnes (2013)

15. Schacht, W.H., Reece, P.E.: Impact of livestock grazing on extensively managed grazing lands. In: Environmental Impacts of Pasture-Based Farming, pp. 122–143 (2008). https://doi.org/10.1079/9781845934118.0122

16. Soupir, M.L., Mostaghimi, S., Yagow, E.R., Hagedorn, C., Vaughan, D.H.: Transport of fecal bacteria from poultry litter and cattle manures applied to pastureland (2006)

17. Wang, H., Aguirre-Villegas, H.A., Larson, R.A., Alkan-Ozkaynak, A.: Physical properties of dairy manure pre- and post-anaerobic digestion. Appl. Sci. **9**, 2703 (2019)

18. Walter, M., Walter, M., Brooks, E., Steenhuis, T., Boll, J., Weiler, K.: Hydrologically sensitive areas: variable source area hydrology implications for water quality risk assessment. J. Soil Water Conserv. **55**,277–284 (2000)

A Functional Subnetwork Approach to Multistate Central Pattern Generator Phase Difference Control

Cody Scharzenberger[✉] and Alexander Hunt

Portland State University, Portland, OR 97207, USA
cscharz2@pdx.edu

Abstract. Central pattern generators (CPGs) are ubiquitous neural circuits that contribute to an eclectic collection of rhythmic behaviors across an equally diverse assortment of animal species. Due to their prominent role in many neuromechanical phenomena, numerous bioinspired robots have been designed to both investigate and exploit the operation of these neural oscillators. In order to serve as effective tools for these robotics applications, however, it is often necessary to be able to adjust the phase alignment of multiple CPGs during operation. To achieve this goal, we present the design of our phase difference control (PDC) network using a functional subnetwork approach (FSA) wherein subnetworks that perform basic mathematical operations are assembled such that they serve to control the relative phase lead/lag of target CPGs. Our PDC network operates by first estimating the phase difference between two CPGs, then comparing this phase difference to a reference signal that encodes the desired phase difference, and finally eliminating any error by emulating a proportional controller that adjusts the CPG oscillation frequencies. The architecture of our PDC network, as well as its various parameters, are all determined via analytical design rules that allow for direct interpretability of the network behavior. Simulation results for both the complete PDC network and a selection of its various functional subnetworks are provided to demonstrate the efficacy of our methodology.

Keywords: Multistate central pattern generators · Functional subnetwork approach · Phase difference control

1 Introduction

As one of the fundamental neural units that contributes to a myriad of rhythmic behaviors throughout the animal kingdom, central pattern generators (CPGs) have seen a plethora of academic research over the past several decades. Thanks to these efforts, there is strong evidence for the existence of CPGs in a wide

Supported by Portland State University and NSF DBI 2015317 as part of the NSF/CIHR/DFG/FRQ/UKRI-MRC Next Generation Networks for Neuroscience Program.

© The Author(s), under exclusive license to Springer Nature Switzerland AG 2022
A. Hunt et al. (Eds.): Living Machines 2022, LNAI 13548, pp. 378–389, 2022.
https://doi.org/10.1007/978-3-031-20470-8_37

variety of animals, including but not limited to insects [10], fish [9], mollusks [15], amphibians [8], and mammals [6], as well as numerous studies detailing their role in various animal behaviors from respiration [11] to swimming [15], flying [12], and ambulation [3]. At the same time, we have seen numerous examples of biologically inspired robots that incorporate CPG elements into their broader control schemes in attempts to study the underlying neuromechanical basis for locomotion [7]. Given their wide applicability to disparate fields of academic research from biology to robotics, it is difficult to overstate the importance of these ostensibly elementary neural circuits; yet, despite the abundance of research in this field, several fundamental areas of inquiry still remain open. Of particular importance to locomotor robotics applications is the question of how best multiple CPGs may be coordinated via descending commands to achieve desired activation patterns. More specifically, since many practical applications require the ability to modify the phase relationship between several interacting CPGs, such as in legged locomotion where the relative timing of individual legs segments varies by gait, it is necessary to be able to design systems of coupled CPGs whose phase difference may be adjusted by simple descending commands. This is precisely the feat that we set out to accomplish in this paper.

1.1   Our Contribution

We present a novel method for controlling the phase difference between several multistate CPGs using a non-spiking functional subnetwork approach (FSA). These CPGs are "multistate" in that they permit arbitrarily many neurons to become maximally excited in a specific, predetermined order. Similarly, the "functional subnetwork approach" refers to the analytical non-spiking network design techniques developed in [14], which we extend and apply extensively in this work to the design of our phase difference control (PDC) network. Our PDC network operates by: (1) computing the existing phase lead/lag between two multistate CPGs, (2) computing the difference between the computed phase lead/lag and the desired phase lead/lag represented by a single descending command, and (3) adjusting the relative excitation of the two CPGs to modify their oscillation frequency and thus adjust their phase difference based on a simple proportional control scheme. Compared to existing techniques such as [1], this method is novel not just in the analytical approach that we take to designing our PDC network, but also in the fact that we are able to control the relative phase difference between two multistate CPGs with a *single* descending command, as opposed to having a specific, pre-determined desired phase difference built into the network parameters themselves. Furthermore, the technique that we present here is applicable to controlling the relative phase of multistate CPGs arranged in arbitrary patterns, including both sequential chains of CPGs such as those found in lamprey [9] and salamander [8] applications, as well as configurations where multiple CPGs utilize a single reference CPG such as when pattern generating CPG layers connect to higher level rhythm generating CPG layers in walking applications [2].

2 Background

The two fields of information that are required to understand our PDC network formulation are those pertaining to central pattern generators (CPGs) and the non-spiking functional subnetwork approach (FSA).

2.1 Central Pattern Generators (CPGs)

As has perhaps already been made clear by the abundant selection of aforementioned studies, a thorough treatment of the history of CPGs and their development is beyond the scope of this work. For a summary, refer to works such as [6] and [10] that provide animal specific overviews. To meet our ends, it is sufficient to instead focus on the mathematical description of these dynamical systems.

Consider a CPG comprised of $n \in \mathbb{N}$ neurons. Let $\mathbb{N}_{\leq n} = \{1, \ldots, n\}$. Then $\forall i \in \mathbb{N}_{\leq n}$ the membrane voltage U_i of the ith neuron with respect to its resting potential $E_{r,i}$ with leak, synaptic, sodium channel, and applied currents satisfies

$$C_{m,i} \dot{U}_i = I_{leak,i} + I_{syn,i} + I_{Na,i} + I_{app,i} \tag{1}$$

where $C_{m,i}$ is the membrane capacitance and the constituent currents are defined as

$$I_{leak,i} = -G_{m,i} U_i, \tag{2}$$

$$I_{syn,i} = \sum_{j=1}^{n} G_{syn,ij}(\Delta E_{syn,ij} - U_i), \tag{3}$$

$$I_{Na,i} = G_{Na,i} m_{\infty,i} h_i (\Delta E_{Na,i} - U_i) \tag{4}$$

with membrane conductance $G_{m,i}$, synaptic reversal potential $\Delta E_{syn,ij}$, sodium channel conductance $G_{Na,i}$, and sodium channel reversal potential $\Delta E_{Na,i}$. Likewise, the synaptic conductance of the ijth synapse $G_{syn,ij}$ is defined by

$$G_{syn,ij} = g_{syn,ij} \min\left(\max\left(\frac{U_j}{R_j}, 0\right), 1\right) \tag{5}$$

where $g_{syn,ij}$ is the maximum synaptic conductance of the ijth synapse and R_j is the operating voltage domain of the jth pre-synaptic neuron. Note that h_i is a second dynamical variable that describes the sodium channel deactivation of neuron i and satisfies

$$\dot{h}_i = \frac{h_{\infty,i} - h_i}{\tau_{h,i}} \tag{6}$$

where the sodium channel deactivation time constant is

$$\tau_{h,i} = \tau_{h,max,i} h_{\infty,i} \sqrt{A_{h,i} e^{-S_{h,i}(\Delta E_{h,i} - U_i)}} \tag{7}$$

with maximum sodium channel deactivation time constant $\tau_{h,max,i}$, and sodium channel deactivation parameters $A_{h,i}$, $S_{h,i}$, and $\Delta E_{h,i}$. The final remaining variables of these equations are the steady state sodium channel activation and deactivation parameters defined by

$$m_{\infty,i} = \frac{1}{1 + A_{m,i}e^{-S_{m,i}(\Delta E_{m,i} - U_i)}},\tag{8}$$

$$h_{\infty,i} = \frac{1}{1 + A_{h,i}e^{-S_{h,i}(\Delta E_{h,i} - U_i)}}\tag{9}$$

where $A_{m,i}$, $S_{m,i}$, and $\Delta E_{m,i}$ are sodium channel activation parameters.

2.2 Functional Subnetwork Approach (FSA)

The functional subnetwork approach (FSA) refers to the analytical methods developed by [14] for designing subnetworks of non-spiking neurons to perform basic tasks, including: (1) signal transfer such as transmission and modulation; (2) arithmetic operations such as addition, subtraction, multiplication, and division; and (3) calculus operations such as differentiation and integration. One of the main attractions of this work lies in the fact that it combines *simple* neural architectures with *analytical* design rules constrained by biological limitations, a combination of features that ensures that the resulting subnetworks are both meaningful and easily interpretable. This is in contrast to the often "black-box" nature of networks whose architectures and other hyper-parameters are tuned via genetic algorithms [4] or Bayesian optimization [5], and whose lower level parameters are determined via any number of popular optimization schemes. In order to construct our phase difference controller subnetwork, we apply many slight variations of the different FSA subnetworks. For a thorough explanation of their original FSA design rules refer to Tables 1 and 2 in [14].

3 Methodology

Having established the context for this work, we now present the computational algorithm that our PDC network performs, as well as the mathematical formulations necessary to design each of its constituent subnetworks. Since the same PDC network architecture is used to control the relative phase between any pair of multistate CPGs, we can assume that we have $N = 2$ multistate CPGs with $n \in \mathbb{N}$ neurons each without loss of generality. Let the subscripts A and B refer to the properties of the first and second multistate CPGs, respectively. In this case, we wish to construct a PDC network that controls the phase difference $\Delta\phi_{AB} = \phi_A - \phi_B$ according to the desired phase difference encoded as an applied current. To accomplish this task, we: (1) create the two multistate CPGs whose relative phase we will control; (2) design a subnetwork that estimates the phase difference between these two CPGs; (3) compute the phase error relative to the desired phase reference; and (4), use a simple proportional control scheme to eliminate the error.

3.1 Designing Driven Multistate CPGs

The first step in designing our PDC subnetwork is to actually create the two multistate CPGs whose relative phase we will be controlling. To accomplish this, we draw significant inspiration from [13], extending their methodology to work for CPGs comprised of arbitrarily many neurons.

Sodium Channel Conductances $G_{Na,i}$. While the sodium channel reversal potentials $\Delta E_{Na,i}$ are determined based on biological constraints, the sodium channel conductances $G_{Na,i}$ are CPG exclusive parameters that must be set to ensure adequate intrinsic excitation of the CPG neurons. Fortunately, the use of arbitrarily many CPG neurons does not complicate [13]'s design rule beyond additional indexing, so no additional derivation is required.

Maximum Synaptic Conductances $g_{syn,ij}$. To compute the required maximum synaptic conductances $g_{syn,ij}$ for each synapse in our multistate CPG, we once again take inspiration from [13]. Szczecinski et al. point out that the oscillatory behavior of a two neuron CPG depends strongly on the bifurcation parameter δ, which represents the steady state membrane voltage of the inhibited neuron when the other neuron is excited. If $\delta \leq 0$, the system operates in a bistable mode. If instead $0 < \delta < \delta_{max}$, the system oscillates with increasing frequency as $\delta \to \delta_{max}$. Finally, once $\delta \geq \delta_{max}$, the system settles into a single stable equilibrium point.

For the purposes of our multistate CPG comprised of $n \in \mathbb{N}$ neurons, we will have $n(n-1)$ total δ_{ij} values to set, where each δ_{ij} represents the desired steady state membrane voltage U_i^* of neuron i when neuron j is maximally excited $\forall i, j \in \mathbb{N}_{\leq n}$ such that $i \neq j$. In other words, when $U_j^* = R_j$ we want $U_i^* = \delta_{ij}$ $\forall i \neq j$. Let $(k_j)_{j=1}^n = (k_1, \ldots, k_n)$ be a sequence of n indexes $k_j \in \mathbb{N}_{\leq n}$ such that $k_j \neq j$ that defines the order in which we would like the neurons of our multistate CPG to become maximally excited. To ensure that only a single neuron becomes excited at a time and that the system oscillates in the desired order, we require that $\forall j \in \mathbb{N}_{\leq n}$ with $i \neq j$

$$\begin{cases} 0 < \delta_{ij} < \delta_{max}, & \text{if } i = k_j \\ \delta_{ij} < 0, & \text{otherwise} \end{cases} \tag{10}$$

In other words, we require that when each CPG neuron becomes excited, only one other neuron in the network attains a positive (but not too large) steady state membrane voltage $0 < \delta_{ij} < \delta_{max,ij}$ and that this neuron be the one that we desire to become maximally excited next. All other neurons in the CPG subnetwork should attain negative steady state membrane voltages $\delta_{ij} < 0$.

With an appropriate selection of bifurcation parameters δ_{ij}, we can write a system of equations that describes the steady state behavior of the multistate CPG system when each of its neurons is maximally excited one at a time.

Specifically, $\forall i, j, k \in \mathbb{N}_{\leq n}$ with $i \neq j$, $j \neq k$, and $k \neq i$ we have

$$
0 = -G_{m,i}\delta_{ik} + \sum_{j=1, j \neq k}^{n} g_{syn,ij} \min \left(\max \left(\frac{\delta_{jk}}{R_j}, 0 \right), 1 \right) (\Delta E_{syn,ij} - \delta_{ik})
$$
$$
+ G_{Na,i} m_{\infty,i} (\delta_{ik}) h_{\infty,i} (\delta_{ik}) (\Delta E_{Na,i} - \delta_{ik}) + I_{app,i}
$$
(11)

where i indicates the post-synaptic neuron of interest, j indicates the pre-synaptic neuron of interest, and k indicates the neuron that is maximally excited. The previous expression is actually a system of $n(n-1)$ equations with the $n(n-1)$ maximum synaptic conductances $g_{syn,ij}$ being the only unknowns (we do not use self-connections, so $g_{syn,ij} = 0 \; \forall i = j$). Solving this system for the unknown $g_{syn,ij}$ allows us to design a multistate CPG that oscillates in the order determined by our choice of δ_{ij} values.

Designing Drive Synapses. In order to control the phase difference between two of our multistate CPGs, it is necessary that we design a mechanism through which we can adjust their relative oscillation frequency. Since each δ_{ij} represents the steady state membrane voltage U_i^* of neuron i when neuron j is maximally excited, we can temporarily adjust the steady state membrane voltage U_i^* without changing the associated δ_{ij} for which we designed our network by applying an external drive current $I_{dr,i}$ to the ith neuron. When this drive current has a magnitude of zero, the transition between neurons j and i occurs at the frequency determined by δ_{ij}. However, as we increase this drive current up to some maximum value $I_{dr,id}^{max}$, the transition between neurons j and i occurs with an increased frequency beyond that associated with δ_{ij}. Since it is our intention to control the *aggregate* phase difference between these CPGs, we use a single drive current per CPG that increases the transition frequency of all pairs of neurons.

In order to control the CPG phase difference via feedback, this drive current must be created via synaptic connections from a single drive neuron (one per multistate CPG). Let $d \in \mathbb{N}$ be the index associated with the drive neuron. Consider the synaptic currents $I_{syn,id}$ generated by the drive neuron $\forall i \in \mathbb{N}_{\leq n}$

$$
I_{syn,id} = g_{syn,id} \min \left(\max \left(\frac{U_d}{R_d}, 0 \right), 1 \right) (\Delta E_{syn,id} - U_i).
$$
(12)

We want to choose $g_{syn,id}$ such that when $U_d = R_d$ and $U_i = \max_{j \in \mathbb{N}} (\delta_{ij})$ then $I_{syn,id} = I_{dr,id}^{max}$. Making these substitutions into the above equation and solving for $g_{syn,id}$ yields our drive maximum synaptic conductance design requirement

$$
g_{syn,id} = \frac{I_{dr,id}^{max}}{\Delta E_{syn,id} - \max_{j \in \mathbb{N}} (\delta_{ij})}.
$$
(13)

3.2   Estimating Phase Lead/Lag

Estimating the phase lead/lag of the two CPGs is the most involved part of controlling their phase difference. This procedure adheres to the following logic: (1)

subtract the signals from the corresponding neurons in the CPGs, (2) integrate and post-process this difference to get a proxy for the phase difference, and (3) combine the phase difference estimates for each CPG neuron pair into a single phase difference estimate.

Double Subtraction Subnetwork. To begin this process, we first subtract the membrane voltages of the corresponding CPG neurons such that $\Delta V_{AB,i} = V_{A,i} - V_{B,i} \; \forall i \in \mathbb{N}_{\leq n}$. In order to ensure that we can represent both lead and lag conditions, we perform this subtraction in both directions, resulting in two signals (e.g., $\Delta V_{AB,i}$ and $\Delta V_{BA,i}$). The first of these signals, $\Delta V_{AB,i}$, is maximized when neuron i of CPG A is maximally excited and neuron i of CPG B is inactive, while the second, $\Delta V_{BA,i}$, exhibits the opposite behavior.

While these two signals are not direct proxies for the phase difference between the two CPG neurons, they do provide information about the phase of the system. Fortunately, no additional design rules are required here because our double subtraction subnetwork is merely a combination of two of the single subtraction subnetworks from [14].

Voltage-Based Integration Subnetwork. In order to determine the extent to which one CPG leads/lags the other, we must integrate the result of our double subtraction subnetwork using a modification of the integration subnetwork from [14]. Integrating $\Delta V_{AB,i}$ and $\Delta V_{BA,i}$ over time indicates how long the ith neuron of each CPG was held high while the other was inactive. Thus by integrating these signals over the oscillation period T of the CPGs, we can compute a proxy $T_{AB,i}$ for the temporal lead/lag between the ith neurons by

$$ T_{AB,i} = \int_0^T \Delta V_{AB,i} - \Delta V_{BA,i} dt. \tag{14} $$

Note that here we are assuming that the two CPGs have the same oscillation period T, which will not be the case once we start driving them at different oscillation frequencies to control their phase difference. This is not a problem in practice so long as the ith neuron of the lagging CPG does not become inactive while the ith neuron of the leading CPG remains active. Practically speaking, this limits how quickly we can adjust the phase difference of the two CPGs.

Post-Processing Neuron Phase Difference Estimates. Having computed a rough proxy for the temporal lead/lag between the ith neurons of two CPGs, it is prudent to clean up this result before proceeding. In particular, the integration subnetwork result tends to change linearly over time as it accumulates incoming currents. Although such behavior is expected of an integrator, it is not ideal for achieving an accurate phase difference estimate because the temporal lead/lag estimate is only accurate after the integrator has reached a steady state result, not during the transient period wherein it accumulates currents.

To address this problem, we first split the centered integration result into two signals via a second double subtraction subnetwork. The first of these signals is produced by a neuron that is excited when the integration output is above its equilibrium value and the second when it is below its equilibrium value. Once the integration result is split into two signals, the linear ramping portions of these signals are removed via a modulation subnetwork [14] that is setup to suppress the results when either $V_{AB,i}$ or $V_{BA,i}$ are high. We call the signals from this modulatory subnetwork $V_{lead,i}$ and $V_{lag,i}$.

Aggregating Phase Difference Estimates. With clean temporal lead/lag estimates $V_{lead,i}$ and $V_{lag,i}$ for each of the neuron pairs in our two CPGs, we can now aggregate these results into single CPG-based lead/lag estimates V_{lead} and V_{lag}. Due to the fact that only one neuron in each CPG is active at a time and that we remove the integration transients, the act of combining the various neuron-based temporal lead and lag estimates is a simple matter of addition. This means that we can use an addition subnetwork from [14] to perform the calculations $V_{lead} = \sum_{i=1}^{n} V_{lead,i}$ and $V_{lag} = \sum_{i=1}^{n} V_{lag,i}$.

Although we now have neural estimates of the temporal lead/lag for our two CPGs, it is necessary to consolidate these estimates into a single value for the purpose of later computing phase error. To accomplish this, we use a combination of transmission, addition, and subtraction subnetworks that we refer to as a "centering subnetwork." First, the V_{lead} and V_{lag} signals are scaled via transmission synapses, then they are shifted upward using a tonic signal of $\frac{R_{center}}{2}$, and finally the opposing scaled signal is subtracted to produce a single, centered lead/lag estimate. Since all of the subnetworks that comprise our centering subnetwork are discussed in [13], no new design rules are necessary.

3.3   Eliminating Phase Error

Given a reasonable proxy for the phase difference between the two CPGs, the next step is to compare this estimate with the desired phase difference and then to take corrective actions to eliminate any error. To begin, we directly compute the phase error via a third double subtraction subnetwork. This time the first output of the double subtraction subnetwork is high when CPG A leads CPG B by too great of a margin, and visa versa for the second output. Despite the fact that these error signals contain the information that the control system needs, the fact that they are split among two neurons is inconvenient. As such, we implement a second centering subnetwork using the same strategy as discussed in Sect. 3.2. Like before the first output of the centering subnetwork is high when CPG A leads CPG B too significantly, low when CPG A lags CPG B too significantly, and exactly in the middle of its representational domain when there is no error. The second output of the centering subnetwork has an exactly inverse interpretation. Given this representation of the error, we can now implement any number of control schemes to eliminate the error by adjusting the currents to the drive neurons for our two multistate CPGs. This work uses a simple proportional control scheme wherein the greater the phase error the more substantial the adjustment in the current applied to each drive neuron.

4 Results

Given the analytical design rules for our various functional subnetworks in Sect. 3, we now turn our attention to demonstrating that these design rules do in fact yield networks that produce the desired results. Toward this end, Fig. 1 summarizes the architectures and open loop simulation results of each of the main functional subnetworks components in their context as part of the PDC network. Neuron C1 serves as the drive neuron in the CPG shown in Fig. 1 and is set to have a small tonic current in order to achieve slow oscillation.

Figure 2 demonstrates the impact that our PDC network has on the CPGs it controls as the desired lead/lag reference is varied.

5 Discussion

The results presented in Sect. 4 indicate that both our individual subnetworks and the fully assembled PDC network accomplish their stated goals. More specifically, as shown in Fig. 1, our multistate CPGs produce robust oscillations that follow their specified neuron oscillation order and respond well to changes in the drive neuron state. Similarly, our basic subnetworks, including our addition, subtraction, integration, and centering subnetworks all perform their associated mathematical operations in Fig. 1 with similar quality to that reported by [14]. Despite the relative slowness of our PDC network, the results generated by this network 2 do demonstrate its ability to adjust the phase difference of two multistate CPGs using a single descending command.

Although our novel PDC network is successful at controlling phase differences, there are several potential areas for improvement, including: (1) improving the robustness of our phase difference estimate; (2) incorporating numerical optimization techniques; and (3) utilizing a more sophisticated control scheme. The first of these improvements concerns the main limiting factor of our current approach. Since our computational strategy for estimating phase difference requires not only that each pair of associated CPG neurons have over lapping signals, but also that the oscillation period of the two CPGs remain relatively similar, there are significant limitations on how quickly we can adjust the phase of our CPGs. One potential solution to these limitations is to estimate phase differences by detecting the rising and falling edges of our CPG neurons, rather than directly subtracting their voltage signals. Once the phase difference estimate it more robust to changing oscillation frequencies, it should be possible to further refine the accuracy of our functional subnetworks by employing numerical optimization techniques. While each of our individual functional subnetworks have been optimized analytically for their specific operation, it is intractable to perform this same type of analysis on the complete network; hence the value in employing a numerical approach. Finally, a more sophisticated control law, such

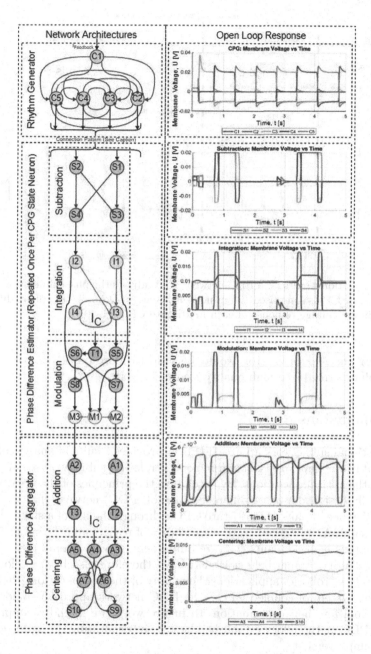

Fig. 1. Selected functional subnetwork architectures and their associated open loop responses in the context of a PDC network. While only a single CPG is shown in the rhythm generator, the other subnetwork responses are selected from a simulation with two multistate CPGs wherein CPG *A* lags CPG *B*. Neurons C2-C5 from CPG *A* connect to neuron S1 from their associated phase difference estimator, while neurons C2-C5 from CPG B connect to S2 from their associated phase difference estimator.

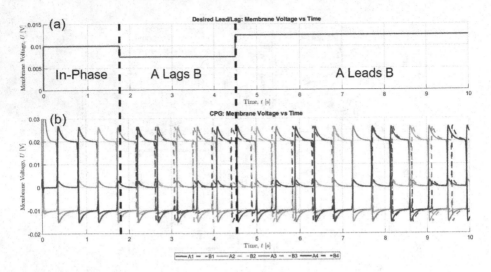

Fig. 2. Simulation results for a PDC network that adjusts the phase difference between two multistate CPGs comprised of four neurons each. (a) Desired CPG phase difference. (b) Membrane voltage response of each multistate CPG.

as PID or state-space control, would be able to more quickly and accurately reduce phase error given high quality feedback.

6   Conclusions

The functional subnetwork approach (FSA) provides a suite of analytical design tools that can be leveraged to build biological relevant subnetworks that perform basic mathematical operations. By extending the principles of the FSA, we have successfully designed a phase difference control (PDC) network that adjusts the phase difference of pairs of multistate CPGs through the use of a single descending command. As evidenced by the large body of research on the subject, CPGs are ubiquitous neural circuits that are fundamental to the proper functioning of many oscillatory animal behaviors and have therefore also been explored in a wide variety of robotics applications. For many of these applications that utilize a complex system of coupled CPGs, the PDC network approach could provide a useful tool for their coordination. In future work, we intend to improve the existing PDC methodology established here by incorporating the aforementioned areas of improvement.

Acknowledgement. The authors acknowledge support by Portland State University and NSF DBI 2015317 as part of the NSF/CIHR/DFG/FRQ/UKRI-MRC Next Generation Networks for Neuroscience Program.

References

1. Cohen, A.H., Bard Ermentrout, G., Kiemel, T., Kopell, N., Sigvardt, K.A., Williams, T.L.: Modelling of intersegmental coordination in the lamprey central pattern generator for locomotion. Trends Neurosci. **15**(11), 434–438 (1992). http://linkinghub.elsevier.com/retrieve/pii/016622369290006T
2. Deng, K., et al.: Neuromechanical model of rat hindlimb walking with two-layer CPGs. Biomimetics **4**(1), 21 (2019). http://www.mdpi.com/2313-7673/4/1/21
3. Duysens, J., Van de Crommert, H.W.: Neural control of locomotion; Part 1: the central pattern generator from cats to humans. Gait Posture **7**(2), 131–141 (1998). http://linkinghub.elsevier.com/retrieve/pii/S0966636297000428
4. Forrest, S.: Genetic Algorithms. ACM Comput. Surv. **28**(1), 4 (1996)
5. Frazier, P.I.: A tutorial on Bayesian optimization. arXiv:1807.02811 (2018)
6. Guertin, P.A.: The mammalian central pattern generator for locomotion. Brain Res. Rev. **62**(1), 45–56 (2009). http://linkinghub.elsevier.com/retrieve/pii/S0165017309000812
7. Hunt, A., Szczecinski, N., Quinn, R.: Development and training of a neural controller for hind leg walking in a dog robot. Front. Neurorobot. **11**, 18 (2017). http://journal.frontiersin.org/article/10.3389/fnbot.2017.00018/full
8. Ijspeert, A.J.: A connectionist central pattern generator for the aquatic and terrestrial gaits of a simulated salamander. Biolog. Cybern. **84**(5), 331–348 (2001). http://link.springer.com/10.1007/s004220000211
9. Ijspeert, A.J., Kodjabachian, J.: Evolution and development of a central pattern generator for the swimming of a lamprey. Artificial Life **5**(3), 247–269 (1999). http://direct.mit.edu/artl/article/5/3/247-269/2322
10. Mantziaris, C., Bockemühl, T., Büschges, A.: Central pattern generating networks in insect locomotion. Develop. Neurobiol. **80**(1–2), 16–30 (2020). http://onlinelibrary.wiley.com/doi/10.1002/dneu.22738
11. Rubin, J.E., Shevtsova, N.A., Ermentrout, G.B., Smith, J.C., Rybak, I.A.: Multiple rhythmic states in a model of the respiratory central pattern generator. J. Neurophys. **101**(4), 2146–2165 (2009). http://www.physiology.org/doi/10.1152/jn.90958.2008
12. Stevenson, P.A., Kutsch, W.: A reconsideration of the central pattern generator concept for locust flight. J. Compar. Phys. A **161**(1), 115–129 (1987). http://link.springer.com/10.1007/BF00609460
13. Szczecinski, N.S., Hunt, A.J., Quinn, R.D.: Design process and tools for dynamic neuromechanical models and robot controllers. Biolog. Cybern. **111**(1), 105–127 (2017). http://link.springer.com/10.1007/s00422-017-0711-4
14. Szczecinski, N.S., Hunt, A.J., Quinn, R.D.: A functional subnetwork approach to designing synthetic nervous systems that control legged robot locomotion. Front. Neurorobot. **11**, 37 (2017). http://journal.frontiersin.org/article/10.3389/fnbot.2017.00037/full
15. Thompson, S., Watson, W.H.: Central pattern generator for swimming in Melibe. J. Exper. Biol. **208**(7), 1347–1361 (2005). http://journals.biologists.com/jeb/article/208/7/1347/16006/Central-pattern-generator-for-swimming-in-Melibe

Time-Evolution Characterization
of Behavior Class Prototypes

Shanel C. Pickard[1,2](✉) (iD)

[1] Case Western Reserve University, Cleveland, OH 44106, USA
sxp671@case.edu
[2] University of Illinois at Urbana-Champaign, Urbana, IL 61801, USA

Abstract. Neuroscientists and roboticists alike are interested in how both the external cues and internal states contribute to determining behavioral sequences. As the motivation drivers change through time, so does the animal switch between alternating activities and outward exhibition of patterned behavior. It is accepted that underlying neural integration of internal states - as well as incoming information of the external environment - give rise to the adaptive abilities of animal behavior in different contexts. Here, the sequences of hunting-motivated behavior of praying mantises were modeled as Markov chains, with each sequence giving rise to a corresponding transition probability matrix. From these transition matrices, three methods of prototype generation were used - cumulative, centroid, and medoid - to produce categorical representatives of the time series data of all five feeding states used in the experiments. Novel to this paper, is the use of Markovian chain metrics to compare the efficacy of these prototypes at capturing the time-evolution behavior unique to each feed state. Results show that the cumulative prototypes best exhibited temporal behaviors most consistent with the real data.

Keywords: Behavioral analysis · Markov chain · Class prototype

1 Introduction

The time series nature of behavior sequences presents interesting opportunities to glean patterns within the order of presentation. Probabilistic-based approaches help capture the stochastic nature [6], but to represent a central tendency of a time series category with a low-dimensional, single representative remains challenging. The goal of a central tendency representative is to capture the breadth of typical properties - the prototypical features - of a category or class. Clustering algorithms, for instance, aim to find this central member (in the case of medoid algorithms) or the central abstraction (as in the case of centroid) as a means to define categorical cluster center [8]. Difficulties arise when time series samples are of different lengths or of irregular sampling intervals, which makes clustering algorithms hard to implement [1]. In this paper, behavior sequences

© The Author(s), under exclusive license to Springer Nature Switzerland AG 2022
A. Hunt et al. (Eds.): Living Machines 2022, LNAI 13548, pp. 390–402, 2022.
https://doi.org/10.1007/978-3-031-20470-8_38

are modeled as Markov chains and used to generate transition probability matrices for each sequence of behavior. Using these transition probability matrices in lieu of the time series behavior allows the issue with variable sequence lengths to be circumvented when trying to compare sequence-to-sequence trends. From the transition probability matrices of each subsequence, three types of prototypes were generated for each feed state: cumulative, centroid, and medoid. Novel to this paper is the comparison of the time-evolution characteristics of the prototypes to the real data. These comparisons were done as a proof-of-concept of Markovian metrics in selecting prototypes that best captured class trends of the five different feed states used in the original experimentation [10].

Introduction to Markov Chains. Markov chains are a widely used to modeling the underlying state dependency for future predictions. Due to its utility in gleaning sequential patterning, Markov chains have been used to quantify processes across a myriad of fields including in the classification and comparison of animal behavior [2, 7]. The underlying assumption of Markov chain is that the behaviors observed in the N previous time steps serve as predictors for the current behavior, with N being the number of time steps in the past (also known as the degree of the Markov model). The possible behaviors belong to a countable set defining the state space of the behavior process and is denoted with the variable x_i, $i \in \{1, ..., k\}$, where i indexes through the list of possible behaviors up through the last, x_k, behavior bin. In the case of the praying mantis behaviors, there are $k = 12$ defined behaviors, including the terminal state of arena resets. The general form of the Markov chain, where the current behavior, x_i, observed in the current time step, n, is expressed as the product rule of joint probability distributions of all the previous behaviors spanning back N steps in the past:

$$p(x_{i_1}, ..., x_{i_N}) = p(x_{i_n}|x_{i_{n-1}}, ..., x_{i_1})p(x_{i_{n-1}}|x_{i_{n-2}}, ..., x_{i_1})...p(x_{i_1}) \qquad (1.0.1)$$

$$\prod_{n=2}^{N} p(x_{i_n}|x_{i_{n-1}}, ..., x_{i_1}). \qquad (1.0.2)$$

If the Markov is first order (as was the case for the Markov chains in this paper), then the assumption is that the current behavior is independent of all past behaviors except for the previous behavior at time step n-1 and the above expression gets simplified to

$$p(x_{i_1}, ..., x_{i_N}) = p(x_{i_1}) \prod_{n=2}^{N} p(x_{i_n}|x_{i_{n-1}}). \qquad (1.0.3)$$

The $p(x_{i_1})$ term is the prior probability used in Bayesian statistical inference to express the probability of observing this initial behavior in the initial time step [3]. By using the property of d-separation, the expression of the conditional distribution becomes

$$p(x_{i_n}|x_{i_{n-1}}, ..., x_{i_1}) = p(x_{i_n}|x_{i_{n-1}}), \qquad (1.0.4)$$

which ultimately expresses the probability of observing the current behavior, x_{i_n}, given the previous behavior $x_{i_{n-1}}$ has occurred.

2 Methods

2.1 Experimental Setup and Data Extraction

Experiments were all done with female *Tenodera sinensis* that were post-eclosion 14–18 days. Healthy animals that were chosen for experimental trials were permitted water but deprived of food 5–7 days prior to the commencement of experiments. Experiment setup entailed a single praying mantis centrally placed within the an arena (37 × 29 cm) followed by four cockroach nymphs (*Blaberus discoidalis*). Confined to the area of the arena, the praying mantis was free to transverse the layout and hunt for prey. Animals were silhouetted by underlit lighting, and behaviors were captured with an overhead video camera. From the videographic data, behavior was binned into one of twelve designated categories by two experimenters. For a more detailed explanation of data collection and behavior designations, please reference Pickard *et al.* [10]. Table 1 provides a summary of the twelve extracted behavior bins and their respective description.

2.2 Generating Prototypes

The behavior sequences that were observed in each feeding state each corresponded to an individual transition matrix. To assemble this $k \times k$ transition matrix (where $k = 1,...12$ possible behaviors), the probability of each behavior transitioning to every other behavior is calculated. Each row of the transition matrix is constrained to add to 1, as expressed in the following equation:

$$\sum_{k=1}^{K} P_{i_k} = \sum_{k=1}^{K} P(x_\mathrm{n} = k|_{\mathrm{n-1}} = i) = 1. \tag{2.2.1}$$

For a discrete Markov chain, as in this paper, each row constitutes a probability mass distribution of probabilities of transitioning out of a behavior, x_i into any of the k behavior bins. The final probability matrix takes the form:

$$P = \begin{bmatrix} P_{11} & P_{12} & P_{13} & \dots & P_{1k} \\ P_{21} & P_{22} & P_{23} & \dots & P_{2n} \\ \vdots & \vdots & \vdots & \ddots & \vdots \\ P_{k1} & P_{k2} & P_{k3} & \dots & P_{kk} \end{bmatrix} \tag{2.2.2}$$

From the transition probabilities matrices, Three transition matrix prototypes were generated using different techniques: 1) cumulative, 2) centroid, and 3) medoid. These three types of metrics were used since they represent three common, yet different ways in which to represent central tendency of a data set. The cumulative transition matrix prototype was assembled as described above, however, a single matrix was generated from the summation of each transition type across all animals *within a whole feeding state*. This was done for each feed state (0,1,2,3, and 4 fed), thereby creating five cumulative prototypes.

Table 1. Summary of behavior bins and their respective descriptions. These behavior bins are the $k = 12$ states that are possible within the Markov model.

Behavior	Description
Successful Strike	*Ballistic extension of the raptorial forearms with successful capture of a cockroach nymph. Hunting specific behavior.*
Missed Strike	*Attempted capture of a cockroach but was unsuccessful. Hunting specific behavior.*
Specific Translation	*Translation towards a specific nymph to close the distance to the prey. Hunting specific behavior.*
Specific Rotation	*Rotation of the head, prothorax, total body, or combination thereof towards a specific nymph in order to centralize prey in the center of the visual field. Hunting specific behavior.*
Specific Monitoring	*Attention to specific prey. This bin is inclusive of slight movements such as leaning towards prey and peering, but excludes rotations and translations. Hunting specific behavior.*
General Monitoring	*Stationary assessment of the arena without specific attention paid towards specific prey. Non-hunting behavior.*
General Translation	*Translation not towards specific prey. Non-hunting behavior.*
General Rotation	*Rotation of head, prothorax, total body, or combination of the above not towards specific prey. Non-hunting behavior.*
Grooming	*Cleaning of the raptorial arms, head, antennae, or legs. Non-hunting behavior.*
Deimatic	*Stereotyped defensive display towards a predator or threatening object, with forearms, wings, and/or abdomen raised in threatening posture. Non-hunting behavior.*
Escape	*Attempting to climb the experimental arena walls. Non-hunting behavior.*
Arena Reset	*Although not a behavior exhibited by the animal, an arena reset is an absorbing bin that signifies the end of a behavior sequence. Absorbing state.*

The centroid transition matrix, C, is assembled from the centroid found at each element across all transition matrices, $C_{i,j}$, within a feed state. the calculation merely becomes the averaged element values [8]:

$$C_{i,j} = \frac{\sum P_{i,j^1} + ... + P_{i,j^n}}{n} \tag{2.2.3}$$

The medoid transition matrix is unique amongst the presented prototypes in that a medoid does not create an abstract element - unlike the cumulative matrix and centroid matrix which are not actual elements of the original data set. In this method, the central tendency is defined as the center of a cluster of the transition matrices belonging to a single feed state which minimizes the sum of squared distances of the members of the group [8]:

$$P_{medoid} = argmin \sum d(P_i, P_j) \tag{2.2.4}$$

The medoid can be defined with many different distance metrics (e.g. Manhattan distance, cosine), however, in this paper, only the Euclidean distance was used. With these three different prototypes, Markovian metrics were used to compare how well they each performed in representing the behavior trends as a correlate of satiety.

3   Results

3.1   Ethograms and Captured Behavior Transitions

The ethograms of the three different prototypes shown in Fig. 1 represent the culminated repertoire of observed transitions captured by the respective prototypes across feed states. The color of the lines correspond to the transition probability as seen in the reference scale at the bottom of the figure. If a behavior was not exhibited, the behavior point was not displayed, as in the case of no escape behavior in Fig. 1Aiii and 1Biii. The cumulative prototypes (Figs. 1Ai-Av) and centroid prototypes (Figs. 1Bi-Bv) show similar transition profiles to one another, indicating that the two prototype methods captured similar transitions that were possible within each feed state. The medoid plots of Figs. 1Ci-Cv show an underwhelming variety of possible transitions as compared to the cumulative and centroid plots.

3.2   Hit Probabilities and Absorption Times

To evaluate the time evolution of behavior of a given Markov chain. Both the hit probabilities and absorption times give insight into how any given state will progress to another state; the former calculates the probability of reaching a downstream behavior given a starting behavior. The absorption time is reported as the number of time steps predicted to reach the absorption state (i.e. the terminating behavior that brings the sequence to an end) from any given behavior.

Hit Probabilities of Prototypes. Hit probabilities represent the probability of hitting a specified target state given a starting state. In Fig. 2, the hit probabilities are shown for select target behaviors: successful strike (Figs. 2Ai, 2Bi, and 2Ci), specific monitoring (Figs. 2Aii, 2Bii, and 2Cii), general monitoring (Figs. 2Aiii, 2Biii, and 2Ciii), and escape (Figs. 2Aiv, 2Biv, and 2Civ). The cumulative and the centroid prototypes (Figs. 2A and 2B) are very similar in calculated hit probabilities. Successful strikes (Figs. 2Ai and 2Bi) show high probability of being expressed regardless of starting behavior. This holds true across feed states (columns within a plot), but the probability is especially high in the more starved feed states 0, 1, and 2 - with the exception of 0-fed and 1-fed general translation. Conversely, the 4-fed behavior seen in the cumulative and centroid prototypes did not show strong tendencies to converge to successful strikes as indicated by the relatively low probabilities of reaching a successful strike from all starting behaviors (4-fed column in Figs. 2Ai and 2Bi).

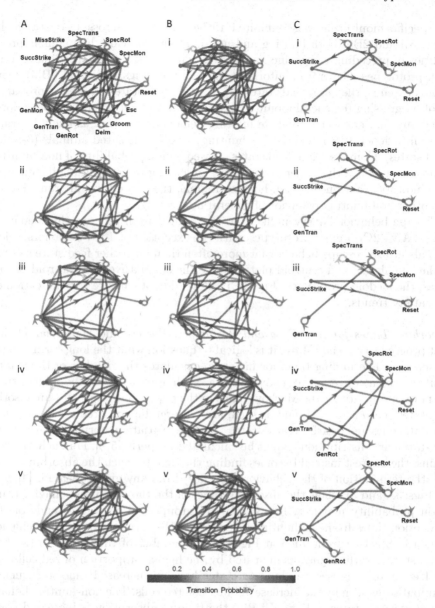

Fig. 1. Ethograms generated from the prototype transition probability matrices across all feed states. Line colors correspond to the probability of transition as shown on the color scale at the bottom of the figure. Cooler colors correspond to lower probability of transition; warmer colors correspond to higher probability of transitional. Each column of ethograms corresponds to the prototypes: (Ai-Av) cumulative for feed states 0–4, (Bi-Bv) centroid for feed states 0–4, and (Ci-Cv) medoid for feed states 0–4. SuccStrike:successful strike; MissStrike:missed strike; SpecTrans:specific translation; SpecRot:specific rotation; SpecMon:specific monitor; GenMon:general monitoring; GenTrans:general translation; GenRot:general rotation; Deim:deimatic; Esc:Escape. (Color figure online)

Specific monitoring was exhibited rather similarly across feed states. In Figs. 2Aii and 2Bii, both hunting and non-hunting behaviors had similar probabilities of preceding to specific monitoring, with weak satiety trending seen in both prototypes. General monitoring target graphs (Figs. 2Aiii and 2Biii) show stronger trends; the lower feed states (0-, 1-, and 2-fed states) show low probability of progressing to general monitoring starting from hunting specific behaviors, indicating that starved animals in hunting behaviors were not as likely to transition into general monitoring (non-hunting) as often as sated animals (3-, and 4-fed states). Conversely, all feed states showed a high probability of non-hunting behaviors significantly higher probabilities of leading to general monitoring and thus indicates that once in non-hunting regime, the animal would transition to this other non-hunting behavior of general monitoring.

Escape behavior is very unlikely to be reached from any starting behavior (Figs. 2Aiv - 2Civ) in all prototypes, with the exception of 4-fed behaviors. 4-fed animals utilized escape behavior far more often than any other feed state as seen in the cumulative and centroid plots. Unlike the cumulative and centroid prototypes, the medoid prototypes (Figs. 2Ci - 2Civ) do not capture any indication of the satiety trends.

Absorbing Times for Real Data and Prototypes. For ergodic Markovian chains that proceed to a steady state, it is logical to question what the long-term behavior may be. The mixing time, for instance, calculates the number of time steps until the chain converges to a steady state. Such approaches as the mixing time are not appropriate for the Markov chains in the paper since they contain absorbing states (i.e. $P_{k \to k} = 1$), and as such, are not ergodic nor irreducible. Because the data does not reach steady-state, the total variation norm distance from the stationary distribution cannot be calculated properly [5,9]. For such Markov chains, the interest instead becomes finding the time to reach the absorbing state (i.e. the termination of the behavior sequence) from any given behavior [4].

Figs. 3A and 3B show the absorbing times of the the *real* date behavior transition probability matrices. Fig. 3Ai-Av are grouped to show the tends of the absorption times from the hunting behaviors to the termination of the behavior sequence. Starting from 0-fed at Fig. 3Ai, the number of time steps to the terminal state is rather quick as indicated by the higher proportion of red cells. As the feed state increases, the hunting states have an increased time to sequence termination as seen by the increase in bluer colored cells. The non-hunting behaviors of starved states in Figs. 3Bi-Biii, the time to absorption is increased compared to hunting behaviors. As the animals became more sated, the non-hunting behaviors showed to be predictive of sequence termination comparable to that of hunting behaviors (see Figs. 3AV and 3BV). This indicates that sated animals had roughly equal time to termination from either hunting and non-hunting behaviors, while starves animals have a clear bias in faster termination from hunting.

The absorption times for the *prototypes* are shown in Figs. 3Ci-Ciii. The cumulative prototypes (Fig. 3Ci), support the trend across feed states, where lower feed states have faster absorption times when compared to sated states. Furthermore, the hunting behaviors showed a faster bias of leading to sequence termination over the non-hunting behaviors. This is further supported by Fig. 3Di that shows the absorption times for each behavior across the feed states for the cumulative prototypes. 0-fed and 1-fed profiles are very similar with all behaviors having faster sequence termination when compared to the progressively sated prototypes. Both the centroid and medoid prototypes don't capture these categorical trends as seen in both Figs. 3Cii-Ciii and Figs. 3Dii-Diii.

3.3   Simulations for Real Data and Prototypes

From each real and prototype transition matrix, 1000 random walk simulations were performed with 2000 simulation steps each. Fig. 4 shows the distribution of states across the 2000 times steps for each behavior. At each time step, the probability of being in each specific behavior is color coded to the reference provided. In Figs. 4Ai-Aiv, the distributions of select behaviors are plotted together across all feed states to show the tendency of reaching these behaviors. Successful strike in Fig. 4Ai shows that lower feed states (0- and 1-fed states) predict faster expression of successful strikes, while higher feed states show greater delays to food capture. Like in the other results sections, specific monitoring in Fig. 4Aii is relatively similar across the feed states, but has a slight increase in probability of expression in the 2-fed state. General monitoring (Fig. 4Aiii) shows increased probability of being expressed as the feed state increases. And lastly, shown in Fig. 4Aiv, escape behavior is not widely used with the exception of 4-fed state runs.

The cumulative prototype simulations in Fig. 4Bi plots showed the best at capturing real data trends across feed states. Successful strikes longer to reach as satiety progressively increased; specific monitoring was relatively similar for all feed states, with a slight increase in 2-fed; general monitoring showed progressively faster expression as satiety increased; and lastly, escape behavior was relatively muted in all feed states. The centroid and medoid prototypes (Fig. 4Bii-Biii) did not perform as well at capturing behavior trends.

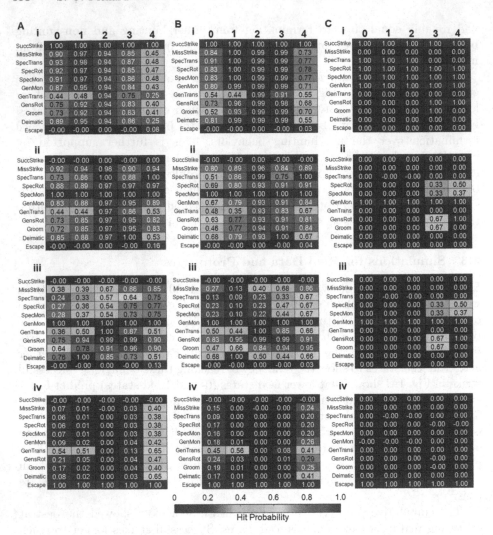

Fig. 2. Hit probabilities to target of all prototypes across feed states. For i-iv, the target was set to be successful strike, specific monitoring, general monitoring, and escape, respectively. The probability of starting in a behavior that will eventually lead to the target is reported in each cell. Color coding is consistent with the legend at the bottom of the figure, where cool colors are low probabilities, while warmer color represent higher probabilities. i-iv targets are consistent across the prototypes: (Ai-Aiv) Cumulative, (Bi-Biv) centroid, and (Ci-Civ) medoid. Each column in a heat plot corresponds to a feed state, consistent with the labeling in the top row. SuccStrike:successful strike; MissStrike:missed strike; SpecTrans:specific translation; SpecRot:specific rotation; SpecMon:specific monitor; GenMon:general monitoring; GenTrans:general translation; GenRot:general rotation; Deim:deimatic; Esc:Escape. (Color figure online)

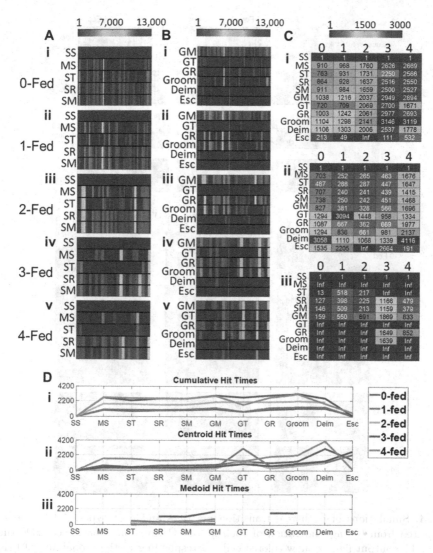

Fig. 3. Absorption times for real data and prototypes. Absorption times are plotted from each behavior to the time of sequence termination. (A) and (B) show the absorption times to the completion of the sequences from the hunting and non-hunting behaviors, respectively. i–iv plots in the (A) and (B) columns are for feed states 0–4, respectively. The color scales are referenced at the top of these columns. (Ci-Ciii) show the absorption times for the three prototypes (Ci) cumulative, (Cii) centroid, and (Ciii) medoid. The color scale for these plots is referenced at the top of the column and does not have as large of a distribution as plots in columns (A) and (B). (D) re-plots the absorption times for each prototype for better comparison of how well each prototype does at distinguishing a trend across feed states. SS:successful strike; MS:missed strike; SpecTrans:specific translation; SpecRot:specific rotation; SpecMon:specific monitor; GenMon:general monitoring; GenTrans:general translation; GenRot:general rotation; Deim:deimatic; Esc:Escape. (Color figure online)

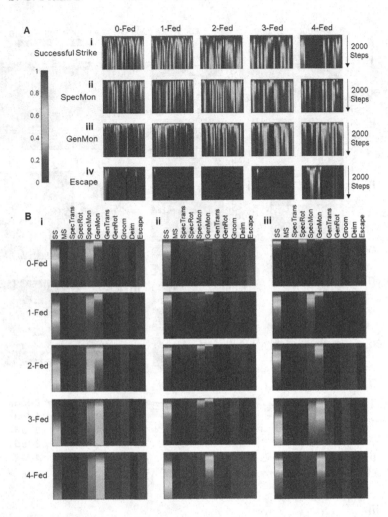

Fig. 4. Simulations of both real transition matrices and prototypes. All figures are generated from the agglomeration of 1000 Monte Carlo simulations, each 2000 time steps. The output figures show colored cells corresponding to the probability of being within a behavior at each time step. (A) The evolution of likely state probabilities of select behaviors. (Ai) Successful strikes are highly probable within 2000 time steps for the starved states, and become less likely to occur within the simulation as the feed state increases. (Aii) Specific monitoring showed greatest probability in the 2-fed runs, however, had similar presentation across the feed states. (Aiii) General monitoring appeared more frequently in sated runs than the starved states, where animals also remained in general monitoring longer. (Aiv) Escape behavior was not used often; it appears the most often in the 4-fed state, where some runs entered escape behavior relatively quickly. (B) The probability evolution of the three prototypes: (Bi) cumulative, (Bii) centroid, and (Biii) medoid. SS:successful strike; MS:missed strike; SpecTrans:specific translation; SpecRot:specific rotation; SpecMon:specific monitor; GenMon:general monitoring; GenTrans:general translation; GenRot:general rotation; Deim:deimatic

4   Discussion

In this paper, cumulative, centroid, and Euclidean medoid prototypes were generated from the transition matrices of freely behaving praying mantis sequences. Markovian metrics were then used to characterize the performance of these three prototypes in capturing time-evolutionary trends across feeding state, which showed the cumulative prototypes best exhibited temporal behaviors most consistent with the real data trends.

In Sect. 3.2, both hit probability and absorption time plots showed trends across feed states best seen in the cumulative prototypes. In the hit probability plots for select behaviors, the cumulative prototype showed starved states had greater probabilities of progressing to successful strikes and thus, prey capture. Conversely, the probability of progressing to non-hunting behaviors was more likely to occur from other non-hunting behaviors. Similar to hit probabilities are the trends seen in time to absorption. The actual data showed that hunting behavior in the starved states lead to sequence termination faster than sated states as well as faster than non-hunting behaviors. Lastly, like the real data in Sect. 3.3, the cumulative prototypes showed starved states to have faster exhibition of successful strike, while more stated states had higher long-term probability of entering into non-hunting behaviors.

References

1. Aghabozorgi, S., Wah, T., Amini, A., Saybani, M.: A new approach to present prototypes in clustering of time series. In: The 7th International Conference of Data Mining, vol. 28, no. 4, pp. 214–220 (2011). http://cerc.wvu.edu/download/WORLDCOMP'11/2011CDpapers/DMI2163.pdf%5Cn.   http://cerc.wvu.edu/download/WORLDCOMP'11/2011CDpapers/DMI2163.pdf%5Cn.   http://www.lidi.info.unlp.edu.ar/WorldComp2011-Mirror/DMI2163.pdf
2. Alger, S.J., Larget, B.R., Riters, L.V.: A novel statistical method for behaviour sequence analysis and its application to birdsong. Anim. Behav. **116**, 181–193 (2016). https://doi.org/10.1016/j.anbehav.2016.04.001. https://doi.org/10.1016/j.anbehav.2016.04.001
3. Bishop, C.M.: Pattern Recognition and Machine Learning (Information Science and Statistics). Springer-Verlag, Berlin, Heidelberg (2006)
4. Ermon, S., Gomes, C.P., Sabharwal, A., Selman, B.: Designing fast absorbing Markov chains. https://www.aaai.org
5. Hunter, J.J.: Mixing times with applications to perturbed Markov chains. Linear Alg. Appl. **417**, 108–123 (2006). https://doi.org/10.1016/j.laa.2006.02.008. www.elsevier.com/locate/laa
6. Johnson, N., Galata, A., Hogg, D.: The acquisition and use of interaction behaviour models. In: Proceedings 1998 IEEE Computer Society Conference on Computer Vision and Pattern Recognition (Cat. No. 98CB36231), pp. 866–871 (1998). https://doi.org/10.1109/CVPR.1998.698706
7. Kershenbaum, A., Garland, E.C.: Quantifying similarity in animal vocal sequences: which metric performs best? Methods Ecol. Evol. **6**(12), 1452–1461 (2015). https://doi.org/10.1111/2041-210X.12433

8. Leon-Alcaide, P., Rodriguez-Benitez, L., Castillo-Herrera, E., Moreno-Garcia, J., Jimenez-Linares, L.: An evolutionary approach for efficient prototyping of large time series datasets. Inf. Sci. **511**, 74–93 (2020). https://doi.org/10.1016/J.INS.2019.09.044

9. Levin, D.A., Peres, Y., Wilmer, E.L.: Markov Chains and Mixing Times (Second Edition) (2017). https://search.ebscohost.com/login.aspx?direct=true&scope=site&db=nlebk&db=nlabk&AN=1627551

10. Pickard, S.C., Bertsch, D.J., Le Garrec, Z., Ritzmann, R.E., Quinn, R.D., Szczecinski, N.S.: Internal state effects on behavioral shifts in freely behaving praying mantises (Tenodera sinensis). PLOS Comput. Biolo. **17**(12), e1009618 (2021). https://doi.org/10.1371/journal.pcbi.1009618

Correction to: Integrating Spiking Neural Networks and Deep Learning Algorithms on the Neurorobotics Platform

Rachael Stentiford⒤, Thomas C. Knowles⒤, Benedikt Feldotto⒤, Deniz Ergene⒤, Fabrice O. Morin⒤, and Martin J. Pearson⒤

Correction to:
Chapter "Integrating Spiking Neural Networks and Deep Learning Algorithms on the Neurorobotics Platform" in: A. Hunt et al. (Eds.): *Biomimetic and Biohybrid Systems*, LNAI 13548, https://doi.org/10.1007/978-3-031-20470-8_7

In the originally published version of chapter 7, the author name Benedikt Feldotto was incorrectly written as Benedikt Feldoto. This has been corrected.

The updated original version of this chapter can be found at
https://doi.org/10.1007/978-3-031-20470-8_7

© The Author(s), under exclusive license to Springer Nature Switzerland AG 2022
A. Hunt et al. (Eds.): Living Machines 2022, LNAI 13548, p. C1, 2022.
https://doi.org/10.1007/978-3-031-20470-8_39

Author Index

Printed in the United States
by Baker & Taylor Publisher Services

Printed in the United States
by Baker & Taylor Publisher Services